Romanticism: A Critical Reader

Romanticism:
A Critical Reader

Edited by

Duncan Wu

BLACKWELL
Oxford UK & Cambridge USA

Copyright © Basil Blackwell Ltd 1995 and as stated in the acknowledgements
Copyright © Introduction and arrangement, Duncan Wu 1995

First published 1995

Blackwell Publishers
108 Cowley Road
Oxford OX4 1JF
UK

238 Main Street
Cambridge, Massachusetts 02142
USA

British Library Cataloguing in Publication Data
A CIP catalogue record for this book is available from the British Library.

Library of Congress Cataloging-in-Publication Data
Romanticism: a critical reader / edited by Duncan Wu.
p.   cm.
"Romantic studies since 1980"—Introd.
Includes bibliographical references and index.

ISBN 0–631–19503–3. — ISBN 0–631–19504–1 (pbk.)

1. English literature—19th century—History and criticism.
2. Romanticism—Great Britain. I. Wu, Duncan.
PR457.R645 1995
820.9′145—dc20   94—25770
                                                                        CIP

Typeset in M Garamond on 10.5/12 pt
by Pure Tech Corporation, Pondicherry, India
Printed in Great Britain by T. J. Press Ltd., Padstow, Cornwall
This book is printed on acid-free paper

...ust a few requests

...NOT write in the book.

...NOT fold down the pages.

...DO NOT leave sticky tabs, paperclips
...marks in the book.

...DO NOT leave any personal items
...s bank cards or receipts in the book.

...e DO NOT eat, drink or smoke over the book.

**Thank you
for helping us
take good care of our books**

Contents

Introduction

Romanticism: A Critical Reader provides a unique overview of romantic studies since 1980, representing most of the movements active during the last fifteen years, including feminism, new historicism, genre theory, psychoanalysis and deconstructionism. It is a kind of progress report, and will be useful to anyone interested in the application of theoretical ideas to literary texts.

The *Reader* brings together a wide range of writers from different schools of thought, dealing, for the most part, with works included in Blackwell's *Romanticism: An Anthology*, which this volume is intended to companion. It includes two essays on each of the six canonical writers – Blake, Wordsworth, Coleridge, Shelley, Byron and Keats – selected from among the most distinguished criticism in the field. Inevitably, space precludes the inclusion of many of those who deserve a place here, but it is hoped the selection will encourage students to read further for themselves. In a number of cases, contributions were drawn from book-length studies of particular subjects. This introduction provides readers not only with a brief account of each essay, but with a summary of the thesis advanced in the volume from which it was drawn, and, in certain cases, an outline of the larger intellectual forces that inspired it. As such summaries cannot help but simplify, they are, emphatically, no substitute for the reader's extended study either of those sources or of their theoretical underpinnings.[1]

Blake

During the 1980s Blake criticism entered a transitional phase in its development. The preceding school of thought, led by Northrop Frye, had achieved its objectives, and the increasing advocacy of theoretical approaches made reorientation inevitable. As a result, this has become one of the liveliest arenas in the field.

Nelson Hilton begins as a meticulous reader of the text, and indeed he emphasizes the importance of encountering each word "in its force-field of sound, etymology, graphic shape, contemporary applications, and varied associations" as a means of revealing the "war/p and woof" of Blake's thought.[2] For Hilton, Blake's principal beliefs are contained in his language – an element of his work distinct from imagery, myths, or symbols. Having rejected the stable, unified, historically-based concept of authorial intention, Hilton prefers to see Blake's work as continually redefining itself through interpretation – itself connected to social structures beyond the poet's control. Hence his assertion that the stories in Blake's works "continually reconstitute themselves even as they tell of structures and figures continually reconstituting themselves."

"Blakean Zen" opens with a demonstration of Hilton's method. Arguing that specific critical interpretations of *Urizen* are essentially discontinuous and unrelated, he finds that the recognition of "levels" of meaning allows us to "play" the text. He goes on to argue for the self-referentiality of *Urizen* in the context of an interpretative "strange loop" by which the work "begins where it left off," as we return to it over and over again. In effect, the poem is a catalyst for change within the reader – not so much a stable, defined artifact as "a process that labors to bring forth processing." What distinguishes Blake from other authors, Hilton argues, is his awareness of this self-referential activity. Readers will wish also to consult Hilton's important volume, *Literal Imagination: Blake's Vision of Words* (1983), and the collection of essays he edited with Thomas Vogler, *Unnam'd Forms: Blake and Textuality* (1986).

Vincent Arthur De Luca's *Words of Eternity* (1991) aims to demonstrate the importance of sublimity to the poetry of Blake. "Blake's Concept of the Sublime," which forms chapter 1 of that book, describes the experience of reading the poetry with characteristic lucidity: "What is a barrier to the faculty allied with sense is an avenue to its more privileged counterpart [Imagination] – and, paradoxically, the avenue becomes available only if the barrier is posed. The sublime stimulus then operates as a kind of psychic traffic light, beckoning one power of the mind to come forth only when another is blocked." This understanding, central to De Luca's thesis, is reflected throughout Blake's major works. One of its most important implications relates to Blake's understanding of the reading experience. After a moment of indeterminacy when the reader's confrontation with the text precipitates a state of disengagement, the corporeal understanding is alternately frustrated while the intellect is released to find satisfaction in the "wall of words." Consequently, our pleasure in reading derives from the "lineaments of gratified desire" – language which has become a friend and companion to the intellect. These linguistic openings contain the promise of that apocalyptic moment when the sign and the human form may become one – a line of thought with important implications for Blakean aesthetics. Because satisfaction arises from our recognition of the creative power of the letter, Blake demands "a total determinacy, or closure of outline" in its portrayal: the sublime of the signifier rests in its determinacy. Thus the Blakean sublime determines not merely tone and content, but the formal artistry of his work. In subsequent chapters De Luca proceeds to identify two modes of vision in Blake: the bardic and the iconic. These produce distinctive forms of sublimity which De Luca explores in detail, and which he uses to define Blake's organizing principles.

This is only De Luca's introduction, but its clarity and sensitivity should encourage students of Blake to read all of his book, as well as those to which he is indebted – particularly Northrop Frye's *Fearful Symmetry* (1947) and Thomas Weiskel's *The Romantic Sublime* (1976).

Wordsworth

Donald G. Marshall has suggested that the publication in 1964 of Geoffrey Hartman's *Wordsworth's Poetry, 1787–1814* "marked an epoch in the study of that poet and of romanticism generally."[3] The sub-genre of books and articles specifically concerned with Hartman's own critical writings testifies to that, and it is further affirmed by the ideological profile of subsequent critical developments in Wordsworth studies, which may be plotted partly by the extent to which they have reacted to Hartman's detailed investigation of what he describes as "the difficult humanising of imagination . . . in Wordsworth."[4] Hartman himself has now moved towards deconstructive methods because, he suggests, Derrida "is renewing our ability to read."[5]

The essays here by James K. Chandler and Alan Liu are representative of the contemporary response to early Hartman insofar as they seek to politicize Wordsworth, though in different ways. Both can be seen as adopting the new historicist assumption that, as Jerome J. McGann puts it, "poems are social and historical products and that the critical study of such products must be grounded in a socio-historic analytic."[6] This idea has a firm foundation in Marxist literary theory, and has proved a powerful force in romantic studies during the last decade. Its implications extend beyond the literary work to such matters as our assessment of the society out of which it came, its first readers, even bibliography. This in turn explains why Marjorie Levinson should argue that "the amassing harmonies of Words-worth's poem ['Tintern Abbey'] effectively muffle the social and political resonance of the date inscribed in the title, of the designated five-year interval, and of the scene of writing."[7] The new historicists set out to unmuffle the resonances in romantic works.

The central argument of James K. Chandler's *Wordsworth's Second Nature* (1984) is that Wordsworth's conservativism was not a product of his middle age, but is evident from 1798 onwards, especially in his adherence to the Burkean tradition of conservative thought. In particular, Wordsworth's theory of a "second nature" is based on Burkean premises. According to this idea, his poetry works on the reader in the same way that the poet himself is affected by the natural world. At the same time, poetry arises from a "second nature" dependent on "habits of association" within Wordsworth himself. Such concepts collapse the opposition between nature and culture, between "natural" and existing political rights – a conflation found also in Burke.

"Wordsworth, Rousseau and the Politics of Education" argues for Wordsworth's familiarity with Rousseau's theory of education, and the Rousseauist scheme adopted by the French government in 1795. Through a careful reading of *Prelude* Book 5 Chandler reveals that the poet of *The Prelude* was fundamentally opposed to the ideas in Rousseau's *Emile*, and that this opposition derived from Burke.

Chandler's conclusions are supported by a detailed scholarly knowledge of the subject – a virtue he shares with Alan Liu. But Liu's thesis is as concerned with psychology as it is with politics: after all, he is interested not so much in what Wordsworth actually wrote, as in what he *denied*. This distinctive view lies at the heart of "The History in 'Imagination'," the introductory chapter to *Wordsworth: The Sense of History* (1989). Against the positivism of earlier critical approaches, Liu offers "a deflected or denied positivism able to discriminate absence." He illustrates his method through analysis of the Simplon Pass episode in *Thirteen-Book Prelude* Book 6. There, he argues, imagination is haunted by the unmentioned Napoleon, who in some sense stands behind the scene described by Wordsworth. Like other Wordsworthians of recent years,[8] Liu is in search of a poet fundamentally altered by the French Revolution. He suggests that whereas the youthful Wordsworth asserted himself as an "I" who could regard nature purely in aesthetic terms, his post-revolutionary self could not escape the influence of history (in the form of revolutionary violence). Thus, in the Simplon Pass episode, history "erupts" into *The Prelude* in the form of the spectral Napoleon. Not everyone will agree with Liu's conclusions, but, as his extensive command of Wordsworth scholarship testifies, he has earned the right to "see through the self and mind in the foreground, through even the nature in the middle ground, to a frightening skeleton in the background." The emergence of Napoleon as an imperial figure of imagination is elucidated in chapter 8 of Liu's book, to which the reader is referred.

Coleridge

Kathleen Wheeler's *The Creative Mind in Coleridge's Poetry* (1981) argues that the poetry composed between 1795 and 1798 exemplified Coleridge's adherence to the 'creative theory of mind' advanced in his later philosophical works. Received opinion sets the formulation of this theory at a later date, *c.* 1801, during his analysis of Descartes, Locke, and Kant. According to Wheeler, Kant was an influence as early as 1795, and led Coleridge to see that "the mind, in its acts, *moulds* experience, and deduces knowledge not only from experience, as Locke maintained, but gains knowledge from those very acts: that is, it thinks about thinking." The act of perception is itself a creative act – and since reading is "like perception," it too is creative. In order to convey this, Wheeler argues, Coleridge framed his poems as dramas in which an unperceiving, literal-minded reader is confronted with a creative, imaginatively vital response to nature.

Her chapter on "Kubla Khan" begins with a discussion of the poem's Preface, which represents the viewpoint of a reductive reader who fails to understand the poem's unity, describing it as no more than a "psychological curiosity" and a fragment.[9] However, the speaker of the poem's "epilogue" (lines 37–54) is also that of the Preface "in a visionary state." At the same time, Wheeler emphasizes that the distinctions between different personae are by no means hard and fast; as she touches on the complex possibilities within the text, she finds the extent of the mind's contribution to the construction of the perceived world to be indeterminate. True to the creative process described by Coleridge, her discussion accommodates contradictions and revisions in a courageous attempt to bring us closer to the "central mystery surrounding artistic creation".

Feminist criticism has proved to be one of the most fertile and productive areas in romantic studies in recent years. Toril Moi has identified two distinct approaches: Anglo-American feminist criticism and French feminist theory.[10] The Anglo-American tradition assumes that the social construction of gender derives from biological sexual difference, and works as the basis of an ideological gender-system. Women thus have physical experiences unknown to men, and their perceptions are shaped by the sex-roles imposed on them. It follows that women write and read distinctively, a notion on which Elaine Showalter has based her theory of "gynocriticism."[11] The critic's function is to identify and analyse these differences, locating them within individual experience and larger cultural ideologies. This approach has been explored recently by Anne K. Mellor, who argues that unless we distinguish between female and male ideologies within romanticism "the gendered dialogue between male- and female-authored texts . . . will go unheard."[12]

French feminists tend to place a higher premium on philosophy than their Anglo-American counterparts; questioning the binary mode of thought that has dominated Western philosophy since classical times, they call for radical change in the cultural practice of identifying the female as the Other. That Other must be accommodated within, they argue, so that the old polarities may be collapsed into a more productive chaos or process. In this context the phallogocentric nature of language itself is a form of oppression which the feminist writer must break down in order to make room for the emergent Other. Theoreticians in this area, whose works the reader may wish to follow up, include Alice Jardine, Toril Moi, and Julia Kristeva.[13]

In " 'Christabel': The Wandering Mother and the Enigma of Form," the Anglo-American feminist, Karen Swann, investigates the significance of genre to a gender-based reading of one of Coleridge's strangest works. Burton's remarks on hysteria provide a keynote to her discussion, in which she argues that hysterical behaviour is both dramatized and provoked by Coleridge: the poem's characters enact it, while the narrators suffer from it. In so doing, they induce a similar response in the reader. Swann finally reveals "Christabel" to be a far more subversive poem than many critics have realized, in its undermining of the laws of gender/genre and in proposing to collapse the positions of patriarch, hysteric, and ironist. For further discussion of these issues as they relate to Keats, Wordsworth, and Coleridge, readers should consult Swann's other publications.[14]

Shelley

James A. W. Heffernan provides an original and helpful introduction to a difficult work with "*Adonais*: Shelley's Consumption of Keats." He argues that, despite appearances, Shelley's poem is not simply an elegy to an admired colleague. In fact, Shelley himself was the source of the myth that Keats was killed by the reviewers: "It gave him the chance not only to get vicarious revenge for the injuries that reviewers had done to him, but also to consume Keats in a myth of his own re-making." Through a close analysis of Keats's "Ode to a Nightingale" and Shelley's *Adonais*, Heffernan demonstrates that the fate to which Shelley condemns Keats – that of being consumed by Nature – "is the very last fate that Keats would have wished for himself," and that Keats is eventually effaced in Shelley's poem by the more dominant figure of Milton.

Eagleton's observation that "The tactic of deconstructive criticism ... is to show how texts come to embarrass their own ruling systems of logic"[15] may go some way to explaining why the romantics have been so attractive to post-structuralists. Romanticism often seems to define itself by its yearning for a "transcendental signifier" ripe for deconstruction; in *Dark Interpreter* (1980), Tilottama Rajan even suggested that Schiller and Schopenhauer were precursors of Derrida. That important volume placed the romantics in dialogue with German philosophers as a means of revealing the discontinuities inherent in their poetry: for her, the romantics were proto-deconstructionists. Rajan's more recent *The Supplement of Reading* (1990) extends this debate by positing that works of the romantic period are distinguished by a hermeneutic which, in her words, "contains the seed of its own deconstruction, because making the reader a mediating element allows for an explicit as well as for an implied reader, and so renders problematical any sentimental reconstitution of text as work." This theme is central to "Deconstruction or Reconstruction: Reading Shelley's *Prometheus Unbound*," from the final section of her book.

Prometheus demonstrates Rajan's belief that reading is a vital supplement to the act of composition. This argument is prefigured, she suggests, by *Alastor* – a highly reflexive poem in that it enacts the processes of making and reading. It is also essentially negative, in that the character of the Poet remains no more than an allegory, a sign of the unfulfilled desire for vision. Rajan suggests that *Prometheus Unbound* is also concerned with the mediation of a visionary ideology, focusing on the dialogue between Asia and Panthea at the beginning of Act II, where Shelley "reflects on the rhetorical problem at the heart of the play: that of whether he can make his vision of a Promethean age convincing, given the lacunae in it." That dialogue echoes Schelling's theory that understanding is reached through a dialogue between the higher, intuitive self, and the mute mediator. It is, in effect, a model for the reading process itself, confirmed by Shelley's logocentric concept of the "written soul" – a hermeneutic intended to reverse the play's inherently deconstructive tendency.

Analysing Asia's dialogue with Demogorgon, Rajan reveals a similar process of mediation. This time, however, the elusive and empty character of Demogorgon turns a vision of hope into no more than a linguistic construct. Rajan concludes by outlining Shelley's representation of the text as drama, with its antimetaphysical consequences.

Byron

Peter J. Manning's "*Don Juan* and Byron's Imperceptiveness to the English Word" comes from his important volume, *Reading Romantics* (1990), which aims "to reconnect literature with the motives from which it springs and the social relations within which it exists." Against the traditionally held view, initiated by Hazlitt, that Byron and Wordsworth are diametrically opposed in their writing, he demonstrates that they share complex affinities.

Manning's title is ironic. Byron was accused of imperceptiveness by T. S. Eliot, but Manning argues that he was highly attuned to the possibilities of language. He reveals this by discussing what he calls Byron's fantasies of fusion – as, for instance, when Haidée nurses Juan, or when Byron describes Juan's enthusiasm for battle. Such moments of intense passion entail the surrender of language, because they consume the individual in a kind of mother–infant dyadic fusion that constitutes the ultimate withdrawal from the social world. In the face of annihilation, such intervening male figures as Alfonso and Lambro compel Juan to assert his independence. This "intermediate space" provides an environment in which Byron's language exists. Necessarily, the indeterminate nature of this space is revealed by the poem's deferral of finality: the work defies aesthetic unities and the illusion of authorial control; it is all middle, without beginning or end; and, in spite of Eliot, Byron's language provokes trains of association that circulate about the entire poem. In fact, Byron shares Wordsworth's dislike of a specialized poetic diction, having composed, in *Don Juan*, the apogee of the conversation poem.

Like Manning, Jerome J. McGann is also concerned, in his "Byron and the Anonymous Lyric," to refine our understanding of Byron's relation to Wordsworthian poetics. For McGann, his poetry constitutes a critique of the romanticism of Wordsworth and Coleridge. Sceptical of the conventions and artifices of romantic expressions of feeling, McGann's Byron is capable of standing outside it. For him, the heightened moments from which Wordsworth makes ethical generalizations are illusory; on the contrary, pain and despair are the controlling agents of his sentimental life. "Fare Thee Well!" strikes a Wordsworthian posture in order to draw attention to its moral and artistic inadequacy.   Byron is for McGann a precursor of the postmodern consciousness, for such characters as Childe Harold are capable of deconstructing, and subverting, the conventions by which romantic poetry was governed. Having passed through a Wordsworthian meditation on nature, Byron can emerge as confirmed in feelings not of love, but of hatred. Against the primal sympathy recommended by Wordsworth, he chooses the elemental – primal conflict, primal energy.

Keats

The poetics of the romantic fragment attracted considerable attention during the 1980s, thanks partly to Thomas McFarland's exemplary study, *Romanticism and the Forms of Ruin* (1981), and its discussion of "diasparactive forms." Balachandra Rajan's *The Form of the Unfinished* (1985) distinguishes between the ruin (the text which was formerly complete, now decayed) and the unfinished – a state that either falls short of finality, or resists it. He goes on to describe an aesthetics of the inconclusive, positing that the long poem's "increasing resistance to its own integrative energies questions not simply the possibility, but the desirability of totalization." Rajan sees this as having culminated with the work of the second generation romantics, and specifically Keats's "The Fall of Hyperion," which treats "understanding as emergent and indefinitely self-revisionary rather than as the progressive inscription of *telos*." This development has socio-political implications, as it "registers the widely recognized alienation of the self from the increasing dehumanization of social and technological aggregates."

His chapter on the two *Hyperions* begins with an examination of the pleasure thermometer lines from *Endymion*, which demonstrate the continuity of the conception behind it. The "cosmic purposiveness" to which *Hyperion* aspires is admirable but incongruous with Keats's temperament. After all, the poem's psychic politics suggest that we must accept "dying into life, disinheritance beyond retrieval, the commitment to self-making rather than self-preservation" – a philosophy at odds with the belief that beauty is truth. The opposition between intellect and imagination is compounded by Keats's view that it is the heart that must authenticate the journey described by the poem towards the formation of an identity. Discontinuity inheres in *Hyperion* partly because the poem never resolves the dejection with which it begins; it can find no justification for pain and suffering.

The Fall of Hyperion deals with this problem by internalizing it through the dream in which Apollo is protected by Moneta against his excessive responsiveness to human misery. Rajan finds the new material so effective that it makes the original fable redundant – as befits the poem of self-formation which "creates its own obsolescence." Keats's myth of the evolving consciousness cannot help but resist closure.

Leon Waldoff's *Keats and the Silent Work of Imagination* (1985) applies Freudian techniques to Keats's poetry in order to show how his work is affected by unconscious fears, desires, and conflicts, and especially by a melancholia exacerbated by the early death of his father and separation from his mother. The female presences which figure in all of Keats's major works arouse powerful, but equivocal feelings, insofar as he wants to reclaim her while harbouring doubts of her fidelity, and even of her existence. "Imagination and Growth in the Great Odes" puts this theory to the test. Having identified the symbols at the centre of each ode as feminine, immortal, and sympathetic, Waldoff argues that the odes extend the project of *Endymion* and *Hyperion* in attempting to express an "ancient longing for restoration and reunion." In the odes on a Grecian urn and to a nightingale, Waldoff argues, Keats is compelled to internalize the symbols when his strategies to reclaim them break down. The nightingale is preserved "in the historical, biblical, and literary imagination," while the urn survives as "an essential part of the collective wisdom of mankind." But this fails to satisfy the libido, which is withdrawn in the process, and with the "Ode on Melancholy" Keats moves away from the desire to restore the symbol, towards "a deeper perception of her presence in all things."

Freudian techniques have also been used with considerable subtlety and sophistication by Wordsworthians; among other studies, readers may wish to consult David Ellis's *Wordsworth, Freud, and the Spots of Time: Interpretation in The Prelude* (1985), and Douglas B. Wilson, *The Romantic Dream: Wordsworth and the Poetics of the Unconscious* (1993).

Other Writers

Against the current of earlier criticism on the subject, Marilyn Butler's "Godwin, Burke, and *Caleb Williams*" reminds us of the "dangerous topicality" of Godwin's novel, and of the part played by "guilt and fear, God and the Old Testament" in *Political Justice*. Just as Godwin's desire to make *Political Justice* "the ultimate answer to the *Reflections*" dictated its tone and content, the use of Burkean rhetoric in *Caleb Williams* can be seen as an element in his critique of Burke's ideas. In fact, Falkland's fall re-enacts Burke's emergence as the servant of the system he seemed to attack. Focusing on "Things As They Are," the novel dares to contemplate the psychological consequences of the establishment of a non-hierarchical system. Butler is the author of a major survey of the period, *Romantics, Rebels and Reactionaries: English Literature and its Background 1760–1830* (1982).

During the last fifteen years or so, gay politics has become an increasingly important influence in romantic studies – one of the most important works to emerge from that movement being Eve Kosofsky Sedgwick's *Between Men: English Literature and Male Homosocial Desire* (1985). Writing as a feminist, Sedgwick's central concern is with homosocial desire. The word "homosocial" refers to bonds between people of the same sex, and can be applied to such phenomena as male bonding – ostensibly an activity characterized by intense homophobia (which she defines as "fear and hatred of homosexuality"). The kernel of her thesis is that, in fact, there is a continuum between homosocial behaviour and "desire" (that is, the affective and social force that holds people together, which may be sexual). This proposition has important implications for political readings of literary works: if a continuum exists between desire and the manner in which societies organize themselves, then we need to be alert to such matters as presented in literary works if we are fully to appreciate the ideology they seek to promote.

This is illustrated by her pioneering discussion of James Hogg's *Confessions of a Justified Sinner* (1824), which she locates firmly within the Gothic paranoid tradition that also includes *Caleb Williams* and *Wuthering Heights*. Even when novels with in this tradition appear ostensibly to be dealing with homosexual themes, she argues that they "have as their *first* referent the psychology and sociology of prohibition and control" – seeking, in effect, to promote heterosexuality within the context of a patriarchy. Having established that male bonding is an organizing factor in the society portrayed by Hogg, she turns to the portrayal of the young Robert Wringhim. He is, she suggests, both feminized and symbolically castrated; at the same time, he is the focus for a good deal of homophobic pressure within the society in which he lives. This in turn makes him "an excruciatingly *responsive* creature and instrument of class, economic, and gender struggles that long antedate his birth." He embodies, in other words, the psychology of prohibition and control operating within the patriarchal society depicted, and implicitly endorsed, by Hogg.[16]

In *Bearing the Word* (1986), Margaret Homans draws together some of the concerns of both Anglo-American and French feminists. Her thesis is that the dominant myth of language, by turning women into "the silent and absent objects of representation," renders them incapable of acts of representation themselves. Because the figurative and metaphorical are reserved for the use of men, women writers were compelled to exploit the literal. "Bearing Demons: Frankenstein's Circumvention of the Maternal" examines these notions as they bear on Mary Shelley's novel. With the creation of the demon, Homans suggests, Frankenstein "perpetuates the death of the mother and of motherhood" to generate a kind of mother-substitute that is "a revision of Eve, of emanations, and of the object of romantic desire." This interpretation provides a metaphor for the myth of language by which the referent (like the mother) must be removed and replaced by "language as figuration that never quite touches its objects." Shelley's novel is therefore a critique of male desire and its circumvention of the mother; at the same time, it literalizes the words of her husband and Byron.

Tom Paulin's critical writing is conditioned partly by his origins as a Northern Irish Protestant – and, as Edward Said has observed, this makes him particularly sensitive to politics as a concrete, intervening force in people's lives.[17] "John Clare in Babylon" provides an essential and evocative reminder of exactly how the English class system operates, and of the effects of such repressive measures as Enclosure. Clare strove to retain the imaginative vitality, the unenclosed power of his language, which "could provoke a class anxiety and fear." Admirers of this essay will want to consult Paulin's *Ireland and the English Crisis* (1984), and *Minotaur: Poetry and the Nation State* (1992).

Does romanticism have a gender? Anne K. Mellor, a leading romantic feminist, believes that it does. Her *Romanticism and Gender* (1993) argues that women writers of the period tended to celebrate not the transcendental imagination but the workings of the rational mind, thus insisting on the innate equality of the sexes. Their intellectual pioneer was Mary Wollstonecraft, whose work Mellor discusses in " 'A Revolution in Female Manners.' " Wollstonecraft argued that the needs of society would be best served if the female capacity for rational thought was fully developed by a comprehensive education – a proposal echoed and amplified by her successors.

Edward Said's introduction to *Culture and Imperialism* (1993) deplores the traditional isolation of literature and philosophy from "the prolonged and sordid cruelty of such practices as slavery, colonialist and racial oppression, and imperial subjection." "Jane Austen and Empire" begins by observing that during the last century the great humanistic ideas of British culture coexisted with imperialism. Turning to *Mansfield Park* (1814), Said reminds us of the political and economic background to Austen's novel. Specifically, Sir Thomas Bertram rules his sugar plantations in Antigua with the same firm discipline which he applies to Mansfield Park: "What assures the domestic tranquillity and attractive harmony of one is the productivity and regulated discipline of the other." These qualities have implications for our understanding of Fanny Price – a poor provincial relative of the Bertrams whose absorption into their world is analogous, Said believes, to the trafficking of wealth derived from the Bertrams' West Indian plantations. For Austen, morality is underpinned by imperialism, with its ensuing business of trade, production, and consumption. And yet, for Said, the novel's greatness rests in its encoding, as opposed to its admission, of ideology. *Mansfield Park* is not a manifesto; it is, rather, a great work of fiction embodying a range of political assumptions to which we must remain sensitive.

All these essays contain insights of permanent interest to those engaged in the study of British literary romanticism, and, as a group, they reflect a vigorous and lively community of critical thought. At the same time, they are occasionally in disagreement, and often in dialogue: Paulin and Sedgwick are both concerned with class, but in different ways; Manning traces a line of thought pursued differently by McGann, and so forth. Readers should remain alert to these distinctions, and the various critical approaches ought to provoke debate rather than assent.

A Note on Texts and Abbreviations

Editorial interventions have been kept to a minimum, and are restricted mainly to minor copy-editing alterations. Brief citations in the text and notes give author and date; full references may be found in the bibliography, pp. 437–56. However, frequently used sources are abbreviated, without dates, and full details of these will be found, in alphabetical order, in the list of Abbreviations on pages xxiv–xxvi.

NOTES

1 Those requiring a fuller account of the theoretical background are advised to consult, as a first step, Terry Eagleton's *Literary Theory* (Oxford, 1983), Jerome

J. McGann's *The Romantic Ideology* (Chicago, Ill., 1986), and Mary Eagleton's *Feminist Literary Criticism* (London, 1991).

2 Nelson Hilton, *Literal Imagination: Blake's Vision of Words* (Berkeley and Los Angeles, Calif., 1983), p. 7.

3 Geoffrey H. Hartman, *The Unremarkable Wordsworth*, Foreword by Donald G. Marshall (London, 1987), p. vii.

4 *Wordsworth's Poetry, 1787–1814* (2nd ed., New Haven, Conn., 1987), p. xi. Alan Liu deals frankly with his relation to Hartman, pp. 113–15, below.

5 Imre Salusinszky, *Criticism in Society* (London, 1987), p. 89.

6 *The Romantic Ideology*, p. 3.

7 *Wordsworth's Great Period Poems* (Cambridge, 1986), p. 2.

8 See, for instance, Nicholas Roe, *Wordsworth and Coleridge: The Radical Years* (Oxford, 1988).

9 Other critics of recent years concerned with the "fragmentary" status of "Kubla Khan" include Anne Janowitz, "Coleridge's 1816 Volume: Fragment as Rubric", *SiR* 24 (1985) 21–39, and Timothy Bahti, "Coleridge's 'Kubla Khan' and the Fragment of Romanticism", *MLN* 96 (1981) 1035–50. In *The Romantic Fragment Poem* (1986), Marjorie Levinson devotes an entire chapter to an analysis of "Kubla Khan".

10 Toril Moi, *Sexual/Textual Politics* (London, 1985).

11 See Moi, pp. 75–80.

12 *Romanticism and Gender* (London, 1993), p. 211.

13 For a lucid and comprehensive account of these matters, see Mary Eagleton's Introduction to *Feminist Literary Criticism*.

14 "Suffering and Sensation in 'The Ruined Cottage'", *PMLA* 106 (1991) 83–95; "Harrassing the Muse", *Romanticism and Feminism* ed. Anne K. Mellor (Blooming-ton, Ind., 1988), pp. 81–92; and "Literary Gentlemen and Lovely Ladies: The Debate on the Character of Christabel", *ELH* 52 (1985) 394–418.

15 *Literary Theory*, p. 133.

16 Other writers who have explored homosexuality in romantic literature include Louis Crompton, *Byron and Greek Love: Homophobia in Nineteenth-Century England* (Berkeley, Calif., 1985), and Wayne Koestenbaum, *Double Talk: The Erotics of Male Literary Collaboration* (London, 1989).

17 Edward Said, "Paulin's People", *London Review of Books* (9 April 1992), p. 11.

Acknowledgements

Thanks are due to the readers consulted by Blackwell while this book was in preparation: Jerome J. McGann, Andrew Elfenbein, and Keith Hanley. Andrew McNeillie, my editor at Blackwell, has been a constant source of encouragement and advice. I am grateful to my fellow contributors for generous help and co-operation.

I edited this book while a postdoctoral Fellow of the British Academy and a Fellow of St Catherine's College, Oxford. I thank both institutions for their kind support.

The editor and the publisher wish to thank the following for permission to use copyright material: Marilyn Butler, for "Godwin, Burke, and Caleb Williams,' *Essays in Criticism*, 32 (1982) pp. 237–57, by permission of *Essays in Criticism*; James K. Chandler, for "Wordsworth, Rousseau and the Politics of Education" in *Wordsworth's Second Nature* (1984) pp. 93–119, by permission of The University of Chicago Press; Vincent Arthur De Luca, for "Blake's Concept of the Sublime" from *Words of Eternity: Blake and the Poetics of the Sublime* (1991), pp. 15–52. Copyright © 1991 by Princeton University Press, by permission of Princeton University Press; James A. W. Heffernan, for "*Adonais*: Shelley's Consumption of Keats," *Studies in Romanticism*, 23 (1984) pp. 295–315. Copyright © The Trustees of Boston University, by permission of *Studies in Romanticism*; Nelson Hilton, for "Blakean Zen," *Studies in Romanticism*, 24 (1985) pp. 183–200. Copyright © The Trustees of Boston University, by permission of *Studies in Romanticism*; Margaret Homans, for "Bearing Demons: Frankenstein's Circumvention of the Maternal" in *Bearing the Word: Language and Female Experience in Nineteenth-Century Women's Writing* (1986) pp. 100–19, by permission of The University of Chicago Press; Alan Liu, for "The History in 'Imagination'," *English Literary History*, 51 (1984) pp. 505–48, updated in Alan Liu, *Wordsworth: The Sense of History*, Stanford University Press, by permission of The Johns Hopkins University Press and Stanford University Press; Peter J. Manning, for "*Don Juan* and Byron's Imperceptiveness to the English Word," *Studies in Romanticism*, 18 (1979) pp. 207–33. Copyright © The Trustees of Boston University, by permission of *Studies in Romanticism*; Jerome J. McGann, for "Byron and the Anonymous Lyric," *The Byron Journal*, 21 (1993) pp. 27–45, by permission of *The Byron Journal*; Anne K. Mellor, for "A Revolution in Female Manners" from *Romanticism and Gender* (1993) pp. 31–9, by permission of Routledge; Tom Paulin, for "John Clare in Babylon" from *Minotaur: Poetry and the Nation State* (1992) pp. 47–55, by permission of Faber and Faber; Balachandra Rajan, for "The Two *Hyperions*: Compositions and Decompositions" from *The Form of the Unfinished: English Poetics from Spenser to Pound* (1985) pp. 211–49. Copyright © 1985 by Princeton University Press, by permission of Princeton University Press; Tilottama Rajan, for "Deconstruction or Reconstruction: Reading Shelley's *Prometheus Unbound*" from *The Supplement of Reading: Figures of Understanding in Romantic Theory and Practice* (1990) pp. 298–322. Copyright © 1990 by Cornell University, by permission of Cornell University Press; Eve Kosofsky Sedgwick, for "Murder Incorporated: *Confessions of a Justified Sinner*" from *Between Men: English Literature and Male Homosocial Desire* (1985) pp. 97–117, by permission of Columbia University Press; Edward Said, for "Jane Austen and Empire" from *Culture and Imperialism* (1993) pp. 95–119, Chatto & Windus, by permission of Random House UK Ltd. and Aitken, Stone and Wylie Ltd. on behalf of the author; Karen Swann, for " 'Christabel': The Wandering Mother and the Enigma of Form," *Studies in Romanticism*, 23 (1984) pp. 533–53. Copyright © The Trustees of Boston University, by permission of *Studies of Romanticism*; Leon Waldoff, for "Imagination and Growth in the Great Odes" from *Keats and the Silent Work of Imagination* (1985) pp. 99–162, by permission of The University of Illinois Press; Kathleen M. Wheeler, for " 'Kubla Khan' and the Art of Thingifying" from *The Creative Mind in Coleridge's Poetry* (1981) pp. 20–41. Copyright © 1981 by K. M. Wheeler, by permission of Harvard University Press and the author.

Every effort has been made to trace all the copyright holders but if any have been inadvertently overlooked the publishers will be pleased to make the necessary arrangement at the first opportunity.

Oxford
April 1994

Abbreviations

AR	*Annual Register*
Aids	S. T. Coleridge, *Aids to Reflection*
Ages	F. W. J. Schelling, *The Ages of the World* tr. F. de Wolfe Bolman (New York, 1946)
Bate	Walter Jackson Bate, *John Keats* (Cambridge, Mass., 1963)
Bate and Engell	S. T. Coleridge, *Biographia Literaria* ed. Walter Jackson Bate and James Engell (2 vols, Princeton, NJ, 1983)
Birdsall	William Wordsworth, *Descriptive Sketches* ed. Eric Birdsall (Ithaca, NY, 1984)
BNYPL	*Bulletin of the New York Public Library*
BW	*The Works of the Rt. Hon. Edmund Burke* (12 vols, Boston, Mass., 1865–7)
CEY	Mark L. Reed, *Wordsworth: The Chronology of the Early Years: 1770–1799* (Cambridge, Mass., 1967)
CMY	Mark L. Reed, *Wordsworth: The Chronology of the Middle Years: 1800–1815* (Cambridge, Mass., 1975)
Coburn	S. T. Coleridge, *Notebooks* ed. Kathleen Coburn *et al.* (5 vols, New York, 1957–)
EHC	S. T. Coleridge, *The Complete Poetical Works of Samuel Taylor Coleridge* ed. E. H. Coleridge (2 vols, Oxford, 1912)
EiC	*Essays in Criticism*
ELH	*English Literary History*
ELN	*English Language Notes*

Erdman	*The Complete Poetry and Prose of William Blake* ed. David V. Erdman (Berkeley and Los Angeles, Calif., 1982)
Essays	S. T. Coleridge, *Essays on his Times* ed. David V. Erdman (3 vols, Princeton, NJ, 1978)
EY	*The Letters of William and Dorothy Wordsworth: The Early Years 1787–1805* ed. Ernest de Selincourt, revised Chester L. Shaver (Oxford, 1967)
Friend	S. T. Coleridge, *The Friend* ed. Barbara Rooke (2 vols, 1969)
Griggs	*Collected Letters of Samuel Taylor Coleridge* ed. E. L. Griggs (6 vols, Oxford, 1956–71)
Howe	William Hazlitt, *Works* ed. P. P. Howe (21 vols, London, 1930–4)
JEGP	*Journal of English and Germanic Philology*
Jones	*The Letters of Percy Bysshe Shelley* ed. Frederick L. Jones (2 vols, Oxford, 1964)
Lects. 1795	S. T. Coleridge, *Lectures 1795 on Politics and Religion* ed. Lewis Patton and Peter Mann (Princeton, NJ, 1971)
Lay Sermons	S. T. Coleridge, *Lay Sermons* ed. R. J. White (Princeton, NJ, 1972)
McGann and Weller	*The Complete Poetical Works of Lord Byron* ed. Jerome J. McGann and Barry Weller (7 vols, Oxford, 1980–93)
Marchand	*Byron's Letters and Journals* ed. Leslie A. Marchand (12 vols, London, 1973–82)
Masson	*Collected Writings of Thomas De Quincey* ed. David Masson (14 vols, Edinburgh, 1889–90)
MLN	*Modern Language Notes*
MLQ	*Modern Language Quarterly*
Moorman	Mary Moorman, *William Wordsworth: A Biography* (2 vols, Oxford, 1957–65)
MY	*The Letters of William and Dorothy Wordsworth: The Middle Years* ed. Ernest De Selincourt, *i: 1806–11*, rev. Mary Moorman (1969); *ii: 1812–20*, rev. Mary Moorman and Alan G. Hill (1970)
Norton *Prel.*	*The Prelude: 1799, 1805, 1850* ed. Jonathan Wordsworth, M. H. Abrams and Stephen Gill (New York, 1979)
Owen and Smyser	*The Prose Works of William Wordsworth* ed. W. J. B. Owen and Jane Worthington Smyser (3 vols, Oxford, 1974)

PJ	William Godwin, *An Enquiry Concerning Political Justice* (2 vols, London, 1793)
PL	John Milton, *Paradise Lost*
P. Lects.	*The Philosophical Lectures of Samuel Taylor Coleridge* ed. Kathleen Coburn (London, 1949)
PMLA	*Publications of the Modern Language Association of America*
Prel.	*The Prelude, or Growth of a Poet's Mind* ed. Ernest de Selincourt, revised by Stephen Gill (Oxford, 1970)
RES	*Review of English Studies*
Rights of Man	Thomas Paine, *The Rights of Man, Part One and Part Two* ed. H. Collins (Harmondsworth, 1969)
Rollins	John Keats, *The Letters of John Keats, 1814–1821* ed. Hyder E. Rollins (2 vols, Cambridge, Mass., 1958)
SC	*Shelley and His Circle* ed. K. N. Cameron and Donald H. Reiman (8 vols, Cambridge, Mass., 1961–86)
Shawcross	S. T. Coleridge, *Biographia Literaria* ed. J. Shawcross (2 vols, Oxford, 1907)
Shelley's Friends	*Maria Gisborne and Edward E. Williams: Shelley's Friends* ed. Frederick L. Jones (Norman, 1951)
SiR	*Studies in Romanticism*
SPP	*Shelley's Poetry and Prose* ed. Donald H. Reiman and Sharon B. Powers (New York, 1977)
Stillinger	*The Poems of John Keats* ed. Jack Stillinger (Cambridge, Mass., 1978)
T	*The Times*
TLS	*Times Literary Supplement*
Weiskel	Thomas Weiskel, *The Romantic Sublime: Studies in the Structure and Psychology of Transcendence* (Baltimore, Md., 1976)
WP	Geoffrey H. Hartman, *Wordsworth's Poetry, 1787–1814* (2nd ed., New Haven, Conn., 1987)
WPW	*The Poetical Works of William Wordsworth* ed. Ernest de Selincourt and Helen Darbishire (5 vols, Oxford, 1940–9)

Blake

1

Blakean Zen

NELSON HILTON

It is essential to understand that the level of information which escapes the observer is largely left to [her or] his own discretion.

Jean-Pierre Dupuy, "Myths of the Information Society"

Johnson's *Dictionary* defines "system" as "any complexure or combination of many things acting together." For Blake, the word could be synonymous with "monotony," but, nonetheless, the state of the world drives Los to "Create a System or be enslav'd by another Mans" (*Jerusalem* 10.20).[1] A system, evidently, is greater than its particular creator, for we also read of Los "Striving with Systems to deliver Individuals from those Systems" (*Jerusalem* 11.5). And here we find ourselves already in the mental strife of Blake's systems, hearing Los both "strive" or contend *with* (against) enslaving systems and, at the same time, "strive" or labor *with* (by means of) them – striving, in the latter instance, to deliver individuals from his own several systems.[2] Considering the implied dynamic, we see that Blake's "system" will be processed by our own, that the work of systems is to process, or strive with, each other. These processing systems can be characterized as intentional, since we ascribe to them beliefs, desires, and epistemic horizons: we read Blake for some reason, and well-known passages from his texts generate a sense of intention on their part. Finally, we see that the interactions or processings themselves take place within the frame of another system, and so on in infinite extension and regression.

Even before opening Blake's books we are, already, deep in the folds of some structure of interrelations, and the seemingly straightforward task of description grows difficult indeed if we hope to describe levels "acting together" – not to mention describing the systems acting against each other and the role of our own system(s) in the melee. A level lies within a given horizon or frame; as a continuum of internal *in*difference, it offers, at least, a respite from continual shifting between different levels. Like the horizon, a level exists as a function of perception; when, for analogy, we leave the plane of the planet earth, the terrestrial horizon first expands, then contracts as the shrinking earth englobes itself behind us and different kinds of "horizons" become more important (like the speed of light). The idea of "levels" is borrowed here from work in cognitive science, where it dominates the conceptualization of information and information-processing. For one laborer in those fields, "a level can be defined objectively as a particular description of input, contrasting with other possible descriptions"; a level may also be treated "as the output available from a particular stage of processing."[3] Given levels of input and output, the processing itself appears to work through parallel "levels" as well (these are levels of levels) – hence we can speak of the simultaneous affect of multiple dimensions of a stimulus. To stave off the madness of proliferating extensions and regressions, we "chunk," or shrink, together the levels not directly before us (this "chunking" or shrinking itself manifesting a move to another level). The mode of chunking, however – the "axis" or logic of subordination – is as arbitrary as the signifier/signified relationship and, like it, reflects learned response (feedback of some kind). As words have no direct relation to things, so the "chunks" of image, belief, perception, and so on have no direct relation to reality; perception becomes a localized function of past and present environment. "Once we see perception as depending on rules of [usually unconscious] inference and knowledge," writes R. L. Gregory, "it is hardly possible to hold that perception is directly related to the reality that we perceive" – or to the text that we read, for that matter.[4] Just so Blake scorns Wordsworth's mentalist fantasy of an exquisite fit between the external world and the mind (Erdman 667): exquisite fit, rather, between projector and projected.

Blake's word for level is "fold," which denotes both an enclosure or yard (the primary entry in Johnson and the *OED*), and a ply, bend, or leaf of some material that may be doubled on itself. The word nicely balances the principal conceptual issue concerning levels: are they discontinuous, like so many cowpens and sheepfolds scattered in isolation over the surface of the earth? Or are they continuous, joined somewhere like folds of fabric (or text) along a crease? Or are they both continuous and discontinuous, depending on the level of perception, which itself may be either or both?

Consider again the folds of Blake's texts. On one level, we experience their brute materiality: paper printed with ink, the very words indenting the surface.[5] Even on this level they differentiate themselves from other objects of their general class (printed books) in being lettered by hand and printed by relief-etching; furthermore they differentiate themselves as well from their own specific class, so we have (the description establishes the violation) seven *unique copies* of *The [First] Book of Urizen*. Within each work, we recognize a level of physical textual organization: the words, for instance, placed in a certain order, bearing certain shapes. And here, again, many other, different levels – are the little rearing horses and flying birds "words" (or are the words "pictures")? The physical textual level (like any other level) constantly interacts with the folds "around" it, as illustrated by *Urizen*, pl. 4, line 24, which no editor adequately transposes to the typographical level:

> 6. Here alone I in books formd of me-
> —tals

On one level, we see that material constraints of space force this long line to hyphenate the final word (though these constraints do not occasion similar measures in equally long, or longer, lines elsewhere in the same plate!). *On another level*, it is logical in this book *of* Urizen for the protagonist, speaking of his books, to describe them and himself as "I in books formd of me–." Logical, at least, to raise that possibility. Such a conjunction of levels of explication ("unfolding") produces an experience of overdetermination; that is, awareness that the particular operant level of interpretation or mode of understanding is inadequate to a perception of the whole phenomenon in question (i.e. the phenomenon is more whole than our perception). This zen-like experience, more arresting than a thought or a reflection, becomes Blake's inestimable gift to the reader ("because it rouzes the faculties to act" [Erdman 702]). In terms of the reader, we can say that Blake's heuristic program continually overloads his or her system, vividly indicating that that system needs reorganization. In terms of Blake's text, we can agree with Umberto Eco that "there is no openness at a given level which is not sustained and improved by analogous operations at all other levels."[6]

Returning to the labelling of folds in the text, we also recognize a level of narrative: the textual elements assembled sequentially suggest a story or series of events. But any story makes sense only as much as we (think we) understand it, as much as we can relate and add it to stories already known. And hence the established industry of finding parallels, allusions, analogies to make Blake's stories safe in terms of the already known (*Paradise Lost*, or Genesis, for example). This produces many levels of symbolic interpretation, some of which, like *Fearful Symmetry*, succeed for a while even in displacing the text. The "symbolic" reading reflects, in a sense, the opposite to the experience of overdetermination: imposing an understood field, such a reading predetermines experience of the text. But now, the very fact of the divergent symbolic determinings of Blake attests to the overdetermination of the stories themselves, and for any thoughtful reader the idea of some convincing symbolic interpretation of anything called "Blake's myth" is impossible. Instead, we grow increasingly at ease with the consummate *bricolage* which has welded together units and symbols, chunks, from wildly divergent discourses to fashion Blake's works. The very stories themselves, as Donald Ault finds in *The Four Zoas*, continually reconstitute themselves even as they tell of structures and figures continually reconstituting themselves.[7]

Let us look again at *The Book of Urizen*, acknowledging the rich processings of the text by Robert E. Simmons, W. J. T. Mitchell, Harald A. Kittel, Kay and Roger Easson, and Leslie Tannenbaum, among others.[8] These readers testify that the text has a powerful effect – that it "compels creation, rather than conveying a copy"; that it "requires us to mediate"; and that it exercises a "kind of manipulation of our perception."[9] Such various individual encounters with the text also leave the new reader a wealth of association, including, for example, "The identification of Los with the sun and Urizen with the earth," Los "playing the roles of Abraham, Laius, and Jupiter," Urizen as "both God and Satan"; an "Urizen-Elohim" and a "Los-Jahweh," along with a "Los-Cain" and an "Urizen-Abel"; and the idea that Urizen is both the "poetic embodiment of Locke's *self*" and "the Lockean *cause*."[10] One processing concludes that "The general structure of *Urizen* is modeled after the three-phase time sequence which lies behind the narrative of *Paradise Lost*"; another, that "Blake transforms the first three chapters of Genesis into a coherent and dramatic narrative that condenses all that is contained in that book"; still another, that "The imagery of the nine chapters . . . is derived from the nine-month gestation cycle."[11] And we hardly need to compare accounts to come up with such an *embarras de richesse*, since each processing can generate its own surplus:

> The central event of Chapter v . . . alludes not only to the Narcissus myth but to the growth of an embryo from a placenta, the division of male and female as recounted in Plato's *Symposium*, the birth of Athena from Jove's forehead, the origin of the moon thrown off from the sun, the beginning of courtly love, the growth of Los's testicles, the fall in the garden, the oozing of a single drop of blood from a wound, Adam's (wet) dream of Eve, the crucifixion, Milton's view of the earth as a ball hanging beneath heaven, and a simple fainting spell, probably from vertigo (Simmons (1970) 172).

Another reader's system with a slightly different intertextual orientation adds other associations. It senses, for example, that Blake adapts Erasmus Darwin's late eighteenth-century version of the big bang: "If these innumerable and immense suns thus rising out of Chaos are supposed to have thrown out their attendant planets by new explosions, as they ascended; and those their respective satellites, filling in a moment the immensity of space with light and motion, a grander idea cannot be conceived by the mind of man."[12] Or it feels that the mysterious lines, "5. The dead heard the voice of the child / And began to awake from sleep" (*Urizen* 20.26–7), echo Jesus in John 5:25: "The hour is coming, and now is, when the dead shall hear the voice of the Son of God," and "all that are in graves ... shall come forth." But does this association make the lines less mysterious? Or would they be less odd if we created a context to argue that the child is the sun (the son of the Son) who "speaks" to vegetable nature? Did those who read the lines before, without the echo, "really" read them? Do we read them now?

All these associations, allusions, analogies, correspondences, echoes, parallels, indicate that there are at least several layers making up Urizen's multi-storied text.[13] Are these levels related to one another in some way such that we can actually imagine an horizon to the text of Urizen? Annotating Swedenborg's *Divine Love and Divine Wisdom*, Blake suggests that the relationship between levels cannot be demonstrated, that the folds are discontinuous. Rather than "level" or "fold," Swedenborg uses the term "degree" to distinguish between Natural, Spiritual, and Celestial levels in man. Blake picks up the term and writes:

> Is it not evident that one degree will not open the other & that science will not open intellect but that they are discrete & not continuous ... you cannot demonstrate one degree by the other for how can science be brought to demonstrate intellect, without making them continuous and not discrete[?] (Erdman 605–6)

Given such a "discrete and not continuous" world, for the reader as for Urizen-Los:

> All the wisdom & joy of life:
> Roll like a sea around him,
> Except what his little orbs
> Of sight by degrees unfold.
>
> (*Urizen* 13.29–32)

Everything rolls like a sea, except what we see: the degrees, folds, or levels we project become a form of blindness and obscurity.[14] To unfold – literally, to *explicate* – wisdom and joy produces shadows ("unfold ... dark visions," "unfold ... darkness"), and by the end of the poem the original waters of wisdom and joy are seen/tasted to have turned to salt ("and the salt ocean rolled englob'd"). If our processing of *Urizen* does not "unfold" or organize the levels into some unified field, then we ought to study what it does do –

how that processing jumps between levels, emitting, through its varying attention, the light by which we perceive its shifting. Take, for example, the lines describing "the immortal" in plate 10. One assumes at first that the subject is Urizen – yet it is the "Eternal Prophet" who "turn'd restless" fifteen lines before:

> 5. Restless turnd the immortal inchain'd
> Heaving dolorous! anguish'd! unbearable
> Till a roof shaggy wild inclos'd
> In an orb, his fountain of thought.

> (10.31–4)

Normal processing may level the attribution "restless turnd" into coherence, but what happens with "unbearable"? Unbearable to whom? and who writes this? This continual wrenching of *Urizen* heals not, and it opens profound narrative anomalies. From the moderately strange cartoon of some "Eternal Prophet" chaining (whatever that may signify!) some lower-case "immortal," we move to the apparently direct – and so, more strange – declaration that, whatever it was, it was "unbearable" until "inclos'd," as "it" must be still at present. Yet that unbearable state is what, up to that point, we were bearing, at least in our inclosed mind/brains. The micro-structures keep contradicting our memory of the text, our "propositional representation of its meaning ... plus the inferences necessary to assure the coherence of this propositional network."[15]

Once we begin to see Urizen in terms of "levels" (or different orders of levels), possibilities proliferate. We no longer devour the text, but begin to produce it, to play it. The "genesis" that many see in *Urizen* dissolves into just so many various stories, including ones that could be labelled the "anthropological" (4.1 ff., thunder suddenly perceived as "words articulate" of some mighty Other leads, eventually, to morality through conceptions of "Sin"); the "biological" (5.28 ff., the womb; 10.37 ff., the seven Ages; 18.1 ff., "the globe of life blood"); the "psychological" (20.8 ff., the chain of Jealousy); the "parodic" (25.34 ff., "Six days they. Shrunk up from existence"); the "cosmological," including the "solar"; and the "self-referential." The book of origins (from Latin *origin-em*, rise) turns into the book of you, (already) risen, and your reasoning about "origin" through various such closed accounts (*Urizen* seems to have beheld what we became). But, as J. Z. Young observes, "the fact that we want to know about origins may tell us much about the way our brains work." He adds – words that could serve as *Urizen*'s epigraph – "the real question is not 'What is the universe and who made it?', but 'what are we humans and what is it possible for us to know?'"[16] It might even seem that *Urizen* offers as many "origins" as it does levels of reference, as many levels of reference as there are accounts of the book itself. The question *Urizen* poses is, then, "What are we readers, and how do we make sense?"

The cosmological-solar and self-referential offer exhilarating levels of play. The first has already appeared with our earlier reference to Blake's use of Darwin's big-bang to characterize one aspect of urizenation. Blake's fascination with the sun and light can be detailed in his reading of Swedenborg, who argues "That without two Suns, the one living and the other dead, there can be no Creation" (Erdman 605). To this Blake adds, "False philosophy according to the letter, but true according to the spirit." For Swedenborg, the dead, material sun is our visible natural sun, which serves to suggest a correspondence to the spiritual sun. To conceptualize the advent and nature of this dead sun, Blake also gave close attention as well to treatments of the origin of sun and light in Milton, Genesis, and Boehme – with the post-Newtonian insight that the birth of the sun also saw the institution of gravity, or "attraction" (for Newton and Einstein as well, the nature of light is a central theoretical problem). The sun appears to be identified with the figure of Los – or, as the engraver reads, sol – and many readers see Los as some kind of emissary from "Eternals," as the figure of imagination who arrives after and in opposition to Urizen. So began the old reading of Blake's myth. But in the minute texture, the primary process of the language, the arrival of Los is well cued by a dense array of nearly subliminal anagrams, paragrams, paronomasias:

Obscure, shadowy, void, *sol*itary	(2.4)
Lo, a shadow of horror is risen	(3.1)
Self-c*los*d, all-repelling: what Demon	(3.3)
. . . Urizen, *so* *n*am'd	
That *sol*itary one in Immensity	(3.41–2)
from the depths of dark *sol*itude	(4.6)
for a *sol*id without fluctuation	(4.11)
a wide world of *sol*id obstruction	(4.23)
3. *Sun*d'ring, dark'ning, thund'ring	(5.3)
wide a*sun*der rolling	(5.6)

Finally, "the vast world of Urizen" appears, "like a black globe / View'd by sons of Eternity" (5.33–4),

8. And Los round the dark globe of
Urizen

So the line appears in Blake's text (not in any editor's), literally posing Urizen as the "ground" of Los's "figure." What appears is, on one level, a *round Los* or sol as *the dark globe* of Urizen, the sun of reason. Plate 9 shows this agonized Los about to lose a conspicuously spherical head, to become, no doubt, what looks to cold Earth wanderers like the sensual, smiling sun.[17] This emphasis on the sun, which permutates through the book, "connects" (we could say, rather, vortexes) to other levels. For to focus on the sun, as Jacques Derrida illuminates in "La Mythologie Blanche," means opening the idea of metaphor itself: the idea of crossing from one level to another.[18] Discontinuity becomes relative (it might be useful to slow down the vortex of Derrida's thought to realize that [on one level, as always] here, as elsewhere, he mines and metaphorizes the insight that perception is an hypothesis grounded in some code; hence, perhaps, his Delphic observation that "perception does not exist"). The sun, or Los, becomes an important image of the energy, the unknown informing power, which the other levels need to begin operation: the anthropological, biological, psychological, and parodic *Urizens* are all sons of the sun. But the sun itself is a son. The "sons of Eternity" end as Urizen's "eternal sons": "Flam'd out!" (23.13–19), mere "sons of Urizen" (28.11). "Shrinking" in one level becomes "rising" in another.

The second delightful level of play is the self-referential; together with the cosmological fold, the self-referential can be thought of as the last consciously-recognizable bracket of *Urizen*. As brackets, these two levels represent inversions of each other, working together to inclose the text for the reader: at *Urizen*'s center, self-referentiality – at its circumference, cosmological metaphorization (or vice versa). Urizen's self-referentiality takes several forms, beginning with the multiple attributions of "of" in the title: Urizen's book? A book about Urizen? A book made from some material called "Urizen" ("books formd of me- / -tals")? A slight cross to the "l" of "sleep" in plate 7 (copy G) pushes the strange transitive or equally odd passive, "laid," to a textual comment on *Urizen*'s own metal existence: "10. But Urizen laid in a stony steep / Unorganiz'd. rent from Eternity." This location borders on the "home" of *The Marriage of Heaven and Hell*: "on the abyss of the five senses, where a flat sided steep frowns over the present world. I saw a mighty Devil folded in black clouds, hovering on the sides of the rock, with corroding fires he wrote . . ." (Erdman 35). Being "rent," our admittedly "unorganiz'd" work (Urizen) declares itself broken from the beginning of time, freshly torn from "Eternity," and a kind of return rendered from Eternity for this particular flat or storey – these plates which give Eternity a temporary home. *Urizen* instantiates such different possibilities (*OED*, "rent": v.^{2}, ppl. a; v.^{2}; sb.^{1}). The paradox deepens as we see Urizen,

> His prolific delight obscurd more & more
> In dark secresy hiding in surgeing
> Sulphureous fluid his phantasies

> (10.12–14)

When, before, Urizen had "written the secrets of wisdom / The secrets of dark contemplation" (4.25–6), "Rage siez'd the strong" and expressed itself "in whirlwinds of sulphurous smoke" (4.47). Then Urizen itself became "the surging sulphureous / Perturbed Immortal mad raging / In whirlwinds" (8.3–5). Creation on one level is decreation on another ("continually building & continually decaying"); prolific delight is hardened and obscured (the term is usually associated with Los) into mundane form in the light of a Boehme-influenced "sulpher Sun" (*America* b.7). *Urizen* is only Urizen's phantasy, or shadow ("The representation of a body by which light is intercepted," writes Johnson). Reaching the formulation "that life liv'd upon death," Urizen recognizes that life lives upon him/it/self (23.37): he/it is the ground for life's figure, a part of a larger dialectic. The layout and coloring of plate 23 emphasize the word "death" as a kind of caption to the figure of Urizen directly beneath it; elsewhere we see the Eternals identify Urizen with "death" ("The Eternals said: what is this? Death / Urizen") and we read of "the death image of Urizen."[19]

Self-referentiality in *Urizen* is also signalled by the first and last illustrations. In the first, under "URIZEN," we see the familiar sad figure, his face bound into a tree-trunk-like beard that grows from (and flows as a river of tears down to) his ground of a book. On the last plate, eyes now cracked open, shoulders and arms slightly raised, the aged figure ponders the thick net that he both holds and sunders. But this plate – the point can be made *because* of the deliberately reversed left-right images of the figure's visible foot – is not a mirror of the first, however much it leads us to reflect on the beginning. Rather than standing transfixed between two mirrors, we find ourselves processing a strange loop, where, as Douglas Hofstadter imagines it – "by moving upwards (or downwards) [or toward 'the end'] through the levels of some hierarchial system, we unexpectedly find ourselves right back where we started."[20] "Self"-referentiality becomes a curious twist in the ongoing, varying (sliding) reflection of one level in another by means of a third:

$$\text{reflection} : \frac{\text{reflector}}{\text{reflected}} \; :: \; \text{self} : \frac{\dfrac{\text{reflector}}{\text{reflected}}}{\text{REFLECTION}}$$

Self-referentiality manifests *Urizen*'s oft-cited "ironic satire" taken to another level – a level where irony's aporia or abyss appears as just a boring infinite regress (or worse, closed loop) in an overly rigid system. In Hofstadter's view, the "strange loop" represents "an interaction between levels in which the top level reaches back down towards the bottom level and influences it, while at the same time being itself determined by the bottom level." The "level-crossing" entailed by the strange loop usually takes the shape of an undecidable proposition, which, in turn, asserts "its own nontheoremhood [or, undecidability] in some system via some code" (these would be the meta-system and meta-code to those in which the undecidability occurred); it was the goal of deconstruction to point out that undecidable proposition as embodying the nexus where the text is unconsciously, umbilically linked to the privileged meta-system of deconstructive reference, language. But (theoretically) through its invocation of the inscribing powers of physics and biology, and (practically) through its non-verbal pictorial discourse, *The Book of Urizen* precludes any such single-minded unravelling. And we are delivered into the urizenic strife of system and (meta?) system most dramatically with the Preludium.

The Preludium offers *Urizen*'s most emphatic moment of internal difference; as Mitchell nicely observes, it is the one plate where "the text is *not* divided into two columns . . . the only plate where text interpenetrates design . . . and the only plate where human figures make positive contact."[21] The seven lines of text bear many constructions. For example: is to write "of Urizen" to write, as the Preludium announces, "Of the primeval Priests assum'd power"? or is it "Of" that power, as the text continues, "When Eternals spurn'd back his religion"? What "power" is in question? (Urizen, in Chapter 1, is "the dark power," "An activity.")[22] What assumptions go into the reader's determination of the priestly "assum'd power"? (Johnson defines "assume" as: "1/ To take; 2/ To take upon one's self; 3/To arrogate; to claim or seize unjustly; 4/ To suppose something granted without proof;" and "5/ To apply to one's own use; to appropriate.") And then, what kind of "Eternals" *spurn?* (and if they "spurn," surely they can "rent"). What kind of "place" can be "Obscure, shadowy, void, solitary"? This interaction of minute verbal particulars and vast mental possibilities illustrates one strange loop of mutual interdetermination between levels. Some power crafted these multiplexed significations, a power that seems to speak most nakedly in (or is it through?) the Preludium's concluding lines:

> Eternals I hear your call gladly,
> Dictate swift winged words, & fear not
> To unfold your dark visions of torment.

The more we reread, the more the lines come apart at the seams. The Book purported to be "of" Urizen, of the "Priests" assum'd power, but addresses instead the Eternals who spurned it. These same "Eternals" are "heard," then commanded and cajoled with standard formulae from Homer ("winged words") and the Bible ("fear not").[23] And, to cap things off, the speaker – or, rather, staging-power – already knows that what will be unfolded are "dark visions of torment." But who is this speaker?

Only one speaker in the text addresses Eternals ("Why will you die O Eternals") and uses singular self-reference, not to mention diction close to that of the power in the Preludium ("Lo! I unfold my darkness"). Of course, "'It is Urizen,'" who, this suggests, is at the omega and alpha of its book's strange loop. Only "it" could speak the Preludium, and only after the involution it records. As reader-processors, we reach the end of the book, with its proffered jump to Genesis 1 and *Paradise Lost* I, only to realize that in comprehending the possibility of that jump we have already made it. *Our* continuation is the Preludium, which we now recognize as the final offering, before the whole, of the tragic insight of the end.[24] The book begins where it left off. But as we keep cycling through the loop, through time, we find ourselves each time slightly changed and each passage slightly different because of the richness of the text.

We perceive new connections within the text and, as we return from other readings elsewhere, new connections between the text and other texts. These new perceptions constitute our ongoing processing of the text – a strange loop which shows the committed reader that it is not quite the same "self" who first looked into Urizen with wild surmise. The experience is not just a matter of grasping new data to be filed away toward a unified view of Urizen – the experience increasingly leads us to discontinuous forms in our understanding. We become more sensitive to the forms of allusion, to the quantum-mechanics of Blake's letter shapes and punctuation, and to the disruption caused by our own too-close observation (perhaps no closer than the engraver's concentrated attention); so we bring more and more to the text, but, at the same time, the text becomes increasingly out of focus, or, rather, multi-focused. "The system's own richness," remarks Hofstadter, "brings about its own downfall. The downfall occurs essentially because the system is powerful enough to have self-referential sentences." The system has enough power, because, in fact, there is neither "self" nor center but, rather, an interacting structure of cells coded into levels which in some places are *both same and other* or are at the moment of change: "self"-reference happens in a difference of time and identity of space. The space within the horizon of the book (to use Paul Mann's phrase[25]) refers, finally, to its annihilation in the reader, who is, in time, to be "you rizen."

Such plays on words – does "Urizen" in his/its text name "character" or "book"? – have a large role in Blake's continual destabilizing (temporalizing) of the sign. The pictures, as well, illustrate instability. Apparent destabilization can, however, also be considered as an effect of multichannel encoding, much as the brain system is thought to work: "current thoughts, it seems, coexist not *serially* in a stream of consciousness, not as distinct episodes . . . but in parallel, in the processes of control."[26] Instability of one level can be the indicator of multi-stability of a larger system which we cannot grasp at once (on its several levels, in parallel). From yet another level, our hard-won vision of multi-stability resolves into one of mere redundancy. But for now we need to see "Urizen" as layered, in part, by the elements $Urizen_1$ (title of work in hand), $Urizen_2$ (name or epithet of apparent "protagonist"); $Urizen_3$ (the association "horizon"); $Urizen_4$ (the association "your reason"); $Urizen_5$ ("death"); $Urizen_6$ ("An activity unknown"); etc. "Decoding" or "understanding" the permutations of inter-interactions between such complex verbal cells poses a formidable problem, for, as J. Z. Young says of messages processed by the brain, "we must be careful to avoid the conception that there is some final stage where the message is 'understood'. There is no central place in the brain where this occurs. The 'decoding' is completed only by action. A dog recognizes a bone by gnawing it" (p. 57). The Eassons act out the paradox involved in the reader's recognition of *Urizen* when they say that "It is a book written to liberate us from books," only to add that the allusions "stimulate us to read further" (pp. 88, 91).

Urizen is a process that labors to bring forth processing, an activity attempting to produce action. Reading *Urizen* today we confront the cognitive truism that "for both perception and meaning of language, we have to give far more weight to processes – thinking and perceiving processes.... The problem is to discover just what these internal processes of language and of perception may be" (Gregory (1981) 422). Such concerns invite us to call the dull mill of literary appreciation "Egypt" and leave it, seeking instead the fresher fields of signs and Science. As we behold the weird and complicated structure of Blake's texts, like *The Book of Urizen*, we become not only what we behold, but our rich and strange ways of making their sense as well. This arduous process of becoming to ourselves appears in *Urizen*'s pervasive "brooding" and "labouring," as though the very work were to induce both our birth of intellect and Urizen to go forth, as once he did, "On the human soul to cast / The seed of eternal science" (*Ahania* 5.33–4). *Urizen* helps us, finally, to appreciate the power and will of an Original Poetic Genius that went into its creation and that goes into our creating of it. For Original Poetic Genius (that triple redundancy) must lie in those obscure internal processes that we cannot monitor ("unknown, obscure") – it is, to use the pertinent description Hofstadter emphasizes at the conclusion of his book: "A Vortex Where All Levels Cross."

In his "Preface to Homer," Pope identifies the poet's fancy or power of invention as the "Poetical Fire" which is the principal quality of a great work ("in *Homer*, and in him only, it burns every where clearly, and every where irresistibly").[27] But the "dark power" or "activity" named Urizen describes his laboured self-creation as a struggle with those same flames: "First I fought with fire; consum'd / Inwards, into a deep world within" (4.14–15). That inner world redounded as his "wide world of solid obstruction," a world which then "teemed vast enormities" (23.2). These disconnected (yet yoked) enormities, "similitudes / Of a foot, or a hand, or a head / Or a heart, or an eye," take us close to the infancy of Science in echoing the distinctly unscientific projection of a Lord God who, Newton writes in the conclusion to *his* "System of the World," is "all similar, all eye, all ear, all brain, all arm, all power to perceive, to understand, and to act; but in a manner not at all human, in a manner not at all corporeal, in a manner utterly unknown to us."[28]

It is the penultimate moment in the history of Urizen, the darkness before the recognition of that earlier shrinking when in the beginning man chunked inaccessible levels into God(s), then repressed that knowledge in order to secure a meta-reference to ground our fearful subjectivity. But, whatever the errors and reasons, Urizen hungers for knowledge and so prompts the creation of the enlightenment world of Science, with "the new *function* which it attributes to the mind of man."[29] Remarkably enough, it is the Eternals who weave the woof of Science after the Old Testament model of the veil for the Tabernacle, or "Tent," "with golden hooks fastend in the pillars" ("pillars ... their hooks were of gold," Ex. 26.32; 36.36).[30] The strangeness of this scene needs to be absorbed more fully than it has been, for it is no simple allegory of "good," unfallen "Eternals" acting to complete man's fall through his creation of Science. Rather, where man, following the instructions of his projected God, made a veil to curtain off and so define a Holy of Holies, now the Eternals, following the instructions of some unidentified speaker(s), curtain off another Holy of Holies, the space of the rest of *Urizen*. The "infinite labour" of the Eternals also links them to Urizen, "In enormous labours occupied," and to "the falling Mind" which "Incessant ... labour'd / Organizing itself" (*Urizen* 3.22; *Los* 4.49). Like man before his projected Eternals, the Eternals are "petrified" with human, all too human, "Wonder, awe, fear, astonishment" (18.13). Ergo: we have met the Eternals, and they are we. And, to conclude their and our "intention," we read (beginning with a curious comma),

> 10. The Eternals, closed the tent
> They beat down the stakes the cords
> Stretch'd for a work of eternity;
> No more Los beheld Eternity.
>
> (19.46–20.2)

Of course, the intertext in Isaiah sees this as a happy state:

> ... thine eyes shall see Jerusalem a quiet habitation, a tabernacle that shall not be taken down; not one of the stakes thereof shall ever be removed, neither shall any of the cords thereof be broken. (33.20)

So we see "eternity," not "Eternity" – or its mercy, time.

We move daily further into the mind's expanding imagination of itself and its situation – through Derrida's strictures on the inescapable logocentrism of language and Suzanne Langer's thesis that "the limits of language are not the last limits of experience, and things inaccessible to language may have their own forms of conception," through the paradoxical multiple worlds of quantum mechanics and R. L. Gregory's conclusion that "all observation depends on assumptions and that no assumptions can be independently justified."[31] We move, with the evolution of Science, further into the study of the mind and the observer, the status of observations, descriptions, and language. And while much of "literature" begins to shrink to a level of entertaining or archaeologically-interesting traces of mimesis, *The Book of Urizen*, like the rest of Blake's experiments in and parables of perception, comes increasingly into view. The reason is not just Blake's prophetic sense of "U," that is, you and I, readers; and not just his involvement with Science, or his genuinely meta-linguistic imagination; most of all the reason today is "his" selfless (which embraces "ironic" and "satiric") exploration and awareness of self-referentiality (which includes irony and satire). As Science begins to look at itself, it assumes the dimensions and the power of Blake's "Imagination" and "Intellect." As Blake suggests in an annotation already quoted, "Science" ("Knowledge" would be the dominant late-eighteenth-century denotation) cannot demonstrate intellect – but through self-referentiality it can become it. Hofstadter writes that once the "ability for self-reference is attained, the system has a hole which is tailor-made for itself; the hole takes the features of the system into account and uses them against the system." So, perhaps, do Blake's systems strive with themselves to deliver, which is to annihilate, ourselves. The "hole" is not torn into the book by an ideal reading; rather, any responsive, empirical reading finds the hole already there. And enters. Urizen's self-referential activity insures that his system can never represent itself totally; it is, irreducibly, open to the present process. Like "Reason or the ratio of all we have already known," *Urizen* "is not the same that it shall be when we know more" ("There is no natural religion"b), when "we" are no more:

> Thus, like the creatures of the coral reef, each reading contributes its lifeless carapace to the body of tradition on which its successors will move.[32]

NOTES

1 Blake is quoted from Erdman.
2 On the phrase "striving with systems" as "an emblem for the contradictory determinations of Blake's poetry" see also Shaviro (1982) 229–50.
3 Treisman (1979) 302.

4 Gregory (1981) 395.

5 The importance of this level is evident when we contrast the work of Roman Ingarden, who conceives of the artistic work as a "many-layered formation" or "stratified structure." For Ingarden, the base level is "the stratum of verbal sounds and phonetic formulation." The printed text "does not belong to the elements of the literary work of art itself . . . but merely constitutes its physical foundation." The "printed format," he admits, does play a "modifying role," but in his ideal phenomenology of reading, that may be discarded as "a certain contamination." Such an attitude serves to remind us at the outset – at the ground level, as it were – of the radical orientation of Blake's project (see Ingarden (1973) 12ff.).

6 Eco (1979) 39.

7 Ault (1986).

8 See Simmons (1970); Mitchell (1969) and (1978), esp. 107–64; Kittel (1978); Blake (1978); and Tannenbaum (1982), esp. 210–24.

9 Simmons (1970) 172; Mitchell (1978) 164; Blake (1978) 90.

10 Simmons (1970) 153; Mitchell (1978) 127, 131; Tannenbaum (1982) 294, 213; Kittel (1978) 120, 123.

11 Mitchell (1978) 123; Tannenbaum (1982) 201; Blake (1978) 71.

12 Darwin (1791), note to i. 107. One might compare Darwin's image to the recent account by Weinberg (1977) 5: "In the beginning was an explosion . . . which occurred simultaneously everywhere, filling all space from the beginning, with every particle of matter rushing apart from every other particle."

13 The Eassons, for two, point to "Blake's extensive, interconnected layering of allusion" (Blake (1978) 94).

14 Compare Davies (1982) 87: "What we normally regard as empty space is in fact a sea of restless activity, full of all sorts of impermanent matter; electrons, protons, neutrons, photons, mesons, neutrinos, and many more species of matter, each existing for only the briefest fraction of time." Note also the speaker in Blake's poem to Butts: "My eyes more & more / Like a Sea without shore / Continue Expanding" (Erdman 713).

15 Kintsch (1979) 221.

16 Young (1978) 31, 33.

17 Copy G emphasizes the idea through the flaming red circle of Los's lips and the fiery orb of a tongue within, his glowing solar irises surrounding black spots of pupils, and his flaming hair.

18 Derrida (1974). Derrida writes, "Everything in talk about metaphor which comes through the sign *eidos*, with the whole system attached to this word, is articulated on the analogy between *our* looking and sensible looking, between the intelligible and the visible sun" (55).

19 *Urizen* 6.9–10, 15.1–2; Erdman continues the oddity of adding a hyphen to make "death-image" (if one were going to add anything, it should be a dash!).

20 Hofstadter (1980) 10; following quotations are from 709, 708, 470 and 713.

21 Mitchell (1978) 111.

22 "Power" is a key word, and Kittel does not go far enough in exploring the possibilities of Blake's response to this important Lockean term. In describing the second and third of the "Three sorts of qualities in bodies," Locke offers

one instance of "assumed" power. He writes, "*sensible* qualities" reflect "the power that is in any body by reason of its insensible primary qualities, to operate after a peculiar manner on any of our senses". Power recurs through the discussion, and the reader is never quite sure if the power is in the body (material) or in our senses. See Locke (1975) Bk. 2, ch. 8, sect. 23.

23 The formula "epea pteroenta" appears over fifty times in the *Iliad*, over sixty times in the *Odyssey*. It is, however, very rarely translated "winged words" in the seventeenth and eighteenth centuries; indeed, Pope never uses the phrase, and Cowper prefers "wing'd accents." I suspect that Urizen's "winged words" points to Blake's close friendship at that time with Fuseli, who had just completed revising Cowper's Homer for Joseph Johnson. "Fear not" appears over seventy times in the Bible, often spoken by or attributed to the Lord in the Old Testament: "fear not, for I am with thee" (Gen. 26: 24, *et al.*). In the New Testament, Joseph is told to "fear not to take to thee Mary"; the shepherds outside Bethlehem at the Nativity are told, by an angel: "Fear not: for, behold, I bring you good tidings of great joy"; and, for a last example which sounds particularly apropos of *Urizen*, an angel tells the women coming to the sepulchre: "Fear not ye: for I know that ye seek Jesus, which was crucified. He is not here: for he is risen" (Matt. 1: 20; Luke 2: 10; Matt. 28: 5–6).

24 Nietzsche writes in *The Birth of Tragedy*,

...the periphery of the circle of science has an infinite number of points; and while there is no telling how this circle could ever be surveyed completely, noble and gifted men nevertheless, reach, e'er half their time and inevitably, such boundary points on the periphery from which one gazes into what defies illumination. When they see to their horror how logic coils up at these boundaries and finally bites its own tail – suddenly the new form of insight breaks through, *tragic insight*... (Nietsche (1967) 97–8).

25 Mann (1989).
26 Dennett (1981) 38.
27 Pope (1967) 5.
28 "General Scholium," Newton (1934) ii. 545.
29 See Cassirer (1955) 37 (beginning the chapter on "Nature and Natural Science").
30 Compare Isaiah 54: 2, where the Lord, "The God of the whole earth," sounds suspiciously like Eternals as he says to Israel: "Enlarge the place of thy tent, and let them stretch forth the curtains of thine habitations; spare not, lengthen thy cords, and strengthen thy stakes."
31 Langer (1951) 265; Gregory (1981) 556.
32 Rosen (1982) 20.

2

Blake's Concept of the Sublime

Vincent Arthur de Luca

Sublime Wonder: The Moment of Astonishment

Terrified at the sublime Wonder, Los stood before his Furnaces.
And they stood around, terrified with admiration at Erins Spaces
For the Spaces reached from the starry heighth, to the starry depth.

(*Jerusalem* 12.21–3)

It is not consistently easy to know what Blake means when he speaks of the sublime. The term appears often enough in his work (as either adjective or noun), although not always in clarifying contexts. Yet it turns up prominently on those occasions when he seems most profoundly stirred to define and explain the principles of his own craft – such as the passage in the *Descriptive Catalogue* in which he declares himself to be a "sublime Artist" (Erdman 544); or when, writing to Butts about his newly finished "Grand Poem," he offers his "Definition of the Most Sublime Poetry" (Erdman 730); or in his annotations to Reynolds's *Discourses*, where he specifies the conditions that establish the "Foundation of the Sublime" (Erdman 647); or when he begins an early version of the first plate of *Jerusalem* with comments on the separation of the sublime and the pathetic. Although Blake offers no systematic theory of the sublime such as we find in Burke or Kant or even in the incipiently theoretical writings of, say, Addison or John Dennis, we should not therefore assume that he lacks a cogent and complex idea of the subject. Like any developed body of thought, Blake's concept of the sublime arises out of a historical context of competing concepts – which, in an ongoing dialogic process, it assimilates, contests, modifies, or completes. We are certain that Blake read Burke's *Philosophical Enquiry into . . . the Sublime and Beautiful*, and there is a strong likelihood that he was familiar with contributions to the developing theory of the sublime made by such writers as Dennis, Addison, Hugh Blair, and Robert Lowth. Even where influence is not specifically demonstrable, it remains a simple matter to observe how thoroughly suppositions about sublimity general to his age pervade his own ideas and creative work.

The passage in *Jerusalem* quoted above is a case in point. It encapsulates a Burkean scenario, and in it several crucial terms in eighteenth-century discussions of sublimity gel. Los and other observers catch sight of something exceedingly vast, perceiving it less as an object than as an affect (a "Wonder"). The sight is both uplifting (sublime) and terrifying, and part of the terror is directed toward the observers' own powerful response of awe ("admiration," the Latinate cognate of "wonder"). The outer vastness somehow modulates into an inner power, mediated by a feeling labeled "terror" (but mixed up with awed surprise and uplift) that attaches itself to both the outer and the inner state. Here is an exemplary instance of what Thomas Weiskel, codifying a scheme out of the speculations of Burke, Kant, and Wordsworth, has termed "the sublime moment," a threefold episode of consciousness, in which a state of radical disequilibrium intervenes between a prior state of ordinary awareness and a final state of transcendent exaltation.[1]

In eighteenth-century parlance, the favorite technical term for this state of disequilibrium is "astonishment." Burke begins the second part of his *Philosophical Enquiry*, an analysis of the sublime proper, with a definition of this term:

> The passion caused by the great and sublime in *nature*, when those causes operate most powerfully, is Astonishment; and astonishment is that state of the soul, in which all its motions are suspended, with some degree of horror. In this case the mind is so entirely filled with its object, that it cannot entertain any other, nor by consequence reason on that object which employs it. Hence arises the great power of the sublime, that far from being produced by them, it anticipates our reasonings, and hurries us on by an irresistible force.[2]

Writers throughout the century refer to astonishment in similar terms.[3] But however much these formulas are repeated, perplexities abound. The psychological state itself seems curiously resistant to straightforward discursive explanation, as Burke's own highly figurative language demonstrates. There is a marked ambiguity in the play of these figures. At the moment of astonishment, when the power of the sublime manifests itself, the mind becomes utterly open to the influx of what it beholds ("filled with its object"), and yet this flood of power into the mind produces no kinetic transfer of energy to the mind's faculties, but rather the reverse – a suspension of internal motion, a total arrest. At first appearing entirely permeable, the mind instantly becomes impenetrable, like a container packed to the choking point ("so entirely filled with its object, that it cannot entertain any other"). The mind is quite stopped ("suspended"), only to be "hurried"; its internal density becomes crushing, and yet finally it is easily carried along. "Astonishment," then, cannot be described so much as circumscribed by a ring of mutually canceling figures such as motion/arrest, penetration/resistance, heaviness/lightness. The figures are drawn from physical mechanics, but they compose no mechanics that Newton would recognize. Here the continuum of cause and effect breaks down; outward forces have unpredictable inward consequences. As Burke presents it, "astonishment" marks the intervention of sharp discontinuities in the spheres of both nature and mind: nature suddenly manifests itself in so overwhelming a fashion that normal relations of subject and object are abolished; at the same time, the mind loses its consistency of operation and becomes a thing of paradox, of self-contradictory extremes.

The "terror" that Los feels at the "sublime Wonder" of Erin's Spaces is probably not any sort of conventional fear, but rather a form of astonishment. Blake displays a surprisingly persistent allegiance to Burkean conceptions and diction, revealed in his willingness to link sublime wonder with terror,[4] and in his attachment to the term *astonishment* and its variant forms. Terror and astonishment are kindred states, as Burke makes clear in an etymological aside: "The Romans used the verb *stupeo*, a term which strongly marks the state of an astonished mind, to express the effect either of simple fear, or of astonishment; the word *attonitus*, (thunderstruck) is equally expressive of the alliance of these ideas; and do not the french *étonnement* and the english *astonishment* and *amazement*, point out as clearly the kindred emotions which attend fear and wonder?"[5] Being struck by lightning is literally a form of astonishment, for etymologically the word means "thunderstruck." Perhaps the prestige of the term "astonishment" in eighteenth-century aesthetics derives ultimately from Longinus, who tells us that "the Sublime, when seasonably addressed, with the rapid force of Lightning has born down all before it, and shewn at one stroke the compacted Might of Genius."[6] The two metaphors that Longinus employs here for the onset of the sublime, the stroke of natural lightning and the blow of intellectual power, imply a hidden and prior third, one that connects the forces of nature to the forces of mind. This mediating figure is of course that of a divine being, like the Jove and Jehovah of myth and scripture, at once the author of both natural thunder and human inspiration. Hence, the word *astonishment* encompasses two contradictory aspects of the sublime that shall remain with us throughout this study; it immobilizes or releases, destroys or raises up. One is either struck by the divine power and "hurried" on to participate in its glories, or one is struck dead as a stone.

Blake uses the term *astonishment* more frequently than any other major poet in the period from 1660 to 1830,[7] but always with careful discrimination. Extraordinarily sensitive to the possibilities of wordplay,[8] he is quick to see the "stone" in *astonishment*,[9] a word that could thus easily encompass the whole program of Urizen, armed with "his ten thousands of thunders" (*Urizen* 3.28), to bring about a "solid without fluctuation," "a wide world of solid obstruction" (4.11, 23). Hence to experience astonishment means, in one sense, to turn to stone, to be "filled," as Burke would say, with the inducing power – and filled solid. Thus in *Urizen*, "Wonder, awe, fear, astonishment, / Petrify the eternal myriads" (18.13–14). Since it is the fate of overweening deities in Blake to be struck by their own thunder, as soon as Urizen manifests himself in all his pride, he is struck down and stunned (from *étonnement*) into "*a stony* sleep" (6.7) or, elsewhere, into "*a stoned* stupor" (*Four Zoas* 52.20). The moment of astonishment is, then, the moment *par excellence* when, in Blake's famous formula, one becomes what one beholds. Beholding Urizen's stony sleep, mentioned previously, Los is "smitten with astonishment" (*Urizen* 8.1). But whose astonishment is alluded to here? Los's own or that of Urizen, whom he beholds lying stunned? There is no meaningful way of sorting out distinctions of this nature. Astonishment astonishes, and the petrified petrifies. Thus in *Jerusalem*, seeking the Minute Particulars, Los is again "astonished he beheld only the petrified surfaces" (46.5); two lines earlier, we read that "Los was all astonishment & terror: he trembled sitting on the Stone." Los is now filled with his stony object and is *all* astonishment; we see all as stone in these regions. From becoming all astonishment it is easy to become a thing that *causes* astonishment, as in Los's statement, "I now am what I am: a horror and an astonishment" (8.18). The abstract noun becomes a stony particular, substituting itself for an individuality now petrified and soon to petrify others.

But as there is a thunder that immobilizes and petrifies, there is also a thunder that cracks open the stones, releasing our buried powers to freedom, a "crack of doom" for a sullen old dispensation. In contrast to the "inarticulate thunder" that Urizen booms at his misshapen children in *Vala* (*Four Zoas* 70.39), we have the articulate thunder of that true God who "To Man the wond'rous art of writing gave," and who "speaks in thunder and in fire! / Thunder of Thought, & flames of fierce desire" (*Jerusalem* 3.4–6). There is also the awakened Albion, "Loud thundring, with broad flashes of flaming lightning & pillars / Of fire, speaking the Words of Eternity in Human Forms" (95.8–9). And there are the Zoas, fraternal at last, who "conversed together in Visionary forms dramatic which bright / Redounded from their Tongues in thunderous majesty" (98.28–9). In contrast to the obliterating power of the Urizenic thunder, the power of this thunder resides in its incisive capacity to clarify and reveal. It does not stun with an avalanche of sound, but rather cleaves through darkness and obstruction, employing as its cutting tools those instruments that inscribe the definite lines of Blake's "writing," "Words," and "Forms."

It follows that the "astonishment" produced by this clarifying thunder encompasses the moment when surfaces and opacities are burst to reveal an infinite potential within. Thus, when Eno in *The Four Zoas* "took an atom of space & opend its center / Into Infinitude & ornamented it with wondrous art / Astonishd sat her Sisters of Beulah to see her soft affections" (*Four Zoas* 9.12–14). A similar response to visionary revelation appears in Blake's ecstatic report of his first days at Felpham:

> In particles bright
> The jewels of Light
> Distinct shone & clear–
> Amazd & in fear
> I each particle gazed
> Astonishd Amazed
> For each was a Man
> Human formd.
> (Letter to Butts, 2 October 1800, lines 15–22, Erdman 712)

If visions of nature humanized bring astonishment, then so too do the recognition and recovery of unfallen portions of humanity within the self: "Los embracd the Spectre first as a brother / Then as another Self; astonishd humanizing & in tears" (*Four Zoas* 85.29–30).

Images of barriers broken, of visions glimpsed through sudden openings, of obdurate forms melting down and flowing together, attend this form of astonishment: "Then Los said I behold the Divine Vision thro the broken Gates / Of thy poor broken heart astonishd melted into Compassion & Love" (*Four Zoas* 99.15–16). Finally, in the single instance in Blake's poetry where astonishment is modified by the adjective *sublime*, Jerusalem recalls ancient days before Albion's dreadful separation: "I taught the ships of the sea to sing the songs of Zion. / Italy saw me, in sublime astonishment: France was wholly mine" (*Jerusalem* 79.38–9). The response of the nations embraces the full paradox of the sublime moment; arrest is freedom here, for to be filled with the object, is, in this case to be filled with a being who is "called Liberty among the Children of Albion" (*Jerusalem* 54.5).

Blake's wide-ranging use of the term *astonishment* provides a good index of his understanding of the problematic dynamics of the eighteenth-century sublime. Not only does astonishment occupy a gap between polarized states of experience, but it also unfolds within itself alternate destinies of the sublime moment. Two possible sublimes quiver in the indeterminacy of the moment of astonishment: one, the sublime of terror and deprivation most closely associated with Burke, and the other, a sublime of desire and plenitude. Blake's imagination is repeatedly drawn to the Burkean sublime, but he appears skeptical that it can serve as a mode of genuine elevation and access to a liberating power. Burke would have us believe that the moment of disequilibrium, suspension of faculties, and immobilization of will arises from the access of an overwhelming external power or magnitude. Blake reads such scenes otherwise: encountering "terrific" objects, his protagonists reel not at a magnitude of power made present, but rather at the magnitude of power lost, at the degree of petrifaction revealed in so-called powers by the time they present themselves as natural "terrors."

Blake seeks a less melancholy sublime, and if as a poet he is to gratify desire and recover plenitude, he must attempt some sort of redemption of astonishment. As his own usage of the term clearly indicates, he has no intention of abandoning the drama, the clash of oppositions, and the suspense inherent in Burke's account. Blake is willing to exploit Burke's evocations of giddiness and irresistible rush since they so easily consort with his own imagery of centers opening up, gates broken down, and forms melting. There is a need, however, to relocate the scene of this drama, away from a point of humiliating encounter between the experiencing mind and some thunderous externality. As Blake's own notions of the sublime become more fully articulated, the encounter is seen to take place between a lesser and a greater faculty of the mind, made manifest through the mediation of the poetic text. Blake not only represents scenes of astonishment in his work, but also seeks to create fresh moments of astonishment in the encounter of poem and reader, offering a petrific text to stony understandings and a field of openings for the receptive. The space of the poem itself becomes the site of sublime wonder.

"The Most Sublime Poetry": Corporeal Limits and Mental Infinities

Blake uses the phrase *sublime poetry* only once in his writings, but it is on a momentous occasion. In the famous letter to Thomas Butts of 6 July 1803, he defines his idea of "the Most Sublime Poetry," asserts his highest literary aspirations, and announces the completion of "the Grandest Poem that This World Contains." The letter is, by any standard, the *locus classicus* for any extended consideration of Blake's idea of the sublime. Its central passage is justly familiar:

Thus I hope that all our three years trouble Ends in Good Luck at last & shall be forgot by my affections & only rememberd by my Understanding to be a Memento in time to come & to speak to future generations by a Sublime Allegory which is now perfectly completed into a Grand Poem. I may praise it since I dare not pretend to be any other than the Secretary the Authors are in Eternity I consider it as the Grandest Poem that This World Contains. Allegory addressd to the Intellectual powers while it is altogether hidden from the Corporeal Understanding is My Definition of the Most Sublime Poetry. it is also somewhat in the same manner defind by Plato. (Erdman 730)

Several of the key terms in this passage are problematic, *Allegory* perhaps the most conspicuously so, if the attention it has received from Blake's critics is indicative. But we are not likely to understand what Blake means here by Allegory unless we have come to understand the meaning of the twice-repeated word *sublime*. Is it merely a vague term of superlative praise, or does it have technical and theoretical specificity? If the latter is true, what is the theoretical import of making the definition of "the Most Sublime Poetry" turn on the issue of reception? In particular, why is a division in the audience or faculties of reception a necessary condition for sublimity? And what does concealment (the "altogether hidden") have to do with this division?

As he writes to Butts, Blake is of course much preoccupied with Hayley's response to the "Grand Poem," probably an early version of *Milton*. It is undoubtedly gratifying to Blake's self-esteem to find in Hayley's incomprehension, or "Genteel Ignorance" (Erdman 730) as he calls it, evidence of the poem's authorship in Eternity. In an earlier letter, Blake had made a similar response to objections of the benighted Dr Trusler: "You say that I want somebody to Elucidate my Ideas. But you ought to know that What is Grand is necessarily obscure to Weak men. That which can be made Explicit to the Idiot is not worth my care The wisest of the Ancients considerd what is not too Explicit as the fittest for Instruction because it rouzes the faculties to act. I name Moses Solomon Esop Homer Plato" (Erdman 702). In the letter to Butts, however, distinctions among classes of men – the weak and the strong, ignorant and wise, idiots and geniuses – are not at issue. The Corporeal Understanding and the Intellectual Powers are faculties within any mind, and not designations for the minds of different persons. Blake strives not to separate the elite from the vulgar as social groups, but rather to uncover the intellectual gifts that we all potentially possess. This is to be done by presenting to the mind artifacts that sift it, separating out the dull from the bright, the stony from the buoyant, so that what is imaginative and visionary within us can outwardly manifest itself. The sublime poem, then, is a thing that can effect a sharp division of the mind into two faculties of opposing capacities. The term *sublime* is precisely appropriate here, for a similar act of division is central to every sophisticated theory of sublimity in Blake's period.

Within the tripartite structure of the sublime moment, discussed earlier, a hiatus of indeterminacy or discontinuity divides a prior moment of normal consciousness from a subsequent moment of idealized restoration or elevation. But it appears that the indeterminacy of the central hiatus is itself the product of a nascent division of emotions and faculties. In Burke, the dichotomy is one of pain and fear on one hand and "delight" on the other, the delight arising from a secondary recognition of our actual safe remove from the sources of apparent pain.[10] Dr. Johnson's sequential formulation is similar: "the first effect [of the sublime encounter] is sudden astonishment, and the second rational admiration."[11] But astonishment itself, as we have seen from Blake's own usage, tends to divide into a phase of incapacity and paralysis, and a phase of momentum and revelation. When the visionary aesthetician James Usher tells us that the passion that the sublime "inspires us with is evidently a mixture of terror, curiosity, and exultation,"[12] we recognize a tripartite structure opening up; the first phase is attached to incapacity and repulsion, the last to the attained height of the sublime proper, and the middle is an indeterminate state of attraction toward the object (and therefore the antithesis of terror), without a fully acquired comprehension of it. In short, within the moment of astonishment are born two states of mind – one that wants to go forward and one that wants to hold back. In more drastic versions of this dialectic, the second state is one that is *held back* whether it wants to go forward or not. In these versions, the division of the mind falls into two unequally privileged faculties – one consigned to pain and deprivation, the other admitted to an exalted sphere of delight.

This division of powers entered the discourse of the sublime as a scene of theophany, in which the unequally privileged powers are those of God and man in confrontation. One of the clearest expressions of this confrontation comes from the Hebraist Robert Lowth, in his *Lectures on the Sacred Poetry of the Hebrews*. Speaking of a description of God's attributes in the Psalms, he comments:

> Here the human mind is absorbed, overwhelmed as it were in a boundless vortex, and studies in vain for an expedient to extricate itself. But the greatness of the subject may be justly estimated by its difficulty; and while the imagination labours to comprehend what is beyond its powers, this very labour itself, and these ineffectual endeavours, sufficiently demonstrate the immensity and sublimity of the object.... Here the mind seems to exert its utmost faculties in vain to grasp an object, whose unparalleled magnitude mocks its feeble endeavours.[13]

This passage revels in the language of human abasement, as Lowth stretches himself to find terms sufficient to express how overwhelmed, vain, incapacitated, ineffectual, enfeebled, and mocked our condition is when compared to God's. Burke abbreviates and intensifies the same scenario, stating that when we contemplate the attributes of God, "we shrink into the minuteness of our own nature, and are, in a manner, annihilated before him,"[14] and this language of humiliation becomes part of the standard idiom of the sublime.[15]

In certain more sophisticated theories of the sublime, this drama of unequal outward confrontation moves inward, with one part of the mind taking on the role of incapacitated humanity while another is substituted in the position of God. Wordsworthians are intimately familiar with that moment in *The Prelude*, Book 6, when the poet, "halted, without an effort to break through" records the failure of the "light of sense," while simultaneously Imagination, "that awful Power," rises up to reveal its home in infinitude.[16] The most radical formulation of this separation of faculties, one curtailed in powers, the other unrestricted, appears in Kant's *Critique of Judgment*, in his discussion of the sublime of magnitude: "The feeling of the Sublime is therefore a feeling of pain, arising from the want of accordance between the aesthetical estimation of magnitude formed by the Imagination and the estimation of the same formed by Reason. There is at the same time a pleasure thus excited, arising from the correspondence with Rational Ideas of this very judgment of the inadequacy of our greatest faculty of Sense."[17] For Kant, an intuitive comprehension of the infinite is "altogether hidden," as Blake would say, from the Imagination, the "greatest faculty of sense" – but it is precisely this inaccessibility that provokes the mind to recognize its possession of transcendent powers that can so intuit: "that magnitude of a natural object, on which the Imagination fruitlessly spends its whole faculty of comprehension, must carry our concept of nature to a supersensible substrate (which lies at its basis and also at the basis of our faculty of thought)."[18] One need only substitute the term "Intellectual Powers" for Kant's Reason, "Corporeal Understanding" for Kant's incapacitated Imagination, and "Sublime Allegory," for the "magnitude of a natural object," in order to recognize that Blake's and Kant's defining conditions for the sublime have, *mutatis mutandis*, an identical structure. What is a barrier to the faculty allied with sense is an avenue to its more privileged counterpart – and, paradoxically, the avenue becomes available only if the barrier is posed. The sublime stimulus then operates as a kind of psychic traffic light, beckoning one power of the mind to come forth only when another is blocked. Such a principle would explain why, in the letter to Butts, Blake deems a privilege afforded to one of the two faculties more sublime than privileges afforded to both ("My Definition of the *Most* Sublime Poetry" [my emphasis]). Without the thwarting of the Corporeal Understanding, there apparently can be no manifestation of the Intellectual Powers as such, for the latter do not always know themselves in an unmediated fashion. A terminal failure of the understanding is required to throw the intellect into relief, and that sudden manifestation serves to replenish man's sense of his own greatness.

These Kantian conceptions are important to the study of Blake's sublime, not because Kant's thought is interchangeable with Blake's (which is hardly the case), but because it indicates so clearly the particular theoretical tradition in which Blake operates. Kant is useful here because he posits with such uncompromising rigor a mental sublime that rests on a dialectic of plenitude and deprivation for its dynamics. By attacking Burke, who did most to establish this dialectic, Blake has obscured his own adherence to it. More recently, Thomas Weiskel has attempted to divorce Blake rigorously and entirely from the whole Burkean–Kantian–Wordsworthian conception of the sublime, but the fact of the similarity remains.[19] The arguments for Blake's repudiation of the tradition are based on partial evidence, or evidence not fully considered in a comprehensive context. A more judicious account would stress how Blake manages to reinvest the deprivation–plenitude structure with new emphases, and adapt it to new ends. For instance, he shows little interest in applying his formulation of the sublime to any object connected with nature, with material power or magnitude. Rather, he slips the poetic artifact into the privileged position of the sublime object or stimulus. But he undertakes no quarrel with the opacities, bafflements, and deprivations endemic to the sublime tradition, and, in his scheme, the mental faculties continue to divide into unequally endowed portions.

Blake also shares with such contemporaries as Kant and Wordsworth the notion that the sublime resides in an identification of a desired infinite with the quester's own intellectual being. Blake's grasp of this concept may be illustrated in some of his earliest etched lines, the last three propositions of *There Is No Natural Religion*:

V   If the many become the same as the few, when possess'd, More! More! is the cry of a mistaken soul, less than All cannot satisfy Man.

VI   If any could desire what he is incapable of possessing, despair must be his eternal lot.

VII   The desire of Man being Infinite the possession is Infinite & himself Infinite. (Erdman 2–3)

If man is infinite, it must be because he *is* capable of possessing the "All" that alone satisfies. Indeed he does possess it, for despair does not in fact rule human life. "Mistaken souls" cry "More! More!" when they in fact already have "All." Their mistake is that of the Corporeal Understanding, which grasps at finites and seeks to accumulate them. But in comparison with the infinite, no amount of accumulation will seem anything but immeasurably small: "the many become the same as the few, when possess'd." As Kant remarks, "the infinite is absolutely (not merely comparatively) great. Compared with it everything else (of the same kind of magnitudes) is small."[20] An infinite possession therefore cannot result from any process of accumulation, no matter how extended, but must exist in the mind whole and a priori. In the same passage as that just quoted, Kant continues: "And what is most important is that to be able to think it as a whole indicates a faculty of mind which surpasses every standard of Sense. . . . Nevertheless, *the bare capability of thinking* this infinite without contradiction requires in the human mind a faculty itself supersensible." Blake's "All," like Kant's "whole," is an object of desire that only the mind of the desirer can furnish.

Blake's letter to Butts about the Intellectual Powers is only one instance of his habitual association of the sublime with a manifestation of intellect and a flight from the corporeal. Thus in the Proverbs of Hell, "Pathos," "Beauty," and "Proportion" are assigned to the heart, genitals, and limbs respectively, but "the head [is] Sublime" (*Marriage* 10.61). Elsewhere, the images in the "Writings of the Prophets" are "sublime & Divine" because they illustrate how "the Imaginative Image returns by the seed of Contemplative Thought" (Erdman 555). In stressing the sublime as a mental greatness, Blake aligns himself with a venerable tradition of thought, beginning with Longinus, who tells us that "the Sublime is an Image reflected from the inward Greatness of the Soul."[21] In the eighteenth century, there are many echoes and variations of this idea before it reaches the extreme subjectivity of self-apotheosis suggested by Kant when he tells us that "sublimity does not reside in anything of nature, but only in our mind."[22] James Usher expresses the concept as well as any: "at the presence of the sublime, although it be always awful, the soul of man seems to be raised out of a trance; it assumes an unknown grandeur; it is seized with a new appetite, that in a moment effaces its former little prospects and desires; it is rapt out of sight and consideration of this diminutive world, into a kind of gigantic creation, where it finds room to dilate itself to a size agreeable to its present nature and grandeur."[23] We are reminded here of James Beattie's quirky derivation of *sublime* from *super limas*, "above the slime or mud of this world,"[24] which in turn glances ahead to Blake's assertion that "I do not behold the Outward Creation & that to me it is hindrance & not Action it is the Dirt upon my feet No part of Me" (Erdman 565).

Closer still to Blake in his view of a sublime that resides in a power of mind is John Dennis, earlier in the century. When Blake tells us that "The Nature of my Work is Visionary or Imaginative it is an Endeavour to

Restore what the Ancients called the Golden Age" (Erdman 555), he may be echoing Dennis, who also has a restorative notion of the arts: "The great design of Arts is to restore the decays that happen'd to Humane Nature by the Fall, by Restoring Order."[25] From Dennis, too, Blake probably acquires his illustrative example of what it means "not [to] behold the Outward Creation," when he contrasts the Corporeal view of the sun as "a round Disk of fire somewhat like a Guinea" with his own view of it as "an Innumerable company of the Heavenly host crying Holy Holy Holy is the Lord God Almighty" (Erdman 565–6). According to Dennis, "the sun mention'd in ordinary Conversation, gives the Idea of a round flat shining Body, of about Two Foot Diameter. But the Sun occurring to us in Meditation, gives the Idea of a vast and glorious Body, and the top of all the visible Creation, and the brightest material Image of the Divinity."[26] Such a transformation of the outward creation, according to Dennis, is a product of Enthusiasm, "a Passion which is moved by the Idea's [*sic*] in Contemplation or the Meditation of Things," and the Enthusiastic passions are noteworthy because "the greater and more violent they are, the more they show the largeness of Soul, and greatness of Capacity of the Writer."[27] Dennis here narrows or virtually effaces the gap between the imagining perceiver and the imagined percept; to recognize the divinity inherent in the image of the sun is tantamount to asserting the divinity of the self that has conceived the image. The sublime becomes the comprehensive term for the state in which this narrowing occurs: "The sublime is . . . never without Enthusiastic Passion. For the Sublime is nothing else but a great Thought, or Great Thoughts moving the Soul from it's Ordinary Scituation [*sic*] by the Enthusiasm which naturally attends them."[28] It is next to impossible to distinguish here between the reader moved and the poet who moves, embraced as they both are by the unifying and apparently free-floating entity of "Great Thought," which generates passions as its operative mode. Dennis takes the terminology of abstract intellect, "Thought," "Contemplation," and "Meditation," to describe a source of the passions and enthusiasm, and it is here that his theory of the sublime is most relevant to Blake.

In Blake's thought, intellect in its fine essence is always connected to the passions. It is through this connection that the Intellectual Powers discover themselves with that total cognition defined as sublime by its idealist theoreticians. In *A Vision of the Last Judgment* Blake declares that "The Treasures of Heaven are not Negations of Passion but Realities of Intellect from which All the Passions Emanate Uncurbed in their Eternal Glory" (Erdman 564). Intellect, then, is the matrix of desire, and generates those passions that, when "uncurbed," are the Alpha and Omega of human happiness. Blake's Intellectual Powers may resemble Kant's supersensible Reason in that both altogether transcend corporeal modes of understanding, but there is this crucial difference: Blake's supreme faculty discovers itself not in the attainment of some cool, absolute rationality but, as the propositions of *No Natural Religion* show, in the infinitude of its desire. An intellect that fails to quicken Enthusiastic Passions – in short, to emanate as love – would be, for Blake, no intellect at all. It is not enough for the Intellectual Powers to possess plenitude; they must be stirred by that plenitude, and seek its realization in an infinite variety of particular forms, such as Dennis's transfigured sun. These forms are "Realities of Intellect" – that is to say, forms made real by intellect to be the objects of its desires.

It follows from this eroticized conception of intellect that "the Most Sublime Poetry" only begins its task when it separates the Intellectual Powers from the Corporeal Understanding. It is not enough for the poem to operate on a logic of negative inference, relying on assumptions that if one faculty is thoroughly baffled, there must be a residual one rising in hidden strength.[29] Merely to posit this other faculty, to display intellect like a statue unveiled, is in no way to "address" the Intellectual Powers. An address manifests itself as such to the extent that it implies a response and provides the opportunities for such response. Sublime poetry addresses the Intellectual Powers by furnishing them with forms of desire, with an ongoing enticement that releases the uncurbed emanation of passion. Intellect is thus revealed not in some abstract fashion but in its desire to read and in the manner of its reading. Similarly, the Corporeal Understanding reveals itself to be that which cannot read. "The Most Sublime Poetry" is, after all, poetry, and if it aims to sunder the faculties so as to manifest them both in their unalloyed forms, then the means for doing so must reside in the text itself.

The Sublime of Reading: Barriers and Disclosures

The Intellectual Powers and the Corporeal Understanding essentially represent two different states of reading, or perhaps more accurately, two choices of reading. The same act of reading may summon both states in varying proportions, and every reader will pass through each state at different times. For the purpose of argument, however, it is more convenient to consider the Intellectual Powers and the Corporeal Understanding as simultaneously presented to the mind, locked in dubious battle, a crisis in reading. Blake's program of displacing the natural sublime object with a text makes manifest what is, according to some recent critics, latent all the time in eighteenth-century and romantic theories of the sublime. Given our recent critical climate, in which all readings are said to be problematic, and in which we as readers are all situated in an abyss between opacity and translucence, between putative presence and actual deferral, it is not surprising that the sublime experience has attracted attention as a displaced experience of reading and as an exemplary instance of its difficulties.[30] Conversely, modern theory has often used the language of the natural sublime (high barriers, gaps, abysses, labyrinths) as metaphors for certain textual events.

Needless to say, there is nothing new in this displaced usage, since the natural sublime itself merely takes over the language that had long been used to describe a rhetorical effect.[31] Blake's textual sublime derives in part from the tradition of Longinus, in which the sublime is a trope of rhetoric designed to move an audience,[32] in part from traditions of hidden gnosis, scriptural hermeneutics and allegoresis, and their medieval and Renaissance secular derivatives.[33] The latter traditions seek less to transport the reader than to make his path difficult and obstacle-ridden; they are designed to exclude the unworthy, and to discipline the worthy and make them hungry for full truth.[34] Elements of this ancient heuristic function undoubtedly figure in Blake's choice of the term *Allegory* to describe the sublime text. But as we shall see, it is the *sublime* of "Sublime Allegory" that bears the heaviest stress in his conception.

The word *allegory*, etymologically an "other-speaking," suggests in its own compound terms "otherness," alienation, and opacity on one hand, and address and disclosure on the other – in short, the different destinies of the divided mental faculties. The text poses itself as a barrier, but at the barrier there is a point of indeterminacy, a state of incomplete disengagement between the Corporeal Understanding and the Intellectual Powers. The barrier seems to flicker equivocally before the eyes, now opaque, now translucent, now forbidding, now yielding. The sublime text must be capable of provoking despair and desire simultaneously, stunned retreat and joyous elevation. Such a text must appear hard to read; it cannot disseminate its meanings easily or transparently. But at the same time that it appears hard to read, it must also present itself as *almost easy* to read – that is to say, it must be filled with all sorts of glancing lusters of language, moments of eloquent simplicity, accessible dicta, and most important of all, innumerable tantalizing hints and tokens of a comprehensive wisdom or *gnosis*, whose full apprehension awaits us, so to speak, just around the bend. It is a text that labors as hard to forestall our indifference to it as it does to hinder its self-disclosure. Such a text may contain "sublime" events, in the conventional sense of the term, as part of its content, but this is not crucial. The crucial sublime event takes place in the actual difficulties of the reading experience.

First, there is the difficulty faced by the Corporeal Understanding. That which is already "altogether hidden" to the Understanding can never be found – and because it is never found, it must be perpetually sought or guessed at. Hence, difficulties come into being only after the Understanding has been denied access to the infinite. After the brief episode of "indeterminacy," the episode of attraction/repulsion, invitation/rebuff, and arousal/despair, issues of blockage and disclosure become decided; barriers are then transcended all at once or not at all. But it is the fate of the Corporeal Understanding to conceive none of this. By definition capable only of understanding bodies, it knows nothing of the infinite and hence nothing of the fact that the infinite is "altogether hidden" from it. The fact of its blockage registers only as the experience of "difficulties" and the necessity of laborious reading.

How does the Corporeal Understanding try to read? Alexander Gerard describes this fruitless labor as succinctly as any writer in the period: "The mind contemplates, not one large, but many small objects: it is pained with the labour requisite to creep from one to another; and is disgusted with the imperfection of the idea, with which, even after all this toil, it must remain contented."[35] Anyone who has ever grappled seriously with Blake's text can supply further instances from his or her own experience, for not even the fittest Blake scholar can honestly claim a plenary exemption from lapses into this state. We have all puzzled over recondite terminology, narrative instability, inconsistencies among utterances or between stubborn details and "the system as a whole." In what seems to be an endless task, our procedures are additive, as we move painfully from line to line exploring the dens of the text. Unlike the Los of *Jerusalem*, we "Reason & Compare" (*Jerusalem* 10.21), accumulating much that is useful to our understandings. But the useful is not the sublime. For all our accumulating, it is number, weight, and measure in a year of dearth, the "More! More!" of the mistaken soul who cannot ever find satisfaction thus; in such a state, despair must be our eternal lot.

Against this dire prospect, we can more effectively estimate the privilege afforded to the Intellectual Powers. For the Corporeal Understanding, the text is a kind of wall, against which it presses itself, groping along, trying in vain to peer through chinks in the hard, opaque surface. How, then, do the Intellectual Powers read? Not, as may be imagined, in some imperious act of untroubled seeing, in which the text becomes a wall of glass, a thing annulled before the glory of some "supersensible" totality lying beyond. Again, our personal experience as readers of Blake must be our guide, and it does not ratify such a serenely grandiose scenario. When we find ourselves first attracted and responsive to Blake's text, it is certainly not because we have been afforded a comprehensive a priori vision of its meanings, but rather because we sense the fullness of its potential. The wall of words is still there, but something within us responds to the shifting, captivating lusters that glance off it, points of eloquence and concentrated wisdom, atomies of beauty and pathos. The more these are perceived, the more they cast light on others, until the wall as a whole becomes luminous. The Intellectual Powers seek not to abolish the wall of words but to find satisfaction in it.

The wall as an image of a text is of course Blake's own, established in a moment at which the drama of blockage and disclosure becomes aware of itself as a trope:

> I give you the end of a golden string,
> Only wind it into a ball:
> It will lead you in at Heavens gate,
> Built in Jerusalems wall.
>
> (*Jerusalem* 77 Erdman 231)

The end of the string is here in these four lines themselves, for the interpretive clues that the reader needs rest in the metaphors "wall" and "gate," which of course represent the sublime alternatives of blockage and disclosure. The key to reading a poem such as *Jerusalem* is to realize the very fact that it provokes opposed modes of reading. The "golden string" offers no decoding device for a deprived Corporeal Understanding. It merely tells us that the text yields itself to the force of trust, curiosity, and desire, and that it fastens itself to the reader at points of little details, felicities tucked away in the crannies of the wall. Each is Heaven's gate, and there are as many golden strings as there are points of entrance, varying from reader to reader.

We are dealing here not with the meaning of the text but with the pleasure of the text: "If the Spectator could Enter into these Images in his Imagination approaching them on the Fiery Chariot of his Contemplative Thought if he could Enter into Noahs Rainbow or into his bosom or could make a Friend & Companion of one of these Images of wonder ... then would he meet the Lord in the Air & then he would be happy General Knowledge is Remote Knowledge it is in Particulars that Wisdom consists & Happiness too" (Erdman 560). Happiness consists in particulars, and the particulars are to be approached as "friends" or "companions," or as emblems of good faith and trust, like the rainbow that God presented to Noah as a guarantee that there would be no second flood (see Gen. 9.12–17). "Contemplative Thought" approaches on a "Fiery Chariot," an emblem associated with fierce desire (see *Milton* 1.10–12). The Intellectual Powers are involved in what seems like a kind of Barthian lover's discourse with the text.

To make a friend of the artist's images (and by image, one must include words in their semantic and graphic dimensions as well, for Blake speaks of the principles of verbal art and visual art interchangeably)[36] is, then, to become their familiar, to embrace them as Los does his Spectre in *The Four Zoas*, "first as a brother / Then as another self" (85.29–30). The image becomes, like the ash on Coleridge's grate in "Frost at Midnight," a "Companionable form" to the Intellect, "every where

/ Echo or mirror seeking of itself,"[37] for the Intellect, as we know, desires an "All" that can only be found within. As a tangible companion, the text is intellect crystallized into visible and particular form. "The Beauty proper for sublime art," Blake tells us in a definitive statement, "is lineaments, or forms and features that are capable of being the receptacles of intellect" (Erdman 544). Such lineaments are as much "lineaments of Gratified Desire" as those that "men in women do require" (see Erdman 474). What satisfies intellect best, apparently, is to lodge itself in a defined space (the overtones of a lover's discourse remain in effect here), while remaining free to exercise "uncurbed" its infinite potentialities.

These requirements are met by language itself, "that system of signs," as Maureen Quilligan puts it, "which retrieves for us the process of intellection."[38] Thus a sublime text is one in which the Intellect recognizes (reads) a glory that the same faculty has put (written) into it. The glory is that of the unrestricted majesty and power of human expressiveness and creativity, exemplified in the gift of language, and made manifest in the immense resources of its signifiers.[39] What Thomas Weiskel has said of Wordsworth's celebration of the power of words in Book 5 of *The Prelude* is applicable to Blake: "The passage is evoking the penumbra of words, the power inherent not in what they mean but in that they mean; or, in what they are, independent of their meaning – in earlier language, the *how* and not the *what* of sublimity.... Power inheres not in the perceptional form but in language or symbolicity itself."[40] For Blake, language is not only the glory of our humanity but its essence, and in the apocalypse described at the end of *Jerusalem*, the form of the sign and the human form become one. Albion speaks "Words of Eternity in Human Forms," and "every Word & Every Character / Was Human" (95.9; 98.35–6). The attraction of the intellect to the text, then, is an attraction to one's native place, and the feeling of sublime elevation comes from the joy of homecoming.

It becomes increasingly apparent that the phrase "Allegory addressed to the Intellectual powers" refers to a scene of self-recognition. "Allegory" means "other-speaking," but in such a state of sublimity as we get at the end of *Jerusalem*, "Sublime Allegory" becomes an "other-speaking" that cancels its own otherness and becomes simply speaking; the only "other" here is the text itself.[41] The text, the signified of its own signifiers, should not be conceived as a shell covering the meaty kernel of meaning, to use a favorite trope of traditional accounts of the allegorical relation. Even the most profound of his critics can lapse into talk of cracking shells and extracting kernels,[42] but Blake never speaks in such terms. Although Blake's works are full of conventional allegorization,[43] Sublime Allegory is not a conventional system of obscured referentiality. Rather, we are to understand it as a discourse that, when it is at its "Most Sublime," addresses itself to a faculty that seeks "companionable forms," not hidden meanings. To be companionable, such forms must be *seen*, must be apprehended in their specific individualities. It is natural, therefore, that in his most extended series of dicta on the requirements of the sublime, Blake makes this particularity the cornerstone of his thought.

Singular and Particular Detail: The Sublime of the Signifier

Blake's best-known remarks on the aesthetics of the sublime are contained in his annotations to the *Discourses* of Sir Joshua Reynolds. Here we observe him engaged in a running argument that focuses on the grand style itself, in which he is forced consciously to stake out positions on the subject in response to alternatives actually posed before him.[44] It is particularly significant, therefore, that Blake's only recorded reference to Edmund Burke and to the *Philosophical Enquiry into ... the Sublime and Beautiful* should occur in these marginal jottings. These notes often seem to use Reynolds as the occasion for an attack directed specifically against Burke. While we have observed elements in Blake's views that are compatible with a Burkean framework, or at least with a tradition in which Burke's voice is conspicuous, the radical differences between the two writers' ideas of the sublime inevitably demand consideration.

Blake more or less identifies Burke as the baleful shadow behind Reynolds's own aberrations:

> Burke's Treatise on the Sublime & Beautiful is founded on the Opinions of Newton & Locke on this Treatise Reynolds has grounded many of his assertions in all his Discourses I read Burkes Treatise when very Young at the same time I read Locke on Human Understanding & Bacons Advancement of Learning on Every one of these Books I wrote my Opinions & on looking them over find that my Notes on Reynolds in this Book are exactly Similar. I felt the Same Contempt & Abhorrence then; that I do now. They mock Inspiration & Vision (Erdman 660)

It is scarcely necessary to dwell here on the obvious revulsion that Blake would feel toward the empiricism, associationism, physiological reductivism, and the psychology of self-interest that underpin Burke's theory of the sublime.[45] These, however, are not Blake's main objects of attack in the Annotations to Reynolds. He is more concerned with the epistemological character of Burke's sublime object itself. Burke's conception of sublime poetry as a form of deliberate indeterminacy seems very much on Burke's mind all along as he reads Reynolds. When Reynolds offers obscurity as "one source of the sublime," Burke's famous argument inevitably rises up before us:

> Poetry with all its obscurity, has a more general as well as a more powerful dominion over the passions than the other art [i.e., painting]. And I think there are reasons in nature why the obscure idea, when properly conveyed, should be more affecting than the clear. It is our ignorance of things that causes all our admiration, and chiefly excites our passions. Knowledge and acquaintance make the most striking causes affect but little. It is thus with the vulgar, and all men are as the vulgar in what they do not understand. The ideas of eternity, and infinity, are among the most affecting we have, and yet perhaps there is nothing of which we really understand so little, as of infinity and eternity. . . .
>
>   But let it be considered that hardly any thing can strike the mind with its greatness, which does not make some sort of approach towards infinity; which nothing can do whilst we are able to perceive its bounds; but to see an object distinctly, and to perceive its bounds, is one and the same thing. A clear idea is therefore another name for a little idea.[46]

These remarks are tantalizing because they mingle concepts that would be anathema to Blake with formulations that sound rather like some of his own. Blake would endorse the notion that poetry is a prime locus of the sublime experience. He would agree that "to see an object distinctly, and to perceive its bounds, is one and the same thing"; indeed the terminology is virtually his own. Moreover, according to a dictum from one of his early tractates, "The bounded is loathed by its possessor" (Erdman 2); there is an implied antagonism between the bounded and man's desire for the infinite that consorts comfortably with Burke's view.

A profound gulf, however, separates Burke's notions of infinity from Burke's. As a Lockean empiricist, Burke must insist on our ignorance of infinity and eternity and restrict the understanding only to finite bodies. The infinite, for Burke, is precisely the absence of what we can know. Sublime objects, then, are merely knowable objects that pose as unknowable. They "make some sort of approach towards infinity" by a process of subtraction, by strategically placed concealments of their bounds. Through the mediation of the indeterminate object, at once accessible and inaccessible, the void of the infinite becomes an implied plenum.[47] An undifferentiated vagueness or generality is therefore useful to Burke's sublime, "because any difference, whether it be in the disposition, or in the figure, or even in the colour of the parts, is highly prejudicial to the idea of infinity, which every change must check and interrupt, at every alteration commencing a new series."[48] An alternative mode of sublimity is to crowd the perceptual field excessively, so that it is all broken lines and broken masses: the poetic equivalents are the "many descriptions in the poets and orators which owe their sublimity to a richness and profusion of images, in which the mind is so dazzled as to make it impossible to attend to that exact coherence and agreement of the allusions."[49]

Blake will have none of this. The "bounded" is indeed to be "loathed" when what is bounded is the understanding itself, conceived by the empiricist as situated in a limited perceptual field of knowable objects circumscribed by a vast unknowable darkness. For Blake, "some sort of approach towards infinity" from this perimeter is no approach worth speaking of; less than all cannot satisfy man. Taken together, Blake's comments on the sublime in the Reynolds Marginalia make the case for a plainly accessible infinite. They all revolve around the principles of particularity, determinacy, and discrimination – qualities essential for making the forms of the artistic surface distinctly visible to the Intellectual Powers:

Minute Discrimination is Not Accidental All Sublimity is founded on Minute Discrimination (Erdman 643)

Without Minute Neatness of Execution The Sublime cannot Exist! Grandeur of Ideas is founded on Precision of Ideas (Erdman 646)

Singular & particular Detail is the Foundation of the Sublime (Erdman 647)

Broken Colours & Broken Lines & Broken Masses are Equally Subversive of the Sublime (Erdman 652)

Obscurity is Neither the Source of the Sublime nor of any Thing Else (Erdman 658)

Blake's stress on particularity and distinctness as productive of the sublime may seem, as Weiskel has said, merely "perverse," an attempt to overthrow Burke by depriving his key terms of their ordinarily understood meaning.[50] Hence, it is important to note that within the general aesthetic debates of his time, Blake speaks from a position of relative strength and within a widely established context. Burke's stance provoked opposition from many quarters, both when the *Philosophical Enquiry* first appeared and several generations thereafter. "Distinctness of imagery has ever been held productive of the sublime," insisted one of the reviewers in response to Burke's famous celebration of obscurity.[51] Similarly, in his "Critical Dissertation on the Poems of Ossian," Hugh Blair tells us that "simplicity and conciseness, are never-failing characteristics of the stile of a sublime writer," and that "to be concise in description, is one thing; and to be general, is another. No description that rests in generals can possibly be good; it can convey no lively idea; for it is of particulars only that we have a distinct conception."[52] Bishop Lowth presses much the same point repeatedly: "the Hebrew poets have accomplished the sublime without losing perspicuity"; their "imagery is well known, the use of it is common, the signification definite; they are therefore perspicuous, clear, and truly magnificent." Lowth goes so far as to make perspicuity part of his definition of the sublime: "that force of composition, whatever it be, which strikes and overpowers the mind, which excites the passions, and which expresses ideas at once with perspicuity and elevation"; and elsewhere he praises a passage in Deuteronomy on the grounds that it "consists of sentences, pointed, energetic, concise, and splendid; that the sentiments are truly elevated and sublime, the language bright and animated, the expression and phraseology uncommon; while the mind of the poet never continues fixed to any single point, but glances continually from one object to another."[53] Lowth senses in Hebrew style a kind of scintillating restlessness, a supercharged *pointillisme* ("sentences pointed, energetic, concise") that reminds us of effects rendered by the Blakean wall of words, discussed earlier, as well as of the luminous potential that Blake tells us resides in particular and determinate forms.

The opinions on this topic of Blake's contemporary, the antiquarian and mythographer Richard Payne Knight, are particularly worth pausing over for their relevance to Blake's own views. Knight's *Analytical Inquiry into the Principles of Taste* directs a stream of argument against Burke's *Philosophical Enquiry*:

> The peculiar business of poetry is so to elevate and expand [its objects] that the imagination may conceive *distinct* but not *determinate* ideas of them; and thus have an infinite liberty of still exalting and expanding, without changing or confounding the images impressed upon it....
> All obscurity is imperfection; and indeed, if obscurity means indistinctness, it is always imperfection. The more distinct a description; and the more clearly the qualities, properties, and energies intended to be signified or expressed, are brought, as it were, before the eyes, the more effect it will have on the imagination and the passions: but then, it should be *distinct* without being *determinate*. In describing for instance, a storm at sea, the rolling, the curling, the foaming, the dashing, and roaring of the waves cannot be too clearly, too precisely expressed: but it should not be told how many yards in a minute they advanced.[54]

In opposing "distinct" to "determinate" ideas, Knight appears from a Blakean standpoint to be taking with one hand what he gives with the other, but the example supplied at the end of the passage alleviates this impression. By "determinate," Knight appears to mean "measured" or "quantifiable" rather than closed or definite. Knight's distinctness is indeed close to Blake's determinacy – and, like Blake, he stresses those elements in the sublime image that give it its *character*, or special form, and eliminates those elements that limit the object to the occasional, the material, or what Blake calls the "Accidental," the stuff of "number, weight, & measure" (*Marriage* 7.14). For Knight, the mind is not exalted and expanded by confronting a bloated indefiniteness. Rather, it must be pierced by the sharpness of the image, and only then can it expand in an indefinite liberty.

These various formulations – Lowth's splendid and pointed sentences, Blair's "lively" ideas, or Payne Knight's distinctly clear rolling waves – all pose a sublime based on salience or concentrated force against the Burkean sublime of perceptual deprivation and diffusion. This sublime substitutes intensity for extensiveness – it cuts more sharply and more deeply, vibrates more intensely, and compresses its power more minutely than anything that our ordinary senses provide.[55] This mode subsumes what Morton Paley has called "the sublime of energy,"[56] and it operates not only in energy's domain of the body but also in the domain of the text, or wherever the multiple and the multifaceted are made altogether manifest in a little moment or a little space. In his Annotations to Reynolds, Blake provides the most articulate and cogent formulation of this notion of the sublime. When Lowth or Payne Knight call for perspicuity and distinctness in sublime poetry, they do so in part because they think that it will bring the object more sharply into focus; the poet's style is like a pair of new eye-glasses for the myopic imagination. Blake goes beyond such writers in proclaiming the sublimity of determinacy, particularity, and discrimination for their own sake. They are valued not because they make objects more clear, but because they are the "real" constituents of objects. Indeed, Blake's prescriptions are too rigorous for even the most sharp-edged mimesis of objects to satisfy. Blake calls for a total determinacy, or closure of outline; a total particularity, or representation of all the parts – indeed, all the particles of the image; and a total discrimination or singularity – that is, the separation and differentiation of the image from every other contiguous image. No ordinary perception or ordinary description, however acute, can meet such requirements. In three-dimensional space, objects hide portions of themselves, crowd on one another's outlines, and break their masses, those nearby obscuring those farther away, all distorted by perspective. Nothing in this space can supply the "lineaments, or forms and features that are capable of being receptacles of intellect." There are only crowded absences here, not presence.

In his visual art, Blake's stylistic manner of flattening the picture plane and disposing his figures in a "symmetrical frontality" serves, as W. J. T.

Mitchell has pointed out, to minimize these defects of natural seeing. Blake is striving "to undercut the representational appearance of particular forms and to endow them with an abstract, stylized existence independent of the natural images with which they are identified." In essence, as Mitchell's study has effectively shown, "Blake's visual images move toward the realm of language, operating as arbitrary signs, emblems, or hieroglyphics."[57] All lines, pictorial and otherwise, are absorbed into the idea of text, an autonomous structure of writing that is anterior to possible referentiality. The particularity, determinacy, and singularity of language are to be found in its signifers, not in the indefinite plurality and ambiguity of its signifieds. The signifier is finite and, at the same time, "polyvalent," or endowed with a surplus of signifying potential in relation to any given signified.[58] "Not a line is drawn without intention & that most discriminate & particular as Poetry admits not a Letter that is Insignificant so Painting admits not a Grain of Sand or a Blade of Grass Insignificant" (Erdman 560). Every line, letter, or grain is "significant" in the sense that it is impressed with a self-subsistent signifying power, which is its principal glory. Blake's reference to the letter indicates that his interest here is in the forms as signifiers, and not in what they signify (see the famous crux in *Jerusalem* 3, Erdman 146: "every letter is studied"). The world of artifacts affords nothing more absolutely and exclusively linear, minute, determinate, particular, individuated, and differentiated than a graphic sign or letter. Because it imitates nothing and cannot be represented at all unless all its parts are inscribed completely, the form of a letter is both perfect and particular, definite and yet open to countless participations in potential reference. We may speak of the determinate sublime, then, as a sublime of the signifier, one in which exhilaration comes from recognition of the creative power of the letter. Behind the letter resides an unnamed and, to fallen eyes, unseen exactitude, for which the abstract term "human intellect" passes as a secular designation.[59]

Problems remain, however, in this account of Blake's sublime. How is one to reconcile, after all, the "indeterminacy" of the sublime moment with the specification that the sublime image must be "determinate"? How indeed does a sublime that requires something "altogether hidden" consort with one that banishes obscurity as its source? For all the harsh attacks on Burke, we may still sense the presence of a Burkean magnetic field tugging at the needle of Blake's aesthetic compass. Conversely, if Burke were to scan some knotty, congested passages from Blake's Prophecies, he certainly could not fault them for lack of obscurity or for a display of "little ideas." Even the characters of Blake's script sometimes fall short of an absolute formal determinacy, so that it is not always easy for an editor to decide what letter or mark of punctuation in a given passage is intended. While Blake's poetic and artistic practice is intellectually directed against Burkean assumptions and precepts, it often betrays a certain fondness for Burkean effects. Compared to Addison, for example, who finds the Roman Pantheon more sublime than a Gothic cathedral,[60] Burke and Blake seem to belong to the same camp: they are unavoidably allied as advocates of a problematic and agonistic sublime.

It is not in the matter of occasion or of agency that Blake and Burke differ in their conceptions of the sublime. They both provide a structure that includes a moment of discontinuity – the episode of "astonishment" – and a psychic effect in which the mind becomes self-divided. They differ in that Blake recognizes the means for a *more thorough* discontinuity and a more radical division of the faculties. Nothing can be more discontinuous with its surroundings than what is altogether determinate, particular, and distinct in itself. The more that Blake withholds from his texts those concessions to referentiality that create the illusion of representing objects known to our understanding – such as syntactic and narrative continuity, familiarity of allusion, and the like – the more his words, letters, and lines take on a distinct intensity of their own, and the more thoroughly they recede from the grasp of the Corporeal Understanding. Yet they do so without any scarifice to their intrinsic clarity of form. The sublime text must be a clear yet difficult text, its clarity based not on mundane simplicities, but indeed turned severely against them. The element of indeterminacy in the sublime of the text rests not at all with the sublime image itself, but with the expectations of the perceiver, conditioned to encounter signifiers that efface their own presence, the better to operate as servants of referentiality. This is one element of the difficulty involved in the determinate sublime, but obscurity, in the Burkean sense, is not the producer of this difficulty.[61] There is a difference between the obscurity that hides outlines like a formless vapor, demanding difficult and ultimately frustrated labor of attempted penetration, and the burden of a text that imposes on the perceiver the difficulty of apprehending many condensed visions of clarity all at once, none of them hidden; if there is blinding here, it is from an overdeterminate clarity of *presence.*[62] What are present, of course, are the seeds of meaning, not the external meanings themselves. Interpretive labors are still required to fetch these, but if the text is truly efficatious, the sublime event will have occurred before these labors begin. There is difficulty in this event too, perhaps greater than that involved in any of the subsequent labor. This is the struggle with a self that is impatient with discontinuity and paradox, demanding a servitude of language to familiar referentiality. Self-annihilation is the key here, as it is with so much else in Blake. When that is accomplished, paradox becomes visionary freedom and the recalcitrance of the text becomes the autonomy of a respected friend, a companion in the dialectic of desire.

The Poet's Work: His Sublime and His Pathos

"When that is accomplished": it is a tall order. Self-annihilation presumably provides the bridge between "the Most Sublime Poetry" and the altruism of "The most sublime act," which, as Blake states in the Proverbs of Hell, "is to set another before you" (*Marriage* 7.17). The sublime *experience* must eventuate in a sublime *doing*, or else the interplay of intellect and its self-satisfying desire remains a sterile and narcissistic exercise, quite alien to anything we know of Blake's program. But the subjugation of self and the act of setting another before oneself are problematic processes; to an observer they may as easily provoke a new sublime of terror as provide intimations of altruistic love. Take, for example, Los's famous *agon* with his Spectre in the first chapter of *Jerusalem*:

> Yet ceased he not from labouring at the roarings of his Forge
> With iron & brass Building Golgonooza in great contendings
> Till his Sons & Daughters came forth from the Furnaces
> At the sublime Labours for Los. compelld the invisible Spectre
> To labours mighty, with vast strength

(10.62–11.1)

Los labors here not in order to achieve the sublime experience but because he has already experienced it; he has had access to the Divine Vision and, indeed, keeps it (see 95.20). His work is both productive and altruistic, simultaneously paternal and maternal, as Blake suggests by projecting from the word "Labours" both the products of the womb ("Sons & Daughters") and those of the wage-earning factory artisan. The language of the passage, however, rigorously excludes any overt hint of the loving, the maternal, the soft, the yielding; it is redolent of the hard, muscular, contentious imagery of a masculine world ("roarings," "iron & brass," "great contendings," "compelld," "mighty," "strength"). If this is a sublime, it is a sublime that meets Burkean prescriptions – or, to use Blake's own words, a "Sublime . . . shut out from the Pathos" (90.12).

My general point is that Blake often finds it difficult to depict his actors in anything other than a sublime mode that they themselves are ostensibly trying to transcend. This is part of a larger problem attendant upon any production of sublime poetry that has a redemptive purpose: the recalcitrance of corporeal existence in time to which the poet must return after his own moment of astonishment and transformation. Ideally, "the Poets Work is Done . . . Within a Moment: a Pulsation of the Artery" (*Milton* 29.1–3), but after that moment has passed, the poet must face the fact that although "the Work" is done, the necessity of further labor is ongoing and unremitting ("yet ceased he not from labouring"). A posture of heroic endurance is required, which tends to bring with it, in what is supposed to be a labor of love, a disquieting rhetoric of force and compulsion. What goes for poets goes for readers alike; too often, after their own sublime encounter with the Blakean text, in their eagerness to spread the good news they turn into aggressive banner-wavers, relentless explicators, or imperious system builders, as anyone acquainted with the history of Blake criticism can easily attest. The essence of the sublime experience is that it offers *all*, a total gratification of desire to the Intellectual Powers, but the communication of that experience (whether by poets or by readers) too readily operates on a principle of *exclusion*, a casting out of the indulgent, the accommodating, the softer "feminine" affections.

Blake is thoroughly aware of this disturbing paradox and the shadow it casts on the efficacy of a "Most Sublime Poetry," and we may conclude this chapter on his conception of the sublime by examining the ways in which he articulates the problem. We are sometimes told that Blake has no distinct concept of the sublime as a separate category of aesthetic experience, that he uses the term as an indiscriminate epithet of praise, and that he conflates the categories of the sublime and the beautiful at will.[63] Although conflations of this sort do occur at certain points in his work, the fact remains that Blake displays a perfect conversance with the terminology of aesthetic categorization in his day. The categories are listed, for example, with their anatomical seats of origin, in this Proverb of Hell: "The head Sublime, the heart Pathos, the genitals Beauty, the hands & feet Proportion" (*Marriage* 10.1). Later in his career he develops a strong preoccupation with these categories, particularly the two chief contraries, the sublime and the pathetic (often subsumed in contemporary accounts by the beautiful). Thus we may infer from some cancelled lines on the frontispiece to *Jerusalem* that he originally intended to make the separation of sublimity from pathos the very argument of his great poetic *summa*. This inference is corroborated by a remarkable account in *A Descriptive Catalogue* of a "voluminous" work on "a subject of great sublimity and pathos" (almost certainly *Jerusalem*), which his painting "The Ancient Britons" was designed to illustrate. It is worth pausing over this account, for it reveals more clearly than anything else in Blake's work a sense of the sublime as a category of limitation or exclusion – not an *all*, but a residue of something prior and greater, for which no aesthetic term is available.

The discussion of the Ancient Britons strangely converts a myth of the origins of history into an allegory of the genesis of aesthetic categories; the myth not only projects "sublimity and pathos," it is *about* sublimity and pathos:

> The three general classes of men who are represented by the most
> Beautiful, the most Strong, and the most Ugly, could not be repres-

ented by any historical facts but those of our own country, the Ancient Britons; ... They were overwhelmed by brutal arms all but a small remnant; Strength, Beauty, and Ugliness escaped the wreck, and remain for ever unsubdued age after age .... The Strong man represents the human sublime. The Beautiful man represents the human pathetic, which was in the wars of Eden divided into male and female. The Ugly man represents the human reason. They were originally one man, who was fourfold; he was self-divided, and his real humanity slain on the stems of generation, and the form of the fourth was like the Son of God. How he became divided is a subject of great sublimity and pathos. (*Descriptive Catalogue* Erdman 542–3)

We are uneasily aware that the "human sublime" offered to us here is something different from notions of the sublime discussed earlier in this chapter, as deduced from the letter to Butts or the annotations to Reynolds. In those instances, the sublime appears to be a term for an absolute height of value toward which all art must tend; here, it merely connotes one *kind* of aesthetic value among others, existing on a par with other competing values, such as those of the beautiful and the pathetic. In the latter case, the sublime serves as a term of differentiation, just as the terms "male" and "female" differentiate subsets of humanity. Some background is useful at this point. Throughout the eighteenth century, ideas of the beautiful and the pathetic tend to separate out from the idea of the sublime.[64] At the same time, as Monk has shown, the pathetic comes increasingly to signify the softer affections aroused by the pitiable and the endearing.[65] Meanwhile, the beautiful tends to lose its ancient conventional association with harmony and proportion, and to acquire feminine sexual connotations. Burke's treatise on the sublime and the beautiful is particularly influential in this latter development. He specifically rejects proportion as the source of beauty and locates it instead in the small, the physically unthreatening, the smooth, and the gently curvaceous, all essentially female attributes that, he writes, comprise "the physical cause of love." The pathetic and the beautiful thus converge upon a common eroticized femininity. Massive, strong, threatening, rugged, and angular, the sublime is obviously conceived as a contrasting male counterpart.[66] Blake himself shows a post-Burkean understanding of beauty when, in the Proverb from the *Marriage* quoted previously, he specifically divorces proportion from beauty, and locates the latter in the genitals. Likewise, in the account of the Ancient Britons, he accepts the assimilation of pathos and beauty: "The Beautiful man represents the human pathetic," and in the fall, this Ancient Briton evolves a female double. Blake substitutes *pathos* for Burke's beauty as the effective contrary term to the sublime ("the human *sublime*," "the human *pathetic*"), but he perpetuates the identification of the contraries as masculine and feminine principles.

In his account of the Ancient Britons, Blake categorizes these principles, yet tends to blur the distinctions between them. Among the Ancient Britons there are, after all, no separate females; all three are men. Moreover, some of their attributes tend to slide into one another: the human pathetic is Beautiful, and there is a Beauty "proper to sublime art" – namely, "lineaments, or forms and features that are capable of being the receptacles of intellect" (Erdman 544). Blake describes his Strong man, the human sublime itself, "as a receptacle of Wisdom, a sublime energizer; his features and limbs do not spindle out into length, without strength, nor are they too large and unwieldy for his brain and bosom. Strength consists in accumulation of power to the principal seat, and from thence a regular gradation and subordination; strength is compactness, not extent nor bulk" (Erdman 545). Strength is, of course, a conventional attribute of the Burkean sublime, but here it is difficult to distinguish from Beauty; if one is a "receptacle of intellect," the other is a "receptacle of Wisdom." Moreover, the description of Strength focuses, oddly enough, almost entirely on classical proportion ("regular gradation and subordination") – the traditional criterion for beauty itself, until Burke banished it in favor of a quasi-feminized form. Beauty is thus defined in terms that belong properly to the sublime ("the head Sublime"), and the human sublime is described in terms traditionally proper to beauty. They interpenetrate in a latently erotic union, as compact strength energizes itself within a receptacle of lineaments – lineaments of gratified desire, perhaps.

They interpenetrate, and yet they do not. If the sublime, the beautiful, and the pathetic are one, why establish them as separate personifications in the first place? And why attach these figures to a myth that discovers them to be already diminished forces? For the Strong man, the Beautiful man, and the Ugly man "were originally one man, who was fourfold; . . . and the form of the fourth was like the Son of God." If the Strong man is the human sublime, who is this fourth, who, according to the myth, vanished "In the last Battle of King Arthur [when] only Three Britons escaped" (Erdman 542)? Indeed, who is the "one man" whose "real humanity" was slain? The "human" of the terms "human sublime" and "human pathetic" appears to be something less than "real humanity," just as three is an inescapable reduction of four.

Blake would like to have it both ways on this matter. He would like to imagine the three Britons as a small, indefatigable remnant, perpetuating in corporeal time and space the plenary powers of humanity that existed before the fall: "a small remnant; Strength, Beauty, and Ugliness escaped the wreck, and remain for ever unsubdued, age after age" (Erdman 542). Thus when he comes to "say something concerning his ideas of Beauty, Strength and Ugliness," (Erdman 544) he presents at least two of these in the interchangeable terms that would have been proper to their ideal status in eternity. The Ugly man, meanwhile, has already taken on the look and actions of lupine or tigerish savagery prominent in the eighteenth-century sublime of terror: "approaching to the beast in features and form, his forehead small, without frontals; his jaws large; nose high on the ridge, and narrow; . . . The Ugly Man acts from love of carnage, and delight in the savage barbarities of war" (Erdman 544–5).[67] Clearly, there is no perpetuation of a prelapsarian sensibility here. Blake's painting of the ancient Britons thus depicts gradations of fallenness; some residues of the fall have separated farther from the lineaments of intellect and gratified desire than others, but all are separate and diminished to some degree. It is only a matter of time before the Strong man, the human sublime, becomes no more than the brawny, cavern-dwelling "*strong* Urthona" (*Europe* 3.10) depicted in the early Lambeth books, or the raging, despairing, indefinitely formed Tharmas, "Parent *power* darkning in the West" (*Four Zoas* 4.6). These are mock strengths and mock powers – for the human sublime when it is cut off from pathos, or the love of intellect for form, becomes an elaborate masquerade for despair.

This latter stage of separation is presented in two important passages from *Jerusalem*, briefly cited previously. One of these is from the cancelled inscription on the frontispiece:

His Sublime & Pathos become Two Rocks fixd in the Earth
His Reason his Spectrous Power, covers them above
Jerusalem his Emanation is a Stone laying beneath

(1.4–6)

Another version of this scene appears late in the poem:

no more the Masculine mingles
With the Feminine, but the sublime is shut out from the Pathos
In howling torment, to build stone walls of separation, compelling
The Pathos, to weave curtains of hiding secresy from the torment.

(90.10–13)

These passages raise the paradoxical idea of a *deprived* sublime, one that is "shut out" from other forms of sensibility, a sublime that is petrified and, in short, fallen. In the first of these passages, the human reason has advanced to sovereignty over the other faculties. In the second, the "stone walls of separation" and the curtain of secrecy that the sublime and the pathos place before one another look suspiciously like those thwartings, or barriers, or obscurities that figure so largely in eighteenth-century accounts of the sublime as a mode of deprivation – a view found in its most rationalist form in Burke. A sublime of deprivation becomes automatically a sublime that puts itself in reason's spectrous power, for it requires that we reason the idea of strength or power into being through negative tokens – withdrawals, resistances, incomplete disclosures. But what has really withdrawn is not "the great" (as Addison called the sublime experience), but rather something so deeply hidden that its absence is unremarked because its appeal is buried (like the Emanation Jerusalem "laying beneath") or forgotten. The mind's deep quest is for receptacles of intellect, the total gratification of desire in definite, permanent form.

Weiskel has found anxiety at the core of the eighteenth-century fascination with the sublime, "the anxiety of nothingness, or absence. In its more energetic rendition the sublime is a kind of homeopathic therapy, a cure of uneasiness by means of the stronger, more concentrated – but momentary – anxiety involved in astonishment and terror."[68] But the unease is never really cured, which is why sublime poems of the period often have to repeat their heightened moments again and again.[69] It is not cured because the true source of the mind's deprivation is concealed from it. The mind is induced into believing that it is deprived from access to "the great," and so it dreams up strategies for discovering itself equal or superior to this "great" – empty strategies from Blake's point of view, for this great does not exist, it is "not extent nor bulk." All the while, however, the anxiety, the unease, the stirrings of an unacknowledged desire continue, prompting the mind to ever-renewed feats of grandeur, new "highs." The Burkean sublime is despair ("howling torment") that thinks itself to be a plenitude of strength.

The masculinist language of the Burkean sublime is important in this context. When Blake paraphrases the separation of the sublime and the pathos as "no more the Masculine mingles with the Feminine," he refers, of course, not to actual men and women. If the masculine mingles no more with the feminine, it is not for lack of physical congress, but rather for lack of something more truly fulfilling. The masculine and feminine principles within the self, which comprise the love dialogue between creative intellect and formal lineaments, have become sundered, so that love is sought in one place and transcendence or the sublime in another, in a masculinist framework divorced from the fulfillment of erotic desire. More accurately, the desires are not quelled, but simply shifted elsewhere. Burke speaks of the softer affections with considerable condescension: "love approaches much nearer to contempt than is commonly imagined," and Frances Ferguson has noted Burke's oddly enervating conception about sexual arousal and the effects of beauty.[70] One reason for this is that the full language of Eros is transferred to another encounter – that with the masculine sublime. Admiration, and then erotic intensity, become attached to strength and bulk. When Burke, describing "the passion caused by the sublime," tells us that it "hurries us on by an irresistible force" and leaves a mind "entirely filled with its object,"[71] he employs the language of ravishment and reveals the latently homoerotic discourse that underpins much of his aesthetics. In the fall, one forgets what one loves – even though the desire for it remains. To vie in muscular, rocklike strength against the vast rock-face of "the great" allows one to forget one's loss; it is a transaction that can assimilate desire in a form in which it need not be recognized as such.

As is frequently noted, Blake, too, privileges masculine imagery in his designs and masculine forms of action in his poetry. Even his type of the human Pathetic, is, before an unfortunate postlapsarian division into sexes, a Beautiful *man*. Some recent critics have called attention to homosexual imagery in certain of Blake's designs. Perhaps one purpose of these displays of eroticized male forms in his work is to expose the latent argument of conventional eighteenth-century sublime aesthetics to plain sight.[72] The object of the exposé is not the homoeroticism per se of the Burkean sublime, but rather its structure of subterfuge and displacement. Blake decodes the attraction to male dominance, cloudily concealed in an abstract discourse about "the great," by offering clearly delineated, unadorned masculine images of potency and action.

But there is also a more positive impulse at work in Blake's privileging of male form. Strength, struggle, and contest all play a genuine part in the constellation of qualities that he values, because they are all necessary to break down conventional modes of understanding. In the Edenic state, the sublime and the pathetic presumably disappear as separate modes of aesthetic experience and reappear joined in an intellectual form neither male nor female. But few readers are already in the Edenic state when they come to Blake, nor would they need the mediation of his art if they were so. The figure of the eroticized male mediates by destabilizing conventional norms of gender polarization, and hence it starts to undo the fall. It thus functions like the Blakean text itself. Blake requires a text that evokes a psychology of response similar to that of the Burkean sublime while presenting an altogether different set of rewards. Hence, he is willing to let a kind of separatist or masculinist aesthetic prevail provisionally in his work, one that defers easy gratification and subjects the reader to various forms of muscular rough treatment – assault on the senses, indecorum, deprivation of the corporeal understanding, unending challenge. The well-delineated muscularity of his masculine images thus serves as a visible epitome of this textual activity.

These images, as images, remain nonetheless a mode of sublimity shut out from the pathos. Yet it is not a sublimity that we can afford to pass unalarmed – as Wordsworth, to Blake's dismay, claimed to do with Jehovah and his shouting angels.[73] The human sublime needs the sublime of greatness and potent terror as a necessary foil, as a first term in a process of educative reading. Let us recall the scene from the cancelled frontispiece of *Jerusalem*, in which a spectrous reason hovers over the two rocks of the sublime and the pathetic, imposed on top of a buried Jerusalem. Once located in the position of the keystone over the arch whereby we enter the poem, the lines plausibly may contain hints to direct our own reading of the poem. We are allowed to see the spectre hovering over the rocky landscape as a rationalist reader might pore over the plates of Blake's sublime allegory. What this reader sees are isolated and ill-defined shapes that he can recognize from the context of eighteenth-century aesthetics – a knottily muscular, surly sublime and an unrefined mass of pathos, a bundle of soft, ineffectual emotions. Both forms emerge murkily from the *Jerusalem* text itself, a stone slab, a plate of scratched metal, a table impressed with a crowd of dead signs. What the spectrous reader does not see is Jerusalem the Emanation, the form of gratified desire, which is a living text.

When Blake cancelled this passage from the frontispiece, so that in all extant copies we enter the gate of the poem wordlessly, he deprived us of these emblematic hints of how to read it. It is one thing to be shown the reasoning spectre reading badly, and quite another to be catapulted directly into the work without posted warnings regarding the spectrous reader in ourselves. This spectrous reader must be conjured up time after time until at last, in our floundering reading of the text, we read *him* and read his sublime (which has been ours until this point) as the vast funerary monument to a displaced erotic desire. Blake forces us to reenact these spectrous readings, to relive these ravishments by "the great," or finally to reject them. The arena for these choices and challenges is in that sum of particular signifying acts and forms that we call the poet's style. On the level of style, as well as of idea, there are two sublimes, one darkly mimicking the other – or, rather, in its rough, separately masculine fashion, memorializing the other, namely the lost but potentially recoverable sublime of intellect. Blake treats the Burkean style of the sublime as Los might treat his spectrous brother; it is appropriated, assimilated, hated, and perhaps secretly loved, but ultimately made present as a negation, the better to reveal the outlines of a new, emergent style.

NOTES

1 See Weiskel 11 and 23–4. Paley (1983) 61 notes elements of the Burkean sublime in the "sublime Wonder" passage of *Jerusalem*.
2 Edmund Burke (1958) 57.
3 Addison, for example, tells us that "our imagination loves to be filled with an object, or to grasp at anything that is too big for its capacity. We are flung into a pleasing astonishment at such unbounded views"; according to Johnson, "[The sublime is] that comprehension and expanse of thought which at once fills the whole mind, and of which the first effect is sudden astonishment, and

the second rational admiration." Here is a sampling of similar contemporary opinions: "The sublime . . . takes possession of our attention, and of all our faculties, and absorbs them in astonishment"; "[the sublime] imports such ideas presented to the mind, as raise it to an uncommon degree of elevation, and fill it with admiration and astonishment"; "objects exciting terror are . . . in general sublime; for terror always implies astonishment, occupies the whole soul, and suspends all its motions." See, respectively, Addison (1811) iv. 340; "The Life of Cowley" in Samuel Johnson (1905) i. 20–1; Usher (1769) 102; "A Critical Dissertation on the Poems of Ossian," in Blair (1773) ii. 422; and Gerard (1759) 19.

4   It is worth recalling Burke's well-known formulation here: "whatever is in any sort terrible, or is conversant about terrible objects, or operates in a manner analogous to terror, is a source of the *sublime*; that is, it is productive of the strongest emotion which the mind is capable of feeling" (Edmund Burke (1958) 39). Just as Burke's sublime rides on an aesthetics of darkness and deprivation, pain and terror, so in Blake's vocabulary *dark* prevails numerically over *light*, *night* over *day*, *death* over *life*. More notably, the word *terror(s)* and its co-derivatives *terrible, terrific*, and *terrified*, taken as a collectivity, would rank within the dozen most frequently used words in his concorded vocabulary (Erdman (1967) records a total of 393 appearances of these terms). Despite his stated aversion to Burke, Blake so closely associates the sublime with the terrific that the terminology of the latter often acquires an honorific luster in his work. Thus we have such phrases as "Terrified at the sublime Wonder," cited previously (the Spaces of Erin are beautiful to Los – see *Jerusalem* 11.8–15), "terrible Blake in his pride" ("When Klopstock England defied," line 2), an uncharacteristically affectionate Enitharmon's "Lovely terrible Los wonder of Eternity" (*Four Zoas* 90.15), the "terrors of friendship" (*Jerusalem* 45.4), and the "terrific Lions & Tygers" that "sport & play" before the Great Harvest at the end of *Milton* (*Milton* 42.38). In these instances *terror* loses most of its terrors, and one gets the sense that in such cases Blake is paying tribute less to the signified *feeling* of terror than to the signifier, a vocabulary of the sublime fondly preserved from the fashions of his youth.

5   Edmund Burke (1958) 58.

6   Longinus (1756) 3.

7   There are fifty-one uses of terms from the collectivity *astonish(ed)(es)(ing)(ment)* in Blake's poetry. Among poets of comparable stature, range, and sublime interests, Milton's poetry yields only six instances; Wordsworth's, seventeen; and Shelley's, eleven. Pope draws upon this cluster of terms sixteen times, almost entirely for his translations of Homer, and Dryden, eleven times, mostly for the *Aeneid*.

8   See Hilton (1983) 16–17, and especially 239–57.

9   This connection is reinforced by the older sense of *astonished* (or its variant *astonied*) to connote deathlike paralysis and insensibility; thus the *OED* on *astonished*: "Stunned; made insensible, benumbed, paralyzed (1611)"; cf. also Milton on Satan's legions, who "lie thus astonisht on th' oblivious Pool" (*PL* i. 266).

10   See Edmund Burke (1958) 37 and 40.

11 Samuel Johnson (1905) i. 21.

12 Usher (1769) 102.

13 Lowth (1787) i. 353.

14 Edmund Burke (1958) 68.

15 Thus Usher remarks in *Clio* that the more violent manifestations of nature cause in us "an humiliating awe, surprise, and suspense: the mind views the effects of boundless power with still amazement" (Usher (1769) 111). Decades later, in his MS treatise "The Sublime and the Beautiful," Wordsworth speaks in similar fashion of "a humiliation or prostration of the mind before some external agency which it presumes not to make an effort to participate but is absorbed in the contemplation of the might in the external power" (Owen and Smyser ii. 354).

16 *The Prelude* (1850), 6. 592–605.

17 Kant (1914) 119–20. The best compact exposition of Kant's views on the sublime remains that of Monk (1935) 6–9.

18 Kant (1914) 117.

19 Weiskel, the most acute and unsparing critic of the Kantian sublime, would have it otherwise: "Blake hated the indefinite, rejected the numinous, and insisted on the primacy of the imagination. His work makes a profound critique of the natural sublime"; in particular, Blake is an enemy "to the inscrutability which always attends the numinous" (Weiskel 7). In making these claims, Weiskel ignores Blake's definition of "the Most Sublime Poetry" as involving something "altogether hidden." He also passes over those occasions in Blake on which the poet celebrates the incomprehensible (e.g., "The Four Living Creatures Chariots of Humanity Divine Incomprehensible / In beautiful Paradises expand" [*Jerusalem* 98.24–5]) or insists on numinous awe (Blake takes Wordsworth himself to task, for example, for not showing *enough* awe when the latter speaks of passing "Jehovah . . . unalarmed" [Erdman 666]). Weiskel appears, moreover, to discount the fact that the terms "Imagination" and "Reason" have mutually reversed connotations in Kant and Blake. That Blake attacks certain emphases on humiliation and deprivation in contemporary theories of the sublime is not in dispute, and Weiskel offers keen insights concerning this critique (Weiskel 63–79). But a critique of a tradition by no means indicates a divorce from that tradition, particularly in the case of one so dialectically motivated as Blake.

20 Kant (1914) 115–16.

21 Longinus (1756) 18.

22 Kant (1914) 129.

23 Usher (1769) 103.

24 Beattie (1783) 606; quoted Monk (1935) 129.

25 Dennis (1704) 6.

26 Ibid., 17. The resemblance has been noted by Beer (1978) 248–9.

27 Dennis (1704) 16 and 21.

28 Ibid., 78.

29 Cf. Roger R. Easson's comment that "Sublime allegory is designed to arouse the intellectual faculties by its grandly manipulative obscurity so that the individual's humanity may awake and cast off the dominance of reason"

(Easson (1973) 316). This insight has much validity, but it disregards elements of attraction built into the sublime text and assigns too much of a purely negative function to its difficulties, which, in Easson's account, work more by anarchic destructiveness than by love: "Sublime poetry . . . threatens to disorient the reader, to overthrow reason, and to let loose the disintegrating forces of chaos" (ibid.).

30 See, e.g., Hartman (1975) 120: "The structure of the act of reading . . . is the structure of the sublime experience in a finer mode"; in Hertz (1978) 70, we hear of an "ascesis of reading"; Frances Ferguson (1981) 67 notes that Burke places poetry at the summit of his "ordering of the arts" because he recognizes language as the preeminent site of difficulty and alienation from apprehensible nature; Weiskel 26–31 speaks of sublime objects and perceivers in terms of "signifiers" and "signifieds" and calls the sublime of difficulty and indeterminacy a "hermeneutic or 'readers's' sublime."

31 R. S. Crane, in his important review of Monk's book on the sublime, was the first to distinguish the naturalized or psychological sublime from the older tradition of the rhetorical sublime (*Philological Quarterly* 15 (1936) 165–7); Weiskel begins his own approach to his subject "with the hypothesis that the encounter with literary greatness – the so-called rhetorical sublime – is structurally cognate with the transcendence, gentle or terrible, excited in the encounter with landscape, the 'natural' sublime" (Weiskel 11).

32 See Longinus (1756) 3: "the Sublime is a certain Eminence of or Perfection of Language, and . . . the greatest Writers, both in Verse and Prose, have by this alone obtain'd the Prize of Glory, and fill'd all Time with their Renown." A remnant of this view survives in Burke, who, after all, strews his *Philosophical Enquiry* with examples from literary texts, and who, despite his stress on the natural sublime, concedes in the final sentence of his treatise that "words" have a power to "affect us often as strongly as the things they represent, and sometimes much more strongly" (Edmund Burke (1958) 177).

33 The most useful account of Blake's debt to these traditions appears in Wittreich (1975) 171–88. Both Hertz (1978) and Weiskel 30–1 touch on the connection between the hermeneutic difficulties of sacred allegory and the bafflements of the sublime, but the richest treatment of the connection is that of Fletcher (1964) 233–61. Fletcher argues, in effect, that the sublime sensibility is simply the eighteenth-century continuation of allegorical modes of thought. If this is true, then Blake's term "Sublime Allegory" epitomizes the transition. The term itself, as has been variously noted, perhaps derives from Lowth (1787) i. 203: "that sublimer kind of allegory," which under a literal meaning "conceals one interiour and more sacred."

34 As Michael Murrin succinctly puts it, "The allegorical poet affects his audience more in the manner of a Hebrew prophet than in that of a classical orator. Instead of appealing to all the people and attempting to win them over to a particular point of view, the poet causes a division in his audience, separating the few from the many, those who can understand from those who cannot . . ." (Murrin (1969) 13).

35 Gerard (1759) 15–16.

36   For example, in describing his painting of the Last Judgment, Blake drifts easily into talking about poetry: "The Last Judgment is not Fable or Allegory but Vision Fable or Allegory are a totally distinct & inferior kind of Poetry" (*Vision of the Last Judgment*, Erdman 554); conversely, when he praises Chaucer's characters, he does so in the pictorial terms of his own aesthetic: "the characters themselves for ever remain unaltered, and consequently they are the physiognomies of lineaments of universal human life, beyond which Nature never steps" (*Descriptive Catalogue*, Erdman 532–3).

37   "Frost at Midnight" 19 and 21–2.

38   See Quilligan (1979) 42.

39   As Heppner puts it, "it is the human power to signify that is the basis for the sublime, not the sensory properties of the material world" (Heppner (1983) 56).

40   Weiskel 180–1; see *Prelude* (1850) 5. 595–605.

41   Some recent treatments of allegory view the entire mode generally in a similar perspective. For example, Quilligan observes that "the 'other' named by the term *allos* in the word 'allegory' is not some other hovering above the words of the text, but the possibility of an otherness, a polysemy, inherent in the very words on the page; allegory therefore names the fact that language can signify many things at once" (Quilligan (1979) 26).

42   See Frye (1947) 380. In the same passage in which he speaks of a "sublimer kind of allegory," Lowth refers to the surface subject as a "rind or shell" hiding the deeper and more important meaning (Lowth (1787) i. 203).

43   "Note here that Fable or Allegory is Seldom without some Vision," Blake concedes in a famous passage of *A Vision of The Last Judgment* (Erdman 554), in which "Vision" replaces the earlier "Sublime Allegory" as the term for the highest reach of art. But the reverse is also true, as Blake makes obvious in the same essay when he identifies the figures of his painting of the Last Judgment in terms that correspond altogether to the conventional notion of allegory; e.g., "it ought to be understood that the Persons Moses & Abraham are not here meant but the States Signified by those Names the Individuals being representatives or Visions of those States"; "The Figure dragging up a Woman by her hair represents the Inquisition"; "they strip her naked & burn her with fire it represents the Eternal Consummation of Vegetable Life & Death with its Lusts" (Erdman 556, 557–8, 558). Frye (1947) 9–11 is useful in distinguishing the two opposing senses in which Blake uses the term "allegory."

44   It is always important to keep in mind the degree of serious deliberation involved in Blake's annotations to Reynolds. The annotated British Library copy of Reynolds's *Works* (the first volume of the three-volume second edition of 1798) contains page after page on which Blake's comments are drafted lightly in pencil and then retraced carefully in ink. Blake presumably considered his marginalia an "official" combat against Reynolds's errors, waged on the very site of their perpetration.

45   E.g., as the agency of the sublime experience, Burke proposes "an unnatural tension and certain violent emotions of the nerves," and he accounts for the delight produced by the sublime as "a sort of tranquility tinged with terror; which as it belongs to self-preservation is one of the strongest of all the

passions" (Edmund Burke (1958) 134, 136). Blake is perhaps indebted directly to Burke for his phrase "Corporeal Understanding": "It is probable," Burke writes, "that not only the inferior parts of the soul, as the passions are called, but the understanding itself makes use of some fine corporeal instruments in its operation" (ibid., 135).

46 Ibid., 61 and 63.

47 As Weiskel summarizes it, "The soul is a vacancy, whose extent is discovered as it is filled. Inner space, the infinitude of the Romantic mind, is born as a massive and more or less unconscious emptiness, an absence" (Weiskel 15). Tuveson (1951) traces the eighteenth-century tendency to identify the physical preserves of God with outer space itself.

48 Edmund Burke (1958) 75.

49 Ibid., 78.

50 Weiskel 67.

51 See *Monthly Review* 16 (1757) 477n.

52 Blair (1773) ii. 423 and 385.

53 Lowth (1787) i. 120, 131, 307, and 325.

54 Knight (1808) 391–2.

55 Cf. Knight on Greek poetry: "The obscurity of the lyric style of Pindar and the Greek tragedians does not arise from any confusion or indistinctness in the imagery; but from its conciseness and abruptness, and from its being shown to the mind in sudden flashes and corruscations, the connexion between which is often scarcely perceptible" (Knight (1808) 401).

56 See Paley (1970) 3–11.

57 Mitchell (1978) 19, 37, and 4.

58 The best discussion of polyvalence or "polysemy" of signification in Blake may be found in Hilton (1983) 10–18.

59 Eaves observes that "metaphors of precision have very close relatives ... in teleological metaphors of ultimate truth, of final distinctions, in Christian theology. A universal man – a man who is the universe, such as the figure of Christ who appears at the beginning of Revelation as a conglomerate of divinity–humanity–animal–vegetable–mineral – carries out the Last Judgement with a two-edged sword as his organ of discourse" (Eaves (1982) 20). Speaking more specifically of Blake's small units of language – words – Hilton says that "the more deliberately the word is perceived, the more it begins to assert itself – to spell itself out – in all its associations and etymology, its eternal human form ... Every word is a parable about linguistic structure as incarnate human imagination" (Hilton (1983) 7).

60 Addison (1811) v. 350ff.

61 See Wittreich (1975) 188. Wittreich tells us that Blake rejects "obscurity as opacity," the obscurity of the Burkean sublime (187). Blake's work demands a complexity of seeing, but this is not the same thing as hindered seeing, which the term "obscurity" implies. The Corporeal Understanding is hindered not so much by obscurities that the poet imposes as by its own false presuppositions.

62 Price (1969) 211, speaking of Blake's occasional pileups of small, sharply visualized details, comments on "the closeness of attention that all but obliterates the outlines of the natural object in its familiar form, finding in it

the effluence of vast powers and rising in wonder to a contemplation of those powers through the object."

63 See Weiskel 67.

64 For Longinus, the Pathetic "or the Power of raising passions to a violent and even enthusiastic degree" was an extremely important, though not a necessary, constituent of the sublime (see Longinus (1756) 17–18). By the first decade of the eighteenth century, Dennis so fully identifies the sublime with the "Enthusiastick Passion" that he even takes Longinus to task for suggesting that the sublime can do without it (Dennis (1704) 78). Late in the century, however, the sublime and the pathetic have become quite distinct, as Johnson's comment on the Metaphysical poets serves to indicate: "Nor was the sublime more within their reach than the pathetick" (Samuel Johnson (1905) i. 20).

65 See Monk (1935) 13 and Paley (1983) 58. Paley provides a good account of Blake's references to the pathetic, particularly with regard to *Jerusalem*.

66 On female beauty, physical love, and masculine traits, see, respectively, Edmund Burke (1958) 115, 151, and 124–5.

67 Dennis is seminal in considering ferocious wild beasts – "Monsters, Serpents, Lions, Tygers" – as appropriate subjects for arousing "Enthusiastick Terrour" and, hence, the sublime (Dennis (1704) 87–8). The sublime, Burke tells us in remarks perhaps not lost on the author of "The Tyger," "comes upon us in the gloomy forest, and in the howling wilderness, in the form of the lion, the tiger, the panther, or rhinoceros." He adds that "on account of their unmanageable fierceness, the idea of a wolf is not despicable; it is not excluded from grand descriptions and similitudes" (Edmund Burke (1958) 66 and 67). Burke may have in mind the famous and bloodcurdling passage on the ravenous mountain wolves, in Thomson's "Winter" 388–413.

68 Weiskel 18.

69 See, for example, Thomson's unappeasable appetite for introducing catastrophe after catastrophe in *The Seasons*, even in the generally benign contexts of "Spring" and "Summer"; on the verbal level, a similar effect is achieved by the jerky, unremittingly exclamatory style of Young's *Night Thoughts*.

70 See Edmund Burke (1958) 67 and Ferguson (1981) 75–6.

71 Edmund Burke (1958) 57.

72 Price notes that the "homosexual fantasy" evident in some eighteenth-century Gothic novels ("sublime beauties coloured by guilt and ambivalent desire") is connected to "the summoning up of titanic energies from their caves of suppression" (Price (1969) 205). Lately some note has been taken of homoerotic elements in Blake's own work; e.g., Fox (1976) 228–9, and Mitchell (1973) 66–7, raise the question of certain designs in *Milton*; and in her sometimes heavy-handed Freudian study *Blake's Prophetic Psychology*, Webster reads these designs as unmistakably homosexual, interpreting them as the poet's quest to acquire the potency of an idealized male muse (Webster (1983) 261–2). *Milton* is, of course, the work par excellence in which the Poet is overtaken by the "irresistible" force of the sublime moment.

73 See the famous passage from Wordsworth's "Prospectus" to *The Excursion* 31–5, and Blake's marginal retort (Erdman 666).

Wordsworth

3

Wordsworth, Rousseau and the Politics of Education

James K. Chandler

All our wisdom consists in servile prejudices. All our practices are only subjection, impediment, and constraint. Civil man is born, lives, and dies in slavery. At his birth he is sewed in swaddling clothes.... So long as he keeps his human shape, he is enchained by our institutions.

Rousseau, *Emile*

"The Old Cumberland Beggar," with its admonishment to "Statesmen," is an explicitly political poem. But although Wordsworth made a point of sending a copy of the two-volume edition of *Lyrical Ballads* to Charles James Fox in 1800, the "Beggar" is virtually the only explicitly political poem to appear in the collection. This fact, curious enough in itself, becomes more curious still when we consider that the "Beggar" was one of the very few of Wordsworth's poems in *Lyrical Ballads* to be composed before the poet's announcement of a new project, one that would occupy his utmost attention through the major period and beyond. "My object," he wrote to James Tobin in the often-quoted letter of 6 March 1798, "is to give pictures of Nature, Man, and Society. Indeed I know not anything which will not come within the scope of my plan" (*EY* 123). Wordsworth probably composed the political passages for the "Beggar" (such as the address to the statesmen) sometime during the six weeks prior to his announcement to Tobin. He would include no similarly explicit political comment in any poem until 1802.

The Prelude, Wordsworth's most important political poem, though not his most explicit, was of course getting well under way in the period from 1798 to 1802. In the full-length version familiar to modern readers, however, *The*

Prelude gives the clearest signs of its ideological orientation in the France books. In the years 1798–1802, as modern scholarship on the poem's genesis has shown, the design called for no treatment whatsoever of Wordsworth's experience of the Revolution. If we look to Wordsworth's work in the years prior to 1798, we find an array of overtly radical poetry and prose. If we look beyond *The Prelude* to *The Excursion* and *The Convention of Cintra*, the political dimension becomes as explicit as it had been in the radical writings of the 1790s. The question, then, is simply this: what happened to Wordsworth's political interests, so evident beforehand and afterward, in the seminal years that comprise the first half of his great decade?

The best lead toward a solution of this problem has emerged from the findings of those scholars who have established a sense of what *The Prelude* was meant to be before Wordsworth decided to expand it into the thirteen-book poem he completed in late 1805. The rough chronology is now fairly clear. Wordsworth began work on the poem in late 1798, and in early 1804 he maintained a view of the poem still probably close to his initial conception: "a Poem on my own earlier life," as he put it to Francis Wrangham in late January or early February, "which will take five parts or books to complete" (*EY* 436). Wordsworth told Wrangham he had three of the books nearly finished. By early March he had completed a fourth and was turning to the last (p. 452). By 12 March he seems already decided on extending the poem (p. 456).[1]

Although the evidence therefore shows that Wordsworth nearly completed the five-book poem before deciding to expand it, the labor of reconstruction has been difficult. Even Jonathan Wordsworth, the five-book *Prelude*'s most ambitious editor, admits that some pieces of the puzzle are probably forever lost or scrambled. Nonetheless, building on the work of those who came before him, he does make a convincing case for his view of the poem's general shape, especially with Books 1 through 4. Books 1–3 correspond roughly to the first three Books of the 1805 *Prelude* – they were in fact copied before Wordsworth's decision to expand. Book 4 evidently fell into two sections, one corresponding to the narrative of the Long Vacation at Hawkshead in Book 4 of the 1805 *Prelude* and the other corresponding to the discussion of books and education in Book 5 of the full-length poem. The final book was probably going to feature the account of the ascent of Snowdon and the famous passage that begins "There are in our existence spots of time."[2] This general outline, whose contours have become increasingly clear since de Selincourt's work of decades ago, quite reasonably leads the most recent editors of the five-book poem to conclude that it is "about a poet's education, by nature and by books, down to the end of his formal education when he was twenty."[3]

This well-supported hypothesis has implications that we should not be reluctant to consider. What Book 5 ("Books") is doing in the full-length

Prelude, for example, is a question that has long exercised Wordsworthians. Book 5's discussion of good and bad educational practice has been a particularly vexing issue. The current view of the five-book *Prelude* provides at least a genetic account of why this material is where it is: in the version of the five-book poem outlined above, the remarks on education would have served the crucial function of discursively summing up the implications of the earlier narrative material on Wordsworth's childhood. Another, more speculative line of inquiry suggested by the five-book *Prelude* relates to Rousseau, whose ideas about education are invariably discussed in commentary on the book on "Books."[4] His *Emile*, probably the period's most widely influential book on education, must acquire a new relevance to Wordsworth's project when *both* works can be described as quasi-philosophical arguments in five books that cover the stages of a child's natural education from infancy to early manhood.

I set these issues momentarily aside because I would like to consider them in the light of a more general consequence of the hypothesis about the five-book *Prelude*. Our sense of it may be sketchy, but this poem would have been the most substantial work Wordsworth produced in the years immediately following 1798. Understood as the design for a work about education, I will argue, the plan for this poem furnishes a key to the nature of the larger plan of which it formed a part. To see how requires another look at the circumstances of the larger plan's conception.

I

Apart from possible work on the lines that became the Prospectus, most of Wordsworth's time during the six weeks preceding his announcement to James Tobin was probably occupied by just two tasks. One, as I have mentioned, was the expansion of "The Old Cumberland Beggar" to include its explicitly political dimension. The other was the expansion of *The Ruined Cottage* to include a detailed history of its main character's education. In this compact *Bildungsroman*, Wordsworth worked out ideas, images, and phrases on which he drew heavily in subsequent writings. Nothing else he wrote compares with the power of these 250-odd lines to feed Wordsworth's future years.

Nor is it difficult to see why this exercise proved so valuable to him. He had composed *The Ruined Cottage* in the previous summer, and now he found himself returning to it. Although the central narrative of the poem relates the pathetic story of Margaret, the last human tenant of the cottage, the ideological center of the poem is the character of the Pedlar, who tells Margaret's story to the speaker. He wields the poem's moral authority. The education Wordsworth wrote for the Pedlar therefore had to establish the old man's character on the strongest possible grounds, a requirement that left Wordsworth with the task of constructing for him the best of all possible educations. As it happened, this perfect upbringing turned out to resemble Wordsworth's own. The poet admitted as much decades later when he told Isabella Fenwick that "the character I have represented in his person is chiefly an idea of what I fancied my own character might have become in his circumstances" (*WPW* v. 373). But the difference in circumstances was no doubt helpful in allowing Wordsworth to draw on his own experience at this trial stage without risking the charge of self-aggrandizement. It is only one measure of the importance of these lines on the growth of the Pedlar's mind that Wordsworth could later incorporate many of them, sometimes changing only third-person pronouns to first-person, into the poem on the growth of his own.[5]

Since the influence of the Pedlar's educational biography pervades so much of the writing undertaken in the service of Wordsworth's great plan, and since the announcement of the plan itself comes so quickly on the heels of this passage's composition, it would seem that Wordsworth's work on a model education is the immediate context of the invention of the plan. But what would lead Wordsworth to think that a character's moral authority is best established by showing the quality of his education? The answer to this question lies, in turn, in the immediate context of the work on the Pedlar's education. This story, which was first told by David Erdman, has to do with Wordsworth's and Coleridge's involvement with the educational schemes of Thomas Wedgwood in late 1797.[6] "Vistas of considerable reach," Erdman argued, "are opened by the discovery that when Tom Wedgwood visited Coleridge and Wordsworth in September 1797 he had it in mind to sound them out as candidates – 'the only persons that I know of as at all likely' – for superintendents of a Nursery of Genius" (p. 487). Erdman does see far-reaching implications in his discovery. He believes that "Wedgwood's ideas about systematic growth" provided a polemical target and a suggestive source for much of Wordsworth's subsequent writing. For although Book 5 of the completed *Prelude* "satirize[s] the whole idea of artificial tutelage," Erdman contends that Wedgwood's ideas proved to be "the most fruitful stimulus of [Wordsworth's] career" (p. 497). The proof is in the writing: "before meeting Wedgwood he had not articulated a single thought upon the subject of *the influence of natural objects on the growth of genius* – nor had he made the slightest attempt at a biographical study of his own or anyone else's mental growth" (pp. 497–8). And to document his claim for the immediacy of Wedgwood's impact, Erdman points to Wordsworth's work on the Pedlar's biography later that winter.

Writing in 1956, Erdman did not have the benefit of either Reed's *Chronology* or the recent reconstruction of the design of the five-book *Prelude*. If he had, he might have seen that the vistas opened by his discovery of Wordsworth's involvement with Wedgwood reach even further than he suggested. There is also a problem internal to Erdman's argument, however, for in demonstrating the role of the Wedgwood plan as a crucial moment in Wordsworth's intellectual biography, Erdman tends to slight the role of other, more momentous educational schemes. For example, against the observations by de Selincourt that Book 5 alludes to *Emile* in making an "explicit criticism of Rousseau's 'tutor,' with his artificial manipulation of Nature's lessons," Erdman apparently feels he has to argue from manuscript evidence that the original passage about modern educators, which dates to 1798–9, "reads rather like a direct attack on such grand improvements in Education as Wedgwood and Beddoes were advocating" (p. 493). Addressing himself chiefly to Erdman's argument, Joel Morkan, in a discussion of the "unity" of Book 5, has argued for the necessity of reading the book "in the light of [Wordsworth's] reaction to current educational ideas" in general and to Rousseau in particular:

> Among the major philosophers, however, Rousseau's educational theory, camouflaging an elaborate set of controls beneath a surface appearance of freedom and spontaneity, would have appeared to Wordsworth the most subtle and insidious of plans. There is an illusion of liberty, but it merely hides the most rigid of limitations. Everything is calculated . . .[7]

While noting the apparent clash between the points of view of Erdman and de Selincourt, Morkan contends that there is no need to choose between them. "It is more useful," he explains, "to focus on the general intention of the satire in Book 5 than on a specific target."[8]

This revision of Erdman is largely salutary, but it fails to see what is finally at stake in this question of educational "freedom." Like Erdman, Morkan locates Wordsworth's writing in the context of educational theory without appreciating the "ideological horizon" circumscribing the educational theory itself. This oversight leads Morkan to represent Wordsworth anachronistically as a Dickensian liberal of the 1840s and 1850s: "He feared that the changes which were taking place in early nineteenth-century educational practice were transforming the world of childhood freedom, symbolized by Hawkshead, into a mental prison with a Gradgrind-like chief warden."[9] But even if the world of *Hard Times* was, in Dickens's pun, "bound to be," it was still several decades away. To understand the purport of Wordsworth's educational program on its own terms, we must look to the world Wordsworth actually knew, to an England influenced by Revolutionary France and a Revolutionary France influenced by decades of philosophical enlightenment. For in this world, educational schemes and political schemes went hand in hand, and the systematic education associated with the name of Rousseau had a well-established political meaning. The five-book *Prelude* could so easily grow into a poem about

Enlightenment and Revolution, in other words, because in some sense that is what it had been all along.

II

It may be true, as some suggest, that a political utopia is implicit in every theory of education.[10] It may be equally true that utopian political schemes, when they are taken seriously, necessarily produce fresh thinking about education. But whether or not the relationship between political and educational theory is necessarily reciprocal, it was certainly thought to be reciprocal in the age of Rousseau, and this view was strongly held by the intellectual leadership of the French Revolution. One reason why the Revolution recognized Rousseau as its natural father was almost certainly that it perceived him to have illuminated the connection between the two domains. In France's public rhetoric during the 1790s, Rousseau was routinely referred to as "the author of *Emile* and the *Social Contract*." And Rousseau himself encouraged the conjunction of the two works (and of the kind of theory each work involved) not only by publishing them within months of one another in 1762, but also by taking pains to show that each followed from the same principles of right, principles derived in the analysis of the State of Nature published six years earlier in the Second Discourse. As the *Social Contract* showed how the just society should be governed, so *Emile* showed how the good citizen should be raised.[11]

Both the public regard for Rousseau and the nature of his perceived legacy to the Revolution can be suggested by the Revolution's official acts of homage to him. The first of these acts occurred in December 1790, a month after Burke's *Reflections* had appeared, when the National Assembly voted unanimously in favor of the following proposal: "Il sera élevé à l'auteur d'*Emile* et du *Contrat social* une statue portant cette inscription: LA NATION FRANÇAISE LIBRE A J.-J. ROUSSEAU."[12] Rousseau was the first individual so to be honored by the revolutionary government, and the action immediately prompted Burke to launch a fresh attack against both the Revolution in general and Rousseau in particular. This attack was published under the title *Letter to a Member of the National Assembly* in May 1791, just months after the Assembly's decree. The Letter shows clearly that Burke understood the French to be honoring Rousseau the educator as well as Rousseau the political writer; its discussion of Rousseau's unfitness as a moral teacher provides the occasion for what is perhaps Burke's only detailed comment on the relation of political concerns to the education of the young.[13]

In spite of the unanimity for the Assembly's first decree, there was no public ceremony in Rousseau's honor until a second decree was carried out three years later in the first months of the Thermidorean period, a time when, as we know from *The Prelude*, Wordsworth was paying special attention to affairs in France. On 11 October 1794, Rousseau's remains were solemnly transported from Ermenonville and enshrined in the newly established Pantheon for Revolutionary heroes.[14] The principal speaker at the dedication ceremony, fittingly, was Joseph Lakanal, the educational theorist who had ushered the proposal for Rousseau's Pantheonization through the Convention a month earlier. His dedicatory address, which circulated in pamphlet form as the "Report on J. J. Rousseau," was delivered "in the name of" the Convention's powerful Committee on Public Instruction.[15] Both this document and its sequel will repay far more attention than we can afford to give them here, where discussion is restricted to matters most relevant to Wordsworth's later enterprise.

Lakanal's speech takes for granted the reciprocity of Rousseau's political and educational views. Sensing that the actual influence of Rousseau's ideas about education has not been fully appreciated, however, Lakanal seeks to redress the balance. He concedes the immense *value* of "the Social Contract and other political writings": "It is true that in these immortal works, and chiefly in that first one, [Rousseau] developed the true principles of social theory, and reached back into the primitive essence of human associations" (pp. 3–4). At the same time, Lakanal wants to argue for what he takes to be the greater *impact* of the *Emile*:

> The great maxims developed in the *Social Contract*, self-evident and simple as they seem to us today, actually produced little effect. One did not sufficiently understand them either to have profited from them or to have feared them.... It was, in a sense, the Revolution that explained them to us. Thus another work had to lead us to the Revolution, elevate us, instruct us, fashion us for it. This work is *Emile*, the only code of education sanctioned by nature (pp. 4–5).

When Lakanal goes on to enumerate some of the beneficial effects of the book, he makes their political consequences apparent:

> The very name of this work immediately recalls great services rendered to humanity. Childhood delivered from the barbarous ties that deform it; the method of reason substituted for that of prejudice and of routine; learning [*enseigner*] rendered easy for him who could receive it, and the road of virtue [*la route de la vertu*] smoothed out like that of science (p. 6).

The many who heeded the command of nature as interpreted by Rousseau in *Emile* had already accomplished "an immense revolution in our institutions and in our manners," so the argument goes, and this revolution is what made it possible, perhaps inevitable, to carry out the political revolution promised in the *Social Contract* (p. 6).

The sequel came two weeks after the Pantheonization ceremony when Lakanal addressed the National Convention on the subject of education, again *"au nom du comité d'instruction publique."*[16] Like the earlier speech, too, it was grounded firmly on the notion of a strong reciprocity between education and politics. "Education," Lakanal told the Convention, "holds so essentially to the primary social institutions of a people – the constitution so needs to be made for education, and education for the constitution – that both will be lacking if they are not the work of the same mind, the same genius, if they are not somehow the correlative parts of one and the same conception" (p. 347). Since Lakanal himself had urged the Convention to approve Rousseau's Pantheonization a few weeks earlier, and since the spectacular tribute to Rousseau as philosopher and educator would still have been fresh in the minds of the Convention's representatives, the single mind, genius, and conception would probably have been understood as Rousseauist. *Emile* and *La Nouvelle Héloïse*, furthermore, are the only two books Lakanal mentions by name.

Lakanal's aim in addressing the Convention was not, however, to praise Rousseau again but to promote an "organizational plan" for a system of national education. When Lakanal and the Abbé Sieyes had proposed roughly the same plan to the Jacobin-dominated Convention in June 1793, Robespierre's forces had squelched it, but now that Robespierre was gone the convention showed a clear willingness to listen.[17] In the Pantheonization, which was conceivably part of a Lakanalian strategy both to test the political waters and to make the Convention more receptive to his Committee's proposal, Lakanal was seeking primarily to raise the prestige of Rousseau as educator. He therefore claimed on that occasion that *Emile* had already effected the revolution in education, had already supplanted the education of prejudice and routine with that of reasoned method. Before the Convention, on the other hand, Lakanal argued that the real educational revolution had hardly begun. And his address relies on a sense of the reciprocity between politics and education somewhat altered from that offered in the Pantheonization speech.

Lakanal prefaces his remarks with an accusation and an apology, both having to do with what he calls the embarrassing failure of the five-year-old Revolution to approve and implement a system of public education. The accusation is aimed at Robespierre and those who accompanied or followed him to the guillotine: "A few months ago, men who had their own motives for wanting to cover everything in darkness were ready to treat as criminals those who would have spoken to you of education and enlightenment" (p. 347). These were men who, perhaps more than the tyrants they helped to oust, "could truly be said to have feared enlightened men as brigands and assassins fear street lamps." But the Jacobins were only part of a larger problem that had not adequately been perceived by Lakanal and his enlightened colleagues. Those who pressed for educational reform during the Terror, he now admits, "had consulted the impatience of our desires rather than the nature of things, and our wishes rather than our means." They had only recently come to recognize certain principles in "the nature of things":

> To succeed in establishing a plan of public instruction on which the human mind can base its grand and legitimate hopes, several conditions are necessary. It is first necessary that the principles of government be such that, far from having anything to fear from the progress of reason, they gain from reason an ever-renewed force and authority. It is then necessary that experience, be it good or bad, should naturally consolidate this government as good; that it be full of life and movement, but that it be no longer tormented by tempests; that liberty have no further conquests to make; and that the entire people should feel that, to push back forever the criminal attacks of the monarchy and the aristocracy, one must submit democracy to reason; finally it is necessary that the human mind have made sufficient progress to be sure of possessing the methods and the instruments that will enable them to enlighten every mind and to make every possible advance (p. 347).

When did these conditions first obtain? "Not until the present time," says Lakanal, "perhaps not even until the present moment."

I won't rehearse the argument by which Lakanal shows how each of these conditions had come to be fulfilled both in the long history of enlightenment that he traces back to Bacon and in the immediate history of the Revolution that he follows up to the fall of Robespierre. It is clear, however, that where the Pantheonization speech presented a simple history of an educational change leading to a political change, the address to the Convention traces a complicated dialectic in which enlightenment and the reconstruction of society on just principles are mutually dependent, mutually reinforcing activities. The fundamental law of this dialectic is that monarchy and pure rational instruction cannot coexist: "Either the instruction would topple the throne, or the throne would corrupt the instruction" (p. 348). In France, instruction had not only toppled the throne, but also survived the Terror, and all Europe now "submits to the power of reason." But Lakanal goes on to warn the Convention that unless this reason is fully refined, the accomplishments of the Revolution will come to a halt. "It is the moment," he says, "when we must gather together in a plan of public instruction worthy of you, worthy of France and of human kind, the enlightenment accumulated by the centuries that preceded us, and the seeds of enlightenment that will be purchased by the centuries that follow us" (p. 348).

The essence of the plan Lakanal proposes lies in the notion of applying to social problems the rational method of scientific inquiry. This is the method – Lakanal calls it "analysis" – that "counts all the steps it takes, but that never takes a step backward or to the side" (p. 348). Analysis is able to carry the "same simplicity of language" and "the same clarity" in the development of social and moral ideas as in scientific ones because "in all kinds of ideas the formation of our ideas is the same, only the objects different." The moral leverage of this analysis is as sure as its procedures are valid:

> By this method, which alone can re-create human understanding, the moral sciences so necessary to people who govern themselves by their own virtues, will be surmised as rigorous in their demonstration as the exact and physical sciences; by this method one spreads over the principles of our duties a light so lively that it cannot be obscured even by the cloud of passions. . . . (p. 348).

Just as political and economic liberty destroyed "the monstrous inequality of riches," so "analysis, applied to all kinds of ideas, will destroy the inequality of enlightenment." Analysis is therefore, according to this argument, "an instrument indispensable to a great democracy" (p. 348).

The goal of Lakanal's plan is to put this indispensable tool into the hands not only of every citizen in France but ultimately of every citizen in an evisioned European republic. On the analogy of fluids affected by gravity, Lakanal imagines enlightenment spreading ("trickling down," we would say now) from the top to the lowest possible levels. The most enlightened philosophers in Europe would be assembled in Paris where they would bring in promising students whom they would teach to teach the method:

> As soon as these courses in the art of teaching human knowledge are terminated, the wise and philosophic youths who have received these great lessons will go and repeat them in all parts of the republic from which they were called: they will open normal schools everywhere; in going back over the art they have come to learn, they will fortify themselves in it, and in teaching it to others, the necessity of questioning their own genius will enhance their views and their talents. This source of so pure an enlightenment, so abundant, when it goes out from the first men of the republic in all forms, overflowing reservoir after reservoir, spreads from space to space through all of France, without losing anything of its purity in its course. To the Pyrenees and to the Alps, the art of teaching will be the same as in Paris, and this art will be that of nature and genius (p. 349).

Lakanal's is a vision of a Continent educated by French philosophes –

indeed a Continent composed of French philosophes. It is a Gallic, enlightened version of Blake's biblical wish that all the Lord's people were prophets. This image of Europe's future was sufficiently pleasing to the Convention that, after a friendly debate and minor revision, they adopted the Committee's plan in early 1795, a decision that marked a new era in the history of French education.

This same plan, with its political implications, is also the chief target of Wordsworth's polemic in Book 5 of *The Prelude* and the unstated subject of his initial five-book poem about education. Ultimately, it must be recognized as embodying the spirit against which Wordsworth developed his own great plan in 1798. Before suggesting how this anti-Rousseauism bears on the interpretation of the poetry in question, I should say something about the likelihood of Wordsworth's familiarity with the ambitions of the Committee on Public Instruction.[18]

III

We know from Book 10 of *The Prelude* (568–86) that, although back in England, Wordsworth watched affairs in France closely during the Thermidorean period that included both the Pantheonization of Rousseau and the Committee's new educational proposal. There is reason to believe that Wordsworth would have taken special note, however, of these particular events. In June 1794, a month before the fall of Robespierre and four months before Lakanal's important speeches, Wordsworth wrote a letter to his friend William Mathews in reference to their intended collaboration on a political journal to be called *The Philanthropist*. Because Wordsworth thinks it appropriate to make a solemn declaration of his political views before entering into such a collaboration, this letter, though it was obviously not, like the *Letter to the Bishop of Llandaff* (1793), intended for print, offers almost as much information as the earlier document about Wordsworth's politics in the first phase of his adult career. And the opening profession of political faith shows that his views are basically unchanged from what he held when he attacked Bishop Watson: he says that he "disapprove[s] of monarchical and aristocratical governments, however modified"; he thinks "Hereditary distinctions and privileged orders of every species ... must necessarily counteract the progress of human improvement," and "hence it follows" that he is "not amongst the admirers of the British Constitution"; he conceives that "a more excellent system of civil policy" might be established in England; and he hails "the changes of opinion respecting matters of Government which within these few years have rapidly taken place in the minds of speculative men" (*EY* 123–4).

These announcements make Wordsworth's stand on the major issues quite clear. In the body of the letter Wordsworth tells Mathews in similarly certain terms what he thinks the magazine should aim to do and what it should contain. After stating his notions about the magazine in a general way, he offers some concrete suggestions:

> It would contribute much to render our work interesting could we have any foreign correspondence informing us of the progress of knowledge in the different metropolises of Europe, and of those new publications which either attract or merit attention. These writings our knowledge of languages would enable us to peruse and it would be well to extract from them the parts distinguished by particular excellence. It would be well also if you could procure a perusal of the french monitor; for while we expressed our detestation of the execrable measures pursued in France we should belie our title if we did not hold up to the approbation of the world such of their regulations and decrees as are dictated by the spirit of Philosophy (p. 128).

Because we have so little documentation of Wordsworth's interests in the years after his graduation from Cambridge, we can easily draw the mistaken conclusion that he simply did not read much then, a conclusion that even finds apparent support in some of Wordsworth's own retrospective accounts. *The Prelude* itself does not name a single writer or book that Wordsworth read at this time – not even Rousseau, who is quoted so knowingly in the Letter to Llandaff. The autobiographical letter to Anne Taylor of 1801 would have its reader believe that the poet had lived in virtual isolation from contemporary intellectual influences (*EY* 326–9). But on those rare occasions when we do hear the twenty-three- or twenty-four-year-old Wordsworth speaking for himself, we are left with a very different impression. In the 1794 letter to Mathews the sentence of particular relevance is of course the one about the "french monitor." The *Moniteur* was the official organ of the French National Assembly and printed its proceedings. Both the September 1794 debate on the Pantheonization of Rousseau and the subsequent discussions of the proposal for the reorganization of the schools appeared in its pages. Lakanal's important address before the Convention, furthermore, was printed in full.[19] Wordsworth's remark to Mathews supplies good reason to believe that he would have been reading the *Moniteur* with considerable care in the early Thermidorean period. Nor are we required to imagine that he merely happened upon the address, for his comment indicates that he would have been combing the pages of the *Moniteur* for just this sort of material.

What could better epitomize what he calls "regulations and decrees... dictated by the spirit of Philosophy" than Lakanal's enlightened proposal, especially if we take as our guide the spirit of Wordsworth's philosophic magazine? Here is Wordsworth's own radical vision of education, the one the *Philanthropist* project was meant to help realize:

> A writer who has the welfare of mankind at heart should call forth his best exertions to convince the people that they can only be preserved from a convulsion by œconomy in the administration of the public purse and a gradual and constant reform of those abuses which, if left to themselves, may grow to such a height as to render, even a revolution desirable. There is a further duty incumbent upon every enlightened friend of mankind; he should let slip no opportunity of explaining and enforcing those general principles of the social order which are applicable to all times and to all places; he should diffuse by every method a knowledge of those rules of political justice, from which the farther any government deviates the more effectually must it defeat the object for which government was ordained. A knowledge of these rules cannot but lead to good; they include an entire preservative from despotism, they will guide the hand of reform, and if a revolution must afflict us, they alone can mitigate its horrors and establish freedom with tranquillity (p. 124).

There are obvious differences between what Wordsworth says to Mathews and what Lakanal would say to the Convention four months later. Wordsworth speaks not in the aftermath of a violent revolution in his country but in the hope of averting one, and he clearly has adult education rather than primary education in view. Nonetheless, the spirit of these remarks is as "Rousseauist" as Lakanal's, and if Wordsworth actually carried out his intention to peruse the *Moniteur*, then Lakanal's systematic application of what he took to be the principles established in *Emile* could hardly have failed to catch the poet's eye. If Wordsworth did take notice of the Committee's project he would surely have greeted it as hopefully as he had awaited it, especially after the Revolution had managed to make an end of Robespierre and his "execrable measures."

Taken in sum, the external evidence for Wordsworth's firsthand know-ledge of what Lakanal said about education in the autumn of 1794 would seem considerable. I believe the internal evidence, especially that associated with the argument of Book 5 of the 1805 *Prelude*, also tends to corroborate this suggestion. But since what Lakanal says about Rousseau, education, and politics is representative of a widely shared view of these matters, my use of Lakanal is also, in part, heuristic. Whether or not Wordsworth knew, say, the October address to the Convention, he probably knew (and held) the widely shared view. What he wrote to Mathews in June of 1794, as we have seen, suggests attitudes already close to the position represented by Lakanal. Prior pronouncements of the Committee on Public Instruction may well

have figured in the early formation of Wordsworth's radical creed – before
the Jacobin period, that is, and therefore before the Committee suffered the
temporary decline in prestige from which it was rebounding in the Thermidorean period.[20] The great forerunner of the Sieyes–Lakanal educational plan
was that proposed in 1792 by Condorcet, the celebrated philosophe who
was the Committee's first leader.[21] Condorcet's plan, which resembled
Lakanal's in points of both theory and practice, was debated in Paris and
circulated in pamphlet form in the spring of that year, precisely the time that
Wordsworth was living on the banks of the Loire and trying to catch up
with the Revolution. Although Lakanal's plan was adopted and Condorcet's
was not, Condorcet's *Report on the General Organization of Public Instruction* is a
text that might also have served the heuristic purposes of contextualizing
Wordsworth's position.[22] It is not far-fetched to think that Wordsworth
knew both texts well. What would be far-fetched is to think that a young
radical so involved in the enlightened Girondist movement of the Revolution could have failed to know about the Committee on Public Instruction,
about its general educational aims and some of its specific recommenda-
tions, and about how, like Rousseau, it considered its educational and
political views mutually translatable.

IV

The answer I am proposing to the initial question should now be clear: in
the first half of his great decade, Wordsworth's political interests found
expression in the poetry he composed on the topic of education. To
understand his political perspective, in other words, we must look to what
he says about education. Since the most explicit poetic comment on
education comes in the lines composed for what became Book 5 of the 1805
Prelude, the best passage to consider first might be the one Wordsworth is
thought to have composed first. It appears in MS. 18a:

> There are who tell us that in recent times
> We have been great discoverers, that by dint
> Of nice experience we have lately given
> To education principles as fixed
> And plain as those of a mechanic trade
> Fair books and pure have been composed that act
> Upon the infant mind as does the Sun
> Upon a flower, in the corrected scheme
> Of modern days all error is block'd out
> So jealously that wisdom thrives apace
> And in our very boyhood we become
> Familiar friends with cause and consequence.

> Great feats have been performed, a smooth high-way
> So they assert has lately overbridged
> The random chaos of futurity.
> Hence all our steps are firm and we are made
> Strong in the power of knowledge. Ample cause
> Why we now living in this happy age
> Should bless ourselves.
>   For briefly 'tis maintained
> We now have rules and theories so precise
> That by the inspection of unwearied eyes
> We can secure infallible results.
> But if the shepherd to his flock should point
> The herb which each should feed on were it not
> Service redundant and ridiculous?[23]

Since this passage dates to 1798–9, it cannot refer to what Morkan calls "early nineteenth-century educational schemes." And while Erdman cites it to support his argument about Wordsworth's debt to Wedgwood, rather than to Rousseau, it stacks up very neatly against the Rousseauist vision of Lakanal and his committee. Certainly the culprits Wordsworth singles out are depicted as making the same kinds of claims the Thermidoreans make under the aegis of Rousseau. Interpreted in light of Lakanal's speech, for example, Wordsworth's "recent times" would refer not to the previous few years but to the Enlightenment, in which we became "discoverers" by virtue of the scientific method that Lakanal says "Bacon, Locke, and their disciples ... found in sounding the depths of nature." After providing this common orientation in intellectual history, the two texts go on to make some strikingly similar observations that are couched in similar terms and metaphors. Wordsworth speaks of the effort to give to education "principles as fixed / And plain as those of a mechanic trade." Lakanal says that the method enables the moral sciences (such as education) to draw conclusions "as rigorous in their demonstration as the exact and physical sciences" and thus to spread over "the principles of our duties" the brightest of lights. Wordsworth suggests that the aim of the destructive educators is to see that "all our steps are firm" and that "we are made / Strong in the power of knowledge" – all error ("wandering") must be blocked – and Lakanal's metaphor is the same when he insists that the method "counts all the steps it takes," but "never takes a step backward or to the side." Even the road metaphor, which is perhaps only an extension of the idea of unerring steps, is common to both accounts.[24]

Because MS. 18a dates to 1798–9, we must not fail to notice how substantially it anticipates the most directly topical lines from Book 5 of the completed *Prelude*, which were not composed until five years later:

These mighty workmen of our later age
Who with a broad highway have overbridged
The froward chaos of futurity,
Tamed to their bidding – they who have the art
To manage books, and things, and make them work
Gently on infant minds as does the sun
Upon a flower – the tutors of our youth,
The guides, the wardens of our faculties
And stewards of our labour, watchful men
And skilful in the usury of time,
Sages, who in their prescience would controul
All accidents, and to the very road
Which they have fashioned would confine us down
Like engines – when will they be taught
That in the unreasoning progress of the world
A wiser spirit is at work for us,
A better eye than theirs, most prodigal
Of blessings, and most studious of our good,
Even in what seem our most unfruitful hours?

(ll. 370–88)

This later passage is somewhat less strident in its irony and perhaps a shade subtler in its implication: here the modern instructor's problem is that he himself needs to be taught by the most studious educator of all, divine providence. Much of the passage, however, is just a recasting of the ur-passage from MS. 18a. Further, in both that early manuscript and in Book 5, these passages introduce the famous lines that begin "There was a boy." We can infer, therefore, not only that Wordsworth's polemic against contemporary education runs back to the period of his earliest work toward *The Recluse*, but also that this polemic is associated from the start with the (superficially) nonpolitical poetry that marks Wordsworth's most characteristic accomplishment in this early major period. It was a pair of lines from "There was a boy," we must recall, about which Coleridge said: "had I met these lines running wild in the deserts of Arabia, I should have instantly screamed out 'Wordsworth!' "[25]

In what would become Book 5 of the completed *Prelude*, the Boy of Winander serves as a natural foil to set off the deformities of the child raised according to the new system; and there, the portrait of system's child (no child at all, according to Wordsworth, "But a dwarf man") comprises the central section of Wordsworth's polemic against modern education. Although the lines from MS. 18a show no evidence of Wordsworth's early work on this portrait, its main features conform with his early criticisms of those who propound "the corrected scheme/Of modern days." If Rousseau is in some refracted way the target of Wordsworth's remarks, therefore, we should expect to find a resemblance between this monster child of the mighty workmen and Rousseau's own ideal pupil Emile – sufficient resemblance, anyway, for the purposes of parody.

In certain respects, the monster child does bear a striking and straightforward resemblance to Emile. Consider for example the first half of Wordsworth's description of the child. He is said to be

> Not quarrelsome, for that were far beneath
> His dignity; with gifts he bubbles o'er
> As generous as a fountain; selfishness
> May not come near him, gluttony or pride;
> The wandering beggars propagate his name,
> Dumb creatures find him tender as a nun.
>
> . . . .
>
> Arch are his notices, and nice his sense
> Of the ridiculous; deceit and guile,
> Meanness and falsehood, he detects, can treat
> With apt and graceful laughter; nor is blind
> To the broad follies of the licensed world;
> Though shrewd, yet innocent himself withal,
> And can read lectures upon innocence.
> He is fenced round, nay armed, for aught we know,
> In panoply complete; and fear itself,
> Natural or supernatural alike,
> Unless it leap upon him in a dream,
> Touches him not.
>
> (ll. 299–318)

Both in its overall tone and in a number of its particulars, I believe, Wordsworth's satiric set-piece description alludes to those passages in *Emile* where Jean-Jacques pauses to sum up the virtues his protégé has acquired at the various stages of his moral development:[26]

> Emile is laborious, temperate, patient, firm, and full of courage. His imagination is in no way inflamed and never enlarges dangers. He is sensitive to few ills, and he knows constancy in endurance because he has not learned to quarrel with destiny. . . . In a word, of virtue Emile has all that relates to himself. To have the social virtues, too, he lacks only the knowledge of the relations which demand them. . . . [At this stage,] he counts on himself, for he is all that one can be at his age (p. 208).

> Opinion, whose action he sees, has not acquired its empire over him. The passions, whose effect he feels, have not yet agitated his heart. He

is a man; he is interested in his brothers; he is equitable; he judges his peers. Surely, if he judges them well, he will not want to be in the place of any of them; for since the goal of all the torments they give themselves is founded on prejudices he does not have, it appears to him to be pie in the sky.... He pities these miserable kings, slaves of all that obey them. He pities these false wise men, chained to their vain reputations. He pities these rich fools, martyrs to their display. He pities these conspicuous voluptuaries, who devote their entire lives to boredom in order to appear to have pleasure (p. 244).

Emile dislikes both turmoil and quarrels, not only among men but even among animals. Never did he incite two dogs to fight with one another, never did he get a dog to chase a cat (pp. 250–1).

What great views I see settling little by little in his head! What sublime sentiments stifle the germ of the petty passions in his heart! What judicial clarity, what accuracy of reason I see forming in him, as a result of the cultivation of his inclinations, of the experience which concentrates the wishes of a great soul within the narrow limit of the possible and makes a man who is superior to others and, unable to raise them to his level, is capable of lowering himself to theirs! The true principles of the just, the true models of the beautiful, all the moral relations of beings, all the ideas of order are imprinted on his understanding. He sees the place of each thing and the cause which removes it from its place.... Without having experienced the human passions, he knows their illusions and their effects (p. 253).

Granting that the lines about the monster child point to these summaries of Emile's attributes, one must not draw the wrong conclusions. Wordsworth is interested in exposing the general attitude of the teacher, not the specific characteristics of the pupil. Indeed, none of the particular virtues he ascribes to the monster child is under attack. Though the author of *The Prelude* depicts himself invading a raven's nest as a boy, we cannot assume that he is opposed to tenderness toward animals. And we know from "The Old Cumberland Beggar" that he approves of kindness toward wandering mendicants. Wordsworth's particulars are intended to recall the overall impression conveyed by Rousseau's description of Emile, the sense that, in Wordsworth's mocking phrase, "Briefly, the moral part / Is perfect" (ll. 318–19). The chief target is a delusive fantasy of moral perfectionism, the notion that virtue can be systematically taught. And we must also be careful not to confuse Wordsworth's objection with the one Rousseau tries to anticipate. "I know," he wrote of (and to) his readers, "that they will take the young man whom I evoke to be an imaginary and fantastic being because he differs from those with whom they compare him. They do not stop to think that he must certainly differ from these young men, since he is raised quite differently, affected by quite contrary sentiments, and instructed quite otherwise from them" (p. 253). Wordsworth's position is not, however, that one child cannot be made "different" from others by dint of training. He would concede that the peculiarity of the child is real enough; the child's ethical superiority is what he thinks illusory.[27]

In respect to the "moral part," then, the portrait of the monster child tallies quite closely with Rousseau's depiction of Emile. But other problems emerge in the second half of the portrait, where Wordsworth depicts the child's intellectual part. "In learning and in books," the passage continues, the child "is a prodigy." His discourse is "embossed with terms of art." He is supposed to be knowledgeable in astronomy, chemistry, geography, navigation, geology, foreign policy; he can "string you names of districts, cities, towns, / The whole world over." And he must live

> Knowing that he grows wiser every day,
> Or else not live at all, and seeing too
> Each little drop of wisdom as it falls
> Into the dimpling cistern of his heart.
>
> (ll. 319–45)

These remarks have probably been a further obstacle to the appreciation of Rousseau's symbolic importance for Book 5, for *Emile* might be cited in any number of places in support of the claim that Rousseau was as suspicious as Wordsworth of a child's early acquisition of too much information and "book learning." Jean-Jacques's dictum that his pupil must "Know how to be ignorant" typifies this apparently anti-intellectual strain in *Emile*.

To resolve this difficulty we must first recognize that in dividing his description of the monster child into two components, Wordsworth is heeding a distinction that was commonplace among the mighty workmen in France's Revolutionary legislature: the distinction between *éducation* (moral training) and *instruction* (intellectual training).[28] For those who made a sharp distinction between the thought of Rousseau and that of the philosophes, *éducation* was usually associated with the former and *instruction* with the latter. But some leaders of the 1790s saw Rousseau as both moralist and scientist – in effect, as the philosophe par excellence – and they saw *Emile* as a book concerned with both *éducation* and *instruction*. Lakanal is a case in point. Certainly his addresses in behalf of the Committee on Public Instruction suggest that in the Thermidorean period Rousseau had come to stand for both kinds of training.

Emile itself, furthermore, offers definite support for this view. Rousseau may have placed Emile's moral education first, but the boy's intellectual training was attended to as soon as he was deemed ready for it. And some of the specific intellectual traits to be cultivated in Emile were characteristic of the Enlightenment mentality attacked by Wordsworth. Another of Rousseau's dicta, for example, "that no authority govern [Emile] beyond that of his own reason" (p. 255) corresponds to the monster child's penchant for putting "All things... to question (1. 341). The monster child "shifts, weighs, / Takes nothing upon trust" (ll. 337–8), and Rousseau's pupil, similarly, does "nothing on anybody's word" (p. 178). Even some of Rousseau's apparently anti-intellectual statements – "Were he to know nothing it would be of little importance to me..." – are qualified by his insistence on rational method – "... provided he made no mistakes" (p. 171).

Taken in context, then, the portrait of the monster child does appear to be a reasonably coherent satire of the revolution's Rousseauist dream of an ideal pupil. But when Wordsworth goes on to say what lies at the heart of the child he has pictured, his analysis seems to substantiate still another sort of potential objection to the claim that Rousseauism is his target:

> Now this is hollow, 'tis a life of lies
> From the beginning, and in lies must end.
> Forth bring him to the air of common sense
> And, fresh and shewy as it is, the corps
> Slips from us into powder. Vanity,
> That is his soul: there lives he, and there moves –
> It is the soul of everything he seeks –
> That gone, nothing is left which he can love.
> Nay, if a thought of purer birth should rise
> To carry him towards a better clime,
> Some busy helper still is on the watch
> To drive him back, and pound him like a stray
> Within the pinfold of his own conceit,
> Which is his home, his natural dwelling-place.
>
> (ll. 350–63)

The objection here is simple. In *Emile* Rousseau clearly states that vanity is for him the worst of human foibles, "the sole folly of which one cannot disabuse a man who is not mad" (p. 245), and Rousseau's method is specifically aimed at making his pupil the least vain of creatures. He describes Emile again and again as unaffected, sincere, and heedless of the superficial judgment of others. If Wordsworth's satire is indeed aimed at *Emile*, his calling this trait the key to Emile's character requires some explanation. Perhaps the first thing to say is that, according to proverbial wisdom, the effort to become, or to produce, the world's humblest person is likely to backfire egregiously. Himself breathing what he calls "the air of common sense," where such wisdom thrives, Wordsworth might simply have concluded that Rousseau's attempt to block all vanity in Emile was itself a colossal act of vanity. Some such commonplace may well be enough to account for the remarks about vanity in Book 5. It is worth bearing in mind, however, that the most celebrated discussion of Rousseau to appear in England during the Revolution – Burke's *Letter to a Member of the National Assembly* (May 1791) – was in fact an attack on him as a teacher of vanity.

Burke's *Letter* was his first work to appear after the publication of the *Reflections*, six months earlier, and is best understood as a sequel to it. Speaking of the October march on Versailles in the *Reflections*, Burke had said that "the most important of all revolutions, which may be dated from that day [was] a revolution in sentiments, manners, and moral opinions" (*BW* iii. 337). In respect to this revolution, Burke's primary aim in the *Reflections* had been to show the meaning and cost of overturning the "mixed system of opinion and sentiment" that dated back to the age of chivalry. In the *Letter*, on the other hand, Burke turned his attention to France's effort to construct a new system of opinion and sentiment, and thus he addressed himself to such topics as the National Assembly's "scheme of educating the rising generation, the principles which they intend to instil and the sympathies which they wish to form in the mind at the season in which it is the most susceptible" (iv. 23–4). The "great problem" facing legislators in this position, as Burke sees it, is "to find a substitute for all the principles which hitherto have been employed to regulate the human will and action." And what he claims the French have chosen in the place of "plain duty," which for him sums up the older, chivalric principles, is "a selfish, flattering, seductive, ostentatious vice." Their object, he says, is "to merge all natural and social sentiment in inordinate vanity" (pp. 25–6).

Burke suggests that the members of the Assembly chose vanity as their guiding principle because of the kind of men they are: "Statesmen like your present rulers exist by everything which is spurious, fictitious, and false, – by everything which takes the man from his house, and sets him on a stage, – which makes him up an artificial creature" (p. 28). But his more central claim in the *Letter* pertains to the choice he sees following from their choice of this "principle": the singling out of Rousseau, in the decree of December 1790, as the patron of their "regeneration of the moral constitution of man" (p. 28). Burke's argument, indeed, makes the Assembly's act of homage to Rousseau seem inevitable. "They chose Rousseau," he says, "because in him that peculiar vice which they wished to erect into ruling virtue was by far the most conspicuous" (p. 26). Rousseau entertained "no principle, either to influence his heart or to guide his understanding, but *vanity*"; he is the "philosophic instructor in the *ethics of vanity*," nay, the "great professor and founder of *the philosophy of vanity*" (pp. 26, 28; Burke's italics).

No one is quicker than Burke to point out that building a system of opinion and sentiment is a difficult task. But he does offer sarcastic praise to the "practical philosophers" of the National Assembly for the speed of their work. The initial choice of vanity was an expeditious one, he points out, since "[v]anity is too apt to prevail in all of us" even without deliberate effort. But of course the Assembly's work is nothing if not deliberate. "Systematic in everything," he says, they "have wisely begun at the source," the relation of the parent to the child. And with the same *esprit de système*, the "next relation which they regenerate by their statues to Rousseau is that which is next in sanctity to that of a father," that of a teacher. Given its initial attractiveness, vanity attains its mature form when two such powerful institutions are pressed into its service. It then becomes a truly formidable adversary:

> In a small degree, and conversant in little things, vanity is of little moment. When full-grown, it is the worst of vices, and the occasional mimic of them all. It makes the whole man false. It leaves nothing sincere or trustworthy about him. His best qualities are poisoned and perverted by it, and operate exactly as the worst (p. 26).

Such an account of vanity helps to explain, I think, why Wordsworth can list a series of genuinely good qualities in his description of the morally deformed child of modern education. No matter how good a quality may be in itself, vanity makes it operate as an evil. For Burke, as for Wordsworth, moral judgment must consider the feeling attached to the quality; vanity, says Burke, "finds its account in reversing the train of our natural feelings" (p. 28).

How closely we should link Wordsworth's analysis of vanity in modern education to Burke's *Letter* is difficult to say. I believe that the author of the Letter to Llandaff would have read Burke's attack, and amid the slim documentation of Wordsworth's reading at this time we find some evidence that he did.[29] It is certainly *possible* that Book 5's remarks about vanity come from somewhere other than Burke and that they have nothing to do with Rousseau. But such a view does not seem *probable* to me in view of the circumstances I have described. We must not fall back into the common error of underestimating the extent of Burke's influence on English opinion in these years. The range of this influence has certainly not been lost on those scholars who have traced the history of Rousseau's reputation in England through this time. Each reaches some version of the conclusion that for decades afterward Burke's *Letter* all but determined "*la fortune de Rousseau dans l'opinion anglaise.*"[30] When these same scholars discuss Wordsworth's major work, I should add, they tend to see it as Rousseauist rather than anti-Rousseauist. And none suspects that this work bears what I have been describing as the stamp of Burke's writings. Since they regard Wordsworth from the distance of a general survey, their oversight is quite understandable. After all, five years before composing his ideal education for the Pedlar, Wordsworth had engaged Burke in intellectual combat with weapons forged by Rousseau.

V

In the lines that introduce the long discussion of education in Book 5, Wordsworth writes that what we are reading "is dedicate to Nature's self / And things that teach as Nature teaches" (ll. 230–1). Like much else in *The Prelude*, this comment encourages us to think that Wordsworth opposed Rousseauist education in the name of natural education. We have already seen, however, that when Wordsworth opposes Rousseauist politics with a politics of nature, he is attacking a writer who himself advocated a politics of nature. Careful analysis of the France books of *The Prelude* shows that Wordsworth sought to maintain a different sense of "nature" in his political critique, a sense closer to Burke's sense of (second) nature. A similar distinction must be observed with respect to Wordsworth's advocacy of natural education.

The need for such a distinction becomes clear as soon as we recall that *Emile* was perceived by revolutionaries like Lakanal as offering "the only code of education sanctioned by nature." Furthermore, Rousseau specifically represented his project as a casting out of artificial education in favor of natural. Even Wordsworth himself seems to acknowledge that modern educators held some such view of their work when he says that they "have the art / To manage books, and things, and make them work / Gently upon infant minds as does the sun / Upon a flower" (ll. 373–6). What evidently has to be established is how this kind of teaching-as-Nature-teaches differs from the teaching-as-(second)-Nature-teaches that Wordsworth would oppose to it.

The Rousseauist position is concisely articulated in the very first paragraphs of *Emile*, where Jean-Jacques announces his concern about man's contamination of the world providence intended for his natural development. Here are the bold opening sentences:

Everything is good as it leaves the hands of the Author of things; everything degenerates in the hands of man. He forces one soil to nourish the products of another, one tree to bear the fruit of another. He mixes and confuses the climates, the elements, the seasons. He mutilates his dog, his house, his slave. He turns everything upside down; he disfigures everything; he loves deformity, monsters. He wants nothing as nature made it, not even man; for him, man must be trained like a school horse; man must be fashioned in keeping with his fancy like a tree in his garden (p. 37).

These are familiar Rousseauist sentiments, and the account to this point offers nothing to which Wordsworth would object, least of all its claim for the vast superiority of divine agency over human. Wordsworth criticized the "mighty workmen," we recall, for disbelieving that "a wiser spirit is at work for us, / A better eye than theirs." With respect to this issue of providence as well as to other related issues, however, Rousseau's argument now takes a turn that marks a crucial parting of ways between the two writers. For Rousseau immediately asserts that if man were not actively to train and fashion man, "everything would go even worse"! "Our species," he explains,

> does not admit of being formed halfway. In the present state of things a man abandoned to himself in the midst of other men from birth would be the most disfigured of all. Prejudices, authority, necessity, example, all the social institutions in which we find ourselves submerged would stifle nature in him and put nothing in its place. Nature there would be like a shrub that chance had caused to be borne in the middle of a path and that the passers-by soon cause to perish by bumping into it from all sides and bending it in every direction (p. 37).

A man who lives in the midst of other men from birth necessarily suffers the influence of human institutions – what Rousseau calls prejudice, authority, example, and so on. These institutions are not a part of nature and, by a law that Rousseau claims to "have proved... countless times," "everything that is not nature is against nature" (p. 405).

On Rousseau's account, therefore, these institutions constitute a kind of antinature, which, if left to operate haphazardly on the individual, tends to stifle natural growth and eventually to produce a monster. One's only recourse, so the argument runs, is to regularize these institutions according to the laws of nature, the rational scheme established by the Author of things. Rousseau's "plan" or "method" (both his terms) is nothing other than the set of rules and maxims for which he claims such rational and natural foundation. This is the essence of what Lakanal calls the substitution of rational method for the influence of prejudice and routine.

The speaker of "Lines Written in Early Spring" (lines in fact written soon after Wordsworth's announcement to Tobin on 6 March 1798) may sound Rousseauist in suggesting that he has "reason to lament / What man has made of man" (ll. 23–4). But Wordsworth's reason proves to be the reverse of Rousseau's. If the latter's worries about man's corruption of man stem from his view that human culture, unguided by systematic human planning, lacks the order of divinely created nature, Wordsworth's worries stem from his fear of the very effort to systematize culture – an effort he indeed represents as a failure of confidence in the providential scheme that the human system claims for its authority. Rousseau says that "the child is at birth already a disciple, not of the governor, but of nature" and that the governor himself "only studies under this first master and prevents its care from being opposed" (p. 61). Wordsworth sees no reason to suspect that nature's care *would* be opposed, except in those cases where someone like a Rousseauist governor interferes. At its best, Wordsworth suggests, such meddling amounts to nothing better than "service redundant and ridiculous." At its worst, it meets the harsher judgment implied in Book 5's Miltonic allusion to the bridge over Chaos, the charge of Satanic usurpation of divine prerogatives.

For Rousseau, we might say, there is nature and derivative rational method on the one side and the antinature of human institutions on the other. For Wordsworth, there is nature and derivative second nature on the one side and rational method on the other. But is it fair to identify Wordsworth's second nature with the human institutions singled out by Rousseau? And how are we to understand the agency of second nature's teaching in Wordsworth's account? What are its normal circumstances, its characteristic forms and procedures? What, in short, serves Wordsworth's natural teaching as the knowledge and application of a method serve Rousseau's?

NOTES

1   One point of controversy in this chronology might be the suggestion that the five-book plan was close to the initial conception of 1798–9. The issue has to do with the status of the two books that survive from that early period, whether they were meant to stand alone as a "two-part *Prelude*" or to begin a multibook work. Reed's arguments against the former position seem to me compelling (*CMY* 135n3). And while the first two books of the five-book poem are not identical with the two books of 1798–9, they are similar. Further, there is the discursive material from MS18a, also dating to 1798–9, whose significance for the five-book poem I discuss below.

2   For a full exposition of the matter see Jonathan Wordsworth (1977).

3   MacGillivray (1964) 242; the description is cited with approval in Jonathan Wordsworth's later essay.

4   Hartman's assumption that Book 5 is about "the presumptuous followers of Rousseau" is representative in this repect (*WP* 19).

5   De Selincourt and Darbishire gloss the lines that reappear in *The Prelude* in their text of the passage on the Pedlar's education (*WPW* v. 381–8).

6   Erdman (1956).

7   Morkan (1972) 251.

8   Erdman (1956) 429.

9   Morkan (1972) 249.

10   See Frye (1970) 122.

11 For a discussion that clarifies the relationship of Rousseau's concerns in the *Second Discourse*, the *Social Contract*, and *Emile*, see Boyd (1963) 126–7, and Masters (1968) 6–15.

12 The proposal was published in the *Gazette nationale ou Le Moniteur universel*, no. 356 (22 December 1790) 88; reprinted *Réimpression de L'Ancien Moniteur* vi. 697.

13 *BW* iv. 3–55, esp. 25–35. Burke represented the commitment of the National Assembly to Rousseau as obsessive in its rigor:

> The assembly recommends to its youth a study of the bold experimenters of morality. Everyone knows that there is a great dispute among their leaders, which of them is the best resemblance of Rousseau. In truth, they all resemble him. Him they study; him they meditate; him they turn over in all the time they can spare from the laborious mischief of the day or the debauches of the night. Rousseau is their canon of holy writ; in his life he is their canon of Polycletus; he is their standard figure of perfection. To this man and this writer, as a pattern to authors and to Frenchmen, the foundries of Paris are now running for statues, with the kettles of their poor and the bells of their churches (iv. 25).

14 Both the ceremony and its genesis have been carefully documented in McNeil (1937).

15 Lakanal (n.d.). The passages cited below from this document are my translations and are cited by page number in the text. In view of Erdman's recent suggestions about Wordsworth and regicide, it may prove to be of interest that Lakanal the educational theorist had first made a name as one of the publicists for the cause that sought and gained the execution of Louis XVI. His *Opinion ... sur la question de savoir: Si Lous XVI peut être jugé?* was printed by order of the National Convention in late 1792. See Dawson (1948).

16 Published in the *Moniteur*, 28 October 1794, cited below by page number in the Plon edition, my translations.

17 See Vignery (1965) 127–8. Vignery points out that Lakanal's address was actually drafted by another member of the Committee, Joseph Garat, a point which ultimately has little bearing on my argument here, though it may help to explain the differences between Lakanal's tactics then and two weeks earlier in the Pantheonization address.

18 As to the question of the *Moniteur's* availability in England, I am told by Professor Jack Censor, the historian of Anglo-French press relations in the 1790s, that the circulation of the *Moniteur* would have been roughly 8,000 and that some copies would inevitably have circulated across the Channel, but that the number of such copies would be difficult to estimate.

19 Vignery (1965) 128–9.

20 The earlier work of the Committee is usefully summarized in Duzer (1935) 84–114, a chapter on "The Spirit of Ideology in Education." For a general review of the Revolution's educational projects through 1793, see also Duruy (1882) 67–99, and L. Pearce Williams (1959) 291–308. The proceedings of the Committee are available for this period in one volume, *Procès-verbaux du Comité d'instruction publique* ed. M. J. Guillaume (Paris, 1889).

21 See Keith Baker (1975) 293–303. What Baker says about Condorcet's development of a "social art" on scientific principles shows how important a forerunner he was for the likes of Lakanal.

22 Unlike Lakanal's addresses of 1794, Condorcet's *Report on Public Instruction* has been translated and is available in a collection of such writings, Fontainerie (1932).

23 This text is included among the notes for *The Prelude*, ed. Ernest de Selincourt and Helen Darbishire (1959), 545–6.

24 In this case, however, the parallel is with the Pantheonization speech where Wordsworth's "smooth high-way" is anticipated by Lakanal's smooth "road to virtue."

25 Griggs i. 453.

26 Citations from *Emile* are to Allan Bloom's translation (1979) and will be noted by page number in the text wherever possible.

27 Though she does not mention the monster child of *The Prelude*, Patterson does point to the "perceptible influence of Rousseau on the notion of the totally good child" in the literature of this period (Sylvia W. Patterson (1971) 158).

28 For more on this distinction see Baker (1975) 285–93, and Vignery (1965) 17, 125.

29 Owen and Smyser have pointed out that in the letter to Llandaff Wordsworth's linking of the names Maury and Cazales may derive from a comment of Burke's in the *Letter to a Member of the National Assembly* (Owen and Smyser i. 65).

30 "Le contenu de cinq ou six pages, repartie dans deux écrits de Burke, a déterminé pour un siècle la fortune de Rousseau dans l'opinion anglaise" (Voisine (1956) 137). Voisine's discussion of the entire Burke–Rousseau controversy is comprehensive and astute; see 127–54. On Rousseau's reputation in England as the "philosopher of vanity," see 241–58. Voisine is less accurate, but still informative, in his treatment of Rousseau's reception by the first-generation English romantics, 157–240. See also Roddier (1947) 307–80, and Duffy (1979) 54–85. For contemporary responses to Burke's attacks on Rousseau, see Lofft (1791) and Boothby (1791) 71–3.

4

The History in "Imagination"

ALAN LIU

At the point of discovery in James Bruce's *Travels to Discover the Source of the Nile*, which Wordsworth knew about by 1803 but may not have read until 1807,[1] there is an agony that must fill any reader of Wordsworth with déjà vu. Bruce believes that he has found the fountains of the Nile, but, strangely, feels disappointment:

> I was, at that very moment, in possession of what had, for many years, been the principal object of my ambition and wishes: indifference, which from the usual infirmity of human nature follows, at least for a time, complete enjoyment, had taken place of it. The marsh, and the fountains, upon comparison with the rise of many of our rivers, became now a trifling object in my sight. I remembered that magnificent scene in my own native country, where the Tweed, Clyde, and Annan rise in one hill; three rivers, as I now thought, not inferior to the Nile in beauty.... I had seen the rise of the Rhine and Rhone, and the more magnificent sources of the Soane; I began, in my sorrow, to treat the inquiry about the source of the Nile as a violent effort of a distempered fancy: –
>
> > What's Hecuba to him, or he to Hecuba,
> > That he should weep for her? –
>
> Grief or despondency now rolling upon me like a torrent; relaxed, not refreshed, by unquiet and imperfect sleep, I started from my bed in the utmost agony; I went to the door of my tent; every thing was still; the Nile, at whose head I stood, was not capable either to promote or

to interrupt my slumbers, but the coolness and serenity of the night braced my nerves, and chased away those phantoms that, while in bed, had oppressed and tormented me.

It was true, that numerous dangers, hardships, and sorrows had beset me ... but it was still as true, that another Guide, more powerful than my own courage, health, or understanding, if any of these can be called man's own, had uniformly protected me. (iii. 640–1)

Like Wordsworth at the peak of experience in Simplon Pass, Bruce at the source of experience discovers deep emptiness. His true discovery is that he has been led all the while by distempered fancy and a Guide, a pair whose conflation might yield Wordsworth's own spirit of worldly denial at Simplon: "Imagination! ... Strong in itself, and in the access of joy / Which hides it like the overflowing Nile" (*Prel.* 6. 525–48).

The readings we now have of the Simplon Pass episode, among which Geoffrey Hartman's is in the vanguard, are so powerful that the episode has become one of a handful of paradigms capable by itself of representing the poet's work.[2] I seek in this chapter to reimagine Wordsworth's 1790 trip and *The Prelude*'s insertion of Imagination into that trip. To do so, I take as my thought-vehicle the framework of the contemporary touring experience itself. One implication of the comparison to Bruce is that the disappointment at the origin of Imagination in the Alps inheres in any tour aimed toward a goal. Bruce's reflections at the point of discovery show that there are really two models underlying his travels: the voyage of exploration, which points toward an exotic goal, and the tour, which allows only passage through the already known (the Tweed, Clyde, Annan, Rhine, Rhone, and Saône). At the moment of discovery, suddenly, it is tour that dominates and exploration that seems out of place. A tour is designed only to make sense of passage, not of a goal. If an exploration were a sentence, its goal would be the last word. But in a tour, the real goal is the sense of the sentence's overall completion, a sense that cannot appear within the sentence but only on the plane of the grammar framing sentences. From a viewpoint within a tour, therefore, any sense of completion posited at the terminus can only appear a gap, an absence.

In Hartman's reading, Wordsworth's "self" forms in this gap as a self-knowing displacement of nature's sourcehood balanced dialectically against restitution to nature. Holding fast to the tour model with its worldly concerns, as opposed to Hartman's model of the mystic pilgrimage,[3] I offer a reformulation, which, if formally only an addition, ultimately declares something quite different about what we believe the self to be. It seems to me that the self arises in a three-body problem: history, nature, self. In *The Prelude* – as in the nineteenth century with its historicist and evolutionist concerns generally – history is the base upon which the issue of nature's sourcehood is worked out. *The Prelude* organizes the 1790 tour so that "nature" is precipitated in Book 6 only as a denial of the history behind any tour, and the goal of the denial – not fully effective until the purge of Books 9 and 10 – is to carve the "self" out of history. The theory of denial is Imagination.

What is history, whose early detail for Wordsworth is the French Revolution? Let me simply gesture for the moment. Something must rush into the gap discovered on a tour with a determined goal, something whose essence will be a sourcehood *elsewhere*. Such is a preliminary, ad hoc definition of history at its contact point with experience: a sense, not yet formulated into idea, that the completion of the present depends perpetually upon something beyond – whether that force of beyond will ultimately be thought as Hegelian *Geist* (anchored in a future sense) or the later Wordsworthian "realities" of people, nation, and church (rooted in the past). We might think here of the anthem of historical sourcehood in Book 8 of *The Prelude*:

>   Great God!
> That aught *external* to the living mind
> Should have such mighty sway! yet so it was
> A weight of Ages did at once descend
> Upon my heart; no thought embodied, no
> Distinct remembrances; but weight and power,
> Power growing with the weight.
>
>   (8.700–6)

The Motive of Description: The 1790 Letter

It will be useful first to view Wordsworth's 1790 trip as much as possible from the perspective of 1790 itself. After shipping to Calais on 13 July, Wordsworth and Robert Jones spent the summer walking through France, the Savoy, Switzerland, and upper Italy along a route with three segments: *1790a*, a beeline south through France to St Vallier, highlighted by a boat trip on the Saône (13 July to 1 August); *1790b*, a winding, looping, and at times backtracking passage from St Vallier through the Savoy, Switzerland, and Italy back up to Basel (1 August to 21 September); and *1790c*, a beeline by boat up the Rhine to Cologne and then home (22 September to sometime in October).[4] The vertical legs of the tour – each straightforward, each undertaken partly by boat, and each immersed in the sights of Liberty (the celebrations of the French *fédérés* and preparations of the Belgian Republican armies, respectively) – flank the divagations of 1790b as if between facing mirrors.

As will be reported by Book 6 of *The Prelude*, the "variegated journey step by step" of 1790a has the contour of seriality:[5]

> Day after day, up early and down late,
> From vale to vale, from hill to hill we went
> From Province on to Province did we pass.

(6.431–3)

So, too, "The Author's Voyage Down the Rhine (Thirty Years Ago)" (probably composed 1820 or 1821) will describe 1790c as a propagation of scenery by repetition:

> We saw the living Landscapes of the Rhine,
> Reach after reach, salute us and depart;
> Slow sink the Spires, – and up again they start!

(*WPW* iii. 409)

Between the mirrors of 1790a and 1790c stands the less clearly defined progress of 1790b. Yet our best direct record of the 1790 tour, Wordsworth's long letter to Dorothy written during 1790b from September 6 to 16, also casts this leg of the tour as simple seriality:

My Spirits have been kept in a perpetual hurry of delight by the almost uninterrupted succession of sublime and beautiful objects which have passed before my eyes . . . . It was with regret that we passed every turn of this charming path, where every new picture was purchased by the loss of another which we would never have been tired of gazing at (*EY* 32, 34).

Seriality reduces at base to duplication, the substitution of one point-scene for another. By point-scenes I mean precisely the pictures Wordsworth sketches: landscape paintings of the mind, each composed as if the perceiver were at total rest and as if human vision permitted only a single-recession system with one vanishing point. Observe, for example, the absolute point of view and bilateral symmetry in this sketch: "The lake is narrow and the shadows of the mountains were early thrown across it. It was beautiful to watch them travelling up the sides of the hills for several hours, to remark one half of a village covered with shade, and the other bright with the strongest sunshine" (*EY* 33). But how does the traveler move from one such point to the next? The point-scene pictured in this passage assumes the petrification of the perceiver: motion has to be projected outward into landscape itself as the "travelling" of shadows. Here we arrive at the paradigm structure, and dilemma, behind a tour's seriality: a tour reduces to two points between which a break poses the problem of continuity.

Of course, a traveler overcomes the break by physically moving. But physical motion, analyzable variously as muscle contractions, steps, whole days' journeys, and so forth, has no innate continuity unless *thought* as continuity. Faced with the gap between points of scenery, a tourist may exert certain muscles in a certain sequence, but he cannot "move" from one point to the next unless the logical relationship between those points is formed in his mind as an accompanying aura of ideas called "description." As emblematized by the fact that Wordsworth probably read, and was guided by, William Coxe's *Travels in Switzerland* before his 1790 trip (Coe (1953) 47–8; Wildi (1959) 225; D. Hayden (1983) 107–10),[6] no tour can exist as a connected movement unless that movement occurs in a space already described.

It is difficult, however, to discover the real logic of connection in description. The elusiveness of such logic is illustrated in the sketch of the "variegated journey" quoted from *The Prelude* earlier. Wordsworth glosses over vague predication – the connective motion sketched by "went" and "pass" – with a cloud of adverbial prepositional phrases that are themselves vague ("From vale to vale . . .") but so conventional that the reader merely assumes the kind of motion meant. The underlying logic of a tour is always unrecoverable behind the conventional, behind modifiers that narrate the relationship between any two point-scenes according to a plot ready-made. With astonishing frequency in the letter, as in the sentence "My Spirits have been kept in a perpetual hurry of delight by the almost uninterrupted succession of sublime and beautiful objects," Wordsworth adopts the most conventional modifier of all locodescriptive tourist experience: a logic of aesthetic movement (as in "I am moved") expressible in the formula, "sublimity" ← ("delight") → "beauty". As in Denham's "Cooper's Hill," movement between scenes of the sublime and the beautiful transforms into a convention of affective movement, delight.[7] One moves from the mountain to the river in a trajectory that is pleasure.

The root modifier of experience to which aesthetics points may be generalized as motivation, or the psychology of movement. Faced with the gap between point-scenes, a tourist cloaks his physical motion and its logic of relationship behind a calculus of affect, a never-ending effort to convince himself, or someone, that even though, as Wordsworth says, "every new picture was purchased by the loss of another which we would never have been tired of gazing at," there is indeed a conventionally understood motive for forward momentum. But such motivation for tours is never fully convincing. Tours, as opposed to journeys or explorations, always seem undermotivated; they always seem to be impelled by someone else's motive.

A tour's conventional motivation, perhaps, always represses something indescribable at home – whether ennui or something stronger. This is especially clear in such works as William Lisle Bowles's tour sonnets (or, as we will see, Wordsworth's own *Descriptive Sketches*, composed 1791–2), where motivation for touring is conventionalized as a romantic problem at home – as a heartbreak whose veiled eroticism cannot be addressed except in the tour's vocabulary of aesthetic pleasure.[8]

We might sum up by saying that a tour is motivated by desire for some special *significance* (whether conceived as meaning or feeling) missing at home: a sense of eventfulness whose site is inherently "out there," other, or elsewhere and so from the first adapted to the form of convention. Convention is the sense of a meaningfulness described by someone prior and other, a significance whose mere redescription in any itinerary will result in a feeling of complete eventfulness.

When Wordsworth models 1790b as if it simply mirrors 1790a or 1790c, then, he follows convention, the form of a tour's meaning. Like Bruce, however, he also wants 1790b to localize a goal in a particular segment of the tour rather than on the plane of the tour's overall completion. But since a tour's real goal of convention can never be focused adequately on a segment (conventional expressions of ecstasy at any Alp or Niagara thus show the thinness of conventionality), the stopgap of convention begins to hollow out in Switzerland. In Wordsworth's 1790 letter, the gap between Alpine point-scenes becomes increasingly difficult to fill with modifiers premising behind aesthetic cliché a meaningfulness, a sense of motivated connection, to be acquired merely by redescribing the scene. And as the gaps become ever more insistent, ever more empty of motivated connection, there begins to come to view the fundamental undermotivation of the 1790 tour. Wordsworth, after all, had no good reason to leave England and the chance of a fellowship behind* – an embarrassing circumstance that his letter deals with by emphasizing how frugal he has been (how much money he has *not* spent) and by apologizing to his Uncle William ("I should be sorry if I have offended him"; *EY* 32, 37). What can fill the gap in motivation in lieu of the conventional?

Observe the gap in pleasure between lower and upper Lake Geneva in the following passage, a space of desire that conventional aesthetics will not explain and that demands "amends," a sort of scenic version of apology to Uncle William:

> The lower part of the lake did not afford us a pleasure equal to what might have been expected from its celebrity. This was owing partly to

* The 1790 letter mentions that he had acquainted his uncle, William Cookson, "with my having given up all thoughts of a fellowship" (*EY* 37).

its width, and partly to the weather, which was one of those hot glaring days in which all distant objects are veiled in a species of bright obscurity. But the higher part of the lake made us ample amends, 'tis true we had the same disagreeable weather but the banks of the water are infinitely more picturesque, and as it is much narrower, the landscape suffered proportionally less from that pale steam which before almost entirely hid the opposite shore (*EY* 33).

We recognize here the two-point model of touring in which description, after a strenuous effort, finally orders the point-scenes as a hierarchy of "low" to "high," as a structure with an innate motive for forward momentum. First there is a lower view felt as insignificant: the goal does not match its celebrated description. Then, after a gap, a higher view repeats the former in a key of greater significance. In the interstice is an ill-defined, ambivalent medium of signification apparent only as a confusion of sensation: a hot glare, veil, or bright obscurity. Considered one way, this obscurity projects Wordsworth's difficulty in description, his lack of aesthetic cliché with which to explain the difference/sameness between lower and upper lakes. We almost hear a sigh of relief when, in the last sentence, he resumes the conventional with the word "picturesque."[9] Considered another way, "bright obscurity" attests to dependence on an *alternate* resource of convention even more banal: talking about the weather. "Bright obscurity" is an atmospherics or ambience, something in the air "out there" in which connection can still be posited as commonly understood.

Following the description of Lake Geneva is a more immense bright obscurity. Wordsworth cloaks the sights later to be monumentalized in Book 6 of *The Prelude* within inexpressibility *topoi* and other clichés of circumvention:

> We left our bundles and struck over the mountains to Chamouny to visit the glaciers of Savoy. You have undoubtedly heard of these celebrated s[c]enes, but if you have not read of them any description which I have here room to give you must be altogether inadequate. . . .
> At Brig we quitted the Valais and passed the Alps at the Semplon in order to visit part of Italy. The impressions of three hours of our walk among the Alps will never be effaced (*EY* 33).

Wordsworth says to Dorothy: only *if* you know the description of the Chamonix could I describe it to you. Description only gestures toward a pleasure of description "out there," hanging in air between brother and sister. Just so, when he says that the impressions of the Simplon Pass will never be effaced, it is unclear what impressions were etched in the first place. Impressiveness also hangs in air, in a pleasure of convention.

Let me borrow a reading from Erich Auerbach's *Mimesis* to frame "bright obscurity," the veil under which Wordsworth shifts conventions at his goal. Examining Hebraic narrative as epitomized in the story of Abraham and Isaac, Auerbach probes at the lack of connection between any two points of narrative, at the "paratactic" magic by which characters simply appear on a new scene or enact new deeds without any movement being described. In the gap between points is Auerbach's "background" (pp. 3–23). Traversing the Alps, Wordsworth is Abraham-his-own-Isaac; motion, or motive, between any two points hides in background ambience.

Talking about the weather is always a way to talk about something else. What alternative to the eroticism of aesthetics hangs suspended in the background? What is in the air?

Federation and Convention

Auerbach's "background" houses the Protean spirit of his work, "history." Here the bonus of entering our problem through the worldly tour shows itself. An entire volume of Bruce's five-volume work is devoted to the "Annals of Abyssinia." So, too, Coxe's splendid reportage of his travels is backed up by an enormous amount of Swiss history – synopses whose focus on tyranny overthrown or liberty defended will be footnoted in later editions with ironic reference to the French occupation of Switzerland.[10] Tours always describe motion through a land written over by history, even though they also carefully keep history – however many pages are devoted to it – in the background as if it were supplemental to the delights of the present tour, as if, in other words, it were merely a flourish complementing foreground appreciation. As a convention of tours, history is ornamental.

The notion of the supplement or ornament is very difficult. We say that an ornament beautifies its object; but the object of ornamentation – as is clear in the tradition of courtly love sonnets – is always presumed to be the *ne plus ultra* of beauty: therefore, why does Beauty need the eroticism of ornamentation? In the face of this paradox, theories of ornamentation must enroll it in a structure of signification – whether Platonic (the ornament represents imperfectly the inaccessible beauty of the true), Aristotelian (the ornament expresses an inner beauty), or Chain-of-Being (everything in the universe is part of a necklace allegorizing the prime mover of beauty). Ornament is a mark, a writing. The shyness of its signified, Beauty, can be accounted for by thinking along the lines Angus Fletcher develops in his study of ornament and its Greek form, *kosmos* (pp. 108–46): ornaments mark on the foreground plane (through tokens of place such as dress or the proper accent) a cosmic order of fitness, a total rule of Beauty, otherwise invisible in the background.

Application: tours *require* the ornament of historical synopses in order to provide visible marks for an immense historical, rather than cosmic, order in the background. Background history composes the overall orbit of signification in which tours participate, an orbit that is no other than the social equivalent of cosmos: "conventionality" itself – the very form of shared meaningfulness out of whose mechanism for positing total fitness the individual tourist draws aesthetics or other specialties of appreciation with confidence that they will fit his experience to the understandings of others. Imagine this composite painting of a tour: nature dominates the foreground, toward the back of the foreground, there is a mark composed of historical synopses, a mark like Brueghel's Icarus that seems ornamental because it points to no signified in the foreground; but the mark is crucial because its conventionality establishes the very perspective system, the social history or overall conventionality of vision within which foreground nature can be seen as a "delightful" beauty in the first place. No jewel without its setting: without history in the background, after all, a landscape is not a landscape; it is wilderness.

The conclusion to be reached so far, then, is that history in a tour ornaments nature in order to limn nature's participation in the true background signified: conventionality or civilization. But something is missing in the picture. If we compare a locodescriptive or prospect *paysage moralisé* such as Denham's "Cooper's Hill" or Pope's "Windsor-Forest" with Wordsworth's tour, we notice a striking contrast. History in "Cooper's Hill" and "Windsor-Forest" decorates nature, but points toward the background signified of civilization so unambiguously that it is as if natural landscape itself were the ornament. In a Wordsworthian tour, the arrow of signification from historical ornament toward the background is curiously blunted: historical markers point nowhere and decorate nature to no purpose.

In order to explain the deflection, Wordsworth's tour should be unfolded into three planes instead of two: history marks the background, nature stands in the *middle* ground, and the real foreground stages the tourist himself, or "I" of description. Lawrence Manley's study of convention in the history of criticism suggests a way to approach the tension in this structure causing historical signification to bend. Manley argues that the ancients saw convention as an order of change or of epiphenomena poised against the universal truth of nature. But by the time of the romantics, convention had enthroned itself so massively as humanistic science and "history" that the relativistic understanding of reality it sponsored made unconvincing the ancient truth of universal nature. Consequently, the romantics reasserted nature's universal truth against that of history in the new form of individuality: the "original" or transcendentally non-conventional self. If Nature now meant the outdoors specifically, the outdoors was only a setting in which the ancient, universal nature could reappear as the individual.

Extending such an analysis, I suggest that in the threefold "painting" of a tour, the middle ground of nature is merely a mediation within the real antithesis of the time between background historical convention and foreground self. Nature, the boundary, is the real mark in the painting. The historical signifier seems to point to no background signified because an interposed veil of nature — really only an idea or mark of naturalness — deflects the arrow of signification so that it points invisibly to the foreground self, which thus originates as if from nowhere, or from nature itself. A tourist in Wordsworth's mold is a historical man who, as soon as he spots scenery, thinks himself primitive and original.

We notice that whether or not guided by Coxe or other tour works specifically, Wordsworth takes care to round out his 1790 letter with homage to social and historical action in France during *l'année heureuse.* Landscape is supposed to be the foreground ("Among the more awful scenes of the Alps, I had not a thought of man"; *EY* 34). Historical background is the supplemental delight or ornamental interest: "But I must remind you that we crossed it at the time when the whole nation was mad with joy, in consequence of the revolution. It was a most interesting period to be in France, and we had many delightful scenes where the interest of the picture was owing solely to this cause" (*EY* 36).

But I suggest that the letter's perspective should be read in reverse: it is history in 1790 that is the sufficient motive and nature the real supplement or mark. The slightly "mad" truancy of 1790 (the letter mentions those who thought the trip "mad and impracticable," *EY* 37) is sanctioned not so much by nature as by the fact that now a "whole nation was mad with joy." History, whose very icon is the Federation, or convention, of a nation, is the common convention of meaningfulness from which the individual with shortcomings in specific motive, in "selfhood," can differentiate himself only by using a province of history — the history of aesthetic taste — to mark a boundary in the middle ground. Only through a flourish of nature can Wordsworth's tourist "I" then appear in the foreground as an "original" denying history and conventionality. An aesthetic tour through France in 1790, after all, is not the same as a tour at other times. Wordsworth's core statement might be phrased as follows: "In 1790, Federation and political spirit are 'in the air' as everyone else's motivation, but I am individual enough to view it all as a matter of aesthetics." Thus the complacent egotism at his letter's end when he spotlights himself in the foreground as the final object of aesthetics. While everyone else may be a sansculotte, he and Jones have the originality to be gypsies at the center of a genre- or subject-painting:

Our appearance is singular, and we have often observed that, in passing thro' a village, we have excited a general smile. Our coats which we had made light on purpose for our journey are of the same piece; and our manner of bearing our bundles, which is upon our heads, with each an oak stick in our hands, contributes not a little to that general curiosity which we seem to excite. But I find I have again relapsed into Egotism (*EY* 37).

The Ego dresses as a "natural" to mark itself off from the historical.

In order to study self-demarcation further, we need to shift at this point from 1790 to the later perspective of Book 6 of *The Prelude*. The description of the 1790 tour in Book 6, read in its own context, is a sustained effort to deny history by asserting nature as the separating mark constitutive of the egotistical self. It may be helpful to think of nature in its deflective capacity here as a mirror. The aim of Book 6 is to prevent the self from looking through nature to underlying history. Nature must instead reflect the self.[11]

Book 6 creates a mirror denying history in two phases. Instigating the first is a moment of insecurity in the balance between nature and history. Wordsworth begins describing his 1790 trip by confessing his younger self's undermotivation, and then immediately compensates with the main motive, Nature:

> An open slight
> Of College cares and study was the scheme,
> Nor entertain'd without concern for those
> To whom my worldly interests were dear:
> But Nature then was sovereign in my heart,
> And mighty forms seizing a youthful Fancy
> Had given a charter to irregular hopes.
>
>   (6.342–8)

But there is a curious flicker in his main motive, a doubling of viewpoint akin to that in a Renaissance "perspective picture" where, as in Holbein's *The Ambassadors*, we see an attenuated construction to be deciphered only by looking at the picture from the side. By a conceit carried in diction – sovereign, seizing, charter – Wordsworth already allows history to infiltrate the very core of nature. Nature is the ground, but the figure – the Revolution – tends to usurp the status of the ground with the same hidden *virtù* (in Machiavelli's sense) by which the trick-image of death in *The Ambassadors* seizes every viewer.[12] Book 6 then compounds the danger by declaring the supplemental motive, history, with such enthusiasm that the Revolution's ornamental gilding threatens to distract the eye entirely:

> In any age, without an impulse sent
> From work of Nations, and their goings-on,

I should have been possessed by like desire:
But 'twas a time when Europe was rejoiced,
France standing on the top of golden hours,
And human nature seeming born again.
Bound, as I said, to the Alps, it was our lot
To land at Calais on the very eve
Of that great federal Day.

(6.349–57)

The implication is that idleness, a perennial concern in Wordsworth's poetry,[13] has the best excuse it will ever have at this time when history supplements scenic holiday with the "work" of nations. History's background helps nature license personal holiday so nicely, indeed, that Wordsworth's oddly passive phrasing of desire ("I should have been possessed by like desire") culminates in the thesis of agency by lottery: "it was our lot / To land" at a particular time in history. The undermotivation with which the 1790 tour begins in Book 6 thus incites overmotivation, a double sufficiency of natural and historical motive only precariously organized so that history is subordinate. If history is work, after all, desire for nature must be indolence.

It is now that Book 6 launches its first defense against history, its initial use of nature as a screen by which overmotivation can seem to mirror the self rather than transmit the historical whole: the great set piece describing the ambience of the Fete of Federation. To appreciate the vanity of this piece, we need to recover with some precision the ambience of 1790. Wordsworth and Jones spent the actual day of Federation, 14 July, first at Calais and then on the road to Ardres, and so did not reach the site of the nearest large fete in Arras until late on 16 July (D. Hayden (1983) 9–12). They then passed belatedly through the sites of other major fetes in the department capitals of Troyes, Dijon, and Lyons. In one sense, it did not matter that they missed the celebration of significant fetes. Secondary celebrations in thousands of smaller towns and villages promulgated the spirit of the larger ones in Paris and the local capitals, and preliminary celebrations such as the Federation of the Pas de Calais, Nord, and Somme at Lille in June, as well as subsequent holidays such as the 18 July *Fête Exécutée en Mémoire de la Fédération Générale* at Champs Elysées, further dispersed Federation Day in time. Altogether, the Federation was a month-long background of celebration to be encountered anywhere. "Southward thence / We took our way direct through Hamlets, Towns, / Gaudy with reliques of that Festival" (6.360–2), Wordsworth says, and adds that on the boat trip to Lyons, he met

> a host
> Of Travellers, chiefly Delegates, returning

From the great Spousals newly solemniz'd
At their chief City in the sight of Heaven.

(6.394–7)

But in another sense the poet must have been at a crucial distance from
the spirit of the fetes. It is significant that his French at the time was far
from fluent.* We have to be aware of two different views of Federation
Day: that of the French themselves, whose architectural, sculptural, visual,
pantomimic, and ritual representations of confederation were conventionalized by verbal meaning – by words inscribing ritual in time – and that of
Wordsworth, whose access primarily, or only, to the panorama of ritual,
"reliques", and the physical behavior of *fédérés* resulted in the need for
surrogate verbalization.[14]

We can begin to approximate the French view by noting that the Fete of
Federation occurred at a time when the new machinery of state, though
already largely operative, hung in suspension between the verbal principles
stated by the 1789 Declaration of Rights and the verbal codification still to
be completed in the 1791 Constitution. The hollow between declaration and
enactment, the gap in the Revolution's own "description," was the space of
oath – the Oath of Federation – and the pithiness of the Oath (epitomized
in Louis XVI's one sentence)* was such that it had to be supplemented
immediately by nonverbal representations – by forms of ritual that were
actually all the oath had of substance. An oath is a promise of being, a
nation's description to itself of desire fulfilled. Like an *assignat*, the promise
had to be seen to be secured upon something tangible, and that security –
the visible picture of being – took the form of architecture, sculpture,
painting, and performing arts both genteel and vulgar. Most immediately,
the oath found visual expression in the relief sculpture on the altar at the
Paris Fete imitating David's *Oath of the Horatii*.[15] More generally, it metamor-
phosed into an astonishingly fertile array of "revolutionary" forms, all
cross-referring to each other in unfathomably complex ways. As contemporary engravings show, for example, there was a flow of allusion between the
circular towers of the fallen Bastille, the dances in the round or *Carmagnol*
performed upon them (the Bastille became a *salle de bal en plein air*) for the
July 14 and 18 fetes), the spontaneous Liberty Dances in the round at the
Paris Fete on 14 July, and the evolutions of the military columns at the same
Fete. All these demonstrations of revolution were in turn encapsulated

---

* During his second trip to France in 1791–2, he wrote his brother Richard, "I am not yet
able to speak french with decent accuracy but must of course improve very rapidly" (*EY* 70).
* After Lafayette's oath binding the *fédérés* to the nation, law, and King, Louis rose and
answered: "*Moi, roi des Français, je jure d'employer tout le pouvoir qui m'est délégué par la loi
constitutionnelle de l'état à maintenir la constitution décrétée par l'assemblée nationale et acceptée par moi,
et à faire exécuter les loix*" (*Collection Complete* i. 159).

within the French version of Shakespeare's Globe, the Paris Champ-de-Mars amphitheater (or such similar concourses as the Grand'Place in Arras).[16]

If this labyrinth of visual and ritual representations provided the Oath with substance, it in return received from verbalization the convention of directed form, of a single, motivated flow of prophecy renouncing the past and pointing toward the future. The Declaration, Oath, and Constitution were the official seals of a massive under-narrative of popular verbalization whose epic was the encyclopedic lists of grievances collected for the Estates General in 1789 and whose episodes were such actions as the Fall of the Bastille collectively described in newspapers, pamphlets, memoirs, and gossip. It was the task of the under-narrative to make sure that the meaning carried in ritual or pantomime would read, destruction → construction, rather than the reverse.

The Fete on the Paris Champ-de-Mars is a telling example of such historicization of visual representation. In her fine study, Mona Ozouf suggests that revolutionary fetes situated themselves on open amphitheaters and other panoramic spaces designed to project openness to nature, to a new social decorum of fraternity, and – most generally, perhaps – to new meaning.[17] The key point is that open space for meaning, especially in an urban center such as Paris, could only be created by destruction of the old. Nature could not be introduced into a metropolis without displacing something artificial; a fraternal social decorum could not be achieved without tearing down the divisive etiquette of aristocratic fetes; and old symbols could not be written over until erased. Generally, the symbolic actions of the Revolution thus took place either in angry dislocation from traditional sites of meaning (to such peripheral spaces as a Tennis Court, for example) or in violent erasures of meaning on such old sites as the Bastille.

The Champ-de-Mars site incorporated both dislocation and erasure. First, the center of the nation shifted across the river from the Tuileries and Palais Royal to a relatively blank slate. Then the slate was made even cleaner by modeling it upon the violent erasure at the Bastille a year ago. The correspondence between the Paris Fete and the Fall of the Bastille was clinched by a relief of the Bastille at the center of the Champ-de-Mars amphitheater,[18] but such correspondence had already been enacted in the very construction of the amphitheater. The preparation of the site required the labor of thousands of men soon joined, in a famous action, by some two hundred thousand Paris citizens of all descriptions, and involved excavating the flat parade ground in order to build a high ramp all around (as was seen in the splendid watercolor of *La Journée des Brouettes* by Etienne-Charles Le Guay in the Musée Carnavalet). The mood during excavation was festive, but the meaning was violent. As the crowds dug, they sang: "He that is raised up will be humbled, and he that is humble will be raised up."[19] The digging on the Champ-de-Mars reenacted the violent undermining signalized by the destruction of the Bastille. Or, in a secondary allusion, it reenacted the forced removal of the King from Versailles during the October Days – the key act making possible the King's symbolic union with the nation on Federation Day. On 5–6 October, 1789, the March of Women broke in upon the royal family at Versailles and brought them to Paris virtually as prisoners (Soboul (1975) 156). As Ronald Paulson points out, this action – especially as seen by Burke – had the symbolic form of a rape or penetration (pp. 60–2). The rape finishes on Burke's pages in a splash of "piercing," "scattered limbs," and "mutilated carcases," as a dismemberment and puncturing – a sort of excavation – of the body politic (p. 164).

How to make something constructive out of violent excavation? Just as contemporary paintings of patriots planting Liberty Trees depended upon a left-to-right convention of "reading" to specify that the Tree, held at a diagonal, is being planted and not uprooted,[20] so the digging at the Champ-de-Mars required convention-making verbalization, epitomized by the popular song, to show that destructive excavation (humbling) merely prophesies construction (raising up). So, too, the "excavation" of the body politic at Versailles on 5 October required its own verbalizations showing that violent evacuation was really a filling, a reunion in which the King filled the emptiness in Paris. Marat spoke of the event in these terms: "It is a source of great rejoicing for the good people of Paris to have their King in their midst once again. His presence will very quickly do much to change the outward appearance of things, and the poor will no longer die of starvation" (quoted Soboul (1975) 157). It was as if the nation experienced a hunger, an evacuation at its center, that the kidnapping of the King magically filled (the filling was then to be emptied again, of course, in the 1791 flight to Varennes completing this diptych of representation).

As Burke knew, no enactment is complete without such propaganda, or historicizing description, accompanying the very spadework of action. Once excavation had created the amphitheater at the Champ-de-Mars, there arose at the center a large, pyramidal altar – the podium for the nation's ultimate piece of propaganda or descriptive convention enlisting the Fete in a historical process of construction. On this altar, on 14 July, the Bishop of Autun (Talleyrand), surrounded by hundreds of white-robed priests, said mass preparatory to the King's Oath. Thus despite the fact that the Fete built itself on undermining the Bastille, on emptying Versailles, and on evacuating religion itself, and despite even the ill omen of unrelenting rain that day, the verbalization peaking in the Bishop's blessing made a totally conventional, but profoundly historical, promise that the explosion of energy seen everywhere in visual form and symbolic action pointed forward to the millennium rather than backward to hell. The blessing transformed the famous rain from ill omen to covenant, a sign of fertility prophesying something like that ultimate celebration of fraternity and nature-become-religion in the Champ-de-Mars: the 1794 Fete devoted to the "Supreme Being and Nature."

We can sum up for our purposes by calling the Fete of Federation the French imagination of history operating under the badge of Reason. The French reimagined the conventions of the past into a convention for the future, and the intersection of past and future was the millennial "now," when the Revolution's transcendental signifieds – Fraternity and Nature – seemed immanent within artistic clichés.[21]

Now we can turn to the alternative verbalization of Book 6 by which Wordsworth takes to an extreme his younger self's aestheticization of Revolution: georgic – the genre closely associated in the eighteenth century with locodescription and the tour but not yet realized in the 1790 letter (even though Wordsworth studied Virgil's *Georgics* closely – especially the third and fourth – at Cambridge soon before the 1790 trip).[22] In *Prel.* 6.355–425, he describes the Revolution as merely a season in vegetable landscape, a "benevolence and blessedness . . . like Spring" that flowers as a rustic May Day or perhaps a harvest festival among "the vine-clad Hills of Burgundy." In this world, the "reliques" of the Fete – "Flowers left to wither on triumphal Arcs, / And window-Garlands" – are not so much garnishes as integral parts of the landscape of growth and decay. Here the very roads along which the young traveler walks appear only as files of "Elms . . . With their thin umbrage." "Enchanting" were "those woods, and farms, and orchards" exclaims the poet-as-*agricola*. In the spirit of the fourth *Georgic*, Wordsworth then inserts within agrarian landscape a simile comparing the *fédérés* to bees that "swarm'd, gaudy and gay." Finally, the set piece of Book 6 reaches its climax in descriptions of *Carmagnol* dances that now, however, appear merely a country dance. "We rose at signal given, and form'd a ring / And, hand in hand, danced round and round," Wordsworth says, and seems so taken with this image of rustic revolution that he repeats it: "round, and round the board they danced again."

Two "snapshots" from the *Georgics:* (1) a plowman working in the field at the end of the first *Georgic* suddenly turns up rusting armor and heroic bones in his fields;[23] (2) Virgil himself, digging for the story behind the spontaneous generation of bees in the fourth, suddenly turns up an entire epyllion, or contained epic, buried in his narrative. Keeping in mind the historical milieu so profoundly in the background of Virgil's work, I offer this preliminary understanding of georgic based on these snapshots: georgic is the supreme mediational form by which to bury history in nature, epic in pastoral. Like the tour mode, it is the form in which history turns into the background, the manure, for landscape. Through georgic, Wordsworth is able, at least at first glance, to make the entire under-narrative of the Revolution sink into unbroken invisibility. In a sense, the young traveler he depicts walks through a landscape that is natural only because it is prehistorical; the possibility of history has not yet evolved. Contemporary engravings depict Liberty pointedly as a woman carrying a broken yoke (Henderson (1912) 314); if France was "georgic" in 1790, after all, such fertility harvested the mass destruction of the agrarian Great Fear of 1789 (on *la Grande Peur*, see Lefebvre (1982)). But in his georgic, Wordsworth appreciates joy without the haunt of historical fear, the yoke of rustic labor without the jagged edge of break with past oppression.

The purpose of the mirror of georgic nature is to hide history in order, finally, to reflect the self. At the beginning of his "vanity," Wordsworth recounts "How bright a face is worn when joy of one / Is joy of tens of millions" (6.359–60). In the mirror of nature, this proportion is reversed: history's tens of millions focus to foreground the poet's joy of one. Halfway through the set piece, external observation of vegetable process thus deflects momentarily into self-absorption:

> 'Twas sweet at such a time, with such delights
> On every side, in prime of youthful strength,
> To feed a Poet's tender melancholy
> And fond conceit of sadness.
>
> (6.375–8)

The tour's original undermotivation becomes melancholy, the convention in locodescription framing the subjective self. Subjectivity then steps even more vainly into the foreground when Wordsworth elevates his younger self above the celebrating *fédérés*:

> In this blithe Company
> We landed, took with them our evening Meal,
> Guests welcome almost as the Angels were
> To Abraham of old.
>
> (6.401–4)

As in Genesis 18:1–15, where angels prophesy the birth of Isaac to Abraham, the blessed tourist steps momentarily out of history altogether in prophetic anticipation of his own self, of an "Isaac" that then appears as the deus ex machina of the whole set piece. What is the specific point of rustic festivity and dancing? Says Wordsworth,

> All hearts were open, every tongue was loud
> With amity and glee; we bore a name
> Honour'd in France, the name of Englishmen,
> And hospitably did they give us Hail

As their forerunners in a glorious course,
And round, and round the board they danced again.

(6.408–13)

Suddenly, the Revolution hails the English poet at the focus of its circle.

Such is the first mirror in Book 6, screening background history from view. Yet, despite its gorgeous polish, the mirror is inadequate because of a basic undecidability in georgic making it at all times, and especially in Wordsworth's time, just as likely to exhume history as bury it. The genres of tour work and georgic, which the Preface of 1815, will call "Idyllic" and "Didactic" respectively, are alike problematic because they tend to fall between the three master genres of Narrative, Drama, and Lyric composing Wordsworth's and literary history's trinity, on the one hand, and true servant genres with clearly defined formal traits (such as Ode as opposed to Elegy), on the other. The generic field in any age, I suggest, distributes itself between master and servant genres with some unstable mediator always filling the role played by tour and georgic in Wordsworth's time. Tour and georgic are preeminently mixed genres in which the stability of genre as a convention is threatening to come apart under the pressure of the times. Tour and georgic in the late eighteenth and early nineteenth centuries are the pressure points where the entire generic field is beginning to rearrange around the massive intrusion of specifically historical reality and the form jury-rigged to imitate it: the novel.

In the era soon to produce a novelist like Scott, history became *the* subject of mimesis, and the georgic mediation of nature projected in Book 6 of *The Prelude* can only bury history out of sight provisionally before turning it up once more. There are, after all, those protruding "bones" in the soil, which, because gothic romance is denied to georgic as an escape valve, cannot be easily covered. Too much energy of repression must be expended to keep the georgic mirror from turning transparent to history. If Wordsworth's simile likening the *fédérés* to bees alludes to the *Georgics*, after all, it certainly also points to the epic use of bees in Homer and in Virgil himself, as well as to the brilliant problem georgic at the close of Book 1 of *Paradise Lost* where Satanic history threatens to swarm into the pastoral tranquillity of the "belated peasant."

The climactic second phase of the defense against history in Book 6 then begins at Mont Blanc precisely upon the discovery that georgic is transparent. The demands Wordsworth makes at this point upon georgic to bury history create such tension in the convention that the epic pole first seems to disappear entirely, leaving an exaggerated insistence upon pastoral. The Mont Blanc episode begins as a fond, georgic look homeward to pastoral: "Sweet coverts did we cross of pastoral life, / Enticing Vallies" (6.437–38). But like Milton's belated peasant, the young traveler suddenly experiences a near eruption of the demonic in the harvest world: the peak of Mont Blanc discovers itself as a gap in georgic fertility, as a "soulless image ... Which had usurp'd upon a living thought" (6.454–55). There is some strange devil of history, I suggest, behind usurpation that the poet-as-*agricola* would rather not see. The whiteness at Mont Blanc – like that in *The White Doe of Rylstone* – is the space in which history can ghost into the present; it is not no meaning but a panic of too much possible meaning. Whiteness is the page for a possible epic whose stern mood must either be recognized or thwarted. For the time being, the whiteness at Mont Blanc – protruding like a heroic bone – is simply ploughed under again. In an effort to make "amends" (6.460) akin to that at Lake Geneva in the 1790 letter, Wordsworth returns from intimations of usurpation to fertility in the Vale of Chamonix by means of a suspiciously hyperbolical pastoral:

> There small birds warble from the leafy trees,
> The Eagle soareth in the element;
> There doth the Reaper bind the yellow sheaf,
> The Maiden spread the haycock in the sun,
> While Winter like a tamed Lion walks
> Descending from the mountain to make sport
> Among the cottages by beds of flowers.
>
> (6.462–8)

Not a trace of grimness does the Reaper seem to betray. But notice the suppression of narrative necessary to screen grimness. Arranged around the hinge of the Reaper are two diptychs: the small birds with the Eagle, and the Maiden with the Lion of winter. There is a muted story of predation here, of some spoliation or usurpation in the area of Chamonix that the 1805 Book 6 (still without the Convent of Chartreuse excursus) must prettify.[24]

It is the near eruption of history at Mont Blanc that provokes the climactic veiling at Simplon Pass. It will be useful to retain Hartman's labeling of the sequence: 6a, the ascent ("Yet still in me, mingling with these delights / Was something of stern mood ..." 6.488–524); 6b, the halt ("Imagination! lifting up itself ..." 6.525–48); and 6c, the descent through Gondo Gorge ("The dull and heavy slackening that ensued ..." 6.549–72). Ascent and descent form the paradigmatic two points of the tour, and the halt is the gap. So much work has been done on the sequence that I will offer at present only a schematic of 6a and 6c in order to move quickly to 6b. In 6a we find a trajectory of serial repetition guided at the end by the Peasant, or holdover *agricola* from the georgic universe. More specifically, 6a pictures an implicit struggle between the vectors of the horizontal and vertical. The horizontal, intoned in the tedious diction of "A length of hours," "Ere long we follow'd," and "at length," is the progress of pure repetition, of one foot after another without describable motive. The vertical, heard in the verbs of "we had clomb," "the Travellers rose," and "climb'd with eagerness," is the vector of significance and motivation. Disappointment, first sounded in Wordsworth's and Jones's request that the Peasant *repeat* his message, but fully realized only in the descent pictured by 6c, arrives upon the discovery that verticality is itself simply a disguised form of flat repetition: "downwards we hurried fast," 6c begins in its record of descent chiastically opposed to ascent. "Downwards" merely repeats without meaningful connection the previously upward climb. Indeed, 6c is a microcosm of the disconnected repetition disappointing Wordsworth so gravely. Gondo Gorge appears as a landscape of binary points separated by oxymoronic divide: "The immeasurable height / Of woods decaying, never to be decay'd ... Winds thwarting winds ... Tumult and peace, the darkness and the light."

What radical of motivation can connect the "two points" whose disconnection images the undermotivation of the whole tour? Here we reach the goal of this chapter, Wordsworth's addition of 6b and the "bright obscurity" of Imagination:

> Imagination! lifting up itself
> Before the eye and progress of my Song
> Like an unfather'd vapour; here that Power,
> In all the might of its endowments, came
> Athwart me; I was lost as in a cloud,
> Halted, without a struggle to break through.
> And now recovering, to my Soul I say
> I recognise thy glory; in such strength
> Of usurpation, in such visitings
> Of awful promise, when the light of sense
> Goes out in flashes that have shewn to us
> The invisible world, doth Greatness make abode,
> There harbours whether we be young or old.
> Our destiny, our nature, and our home
> Is with infinitude, and only there;
> With hope it is, hope that can never die,
> Effort, and expectation, and desire,
> And something evermore about to be.
> The mind beneath such banners militant
> Thinks not of spoils or trophies, nor of aught
> That may attest its prowess, blest in thoughts
> That are their own perfection and reward,
> Strong in itself, and in the access of joy
> Which hides it like the overflowing Nile.

(6.525–48)

Here is the great mirror into which Wordsworth looks to reflect upon his "self." The process of this reflection is complex and sums up the entire pathway of deflection I have sketched so far.

Crucial is the passage's initial flicker from first person singular ("I was lost," "I say," "I recognise") to first person plural ("shewn to us," "whether we be young or old," "Our destiny, our nature, and our home") and then to the impersonal ("its prowess," "Strong in itself," "hides it"). Looking outwards, the "I" perceives "we's" and "our's" that are the pronouns of convention and collectivity. "We" and "our" are signifiers of background that, given a chance, would point directly into the history heard with such frightening force and precision in the vocabulary of 6b as a whole: "Power . . . all the might of its endowments . . . struggle to break through . . . glory . . . strength / Of usurpation . . . Greatness . . . banners militant . . . spoils or trophies . . . prowess . . . Strong in itself." But there is a deflection here, and the arrow of signification bends, in an extraordinary sentence, to point perpetually "there" into a historically ungrounded "being" we might call objectified subjectivity:

> Our destiny, our nature, and our home
> Is with infinitude, and only there;
> With hope it is, hope that can never die,
> Effort, and expectation, and desire,
> And something evermore about to be.

The perpetual "out there" of such desired "being" is propped up, we notice, upon reference to external nature as pure figure. The "I" comes to see nature as if in quotes: "*like* the overflowing Nile." Anointing itself with a figure of externality as groundless in origin as the Nile itself, which in the 1850 poem pours from a "fount of Abyssinian clouds," the "I" thus comes into the majesty of objectivity seemingly without any further need for the mediation of the most human approach to objectivity: collectivity. History is denied, and the "I" engenders itself autogenetically as the very crown of what I have called objectified subjectivity: a mind knowing itself only in the impersonal – "strong in *it*self."

The "I," in sum, looks into the background of collective history, deflects upon nature's polish of objectivity, and at last sees itself reflected as the awesome, historically free personality of "*The* mind."

Imagination and Napoleon

But Book 6 cannot be read wholly on its own. Let me now open the aperture completely to view Simplon Pass in the overall context of *The*

Prelude and 1804, when Book 6 and much of the rest of the poem were composed.[25] In this context, it becomes important to stare fixedly into, and *through*, the mirror of the Imagination. In the construction of the total *Prelude* in 1804, I believe, Wordsworth inserted background reminders of historicity in the Imagination passage as avenues toward a realization that "the mind" must finally enroll (literally enlist, as Wordsworth did in the Grasmere Volunteers in 1803; see Moorman i. 602–3) in a collective system authorized from some source "elsewhere" than the self: in the grounded or demystified Nile that is history.[26] Specifically, Book 6 and the Imagination passage look forward to the direct concern of the Revolution books (Books 9 and 10) with a deluge of history. Wordsworth probably began composing much of Books 9 and 10 soon after finishing 6 in late April 1804 (with additional work in October to December of that year; see Norton *Prel.* 518–19; *CMY* 650–3); and there is the possibility that all three books dealing with France were composed in a single manuscript (Norton *Prel.* 519). In the movement of the total poem, the denial (and de-Nile) of history in 6b really warns that the nature and self thus far imagined are antediluvian. Wordsworth is about to go on to open the floodgates in order to let in a ferocious tributary of his Nile: the river of "shapeless eagerness," as we will later see, that rushes us into explicit history at the opening of Book 9.

What preoccupies Imagination in 1804 such that it at once prevents and presages history? MS. WW of *The Prelude*, we know, shows that Wordsworth originally inserted what is now viii. 711–27 – the first part of the simile of the cave – between 6a and 6b (Norton *Prel.* 216n). Imagination, I suggest, is as hollow as this cave. The more we look into it, the more we submit to an interior, self-motivated reality bodying forth (in the language of the simile) "Shapes and Forms and Tendencies to Shape." Specifically, Imagination cavitates nature to show the protruding bones of the historical world of 1804. In 6b, Imagination sees in nature not just its own reflection but that of a firmly *historical* genius of imagination – of the Imaginer who, in a manner of speaking, wrote the book on crossing the Alps. I believe that if we look into 6b, we will see through the self and mind in the foreground, through even the nature in the middle ground, to a frightening skeleton in the background. Whatever else it is, Imagination is the haunt of Napoleon, the great Bone of the time (a standard play on words in the early 1800s; see below). More precisely, if Imagination reflects upon nature as a mirror, the mirror is of magistrates and shows Imagination to itself as a canny double for uncanny Napoleon. Imagination at once mimics and effaces Napoleon in an effort, anticipatory of Books 9–10 and after, to purge tyranny by *containing* tyranny within itself as the empire of Imagination.[27]

We need to be careful here with degrees of certainty. An adequate reading of Wordsworth's texts in their historical context, I will suggest, requires not so much positivistic method as a deflected or denied positivism able to discriminate absence. For the moment, however, we can reach our goal simply by positing a ladder of increasing certainty. No single piece of evidence in the following presentation leads absolutely to the conclusion that Napoleon stands in the background of 6b, but the sum, I believe, has plausibility; and such plausibility in the specific thesis will be sufficient to carry the general argument that 6b is decisively engaged with history. I highlight the most telling specifics in italics, but I also include supplementary suggestions based on circumstances and sometimes wordplay that might appear farfetched in normal times. After reading in the literature and art of British reactions to Napoleon in the years of war fever – including the standard plays on the skeletal nature of "Bone-apart" and the fabulous apocalyptic interpretations of Bonaparte's name as the Number of the Beast[28] – I believe that no accident possible to be interpreted should be omitted in detailing an imagination of Napoleon. In any case, the plausibility I aim for does not rest finally on one-to-one correspondence between history and the Imagination passage, but on the alliance between text and context considered as wholes.

18 Brumaire. In 1799 Napoleon returned unexpectedly to France from his Egyptian campaign, reached Paris on 16 October with massive popular support, and took control of the Directory in the coup d'état of 18 Brumaire (actually 18–19 Brumaire; 9–10 November).[29] *The Annual Register* (years 1758–92, 1794–6, 1800, 1802–11, and 1814–20 were in Wordsworth's Rydal Mount library; Shaver (1979) 9) banners the world's astonishment at this advent as if from nowhere, choosing a style of language – "in defiance of reason ... not any one ... could have imagined" – that we will need to consider later:

> Whether we contemplate the great affairs of nations in a political or military point of view, the return of Buonaparte to France ... is the grand and leading event in the history of 1800. ... Who could have believed that a simple sub-lieutenant of artillery, a stranger to France, by name and by birth, was destined to govern this great empire, and to give the law, in a manner, to all the continent, in defiance of reason? ... There is not any one in the world who could have imagined the possibility of an event so extraordinary (1800: 66).

"Brumaire" is the month of mists in the vividly imagined revolutionary calendar, and Napoleon's takeover climaxed in his famously violent personal appearance before the hostile Council of Five Hundred at Saint-Cloud (spoken of simply as "Cloud" in the early Revolution because of antisacral doctrine; see Robiquet (1964) 62). In the world's eye, we might say, Napoleon burst upon the scene as a kind of "vapour," or cloud, an upstart and illegitimate spirit.

In 6b Wordsworth begins with a coup d'état of Imagination retracing something like the spirit of 18 Brumaire: an "unfather'd vapour" starts up in defiance of all expectation, comes with "Power" upon a poet who, like France in 1799, was "Halted, without a struggle to break through," and changes the regime with such "strength / Of usurpation" that the astonished poet, like France before Napoleon's renewed spectacles of state,* must say, "I recognise thy glory." Such recognition of glory – the great instance of bright obscurity – merely makes official what the poet had unconsciously, in an analogy to French popular support for Napoleon, depended upon all along.

Anchoring the reading of Imagination as coup d'état is Wordsworth's strong use of the figure "usurpation," a use prepared for in the chronicle of Mont Blanc. Usurpation in Book 6 is a figure backed up by allusion to *Macbeth*, the poem's preferred exemplar of the usurper.[30] Just after describing the descent through Gondo Gorge, Wordsworth describes "innocent Sleep" lying "melancholy among weary bones" (6.579–80; *Macbeth* II.ii.33). In one sense, the allusion points ahead in the poem, and backward in time, to Book 10 and the night in 1792 when the poet heard a voice in the Paris hotel quoting the regicide Macbeth: "Sleep no more" (10.77; *Macbeth* II.ii.32). Since Book 10 moves on immediately to the confrontation between Robespierre and Louvet, we can guess that Wordsworth's Macbeth, in the context of 1792, figures Robespierre (who in 10.461–2 is also represented as an offspring of Lear). But in another sense, the allusion to *Macbeth* in Book 6 with its addition of the image of bones points to Old Boney: *in the context of the years immediately preceding 1804, "usurper" cannot refer to anyone other than Napoleon.*

After 18 Brumaire, "usurper" was applied to Bonaparte in English parliamentary speeches, pamphlets, and newspapers with the consistency of a technical term and irrespective of party affiliation or sympathy with French republicanism. Whether he was thought merely to epitomize republicanism or to break with it, the premise was that Napoleon was a usurper.[31] Use of the epithet peaked first in 1799–1800 after 18 Brumaire and Napoleon's subsequent offer of peace to George III, which the Government chose to perceive as an insult because Napoleon took the stance of equal. The *Times* of London, for example, named Bonaparte "usurper" immediately after his coup (18, 20, 22 November 1799). In his forceful speech of 3 February 1800, Pitt then referred repeatedly to Napoleon as "usurper" and his government as a "usurpation" (pp. 273, 276, 278). Similarly, Sheridan spoke of Bonaparte in 1800 as "this ferocious usurper" (quoted in Maccunn (1914) 21). Use of the epithet then peaked a second time in 1803–4 upon

* Beginning with the pageantry of Napoleon's symbolic move to the Tuileries on 19 February, 1800 (Sydenham (1974) 235).

the resumption of hostilities after the Peace of Amiens, when *The Annual Register*, for example, labeled Bonaparte "the Corsican usurper" (1802: 224) and the *Times* similarly issued a virtual litany of "usurpers," "audacious usurpers," and "Corsican Usurpers."[32] Perhaps the best way to suggest the possible impact upon Wordsworth of the usurpation epithet in these years is to read Coleridge in the *Morning Post*. In 1800, Coleridge characterized Bonaparte, his regime, or various French decrees in such barbed phrases as "this insolence in the usurper" and a "low Harlequinade of Usurpation." On 11 March 1800, Coleridge's rhetoric drives the point home: Napoleon's rise is a usurpation, he says repeatedly, and "In his usurpation, Bonaparte stabbed his honesty in the vitals" (*Essays* i. 63, 91, 207–11).*

Marengo and Aboukir. Completing the coup is the "battle" of Imagination. *A Swiss mountain pass in 1804 was first and foremost a military site*: the avenue of the "modern Hannibal," as Coleridge later described Napoleon's forces (*Essays* ii 138). It is even more suggestive that 6b inscribes within the literal setting of the Swiss Alps the figure of the Nile, and so folds into Simplon Pass the two most crucial scenes of battle in the Napoleonic wars prior to Trafalgar in 1805: Switzerland (together with northern Italy) and Egypt. The Alpine region, Wordsworth's model of political independence, was the ground of Napoleon's most brilliant successes, and the mouth of the Nile that of his only major defeat to date. The lamination of the two is interpretive: if 6b begins with coup d'état, such illegality becomes progressively transformed until, by the end, Wordsworth has purged tyranny from Imagination in the flow of the Nile.

To begin with, 6b may be read as the conflation of the several Alpine campaigns: "Halted, without a struggle to break through," the poet is in the position of French troops awaiting the imagination of Napoleon to lead them through the pass. To some extent, Imagination's progress of blockage followed by rapid breakthrough may reflect the 1796 Italian campaign that first made Napoleon famous. Blocked by the numerically superior Austrians and Piedmontese at the Maritime Alps just to the south of Switzerland, Napoleon gestured toward Genoa, stabbed past the Alps to divide and defeat the enemy armies, and created out of Italy the Cisalpine, Cispadane, and Transpadane republics – a creation accompanied by the first of his wholesale "spoliations," as *The Annual Register* terms them, of treasuries and art (1796: 96). To a larger extent, Imagination's progress may reflect France's repeated occupation of Switzerland. Wordsworth later said that this conquest was the culminating factor in his turn of sympathy against France, but linking his various statements on the matter to a specific historical action has proved problematic. J. C. Maxwell argues persuasively that the

---

* In fact, Coleridge's fulminations against Bonaparte as "usurper" in early 1800 coincided with one of his peaks of admiration for him.

interventions of 1798 and 1802 – the former not directly led by Napoleon – are equally likely (or unlikely) to have provoked Wordsworth's turn. It seems that Wordsworth conflated the two invasions in hindsight and attached them both to Bonaparte. The 1798 occupation of Switzerland by French armies (while Napoleon prepared for Egypt) and the consequent declaration of the Helvetic Republic were also accompanied by vast "spoliations" of treasuries (*AR* 1798: 36). The 1802 action occurred during an insurrection against the French-instituted Helvetic Republic when Napoleon, despite promises to the contrary, intervened both by sending troops under General Ney and by transmitting a manifesto that *The Annual Register* says "will ever be memorable for its despotic arrogance" (1802: 233). One of Napoleon's special interests in both the 1798 and 1802 occupations, we may note, was to secure the Valais canton and so the link between Paris and Italy through the Simplon Pass (R. R. Palmer (1972) 171; A. Palmer (1984) 148).

To the largest extent, however, Imagination's progress in 6b reflects Napoleon's most astonishing stroke to date: his 1800 passage through the Swiss Alps leading to the Battle of Marengo. Newly become First Consul, Napoleon set off in May as de facto head of the Italian campaign to take the Austrian army from the rear. *Like Wordsworth, Napoleon arrived at Geneva, followed the northern shore of the lake eastward to the Rhone River, and then turned southward toward Chamonix.* Here he diverged, but only slightly, from Wordsworth's 1790 route. While part of his army crossed at Mount Cenis, Little St Bernard, and Mount St Gotthard, and a demibrigade of approximately 1000 men was sent to demonstrate as loudly as possible that the crossing would be at Simplon, Napoleon himself accompanied the main army through Great St Bernard Pass (about 50 miles southwest of Simplon).[33] In an action comparable to Hannibal's crossing by elephant, he broke down his artillery and sledded it through the snow-blocked defile. *This was the first blockage to be overcome in a march widely reported as a series of halts followed by breakthroughs.* The next blockage occurred at Fort Bard, which seemed to impede a narrow defile just past Great St Bernard. "There was no alternative," *The Annual Register* admires; "the fort must either be taken or another passage sought. Each had its difficulties, but Buonaparte's genius surmounted them" (1800: 191). After some skirmishing, Napoleon raised a cannon on top of a nearby church and battered the fort into surrender.[34] The final, decisive instance of halt followed by breakthrough was the Battle of Marengo itself, which Napoleon turned from defeat into victory. Posted in the rear of the Austrians, Napoleon's inferior forces began retreating under heavy Austrian artillery fire at the village of Marengo. Only with the arrival of Corps Commander Desaix's division from the south could Napoleon mount a charge, supported by all his artillery and cavalry, that broke the Austrian forces.

In the context of 1804, then, any imagination of an Alpine pass would remember the military "genius" of Bonaparte. It seems natural that Wordsworth's halt "without a struggle to break through" at the beginning of 6b should lead to the "banners militant" toward the close. The martial air of 6b, indeed, fairly trumpets itself. If we read in the spirit of the banners, Wordsworth's "visitings / Of Awful promise, when the light of sense / Goes out in flashes that have shewn to us / The invisible world" hint the violence of artillery. Even Wordsworth's great rallying speech has a military ring:

> Our destiny, our nature, and our home
> Is with infinitude, and only there;
> With hope it is, hope that can never die,
> Effort, and expectation, and desire,
> And something evermore about to be.

Whatever else it is, this speech — in its very cadence — is a double of Napoleon's widely publicized rallying speeches to his armies. After the 1796 breakthrough in the Maritime Alps, for example, *The Annual Register* quotes Bonaparte addressing his troops:

> You have precipitated yourselves, like a torrent, from the heights of the Appennines. You have routed and dispersed all who have opposed your progress.... Yes, soldiers, you have done much; but does there remain nothing more to be done? Though we have known how to vanquish, we have not known how to profit of our victories.... Let us depart! we have yet forced marches to make, enemies to subdue, laurels to gather, injuries to revenge. (1796: 91)*

But the parade of banners militant, of course, does not conclude the martial review of 6b. Wordsworth continues:

> The mind beneath such banners militant
> Thinks not of spoils or trophies, nor of aught
> That may attest its prowess, blest in thoughts
> That are their own perfection and reward.

Here, even amid the military anthem, his act of purging Napoleon begins. *Wordsworth's stress in 1804 that the Imagination is its own reward, and so eschews*

---

* Coleridge's comments in the *Morning Post* for 1 January, 1800, on a similar speech of Napoleon's could almost be taken to describe Wordsworth's "egotistical sublime" as well: "Through all these proclamations the fierce confidence, and proud self-involution of a military despot, intoxicated with vanity, start out most obtrusively" (*Essays* i. 63).

spoils and trophies, should be seen to reject precisely Napoleon's famed spoliations. His homage to the overflowing Nile — which enriches, rather than, like the "torrent" of Napoleon's armies, robs — then speaks the final "no" to tyranny. Even as French forces occupied Switzerland in 1798, Bonaparte was preparing to sail for Egypt in an effort to disrupt British commerce with the Far East. Despite great successes on land, victory was robbed from him by Nelson, who destroyed the French fleet at Aboukir on the mouth of the Nile and so left Bonaparte's forces suddenly stranded in Egypt. More important than the actual British victory was the fact that Napoleon's myth of invincibility was for the first time broken. Aboukir was a moral victory, the prophecy of British triumph even in the years of greatest French conquest. Layering the Nile into the Alps, Wordsworth predicts the "Character of the Happy Warrior."*

The Spirit of Imagination. In sum, Wordsworth in 6b makes a preliminary trial of the method by which history can be cleansed of tyranny so that only the shining "genius" figured by Napoleon — and shared by the poet — will reign. Here we reach the most telling point of correspondence between Wordsworth's Imagination and Napoleon — that of pure spirit. While general British reaction to Bonaparte fluctuated from uncertainty before his usurpation in 1800 to enthusiasm during the Peace of Amiens in 1802 and finally to renewed hostility, *one species of reaction was constant, if officially inadmissible: admiration of the "genius," "sublimity," and "imagination" represented by Napoleon.* Bonaparte, as Scott would later call him in his biography, was the "master-spirit" of the age (p. 216). *The Annual Register,* for example, consistently admired Napoleon's gifts of mind until its first notes of distrust in the 1802 volume (published in 1803). In its character sketch of 1800, for instance, it discovers Napoleon's youthful "spark of genius," and then marvels at his mature genius: Bonaparte possesses "a firm and undaunted spirit, and a genius penetrating, sublime, and inventive," and "his letters, his speeches, his actions, all proclaimed a sublimity of courage, imagination, and design, beyond the limits of vulgar conception" (1800: 11). Hazlitt would later take the same approach in his biography, apostrophizing the Battle of Marengo as "the most poetical of his battles," a battle as "romantic and incredible" as if "Ariosto, if a magician had planned a campaign" (p. 177). And Scott's biography will announce Napoleon's imagination in these terms:

No man ever possessed in a greater degree than Buonaparte, the power of calculation and combination necessary for directing such

* Writing in the *Morning Post* for 11 March, 1800, Coleridge similarly "grounded" the Nile by reference to Napoleon: "the Chief Consulate ... pretends to no sacredness; it is no Nile, made mysterious by the undiscoverableness of its fountainhead; it exists, because it is suitable to existing circumstances; and when circumstances render it unnecessary, it is destructible without a convulsion" (*Essays* i. 209).

decisive manoeuvres. It constituted indeed his secret – as it was for some time called – and that secret consisted in an imagination fertile in expedients which would never have occurred to others (p. 216).

In his superb rendering of the Battle of Marengo, Scott then makes it sound as if Bonaparte in Great St Bernard Pass were indeed Wordsworth confronting nature in Simplon Pass:

> [He proceeded] to the little village called St Pierre, at which point there ended every thing resembling a practicable road. An immense and apparently inaccessible mountain, reared its head among general desolation and eternal frost; while precipices, glaciers, ravines, and a boundless extent of faithless snows, which the slightest concussion of the air converts into avalanches capable of burying armies in their descent, appeared to forbid access to all living things but the chamois, and his scarce less wild pursuer. Yet foot by foot, and man by man, did the French soldiers proceed to ascend this formidable barrier, which Nature had erected in vain to limit human ambition . . . in places of unusual difficulty, the drums beat a charge, as if to encourage the soldiers to encounter the opposition of Nature herself. (pp. 336–7)[35]

Recall the diversionary force that Napoleon sent to demonstrate in Simplon Pass. If my presentation has even the barest plausibility, it will appear that Wordsworthian nature is precisely such an imaginary antagonist against which the self battles in feint, in a ploy to divert attention from the real battle to be joined between *history* and self. Whatever the outcome of the skirmish (called dialectic) between nature and self, history, the real antagonist, is thus momentarily denied so that when it debouches at last, it will be recognized with shock by the feinting mind as the greatest power of the Wordsworthian defile. As envisioned in the framework of the total *Prelude* – where the books of unnatural history then come at the point of climax rather than, as in *Paradise Lost*, of denouement – denial is the threshold of Wordsworth's most truly shocking act of Imagination: the sense of history. The true apocalypse will come when history crosses the zone of nature to occupy the self directly, when the sense of history and Imagination thus become one, and nature, the mediating figure, is no more.

NOTES

1 Bruce's long-awaited work appeared in 1790 in time for the *European Magazine* to review it in its issues from May through August (with many excerpts including the passage I quote). But it is unlikely that Wordsworth read Bruce or the reviews before he embarked in July of the same year on his Continental tour,

which I will compare to Bruce's journey. Coe (1953) does not mention Bruce, and there is no direct evidence that Wordsworth read Bruce before working on the 1805 *Prelude*. We surmise that Wordsworth at least knew of the *Travels* by this time, however, because he and Dorothy visited "the residence of the famous traveller Bruce" during their 1803 tour of Scotland (Dorothy Wordsworth (1940) i. 364–5). The first direct mention of the *Travels* occurs in a letter from Dorothy to Lady Beaumont on 24 January 1807, which mentions Coleridge's recommendation of the 1804 edition and petitions, "If you purchase it we should be very glad to have the reading of it" (*MY* i. 129). The 1790 first edition of the *Travels* was later among Wordsworth's books at Rydal Mount (Chester L. and Alice C. Shaver (1979) 36).

2 *WP*, esp. pp. 31–69. I should also mention Weiskel's work, which, through its phrasing of the Imagination in Simplon Pass as amnesia, resistance, and rejection, has guided my description of Imagination as denial.

3 Hartman's description of the poet's "turn" of mind in Simplon Pass models itself on a Pauline, Augustinian, or "mystic" conversion (*WP* 33) whose external manifestation as pilgrimage is directly contrasted to the experience of the revolutionary in 1790 France (56). My insistence upon "turn" as wordly tour implies in part that being a pilgrim in 1790 does not distinguish Wordsworth from the thousands of French *fédérés* journeying to and from the Fete of Federation; cf. Ozouf (1976) 71: "La Fédération en prend son caractère singulier d'être plus et moins qu'un pèlerinage."

Since Hartman's book is the landmark work in Wordsworth studies, it may be useful at the start to chart my intended navigation relative to it. A bare paraphrase of Hartman's argument might run as follows: in the beginning, there is a radical of consciousness whose very condition of being is its effort to emerge as self-consciousness. Emergence involves a dialectic between "apocalypse," in which the self moves toward imaginative independence from nature, and "humanization," in which the self restores nature to primacy through the "myth" that nature guided mind beyond itself in the first place. The final outcome is "humanized imagination," reached by 1805 in the Simplon Pass and Snowdon episodes: a consciousness aware of self as the "borderer" subsuming both the powers of mind and nature. Such imagination may be called humanized because nature is the common medium through which mind allies itself to everyday human existence (esp. 140).

Yet, of course, such a bare reading of Hartman misses his book's very pulse: the tremendous pathos with which it watches over, as if over a dead body, the empiricist component in the dialectic of self – the return to nature. Hartman is never more moving than when describing this return, and it soon becomes clear that his dialectic was never a balance but a master–slave relation of apocalypse to humanization, respectively, in which the traitorous slave binds the master. For Hartman, nature is Wordsworth's tragic flaw, and the return to nature his Prometheus bound. Apocalyptic imagination appears in a cloak of connotation – "apocalyptic vigour" and bravery in the face of "dangers," for example – dramatizing its heroic priority as the origin of phenomena (61, xiii). By contrast, humanizing nature is "pedantically faithful" (39), an "avoidance of apocalypse" (61), an "evaded recognition" (61), an effort to "retard" or "beguile" (147), a "displacement" (257), and a "flight" (293) by which Wordsworth "dooms himself" (187). If apocalypse is phenomenal, in other words, humanization can only be epiphenomenal "myth" (135), "superstition" (330), or "illusion" (330).

In sum, Hartman's argument consists not only of an analytic – the dialectic explaining Wordsworth's development up to about 1805 – but of a genuinely critical act: the shaping of that analytic into a sort of divine tragedy in which the poet's guiding Virgil, nature, misleads him. But there is no innate reason why the analytic should privilege apocalypse. Blake, to whom Hartman consistently alludes, is one demon behind such twist of dialectic. The real demon is Hegel – or, perhaps, a Paulinized Hegel. The terms "Akedah" and "Apocalypse," after all, are not ideologically neutral: they contain in seed the entire teleology by which the Old Testament opens out into the New, or – in the Pauline vision to which Hartman sometimes refers (50, 56) – the "natural" man (*psychikos*) into the "spiritual" (*pneumatikos*). And as Abraham opens out into Paul, so Paul at last opens out into Hegel, whose method deeply, and sometimes explicitly, underlies Hartman's turn of mind. As Hartman implies in his Critical Bibliography for the chapter "Via Naturaliter Negativa," his attempt to unite two strands of criticism, one for which Wordsworth is the poet of nature and the other for which he is the poet of consciousness opposed to nature, proceeds "in a genuinely dialectical manner" (349). The precedent Hartman endorses for such an approach is Hegel's – as opposed, for example, to Heidegger's (see *WP* 366n3 on the latter). Arguing the movement of the soul in *The Borderers* "toward individuation, or from a morality based on 'nature' to one based on the autonomous self" (129), he adds in a note: "This transition is studied exhaustively in Hegel's *The Phenomenology of Mind* . . . (especially the chapters on lordship and bondage, and stoicism, skepticism, and the unhappy consciousness); it also has affinities with sections Hegel wrote with the cataclysm of the French Revolution in mind, such as 'Reason as Lawgiver' and 'Reason as a Test of Laws' " (369n26).

Hegel's work balances the mind's effort to "annul and transcend" reality against its contrary dispersion into reality "as an object" (Hegel (1967) 86) and so predicts Hartman's dialectic of apocalypse and humanization. But it weights that balance teleologically such that originating consciousness points inexorably to terminating self-consciousness. In this field of idealism, dialectic cannot but privilege the mastery of pure mind over objectivity. Thus the overall process of Hegelian dialectic is progress: the world-mind transforms reality into ideologies or philosophies, and then climbs the peak of self-consciousness when it reviews and subsumes philosophies so as to project itself, at last, as the world-mind direct. With this dynamo powering his method, Hartman cannot avoid viewing Wordsworth's return to nature as tragic – not unless the poetry after 1805 or so is made to vanish. Wordsworth's Snowdon-consciousness is aware of itself as the totality of the mind-nature dialectic and so measures up to Hegel's epiphanic Absolute Knowledge. But the "late" poetry after this peak from 1805 to the 1814 *Excursion* then appears a fall because post-self-consciousness is unimaginable in the Hegelian method. It is the tragedy of post-self-consciousness that casts its long shadow over the early corpus.

My own book is meant to place consciousness and nature alike in history. Only a historicization of dialectic can deploy what Hartman calls the Hegelian "affinities" between consciousness and the French Revolution (together with other cultural phenomena) in such a way that the power of the apocalyptic reading can be extended integrally into the whole of Wordsworth's corpus. The alpha and omega of Wordsworth's apocalypse, I believe, is the recognition that history was there before, and will be there after, the agony of consciousness.

4 The best work on the 1790 tour is now Donald E. Hayden (1983), which appeared too late for me to make full use of it. In grasping the details and total shape of the 1790 trip, I am indebted primarily to Havens (1941) 418–34; Moorman i. 128–49; and *CEY* 97–115. D. Hayden (*passim*) and Havens (pp. 420–3) include maps of the trip.

5 I have written elsewhere on the problem of linear repetition ("Toward a Theory of Common Sense") and have noted that my mediate guide is Continental thought on repetition, most notably the work of Derrida, and my primary immediate guide, J. Hillis Miller (1978) and (1982). I should add in my current context a secondary – but more specific – immediate guidance: Stuart Peterfreund's fascinating "Seriality and Centred Structure in Wordsworth's Later Poetry" (paper read at MLA Conference, New York, 28 December 1981). In the view I express here, the seriality of the later poetry is built into the structure of tour experience itself.

6 On other travel literature that may have guided Wordsworth's trip, see Moorman i. 128, 135; Donald E. Hayden (1983) 103–7; Birdsall 5.

7 Describing "the steep horrid roughness of the Wood" and "the gentle calmness of the flood," Denham observes, "Such huge extreams when Nature doth unite, / Wonder from thence results, from thence delight" (Denham (1928) 79).

8 Bowles explains the melancholy cast of his sonnets in his 1800 Preface by saying: "They who know [the author], know the occasions of [his poems] to have been real; to the publick he might only mention the sudden death of a deserving young woman" (Bowles (1800) vii).

9 On Wordsworth's 1790 letter in the context of the picturesque, see Heffernan (1969) 17–18; Spector (1977) 92–3.

10 Coxe's attention to Swiss history is too extensive to be fully documented; an example of his commentary, matched by a note on the post-revolutionary situation, is Letter 17 as published in the 1812 edition. Here description of the 1444 battle between the Swiss and French near Basel is compared to the French-instigated Revolution in Basel leading ultimately to the Helvetic Republic.

11 I follow the lead of Weiskel 150–1 and *passim*, in allowing myself to be influenced here by Lacan, whose mirror paradigm and concept of the imaginary hold out enormous potential for extending psychoanalytic study of Wordsworth beyond the elementary Freud. In Lacan's terms, Wordsworth's nature becomes a mirror rejecting the order of the "symbolic" in favor of the "imaginary." The "imaginary" is epitomized in the moment the infant first identifies itself with its image in the mirror/mother of objective existence without awareness of difference (the self "out there" becomes a more definite version of the uncoordinated subject standing before the mirror). The specular, external "self," in other words, is not known to be merely a signifier and so subordinate to a collective convention of signification, to history. By contrast, the symbolic,

in Lacan's generalization of the Oedipal crux, is the realm in which acceptance of a collective authority (named the Father, or Law) demonstrates to the subject standing before the mirror that his external image is indeed a signifier like all other social selves, enrolled in a system over which individuals have little control. The self sees itself in history, and knows that the "I" it enacts "out there" is alienated by convention from the true subject who does the enacting. In Book 6 it is not so much that Wordsworth has not yet glimpsed the collective authority of history as that he denies it, represses it behind an "imaginary" mirror/mother of nature, a one-way mark, veil, or boundary. I draw generally upon Lacan (1977), with special reference to pp. 1–7. Lemaire (1977) has been especially helpful in elucidating Lacan's difficult writing.

12 I wrote this chapter before the advent of the New Historicism and before I read Greenblatt's excellent *Renaissance Self-Fashioning.* Any discussion of Holbein's *Ambassadors* in a literary or cultural studies context must now take account of Greenblatt's suggestive use of this picture, which he reproduces on his cover and applies as a crucial paradigm (esp. 17–27). Greenblatt's focus is on the disruptive and estranging power of the anamorphic skull in the foreground: "To see the large death's-head requires a . . . radical abandonment of what we take to be 'normal' vision; we must throw the entire painting out of perspective in order to bring into perspective what our usual mode of perception cannot comprehend" (19). A curious fact is that in teaching the painting in my British Studies course over the years, I have noticed that students seeing the painting in a slide presentation consistently and immediately identify the skull without any prompting or desire to look at the painting from the side (unless this is suggested to them) or real surprise. ("That's a memento mori, isn't it?" is a stock response.) Does Holbein's picture appear less tricky to modern viewers accustomed to inventive video techniques, or was the picture ever as radically unsettling as Greenblatt suggests? The whole issue of what constitutes the "trickiness" of trick pictures in any age is of interest. Besides the approaches of Arnheim or Gombrich, it would be useful to inquire into the social, political, and economic determinations of trickiness. When and for what reasons, for example, did Machiavellian *virtù* acquire its modern connotations of political trickiness so that viewers of statecraft on television news, a sort of modern *Ambassadors*, now often *look* for signs of cosmetic and other trickiness?

13 See Jeffrey Baker (1980) 113–43.

14 Paulson has studied the representational structure of contemporary British reactions to the Revolution in his *Representations of Revolution.* Paulson's work here and elsewhere has particularly made me aware of the richness in the verbal/visual seam. I regret that Lynn Hunt's *Politics, Culture, and Class in the French Revolution,* with its suggestive discussion of the rhetoric, symbolism, and imagery of revolution, did not appear in time for me to draw upon it in the argument below.

15 See Herbert (1972) 71 and accompanying illustration; see also Paulson (1983) 28–36, 260, on David. The oath motif of upraised arms was standard in the Revolution's visual representation of itself, appearing also, for example, on the

medal commemorating the Federation (see the design in Sagnac and Robiquet (1934) 230).

16 For the congruence between the towers of the Bastille and dances in the round, see the illustrations in Hampson (1975) 72–3. For the Bastille as an open-air dance hall, see the illustration in Henderson (1912) 144. Contemporary engravings of the 14 July Fete on the Champ-de-Mars are plentiful; for ones displaying the dance-like military evolutions, see Hampson (1975) 86; Henderson (1912) 141. See also Henderson (1912) 142, for a contemporary report of the circles formed by cavorting soldiers at the Champ-de-Mars. For a view of federation in the Arras square, with its central altar resembling that at the Paris fete, see the engraving in DHotel (1934) 197.

17 I abbreviate considerably the conclusions in Ozouf's chapter, "La fête et l'espace" (Ozouf (1976) 149–87).

18 *Collection Complète des Tableaux Historiques de la Révolution Française* i. 155. The narrations of the Paris Fete of Federation and preceding events in this work and in Sagnac and Robiquet (1934) 222–34, are particularly vivid.

19 "Celui qui s'élève, on l'abaissera; / Et qui s'abaisse, on l'élèvera" (Sagnac and Robiquet (1934) 224). On the festivity coupled with "contained violence" of the preparations for the Paris Fete, see Ozouf (1976) on "La fête de la Fédération: le modèle et les réalités."

20 See the reproduction of *The Tree of Freedom, 1789* on the cover of Edmund Burke (1969).

21 Such collective imagination was not imaginary in Lacan's sense because revolutionary propaganda was not innocent of awareness that the Fete was a grand signifier rather than uncontaminated reality. From the first, the Revolution's undernarrative of verbalization was grounded in historical process, in an Oedipal rather than pre-Oedipal struggle to destroy the fathering conventions, fetes, decorums, and art works of the *ancien régime* so that the collective Law behind society could be renamed "People" instead of "Father/King." As seen in the time's prodigious experiments in costumes, personal names, names of streets, and so forth, the Revolution took place in the sphere of the historically activated signifier rather than that of the referential sign identified timelessly with reality. Until the 1803 legislation regulating the explosion of names, for example, one named oneself Betterave, Raisin, or Tournesol (Garaud and Szramkiewicz (1978) 16) not in naive imagination of man as nature but in rejection of the oppressive past and its restrictions binding names to place, class, and religion. (On naming and renaming, see Robiquet (1964) 55–64; and Garaud and Szramkiewicz (1978) 9–19; see also Paulson (1983) 15–16).

22 Schneider (1957) 165–6. Schneider notes Wordsworth's particular attention to the description of beehive society in the fourth *Georgic*.

23 Paulson remarks with regard to Constable, "It is well ... to remember the political dimension of the georgic poem: the symbol of regeneration becomes the rusted sword or the soldier's rotting corpse turned up by the plough, and civil war always casts a shadow over harvest" (Paulson (1982) 131). My understanding of the historical implications of georgic is greatly enriched by Wilkinson (1969).

24   Coleridge's criticism of the line, "Descending from the mountain to make sport," helps confirm that there is some instability in the text here: "This line I would omit; as it clearly carries on the metaphor of the Lion, and yet is contradictory to the idea of a 'tamed' Lion, 'to make sport' *etc.* is here at once the proof of his having been 'tamed' and the object of his 'descending from the mountains,' which appear incompatible" (*Prel.* 276–7 n). Wordsworth's Lion is only insecurely tame.

25   As Reed notes, there is a slight possibility that 6c was "composed," if not actually written, in 1799, the date given upon publication of the passage as "The Simplon Pass" in 1845. But other evidence makes it much more likely that 6c was composed with 6a and 6b in 1804 (*CEY* 31, 261 and n). Hartman uses the 1799 date for 6c, *WP* 48, 63.

26   Gates studies Wordsworth's use of rivers as images of history in "Wordsworth and the Course of History." Partly under the guidance of R. G. Collingwood, she also speaks of the historical imagination in "The Prelude and the Development of Wordsworth's Historical Imagination," but her approach is to make historical imagination a secondary faculty, in addition to "apocalyptic imagination."

27   Turner's *Snowstorm: Hannibal and His Army Crossing the Alps*, exhibited in 1812, provides an analogue of the combined mimesis and effacement of Napoleon I indicated here. Napoleon is nowhere to be seen in Turner's celebrated landscape of human diminishment – no more so than Hannibal himself. But as Lynn R. Matteson shows, such invisibility is not simple absence. Relevant are Turner's earlier sketches on the Hannibal theme and the link between *Hannibal and His Army Crossing the Alps* and ancient British, as well as contemporary French, history (made more pointed, perhaps, by Turner's private viewing of David's *Napoleon at the St Bernard Pass* in Paris in 1802, coupled with general British interest in the 1809 uprising against Napoleon in the Tyrolean Alps; Matteson (1980), esp. 393–6). These factors allow us to posit – i.e., to hypothesize and further confirm or disprove – the absence of Napoleon with a precision we usually reserve for positive fact. The absence of the Emperor known as the contemporary Hannibal may be firm enough, indeed, to shape the very landscape: imperial absence is the vortex, or revolution, that is Turner's totalitarian vision of nature. With assured relevance, then, we see in *Hannibal and His Army Crossing the Alps* the fact that the man who would cross nature – in more than one sense – is definitively *not* there. He has been crossed out. (On the link between Turner's painting and Napoleon, see also Lindsay (1966) 118; Butlin and Joll (1984) 89; Kroeber (1974) 329; and Heffernan (1985) 85. Heffernan compares Rousseau's account of his Alpine passage, which invokes Hannibal, with Wordsworth's account of Simplon; Heffernan's comments about the intimations of history at Simplon – specifically the history of Hannibal's crossing – are consonant with my own views; Heffernan (1985) 65–7).

28   See, for example, Ashton (1968) 5–11 and *passim.*

29   Contemporary accounts of Napoleon and the Napoleonic years will be cited when used; I have also benefited from modern accounts, the two most helpful for my purposes being those by Sydenham and David Chandler.

30 Since publishing an early version of this chapter in 1984, I have discovered
    Mary Jacobus's excellent 1983 essay, "'That Great Stage Where Senators
    Perform': *Macbeth* and the Politics of Romantic Theater." In arguing the
    "dangerous theatricality of the imagination," Jacobus anticipates many of the
    points I make in the following discussion about Wordsworth's use of Macbeth,
    including the linkage between Macbeth and the concept of usurpation (356) and
    between Macbeth and Robespierre (363).

31 On political differences in British attitudes toward Napoleon after the usurpa-
    tion, see Maccunn (1914).

32 The 1802 volume of *AR* appeared in 1803. For the usage of "usurper" and
    "usurpation" in *T* in 1804, see the issues of 16 and 20 April; 30 May; 2 June;
    19 November. (The 19 November issue brands Napoleon a "usurper" five
    times within the space of a single column.)

33 On the troops at Simplon, see David G. Chandler (1966) 276 and 168 map;
    also Thiers (1845) 214. *AR* for 1800 (published 1801) gives a brief contempor-
    ary notice of the movement through Simplon (190). Bonaparte had originally
    designed his main crossings for Simplon and Mount St Gotthard (David G.
    Chandler (1966) 274). For an appreciation of the strategic concerns that caused
    him to shift his emphasis from these two most northern passes, see Thiers
    (1845) 201–2. Simplon was one of the passes Napoleon continued to hold after
    his crossing in order to secure his avenues of retreat (Thiers (1845) 211, 221).
    Convenient maps of the campaign may be found in David G. Chandler (1966)
    168, 272–73; Sydenham (1974) 245. There is also one other intriguing resem-
    blance between Napoleon's and Wordsworth's crossings that I have not
    pursued. This is the extent to which Napoleon at Great St Bernard was
    precisely a tourist. Besides the breaking down of the artillery, the most famous
    episodes from the crossing in nineteenth-century lore concerned Napoleon's
    conversations with his native guide and with the monks at the hospice in Great
    St Bernard. See, for example, the highly novelistic rendering of Napoleon and
    his guide in Abbott (1883) 320.

34 According to *AR* (1800) 192. But David G. Chandler notes that the Fort,
    though essentially bypassed, held out until June (280).

35 Abbott's biography of Napoleon shows the influence of romanticism even
    more strikingly. Relating the superhuman devotion and love of the cannoneers
    for their guns in the Great St Bernard pass, Abbott writes: "It was the genius
    of Napoleon which thus penetrated these mysterious depths of the human soul,
    and called to his aid those mighty energies. 'It is nothing but imagination,' said
    one once to Napoleon. 'Nothing but imagination!' he rejoined. 'Imagination
    rules the world'" (Abbott (1883) 318).

Coleridge

5

"Kubla Khan" and the Art of Thingifying

KATHLEEN M. WHEELER

The Preface to "Kubla Khan"

An analysis of "Kubla Khan" is complicated by its extraordinary preface,[1] and also by the way the verse seems to fall into two sections, or two separate visions, the "body" of the poem (lines 1–36), and the last eighteen lines. For the sake of brevity one might refer to these final lines as the "epilogue."

The preface to "Kubla Khan" acts to highlight specific formal aspects of the poem as opposed to the substantial content – the landscape descriptions and the Khan's activities – aspects such as the origins of the poem in subjective visionary experience, the nature of the composition processes, and the ultimate failure to complete the composition due to certain circumstances. The preface distances the reader from the specific imagery and content of the poem by explicitly focusing his attention upon the poem as an instance of poetic creation, while raising a host of subsidiary issues for the reader to grapple with: the relation of art to dream and extraordinary states of consciousness generally, sources of art in the unconscious, the relation of images seen with the inward eye and the correspondent expressions, the relation of the resulting poem to the original vision, and the role of memory in imaginative activity. In addition, there are more formal aspects of the preface to which the reader may attend, a shift analogous to the shift that the preface encourages with regard to the poem, away from factual details and concern for their accuracy, toward structural properties, narrative voices, and the relation of the preface to the verse.[2]

The preface, like the verse, seems to fall into two sections,[3] the first short paragraph (often left out in modern editions, and deleted from that of 1834), and the main body of the prose account. The first sentence reads somewhat like an advertisement to the poem, and makes two statements crucially affecting the reading of the poem: for it would never occur to a reader to approach the poem as a "psychological curiosity," instead of for its poetic merit, unless he had been so instructed (see moreover the prefatory remarks to "The Three Graves": "Its merits, if any, are exclusively psychological"). Nor does it seem likely that a reader would have thought "Kubla Khan" any more a fragment than any other poem, if he had not been told that it represented only a portion of a vision which inspired it.[4] The preface suffers from a somewhat similar over-determination: one assumes that it is separate from the verse in an absolute way, and not integrally related to the poem as a work of art; and one assumes the author to be Coleridge reporting directly his own views about the poem.

Two points militate against these assumptions; the preface is composed in the third person narrative, so that the writer of the verse and the author of the preface seem to be distanced aesthetically; a persona is created for the preface writer, an alternative authority responsible for the views presented, and this indirect discourse immediately alerts the reader to the possibility of irony. Such a gesture is not unknown to Coleridge readers: in his two other most important works, "The Ancient Mariner" and the *Biographia Literaria*, he invents in the former a persona who glosses the poem, and in chapter thirteen of the *Biographia* he incorporates a letter "from a friend" at a critical moment, also to explain a fragment, namely chapter thirteen. The friend is of course Coleridge himself, and the effect is an ironic detachment toward the content of the fragment in order to emphasize another level of content and another attitude. The existence of the preface persona in "Kubla Khan" is further suggested by the sudden shift from third to first person in the last paragraph of the preface, and the statement of this persona suggests that he is meant to be taken as an editor: "As a contrast to this vision, I have annexed a fragment of a very different character describing with equal fidelity the dream of pain and disease." He refers to "Pains of Sleep." This last sentence is also frequently left out of the best modern editions, as for example I. A. Richards's edition for Viking Press, or John Beer's Everyman edition. One loses the shift from the third to the first person, and by this omission is lost the equally important comment about the "Pains of Sleep" – namely that it too is called a fragment, and that it too is supposed to describe a dream. This puts a very different meaning on the use of the words "fragment" and "dream" in the early sentences of the preface, when the terms are used so broadly. For in what sense can one understand "Pains of Sleep" as a fragment or as a dream poem?

Not only is a persona created in the preface by the third person narrative; the referent of this "Author" is also not altogether clear. For instance, in the advertisement section of the preface, the persona uses the phrase, "as far as the Author's own opinions are concerned." But it is uncertain who "the Author" refers to in this first occurrence of the phrase. The tendency to assimilate this referent to the referent of future occurrences of the phrase "the Author" is admittedly strong, but not compelling. In the first instance it may mean "that Author," referring to Lord Byron,[5] the "poet of great and deserved celebrity"; it may mean the author of the advertisement, "this Author"; or it may mean the author–poet of the verse lines. If we take seriously the idea that personas are important distinctions, whose perspectives are not to be confused with that of the "omniscient," physical man to whose identity we ascribe poetic productions, such discriminations are not unimportant. Taking Coleridge to be this omniscient author we must nevertheless grapple with the problems he creates for the reader in creating his third person persona. That is, is his account to be taken seriously, or literally, and does *he* really believe that "Kubla Khan" is a fragment, and important not primarily as a poetic production, but rather as a "psychological curiosity"? Or does the ambiguity of "the Author" not throw into question the authority of these "opinions"?[6]

The creation of a persona (or perhaps more than one) in the preface lends the prose a literary–fictional quality which is not out of keeping with its general style; its Gothic evocation of summers, ill-health, lonely farmhouses on Exmoor, confines, anodynes, travelogues, sleep and dreams, visions, and finally the extraordinary imagery of the last several lines before the lines from "A Picture." In comparison with the poem, the language is distinctly prose, and not as rich in imagery or as intensely compressed; but the wholly unnecessary detail of the description almost makes up for the imagery absent.

Such details are meant as, for example, "lonely" farmhouse, the sleep of "three hours," the "2–300 lines," "pen, ink, and paper," the person "on business from Porlock," being detained "above an hour," the "eight or ten scattered lines," and so forth. The informative detail is indeed more appropriate to the prose than a corresponding intensity of imagery might have been. A glance at the note attached to a manuscript copy of the poem raises questions as to the factual and fictional content of the longer account:

> This fragment with a good deal more, not recoverable, composed, in a sort of Reverie brought on by two grains of Opium taken to check a dysentery, at a Farm House between Porlock & Linton, a quarter of a mile from Culbone Church, in the fall of the year, 1797.[7]

With reference to the preface, the note adds some detail but leaves out much more than it contributes. The information in the preface conflicts with this cursory account in several respects, the most important perhaps being that the note reports merely a reverie of sorts, in which the poem actually was *composed* – there is no qualification on the idea of "composition," "images rising up in a dream with all the correspondent lines and no consciousness of effort." Contrasting this relatively factual, literal, and dry account of the circumstances surrounding the birth of the poem with the actual published preface, one illustrates what the latter is not: it is not a literal, dry, factual account of this sort, but a highly literary piece of composition itself, providing the verse with a certain mystique. The preface itself is problematic in view of the extensive expansion from the note: to what extent are the additions to the preface mere interpolations and fanciful elaborations?

Although this question is probably unanswerable, it may not even be the important one to ask. Perhaps it is more pertinent to ponder why Coleridge chose to write a preface, and why he chose to include the details, facts or fancy, so minutely described.[8] For example, there may be some more profound significance to the statement that the poet fell asleep while reading the quoted lines from *Purchas his Pilgrimage* (lines closely related in factual content to the first lines of the poem), than merely that it was the occasion of the dream. Coleridge may be ironizing by playing on the tradition that the Khan fell asleep and dreamt the plan of the palace to be built.[9] Some connection between explicit sources and original transformation of those sources from other authors into new creations might be implied. Perhaps the chasm between such sources and the original use of them emphasizes the mystery surrounding the passage from ordinary consciousness into creative states.

Thus Coleridge himself would be giving the first hint that a tracing of the sources of his imagery would prove to be a fascinating way of becoming aware of the richness of the poem's meanings, as Lowes initially showed. But the problematic relation between the external world as stimulant, and inspiration, is being broached, as it is broached also in "This Lime-Tree Bower." Indeed the quotation in the preface of the lines from the travelogue relates to the first section of the poem as the manuscript note quoted above relates to the expanded preface. That is, the preface is a literary and poetic expansion of the manuscript note, dry and factual as it is, just as the quote from *Purchas his Pilgrimage* is expanded into the body of the poem. Did Coleridge then change "a sort of Reverie" to "a profound sleep, at least of the external senses," in order to emphasize and draw attention to the difference between *waking* consciousness and states of poetic vision, since the latter are more closely associated with the subconscious than mere reverie?[10] The connection between dream-consciousness and poetic vision is of course an ancient allegory which recurs in medieval dream poetry, and which Shakespeare and then all the romantics take up. Of the romantics, Keats most persistently relates sleep or dream and poetry.

Coleridge might also have qualified the notion of composition in order to suggest the problematic nature of composition and its mysterious connections with the will and memory, and with the original vision of images seen with the inward eye, but translated into linguistic expressions. The addition to the account of the "person on business from Porlock"[11] may be a fictional personification of the inhibiting factors interrupting the recovery of the whole: the likening of this person to a stone in the last sentence before the excerpt from "A Picture" may well cause a smile. The phrase "Person from Porlock" could certainly be a designed alliteration of "Purchas's Pilgrimage," the one marking the beginning, the other the end of the poem. The word "business" also had for Coleridge a very special connotation at the time (see Griggs i. 340–1); the "business" has to do with the spying to which Wordsworth and Coleridge were subjected by the "Aristocrats" (see also Shawcross i. ch. x). This took place at the time Coleridge says he composed "Kubla Khan," and at a time when he was trying to decide whether it would be wise to encourage John Thelwall to come to settle near him and Poole and Wordsworth. But the idea of spying might be applied to the faculty of reason as a censor of the imaginative faculty; thus the person on business personifies the spying, censorious reason interruptive of the imagination, the faculty uppermost in the minds of the "Aristocrats."

The Preface and the "Epilogue"

Apart from the creation of personas and the addition of details which romanticize the account and lend to it symbolic associations which turn the preface into a literary prose, instead of a factual, direct communication, (a prose riddled with possible ironies and explicit metaphors), the second major factor suggesting that the preface is to be intimately associated with the poem in an aesthetic sense is its connection with the "epilogue," that is, lines 37–54. In function, the preface and the epilogue exhibit strong similarities: both mention a prior experience in which some aesthetic activity is being described (the damsel sings and makes music, the poet dreams and makes a poem), and both make explicit reference to the loss of vision and the intense longing to revive it, and to build from it a "dome in air" in one case, and the poem's remaining sections in the other. In both the preface and the epilogue the presence of a narrator is much more evident, as distinguished from the omniscient, unobserved narrator of lines 1–36.[12] The juxtaposition of seen images and heard sounds in the epilogue is very like the images and "correspondent expressions" mentioned in the preface: in neither case is this problematic relationship explained. It seems correct to say that both preface and epilogue are distinct from the body of the poem in that both seem to refer to it; both are meditations upon visionary activity itself, whereas the body of the poem does not directly communicate these issues. It has a distinct and explicitly literary content. Neither the preface nor the epilogue contributes to the landscape description of the three sections of the verse which constitutes the body of the poem.

Some subsidiary complications arise from this comparison of the preface with the epilogue, and from the aesthetic distance of the epilogue to the body of the poem. When in the preface it is stated that "the Author . . . wrote down the lines that are here preserved," as a consequence of a profound sleep, one may wonder whether the phrase "these lines . . . here preserved" refers to all fifty-four lines of verse, or only to the first thirty-six, thus excluding the epilogue from the vision. In fact, it is only the first thirty-six lines which relate to the quotation from "Purchas's Pilgrimage" in the preface.[13] There is no mention of an Abyssinian maid, a dulcimer or song, or a visionary and a group of frightened beholders.[14] But the mention of the dome and caves of ice in the epilogue suggests that the epilogue is not simply a second, separate vision, but that the music and song of the maid are connected in some mysterious way with the sunny dome of pleasure and the caves of ice. The intrusion of the narrative "I" in the epilogue contributes to the disassociation of the content of the epilogue from the vision of lines 1–36 described by an omniscient narrator, and makes it almost impossible to include the last eighteen lines in that particular vision. On the contrary, the "I" seems to take up where the preface left off, and to reiterate the concerns expressed there.[15] That is, the "I" of the epilogue seems also to be the poet of the preface, but in a visionary state. In this reiteration, the vision mentioned in the preface seems to be mentioned again, but instead of describing the content of the vision, the vision is given a previously unacknowledged framework, a damsel with a dulcimer, who sings of Mount Abora, but also of Kubla Khan and the River Alph.[16] The visionary then repeats the desire reported by the preface persona for the poet to revive the vision, explaining that a revival of the maiden's song would make it possible for him to build "that dome in air." The connection of the song and the dome suggests that the song is the condition and inspiration for the dome, and "dome in air" may be a way of symbolizing a poem, as "articulated breath," or organized sound, as music itself is.[17] The omniscient narrator of the Khan's activities is not, then, the "I" of the epilogue, of the "Author" of the preface, but the damsel with the dulcimer, a design creating a dream-vision (about the Khan) within a dream-vision (about the damsel) within a dream-vision (about the "I" of the epilogue). That is, the narrator is symbolically the imagination itself, or the ideal poet, the ideal creator, omniscient, mysterious, and unknown.

The absolute distinction between narrators is impossible to maintain, however. The visionary "I" attributes a separateness to the character of the damsel by twice referring to the music as *her* song. He also intensifies her independence by inverting the word order of the sentence in lines 37–40, so that her existence is postulated as more objective than it would be if ordinary word order were preserved. By placing the object, the damsel, first, he foregrounds it and emphasizes her reality, de-emphasizing her visionary subjectivity and distancing her from himself. He "externalizes" her to some extent. However, because she occurs admittedly in a vision, not only has she no independent existence apart from the persona of the "I" in any absolute sense, but her song is equally his song: she is a mere intermediary between the visionary "I" and the music. As an intermediate being, she is probably best understood as herself a personification of imagination, that "intermediate faculty," as Coleridge elsewhere identifies it.[18] By creating such a separate, but not absolutely distinct persona, the poet manages to give poetic expression to the character of the faculty of imagination in its peculiar independence from his conscious control: his imagination is his and yet not his, as the song is his and not his. His control is tenuous at best, if not wholly illusory, and because of this lack of control, the faculty seems to have a will of its own, hence a personality or identity distinct from the poet.

It is precisely this independence and intermediary quality of imagination which Coleridge expresses in the preface. In the epilogue he has given the faculty a character of its own, but in the preface he does not dramatize in this way in order to express the nature of imagination. Instead he creates a dream allegory: he uses states instead of characters, and contrasts the waking state and the dreaming state. It might be correct to say however that although the dominant mode in the preface is the dream myth, characterization also takes place. The faculty interrupting or inhibiting imagination is characterized as the "person on business from Porlock," a vivid and ironic counterpart to the Abyssinian maid as imagination in the epilogue. To liken the "person . . . from Porlock" to a stone is to recall Blake's portrayal of "Urizen" (Your Reason?) as a stony, inflexible authoritarian figure. In addition to this persona, the preface-writer persona is created as a characterization of, perhaps, a "business-minded" or a censorious, literal-minded reader. In the dream state, the self has not conscious control over what it experiences; its creations, that is, its visions, seem "as it were, given." Things produced at the subconscious level almost always seem given, because the conscious ego is unconscious of any active role in their construction. Hence external nature, dreams, inspiration, etc., all seem to be independent of the self as known.[19]

Some independent reservoir or source for these images "which . . . rose up . . . as *things*" is implied, analogous to the damsel in function, but not personified: a myth of mental topography is used instead. The waking self, when it does finally regain some control over the psyche, acts merely as an amanuensis to this other state of being. There is only an implied character in the idea of a being dictating to the waking self, and in fact this "dictator" may best be *contrasted* with the imaginative, dreaming self or state, as memory. It may be in order to express this quality of imagination as beyond conscious control and the dictates of will and memory, and as having sources in the unconscious as suggested by the dream allegory, that Coleridge decided to alter the description of the state from "a sort of Reverie" to "a profound sleep, at least of the external senses," and to qualify the notion of composition as he did in the preface but did not in the manuscript note.

Both the dream allegory and the persona of the damsel act to split the self of the visionary or poet into an imaginative, inspired self, and a self that merely recollects the former self. Indeed a further, more removed stage is indicated, where the poet is neither visionary, nor textmaker (where the memory and imagination seem to act together) but merely a reader, a passive self in comparison to the other two stages. The third person narrative of the preface expresses precisely this latter distinction: the persona who wrote down "the lines preserved" is not only distinct from the visionary self beyond the conscious control, in the persona of the Abyssinian maid; he is also distinct from the merely recuperative self who writes the preface. The aesthetic distance between the two would seem chasmic to the "fallen" poet, and he would seek to represent the distance by the distancing devices of personas and allegories of states. Thus the poem is not only about inspired experience, but also about the fall back into ordinary experience, and the relation between the two.

A further correspondence between the preface and epilogue creates another perspective in the poem for the reader. The complexity of the poem has already been said to include a level representing the poet's consciousness of his process of creation. The level at which the poet is twice removed from vision is the level of the poet as reader of his own creations, his texts, themselves products of vision.[20] The suggestion in preface and epilogue is that the poet cannot remain contented with this relatively passive state, and seeks to become a maker again, or even a visionary. The present is always only a portion or a fragment of experience as long as it is uninspired by imagination. Without the imagination to perceive connections the mind sees not totality, but parts. Hence in "unawakened" consciousness, in ordinary, "third remove" perception, all of the productions of imagination seem only portions and fragments in comparison with what the mind is able to remember vaguely that it once knew: something whole and entire, a vision of eternity. The text is only a portion of that eternity. It is in this metaphorical sense that "Kubla Khan" should be understood as a fragment: as an organic whole it is complete in itself; though, as a plant may grow to a larger size, lines may be added to increase it, but their additions do not imply that in its present size it is imperfect or incomplete in any aesthetic sense.[21]

The poet seeking to become maker again, and to raise himself from his merely passive state of reader or present spectator of past acts and visionary experiences, is a model for the reader who also dares not to remain satisfied with observing someone else's past acts. Thus the "all" who cry "Beware! Beware!", these observers of the poet, seem to be negative models of reading, as they refuse to participate in his activity, and refuse even to allow him to communicate with them. They seem to treat him as a "psychological curiosity," and refuse to "see" his visions of sun and ice. As an audience, referring to the poet–visionary as "He," they repeat the perspective of the writer of the preface referring to "the Author." One must, on the basis of this analogy, wonder if the preface persona may not also be expressive of the limited perspective of a not altogether ideal reader. At the same time, the preface persona operates as ideal-reader, and this paradoxical superimposition, which also affects the "all who cry" (who seem also worshipful), will be discussed below. It is this ambivalence which makes it possible also to relate the preface-persona and the visionary "I," who is certainly *not* a negative model of reading. This "I" is, on the contrary, as positive a model of a spectator–reader as one could imagine, so active as to threaten by his participation to become a poet as well. The preface persona becomes for the moment an example of a not wholly unimaginative, but nevertheless reductionist reader. It is *he*, not Coleridge, the ironical, detached creator of this persona, who believes that the origins of the poem mark it as a literal fragment, lacking in aesthetic wholeness. He cannot see that because the poem is a true part of a greater vision, that it is at the same time a unity, regardless of whether more lines might have been added. One might argue that more lines could always be added: there is no determined correspondence between images and words, and sounds and words. Images and musical sounds are not words, and hence are not exhaustible by them; this is surely why the relation between the two is left problematic in both preface and epilogue.[22] Moreover, the poem "Kubla Khan" may also be understood to be a fragment in the sense that it lacks the correspondent images visible to the inner eye in an experience of eidetic imagery, as the dream-text lacks the wholeness of the dream experience of sights, sounds, and colours.

The literal-minded preface persona fails to see these ramifications of the notion of fragment. He views the poem as of interest primarily not as an aesthetic work, since it is a mere fragment, but as a psychological curiosity, as does the epilogic audience. Thus he not only fails to see the symbolic significance of the notion of fragment; he also fails to see the dream account as a metaphor of poetic creation. This reader allegory is posed in both the preface and epilogue as a model to the reader of how not to respond to the poem, a gesture all too familiar to Coleridge readers.[23] The analogy between poet and reader suggests on the other hand a model of a participatory, creative reading, and is illustrated in the lines from "The Picture," included in the preface, in which it is clear that the poet's perspective and the reader's are analogous at certain times. Is the poor youth the poet or reader, or is he not both? Yet his role appears to be passive. But the stream mentioned in the preface as an allegory of the consciousness sets the stream of these lines in a similar allegorical relation with the consciousness. The passivity of the youth's posture may represent his stilling of the conscious self in order that the sources of genius may become accessible.[24] Thus he gives up any illusion of control over his faculty of vision, and adopts an apparently passive posture, while his active imagination takes over and creates according to principles normally inaccessible to the conscious self.[25] It is clear that the superficially active reader who reduces, paraphrases, chooses amongst ambiguities, decides about paradoxes, and judges, fails to activate his imaginative being, and never closes the gap between the poem and his perceptions of it. The poem remains an absolutely separate and distinct entity, whereas the breakdown of the boundaries of the poem as exhibited by the preface and the epilogue, and the intimate involvement of the preface in the poem, suggest, too, that the reader's "preface," his account of the poem, is also not altogether distinct from some authoritative text, but actually contributes to the text as an entity. The account, then, is an integral part of the text.

In a sense, the preface makes it problematic to determine where the poem begins, and the epilogue prevents the determination of an end point. The epistemological claim being made is that one cannot decide the extent of the mind's contribution to the construction of objects of experience; hence the boundary between independent objects and mind is uncertain. The aesthetic claim corresponding to this epistemological one is that one cannot determine what is description and what is interpretation: the work of art as a work of art exists in the experience and response of the spectator to such an extent that when the reader thinks he is observing or perceiving the artifact purely or objectively, he is as mistaken as the philosopher who believes he can perceive a thing-in-itself. The challenging of the view that thought and thing are absolutely distinct entities is encouraged at both the aesthetic and epistemological levels of the poem. As Coleridge constantly insists, it is not necessary to divide in order to distinguish: thought and thing are different, but not essentially different. Moreover, they may only be facts of experience, not of reality, in the absolute sense (on the "outness prejudice" see Shawcross i. 177–9).

Because of the equally vague boundary between the "vision in a dream," and the meditations about it, the certain line distinguishing illusion and reality is dissolved: the border between art and reality has already been shattered as the reader realizes that he mistakes his responses for the text. The distinction between poet and reader erased in the lines from "A Picture," quoted in the preface, also emphasizes this breakdown between art and reality; and the mixing up of Coleridge and his ironic persona in the preface breaks down the distinction between poet and reader, or at least makes it less than certain where the boundaries lie and what exactly the distinctions in roles are. The *perception* involved, for example, in reading, is suggested to be analogous to the activity of creating artifacts, when reader and poet are mixed up together, an analogy expressed by the distinction between primary and secondary imagination. For in this distinction, Coleridge insists that perceptual processes (such as reading) are fundamentally creative, imaginative experiences.

The Perceptual 'Art of Thingifying'

Coleridge believed that the processes of construction involved in artistic making were analogues of basic perceptual processes, but operating at a secondary level. That is, art uses as its materials the products of perception, and builds out of them new, higher order cultural "things." Because art operates at a secondary level, it in effect mirrors the primary level production of material things, or perceptual objects, and can be a source of knowledge about those primary constructive modes indirectly through an analysis of artistic production. When Coleridge investigates the artistic process of making, he is able to draw an analogy to basic perception, and to psychological production. By adopting a transcendental idealist posture, he insists that the mind is crucially active in the perception of the world, and is not passively receiving already formed objects that impress their fixed, stable and independently existing structures on the mind. Hence, when the preface writer states that "Kubla Khan" is of interest primarily as a "psychological curiosity," it is possible to understand that phrase as an indication that the poem is not only interesting poetically, but also as a source of knowledge about the mysterious processes of perception, which it mirrors as an artifact.

The productions of works of art, that is, the transformation of subjective, internal experiences into external, public objects, is a familiar experience, if not at first hand then at a removed perspective. We do not easily forget that art products were not always things, but results of mind externalizing subjective experiences. In "Kubla Khan" one of the most recurrent themes seems to be this process of "thingifying," a word which Coleridge used to indicate the close relationship between thought and thing (and correlatively process and product, mind and nature, self and other).[26] The main interest in the preface is the process of making the dream or vision into a thing; in the epilogue the visionary wants to make the music into a more permanent "dome in air" by reviving within him the Abyssinian maid's song; the damsel gives expression to her feelings about Mount Abora in "symphony and song"; in the first half of the poem, Kubla Khan has a pleasure dome built according to his idea; and even in the second half of the poem, nature seems to be described as externalizing herself both by flinging up the sacred river on to the surface of the earth for a few miles before it sinks back into her inner world, and also by forcing great fragments, "dancing rocks" into the air. In each case the objects made begin their existence by being "flung forth" or externalized: they were not always there, but are products from another inner world. Not only works of art, but various objects are here presented as erupting from a subterranean world. Nature and culture are described as analogues. Indeed, it is not even clear in lines 1–11 which of the images are part of Kubla's design and which are nature.

In all of these examples there is an ambivalence between activity and passivity, an ambivalence central to a theory of mind as active or passive. Kubla Khan decrees the dome and gardens, but does he actively engage in the construction of it? Does the damsel act merely as the instrument performing an already composed music and song, or is she creating her song? Is the vision of the visionary in the epilogue a creation of his, or is he receiving it in a passive stance; and in what sense would he build the dome from the damsel's music, revived *within* himself? Would she somehow *give* it to him? Clearly this ambivalence is most explicit in the preface in the qualifications surrounding the notion of composition, and more generally in the dream allegory. It is repeated in the quoted lines from "A Picture": for if "now once more/The pool becomes a mirror," then the observer *makes* the image reflected, and thus his function is hardly altogether passive. In each case, the ambivalence between the active and passive roles seems to foreground once again the central mystery surrounding aesthetic creation: to what extent is art the result of inspiration, or forces beyond conscious control, and to what extent must the artist consciously guide this inspiration through decision, judgment, and technique acquired by practice?

The poem makes a gesture at a kind of solution, by seeming to indicate that whatever the degree of interaction, it is evident that the conscious ego must to a large extent remain in a state of stillness in order for unconscious sources of genius to awaken and begin to express themselves through the ego as instrument and not as source of the inspiration. Thus "Kubla Khan" is not to be understood as an anomaly, but as a result of the ideal mode of production. That is, genius speaks so fully and coherently that no completing acts on the part of conscious man are needed. The author's genius is perfectly integrated with his conscious mind in this ideal production, and no arbitrary, merely conscious gestures are made; the conscious is always interpenetrated by an intuition of its appropriateness. By writing the preface, Coleridge emphasized the importance of the integration of the passive and active, of the conscious and the unconscious, and reversed the common notion of what constitutes activity in art.[27] The preponderantly active part must be given to the unconscious, while the conscious accepts a subordinate, though integrated, role. The presence of the preface, however, reaffirms the view of art not as a merely unconscious outpouring of unreflective feeling, but as a highly self-conscious activity. The author is deeply impressed by his paradoxical position: his loss of self-control as he usually understands it; his subjection to this power seeming to be his, and yet more than him; his suspension of conscious intention at the same time that he is observing himself acting, yet not acting, or intending by means of intuition and not arbitrarily.

By bringing out this ambivalence in the meaning of "active" in artistic processes, Coleridge implicates the reader's role as well, as the analogy so vividly expressed in the lines from "A Picture" suggests. The reader as perceiver of the poem must participate and be active or the object will remain an entirely separate entity from him, never assimilated into his fabric of experience. Clearly it must be an activity guided by intelligence and creative response. And for this to occur, the conscious self must in reading subordinate itself to some intuitive guidance, to some genial stillness, while the artifact works upon him to awaken his imaginative faculty. Poet and reader roles are compared in order to emphasize this similarity in the kind of activity required for catching a glimpse of the vision that the work of art tries to embody.

If art mirrors perception, however, this analogy must be drawn out in its implications not only for reading as a type of perception, but for the production of things as products of perception. Coleridge explains that "to think is to thingify." But to perceive was also originally to thingify. When we think, we delimit the boundaries of concepts, and discriminate distinctions. But for Coleridge, culture, the world of thought, of art, of science, and all the objects of culture are no more dependent upon perception than the world of nature, as we know it. Objects perceived by the mind can never be known independently of the perception of them, and this general ontological point is enlightening for an understanding of art from the point of view of both the spectator and the artist. Since there is no way of achieving certainty as to the nature of the object in itself, its familiar objectivity must be understood as a purely inter-subjective independence. Primary imagination, that is, perception, reveals its principles of organization and construction in its products because, like art, it constructs them according to those inner principles.

Landscape and the Imagination

The analogy between art and perception or poet and reader is expressed by the distinction between primary and secondary imagination, and this distinction may be seen to be functioning as an explicit metaphor in the body of the poem, while in the preface and epilogue it is only implied. For in the preface and epilogue the problem foregrounded is the relation of the artist and the spectator to the work of art. In the body of the poem this relationship is generalized to include perception through the metaphor which the landscape provides. The landscape has two contrasting aspects. But in "Kubla Khan" the contrast between the Khan's architectural and landscaping gestures in lines 1–11 and the natural, wild, and unencompassed scene of the "deep romantic chasm," its fountain, and so forth, in lines 12–30, suggests the distinction between the secondary activities of art and culture, which use the materials of nature to create new materials, and the primary activities of perception. The Khan, like the artist, builds out of nature. But the labours of the earth, her flingings of huge *fragments* into air, and her forcing up of the fountain as the source of the river, are analogues of the unconscious mind creating its nature for itself.

An alternative allegory to account for the contrast in landscape presents itself, however, as the distinction between fancy and imagination. Coleridge had not yet articulated either the fancy/imagination distinction or the distinction between primary and secondary imagination. They can only be said to be implicit in the poem, a fact which suggests how much his experiences as a poet must have affected his thinking about art, reality, and the faculties of mind or "powers of knowledge."[28] The Khan's measuring and counting, his erecting of walls, and his decrees suggest a more mechanical construction relying on fancy as its faculty of direction. As a contrast, the natural imagery of stanza II combines both the idea of the truly artistic mode of construction according to organic principles, and the idea that art mirrors nature as an organically unified and naturally produced whole. It also suggests the metaphorical implications of the idea of fragment: not only artifacts, but natural objects are fragments in the sense that they participate in a greater whole: "dancing rocks" is an effective image to combine the two oppositions of culture and nature, and the idea that every part may be both a unity and a fragment of a larger unity. "Dancing *rocks*" may relate to "stony reason" as well, and may imply a theory of language and art as inevitably degenerating through familiarity (as will be further discussed below). Shelley's "dead metaphors," or Coleridge's "worn-out metaphors," would seem to express a similar idea. The image of the earth labouring in "fast thick pants" suggests childbirth, the birth of ideas or works of art, and natural production as all interrelated experiences contrasted with more deliberate, mechanical productions.[29]

The overlapping of these two allegories in the landscape imagery suggests no accidental ambiguity. It suggests that the activity of secondary imagination has a further, ominous aspect to it. It can degenerate from the creation of new metaphors and symbols into a faculty manipulating fixities and determinates, or it can be mistaken for such a faculty. Shelley expressed this sinister aspect when he pointed to the degeneration of metaphors into dead metaphors;[30] Coleridge pointed to truths so true as to lose the power of truth.[31] Thus the ambivalence of the landscape actually seems to function to express this further side of imaginative experience and its gradual change into fancy, and indeed memory. Perception even more than art seems to suffer the degeneration which results in a chasm between thought and thing. Indeed, art is the corrective to the degenerate perceptions of "single vision". The only corrective to degenerate art is art that revitalizes the lost associations. The representation of the cessation of imagination or its change into fancy and memory is a repetition of the preface and epilogue; both bemoan the loss of vision in a much more explicit way, though perhaps less demonstrably, since here we actually have an instance of the difference: the Khan measures and decrees and walls and girdles. He shuts out nature and imagination, and art degenerates.[32]

The preface encourages such a procedure of internalizing the landscape, or making it a topographical metaphor of mental processes.[33] The stream of consciousness of the preface both in the extended metaphor of images on a stream and the lines from "A Picture" provides a model for interpretation of the landscape. The use of landscape as the content to be internalized suggests two applications: first, the landscape we know as nature is revealed as an externalized projection of mind, and secondly the topographical imagery acting as the surface or landscape of the *poem* is equally projected. To understand either nature or art correctly, we must understand them as things, but as things not absolutely external and independent of perception. For as the poem has suggested in preface, epilogue, and body, and in several allegoric levels of all, things originate in the life of the mind and are projected according to its principles and categories of organization. The "prejudice of outness" almost obliterates this awareness of the origins of things: art can remind us of it, and give us a truer view of experience: what is "given" and "external" seems so because its production originates at unconscious levels.

The poem depicts the tremendous desire of the human psyche to create objects and send them out into the world. And it shows nature in the throes of the same intense productivity. The Khan, the damsel, the visionary, and the poet are all making, and nature is making rivers, fountains, and fragments of "dancing rocks." But at the same time as the poem expresses the force and primacy of this making instinct, it also seeks to understand its origins, its conditions for success, its degeneration, and its recurrence. It seeks to analyse the relation of the product made to the maker, and to the experience that inspired the maker.[34] It shows how the familiar devices of personification of forces (e.g., the Abyssinian maid as imagination and the "person on business from Porlock" as ego – two figures additionally effective in their contrast with each other), and the creation of personas either to split the self of the author or to make a caricature of the "sleeping" reader, are instances of "thingifying." But by demonstrating the process of making, things are "dethingified": their origins are shown to be in the creating mind, not in an external substance.

The myths of dream and vision, and the invitation to internalize the landscape as a psychological topography, further act to depict the art of thingifying and the tenuousness of the border between art and reality, mind and nature, creation and perception. The writer makes distinctions between dream and reality, creates distinct characters in the vision, distinct parts to the poem, distinct landscapes, distinct objects, but then builds an uncertainty around them all so that closer examination reveals them to be striving toward a dissolution of distinct selves or boundaries. For example, the maid's song and Kubla's dome are distinct, but are then mysteriously brought together both when we realize that the "second" vision may imply that the song of the maid is about the dome, and when the visionary says that he will build the dome with the song of the maid. The visionary and the damsel are not altogether distinct, as we realize she occurred in a vision; and even Kubla and the visionary are identified in the visionary's claim that *he* will build the dome in air: he takes over Kubla's distinct role.[35]

Nor can we be certain in the landscape and architectural imagery what is built and what is there already as nature, what is part of the enclosure and what is excluded from it. Are we given a description of what was enclosed or of that which does the enclosing?[36] The "forests ancient as the hills" enfold "sunny spots of greenery" but do the walls enclose all, or are they enclosed by the forests? Is the deep romantic chasm within or without the walls? Is it part of or an alternative to the Khan's gardens, and has he surrounded it or walled it out?

The landscape models, and thus enriches, the indeterminacy of the poem's boundaries. Does the epilogue contain the body of the poem as an embedded vision, or is it contained in the Khan's landscape vision? The ambivalence is effectively expressed by the detail of contrasting "here" in line 10 with "there" in line 8. Moreover, the narrator's perspective is subtly indicated as "here," in the ancient forests, as opposed to "there," in the gardens (the 1828 and 1829 editions ignore the distinction; "here" is repeated in line 8). The narrator seems to be located in the natural scenery looking down upon the artifice of the Khan. He might be understood to be singing of the dangers and limitations of uninspired art: of imposing form instead of discovering it. Or he may be emphasizing the important relation of nature to art, thus suggesting the integration of inspiration and intention: art must be produced naturally, but with skill or artifice. This is precisely the dilemma suggested by both the preface and the visionary of the epilogue. In the preface, "the Author" is tempted apparently to try to fashion what he cannot regain from the muse: "Yet from the still surviving recollections in his mind, the Author has frequently purposed to finish for himself what had been originally, as it were, given to him...Σαμερον [Αὔριον] ἄδιον ἄσω [tomorrow I will sing a song]: but the to-morrow is yet to come." This is at least the view of the persona, but perhaps "the Author" is too wise to attempt such an artificial work. Likewise, the visionary knows that his "vague and dim recollection of the general purport of the vision" of the damsel is not enough to build the dome in air (the rest of the poem?); only a *revival*, not a memory, but a genuine imaginative reproduction of the lost vision, will achieve the completion desired: a genuine repetition.

The most extraordinary ambivalence occurs in the last part of the body of the poem, lines 31–6, in which the *shadow* of the dome of pleasure seems to be the referent of "it" in line 35, rather than the dome itself. And both lines 36 and 46 suggest that the miracle is not the dome of pleasure, but a unification of the dome and the caves of ice. But the caves of ice are nature's child; only the dome is Kubla's creation. We tend to forget this distinction and read the lines as if the Khan had created this synthesized miracle "That sunny dome! those caves of ice!" But it seems to arise from the musings of the narrator about the shadow of the dome floating upon the waves midway between fountain and caves.

Lines 31–6 suggest further clues to the perspective of the narrator of the body of the poem as an observer seeking to portray the limitations of "decreed" art. The ambiguous reference of "it" in line 35 to either "the shadow of the dome" or "sunny dome with caves of ice" has Platonic undertones of relations of shadow to substance with the correspondent reversal of the reality of each. The "miracle of rare device" referring either to shadow or to the fusion of dome and caves is something more than the mere dome of the Khan it would seem, and the narrator, by introducing these lines, strangely disconnected from the landscape of lines 1–30, seems to be trying to propose some solution to the opposition between art and nature. The use of the word "measure" to mean song or music contrasts with the literal measurings of the Khan for his garden, and sets up a tension since the source of this "mingled measure" is the "caverns measureless to man," and the fountain. The implication might be that imagination most faithfully captures the nature of human experience not by measuring it deductively or quantitatively; it measures by expressing that nature in outward forms but according to inner principles, and thereby best captures its "dimensions."

Concluding Remarks

A model of ambivalence occurs in the epilogue and is mirrored in the preface. The reported speech of lines 49–54 is attributed to an unidentified group of observers, the "all." But the speech is not direct report, it is the interpolation of the visionary: the words are *his*, the symbols and images are his representations (as the damsel's song was his also). And although this audience at first appears hostile, it is not really clear whether they are ostracizing the poet or worshipping him, and it is far from clear which attitude the visionary is describing. For the revived music heard by the "all" also will enable them to see the dome and caves of ice.

The persona created in the preface suffers the same reversal. His perspective seems limited and narrow, as he brands the poem fragmentary and a "psychological curiosity." He believes the author intends to finish the poem, but is unable to. Indeed there is no limit to the interpolation from the manuscript note that we may ascribe to him. The extraordinary intrusion of an "I" in the last sentence of the preface seems to give further reality to the persona of the preface writer as a mere editor of the poems, and not the author of them. Whatever the author may have told him may have been meant ironically, and he may have taken it all literally. But even this naivety is transcended when one realizes that the persona, as long as he is not distinguished from Coleridge, is the literal-minded reader projecting his own notions of fragment (as literally a fragment) and psychological curiosity (as hence not of poetic merit) on to Coleridge. He assumes Coleridge means the preface literally because the reader cannot see it imaginatively. But the moment he "thingifies" a persona, sees the possibility of indirectness and irony, and takes the hint from the third person narrative and the conflicting "I" in the last line ("I have annexed a fragment of a very different character"), he has actually "thingified" or made an object of awareness his own unimaginative response to the poem, distanced himself from it, and thereby overcome it. He too, then, must personify, as does the artist, his "person on business from Porlock," who restricts his view.

The process comes full circle as the reader realizes now the importance of personification as a model, and the importance of the symbolic and mythic meanings of the dream, the fragment, and so forth. For as he does, he sees that there is no longer a need to maintain the preface persona, with Coleridge as the ironical detached creator of him. The very terms of the preface: the "dream," the "fragment," and the "psychological curiosity," all were meant symbolically anyway. They are not pejorative terms but simply characterizations which identify the nature of all aesthetic products. That is, all poems are fragments, in the sense that they are "portions of one great poem"; all originate in dream-like states or "sleeps of the external senses"; and all are psychological curiosities because all are expressive of the mind's mode of perception by "thingifying" experience into outward forms. Thus Coleridge achieves an aesthetic representation of his philosophy of art: he is not content with mere discursive rendering. He embodies his theory in the practice, and this may partially account for the richness of his poem.

Thus, just as the apparent irreverence of the speakers in lines 49–54 is changed to worship, so the criticisms and belittling comments of the preface are changed into descriptions of what art should be. The persona is dropped when we read the preface as written by Coleridge the genius, who had confidence in his poetry and had the ability to devise every conceivable mode of helping the reader to see its richness, including the risk of making himself a "laughing-stock" in order to make available to the reader the tool of irony and indirectness if metaphor and symbol proved too difficult in the first stages. To sacrifice his right of authorship to the muse and the poem's claim to meaning by originating it in a dream, in order that the reader may be stimulated to a kind of authorship by interpreting the dream, is a gesture of incalculable generosity.[37]

The myriad ambiguities and possibilities discussed throughout this chapter result from the effort to represent the complex, contradictory and multivalent nature of both aesthetic and perceptual experience from several different perspectives. Thus the visionary "I" of the epilogue may be seen as a model reader, striving to respond appropriately to the work of art, the Khan's productions, by means of the damsel, a personification of imagination or inspiration. In this respect the structure of "Kubla Khan" is much like that of "The Ancient Mariner," the Wedding Guest serving a similar function as a model spectator. But the visionary "I" is then complicated by representing, as well as the reader's or spectator's perspective, the act of composition from the poet's point of view. Indeed he has usually been understood only in this way, as ideal poet, though it is arguable that his spectator function is still more interesting and adds a dimension to the poem, for his role as poet is only a repetition of the Khan's representation as a poet. This dual role of the visionary "I" helps to emphasize the essential similarity of the poet's and the reader's roles.

Further complications arise in an effort to grasp the significance of the Khan's activities. For he has been seen to offer an equally contradictory duality like the visionary "I." The Khan's paradoxical nature is slightly different: he offers a split in the artist's nature, rather than a split between artist and spectator. He represents the artist as too purposeful, as conscious, and as uninspired, that is, as talent and artifice, in distinction from genius. And he represents the true artist and his essential integration with nature and natural forces, the word nature drawing on all its other connotations as well, of human nature, the natural, and nature as imagination. The ambivalent relation of the garden to the natural scenery contributes to this paradoxical duality. But this duality further represents the way even true art can become degenerate, through familiarity, habit, and acquiescent approbation, or, for example, unthinking acceptance of certain works as of classic stature. This possibility immediately creates another split, analogous to the split in the artist's nature. That is, the reader is subject to such a split, and he too can be represented as inspired or only artificially responsive. This ambivalence in readership is iterated in the portrayal of the "all who cry," where it is not clear whether the attitude is worshipful or censorious.

But the reader split seems most effectually represented in the preface, and in this, "Kubla Khan" once again repeats the technique of "The Ancient Mariner," with its gloss persona. For the preface persona seems to offer the identity of a reductive and naive reader who fails to see the importance of the artifact as self-imaging. The "person on business from Porlock" may be, like the damsel, a personification of a faculty of the mind, but in this case the faculty personified is not the one instrumental in creative response. That faculty represses and censors, and therefore properly belongs to the reductive reader persona as his habitual state; it belongs to the poet only as an interruptive agent. The complication in the preface persona, not repeated in the gloss persona in "The Ancient Mariner," involves another level of self-awareness; the preface persona as a reductive reader turns out to be a projection caused by the failure of the reader to take the elements of the dream, the fragment, and "psychological curiosity" as metaphors. If taken as metaphors, these elements imply a persona who is not a reductive reader, but who is ironizing that sort of reader.

One final set of complexities must be considered, involving the relation of the epilogue to the body of the poem, and the preface to the verse. It has been pointed out at length that the relation of the last eighteen lines to the first thirty-six is problematic in the extreme. This uncertainty could be taken to represent the obscure relation of the reader to his text and the poet to his creation. The omniscience of the narrator of the first thirty-six lines implies that there is no question of conscious control or volition in this relation. And the contrast of omniscience with first person narrative in the epilogue seems to highlight this difference between conscious and unconscious selves or states. This last section of the verse, like the final stanza of "The Eolian Harp" and the last stanza of "This Lime-Tree Bower," and like the Wedding Guest framework in "The Ancient Mariner" or the ambivalence of the imagery of frost in "Frost at Midnight" in the last stanza of that poem, adds a level of self-consciousness to the poem and without this level the verse would be incomplete, ending at an arbitrary point. An experience would have been portrayed, but without any level of reflection about that experience, and without any reflection about the possibility and nature of communicating it. It would have remained at a remove, as an external object never assimilated, never "seeking echo or mirror of itself," never "making a Toy of Thought." Without such a level of reflection, the poem would have been a literal fragment; but with its epilogue, like all the poems mentioned above, it becomes a complete, rich work of art.

The preface acts as a link between the reader and the poem and as such its relation to the verse is as problematic as is the relation of art to reality or of spectator to art. It is appropriately ironic, as is the gloss, because it thereby renders the inherent irony of the spectator's situation. It gently caricatures the delusion of literal-mindedness, and gives metaphor as the solution to that imprisoning language. And since it engages the reader aesthetically and not discursively, it is proper to consider it as an integral part of the text, not merely as an external prose commentary, though of course it seems to be only that to the unimaginative, reductive reader parodied in the persona. Perhaps it would be correct to conclude that such a negative model of reading as is offered by the preface and the gloss of "The Ancient Mariner" must always appear to be outside the formal structure of a work of art initially. For its function can only be apprehended after a level of critical reflection on the work has been achieved. A positive model, on the other hand, such as the visionary or Wedding Guest, or the speaker in other poems such as "This Lime-Tree Bower," can always be understood as the poet. This viewing of someone else's experience does not require self-conscious reflection, but it should never be mistaken for aesthetic response. As most artists realize, superficial non-integration may be a great stimulus to reflection, enabling the reader to discover the profound unity of a work: it can act as a stepping stone to an understanding of the full implications of the more integrated aspects. Thus the preface helps to lead the reader to see the possibilities of the epilogue and its relation to the body of the poem. The apparent non-integration of the epilogue to the body of the poem reflects the schism in experience between the conscious and the unconscious, or the conscious and the self-conscious. The poem will appear as fragmented and incomplete as the understanding of its readership is; but its beauty, that is, its intuited unity and truth to aesthetic experience, has preserved it as a compelling enigma, and will surely continue to do so.

NOTES

1 The composition of the verse and the preface of the poem are thought to have been separated by perhaps as much as nineteen years; the dating of the preface is even more difficult than that of the poem, for the poem was certainly written between 1797 and 1799. The preface was probably composed only just before the 1816 publication with "Christabel" and "Pains of Sleep." On the dating of the poem dozens of articles have been written; but of especial interest is Chambers (1933) and (1935). Elizabeth Schneider (1953) 153–237 is surely mistaken in dating "Kubla Khan" as late as she does; Margoliouth (1953) 352–4 indicates a more plausible date of about 1 June 1798. However, October 1797 seems the most likely date for a number of reasons, not to mention Coleridge's own comments on two separate occasions; see Griggs i. 349–52 for a number of comments which encourage acceptance of autumn 1797 as the date of composition. While the apparent gap in years between the composition of verse and preface may seem an argument against the close interaction of the

two, not only the nature of the interaction, which does not depend upon a proximity in time of composition, but also the existence of the *Crewe Manuscript* with its preface version, which grew into the published version, would militate against such an argument.

2 In few of the well-known studies of "Kubla Khan" is the preface discussed as of literary significance, nor is its aesthetic relation to the poem considered. Shaffer (1975) sees the importance of the preface as an expression of a theory of inspiration, but discusses it more in relation to higher criticism of the Bible in Germany in the 1790s. Chayes (1966) offers a brief but suggestive account.

   Coleridge's contemporaries differed in their responses to the meaning of the preface. Peacock insisted the preface should be received with a "certain degree of scepticism" (Peacock (1924–34) viii. 290). Alford recorded a similarly sceptical comment by Wordsworth (Alford (1873) 62).

3 The stanzaic structure of the poem differs from edition to edition. The *Crewe Manuscript* has only one major division, occuring between lines 36 and 37; *1829* has three stanzas, with no new stanza after line 36; *1834* is ambiguous, line 36 coming at the bottom of the page may suggest a fourth stanza. Even with these variations in mind, the reader usually senses major division between the first 36 and the last 18 lines.

4 Fogle (1960) argues for the unity of the poem as advancing through a reconciliation of opposites to a unified whole. See also Rauber (1964) 212–21. Meyerstein (1937) discusses the unity of the poem and its genre as a short Pindaric ode, with two main divisions only.

5 According to Leigh Hunt, Lord Byron was "highly struck" with Coleridge's recitation of the poem in 1816 (Leigh Hunt (1928) 345).

6 Coleridge had presented his work under other auspices before, such as Nehemiah Higginbottom (author of a series of sonnets in the *Monthly Magazine*, November 1797), as he pointedly explained in the *Biographia* (see Shawcross i. 17–19, on this and other (anonymous) contributions). Elizabeth Schneider suggests that Coleridge may have been the author of two articles attributed to a "Professor Heeren of Göttingen" appearing in the *Monthly Magazine* of January 1800, a gesture of irony if it were truly Coleridge's work. Is "Heeren" possibly a play on "Herr" and on the German practice of piling up titles before a name? See Elizabeth Schneider (1953) 289 ff.

   Kierkegaard is the most obvious related example of an author creating personas for the sake of ironic communication. Shelley often attached prefaces in the form of advertisements to his poems, sometimes echoing the preface to "Kubla Khan" in tone and style, and in the creation of a persona. See e.g., the advertisement to "Epipsychidion."

7 This note is attached to the *Crewe Manuscript*, now in the British Library, dated 1810 according to Watson (1966) 119. See John Beer's edition of *Coleridge Poems* in the Everyman paperback (1963) 164, for a discussion of the *Crewe Manuscript*.

8 The explanation usually advanced for why Coleridge wrote the preface suggests that the preface was a gesture of self-defence for not having finished the poem. See e.g., Yarlott (1967) 128 for a fairly representative account: "[the preface was written in] self-defence, anticipating the charge of obscurity which the

poem's acknowledged imperfection of organization would produce..." "Acknowledged" by T. S. Eliot perhaps, but see footnote 10. See also Lowes, who, it would seem, had promulgated this basic position some forty years earlier, in *The Road to Xanadu* (1927), chs 18, 19, 20, and esp. 412–13. Elizabeth Schneider (1953) 26 ff. expresses a similar assessment.

9   Lowes (1927) 358 reminds us that "in ancient tradition the stately pleasure-dome of Kubla Khan itself came into being, like the poem, as the embodiment of a remembered vision in a dream." Lowes thinks this point insignificant enough to be relegated entirely to a footnote. But this is just the sort of point Coleridge would have seen fit to turn to his own use by creating a *poem* designed in a dream as an analogue of the Khan's palace or dome, an analogue expressly designed to draw the reader's attention away from the obvious *content* of the poem and toward the composition and reading of the poem. J. P. Collier's report suggests that Coleridge was aware of the legend that the Khan's plan for a palace had originated in a dream (Coleridge, *Shakespearean Criticism* (1930) ii. 47). Coleridge's own comments elsewhere suggest a thorough awareness of the pregnancy of the dream as a metaphor for poetic composition. A marginal note to Eichorn (1787) iii. 38 is pertinent to the preface:

> From the analogy of Dreams during an excited state of the Nerves, which I have myself experienced, and the wonderful intricacy, complexity, and yet clarity of the visual Objects, I should infer the [spontaneity and inspired character of Ezekiel's vision of God]. Likewise, the noticeable fact of the words descriptive of these Objects rising at the same time, and with the same spontaneity and absence of all conscious Effort, weighs greatly with me, against the hypothesis of Pre-meditation, in this and similar Passages of the Prophetic Books.

And see e.g. Coburn iii. 4410: "We are nigh to waking when we dream, we dream." (Cf. Freud who interprets the dream within a dream as closest to reality.) The visionary in the epilogue may be in some such situation. Note in connection with this the statement in Coleridge, *Literary Remains* (1836–9), i. 173: "A poem may in one sense be a dream, but it must be a waking dream." That "one sense" is perhaps best indicated by another comment, in Coleridge, *Miscellaneous Criticism* (1936) 36: "You will take especial note of the marvellous independence and true imaginative absence of all particular space or time in the Faery Queen.... It is truly... of mental space. The poet has placed you in a dream, a charmed sleep, and you neither wish, nor have the power, to inquire where you are, or how you got there." This freedom from the conscious dictates of space and time characterizing the unconscious and art is mentioned also by A. R. Jones quoting House in "The Conversation and other Poems," Brett (1971) 99: "We are also conscious of an 'extraordinary sense of the mind's *very being*, in suspense, above time and space,' that 'arises in the poet himself in the act of composition.'"

10   Critics from Schneider to Watson have discounted the notion that the poem was literally composed in a dream. See Watson (1966) 120, and Schneider

(1953) 22 ff and 45. Yarlott and Lowes seem to assume the dream account to be meant literally only, without any symbolic or ironic significance; see Yarlott (1967) 128 and Lowes (1927), chs 18, 19 and 20. Beer points out that however the poem was composed, it is not a "meaningless reverie [as many have assumed] but a poem so packed with meaning as to render detailed elucidation extremely difficult" (Beer (1959) 202). Eliot's view that the poem lacks the organization needed to complement the inspiration is set to rest by the elucidation of the connections amongst the imagery in Beer (1959), chs 7 and 8; see Eliot (1933) 146.

11 An anonymous contributor to the *TLS* (16 February 1962) says that this omission from the *Crewe Manuscript* "places the whole matter of the circumstances in which 'Kubla Khan' came into existence in a different, more sober light"; see also Coburn i. 278 on a Mr Porson.

12 Lowes briefly notes this point, but does not seem to attach any importance to it. He, moreover, seems to identify the "I" of the epilogue with a tartar youth (Lowes (1927) 408). Schneider recognizes the contrast between the body and epilogue of the poem, but only concludes from that that the poem is an unfinished fragment! (Schneider (1953) 247–8). Watson interprets the break as a distinction between fancy and imagination (Watson (1966) 124–6). Lowes correctly, I believe, divides the poem up into four sections, in the stanzaic divisions of 1816, but makes no claim that the fourth is different from the other three (Lowes (1927) 406). In Yarlott (1967) 147 ff, no distinctions between the parts are drawn at all in any conscious sense, nor is there any significant discussion of how the epilogue content relates to the lines 1–36, or why it varies in narrative perspective, content, and style.

13 The title of the work is actually *Purchas his Pilgrimage*, though Coleridge's version sometimes appears on the bindings of editions and, as E. H. Coleridge has pointed out in his notes, the lines which Coleridge quotes as his source are quite different from the lines in the *Pilgrimage*.

14 Lowes (1927) 362 ff. suggests that a passage in *Purchas* does at least mention damsels and youths and songs. "Abyssinian" and "dulcimer" are traceable to more obscure sources, though Abyssinian is discussed later by Purchas. The damsels and youths were inmates of the Khan's palace, however, a point which serves to connect the singing damsel even more closely with the Khan's activities.

15 Many critics since have disagreed with Lowes's reductive assumption that the "I" of lines 37–54 is a tartar youth. Most postulate him as the archetypal poet, and cite sources as ancient as Plato's *Ion* to mark the connection between poetry, madness, and the corresponding imagery of honey-dew and milk, and the flashing eyes and floating hair. See, e.g., Yarlott (1967) 148 ff., who too simply equates the "I" with Coleridge and not the poet *par excellence* as well. Watson (1966) 122 sees him as the latter, as does Schneider (1945) 800. Beer offers the most satisfactory account of the "I" as visionary, artist, or genius: "the apotheosis of all the 'divine men' who had haunted Coleridge's youthful imagination" (Beer (1959) 261 ff.). He is not Coleridge, but Coleridge's ideal of absolute genius (as contrasted with commanding genius); not Coleridge him*self* but only Coleridge as he transcended himself:

To have a genius is to live in the universal, to know no self but that which is reflected not only from the faces of all around us, our fellow creatures, but reflected from the flowers, the trees, the beasts, yea from the very surface of the sands of the desert. A man of genius finds a reflex to himself, were it only in the mystery of genius (*P. Lects.* 179).

16 That the damsel sings of "Mount Abora" seems to exclude her from being the singer of lines 1–36. But in nearly all of the important passages traced as sources for the River Alph, a mountain was present, from which the river sprang. Thus the river and the mountain are always closely associated in the landscape, so that to sing of Mount Abora would be to sing of the river as well. For the most important mountain – river connection see Beer (1959) 221: "This river, as soon as it issues out from between the cleft of the mountain..." See also 220, for another connection: "...the River Barrady breaks out from between the Mountains: its Gardens extending almost to the very place," and 257 for the religious and inspirational associations of the mountain. Lowes (1927) 361 offers other sources in which the river issues from a mountain. See especially 372 for a description of a mountain full of water that is forced out at the foot to become the river. Still more importantly for the connection, Lowes 373 traces the name Abora not to a mountain but to the names of two rivers, Abola and Astaboras. Lowes concludes, "...Mount Amara – its name merged with the name of the river that flowed by the Mountains of the Moon" (376). See further 382. And see the *Crewe Manuscript* for the variant "Mt Amara."

Beer further associates the maid with the Khan's world by uncovering the explicit sexual and female connotations of the walls and towers and gardens, and their sources in the *Song of Solomon* (see Beer (1959) 270–1). Thus not only might the maid's song be construed as the song of lines 1–36, but the landscape description would be of the "damsel with a dulcimer" described allegorically.

17 Thus the pun on "air" as melody. Cf. "The Eolian Harp" line 32. For Coleridge on music as "articulated breath" see Coburn iii. 4022.

18 See e.g., *Lay Sermons* 29 for Coleridge on the imagination as that "reconciling and mediatory power, which incorporating the Reason in Images of the Sense, ...gives birth to a system of symbols, harmonious in themselves, and consubstantial with the truths, of which they are the conductors." Note the use of "harmonious." Note also the explanation in Shawcross i. 86. All efforts to identify the Abyssinian maid with a specific woman in Coleridge's life seem reductive and quite contrary to the activity of imagination as a producer of *symbols*, not of allegories (see *Lay Sermons* 30).

19 See Coleridge "On the Philosophic Import of the Words Object and Subject," (1821) 247–50, on the given and the external.

20 Jean Paul Richter (1804) places the idea of the poet's observation, his "Schau" or "Betrachtung," of his own work of art, at the centre of the theory of irony as aesthetic distance, since the artist is said to be simultaneously spectator, and vice versa. The artist's ability to maintain a third person perspective *while creating*, is a measure of his achievement of ironic self-consciousness.

21 Watson (1966) 120 says "Kubla Khan" is "wonderfully of a piece." Beer (1959)
     275 also argues with detailed analysis for the completeness of the poem. On
     the poem's metrical unity, see Purves (1962).

22 A further reason for thinking that Coleridge's description of the dream and the
     "images [which] rose up before him as *things*" was a metaphor of poetic
     composition, is to be found in his letters to Southey and Davy, and Godwin as
     well, which Lowes (1927) 66, points to as descriptions of eidetic imagery.
     Coleridge seems to have been unusually adept at this ability to seem actually to
     see scenes before one as external, independent perceptions, at the same time
     that one is aware that they are purely mental productions. But see also the
     Eichorn marginal note quoted above, note 9.

23 See, e.g., the anecdote about reading Plato in Shawcross i. 160–1, or the letter
     from a friend in chapter 13. Both chapters are full of recipes for reading
     imaginatively. The gloss to "The Ancient Mariner," it will be argued below, is
     a fine instance of a parodied reading situation.

24 Yeats writes about the paradoxical relation of active and passive in creative
     experience:

   The purpose of rhythm, it has always seemed to me, is to prolong the
   moment of contemplation, the moment when we are both asleep and
   awake, which is the one moment of creation, by hushing us with an
   alluring monotony, while it holds us waking by variety, to keep us in that
   state of perhaps real trance, in which the mind liberated from the pressure
   of the will is unfolded in symbols (Yeats (1964) 48).

   Yet Yeats never underestimated the conscious role of the poet. See Beer (1959)
   203–4 for Yeats's appreciation of the balance between instinct and intention.

25 Coleridge describes this peculiar passive, receptive state of the conscious mind
     in Shawcross i. 166–7, in his quotation from Plotinus, and in his metaphor of
     the air-sylph or the chrysalis.

26 For Coleridge's use of "thingify," see Griggs iv. 885 to Derwent Coleridge,
     November 1818: "... to think is to thingify." The entire passage on logic is
     relevant.

27 See Shelley, "The Defence of Poetry":

   Poetry is not like reasoning, a power to be exerted according to the
   determination of the will. A man cannot say, "I will compose poetry". ... for
   the mind in creation is as a fading coal, which some invisible influence,
   like an inconstant wind, awakens to transitory brightness; this power arises
   from within, like the colour of a flower which fades and changes as it is
   developed, and the conscious portions of our natures are unprophetic
   either of its approach or its departure [(Percy Bysshe Shelley (1951) 517)].

   Shelley then goes on to make observations expressly relevant to the loss of
   vision of the visionary, and relevant to Coleridge: "Could this influence be
   durable in its original purity and force, it is impossible to predict the greatness
   of the results; but when composition begins, inspiration is already on the

decline, and the most glorious poetry that has ever been communicated to the world is probably a feeble shadow of the original conceptions of the poet." Shelley further notes a point lending support to the hypothesis that Coleridge's dream account is a metaphorical rendering of the poetic process of composition: "I appeal to the greatest poets of the present day, whether it is not an error to assert that the finest passages of poetry are produced by labour and study. The toil and the delay recommended by critics, can be justly interpreted to mean no more than a careful observation of the inspired moments, and an artificial connexion of the spaces between their suggestions by the intertexture of conventional expressions; a necessity only imposed by the limitedness of the poetical faculty itself." And see the important passage on Judgement and instinct in Griggs iv. 898n (to Tulk, 17 December 1818). See also Coleridge, *Shakespearean Criticism* (1930) i. 197–8, and Shawcross ii. 258, "On Poesy or Art." And see *Coleridge's Literary Criticism* (1921) 186.

28 See Walter Jackson Bate and John Bullitt (1945) for sources which could well have influenced Coleridge's early thinking.

29 Most critics see the Khan's activities as unrepresentative of artistic creation, because he seems to decree, measure, and quantify. See Beer's analysis in terms of the commanding genius distinguished from the absolute genius (Beer (1959) 216–17 and 226–7). Watson (1966) 122 agrees that the poem has levels concerned with aesthetic process, but his claim that the first 36 lines of the poem are results merely of the faculty of fancy is inconsistent with the richness of the images and their power as symbols invoking universals. He seems to make the poem into a mere allegory.

30 See Percy Bysshe Shelley (1951) 496. For Coleridge on the degeneration of truth see the appropriate passage in Coburn i. 119 dated only vaguely as 1795–6: "Truth is compared in scripture to a streaming fountain; if her waters flow not in perpetual progression, they stagnate into a muddy pool of conformity & tradition. Milton." The Khan at least showed wisdom in building his dome by a streaming fountain of truth.

31 See further *Aids*, aphorism I, and *Friend* i. 110.

32 See Yarlott (1967) 133 on the Khan shutting out nature. And see also 131 ff. for a general discussion of the Khan's "art" as opposed to truly inspired art. Yarlott (1967) 151 makes an interesting comparison of Kubla's garden with the dell, marriage, and domesticity generally. See Beer (1959) 222–3 for similar observations, and his additional insight that the Khan's garden of earthly paradise and the sun-worship of the poem suggest the pantheistic tendencies which always conflicted with Christianity in Coleridge's thought.

33 The landscape of "Kubla Khan" seems to reflect late seventeenth- and early eighteenth-century interests in gardening as a metaphor for the cultivation of genius. Shaftesbury, and earlier, Sir William Temple, had all written using the garden as a metaphor for genius. The metaphor became more interesting as writers set up the dichotomy between the carefully landscaped garden (geometric garden), the "Chinese" garden (less obviously manicured), and the wild, natural garden. Finally the garden was contrasted with nature itself, and this contrast reflected the changing attitude toward the nature of genius and the relation of instinct to judgement. The poetry of the eighteenth century also

reflected the development of the concept of genius in the imagery, Thomson, and later Chatterton, amongst others, relying more and more upon natural scenery, which culminated in the romantic landscapes of the Gothic novels and romantic poetry.

34 The poem also suggests to many critics a level of creation at the cosmico-religious level; thus Shaffer's relating of "Kubla Khan" to higher Biblical criticism (Shaffer (1975)), and Mercer's relating the poem to Jacob Boehme and the redemptive process, Mercer (1953). The connection of the poem with *Paradise Lost, Song of Solomon,* and *Ezekiel* enriches the religious dimension. For a different, more pagan, interpretation, see Charles I. Patterson (1974).

35 Thus the visionary is distinct from the Khan only in that he possesses the Abyssinian maid – he is artist inspired, while the Khan is perhaps artist, or maker, without inspiration, at least from the visionary's point of view. It is the Khan's dome and garden which are "unfinished" for the spectator: they lack the completing inspiration of imagination. Boundaries seem arbitrary and not expressive of any integral part/whole relationship or of any interaction with nature and with the materials out of which the boundaries are built. It is true, as most critics maintain (Yarlott (1967) 145–6; Beer (1959) 246, but see Watson (1966) 123 and 128 for a contrasting view), that the visionary's "dome in air," the "shadow dome" and the Khan's "pleasure dome" are all different. But they are different only as maid, visionary, and Khan are different: as aspects of the self and, as Blake would put it, as different levels of vision. Or they illustrate the changing function of imagery, from description of an external landscape, to symbolic of the internal organizing mind. It is necessary to stress however that the Khan's activities, his gardens, may also be a model of imaginative, vital art, as well as of degenerate art. This apparently contradictory two-fold significance best expresses the nature of art and metaphor as potentially degenerative from the point of view of spectator and artist. Thus visionary and Khan may have identical roles as artists, or they may be seen as opposite – the Khan as artist, the visionary as spectator wishing to complete for himself by imaginative response the unfinished dome. Thus the poem represents vividly the aesthetic situation of spectator striving to recreate for himself the work of art – the dome – by means of imagination – the damsel.

36 Watson (1966) 123 recognizes the ambiguity of the contained or containing imagery and landscape. Yarlott assumes reductively that the ancient forests are encompassed by the Khan's walls, but not assimilated into the garden effectively. A recognition by Yarlott of the enclosure ambiguity would, however, strengthen his case that art which shuts out or fails to assimilate nature is only artifice; see Yarlott (1967) 137.

37 Contemporary reviewers of "Kubla Khan" did not see it this way. *The Eclectic Review* 5 (1816) 565–72 announced that the poem should never have been published. Hazlitt said it was "nonsense" in the *Examiner* (2 June 1816) 348–9. The most favourable response was to estimate the poem as "not wholly discreditable," as "Christabel" was said to be, *Anti-Jacobin Review* 50 (1816) 632–6. More recently, Eliot felt called upon to protest against "the exaggerated repute of *Kubla Khan*" (Eliot (1933) 146).

6

"Christabel": The Wandering Mother and the Enigma of Form

KAREN SWANN

The first questions Christabel asks Geraldine refer to identity and origins: "who art thou?" and "how camest thou here?" Geraldine's response is oblique; in effect she replies, "I am like you, and my story is like your own":

> My sire is of a noble line,
> And my name is Geraldine:
> Five warriors seized me yestermorn,
> Me, even me, a maid forlorn: ...
>
> They spurred amain, their steeds were white:
> And once we crossed the shade of night.
> As sure as Heaven shall rescue me,
> I have no thought what men they be;
> Nor do I know how long it is
> (For I have lain entranced I wis)
> Since one, the tallest of the five,
> Took me from the palfrey's back,
> A weary woman, scarce alive. ...
>
> Whither they went I cannot tell –
> I thought I heard, some minutes past,
> Sounds as of a castle bell.
> Stretch forth thy hand (thus ended she),
> And help a wretched maid to flee.

(ll. 79–104)[1]

Geraldine's tale echoes and anticipates Christabel's. Christabel is also first introduced as the daughter of a "noble" father; she, too, experiences things she "cannot tell," calls on Heaven to rescue her, crosses threshholds and falls into trances. But in contrast to the story "Christabel," often criticized for its ambiguities, Geraldine's tale presents sexual and moral categories as unambiguous and distinct: villainous male force appropriates and silences an innocent female victim. This difference effects a corresponding clarification of genre. Geraldine translates "Christabel" into the familiar terms of the tale of terror.

Geraldine's translation would appear to establish the identity of the woman. Ultimately, however, her story complicates the issue of feminine identity by suggesting its entanglement, at the origin, with genre. How one takes Geraldine depends on one's sense of the "line" of representations she comes from. For Christabel, but also, for any absorbed reader of circulating library romances, Geraldine's story of abduction works as a seduction – Christabel recognizes Geraldine as a certain type of heroine and embraces her.[2] More guarded readers appropriate Geraldine as confidently as Christabel does, but they see her quite differently. Charles Tomlinson, for example, reads "Christabel" as "a tale of terror," but in contrast to Geraldine's own story casts her in the role of villain, while for Patricia Adair, Geraldine is betrayed by her very conventionality: she tells her story in "rather unconvincing and second-rate verse which was, no doubt, deliberately meant to sound false."[3] Geraldine is "false" because she comes from an ignoble line of Gothic temptresses, or, in the case of other critics, because she can be traced back to the ignoble Duessa and to a host of other predatory figures. Tellingly these sophisticated readers, who employ literary history to read Geraldine as a figure of untruth, are the worst ruffians – they either refuse to hear the woman's story of her own abduction, or assume that her protests are really a come-on.

Geraldine may be Christabel's ghost or projection as many critics have suggested, but only if we acknowledge that Christabel produces herself as a received representation – a feminine character who in turn raises the ghosts of different subtexts, each dictating a reading of her as victim or seductress, good or evil, genuine or affected. I will be arguing in this essay that "Christabel" both dramatizes and provokes hysteria. The poem explores the possessing force of certain bodies – Geraldine's, of course, but also bodies of literary convention, which I am calling "genres." Particularly in Coleridge's day, debates on literary decorum allowed the gendering of structure in a way that seemed to assuage anxiety about the subject's relation to cultural forms. Questions involving the subject's autonomy could be framed as an opposition between authentic, contained "manly" speech and "feminine" bodies – the utterly conventional yet licentiously imaginative female characters, readers, and genres of the circulating libraries. In "Christabel,"

Coleridge both capitalizes on and exposes culture's tactical gendering of formal questions. The poem invites us to link the displacing movement of cultural forms through subjects to the "feminine" malady of hysteria and the "feminine" genres of the circulating library; at the same time, it mockingly and dreamily informs us that hysteria is the condition of all subjects in discourse, and that the attribution of this condition to feminine bodies is a conventional, hysterical response.

I

If Coleridge were thinking of dramatizing hysteria in a poem, he might have turned to Burton's account of "Maids', Nuns', and Widows' Melancholy" in *The Anatomy of Melancholy*, a book he knew well. According to Burton, hysterics "think themselves bewitched":

> Some think they see visions, confer with spirits and devils, they shall surely be damned, are afraid of some treachery, imminent danger, and the like, they will not speak, make answer to any question, but are almost distracted, mad, or stupid for the time, and by fits. . . .[4]

The malady befalls barren or celibate women; among these, Catholic noblewomen who are forced to remain idle are particularly susceptible. Most of the symptoms Burton catalogues are touched on in the passage quoted above. Hysterics have visions and are afraid "by fits" – the "fits of the mother" or womb ("the heart itself beats, is sore grieved, and faints . . . like fits of the mother" (p. 415)). The symptom which most interests Burton, though, is the inability of hysterics to communicate their troubles: they "cannot tell" what ails them. This fact becomes a refrain of his own exposition: "and yet will not, cannot again tell how, where, or what offends them"; "many of them cannot tell how to express themselves in words, or how it holds them, what ails them; you cannot understand them, or well tell what to make of their sayings" (p. 416).

They "cannot tell," and *you* cannot "well tell" what to make of them: the phenomenon of their blocked or incomprehensible speech seems to produce similar effects in the writer. And indeed, Burton's impetuous and fitful prose in many respects resembles the discourse of the hysteric, into whose point of view he regularly tumbles ("Some *think* they see visions," but "they *shall* surely be damned" (my italics). Far from resisting this identification, Burton makes narrative capital from the slippage, as here, when he allows himself to become "carried away" by sympathy for the Christabel-like afflicted:

> I do not so much pity them that may otherwise be eased, but those alone that out of a strong temperament, innate constitution, are

violently carried away with this torrent of inward humours, and though very modest of themselves, sober, religious, virtuous, and well given (as many so distressed maids are), yet cannot make resistance ...

and then, as if shaking off a "fit," comically pauses to reflect on his own indecorous "torrents":

> But where am I? Into what subject have I rushed? What have I to do with nuns, maids, virgins, widows? I am a bachelor myself, and lead a monastic life in a college: *nae ego sane ineptus qui haec dixerim*, I confess 'tis an indecorum, and as Pallas, a virgin, blushed when Jupiter by chance spake of love matters in her presence, and turned away her face, *me reprimam*; though my subject necessarily require it, I will say no more. (p. 417)

Protesting all the while his ignorance of women, the "old bachelor" coyly figures himself as a virgin whose body betrays her when desire takes her unawares. He also takes the part of the apparently more knowing and self-controlled Jupiter, but only to suggest that the latter's fatherly indifference is an act. For whether he is an artful or artless seducer, Jupiter himself appears only to rush into speech "by chance" – the "chance," we suspect, of finding himself in such close proximity to his virginal daughter. The woman whose desire is written on her body is like the man who makes love the "matter" of his discourse: both attempt to disguise desire, and become the more seductive when desire is revealed in the context of their attempts to suppress it.

The story of Pallas and Jupiter is placed at a strategic point in Burton's chapter. It punctuates his resolve to check the torrents of his narrative, a resolve immediately and engagingly broken when, more "by chance" than design, he finds he has to say something more ("And yet I must and will say something more"). This time he is prompted by his commiseration with all distressed women to launch an attack on "them that are in fault,"

> ... those tyrannizing pseudo-politicians, superstitious orders, rash vows, hard-hearted parents, guardians, unnatural friends, allies (call them how you will), those careless and stupid overseers ...

those fathers and parental substitutes (particularly the Church), who "suppress the vigour of youth" and ensure the orderly descent of their estates through the enforced celibacy of their daughters (p. 418). An "old bachelor" who leads a monastic life in a college; whose own discourse, like the discourse of the hysteric, seems to be the product of a strained compromise between lawless impulses and the claims of order; who might himself be said to be possessed by spirits and the dead language in which they wrote, ends his discussion of "maids', nuns', and widows' melancholy" by championing those who "cannot tell" against the ungenerous legislators of the world.

There are suggestive correspondences between Burton's chapter on hysteria and "Christabel." Christabel is a virtuous Catholic gentlewoman whose lover is away, possibly at the behest of her father, out of whose castle she "steals" at the beginning of the poem. Whether or not he is responsible for blighting love affairs,[5] Sir Leoline has affinities with both of Burton's father-figures: like the "pseudopoliticians" he is intimately linked with repressive law; like Jupiter, his relation to his daughter is somewhat suspect. Moreover, the poem's descriptions of Christabel's experiences – first with the possibly supernatural Geraldine and later, with a traumatic memory or scene which comes over her by fits and bars her from telling – and its insistent references to a "mother" who at one point threatens to block Geraldine's speech ("Off, wandering mother!" (l. 205)), follow Burton's account of the characteristic symptoms of hysteria. But Coleridge may have appreciated most the comic slippages in Burton's narrative between the slightly hysterical scholar whose business it is to "tell" and the women who are the matter of his discourse. When he came to write "Christabel," Coleridge told the story through narrators who are as enigmatic as the women they tell about – we cannot "well tell" if they are one voice or two. More than any detail of the plot, the participation of these narrators in the "feminine" exchanges they describe, and the poem's playful suggestion that hysteria cannot be restricted to *feminine* bodies, marks the kinship of "Christabel" and Burton's text.

II

Who is Geraldine and where does she come from? Possibly, from Christabel. In the opening of the poem Christabel has gone into the woods to pray for her absent lover after having had uneasy dreams "all yesternight" – "Dreams, that made her moan and leap, / As on her bed she lay in sleep," we are told in the 1816 version of the poem. In the woods *two* ladies perform the actions of moaning and leaping which, yesternight, *one* lady had performed alone:

> The lady leaps up suddenly,
> The lovely lady, Christabel!
> It moaned as near, as near can be,
> But what it is she cannot tell –
> On the other side it seems to be,
> Of the huge, broad-breasted, old oak tree.
>
> (1816: ll. 37–42)

For a moment we, too, are in the woods, particularly if, like the poem's "first" readers, we already know something of the plot. Does "the lady" refer to Christabel or Geraldine? Is her leaping up the cause or effect of fright? The next lines supply answers to these questions, and as the scene proceeds "it" resolves into the distinct, articulate character Geraldine. For a moment's space, however, we entertain the notion that an uneasy lady leaped up suddenly and terrified herself.

Burton says of hysterics, "some think they see visions, confer with spirits and devils, they shall surely be damned." Geraldine is such a "vision." She appears in response to what Burton implies and psychoanalysis declares are the wishes of hysterics – to get around patriarchal law, which legislates desire. In the beginning of the poem Christabel "cannot tell" what ails her, but critics have theorized from her sighs that she is suffering from romance, from frustrated love for the "lover that's far away," for the Baron, or even, for the mother.[6] Geraldine, who appears as if in answer to Christabel's prayer, "steals" with her back into the castle, sleeps with her "as a mother with her child," and then meets the Baron's embrace, allows the performance of these wishes. Moreover, like an hysterical symptom, which figures both desire and its repression, Geraldine also fulfills the last clause of Burton's formula: although much is ambiguous *before* she appears, it is not until she appears that Christabel feels "damned," and that we are invited to moralize ambiguity as duplicity, the cause of "sorrow and shame" (ll. 270, 296, 674).

As well as answering *Christabel's* desires, however, Geraldine answers the indeterminacy of the narrative and the reader's expectancy. The wood outside the Baron's castle is not the "natural" world, as is often declared,[7] but a world stocked with cultural artifacts. Before Geraldine ever appears it is haunted by the ghosts of old stories: familiar settings and props function as portents, both for the superstitious and the well-read. The wood and the midnight hour are the "moment's space" where innocence is traditionally put to the test, or when spirits walk abroad; other details – the cock's crow at midnight, the mastiff's unrest, the contracted moon – we know to be art's way of signifying nature's response to human disorder. These so-called "Gothic trappings" ensnare us because they mean nothing ("Tu-whit, tu-whoo") and too much: like the sighs we seize on as evidence of Christabel's inner life, they gesture to an enigma, something as yet hidden from view. Geraldine makes "answer meet" to these suspensions of the narrative, not by providing closure, but by representing indeterminacy:

> There she sees a damsel bright,
> Drest in a silken robe of white,
> That shadowy in the moonlight shone:
> The neck that made that white robe wan,

Her stately neck, and arms were bare;
Her blue-veined feet unsandal'd were,
And wildly glittered here and there
The gems entangled in her hair.

(ll. 58–65)

Precipitating out of the Gothic atmosphere, Geraldine promises to contain in herself an entrapping play of surfaces and shadows; with her appearance suspense resolves into a familiar sign of ambiguity.

Geraldine is a fantasy, produced by the psychic operations of condensation and displacement. On the one hand, her function is to objectify: she intervenes in moments of interpretive crisis as a legible representation – a "vision," a story, and a plot. At the same time, though, she, the story she tells, and the plot she seems to set in motion are all displacing performances of ambiguities she might at first promise to "answer" more decisively. After she pops up, two women dramatize the implied doubleness of the daughter who "stole" along the forest keeping her thoughts to herself (l. 31). Very little else changes. Prompted by an uneasy dream one woman "stole" out of her father's castle; two women return to it "as if in stealth" (l. 120), and by the end of Part I Christabel has simply resumed "fearfully dreaming," at least according to the narrator (l. 294). The spell that becomes "lord of her utterance" (l. 268) that night does no more than render explicit the inhibition of her "telling" already operative in the opening scene of the poem, where her silence was obscurely connected to the brooding, dreaming "lord" of the castle, the father who loved the daughter "so well." By the end of the poem we have simply returned to where we began: Christabel is "inly praying" once again, this time at the "old" Baron's feet, and once again Geraldine is on "the other side" (l. 614).

While it proposes an answer to the question "who art thou?" this reading only makes Christabel's second question to Geraldine more problematic: Geraldine is a fantasy, but she does not seem to "come from" any locatable place. The many source studies of the poem have shown that her origins are as much in literature as in Christabel: she first appears to the latter as a highly aestheticized object, and first speaks, many readers think to her discredit, in a highly encoded discourse. A material, communally available representation, she could have been dreamed up by any of the characters to whom she appears in the course of the poem – by the uneasy dreamer Christabel, but also by the Baron, into whose castle she steals while he is asleep, and, Christabel suggests, dreaming uneasily (l. 165), or by Bracy, whose dream of her seems to "live upon [his] eye" the next day (l. 559). She could even be part of *our* dream. For in "Christabel" as in all of his poems of the supernatural, Coleridge plots to turn us into dreamers – to "procure" our "willing suspension of disbelief," our happy relinquishment of the reality principle. In "Christabel" as in dreams there is no version of the negative: questions raise possibilities that are neither confirmed nor wholly dismissed ("Is it the wind...? / There is not wind enough..." [ll. 44–5]). Tags drift from one "lady" to another, suggesting the affinity of apparent adversaries; signs are familiar yet unreadable, laden with associations which neither exclude each other nor resolve into univocality.

Geraldine intervenes into these several dreamlike states as a figure of the imaginary itself – a figure whose legibility derives from its status within the symbolic order. She obeys the laws which structure all psychic phenomena, including dreams, jokes, and hysteria, the malady which allowed Freud to "discover" these very laws. The latter, however, do not explain why *particular* representations become collectively privileged. Why, at moments when they brush with the (il-)logic of the unconscious, do subjects automatically, even hysterically, produce certain *gendered* sights and stories? – produce the image of a radically divided woman, or of two women in each other's arms; and produce the story of a woman who seduces, and/or is seduced, abducted, and silenced by a father, a seducer, and/or a ruffian? This story, including all the ambiguities that make it hard to "tell," is of course the story of hysteria as told by Burton, and later, painstakingly reconstructed by Freud from its plural, displacing performances on the bodies of women. Even the common reader would know it, however, for it describes all the permutations of the romance plot – a form largely, but not exclusively, associated with a body of popular, "feminine" literature.

If a body like Geraldine's pops up from behind a tree when all the witnesses are in the woods, it is no accident: everyone thinks feminine forms appropriately represent the dangers and attractions of fantasy life. Coleridge, who dramatized the highly overdetermined romance/hysteria plot in "Christabel" and happily flaunted feminine bodies when it suited him, was no exception. But I want to argue, first by looking at his generic play, and then by examining his treatment of the family romance, that in "Christabel" he was also mockingly obtruding a conspiracy to view, allowing us to see "feminine" genre and gender alike as cultural fantasy.

III

"Christabel's" narrators are themselves hysterics. The poem's interlocutor and respondent mime the entanglement of Geraldine and Christabel – I call them "they," but it is not clear if we hear two voices or one. Like the women they describe, they are overmastered by "visions." Repeatedly, they abandon an authoritative point of view to fall into the story's present; or they engage in transferential exchanges with the characters whose plot they are narrating. In the opening scene, for example, one of them plunges into the tale to plead to and for Christabel: "Hush, beating heart of Christabel!

/ Jesu, Maria, shield her well!" As if she hears, a stanza later Christabel cries out, "Mary mother, save me now!" (ll. 53–4, 69). Further on, the sequence is reversed when the speaker seems to take up Christabel's speech. She has just assured Geraldine that Sir Leoline will "guide and guard [her] safe and free" (l. 110); although the narrators generally are not as trusting as Christabel, one seems inspired by her confidence to echo her, twice: "So free from danger, free from fear / They crossed the court: right glad they were" (ll. 135–6, 143–4).

These narrators create the conditions and logic of dream: like them, and because of them, the reader is impotent to decide the poem's ambiguities from a position outside its fictions. Furthermore, the poem's "fictions" seem to be about little else than these formal slippages. The repressed of "Christabel's" dreamwork is almost too visible to be seen – not a particular psychic content but literary conventions themselves, like those which demand that narrators speak from privileged points of view, and important for this argument, bodies of conventions or "genres." "Christabel" obtrudes genre to our notice. The Gothic atmosphere of the first stanza, with its enumerations of ominously coincident bird and clock noises, goes slightly bad in the second – partly because of the very presence of the shocking "mastiff bitch," but also because both mastiff and narrator become heady with coincidence: making answer to the clock, "Four for the quarters, and twelve for the hour . . . Sixteen short howls, not over loud," she becomes an obvious piece of Gothic machinery (ll. 10–13). A similar generic disturbance occurs between Part I, told more or less in the "tale of terror" convention, and its conclusion, which recapitulates the story in a new convention, that of sentimental fiction. Suddenly Christabel "means" "a bourgeois lady of delicate, even saccharine, sensibility": "Her face, oh call it fair not pale, / And both blue eyes more bright than clear, / Each about to have a tear" (ll. 289–91). As suddenly, the narrators are exposed in a desperate act of wielding genre, using convention to force legibility on a sight that won't be explained.

Once we become aware of these instabilities, no stretch of the poem is exempt. In life women might faint, dogs might moan, and fires might flare up without anyone remarking it; if these coincide in story, they mean something. When they coincide in the overloaded, tonally unsettling Part I of "Christabel" they simultaneously draw attention to themselves as elements of a code. Although we may think of genres as vessels which successive authors infuse with original content, "Christabel's" "originality" is to expose them as the means by which significance is produced and contained.

This analysis raises the issue of the generic status of "Christabel." What is its literary genre? But also, what genre of psychic phenomenon does the poem aspire to – is it like a dream, as we first proposed, or like a joke? The latter question may not immediately seem important, since jokes and dreams have so much in common: like hysteria, they work by condensation and displacement to bring the repressed to light.[8] But for the poem's first readers, at least, it clearly mattered which was which. The reviewers of 1816 fiercely protested the poem's "licentious" mixing of joke and dream, categories of psychic phenomena which they translated into literary categories: was "Christabel" a bit of "doggrel," a wild, weird tale of terror, or a fantastic combination of the two? (Modern readers, less tuned to genre play, have decided the question by not hearing the jokes.)[9] Coleridge's contemporaries recognized that jokes and dreams demand different attitudes: if one responds to "Christabel" as though it were just a wild weird tale, and it turns out to be a joke, then the joke is on oneself. "Christabel" frightened its reviewers, not because it was such a successful tale of terror, but because they couldn't decide what sort of tale it was.

"Christabel" made its first readers hysterical because it is not one genre or another but a joke on our desire to decide genre. As such, it turned a "merely" formal question into a matter of oneupmanship. Most of the critics responded by redirecting the joke, giving the impression that it was on the poem and the author. Coleridge, they claimed, mixed the genres of joke and dream, not as a joke, but in a dream. What is telling is their almost universal decision to recast these issues of literary and formal mastery into the more obviously charged and manageable terms of sexual difference. According to them, the poem was, after all, just one of those tales of terror which ladies like to read ("For what woman of fashion would not purchase a book recommended by Lord Byron?" asks the *Anti-Jacobin*[10]); the author, variously described as an "enchanted virgin," an "old nurse," a "dreamer" – by implication, a hysteric – simply could not control the discourses that spoke through him like so many "lords" of his utterance.[11]

Gendering the formal question, the reviewers reenact the scene of Geraldine's first appearance: then, too, a variety of characters responded to indeterminacy by producing a feminine body at once utterly conventional and too full of significance. In critical discourse as in fantasy life, it seems, feminine forms – the derogated genres of the circulating library, the feminized body of the author, or the body of Geraldine – represent the enigma of form itself. Female bodies "naturally" seem to figure an ungraspable truth: that form, habitually viewed as the arbitrary, contingent vessel of more enduring meanings, is yet the source and determinant of all meanings, whether the subject's or the world's.

Displacing what is problematic about form onto the feminine gender ultimately serves the hypothetical authenticity and integrity of masculine gender and "manly" language. Look, for example, at the opening lines of the passage Hazlitt selects as the only "genuine burst of humanity" "worthy of the author" in the whole poem – the only place where "no dream oppresses him, no spell binds him"[12]:

Alas! they had been friends in youth;
But whispering tongues can poison truth;
And constancy lives in realms above;
And life is thorny; and youth is vain;
And to be wroth with one we love
Doth work like madness in the brain.
And thus it chanced, as I divine,
With Roland and Sir Leoline.

(ll. 408–15)

Hazlitt was not alone in his approbation: many reviewers of the poem quoted this passage with approval, and Coleridge himself called them "the best & sweetest Lines [he] ever wrote."[13] They are indeed outstanding – the only moment, in this tale about mysterious exchanges among women, when an already-past, already-interpreted, fully-breached male friendship is encountered. For those of us who don't equate "manliness" with universality and authenticity, this unremarked confluence of masculine subject-matter and "genuine" discourse is of course suspicious: it's not *simply* purity of style that made this passage the standard against which all other Christabellian discourse could be measured and found "licentious," "indecorous", "affected" – in short, effeminate.

But here, we are anticipated by the passage itself, which exposes "manliness" as a gendered convention. When the narrator begins this impassioned flight, we assume he speaks from privileged knowledge: why else such drama? Several lines later, though, he betrays that this is all something he has "divined," something that may have chanced. "Chancing" on a situation that really spoke to him – a ruined manly friendship – the narrator has constructed a "divination" based on what he knows – about constancy (it isn't to be found on earth), life (it's thorny), and youth (it's vain). Although he is more caught up in his speech than she, his voice is as "hollow" as Geraldine's. His flight or "genuine burst of humanity" is a fit of the mother, and a mocking treatment of manly discourse on the part of Coleridge, whose later accession to the going opinion was either a private joke or a guilty, revisionary reading of his licentious youth. If this tonal instability was lost on "Christabel's" reviewers, it can only be because, like the narrator himself, they were reading hysterically: a "vision" of autonomous male identities caused them automatically to produce a set of received ideas about manly discourse.

"Christabel" exposes the conventionality of manly authenticity and the giddiness of manly decorum; in the same move, it suggests that attributing hysteria to feminine forms is a hysterical response to a more general condition. In the poem as elsewhere, "the feminine" is the locus of erotic and generic license: this can have the exciting charge of perversity or madness, or can seem absolutely conventional, affected. "Christabel" contrives to have these alternatives redound on the reader, who continually feels mad or just stupid, unable to "tell" how to characterize the verse at any given point. Here is Christabel "imprisoned" in the arms of Geraldine:

> With open eyes (ah woe is me!)
> Asleep, and dreaming fearfully,
> Fearfully dreaming, yet, I wis,
> Dreaming that alone, which is –
> O sorrow and shame! Can this be she,
> The lady, who knelt at the old oak tree?
> And lo! the worker of these harms,
> That holds the maiden in her arms,
> Seems to slumber still and mild,
> As a mother with her child.
>
> (ll. 292–301)

Geraldine's arms, the scene of the close embrace, and the conclusion as a whole, which recasts Part I as a sentimental narrative – all in some sense work to imprison the significances of the text. Yet the scenario only imperfectly traps, and closes not at all, the questions which circulated through Part I. Identity is still a matter of debate, and still hangs on a suggestively ambiguous "she" ("Can this be she?"). Even the women's gender identities and roles are undecidable, their single embrace "read" by multiple, superimposed relationships. Geraldine, a "lady" like Christabel, is also sleeping with Christabel; a "worker of harms," a ruffian-like assaultor of unspecified gender, she is also like a "mild," protective mother. If in keeping with the sentimentality of this section of the poem, the mother/child analogy is introduced to clean up the post-coital embrace of the women, it redounds to suggest the eroticism of maternal attention. These ghostly stories, all already raised in the text of Part I, work to create the compellingly charged erotic ambivalence of "Christabel" – ambivalence about becoming absorbed into a body which may be "the same" as one's own, or may belong to an adversary, a "worker of harms," and which is associated with, or represented by, the maternal body.

Christabel's situation, including, perhaps her feminine situation, is contagious. The narrator, who seems overmastered by the very spell he is describing, can only direct us to a "sight" ("And lo!"), the significance of which he "cannot tell." His speech breaks down before the woman who is "dreaming fearfully, / Fearfully dreaming," before the form that may conceal "that alone, which is."

The narrator circles round but cannot tell the enigma of form, of the body or sign that is at once meaningless and too full of significance. His own discourse repeats the paradox of the "sight," and becomes a locus of the reader's interpretive breakdown. His lament strikes us as coming from "genuine" distress at the remembrance of Christabel's horrible predicament. But particularly in context, the lines —

> With open eyes (ah woe is me!)
> Asleep and dreaming fearfully,
> Fearfully dreaming, yet, I wis,
> Dreaming that alone which is —

raise the ghost of a sentimental style that as a matter of course suppresses all distressing sights and implications, while coyly directing the reader to what's not being said. To decide the narrator's credibility — is he bewildered or merely "affected," effeminate; could he even be camping it up? — it is necessary to bring genre to bear, to decide whether Gothic or sentimental romance is a determining convention. This is simultaneously to recognize that the voice we have been hearing cannot be authentic — if mad, it speaks in the tale of terror's legislated mad discourse; that genres are constructs which produce meaning for the subject; and that genres, like fantasy, reproduce the indeterminacies they at first appear to limit or control. Our relation to Christabel's narrators is like theirs to Christabel: the enigmatic form of their discourse turns us into hysterical readers, subject to the possessing, conventional bodies that that discourse raises in us.

IV

"Christabel's" romance plot suggests that our culture's hysterical relation to feminine forms — or its hysterical feminization of form — has its origins in the family romance. The poem invites us to distinguish between paternal and feminine orders of experience. The father's sphere is the Law — a legislative, symbolic order structured according to a divisive logic:

> Each matin bell, the Baron saith,
> Knells us back to a world of death.
> These words Sir Leoline first said,
> When he rose and found his lady dead:
> These words Sir Leoline will say
> Many a morn to his dying day!

> And hence the custom and law began
> That still at dawn the sacristan,
> Who duly pulls the heavy bell,
> Five and forty beads must tell

> Between each stroke – a warning knell,
> Which not a soul can choose but hear
> From Bratha Head to Wyndermere.
>
> (ll. 332–44)

The Baron's response to a traumatic event is to commemorate it. Every day, punctually, he relives the loss of "his lady," spacing and controlling the recurrences of his sorrow. By institutionalizing the observance, he turns a private grief into a public ceremony. The compulsive becomes the compulsory: the sacristan "duly" pulls his bell, and "not a soul can choose but hear."

Separation is something of a habit with the Baron. Three other times during the poem he attempts to stabilize his relation to a disturbing person or event by opening out a "space between" (l. 349). In the past, the narrator "divine[s]," Sir Leoline had been "wroth" with Lord Roland (ll. 412–13). Wrath and the threat of madness precipitate a separation which leaves each scarred (ll. 421–2). The speaker "ween[s]" these scars will never go away and seems to guess right, since the Baron's memory of that friendship revives when Geraldine appears on the scene and tells her story:

> Sir Leoline, a moment's space,
> Stood gazing on the damsel's face:
> And the youthful Lord of Tryermaine
> Came back upon his heart again.
>
> (ll. 427–30)

For a second time the Baron experiences maddening confusion, here obscurely related to the striking together of "youthful lord" and "damsel," known and new, past and present, revived love and recognized loss. Once again he becomes wrathful ("His noble heart swelled high with rage" [l. 432]), and introduces a "law" of deathly separation: he will "dislodge" the "reptile souls" of Geraldine's abductors "from the bodies and forms of men" (ll. 442–3). Finally, for a third time the Baron meets "[swelling] rage and pain" (l. 638) and "confusion" (l. 639) with division: in the last stanza of the poem, "turning from his own sweet maid," he leads Geraldine off (l. 653).

The Baron's customs and laws divide and oppose potential "sames" or potentially intermingling parts of "the same." In contrast, femininity bewilders the narrator because one can never tell if identities and differences are constant, "the same": "Can this be she, / The lady, who knelt at the old oak tree?" (ll. 296–7); "And Christabel awoke and spied / The same who lay down by her side – / Oh rather say, the same . . ." (ll. 370–1). Tales, glances, and verbal tags circulate between Christabel and Geraldine throughout the poem: each is a "lady," each makes "answer meet" to the other. These exchanges could be said to obey the law of "the mother." Her function has puzzled some critics, who have found it hard to reconcile her angelic guardianship of Christabel with her likeness to Geraldine.[14] Coleridge, however, intended "Christabel's" mother to be a punning, rather than a stable, character. Referring simultaneously to the malady of hysteria, the womb whose vaporish fantasies were thought to block the hysteric's speech, and the female parent, "the mother" is an exemplarily vagrant sign, whose shifts of meaning obey the very "laws" which determine the characteristic displacements of hysteria.

The mother escapes the Baron's divisive categories. Neither opposites nor "the same," Geraldine and Christabel are identically self-divided, each subject to a "sight" or "weight" whose history and effects she "cannot tell." The Baron might attempt to redress such duplicity by dislodging offending "souls" from the "bodies and forms" they occupy. The "mother," however, is neither spirit nor body. Dying the hour Christabel was born, she inhabits her daughter as an already-dislodged form, or in psychoanalytic terms, as an alien internal entity or fantasy.[15] At times Christabel feels this "weight" as the fully external, "weary weight" of Geraldine (l. 131), at times as an inner "vision" which "falls" on her. Where the Baron imagines parenthood bestowing on him all the privileges of ownership ("*his own* sweet maid"), possession by the "mother" breaks down privilege, including that of an original, controlling term. The "weight" or "sight" is both within and without, both the fantasy that cannot be told and the representation that makes it legible.

The Baron also remembers the mother by a weary weight, but he gets someone else to heft it: every morning his sacristan "duly pulls the heavy bell" which "not a soul can choose but hear." Obviously the organizations we have been calling the father's and the mother's exist in some relation to one another. A feminist reading of this relation might charge the Law with producing hysterics, women who "cannot tell" what ails them because the Law legislates against every voice but its own. The *Baron* stifles the daughter by his oppressive, deathly presence: stealing back into his castle with Geraldine, Christabel passes his room "as still as death / With stifled breath" (l. 171). "The mother" – the malady of hysteria – symptomatically represents the daughter's internalization of patriarchal Law. This reading is supported by Burton, who laid the daughter's troubles on the pseudopoliticians, and by Geraldine, who identifies the curse that prevents Christabel from "telling" as masculine prohibition: the sign which seals them both up is a "lord" of utterance and an "overmastering" spell.

A plot as popular as this one, however, is probably overdetermined. "Christabel" invites at least two other readings of the relation between hysteria and the Law. First, that hysteria produces the Law: repeatedly, the Baron opens out a space between himself and perceived threats in order to "shield" himself from overmastering confusion or madness. Second, that the

Law is just one form of hysteria. According to the narrator, the Baron's
cutting efforts leave him internally scarred. The space between is also a mark
within, from which no "shield" can protect him. Like the hysteric he is
always vulnerable to a recurrence of "swelling" confusion, a revival of the
already-internalized mark, to which he responds with another legislative cut.
The Law resembles hysteria in its defenses and effects: it attempts to decide
irresolution by producing something "on the other side," and its cuts leave
the legislator subject to recurrences.[16]

   "Christabel" invites us to decide there is only one significant "sight" –
Geraldine's bosom; and to infer that it is women who can have no discourse
within the Law. But at the same time it allows us to see hysteria as the
coincidence of superimposed fields: as a metaphysical condition of the
speaking subject, as a malady historically affecting women who suffer under
patriarchal Law, and as a fantasy of patriarchal culture – a representation
which figures the subject's alienation from the symbolic order on the bodies
of women. Christabel and Geraldine, who enter the Baron's castle while he
sleeps, enact their 'own' fantasy and his dream.

   To account for the power of this dream, we might try tracing it back to
the origin. At the moment the Baron is about to cast off his only child, a
protesting narrator invokes the mother:

> Why is thy cheek so wan and wild,
> Sir Leoline? Thy only child
> Lies at thy feet, thy joy, thy pride,
> So fair, so innocent, so mild;
> The same, for whom thy lady died!
> O by the pangs of her dear mother
> Think thou no evil of thy child!
> For her, and thee, and for no other,
> She prayed the moment ere she died:
> Prayed that the babe for whom she died,
> Might prove her dear lord's joy and pride!
>   That prayer her deadly pangs beguiled,
>   Sir Leoline!
> And wouldst thou wrong thy only child,
>   Her child and thine?

                                                      (ll. 621–35)

These lines refer us back to the opening of Part II, where custom and law
were instituted in response to a "lady's" death. This "lady" was also a
mother, the narrator reminds us here; her death was simultaneous with a
birth, her "pangs" – at once labor and death pangs – were beguiled by
prayers, her suffering mingled with joy.

The Baron's law is an interpretive moment: he decides to read the occasion as a death only. His action anticipates his later disavowal of Christabel, which occurs almost as if in response to the narrator's reminder that she is "[thy lady's] child and thine"; and it resonates with Geraldine's response when, diverted from her plot for a moment as love for Christabel and longing for the mother rise up in her, she collects herself by flinging off the latter ("Off, wandering mother!" (l. 205)). In each case, a feminine body comes to represent a threat to the wishfully autonomous self. "Christabel," with its punning allusions to "the mother," invites us to speculate that the "law" of gender, which legislates the systematic exclusion of feminine forms, is connected to the experience of maternal attention. In this view, representations of feminine bodies as sites of non-self-identity all take revenge on the maternal body, which, in its historical role as the first "worker of harms," is the agent through which identity is constituted on a split. The mother "wounds" with her love, constituting the subject as originally, irreducibly divided, marked by the meanings and desires of the Other.

This reading, however, may play into the hands of the patriarchs. Historically, they have used maternity to ground a question of origins; they have used gender to naturalize what is in fact a function of genre – of constructs which are only meaningful within an already-originated cultural order. To suggest that misogyny can be traced to experience of the mother, to attribute it to blind revenge for the subject's condition, is to give it a sort of tragic weight. It's also to forget the tone of "Christabel." The urbane ironist and even the apparently less controlled patriarch of that poem suggest that the projects of culture are at once more political and more finessed than what we've just described. The Baron's exclusion and readmission of women amounts to a kind of play. He guards his fantasied autonomy by opening out spaces between – between bodies, genders, generations. He lives in a deathly, "dreary" world, until his "dream" of radically split women reanimates it with desire. With the appearance of Geraldine, the threat of abduction – a threat for every subject in discourse – can be rewritten, flirted with, in dreams of seduction which repeat, at a safe distance, the "confusions" of first love. That night, a fantasized feminine body – single yet double, like the mother's when pregnant with child, or the hysteric's when inhabited by the vaporish conceptions of an origin which is never *her* origin – performs exchanges with another body like her own. These women figure but only imperfectly contain impropriety, allowing its threats and attractions to return to the Baron's world as a taint. Geraldine moves from Christabel's bed to his arms, supplanting the daughter who had supplanted the mother; for a moment, she produces in him the illusion that one can "forget...age" (l. 431) and all that has intervened, and recapture the fantasied past, when exchanges traversed the laws of self-identity and even the laws of gender.

V

Coleridge, who capitalizes on the potential of feminine bodies to eroticize masculine discourse, is himself a pseudopolitician; at the same time, like the hysteric he seems to counter the Law. Drawing together matters of form and desire, his discussion of meter in the Preface to "Christabel" nicely illustrates this double relation to the symbolic order. On the one hand, the principle the author lays down is strikingly consonant with the Baron's tolling "custom and law":

> I have only to add that the metre of Christabel is not, properly speaking, irregular, though it may seem so from its being founded on a new principle: namely, that of counting in each line the accents, not the syllables. Though the latter may vary from seven to twelve, yet in each line the accents will be found to be only four. Nevertheless, this occasional variation in number of syllables is not introduced wantonly, or for the mere ends of convenience, but in correspondence with some transition in the nature of the imagery or passion.

"Christabel's" metrics are figured in the poem as the ringing of the Baron's clock and matin bell. Coleridge's "principle," however, is designed to accommodate, not just the Baron, who would institute unvarying repetition, but also the movement of desire, "transition[s] in the nature of the imagery or passion."

Coleridge's meter, or more broadly, his joking treatment of gender and genre, can thus be seen as a compromise between the Law's reificatory strategies and the potentially wanton, disruptive liveliness of passion – a compromise which ultimately benefits the ironist who acquiesces to the laws he also exposes as interested. Yet Coleridge's play, which mocks the law of gender/genre by too faithfully reinscribing its conventions, also opens up the possibility of a more radical collapse between the positions of patriarch, hysteric, and ironist: it exposes the wantonness of the Law, and allows one to discover the laws of desire; it suggests that the Law itself may be inseparable from the operations of desire. When Bracy the Bard hears the Baron's deathly matin bell, he declares, "So let it knell!"–

> There is no lack of such, I ween,
> As well fill up the space between.
> In Langdale Pike and Witch's Lair,
> And Dungeon-ghyll so foully rent,
> With ropes of rock and bells of air
> Three sinful sextons' ghosts are pent,
> Who all give back, one after t'other,

The death-note to their living brother;
And oft too, by the knell offended,
Just as their one! two! three! is ended,
The devil mocks the doleful tale
With a merry peal from Borodale.

(ll. 348–59)

Bracy's accession echoes Christabel's words at the end of Part I, when she announces her obedience to Geraldine's request: "So let it be!" (l. 235). Bracy is in league with the hysteric, and Coleridge with them all – and all submit to the Law. When Christabel steals into her father's house with Geraldine, we "cannot tell" if her silence is the absolute solicitude of a dutiful daughter or a sign of subversive intent: does hysteria come from too much or too little respect for the father? In a sense it doesn't matter, since the effects are the same for the Baron and us: her very unreadability draws out and mocks his and our possessing desire to decide meaning. Her strategy resembles Bracy's – apparently without doing anything himself, he simply "lets" the Law mock its own voice. It echoes through hollow, rent spaces, which in dutifully returning its knell, elude its efforts to control the significance of an event. "Telling" notes become the occasion of ghostly echoes, which in turn generate Bracy's lively ghost stories; finally, as if by way of commentary, the "devil" makes merry mockery of the whole phenomenon. The passage describes in little the narrative tactics of "Christabel." By too-dutiful accession to the laws of gender and genre, "Christabel" exposes their strategies to view, letting the Law subvert itself.

NOTES

1 Quotations from "Christabel" and its preface are taken from EHC.
2 See Luther (1976) for the argument that Christabel is a reader of romances.
3 Tomlinson (1973) 235; Adair (1967) 146.
4 Burton (1977) 416. Future references to this edition appear in the text.
5 In "Sir Cauline," the ballad from which Coleridge took the name Christabel, this is the case: that Christabel's lover is dismissed by her father.
6 See, e.g., Basler (1948) 41; Enscoe (1967) 44–5; Spatz (1975) 112–13; Schapiro (1983) 61–85.
7 See, e.g., Enscoe (1967) 43; Beer (1977) 187; and Piper (1978) 216–27.
8 Or so Freud claims, Freud (1963) 159–80.
9 For examples of the reviews, see Reiman, *Romantics Reviewed* (1977) ii. 666, 239. Modern critics sometimes notice tonal or generic instability as "falls" into Gothic trickery, into caricature of the Gothic, or into sentimentality; see e.g., Schulz (1963) 66–71; and Edwards and Emslie (1971) 328. The latter suggest these discrepancies are intended to shock.
10 Reiman, *Romantics Reviewed* (1977) i. 23.

11 Reiman, *Romantics Reviewed* (1977) i. 373; ii. 866; ii. 531. I discuss these reviews more fully in Swann (1985).
12 Reiman, *Romantics Reviewed* (1977) ii. 531.
13 Griggs iii. 435.
14 See, e.g., Delson (1980); and Enscoe (1967) 46.
15 My understanding of fantasy here follows that of Laplanche and Pontalis (1968).
16 My argument here is indebted to Richard Rand's discussion of the ubiquitous "mark" in "Geraldine," Rand (1978).

Shelley

7

Adonais: Shelley's Consumption of Keats

JAMES A. W. HEFFERNAN

"Does Shelley go on telling strange Stories of the Death of Kings? Tell him there are stran[ge] Stories of the Death of Poets. . . ,"[1] So wrote Keats to Leigh Hunt in 1817, four years before his own death prompted Shelley to write one of the most remarkable elegies in English literature. *Adonais* is remarkable not simply because it at once reflects and transforms the whole tradition of pastoral elegy from Moschus and Bion to Spenser and Milton, but also because its point of departure is a singularly strange story about the cause of Keats's death. No one now believes this story, but critics normally assume that Shelley did, that he simply took into his poem what had been given to him as a fact. The story that Keats's death was precipitated by a harsh review of *Endymion* provides, says Ross Woodman, the "literal or historical level" on which Shelley builds his visionary poem.[2] But when the "literal or historical level" is itself a piece of fiction, it should be much more thoroughly examined than it has been up to now. Careful scrutiny will show that Shelley himself invented the strange story of Keats's death. It will also allow us to see that in generating *Adonais* from that story, Shelley consumes as well as re-creates the personality of Keats.

I

The difficulty of isolating that personality from Shelley's version of it – or vision of it – is illustrated by Earl Wasserman's observation that "the skeletal form of the Adonis legend provided a nearly exact means of translating Keats's biography into a conceptual pattern."[3] In one sense Wasserman is right. The story of a promising young poet slain by the malice of critics could be readily translated into the story of the youthful Adonis slain by an evil beast. But when Wasserman speaks of the poem as a translation of Keats's "biography," to what biography does he refer? In the spring of 1821, when Shelley wrote *Adonais*, there was none worthy of the name. There were merely a few facts and a number of rumors, and it was Shelley himself who created the most notorious rumor of all. Careful examination of the evidence will reveal that, beyond any reasonable doubt, the strange story of Keats's assassination is merely the first of the fictions with which Shelley deliberately consumed the facts of Keats's life.

This particular fiction was based on a purely second-hand knowledge of Keats's last years. The last that Shelley ever saw of Keats was in the winter of 1818, three years before his death.[4] In July 1820, when Shelley was in Pisa, a letter from John Gisborne brought him news that Keats had burst a blood vessel and was seriously ill with consumption.[5] When Shelley then wrote solicitously to Keats and invited him to come to Pisa, Keats sent his thanks, but indicated that he might not be able to come, and in fact never did come, going instead to Rome, where he died on 23 February, 1821.[6] In place of himself he asked John and Maria Gisborne to bring Shelley his words: a letter and the newly published volume of his poems – *Lamia, Isabella, The Eve of St. Agnes and Other Poems.* Yet it was not from Keats's words that Shelley constructed his version of Keats's ending. On the one hand, with no authorization from Keats, the publishers' "Advertisement" to the new volume apologized for the unfinished state of *Hyperion* by saying that "the reception given to [*Endymion*] discouraged the author from proceeding."[7] On the other hand, Gisborne's letter told Shelley that Keats had burst a blood vessel. After Keats's death, this piece of information gave Shelley the means to literalize the metaphor merely implied by the "Advertisement": the criticism of *Endymion* had killed not merely Keats's ambition, but Keats himself.

To see just how much of Shelley's imagination went into this literalization of a metaphor, we have only to compare what he knew about Keats with what he says about him in his letters and in the Preface to *Adonais*. Shelley knew, first of all, that nearly two years separated the appearance of the reviews of *Endymion* from the bursting of Keats's blood vessel. There were three harsh reviews of *Endymion*, but the only one Shelley cared about appeared in the April 1818 issue of the *Quarterly Review*, belatedly published on 27 September (Bate 366). Since Shelley describes the language of this review in a letter (Jones ii. 252), he must have seen it for himself and must have known at least the approximate date of its appearance. He must also have known the approximate if not the exact date of what he called Keats's "dangerous accident" (Jones ii. 220), since he would surely have learned this from Gisborne's letter or from the Gisbornes in person when they came to Italy in October.[8] Finally, the new volume of Keats's poetry which the Gisbornes brought for him clearly showed that Keats had remained vigorously productive long after the reviews of *Endymion* appeared. Shelley had no way of knowing that the publishers' statement about the effect of the reviews on the writing of *Hyperion* was a lie, and he believed it.[9] But even if the statement were true, even if Keats had managed to write all of *Hyperion* by September 1818, when the *Quarterly's* review of *Endymion* supposedly stopped him, he could hardly have written the entire 1820 volume by that time.[10] Nevertheless, Shelley repeatedly implies in his letters and in the Preface to *Adonais* that the *Quarterly's* review of *Endymion* had left Keats scarcely able to write anything at all.

To read Shelley's statements about Keats's condition is to see a mounting insistence on the suddenness with which the *Quarterly's* review incapacitated him. In Shelley's first known statement about the matter, made in a letter probably written in late October or November 1820, he says, "Poor Keats was thrown into a dreadful state of mind by [the *Quarterly's* review of *Endymion*]. . . . The first effects are described to me to have resembled insanity, & it was by assiduous watching that he was restrained from effecting purposes of suicide. The agony of his sufferings *at length* produced the rupture of a blood vessel in the lungs, & the usual process of consumption appears to have begun."[11] In the second version of the story, which appears in a letter of 17 April, 1821 to Byron, the somewhat protracted process first described is accelerated: "Young Keats," he writes, ". . . died lately at Rome from the consequences of breaking a blood-vessel, in paroxysms of despair at the contemptuous attack on his book in the *Quarterly Review*" (Jones ii. 284). Then, when Byron asks if the story is *"actually"* true," Shelley insists that it is, and accelerates it further. "Hunt tells me," he writes, "that in the *first paroxysms* of his disappointment [Keats] burst a blood-vessel; and thus laid the foundation of a *rapid* consumption."[12]

This last statement is not only inconsistent with the first one, which speaks of a delayed effect; it is also utterly incompatible with what Shelley knew, since a blood vessel that broke in June 1820 cannot possibly have done so "in the first paroxysms" of disappointment over reviews that appeared in September 1818. Furthermore, Shelley's version of what Hunt told him has no relation to what Hunt actually told him. On 12 November, 1818, soon after seeing the *Quarterly's* review of *Endymion* and Keats himself, with whom he undoubtedly discussed it, Hunt wrote Shelley that "they [i.e., the *Quarterly*] have now been abusing Keats at a furious rate," but there is no reference to anything like "paroxysms of despair" in Keats himself. On the contrary, Hunt says only that "it is pleasant, on many accounts, to see how public disgust is increasing against them [the *Quarterly*] every day."[13]

No one can ever know, of course, exactly what Shelley may have been told about Keats and the *Quarterly* in letters now lost or in unrecorded conversations. But nothing that Shelley is known to have learned from others supports his story, and some of what he is known to have learned contradicts it. Furthermore, in telling and re-telling his story about Keats, Shelley willfully ignored what Keats himself had shown him during their brief exchange of letters in the summer of 1820.

As already noted, Shelley wrote to Keats on 27 July, 1820, after learning from John Gisborne that Keats had burst a blood vessel and was seriously ill. Whatever Gisborne said in his no longer extant letter, Shelley's letter gives not the slightest hint that he sees any connection between Keats's present illness and the *Quarterly*'s review of *Endymion* – though Shelley speaks of both the illness and the poem. Indeed, if Shelley ever really believed that Keats could have been fatally wounded by negative reviews of *Endymion*, it is strange that his own letter to a Keats whom he knew to be seriously ill should itself have included criticism of that poem. Shelley speaks of its "treasures," yet also calls them "treasures poured forth with indistinct profusion," which "people in general will not endure."[14] Shelley thus presumes that Keats could take criticism without flinching, could recognize the defects of his own early work and grow beyond them. And in fact Keats did recognize those defects – as he plainly shows in his response of 16 August, 1820 to Shelley's letter. In a free spirit of critical give-and-take, Keats expresses his reaction to *Cenci* by first of all urging Shelley to "curb your magnanimity and be more of an artist, and 'load every rift' of your subject with ore" (Rollins ii 323). But Keats no sooner gives this advice than he catches himself in the irony of doing so: "And is not this extraordina[r]y talk for the writer of Endymion? whose mind was like a pack of scattered cards – I am pick'd up and sorted to a pip. My Imagination is a Monastery and I am its Monk – you must explain my metap^cs to yourself" (Rollins ii 323).

The metaphysics is not very deep, and Shelley was quite capable of fathoming it. The poet who urges self-discipline upon Shelley can plainly perceive the lack of it in his own *Endymion*, and can also remember – as he goes on to say – that Shelley himself advised him not to publish his "first-blights."[15] But the scattered cards of his mind, he says, are now picked up and sorted; he has renounced luxurious extravagance in favor of monastic self-control. With characteristic playfulness, Keats shows that he has withstood the reviewers, that his declining health has nothing to do with them, and that he is more than ever in charge of his own mind.[16] In fact, it was only this steadfast self-possession that enabled him to begin work on *Hyperion* and thus to produce the fragment that Shelley describes in the Preface to *Adonais* as "second to nothing that was ever produced by a writer of the same years."[17]

Yet this same Preface tells us of a pathetically vulnerable mind – a mind so uncontrolled that it could be fatally agitated by a single review. Keats's genius, wrote Shelley,

> was not less delicate and fragile than it was beautiful; and where cankerworms abound, what wonder if its young flower was blighted in

the bud? The savage criticism on his *Endymion*, which appeared in the *Quarterly Review*, produced the most violent effect on his susceptible mind; the agitation thus originated ended in the ruture of a blood-vessel in the lungs; a rapid consumption ensued, and the succeeding acknowledgements from more candid critics, of the true greatness of his powers, were ineffectual to heal the wound thus wantonly inflicted. (*SPP* 390–1)

Enough has been said, I think, to show that this strange story of Keats's death was deliberately fabricated by Shelley. But it is not only a fabrication; it is also an insult. Even before *Adonais* was published, Byron saw that Shelley's story about Keats – if true – showed him to be little more than a feckless narcissist: a man of "inordinate self-love" and without, Byron clearly implies, "powers of *resistance*."[18] The crucial question raised by the Preface to *Adonais*, then, is why Shelley paints this picture: why does he slander Keats in the very act of seeking to defend him against slander?

II

Part of the answer to this question can of course be found in Shelley's long-smoldering feud with Robert Southey, the once radical older poet who had long since turned conservative and who in 1813 had been granted the Laureateship for his pains. Kenneth Neill Cameron long ago showed that although Southey at first befriended and encouraged the younger poet, he antagonized Shelley by covertly attacking his radicalism in the January 1817 issue of the *Quarterly Review*.[19] When Shelley was thereafter slurred in the *Quarterly*'s review of Hunt's *Foliage* (issue of January 1818) and then personally vilified in its review of his own *Revolt of Islam* (issue of April 1819), he incorrectly assumed each time that Southey was the reviewer, and in June 1820, he wrote Southey directly to ask him about the authorship of the second review.[20] Though Southey denied authorship, Shelley's request led to a bitter exchange in which Southey accused him of causing the destruction of his first wife, who had committed suicide in 1816.[21] Shelley never answered this accusation directly, but the letter which conveyed it probably reached him in October 1820, the same month in which he received Keats's last volume from the Gisbornes and doubtless spoke with them about Keats's "dangerous accident." After reading the volume, Shelley then wrote to William Gifford, Editor of the *Quarterly*, a letter in which his long-standing resentment of the *Quarterly*'s attacks upon him first found an outlet in a counter-attack upon it for its maltreatment of Keats.

Self-defeatingly argued, at once barbed and imploring, this letter was apparently never sent. Though Shelley is seeking Gifford's support for Keats's new volume, he begins by calling attention to the *Quarterly*'s "slanderous" attack upon himself; and though he admits that *Endymion* was "defective, & that perhaps it deserved as much censure as the pages of your review record against it," he charges that the *Quarterly*'s review of *Endymion* has made Keats critically ill (Jones ii. 251–2). Southey is not mentioned in this letter, but Shelley's newly exacerbated hatred of him was by now virtually one with his hatred of the *Quarterly*. A few months later, Keats's death gave Shelley the means to express both hatreds publicly in *Adonais* and its Preface, to denounce the *Quarterly* for its "savage criticism" of Keats, and to single out Southey – without mentioning him by name – as Keats's "murderer."[22] In this way, Shelley could at last gain fit revenge for the repeated attacks upon him in the *Quarterly* and for Southey's accusation that he had destroyed his first wife.[23]

Yet it is not enough to say that the facts of Keats's life and death were consumed by Shelley's quest for revenge. Shelley also wished to project onto Keats the vulnerability he felt in himself, and thus to resolve the profound ambivalence with which he regarded the delicacy of his own idealism. The ambivalence is evident in poems such as "Ode to the West Wind," where the speaker represents himself as both the pathetically fragile victim of a crucifying world ("I fall upon the thorns of life! I bleed!") and as the resounding voice of a "Spirit fierce," a spirit "tameless, and swift, and proud." In *Adonais* itself, Shelley presents himself among the mourners as a "frail Form," a dying lamp, a falling shower, a breaking billow, a bacchant holding the thyrsus with a weak and shaking hand, and a stricken deer – in short, as "a Power / Girt round with weakness" (ll. 271–97). Yet as Ross Woodman has recently argued, this picture of helpless vulnerability is not so much an idealized self-portrait as the parody of a posture which Shelley seeks to shed.[24]

In the unsent letter to Gifford – the letter in which Shelley invents his story of Keats – the first thing Shelley does is to assert his own invulnerability. After flatly declaring, "I never notice anonymous attacks," he proceeds to complain about the latest one, and to say that in respect to its author, "I am there sitting where he durst not soar –" (Jones ii. 251). Shelley alludes, of course, to Milton's Satan, who, when caught in Paradise by the angels Ithuriel and Zephon, denounces them for failing to recognize a being once "sitting where ye durst not soar."[25] In thus comparing himself to Satan at his most disdainful, Shelley implicitly attributes to himself the "energy and magnificence" that he explicitly attributes to Milton's Satan in the "Defence of Poetry" (*SPP* 498), written just a few months after the letter to Gifford. But having asserted his own majestic invulnerability, Shelley goes on to say, "That case is different with the unfortunate subject of this letter, the Author of Endymion, to whose feelings & situation I intreat you to allow me to call your attention" (Jones ii. 252). In this first picture of the word-stricken Keats, Shelley begins to create a victim for whom he could solicit the pity that he, like Satan, at once desired and disdained for himself. In *Adonais*, therefore, the strength of character that Keats revealed even in his own letter to Shelley had to be consumed by the weakness projected onto him. To Byron Shelley wrote of the poem: "I need not be told that I have been carried too far by the enthusiasm of the moment: by my piety, and my indignation, in panegyric. But if I have erred, I console myself by reflecting that it is in defence of the weak – not in conjunction with the powerful" (Jones ii. 308).

Defender of the weak is the role Shelley assumes, and that is why he first of all seeks to establish the fragility of Keats in the Preface of the poem. Even in the last paragraph of the Preface, which was based on Robert Finch's account of Keats's final months, Shelley makes no mention of the extraordinary vigor that Finch says Keats displayed in this period.[26] Shelley's celebration of Keats required a poet weak enough to have been killed by the words of a reviewer so that he might be resurrected by the words of Shelley, whose elegy would be a sublime *reviewing*, a visionary transformation of the pastoral dreamer into a Miltonic genius, and hence a demonstration of Shelley's own power. If there is indeed something that does not displease us in the misfortunes even of our dearest friends, the death of one who never quite became his friend could not have been entirely displeasing to Shelley. It gave him the chance not only to get vicarious revenge for the injuries that reviewers had done to him, but also to consume Keats in a myth of his own re-making.

III

The consumption begins with Shelley's portrayal of Keats as scarcely more than a victim in the first half of the poem. Shelley's model for this portrayal was of course the ancient Greek "Lament for Adonis," attributed to Bion, but given the ways in which other poets had used the story of this lament, Shelley's version of it significantly emphasizes the vulnerability of the central figure. In the original "Lament," Adonis is simply a fair and reckless hunter who has fatally pitted himself against a boar.[27] In Renaissance versions of the myth, the hunter is explicitly well-armed: Shakespeare's Adonis runs upon the boar with a sharp spear (*Venus and Adonis*, l. 1120), and in Spenser's elegy for Sidney, which had a demonstrable influence on Shelley's elegy for Keats, Astrophel does considerable damage with spear and sword before he is fatally gored.[28] But Shelley's Adonis is not so much a hunter as a defenseless child: "Oh gentle child, beautiful as thou wert," says Urania in stanza 27,

> Why didst thou leave the trodden paths of men
> Too soon, and with weak hands though mighty heart

Dare the unpastured dragon in his den?
Defenceless as thou wert, oh where was then
Wisdom the mirrored shield, or scorn the spear?
Or hadst thou waited the full cycle, when
Thy spirit should have filled its crescent sphere
The monsters of life's waste had fled from thee like deer.

(ll. 235–43)

In the very next stanza this weaponless child is implicitly compared with Byron, "the Pythian of the age," who at his foes "one arrow sped / And smiled!" (ll. 249–51). Thus Shelley intimates that if Keats had waited before publishing his first long poem, he could have vanquished his detractors as Byron did his. But Shelley must have known that Byron too was young – just twenty-one in fact – when he published *English Bards and Scotch Reviewers* (the "arrow"); and though Shelley apparently thought that Keats was only twenty when *Endymion* appeared, he had no grounds for believing there was any substantial difference between the ages at which Keats and Byron published their two poems.[29] In these two stanzas, then, the facts about Keats and Byron and the details of a myth which Shelley inherited through the Renaissance are alike consumed by his desire to make Keats powerless.

As pure victim, as a weak and immature child, Adonais embodies the very antithesis of that epic-making power which Keats demonstrated in *Hyperion* and for which Shelley salutes him in the Preface. The poem itself implicitly affirms this power but explicitly denies it. By representing Keats as the beloved son of Urania, Shelley implicitly compares him to Milton, who made Urania his muse in *Paradise Lost*, who is "third among the sons of light" in a procession presumably headed by Homer and Dante, and who is now to be followed by Keats.[30] But there is nothing epic-making about the figure Shelley gives us. The poem ostensibly written to celebrate the powers of Keats's maturity is at once repressive and regressive, turning the muse of *Paradise Lost* into the mother of apprentice verse, turning epic ambition into pastoral reverie.[31]

Significantly, the mood of pastoral reverie is reinforced by the way in which Shelley uses Keats's own poetry. Shelley nowhere alludes to *Hyperion*, the one and only poem of Keats he unequivocally admired. His only indisputable allusions are to poems he thought defective or weak, such as *Endymion*, which furnishes some of the imagery used in the description of the hovering Dreams (ll. 73–108), and *Isabella*, which supplies the mawkish image of the pale flower nourished by the maiden's tears (ll. 48–9).[32] But the most revealing of Shelley's allusions to Keats's poetry are those he seems to make to a poem now firmly established as one of Keats's greatest: "Ode to a Nightingale."

I say "seems" because we cannot be sure that Shelley is thinking of

Keats's ode – which he nowhere explicitly commends – when he says to Adonais in stanza 17: "Thy spirit's sister, the lorn nightingale / Mourns not her mate with such melodious pain / ... / As Albion wails for thee" (ll. 145–151). In his painstaking commentary on *Adonais*, Earl Wasserman glosses this passage without even mentioning Keats's ode, tracing Shelley's language solely to Bion's "Lament," which speaks of "nightingales that in the thick foliage complain" as birds "whom once he pleasured, once taught to sing."[33] Nevertheless, Shelley's reference to the nightingale as "lorn" may certainly be read as an echo of Keats's "forlorn": a word that is itself echoed within Keats's poem to link the end of stanza 7 ("fairy lands forlorn") with the opening of stanza 8 ("Forlorn!").[34] In Shelley's poem the "lorn" applied to the nightingale in stanza 17 (l. 145) likewise echoes the "lorn" applied to the Urania in stanza 2, where she is said to be sitting "mid listening Echoes" while one of them "with soft enamoured breath, / Rekindled all the fading melodies" sung by the now departed Keats (ll. 12–18).

Ross Woodman has recently argued that the one rekindling those melodies is Shelley. The "soft enamoured breath" (l. 15) rising up to Urania in her "secret Paradise" (l. 208), he says, corresponds to the "quiet breath" with which Keats in the Ode calls "easeful Death / ... soft names in many a mused rhyme" (ll. 52–4). Such a song cannot be understood by Shelley's Urania, who is not the heavenly muse of Milton's poem but the earthly Venus Genetrix, who is "Chained to time" (l. 234). Woodman therefore reads Shelley's song as a transformation of Keats's, which acknowledges the mortality of the singer even as it proclaims the immortality of the bird. By contrast, Shelley's song places Keats in a timeless realm beyond the time-full world to which Shelley's "lorn Urania" and his "lorn nightingale" are both inescapably bound (Woodman (1978) 63–70).

Essentially, this reading reinforces that of Wasserman, who says that Shelley's "lorn nightingale" represents the earthly poet singing in "the night of time" as distinct from the eternal spirit that emerges in the latter part of the poem (p. 490). But what then are we to make of stanza 42, where Shelley says that Adonais "is made one with nature" and that his voice is heard "in all her music, from the moan / Of thunder, to the song of night's sweet bird" (ll. 371–2)? If Keats's "immortal Bird" becomes a creature who simply signifies the "night of time," the alter ego of a Urania who herself embodies the temporality of nature, how can Keats's immortality be defined in terms of an *identification* with nature and with the sweet bird of night?

A possible answer is provided by stanza 43, where Shelley says that Adonais "doth bear / His part, while the one Spirit's plastic stress / Sweeps through the dull dense world" and irresistibly transforms everything to "its own likeness" (ll. 380–5). Thus Adonais' identification with nature might really be understood as nature's identification with him, or more precisely with a spiritual power that "shapes the Many," as Wasserman says (p. 498).

But whether Adonais is made one with nature or nature is made one with spiritualized power, Keats is merely a part or "portion" of this oneness (l. 379); his particular identity is consumed by it.

To represent Keats as the singer whose voice is blended with that of "night's sweet bird" is not to rekindle Keats's song but to quench its distinctive fire. When Woodman refers to Keats's ode as itself a "plaintive anthem" (Woodman (1978) 68), he confuses the song of the bird with the poet's response to it. The two are not the same. Keats's ode fundamentally questions the possibility of an identification even as it tempts us to believe in it. "Plaintive anthem" is the phrase Keats uses to describe the song of the nightingale in the final stanza of the poem (l. 75), where he projects on to the bird the sense of forlornness that he himself feels at the fading of a song that seemed at first happy and full of summer in its theme. The radical shift in his descriptive terms suggests that he is not so much taking part in the bird's existence – in the words of his well-known letter to Bailey (Rollins i. 186) – as he is making us conscious of his own. Keats knows, in fact, that the sound of the nightingale's song depends on the mood of the listener,[35] and it is chiefly his own mood that concerns him. Indeed, for all the poet's aspiration to union with the bird, the "Ode to a Nightingale" is ultimately a song of himself, of what Randel calls his own "irrevocably separate consciousness" (Randel (1982) 54), of his resistance to absorption by nature or by the song of the bird and most especially by the very thing that Shelley regards as the gateway to transcendence: death. In the world of Keats's ode, to die is to become not a god but a sod.

Embedded in the ode, then, is an unflinching recognition of the price to be paid for the very absorption that its speaker longs to experience by fading away with the bird into the "forest dim." He is "half in love with easeful Death" because it constitutes what Randel calls "the ultimate subtraction from consciousness," the apparent fulfillment of the wish "to approximate nature's pre-conscious unity with itself" (pp. 54, 52). Yet paradoxically, the very numbness that would initiate him into this preconscious state – the "drowsy numbness" of the ode's opening line – is not a relief from pain (the very essence of physiological numbness) but a cause of it. "My heart aches, and the drowsy numbness *pains* / My sense" (italics mine). The loss of sentience, even the loss of the capacity to feel pain, is at once seductive and painful to contemplate.

To be consumed by nature, therefore, or even by a "one" that subsumes nature, is the very last fate Keats would have wished for himself. He knew only too well that he could not escape pain without losing consciousness, nor again consciousness without experience of pain. It is striking to note that the fragment of *Hyperion* for which Shelley expresses so much admiration in the Preface to *Adonais* ends with a kind of death radically different from the "easeful Death" half-heartedly invoked in "Ode to a Nightingale" and sympathetically imputed to Keats in stanza 40 of *Adonais*, where Shelley imagines that "Envy and calumny and hate and pain, / And that unrest which men miscall delight, / Can touch him not and torture not again" (ll. 353–5). The death experienced by Keats's Apollo at the termination of *Hyperion* is not this transcendence of all suffering but precisely its opposite: a painful birth of consciousness, a sudden comprehension of "agonies,/Creations and destroyings," a process

> Most like the struggle at the gate of death;
> Or liker still to one who should take leave
> Of pale immortal death, and with a pang
> As hot as death's is chill, with fierce convulse
> Die into life.
>
> (iii. 126–30)

Truncated though it is, the ending of Keats's *Hyperion* unmistakably reveals a conviction that would permeate all of his writing and poetry to come. By late March 1819, when he wrote the lines on Apollo's agonizing birth, he had come to believe that pain was the very condition of consciousness, identity, and life itself. It is startling to see that in writing of "soul-Making" on 21 April, 1819, Keats at once anticipates and repudiates the pain-transcending form in which *Adonais* will cast his immortality. Shelley represents the soul of Keats as an intense and glowing atom that is quenched in death (ll. 179–80), and then, in a radical shift of vision, as a pure spirit flowing "Back to the burning Fountain whence it came / A portion of the Eternal, which must glow / Through time and change, unquenchably the same" (ll. 339–41). But in the "soul-Making" passage, Keats uses comparable terms for children who die without ever forging an identity in the crucible of pain. God, says Keats, makes intelligences from "sparks" of his own essence, the counterpart of Shelley's glowing atoms. But when a child dies, "the Spark or intelligence returns to God [Shelley's burning fountain] without any identity" and hence without any soul because it has not experienced the "World of Pains and troubles" that is required to form one (Rollins ii. 102–3). In Keats's eyes, pain not only generated identity but sustained it. The ambivalence with which the speaker of the "Nightingale" regards the prospect of an "easeful Death" in May of 1819 can be heard still more poignantly in September 1820 from a Keats now fatally wracked with tuberculosis. "I wish for death every day and night to deliver me from these pains, and then I wish death away, for death would destroy even those pains which are better than nothing" (Rollins ii. 345).

Nevertheless, the question raised by Keats's own "Nightingale" is whether or not death can be turned into life, and the language in which *Adonais* says that it can partly echoes the ending of Keats's ode: "Fled is that vision: Do

I wake or sleep?" Destabilizing the conventional meaning of the contrast between "wake" and "sleep," Keats's question implies or at least raises the possibility that real wakefulness can be experienced only in the midst of dream-like vision, while the act of waking from such a vision may be really a way of putting the imagination to sleep. A similar reversal marks the turning point of *Adonais*, where the prostrate pastoral dreamer becomes the soaring imperishable spirit, or where – as Wasserman has argued – "the season–God Adonis becomes the Hebrew Adonai, symbol of mind and spirit, God of the resurrection" (p. 475). In the pivotal stanza of Shelley's poem, Adonais "wakes *or* sleeps with the enduring dead" (l. 336, italics mine); in stanza 39, "he is not dead, he doth not sleep – / He hath awakened from the dream of life" (ll. 343–4); and in stanza 41, "He lives, he wakes" (l. 361). Shelley thus seems to proclaim the resurrection of Keats in Keats's own language.

But the resurrection Shelley proclaims for Keats is not a dying into life. It is a merging into the "One" that consumes individual entities even as it consumes individual colors, blending them all into the undifferentiated "white radiance of Eternity" (l. 464). Furthermore, the way in which this oneness consumes the identity of Keats is anticipated by the way in which a merely possible allusion to the last line of Keats's "Ode to a Nightingale" is overpowered – in stanza 38 – by an unmistakable allusion to *Paradise Lost*. In this crucial stanza, Keats is resurrected not so much by the power of his own language as by the rhetoric of Milton's Satan: by a language Shelley uses to make Keats embody the Satanic disdain with which Shelley regarded his detractors. To grasp the full complexity of stanza 38, we must realize that it speaks at once to two different audiences: to Keats's unnamed detractor, who has just been denounced in stanza 37, and to the presumably sympathetic reader:

> Nor let us weep that our delight is fled
> Far from these carrion kites that scream below;
> He wakes or sleeps with the enduring dead;
> Thou canst not soar where he is sitting now.

> (ll. 334–7)

The fourth line of this stanza is doubly arresting. Besides alluding to Milton, it creates a sudden shift in audience. The first three lines speak to the sympathetic reader *about* Keats and his detractors; the fourth line speaks *to* the detractor who has just been denounced, but whom Shelley cannot relinquish or forget. Thus Shelley's joyous vision of a resurrected and glorified Keats includes a counter-vision of a condemned reviewer, a day of retribution for Keats's enemy, whose cold embers – in the very last line of this crucial stanza – "choke the sordid hearth of shame."

Yet the superficial orthodoxy in this pattern of reward and punishment is radically undermined when we recognize in Shelley's fourth line an allusion not merely to Milton, but to Milton's Satan, and to the very line with which Shelley expressed his majestic disdain of reviewers in the unsent letter to Gifford. Here this majestic disdain is transferred to the resurrected figure of Keats, who thus becomes a Shelleyan version of Milton's Satan.

The epic defiance of Milton's Satan, then, is invoked precisely at the turning point of the poem, the moment when its pastoral vision of Keats as the fragile and dreaming shepherd turns into an epic vision of the heroic and cosmic voyager, the Luciferian star who rises rather than falls, who is not cast down into the penal fire of hell but rather drawn up into the burning fountain of an eternal light which will beckon to Shelley in the very last valedictory stanza of the poem, where Shelley himself becomes the Luciferian voyager borne darkly and fearfully afar. Yet Milton shadows this light even as he gives Shelley the language with which to glimpse it. Yearning to celebrate the epic-making power promised but still not realized in *Hyperion*, Shelley borrows the muse who inspired *Paradise Lost* and puts her into a pastoral poem, the form in which the epic-poet-to-be traditionally serves his apprenticeship and of course the form in which Milton has served his. Curiously, there is no definite allusion to *Lycidas* in Shelley's poem or in the epigraphic procession of the literary mourners who come before it: Plato, Bion, and Moschus. But the ghostly figure of the pastoral Milton takes his invisible place in that procession, even as the epic-making Milton takes his visible place in the fourth stanza of the poem. Milton encompasses both the pastoral beginning and the epic and between which the infinitely elastic identity of Keats is stretched to the vanishing point.

IV

For Milton, *Lycidas* was the conversion of an end into a beginning, of one poet's death into the birth of another who confidently looks forward at the end of his elegy to fresh woods, and pastures new. For Shelley, *Adonais* is the conversion of the beginning into the end. Shelley seeks not only to envision the fulfillment of the epic promise made by the fragmentary *Hyperion* but also to construct a destiny and destination for himself. The long journey Milton makes from *Lycidas* to *Paradise Lost* becomes in *Adonais* a giant leap from the pastoral of the opening stanzas to the apocalypse of the closing one. Thus, even as the pastoral framework of *Adonais* splits open to reveal an epic vision, the massy earth and sphered skies are in the final stanza "riven" to reveal eternity.

To move from time to eternity is to move from absence to presence, from that which ceases to be to that which is. Shelley begins and ends his elegy with the present tense. In the opening line, he weeps; in the closing line, he is beckoned to an abode "where the Eternal are." But while the present tense of the closing line is at least putatively fixed, the present tense of the opening one is really a passing tense. When Shelley says, "I weep for Adonais," the *I* who weeps has already been displaced by an *I* who writes, and writes in the knowledge that grief itself is mortal, as we are told in stanza 21.

Shelley seeks, then, to convert the passing moment into a moment of passage, the fictive present into the fixed present of eternity, the absent Keats for whom he vainly waited in Pisa into a starry presence that unchangingly awaits him in the sphere of Venus. But the cost of admission to this sphere is a radical transformation of Keats's identity. To reach the place where "Envy and calumny and hate and pain / ... / Can touch him not and torture not again" (ll. 353–5), Keats must *be* tortured by Shelley. From the Greek Adonis to the Hebrew Adonai, from dying god to undying God, from the frail and helpless dreamer to the king of thought, from the pastoral vision to the epic one, from Moschus to Milton, Keats's identity is consumed and recreated by "the one Spirit's plastic stress" that sweeps through it, "torturing the unwilling dross that checks its flight / To its own likeness" (ll. 384–5).

The counterpart of changelessness in time is oneness in space: "the One remains, the many change and pass" (l. 460). As white radiance consumes individual colors, the One consumes individual identities, the separate manifestations of passing moments. It consumes even the identity of Keats, who in a famous letter to Richard Woodhouse said – or seemed to say – that he had no identity at all, who distinguished himself from the Wordsworthian or egotistical sublime by saying that the poetical character in him "is not itself – it has no self – it is every thing and nothing..." (Rollins i. 387). Yet even as he defines himself in opposition to the egotistical sublime, Keats here reveals his own ego, a chameleonic personality whose very life is bound up with the changing colors of its infinitely various moods and ambitions.[36] These are what the One consumes as ambition gives way to submission, and Shelley's original command to weep becomes the ultimate imperative: "Die, / If thou wouldst be with that which thou dost seek!" (ll. 464–5).

Having turned Keats into an artifice of eternity, Shelley longs to be gathered into it himself. Like the command to weep, the command to die is addressed to himself as much as to the reader. The poem that set out to consume a victim of consumption ends by consuming its own author, who offers himself to the fiery light which "now beams on me, / Consuming the last clouds of cold mortality" (ll. 485–6). Yet the prophesied death of Shelley's mortal self leads to a transfiguration that precisely reverses what he has done to Keats. While Keats's epic ambition has been regressively turned into a pastoral dream which is then consumed by the One, flowing "back to the burning fountain whence it came" (l. 339), Shelley turns himself from a frail phantom into an heroic voyager. Though he first represents himself among the mourners as a figure of pathetic weakness, the double of the "defenceless" child he mourns (l. 239), stanzas 31–4 reveal a crucial difference between the two. Adonais was a flower nipped in bloom, a "broken lily" (ll. 48–54); his mourner is considerably stronger. Of his own power he asks, "Is it now broken?" (l. 286) and then answers:

> On the withering flower
> The killing sun smiles brightly: on a cheek
> The life can burn in blood, while the heart may break.
>
> (ll. 286–8)

Here Shelley significantly echoes the way Byron had earlier defined his own capacity to endure the pain of mourning: "And thus the heart will break, yet brokenly live on" (*Childe Harold's Pilgrimage* iii. 32). Shelley thus begins to disclose the resilience and the tenacity which, he clearly believed, distinguished him and Byron from delicate plants like Keats.[37] The succeeding stanzas underscore this difference. While Shelley describes Keats in the Preface to *Adonais* as the victim of a "poisoned shaft" (*SPP* 391), he represents himself as a suffering *survivor*, a deer "struck by the hunter's dart" (l. 297) but not killed by it, a figure branded like Cain or bloodied like Christ (ll. 305–6) but not destroyed. This implicit determination to endure and triumph over his persecutors becomes explicit in stanza 38, where – as we have seen – it is momentarily projected onto a Keats who is made to embody Shelley's own Satanic disdain. But Shelley goes on to recover this projection for himself. In the end it is he – not Keats – who becomes the epic voyager, sailing not *to* earth, as Milton's Satan did, but *from* it:

> The breath whose might I have invoked in song
> Descends on me: my spirit's bark is driven;
> Far from the shore, far from the trembling throng
> Whose sails were never to the tempest given;
> The massy earth and sphered skies are riven!
> I am borne darkly, fearfully, afar:
> Whilst burning through the inmost veil of Heaven,
> The soul of Adonais, like a star,
> Beacons from the abode where the Eternal are.
>
> (ll. 487–95)

Ironically, Shelley's lines recall the mortal end of Lycidas even as they foretell his own. But Shelley will not be content with the posthumous status of Milton's character, who is translated to a heavenly version of the pastoral world which he has left and who becomes "the Genius of the shore" (l. 183), protector of those who sail. In Shelley's final stanza, the pastoral world has been utterly consumed; the earth and skies which enclose it are riven to reveal the starry soul of Adonais: the burning fountain in which the soul of Keats has been all but consumed.

Remarkably enough, however, the consumption is checked by the very last word of the poem, which implicitly re-individuates a personality earlier described as simply "a *portion* of the Eternal" (l. 340, italics mine). The Eternal One which has threatened to consume all identities becomes at last an Eternal many, a pantheon of apotheosized poets. Yet the effect of the final word is just barely to recover the identity of Keats. The star-like soul which beckons Shelley is the infinitely attenuated spirit of a spirit, something distilled from the "flowers of gentle breath" which Keats's leprous corpse exhaled and which were themselves "like incarnations of the stars" (ll. 172–4). Doubly deincarnated, Keats's soul has been virtually depersonalized as well, and even as he yearns for union with it, Shelley himself hesitates to share its fate. "What Adonais is," he asks, "why fear we to become?" (l. 455). The question is not merely rhetorical. We fear it because we – including the speaker, who is talking to himself quite as much as to us – fear the absorption of the many into the one, the annihilation of personal identity, the consumption of personality by impersonal essence – the transcendently inscrutable "what." Shelley is torn between the ambition to perpetuate his own identity as a poet and the desire for a Platonic oneness that consumes identity even as it putatively guarantees permanence. The mourner who earlier "in another's fate . . . wept his own" (l. 300) can now see in Keats's fate a state at once alluring and alarming: the prospect of immortal anonymity. It is the fear of this prospect that finally drives Shelley – borne darkly, fearfully afar – to pluralize "the Eternal" after first singularizing it, and thus to gratify at once his yearning for transcendence and his need for individuation. Shelley now sees that only by envisioning the survival of Keats's identity can he foresee the survival of his own, and hence the permanent achievement of a personal transcendence: a state of being to which his own detractors cannot soar. From the weeping of the first stanza to the lowering wind of the last one, the inexorable flow of the poem has carried its subject, its speaker, and even itself to the brink of annihilation. Up to the very last word, the present tense verbs of the final stanza signify passing and imminent absence rather than presence: the breath descends; I am driven; I am borne; the soul beacons. Yet even as the *I* who writes helplessly transcribes the imminence of its own passing, the eye of the I foresees its transformation into something eternally individuated and eternally present, as fixed as existential prediction can make it. An abode where the eternal *are* is a place where Keats and Shelley may individually co-exist – so long as the words which signify that abode remain alive and unconsumed.

NOTES

1 Rollins i. 139–40.

2 Woodman (1964) 160.

3 Wasserman (1971) 462–3.

4 *SC* v. 410.

5 Gisborne's letter does not survive, but the bursting of the blood vessel, which occurred on 23 June, is recorded in Maria Gisborne's journal for 28 June; and in Shelley's own letter of 27 July to Keats, he says that Gisborne has sent him an account of "the dangerous accident you have undergone," and "adds that you continue to wear a consumptive appearance" (*Shelley's Friends* 35–7; Jones ii. 220). News about Keats's condition may also have come from Leigh Hunt, who in any case wrote to Shelley on 23 August that Keats was "better" (*SC* v. 413).

6 Keats wrote to Shelley: "If I do not take advantage of your invitation it will be prevented by a circumstance I have very much at heart to prophesy" (Rollins ii. 322) – presumably his death.

7 Quoted Bate 650; Keats himself termed this statement "a lie" (Bate 651).

8 Shelley seems to have received Keats's new volume and letter not from the Gisbornes directly but from Claire Clairmont (with whom they left the Keats materials) on 16 October; see Milne (1976) 282n, citing Holmes (1975) 613, and Clairmont (1968) 178–9. But Shelley did see the Gisbornes in Leghorn on 17 October, and in spite of his irritation with them over a money matter, he saw them periodically thereafter until they returned to England the following July; see *Shelley's Friends* 9–10.

9 After seeing Keats's new volume, Shelley urged William Gifford to read *Hyperion*, "the composition of which was checked by the Review in question" – i.e., the *Quarterly* (Jones ii. 252; see also Milne (1976) 279, 284). The publishers' "Advertisement", however, says only that Keats was discouraged by "the reception" of his poem.

10 Curiously enough, Keats himself wanted Shelley to believe that he *had* written most of it by that time. "Most of the Poems in the [1820] volume," he says in his letter of 16 August, 1820 to Shelley, "have been written well above two years" (Rollins i. 323). Since most of the volume had in fact been written *less* than two years before its publication and since some of the poems – including the title piece *Lamia*, first in the volume – had been written less than one year before, I believe with Milne (1976 p. 281) that Keats was disingenuously trying to represent himself as a model of literary self-restraint: as one who kept his poems back instead of rushing them into print like Shelley, with his uncurbed magnanimity. But Shelley took no notice of Keats's backdating. That he believed the 1820 volume to be essentially the product of Keats's full maturity is clear from a notebook dialogue in which a speaker who evidently represents Shelley defends the volume against severe attack – but only after conceding that the first three poems are "very inadequate to . . . what we should expect from the matured & disciplined powers of the writer" (quoted Milne 279).

11 Jones ii. 252; my italics. Jones assigns the letter to November (with a question mark), but since Shelley writes that he has "just seen" the new Keats volume

that he probably received on 16 October (see note 8), the letter could have been written any time after that date.

12 Letter of 4 May, 1821, in Jones ii. 289; my italics. I quote from Byron's letter as given in Jones ii. 284n.

13 I quote from Hunt's letter as given in Jones ii. 65n; Keats called on Hunt on 23 October (Bate 384n). Nine days before, Keats made a comment similar to Hunt's in a letter to his brother George: "Even as a matter of present interest the attempt to crush me in the Quarterly has only brought me more into notice and it is a common expression among book men, 'I wonder the Quarterly should cut its own throat'" (quoted Bate 372n).

14 Jones ii. 221. Shelley is here tactfully re-stating what he wrote to Charles Ollier after first reading *Endymion*: that "much praise is due for me having read [it], the Authors intention appearing to be that no person should possibly get to the end of it" (Jones ii. 117). Ironically, the same complaint is made in the review that Shelley held responsible for Keats's death (see Bate 369).

15 Rollins ii. 323. Shortly after the harsh reviews of *Endymion* appeared, he himself spoke of it as "slipshod," and also said: "In Endymion, I leaped headlong into the Sea, and thereby have become better acquainted with the Soundings, the quicksands, & the rocks, than if I had <stayed> stayed upon the green shore, and piped a silly pipe, and took tea & comfortable advice" (Rollins i. 374).

16 In the letter just quoted, he also says: "Praise or blame has but a momentary effect on the man whose love of beauty in the abstract makes him a severe critic on his own Works" (Rollins i. 373).

17 *SPP* 390. I quote Shelley's poetry from this edition by giving line numbers alone.

18 I quote from Byron's letter of 26 April, 1821, as given in Jones ii. 284. Byron says that "in this world of bustle and broil, and especially in the career of writing, a man should calculate upon his powers of *resistance* before he goes into the arena" (Jones ii. 284).

19 Cameron (1942) 492–503.

20 Ibid., 490–1.

21 Southey charged Shelley to "ask your own heart, whether you have not been the whole, sole, and direct cause of her destruction." Letter of? September 1820 given in Jones ii. 232.

22 *SPP* 391. The unnamed villain is also called "a base and unprincipled calumniator" and a "miserable man." Cameron has shown that all of these epithets were meant for Southey; see Cameron (1942) 509–12 and (1974) 430–1.

23 Cameron suggests that Shelley was avenging himself for Southey's covert attack on him in the January 1817 *Quarterly* (Cameron (1942) 512), but uppermost in Shelley's mind, I think, was the accusation that Shelley had made in his much more recent – and heretofore unanswered – letter.

24 Woodman (1978) 72.

25 *PL* iv. 829. Here and below I quote Milton's poetry from Milton (1965).

26 In a letter forwarded to Shelley by John Gisborne on 13 June, 1821. Finch wrote of Keats in his last months: "His passions were always violent, and his sensibility most keen. It is extraordinary that, proportionally as his strength of body declined, these acquired fresh vigour, and his temper at length became so

outrageously violent as to injure himself, and annoy everyone around him" (as given in Jones ii. 300n). Shelley uses some material from Finch's letter in the last paragraph of the Preface, but gives no hint of what Finch says here.

27 See Bion (1953) 144–7. For useful comment on the Adonis legend and pastoral elegy, see Lambert (1976) xxix–xxxii, 24–5.

28 *Venus and Adonis* 1120; *Astrophel* 103–8. On Shelley's debt to *Astrophel*, see Harrison (1933) 54–63, and Silverman (1972).

29 Byron was 21 when *English Bards and Scotch Reviewers* was published anonymously in March 1809, and, since the Preface to *Adonais* incorrectly states that Keats died "in his twenty-fourth year" (i.e., at age 23), Shelley must have thought that he was only 20 when *Endymion* appeared (in May 1818), though he was actually 22. For more on the relation between *Adonais* and *English Bards*, see Manning (1970) 380–1.

30 Lines 28–36. Since Milton is "the Sire of an immortal strain" (l. 30), and since Keats–Adonais is "the nursling of [Urania's] widowhood" (l. 47), Reiman takes him as Milton's posthumous child (*SPP* 392n).

31 As Wasserman notes, Shelley turns Milton's heavenly Urania back into the earthly and erotic Aphrodite, so that while Keats–Adonais may seem to be the descendant of Milton and the heir to his epic muse, he actually corresponds to the Bion of Moschus' "Lament": to the poet who sang of love and Pan rather than of war, as Homer did (Wasserman (1971) 496n).

32 See *Endymion* ii. 392–427, and *Isabella* 409–32. For Shelley's misgivings about *Endymion*, see note 13. His 19 October letter to Marianne Hunt conveys a low estimate of everything but the *Hyperion* fragment in the 1820 volume. After praising the fragment, he says: "His other things are imperfect enough, & what is worse written in the bad sort of style which is becoming fashionable among those who fancy that they are imitating Hunt & Wordsworth" (Jones ii. 239). Nevertheless, Curran (1983) has recently argued that *Adonais* is strongly influenced by Keats's writings, and particularly by the poems of the 1820 volume.

33 Wasserman (1971) 489–90; Bion (1953) 133–4.

34 Lines 70–1. I quote Keats's poems from Stillinger.

35 On this point see Randel (1982) 51.

36 Though Shelley sees life as a "dome of many-colored glass" that "Stains the white radiance of Eternity" (Jones ii. 462–3), it is notable that Keats – like Melville – uses whiteness as a sign of annihilation: in *Lamia* the richly colored heroine is made to turn a "deadly white" just before she permanently disappears (*Lamia* ii. 276).

37 When Byron questioned Shelley about Keats's sensitivity to criticism and recalled that his own reaction to an attack on *Hours of Idleness* was "rage, and resistance, and redress – but not despondency or despair" (Jones ii. 284), Shelley replied: "Some plants, which require delicacy in rearing, might bring forth beautiful flowers if ever they should arrive at maturity. *Your* instance hardly applies. You felt the strength to soar beyond the arrows; the eagle was soon lost in that light in which it was nourished, and the eyes of the aimers were blinded" (Jones ii. 289).

8

Deconstruction or Reconstruction: Reading Shelley's *Prometheus Unbound*

TILOTTAMA RAJAN

More conspicuously than those of Wordsworth or Keats, Shelley's poems are accompanied by prefaces that place a hermeneutic frame around them, pleading with the reader for their sympathetic reception yet thereby recognizing that what they try to "say" is subject to dissent. The writing of prefaces, however, is only a symptom of a more pervasive awareness that the imagination is not autonomous. The ways in which reading becomes the dialogical supplement of writing are a central concern of the two later poems we shall consider. But the problem of reading, though deferred, is present on the margins of more hermetically visionary poems as well. In this respect *Alastor* can provide us with a pre-text for raising problems that Shelley explicitly confronts in his later work. For its defense of "poetry" is attempted through a hermeneutics of negativity that stops just short of consuming what it struggles to protect and that requires us to reconceive both the role of deconstruction in semiosis and the nature of reading.

Alastor is a highly reflexive poem that enacts simultaneously the processes of making and reading. In conflating these two activities, it nevertheless elides the deconstructive dialogue between them that Shelley must confront in *Prometheus Unbound*. The poem is in the first place about the writing of itself. As a poet himself, resuming his "long-forgotten lyre" (l. 42, *SPP*), the Narrator has the task of animating what reverts at the end to "An image, silent, cold, and motionless" (l. 661, *SPP*). He must give substance to the Poet, who is otherwise an empty sign, threatening to deconstruct a romantic ideology of vision that becomes no more than an intent of consciousness. But this struggle against the counterspirit of language proves to be a troubled one, because the Narrator's attempt to make the Poet speak to us takes form not as the inspired song he originally plans (l. 19, *SPP*), but as poetic narrative: in a form that keeps complicating the drive toward idealization by entangling it in a story of particular facts. Converting lyric into narrative, the text defers the identity of the Narrator with his own mood. For subjective narrative of the kind produced in *Alastor* is caught in a series of differences: in the difference of the Narrator from an alter ego with whom he cannot quite identify, and in this case in the internal differences of a story that must be told twice over and that is eventually abandoned rather than concluded.[1] Moreover, as a text addressed *to* someone rather than simply "overheard," as Frye says of the lyric,[2] such narrative is "poetry" produced at the site of interpretive dissent. It is already aware that its readers might think otherwise, incipiently dialogized by this awareness.

But at the same time the Narrator's attempt to write the figure of the Poet is already a hermeneutic, not a mimetic or creative act; the Narrator does not commemorate someone he has known intimately, like Wordsworth remembering Lucy. Like the speaker of the conversation poems he tries to understand from the outside an experience he has not had but struggles to believe in. That he tells it twice testifies to his persistence in trying to get to the heart of the Poet's story. His attitude to a visionary ideology whose authority is felt only as an absence thus models for us the role of the reader who must overcome doubts that are created by the fact that we live in the twilight of the idols. It is therefore difficult to imagine the Poet except as a "twilight" phantasm (l. 40, *SPP*), and indeed to construct him except as a character without interiority, a mere sign of what he wants to be. Indeed, the hermeneutic modeled here is considerably more negative than that of Coleridge. Where Coleridge is able to invest the experience he would have us recover in another person, the Narrator does not clearly represent the Poet as having had a visionary experience. "Vision" is disturbingly accompanied by fainting (ll. 188–91, *SPP*), and if "meaning" once flashes on the Poet's "vacant mind" (l. 126, *SPP*), it is never represented in language. That the Poet is essentially a representation is marked in the preface, where his life is described as "allegorical" (*SPP* 69). As sign, he posits nothing except the desire to posit. For the preface negates the Poet as "self-centred" but then negates the "meaner spirits" who do not follow his example, so as to signify through this double negation a desire for the visionary that is not embodied in the Poet himself (*SPP* 69–70).

What the Narrator attempts is, however, a hermeneutics of negativity that makes us aware both of a powerful resistance to deconstruction and of the crisis faced by such resistance. Crucial to his strategy is the estrangement of the Poet, whose journey through regions that are culturally and temporally distant draws our attention to a hermeneutic problem, while also putting the Poet in the space of the auratic. Scattered through the poem are references to the Orient that try to make the vacancy repeatedly alluded to in the poem into an occulation of meaning. Nature finally builds a "pyramid" over the Poet's moldering bones (l. 53, *SPP*), and while alive he is represented among obelisks and sphinxes (ll. 111–16, *SPP*), lingering among "memorials / Of the world's youth" in places where "dead men / Hang their mute thoughts on the mute walls around" (ll. 119–22, *SPP*). These images function as signals to the reader which reverse what Geoffrey Hartman has presented as a "westering" movement in romantic poetry[3] and ask us to construct the sublime from within the hermeneutic. But it is not a question of deciphering that cipher which is the figure of the Poet, for the Oriental exists only as the negation of our own world, and thus as a dead world. More helpful than theories that associate hieroglyphs with a lost origin is Hegel's account of Egyptian art as the crystalization of the symbolic phase:

> Egypt is the country of symbols, the country which sets itself the spiritual task of the self-deciphering of the spirit, without actually attaining to the decipherment. . . . But their works remain mysterious and dumb, mute and motionless, because here spirit itself has still not really found its own inner life and still cannot speak the clear and distinct language of spirit (Hegel (1975) i. 354).

Hegel's description helps to explain why the visionary mode in *Alastor* is conceived only negatively, in terms of silence, absence, vacancy. For the visionary is still only a figure of itself. Crucial to the negativity of Egyptian art are the pyramids that take form as "a double architecture, one above ground" and obviously constructed only for the sake of the "inner meaning" it envelops, the other "subterranean" but consisting of an intricate network of labyrinths and hieroglyphs, one might say of further signs. These signs, moreover, construct a world that is dead. According to Hegel, Egypt turned from the phenomenal world to the inward, but conceived "as the negative of life, as death," such that "the immortality of the soul" is still only conceptualized as the "preservation of corpses" (Hegel (1975) i. 355). The "reorientation" of *Alastor* therefore involves grasping the text as the sign of some inner meaning that is absent. It also involves seeing an otherwise nihilistic emphasis on death – on the Poet's moldering corpse – as an embalming of that which remains still (to be) born. Augmenting our sense of the visionary mode as lifeless is the fact that the Poet almost never speaks, spending his days among "speechless shapes" (l. 123, *SPP*). But muteness for Hegel is not the death of the sign, but rather the site of the text's delivery to and by the future. Egyptian art is summed up by the statues of Memnon, which "numb, stiff and lifeless, are set up facing the sun in order to await its ray to touch them and give them soul and sound." Unable to "draw animation from within" like the human voice, these statues require "light from without which alone liberates the note of the soul from them" (Hegel (1975) i. 358).

For the reader outside the text, however, it is difficult not to see the hermeneutics of negativity described here as a mystification. Denying itself the constructive force of prophecy, the poem's elegiac orientation toward the past constantly thwarts our attempts to posit something on the ground of the Poet's absence, by reinscribing them in the Narrator's failure to represent him. The phenomenological recuperation of death as a state of consciousness thus comes up against the materiality of death, against the sense that it is the obliteration of what survives only as a trace. Or to put it differently, the Poet's death still has the force not of transcendence but of a double negation: a negation both of the ordinary and of the visionary. Any attempt to make it into a transcendence is suspended by the way in which this text exchanges author and reader functions so that neither can be self-grounding. For the Narrator's attempt to give the Poet an identity emerges as a hermeneutic act, such that writing is already interpretation and not a reflection or expression of truth. But, on the other hand, the reading of identity emerges as figurative because the muteness of the Poet prevents it from being a reconstruction of something already said or thought. We have seen how such instability can become an occasion for reformulating the relationship between text and reader. Indeed, the double negation of the preface asks that we read beyond the poem and open it to historical reformulations of the dialectic between the visionary and the social. But the poem itself seems committed by its form as a quest (for truth) and by the hermeneutics of elegy to an essentialism that preempts heuristic reading. As elegy, *Alastor* stands at the opposite pole from *The Triumph of Life*, where it is not the living who must turn toward the dead but the past that must encounter the present. Michael Fried has described how painters in the age of Diderot found it necessary to include the beholder as witness to their truth, only to turn away from him as the site of their insertion into a world outside the hermetically sealed enclosure of the canvas.[4] This tension between "absorption" and "theatricality" parallels the ambivalent attitude of traditional hermeneutics toward the reader: an ambivalence particularly evident in the fact that the elegy frames the role of the reader within the death of its subject. Like those paintings that invite us to watch them turning away from us, romantic elegy asks us to join in re-membering its subject, while sealing it against further reading by leaving us with the reproach of the Poet's death. For the dead elicit sympathy but also guilt, such that any understanding that is also critical becomes like a violation of the sacred.

To compare *Prometheus Unbound* and *Alastor* may seem unusual, but the later text is again concerned with the mediation of a visionary ideology. The problem of mediation is raised by the very mode of lyrical drama, which

Shelley defines in the preface to *Hellas* as a difference between vision and history that signals the intentionality of the former:

> The subject in its present state, is insusceptible of being treated otherwise than lyrically.... I have, therefore, contented myself with exhibiting a series of lyric pictures, and with having wrought upon the curtain of futurity which falls upon the unfinished scene such figures of indistinct and visionary delineation as suggest the final triumph of the Greek cause (*SPP* 408).

We can reformulate this by saying that the materiality of narrative and drama, of writing vision into the language of events, inevitably defers the re-visioning of history as the phenomenology of mind. Appealing to futurity, Shelley experiments with the idea of a prophetic hermeneutics that will read beyond the indistinctness of his play. But in transposing lyric into drama, he also submits vision to the theatricalization of which the romantics were so deeply suspicious.[5] We can therefore expect that he will deal much more explicitly with the problematic relation of "poetry" to its audience.

For much of its history, critics have emphasized how *Prometheus Unbound* fails as an act of representation. Such assessments, though insensitive to the ways the play encodes its own textuality, seem more accurate in describing its construction than the organicist readings that replaced them. From the nineteenth century onward, critics have accused the play of being "intangible," "vague and hollow," populated by characters who are "spectral, often formless, sometimes only voices."[6] Some of the gaps in its logic are thematic. The movement of history toward the far goal of time is seen in linear and eschatological terms, but the historical process is also imaged as a cyclic one in which the infirm hand of Eternity may allow Jove to return again. Other gaps are dramatic. Demogorgon, a volcanic and amoral power who sees the deep truth as imageless in the early part of the play, suddenly becomes Olympian and beneficent in a fourth act that lifts the veil and does image ultimate reality. Yet other gaps have to do with the semiotics of the play's characterization, which hovers uncertainly between the external and the internal. For instance, while Prometheus himself remains chained to the rock, two secondary figures carry out the task of ending the Jovian age. Asia, whose ethic of love is consistent with Prometheus' forgiveness of Jupiter, must be seen psychologically as a force within Prometheus, if the latter's change of heart is to be viewed as something active and not merely contemplative. But Demogorgon, whose violent overthrow of Jove re-presses rather than forgives him, is conceived allegorically as a power beyond Prometheus himself. Yet if Asia is internal to Prometheus, can we really dissociate Demogorgon from a Prometheus who is then caught in the paradox of using violence to achieve peace? It is hardly surprising, in view of such contradictions, that the triumphant fourth act seems an aria tacked on to a three-act drama, rather than an organic resolution.

Perhaps the most troubling lacuna in the play has to do with the unilateral nature of Prometheus' forgiveness of Jove, on which the entire action depends. If Promethean love is indeed to inaugurate a new age, then surely this love cannot remain a paradise for a sect. Yet it is only the Jove within Prometheus who is overcome by love. The actual Jove, in a scene reminiscent of *Paradise Lost* where Satan is hurled headlong only to rise again, is cast into the abyss: repressed rather than reintegrated. These local aporias are, moreover, reflected in the text's ambiguous genre. *Prometheus Unbound* is often described as a political allegory. As a political work it assumes the legislative, even the executive, authority of words. But as an allegory it concedes that the world it represents exists at a certain distance from actuality and must be rendered abstractly rather than realistically. Moreover, Shelley himself described *Prometheus Unbound* through another paradox when he subtitled it a lyrical drama. As drama, it claims an objectivity at odds with its often diaphanous language. A dramatic action is concretely, materially present before us. Drama is, moreover, a communal mode: because it communicates to an audience, it assumes a shared ideology and an affective link between words and the world outside them. Yet Shelley's play is a lyrical drama, by definition impossible to stage in the theater of the world, and acknowledging for itself a merely private and subjective status. Interestingly, Shelley himself expected it to be read by no more than twenty people, perhaps as few as five.[7]

Faced with such disjunctures in the play, the response of modern critics has been to use an aesthetic version of the argument from design. K. N. Cameron, for instance, raises the question of why Demogorgon is described as having existed from time immemorial and then is introduced in Act III as the child of Jupiter and Thetis born to overthrow his father. Making Demogorgon the fatal child is necessary to show how tyranny breeds its own destruction. But an awkward by-product of this new parentage is that Demogorgon, previously an abstract force outside time, now becomes historically specified as a revolutionary power within the world of time, liable to be consumed by the future as he has consumed the past. Cameron's response is to argue that this ungrammaticality makes sense on a deeper level. Jove is mistaken when he identifies his fatal child with Demogorgon, and evidently Demogorgon himself, when he identifies himself as Jove's child (III. i. 54, *SPP*), is speaking only metaphorically, although he is speaking literally when two lines earlier he identifies himself with Eternity.[8] This argument, however, seems ingenious. If Shelley simply wanted to have Jove overthrown by his child, we must ask why he had to create confusion by identifying the child as Demogorgon when Hesiod and Aeschylus make no such identification. He wished, of course, to show the revolution as engendered within history. But he could have given the fatal child some other name, except that identifying it with Eternity is also necessary if the Promethean revolution is to have a transcendental guarantee and not to be a purely local event. Moreover, it is not simply Demogorgon's identity as the child of Jupiter but also his identity as "Eternity" which is in question. In Act III he announces that he is Eternity (III. i. 52, *SPP*); in Act IV he refers to "Eternity, / Mother of many acts" (IV. 565–6, *SPP*), as though Eternity is something other than himself, and as though he is not supreme but subject to some other force. Between Demogorgon the first cause who resides in the realm of *res cogitans*, and Demogorgon the effective cause operating in the sphere of *res extensa* or historical events, the link is as unclear as the one Descartes constructs between his two spheres via the pineal gland. Or to put it differently, Shelley cannot make the transition from the sphere of thought to that of actuality, a problem not untypical of revolutionary thinkers, and also fundamental to the status of the play's revolutionary discourse. One could go on, but the point is a simple one. It is that one can construct exits from the interpretive labyrinth of the play if one tries. But any attempt to clarify the play's dramatic syntax simultaneously generates further ungrammaticalities.[9]

Described this way, the play invites scepticism. But *Prometheus* is a consciously metafictional text whose deconstruction is part of the dialogue on aesthetics set in motion by the *Defence*. It includes at least two scenes of understanding which reflect on the process by which a unified truth is constituted, communicated, and confirmed: the dialogue between Asia and Panthea at the beginning of Act II and Asia's visit to the Cave of Demogorgon later in the act. The first of these comes immediately after Act I, which reluctantly recognizes the discourse of hope as hypothetical. The two crucial episodes of Act I – the encounter between the reformed Prometheus and the Phantasm of Jove, and the psychomachia that balances the Furies against the Spirits of hope – do not simply convey the play's optimistic propositions. They also reflect back on themselves and must be viewed semiotically as well as thematically. In Prometheus' revocation of his curse, voice is deliberately decentered. His words are split away from their original speaker and attributed to Jove, himself not a person but a phantasm, an empty schema like the subject in Lacanian psychoanalysis. The words do not seem to come from anywhere or from anyone: they do not belong and are therefore inappropriate. This curious device, which has an effect similar to that which Brecht describes as *Verfremdung* or alienation, suggests that the Jovian element in Prometheus is no longer a part of his thinking. But it is also used to remove from those words the ability to affect the real world that comes from their being centered in a speaking self. Deprived of the validating authority of the emotions that generated them, Prometheus' words become simply words, grounded in nothing outside themselves. But the decentering of the text of hate inevitably makes us aware that its successor, the text of love and forgiveness, is also an intent of consciousness. To put it differently, Prometheus uses the fact that he exists within the prisonhouse of language precisely to argue that the semiotic manacles he has created by perceiving his relationship to Jove in a certain way are mind-forged. But in making the past into a text that he can rewrite, he semiotizes the future, making it, too, into a text that may lose its grounding in reality if it does not find readers with a similar emotional tropology. The result is a displacement of the play's subsequent action from the status of signified to signifier. This displacement will be accentuated throughout the play in the use of aesthetic rather than natural analogies to evoke the process of Promethean renewal.[10]

The summoning up of the phantasm can in fact be seen as mise-en-abime of the larger play. Occurring entirely inside Prometheus' consciousness, it reduces the play's action to a play with images, disclosing the immateriality of what Shelley describes as writing "drawn from the operations of the human mind" (*SPP* 133). Equally problematical is the remainder of the first act. The Furies are depicted as insubstantial phantasms from "the all-miscreative brain of Jove" (l. 448, *SPP*). But the matching of the spirits against the Furies suggests that they may be no different. Not only do the spirits have difficulty envisioning a world in which ruin is no longer love's shadow, the fact that their tenuous vision of a redeemed world takes the form of a dream acknowledges that imagination cannot give a foundation to what it posits except as an intent of consciousness.

It is against this background that we must see the dialogue between Asia and Panthea in which Shelley reflects on the rhetorical problem at the heart of the play: that of whether he can make his vision of a Promethean Age convincing, given the lacunae in it. Again, the vision takes the form of dreams, subliminally felt as Panthea sleeps in Ione's arms in the depths of the sea. The scene focuses on the difficulty she has in articulating her two dreams about the psychological resurrection of Prometheus and the future heralded for the rest of mankind by his transformation. Thus it raises the two problems central to the poetic process: that of expression, the finding of signs to signify the ineffable, and that of persuasion, the creation of an interpretive community that will give assent and solidity to an otherwise esoteric vision. It is the latter alone that can fulfil the imperatives of Shelley's form by translating lyric into dialogue and finally drama, visionary intention into communication and action. Panthea in this scene functions as the implied author, the hierophant of "an unapprehended inspiration" (*SPP* 508), while Asia is the reader desired by the author and one who "produces" the meaning of the text by intuitively grasping his intention. Shelley's essential work, as distinct from his published text, is figured here in the form of the dreams. The word "text," meaning something that is woven together, designates a collection of signs with grammatological but not pneumatological status. Its relationship to the term "work" is, to borrow his own distinction, like that of a mosaic to a painting, a mosaic being a conglomerate of parts and a painting being a unified whole (*SPP* 504). Although Panthea's words (like Shelley's text) serve as conductors of the play's vision, this vision remains scattered as long as Asia attempts to ground it in the words themselves, which are transitory and fragmentary, imaged in terms of winds and air (II. i. 37, 109, *SPP*). In short, at the beginning of the scene we are able to scan the textual mosaic but unable to grasp the work.

The roles of Panthea and Asia correspond almost exactly to those Schelling assigns to the two sides of the self at the beginning of *The Ages of the World.* Schelling conceives of understanding as a dialogical process, but one that culminates in identity rather than difference, the difference being due to the process of articulation and the ultimate identity of questioner and respondent being also a finding of identity. Understanding is first of all a process of recollection and recognition by which we reawaken the "arche-type of things [that] slumbers in the soul like an obscured and forgotten, even if not completely obliterated, image" (*Ages* 85). But this we accomplish through dialogue, which enables us to make conscious what we sense only obscurely, by learning it from another who turns out to be an objectification of ourselves. In the phenomenology of understanding, which can serve as a model for the reading process, there are two participants: "an asking one and an answering one, an ignorant one which, however, seeks knowledge, and a knowing one which, however, does not know its knowledge." The higher, intuitive self, in Schelling's words, "is mute and needs a mediating organ in order to attain expression" (*Ages* 89). Similarly, in *Prometheus Unbound* Panthea, though in possession of what Shelley calls "the uncom-municated lightning" of the play's vision, (*SPP* 134), is ignorant of what she knows and needs Asia to produce her vision. That the vision is inarticulate until it is read is a significant point, and one whose deconstructive consequences will emerge in the visit to Demogorgon. But for the present it is enough to say that the reader here is given the responsibility of recovering and in some sense co-creating a vision that otherwise would "not speak to us, but remain dead" (*Ages* 88).

Communication proceeds only when the internalizing of knowledge described by the German word for recollection, *Erinnerung,* occurs through an identification of author and reader. Suddenly, Asia discovers the right method of reading by gazing into Panthea's eyes and there reading Prometh-eus' "written soul" through a paradoxically "wordless converse" (II. i. 110, 52, *SPP*). The logocentric concept of the "written soul" resolves the paradox of traditional hermeneutics: the paradox that in order to preserve vision one must fix it in writing, but that writing is always external and supplementary to what it transmits.[11] The process of moving beyond the linguistic sign to the language of the eyes suggests how the reader, too, can break the hermeneutic circle by moving beyond a semiological reading that decenters vision to a psychological reading that allows us unmediated access to the inner core of the work. The breaking of this circle serves as a catalyst for the communication of Panthea's second dream, which turns out to have been Asia's also. Thus we can see in this scene the outlines of a Shelleyan hermeneutic designed to reverse the deconstructive potential within a text that fails to confirm itself by meeting the classical criteria for unity. The published text, composed of disjunctive elements that can be brought together only by imaginative leaps, is seen as a product of the semiotic fracture described in the *Defence*, which occurs when inspiration is signified through composition (*SPP* 504). But the scene dramatizes the imaginative project as interpersonal communication rather than simple linguistic intention involving a dyadic relationship between the sign and the thing or concept signified. In other words, it presents reading as a psychological and not just a semiological process. Asia responds to Panthea's dream, not on the level of its fractured signifiers, but through a process of what Dilthey calls "reconstruction" (*Nachbildung*). By translating a language initially "given us only from the outside" in terms of "our own sense of life," Dilthey argues, we center the isolated signs "given to our senses" in a "coherence experienced from within."[12] This coherence, though subjective, is also shared between author and reader. Panthea's attempt to voice her dream is an invitation to Asia as implied reader to re-cognize the dream she herself has had. As such, the dialogue between the two sisters serves as a model for the dialogue intended to occur between author and reader. Critics have often complained that the fourth act is like a castle in the air. But the insubstantiality of the play's action is not the point, because the action cannot become real until we as readers recognize it as the dream we have had. The fourth act, in which Shelley stages an objectively unverifiable outcome in the theater of his own mind, invites us to stage Shelley's vision in the theater of *our* minds and thus bridge the gulf between intention and actuality conceded in the notion of lyrical drama.

As an intratextual allegory of the transmission of text to reader, this scene is of course stage managed. By imaging the author and implied reader as sisters, Shelley assumes a reading based on sympathy, a dialogue that is no dialogue because the Other is the emotional twin of the self. It is this same assumption of psychic affinity which allows him in *The Defence* to construct a hermeneutics of understanding in which reading is the redemption of a fragmentary text through the animation of archetypes that point to the intention in which the text has its genesis (*SPP* 505). But it is necessary to distinguish between the implied and the explicit readers: using the term "explicit reader" as H. R. Jauss uses it to distinguish the actual historically differentiated reader from Iser's idealized "implied reader" whose role is prescribed within the text.[13] Though this reader by definition is not figured in the play, the reader's presence as a potentially negating force is something of which Shelley seems aware even in the dialogue between Asia and Panthea, but more strongly in the visit to the Cave of Demogorgon.

One of the changes that Shelley made in the draft manuscript of the play casts considerable light on the way he problematizes the hermeneutic journey undertaken in the second act. When Asia asks her sister to raise her eyes so that she can read Prometheus' soul in them, the draft shows Asia experiencing an ecstatic communion with the burning image of Prometheus in Panthea's eyes: "It is his spirit in their orbs."[14] This passage is deleted in the published version, which goes straight on to Panthea's troubling question: "what canst thou see / But thine own fairest shadow imaged there?" (II. i. 112–13, *SPP*). Panthea here points out that her eyes may not be a window into some ultimate reality but a mirror in which Asia sees the projected text of her own desire. Read in the light of the deleted passage, the sceptical potential of this question is neutralized, and Panthea's question can be taken positively as meaning that the soul of the work, the vision of Prometheus, is also a reflection of Asia's epipsychic essence, her fairest shadow. It thus guarantees the culmination of the interpretive dialogue between author and reader in a fusion of horizons, accomplished literally through an act of vision. Read without the deleted passage, the question becomes more sceptical and suggests that the supposed essence of the work is a projection by the interpreter of her own self, which is itself a construction, an "image" momentarily constituted in the kaleidoscopic process of communication rather than preceding it. We will return later on to this point about the semiotics of identity: that of author, reader, and character. Suffice it to say that Asia's response to Panthea's question about the nature of the text read in the eyes is contradictory: she at first confirms the hermeneutic myth of transparent communication by paralleling Panthea's eyes to "the deep blue, boundless Heaven" (II. i. 114, *SPP*). But then she suggests that what she reads there is a labyrinth of tropes: "dark, far, measureless, – / Orb within orb, and line through line inwoven. –" (II. i. 116–17, *SPP*), an image for visionary communication that is repeated in the "life of life" lyric, where Asia's eyes are paralleled to mazes (II. v. 53, *SPP*). It is true that Asia here goes on to announce that the hermeneutic circle has been broken when she declares: "The dream is told" (II. i. 126, *SPP*). But the seeds of the later scene have already been sown. We are aware that the notion of a language that is grounded in something beyond language may be itself a linguistic construct and therefore subject to doubt and dismantling.

Even more unsettling for a hermeneutic reading is the second interpretive interlude, Asia's dialogue with Demogorgon. Immediately after their conversation the sisters follow the echoes of voices into a forest that presumably leads into the depths of consciousness and toward the origin of things. This journey is the narrative equivalent of the process that Husserl describes as reduction or epoché, by which one seeks to reach the transcendental subjectivity, in this case, of the author. The shift from dialogue to lyric at the end of the first scene and in the dialogue of the Fauns signals a bracketing of the external world. The voices of the speakers are no longer dramatically differentiated, and their lyrical oneness is an attempt at what Schelling describes as the annulling of "all duality in one's self, so that we would be, as it were, only inwardly, and live altogether in the supramundane, discerning everything immediately" (*Ages* 88). But the sisters' journey ends in the Cave of Demogorgon, where the philosophical foundations of traditional hermeneutics are eroded, as Shelley once again brings into the foreground the problems of communication, interpretation, and reading. Asia's conversant is no longer her sister but Demogorgon, a being who is sexually and ontologically other than her. The scene reflects on the opacities of communication, and though the explicit reader is not figured in the text, the reader's potentially negating presence emerges from the gaps and silences where the dialogue within the text fails to become a meeting of minds and thus reflects back on reading as dialogue. But the scene is only obliquely about the relationship of the implied to the explicit reader, and in fact is about something more radical which subtends this relationship: the relationship of the reader to the work itself. Ostensibly, the scene repeats the earlier one and ends with Asia as implied reader "producing" the meaning of Shelley's work when she acts on her perceptions and perceives in a positive light what is actually a very ambiguous event: the appearance of the two chariots that herald some momentous historical change. Ostensibly, then, it is the active mirror image of its contemplative counterpart: in the first scene Asia understands the work and articulates its vision; in the second scene she translates it from the sphere of expression to the sphere of events. But in fact the scene renders highly problematical the reading for which Asia serves as missionary, by dismantling our earlier security as to what the work says, and what the animating intention behind it is.

Crucial to this second scene is the figure of Demogorgon, a character who again seems an empty schema rather than a tangible personality. If Panthea was the means by which the reader made contact with the essence of the work and the spirit of its author, then Demogorgon is her antithesis: the means by which we recognize that the inner core of the work is absent, its voice "lacking," its cryptic and contradictory text all that there is. "His" eyes cannot be read. "His" curious lack of personality denies the possibility of communication except on a grammatological level, and indeed the inconclusive dialogue between Asia and Demogorgon often revolves around the signifier. It is halted by grammatical problems such as the specification of an antecedent to a pronoun, as in Asia's attempt to find out what is meant by "He reigns" (II. iv. 28, 31, 32, *SPP*), and it is held up by the need to identify an abstraction that stands in place of someone whose identity we are never told, such as the destiny in the chariot (II. iv. 146, *SPP*) or "God" (II. iv. 112, *SPP*). Asia is once again the implied reader who believes in the sacred necessity of hope: the reader we might suppose to be desired by Shelley or by a part of him. As a dramatic character, she seeks a meeting with her creator or his intermediary that will allow her to understand the destiny of the created world. As implied reader, she seeks a fusion of horizons with the author that will enable her to grasp the essence of the work and then act on her intuition. But she succeeds in neither aim, for Demogorgon, apparently the originating or intending force behind the play's events, proves ungraspable. Consequently, what in the earlier scene was the "soul" of the work, the vision of hope discovered behind its flawed form and language, now becomes itself a linguistic construct. Meanwhile, the inner core of the work, which Asia was once able to read in Panthea's eyes, has disappeared, to be replaced by a vacancy. The scene therefore complicates severely a traditionally hermeneutic reading that allows the unity of the work to be potential rather than actual. The reconstruction of the original work encouraged in the dialogue with Panthea is presented as the reconstruction of a unity that may not be there, a passionately optimistic attempt to center something that is decentered and unfocused, having, like Demogorgon itself, neither "form – nor outline" (II. iv. 6, *SPP*).

Crucial to the philosophic dismantling of hermeneutic reading is the rigorously antiphenomenological character of this episode. For the scene probes not only the authority possessed by individual acts and speech acts, but also the semiotics of the self in which action and language have their origin. Traditional hermeneutics assumes the existence of a transcendental ego, an essential core within us which gives value to our words and which is guaranteed by its link to a similar spirit on the level of the macrocosm. It is this ego that we had seemed to grasp in the dialogue between Panthea and Asia, whose shared discovery of identity enabled them also to grasp the Promethean spirit of the age. The figure of Demogorgon, however, deconstructs any notion of history as an organic manifestation of a spirit, a developing SUM or I AM. It casts in doubt the phenomenological notion of a *Geist* or world-historical spirit elaborated by Hegel and also assumed in such catch phrases as "the spirit of the age." Moreover, what this scene does on the level of the world-historical spirit a much earlier passage, which is explicitly linked to this scene by its introduction of Demogorgon, does on the level of the individual self. Close to the beginning of the play, in Earth's enigmatic description of how the Magus Zoroaster met his own image in the garden, Shelley already raises the question of what there is behind the possibly kaleidoscopic formation we call the individual. Ostensibly, the question is raised to dismantle the credibility of Jupiter by phantomizing him. But the implications of Earth's speech resonate through the rest of the play and unsettle our reaction to other characters and hence the authority of what they say and do. We are told by Earth that behind the flesh-and-blood forms of those who "think and live" is an appearance, not a reality: that the essential self is variously an image, a phantom, a "vacant" shade (I. 198, 216, *SPP*).

> For know, there are two worlds of life and death:
> One that which thou beholdest, but the other
> Is underneath the grave, where do inhabit
> The shadows of all forms that think and live . . .
>
> There thou art, and dost hang, a writhing shade
> . . . all the Gods
> Are there, and all the Powers of nameless worlds,
> Vast, sceptred phantoms;
>
> (I. 195–206, *SPP*)

Moreover, as Shelley suggests in a canceled line, the encounter between the self and its other dooms us henceforth to interweave the two worlds of life and death, the ego and its deconstructed image.[15] Thus, it is not only Jove who becomes an echo within this ghost sonata, but Prometheus also, Demogorgon, and indeed everyone who thinks and lives. In Asia's visit to the cave, for instance, the thinking and living Demogorgon who will later overthrow Jove is dismantled before we meet him by our encounter with his vacant image, an encounter that exposes the later, active Demogorgon as a linguistic constitution. Although Prometheus in this play is not similarly dismantled by his shade, he is perplexingly absent from the drama he initiates. With the exception of one scene, Act III, scene iii, he speaks only one line after Act I (III. iv. 97, *SPP*). Critics have sometimes rationalized the disappearance of the play's characterological center by seeing various secondary figures as projected parts of Prometheus, such that he is reassembled, like Albion, from his parts.[16] But this only makes us question whether what we call Prometheus is a holistic entity, or a conglomeration of selves. When he and Asia retreat to the cave at the end of Act III, we must ask, is this the cave that like the hermeneutic circle conceals a potential totality to be brought to light by a sympathetic reader? Or is it, like the Cave of Demogorgon, the site of a return behind what Lacan calls the mirror-stage, to a space where we uncover the original self, a vacant sign as yet untenanted by author or reader?

Asia, indeed, does tenant the space vacated in this episode. The scene ends with Asia acting out her reading by ascending in the chariot of hope, following her own statement that in the absence of any ultimate meaning, one may make one's heart the oracle of its own truth. But this time we must consider more closely the status of the discourse of hope that she offers us as the hermeneutic matrix of the play. The long dialogue between Asia and Demogorgon begins with a theogony in which she places Prometheus' transformation as a moment in the phenomenology of the world-historical mind, thus also accounting for the Jovian Age as a fortunate fall. It ends with her decision to see the arrival of the two chariots positively, which prepares the way for her reunion with Prometheus, and metaphorically for the union of the revolutionary mind with the material world. Thus, the scene might seem to encapsulate and reveal the entire action, the *arche* and *telos*, of the otherwise obscure Promethean drama. But if Asia starts from the assumption we have already encountered in Schelling, that the spirit of the work is a "voice unspoken" (II. i. 191, *SPP*) that emerges in dialogue, the scene disturbingly challenges the hermeneutic conception of understanding. For what it offers us is a dialogue that is Lacanian in structure, a dialogue that does not so much reveal the identity of the text as bring to light its difference from itself. Asia's redemptive theogony, as Stuart Curran has pointed out, is radically different from the cosmic history provided earlier by Earth, who suggests that there "never was a golden age, but only the continuous tyranny of Jupiter."[17] Though it is told in the past tense, Asia's account is no more than an interpretation. Crucial to its tenuous status is its dialogical setting, which in the relative silence of Demogorgon registers the possibility of another side to what is being said. That dialogue can function to accentuate our sense of language as difference was pointed out a long time ago by Harold Pinter, who suggests that "the speech we hear is an indication of that we don't hear. It is a necessary avoidance... which keeps the other in its place."[18] Indeed, Asia cannot quite avoid the other side of what she says, for the very length of her speech gives her space in which to complicate the idea of the Jovian age as a mere interregnum between the Saturnian and Promethean ages. It seems that Prometheus created Jupiter by giving him "wisdom, which is strength" (II. iv. 44, *SPP*), even though Asia also claims that "Jove now reigned;" as though he is an autonomous entity (II. iv. 49, *SPP*). The uncertainty about whether Jove is an external oppressor or a figure for some self-destructive potential within the human race leaves us unclear whether the "speech" and "Science" that Prometheus gives humankind in a second attempt at organized innocence (II. iv. 71–5, *SPP*) will not recreate "Jove." And indeed that doubt is registered in Asia's description of the "legioned hopes" that Prometheus awakens as narcotics that "hide with thin and rainbow wings / The shape of Death" (II. iv. 59–63, *SPP*).

As significant as the insecurity of Asia's theogony is the tenuous way in which the sisters construct a link between signifier and signified in the interpretation of the two chariots. For this scene, after all, initiates the resolution of the plot. Carlos Baker speaks for Asia and for a long critical tradition when he sees the chariots, one dark and one light, as intended for Demogorgon and Asia, respectively.[19] By associating Asia with the light chariot, and by making the force within the dark chariot serve the purposes of good, he sidesteps the possibility that the dark chariot may herald a second coming in which the center no longer holds. He makes destruction a prelude, rather than a Manichaean alternative to, construction. Yet the text is by no means so clear. Asia at first assumes that the dark chariot has come for her (II. iv. 145, *SPP*), a possibility that the spirit never actually denies, as he announces ominously that the reality of what he is, is worse than it appears: "I am the shadow of a destiny / More dread than is mine aspect —" (II. iv. 146–7, *SPP*). Moreover, it is not certain whether "Heaven's kingless throne" (II. iv. 149, *SPP*), which the dark charioteer threatens to demolish, refers to Jove's throne or to the authority of some power higher than Jove, whose overthrow might lead to total chaos. Although the spirit in the light chariot does announce that it has come to bear Asia to Prometheus (II. iv. 168, *SPP*), the spirits, as we know from a canceled passage at the end of the act, may well be voices from a heart that is its own oracle. Again, the positive construction put on the scene's ending is no more than an interpretation, supplied, significantly, by Panthea and eagerly taken up by Asia. And again the silence of Demogorgon makes us aware of another side to this interpretation. Panthea, we recall, was earlier the author who functioned as a medium for "the gigantic shadows which futurity casts upon the present." But the author, to quote Roland Barthes, is now a "guest" in his own text, "inscribed . . . like one of his characters, figured in the carpet."[20]

The deconstructive reading encouraged by Asia's visit to the Cave of Demogorgon would see the play's hiatuses as dismantling its attempt at a transvaluation of values through a logocentric act of mythmaking. For the authority of mythmaking is eroded by the contrivances of which it makes use: by the disjunctive structure and characterization. But the reading urged earlier might see the very disjunctiveness of the text as something that antithetically stimulates the reader to break the hermeneutic circle and grasp the synthetic totality of the work across its negativity. It may seem that the play consumes the hermeneutic reading it offers. Or to put it differently, it may seem that the scene in Demogorgon's cave resists any attempt to reduce it to a concessive clause in the play's dramatic syntax. Indeed, my argument has been that hermeneutics contains the seed of its own deconstruction, because making the reader a mediating element allows for an explicit as well as for an implied reader, and so renders problematical any sentimental reconstitution of text as work. But the presence of the reader similarly complicates a deconstructive interpretation, because the explicit reader may, after all, follow a range of reconstructive options from sympathetic under-standing to demythologization.

The plethora of choices available to us is nowwhere more evident than in the play's method of characterization as it guides us, again equivocally, to seek or resist a phenomenological understanding. It is helpful here to distinguish between allegorical and psychological or symbolic charac-terization, using the distinction between symbol and allegory as de Man uses it with reference to rhetorical figures.[21] Shelley's method of characterization, for the most part, is allegorical. Jove, the Furies, the various spirits, and Earth, are conventionally allegorical characters. Prometheus and Demogor-gon are more complex. They have the abstractness, the hollowing out of "individuality," that Hegel sees as natural to allegorical characters (Hegel (1975) ii. 1177), and the concomitant emphasis on character as actant rather than personality, signifier rather than signified. But if their characterization manifests the split between tenor and vehicle proper to allegory as a figure, the tenor is less clearly specified than in the case of the other characters. Still, they, too, are products of an allegorical characterization that decenters personality, by splitting the discourse in which the subject manifests itself from the originating subjectivity behind the words, and giving us only the former. Allegorical characterization seems the logical extension of the semiotics of selfhood that emerges from the play's two encounters between the magian ego and its empty origin. But Asia and Panthea, on the other hand, are somewhat different: personalities rather than signifiers. Shelley's characterization is nowhere realistic, but these two figures, who are not dramatically fissured in the manner of Prometheus and Demogorgon, are drawn symbolically rather than allegorically. There is no split between discourse and self, and the words of the sisters therefore provide us with immediate access to the inner core of their psyches. The allegorical subject is a schema that we know through a relatively conventionalized discourse and not in its interiority. This method of characterization, which makes the various characters into constructs rather than persons, cuts against the psychological identification between the reader and the central voice(s) in the text crucial to hermeneutic understanding. Allegorical characters can only be read grammatologically, though in a framework that may be either structuralist or poststructuralist. But psychological characters, whether real-istic or symbolic, demand a phenomenological reading. Since it is partly through its characters that one grasps the identity of a dramatic text, the play's ambiguous method of characterization leaves its identity in doubt.

This is not to say that a hermeneutic reading offers us the key to the play. The text itself clearly undermines the epistemological authority of such a reading, though it supports its ethical authority. But the reinscription of the hermeneutic as desire displaces us from any schematic use of deconstruc-tion. Indeed, one might argue that a third approach is suggested in Shelley's representation of the text as drama, as performance: a designation with profoundly antimetaphysical consequences. With Asia's decision to interpret the arrival of the chariot positively, the play seems to move to an optimistic conclusion. Indeed, Harold Bloom complains that in "Act IV the imagination of Shelley breaks away from the poet's apparent intention, and visualizes a world in which the veil of phenomenal reality has been rent."[22] More precisely, it is after Act II, scene iv, rather than after Act III that the play makes its great imaginative leap, electing quite consciously to produce the meaning of the play according to one particular version. Yet if we are to understand the status of the play's discourse beginning with Asia's ascent in the chariot, we must understand its relationship to the earlier part of the play. The second or active half of the play stands in relation to the first reflective or reflexive part rather as a dramatic performance stands in relation to the script that elicits it.[23] The relationship between script and performance is not strictly symmetrical, because a performance is a production of the script, not a reproduction related to the script as a photograph to its negative (as Asia might like us to believe on her emergence from the Cave of Demogorgon). Script and performance exist in different spaces, the former being intentional and complex, the latter being a concrete actualization, which succeeds in being such only by a deliberate act of simplification: by repressing the traces of alternative performances that exist in the intentional space of script. What this means, given that the individual production of a play is personally and historically variable, is that Shelley's *Prometheus* as script is open to the deconstructive production that as performance it chooses to exclude. Or to put it differently, his staging of the Promethean myth in the theater of his mind has, as performance, the status of a concrete possibility: it is more than a merely abstract potentiality, but less than a reality. Shelley himself suggests in the preface that he is aware of his play as a performance. It is in the nature of drama, he argues, to use a certain "arbitrary discretion" in its reworking of inherited subject matter, to produce rather than reproduce an action (*SPP* 132). Moreover, he concedes that his production of the myth is historically limited, being an effect of culturally conditioned tropes of understanding that operate through the individual: "Poets, not otherwise than philosophers, painters, sculptors and musicians, are in one sense the creators and in another the creations of their age" (*SPP* 135). That the Shelleyan version is formed by the spirit of the age (a more romantic term for what we now refer to as "discursive formations") is the source of its momentary authority and also of its vulnerability. But the fact that the gospel according to Asia is performance and not metalanguage has another side to it. For it means that any interpretation of the play is also not metalanguage but performance: or as Josué Harari puts it: "any theory of the text *is itself text*."[24]

That the plot as a performance of the myth cannot be reified into an imitation of an action is a point that can be further clarified if we borrow the distinction between story and discourse made, among others, by Seymour Chatman.[25] The story comprises the actual events of the narrative, while the term "discourse" refers to a telling and thus an interpretation of the events. But the discourse of *this* play is ungrounded in a story. For the story of who invested Jupiter with power and of what the limits and extent of that power are is never clarified, because the various cosmogonic fictions provided only serve to complicate the matter further. Indeed, the story of Prometheus' forgiveness of Jove, the most pivotal event in the play, is also unclear, for all we really know is how Prometheus tells the story of his attitude to Jove from 1.59 onward, but not what actually happens within his psyche. For instance, only a few minutes before he announces that the quality of mercy is not strained, Prometheus vengefully pictures Joves being forced to kiss his bloody feet (I. 49–52, *SPP*). One may argue that this is before the crucial recantation, though the transformation is too instantaneous to be wholly persuasive. But several lines after Prometheus' spiritual transformation, in his confrontation with the Furies, he appears still to feel the darker emotions of which we thought him purged and describes his mastery over these emotions by disturbingly paralleling it to the repressiveness of Jove: "Yet am I king over myself, and rule / The torturing and conflicting throngs within / As Jove rules you when Hell grows mutinous" (I. 492–4, *SPP*). Thus we do not know whether line 59 states an intention or an actuality, and whether the optative mode ("the Curse / Once breathed on thee I would recall") is used because Prometheus has not yet met the phantasm of Jupiter or because he has not yet become fully capable of forgiveness. In other words, we do not know what happens at line 59, and know only how Shelley later stages the meaning of the play. The displacement of the action from story to discourse, from signified to signifier, is crucial to Shelley's emergent recognition that if the text of desire is to be saved, it can be saved only as performance and not as mimesis.

One indication of Shelley's willingness to untie the text he actually published is the curious organization of the manuscript in the Bodleian library, possibly one on which he worked both before and after publication.[26] It begins with Act IV and proceeds to alternate Act I on the left-hand side of the page with the remainder of Act IV on the right-hand side. The manuscript continues up to the middle of II.ii, then alternates part of the third scene on the left side with the remainder of the second scene on the right, and finally places the remainder of the third scene (the song of the Spirits) on the left-hand side alongside the crucial dialogue in the Cave of Demogorgon (II. iv).[27] Textual scholars have explained away the state of the manuscript by suggesting that it is an intermediate draft in which Shelley transcribed the first three acts and then inserted the fourth act, known to be an afterthrought, "wherever there happened to be a vacancy."[28] Yet the mechanical explanation does not entirely clarify why he left several pages at the beginning of the notebook blank, if he was not toying with the idea of putting something there. Still less does it explain why the unweaving of the play's linear succession is continued through the disarrangement of the second act. The redeployment of the parts of Act I, moreover, is not just eccentric. The second and third scenes are split at logical points, and from the middle of the second scene onward the effect is antiphonal. Lyrical scenes are divided from and juxtaposed with dramatic ones. The lyrical segments are separated and transposed to the right-hand side, as if to stage a confrontation between the imaginary world projected by desire and the greater complexities of the linguistic order.

The manuscript is therefore quite different from the published text. For the linear action of the latter may seem to distinguish it from the "open" texts described by Umberto Eco, which "the author seems to hand . . . on to the performer more or less like the components of a construction kit."[29] Indeed, it would be wrong to say that Shelley's text is ever completely open, that he is unconcerned about its "eventual deployment,"[30] and it would be more accurate to say that he places a model for the text's deployment within a structure that exposes it as problematic. Nevertheless, the mobile text that emerges from the manuscript dissolves space and time, juxtaposing different temporal planes and placing the cancellation of the Hours alongside the period of Prometheus' enchainment. One is reminded of Shelley's statement that pronouns and tenses are grammatical intrusions (*SPP* 483), and of the many romantic projects for dissolving boundaries, whether they be between different spatiotemporal orders or between different perceptual modes. Indeed, as in Blake's later prophecies, the impulse behind this aesthetic and temporal syncretism is partly to redeem time by making all time eternally present. But one may also be reminded of Nietzsche's statement that to abolish grammar might finally be to get rid of God.[31] For the cubist disassembling of the text radically upsets our sense of a fixed perspective on events. The interpretive results of placing the last act at the beginning, for instance, are by no means easy to discern. It may occupy a prefatory position and inform us how to read the play. Or it may project a lyrical vision, only to parody the dangers of moving too quickly to the end of the play by exposing the perilous underpinning of this vision in the preceding three acts. That parts of the play can be placed in different spatial positions emphasizes that every event must be viewed in more than one way. For instance, Demogorgon's exuberant addresses to the Earth, the moon, and the "happy dead" (IV. 524ff.) must seem curiously hollow when placed, in a kind of collage, opposite the Magus Zoroaster's encounter with his own shadow and the subsequent disclosure that Demogorgon, too, is no more than a shadow. Similarly, the song of the Spirits, with its movement beyond the veil of life and death, is set against the equivocal conversation between

Asia and Demogorgon, and displaced into the vacant pages used for corrections and afterthoughts. It thus loses its lyrical immediacy and becomes an echo of itself, the object of a Brechtian alienation effect. Again and again, it is as though the play is quoting itself and reducing mimesis and voice to text. But the odd juxtapositions do not necessarily work toward dismantling the Promethean drama. The conjunction of the last and first act, like one of those windows into eternity of which Blake speaks, can also be seen as opening up a vista that Act I by itself denies us, thus reducing Act I to quotation. It is as if copying out the text without preparing it for print freed Shelley to compose and decompose it, so as to dissolve in his mind any illusion that the form he finally gave it was inevitable.

It is appropriate to conclude with some theoretical reflections. The idea of the text as performance, while it accommodates a hermeneutic reading, is philosophically very different from the reading dramatized in the dialogue between Asia and Panthea, which assumes that we can grasp the identity of the text. But as I have already suggested, traditional hermeneutics contains the traces that lead to its own deconstruction, as to some extent does poststructuralism. Both contain tendencies to reify interpretation that are at odds with their insistence that we intertextualize fiction and reality. Hermeneutics, as we have seen, requires that literature enter the world of communication in order to be brought to life, yet clings to a dualism of work and text that makes the work an essence unchanged by its existence in the communicative process. Poststructuralism, on the other hand, de-idealizes the notion of literature as a special form of language, protected by a dualism that privileges it above other forms of discourse. But it often ends by underprivileging literary discourse, thus reverting to a dualism that denies language the power to affect reality. I have suggested here that what *Prometheus Unbound* responds to is an approach that intertextualizes fiction and "reality," and recognizes that they mutually make and remake each other. But the attempt to construct this approach from interpretive interludes in the play and from the theory of the romantic period itself marks a reluctance to engage in the ahistorical and paradigmatic reading that Frank Lentricchia criticized in Yale deconstruction:[32] reading that assumes that the interpretation of a particular text is a paradigm for the interpretation of all other texts. *Prometheus Unbound* is a particular kind of text, and a strictly poststructuralist approach may well be appropriate for a different kind of text such as the French *nouveau roman*. As a play that has elements of political allegory, it belongs with works like Blake's *Songs* and prophecies, the reformist novels of Godwin and Wollstonecraft, even Wordsworth's *Prelude*: in other words, with works that assume the interaction of fiction and sociopolitical reality, fiction and personal life. But as a text that claims some relationship between literature and history, it also recognizes its own vulnerability to having its significance constituted differently by different readers. For the semiotics of theater is not identical with the semiotics of the book, the former being a performance that is subject to change. In choosing the mode of drama, Shelley departs from *Alastor* to set his work in the space of historical difference and forfeits for it the closure of a classic that can codify its message. To adapt a phrase from "Mont Blanc," the text "governs thought" but does not originate it: it remains a presence in the world, but no longer one that can institutionalize meaning.

NOTES

1 I discuss the doubling of the narration and the relationship between lyric and narrative in Tilottama Rajan (1991). For a general discussion of lyric versus narrative modes see Tilottama Rajan (1985).

2 Frye (1957) 249.

3 Hartman (1975) 126–7.

4 Fried (1980) 103–4.

5 Ibid., p. 104.

6 See Percy Bysshe Shelley, *Prometheus Unbound* (1959) 41–2, 44.

7 See Peek (1927) ii. 125; Percy Bysshe Shelley, *Complete Works* (1926–30) x. 354.

8 Cameron (1943).

9 I borrow the term "ungrammaticality" from Michael Riffaterre, who uses it to indicate an element that disrupts the manifest grammar of a text and that thus threatens "the literary representation of reality or mimesis" (Riffaterre (1978) 2). Unlike him, I do not believe that the ungrammaticality is part of "a deviant grammar or lexicon" that is eventually integrated into a unified system of signification.

10 Cf. *SPP, Prometheus Unbound* ll. 661–3; III. iii. 160–6; IV. 153–8, 212–13, 236–40.

11 Dilthey (1971–2) 232–3.

12 Ibid., 231.

13 Jauss (1978) 142.

14 See Percy Bysshe Shelley, *Prometheus Unbound* (1959) 187.

15 See ibid., 143. The canceled line following "For know there are two worlds of life and death" is "Which thou henceforth art doomed to interweave."

16 See, for instance, Pottle (1965).

17 Curran (1975) 40.

18 Pinter (1962) 25.

19 Carlos Baker (1948) 107; cf. also Cameron (1943) 119–20.

20 Barthes (1977) 161.

21 Paul de Man (1983) 187–208.

22 Bloom, *Ringers in the Tower* (1971) 96.

23 For a discussion of the relationship between script and performance see Elam (1980) 208–9; see also Terry Eagleton (1978) 64–6.

24 Harari (1979) 40.

25 Chatman (1978) 1, 19–22. For a critique of the Platonic dualism implicit in Chatman's distinction see Barbara Herrnstein Smith (1980) 209–32.

26   Percy Bysshe Shelley, *Prometheus Unbound* 12.
27   The Bodleian manuscript consists of three notebooks. MS E1 begins with Act
     IV and proceeds for 427 lines, slightly beyond Earth's ode on humanity as "one
     harmonious soul of many a soul" to some lines spoken by the Moon. At this
     point Shelley commences Act I on the left-hand pages and continues to insert
     the remainder of Act IV on the right-hand side. This notebook ends in the
     middle of the scene involving the Furies. MS E2, at least equally confusing,
     begins with the remainder of Act I on the left-hand side. Several pages on the
     right side are left blank, and it is not until he reaches the middle of Act II,
     scene ii, that Shelley again returns to his dizzying practice of dividing the play
     between the two sides of the notebook. Having placed all of the dialogue
     between Asia and Panthea and part of the next scene (II. ii. 1–63: the
     semichorus of Spirits) on the left side, Shelley suddenly shifts the remainder of
     II. ii to the right-hand side. Thus the first part of II. iii, Asia's conversation
     with Panthea as they approach the volcano, is placed on the left side, beside
     the remainder of II. ii (the dialogue between the Fauns: ll. 64 ff.). The second
     half of scene ii does not occupy as much space as the first half of scene iii, and
     Shelley therefore leaves one of the right-hand pages blank as he continues
     scene iii up to the end of Panthea's and Asia's conversation (II. iii. 53). The
     remainder of scene iii is now shifted from the left to the right-hand side. Thus
     the crucial interview between Asia and Demogorgon (II. iv) now occupies the
     left side, while the remainder of scene iii (the song of the Spirits: ll. 54ff.) is
     juxtaposed opposite it. MS E2 ends in the middle of II. iv. MS E3, far simpler
     in its disposition of the play, begins at II. iv. 124 and continues straightforward-
     ly to the end of Act III, sometimes but not always leaving the right-hand pages
     blank for corrections.
28   Locock (1903) 28–9. Zillman also points out that the transcription of Act IV
     begins before that of Act I. But his account of the remaining acts makes them
     sound simpler than they are: "This act (I) was completed on page 20v, with Act
     II following on 21v and continuing to the end of the book (page 43v, line II
     iv. 74). Again Shelley continued directly into the next notebook (E3), with the
     next line of Act II starting on page 1v and ending on 10v" (p. 22).
29   Eco (1984) 49.
30   Ibid.
31   Nietzsche (1968) 38.
32   Lentricchia (1980) 310–17.

Byron

9

Don Juan and Byron's Imperceptiveness to the English Word

Peter J. Manning

In a famous essay which mixes praise and contempt in characteristic fashion, T. S. Eliot observed in 1937:

> Of Byron one can say, as of no other English poet of his eminence, that he added nothing to the language, that he discovered nothing in the sounds, and developed nothing in the meaning, of individual words. I cannot think of any poet of his distinction who might so easily have been an accomplished foreigner writing English.[1]

From this stigma of "imperceptiveness . . . to the English word" Byron and Byron criticism have yet wholly to recover.[2] The condemnation is best challenged by examining the assumptions on which it rests.

Eliot's privileging of the word is true to his symbolist heritage. Implicit in the negative verdict on Byron is the recommendation of an evocative poetry, one that gathers itself into a dense concentration of almost magically suggestive power, a poetry marked by moments at which meaning seems to overflow mere connotation, by nodal points at which meanings accumulated through an entire work converge and are released. The sense of an investment of meaning beyond the capacity of words creates a brief illusion of intensity and inclusiveness. A standard that invokes the word thus tends to acquire the hieratic associations of the Word, the authoritative utterance in which not only meaning but also being seem actually to reside. For Coleridge, the most reflective theorist of this mode among the English romantics, symbolism was, as J. Robert Barth has reiterated, intimately bound up with a sacramental view of the world.[3] At its extreme, however, Eliot's position values the single pregnant phrase, the resonant, gnomic aphorism. Keats's Grecian Urn, animated by the inquiries of its beholder, itself speaks only teasingly or remains silent. Unheard melodies can be judged sweeter than real ones because with them the gap between signifier and signified is widest, and the power of suggestion verges therefore on the infinite.

Other premises for poetry are possible, and attitudes other than awed contemplation are appropriate ends. One could sketch a poetics based not on the word but on words – that is, not on the charge granted the individual word (whether through special diction, or as the focus of an imagistic or narrative pattern, or by an aura of numinous presence), but on the relationship between words in themselves unremarkable. In contrast to Eliot's bias toward the symbolic, hence the static, one might urge the disjunctive and the dynamic; in place of Eliot's favoring of "full" speech, one might posit a discourse based on absence, one that never offers the consolations of climax or comprehensiveness, never holds forth the promise of an order suddenly made manifest. *Don Juan* exemplifies these procedures, and its richness refutes Eliot's judgment of "this imperceptiveness of Byron's to the English word" by revealing the narrowness of Eliot's criteria. I shall argue that it is precisely in proportion to his refusal to exalt the individual word that Byron is able to display the multiple functions of language itself.

I

The language of *Don Juan* can be approached through the role of language as it is conceptualized *in* the poem. The most satisfying starting point is paradoxically a scene in which language is unnecessary, Byron's depiction of the embrace of Juan and Haidée. "They had not spoken; but they felt allured, / As if their souls and lips each other beckon'd," the narrator observes (ii. 187):

> They fear'd no eyes nor ears on that lone beach,
>   They felt no terrors from the night, they were
> All in all to each other: though their speech
>   Was broken words, they *thought* a language there, –
> And all the burning tongues the passions teach
>   Found in one sigh the best interpreter
> Of nature's oracle – first love, – that all
> Which Eve has left her daughters since her fall.

(ii. 189)[4]

This characterization of Haidée's voice presents a familiar romantic figure, at once pathetic and sublime. Voice is here an absolute presence, capable of doing without the agency of words and directly inspiring a response from its hearers. The less Haidée and Juan can talk, the more intensely they share:

> And then fair Haidée tried her tongue at speaking,
>   But not a word could Juan comprehend,
> Although he listen'd so that the young Greek in
>   Her earnestness would ne'er have made an end;
>
>   (ii. 161)

Freedom from language becomes the very mark of intimacy:

> And then she had recourse to nods, and signs,
>   And smiles, and sparkles of the speaking eye,
> And read (the only book she could) the lines
>   Of his fair face, and found, by sympathy,
> The answer eloquent, where the soul shines
>   And darts in one quick glance a long reply;
> And thus in every look she saw exprest
> A world of words, and things at which she guess'd.
>
> And now, by dint of fingers and of eyes,
>   And words repeated after her, he took
> A lesson in her tongue; but by surmise,
>   No doubt, less of her language than her look:
> As he who studies fervently the skies
>   Turns oftener to the stars than to his book,
> Thus Juan learn'd his alpha beta better
> From Haidée's glance than any graven letter.
>
>   (ii. 162–3)

Just before the return of Lambro brings it to an end Byron presents again the preternatural harmony between Juan and Haidée:

> The gentle pressure, and the thrilling touch,
>   The least glance better understood than words,
> Which still said all, and ne'er could say too much;
>   A language, too, but like to that of birds,
> Known but to them, at least appearing such
>   As but to lovers a true sense affords;
> Sweet playful phrases, which would seem absurd
> To those who have ceased to hear such, or ne'er heard.
>
>   (iv.14)

The poem puts forward two analogies to the communion that ordinary language is too clumsy to express. The first is mythical and honorific: "They were alone once more; for them to be / Thus was another Eden" (iv. 10). Byron delineates the privacy of Juan and Haidée as a mutual transparency, a vision of complete reciprocal love seemingly prior to the fall into selfhood. This formulation is co-ordinate with another of differing tenor; the poem continues, "All these were theirs, for they were children still, / And children still they should have ever been" (iv. 15). The second analogy introduces an infantile coloring into the paradisal scene.

Haidée and Juan both appear as children to the narrator enmeshed in a bewildering adult world, but within the story their roles are clearly distinguished: Haidée functions as the mother of the infantile Juan. Famished and half-drowned, Juan is reborn from the sea and nursed back to health in Haidée's warm, well-provisioned, and womblike cave. As the weakened Juan slept, Haidée "bent o'er him, and he lay beneath, / Hush'd as the babe upon its mother's breast" (ii. 148); when he revived, Haidée, "who watch'd him like a mother, would have fed / Him past all bounds" (ii. 158).

These similes and the narrative configuration in which they occur place the ideal wordlessness of Haidée and Juan in parallel to the symbiotic union of mother and infant, at that early stage of human development before the infant comes to see himself as separate from the mother. Language at this level is a secret and subtle bond, a process of ceaseless and delicate adjustment, of needs understood and gratified before they are expressed. The figurative identification of the erotic sublime, as it were, with the dyad of mother and infant has important consequences for the conceptualization of language in *Don Juan*.

Juan participates briefly in a state anterior to the formation of an independent identity, but this fantasy of boundaryless bliss conflicts with the continued integrity of the adult who imagines it. To aspire toward the condition of Haidée and Juan carries the threat of self-abolition: to an autonomous being the idealized fusion is equivalent to a dangerous dissolution.[5] Inevitably, the beloved Haidée is therefore also a figure of death. As many critics have remarked, ominous overtones surround her from the moment of her introduction:

> Her hair, I said, was auburn; but her eyes
>   Were black as death, their lashes the same hue,
> Of downcast length, in whose silk shadow lies
>   Deepest attraction, for when to the view
> Forth from its raven fringe the full glance flies,
>   Ne'er with such force the swiftest arrow flew;
> 'Tis as the snake late coil'd, who pours his length,
> And hurls at once his venom and his strength.
>
>   (ii. 117)

Even Haidée's most maternally protective gestures bear, in exact relation to their nurturing power, vampiric suggestions:

> And then she stopp'd, and stood as if in awe,
> (For sleep is awful) and on tiptoe crept
> And wrapt him closer, lest the air, too raw,
> Should reach his blood, then o'er him still as death
> Bent, with hush'd lips, that drank his scarce-drawn breath.
>
> (ii. 143)

These sinister aspects are reinforced by the two other instances of wordlessness in *Don Juan* with which the episode of Haidée and Juan is thematically connected. The first concerns the grotesque "misshapen pigmies, deaf and dumb" (v. 88), who guard Gulbeyaz's door:

> Their duty was – for they were strong, and though
> They looked so little, did strong things at times –
> To ope this door, which they could really do,
> The hinges being as smooth as Rogers' rhymes;
> And now and then with tough strings of the bow,
> As is the custom of those eastern climes,
> To give some rebel Pacha a cravat;
> For mutes are generally used for that.
>
> They spoke by signs – that is, not spoke at all
>
> (v. 89–90)

Through the seemingly capricious comparison with the verse of Samuel Rogers, Byron links "smooth" writing to muteness and death, while the slant rhyme of "do" with "though" and "bow" makes clear that he himself rates lithe movement above euphony.[6] The conversation between Juan and General Lascy during the battle of Ismail displays a second, but different, linking of speechlessness and death; this exchange, like that between Juan and Haidée, is marked by linguistic incompatibility:

> Juan, to whom he spoke in German, knew
> As much of German as of Sanscrit, and
> In answer made an inclination to
> The General who held him in command;...
>
> Short speeches pass between two men who speak
> No common language; and besides, in time

Of war and taking towns, when many a shriek
  Rings o'er the dialogue, and many a crime
Is perpetrated ere a word can break
  Upon the ear, and sounds of horror chime
In like church bells, with sigh, howl, groan, yell, prayer,
There cannot be much conversation there.

(viii. 57–8)

Byron's description of Juan's enthusiasm for battle recalls several features
of the episode of Juan and Haidée and so brings the two episodes into
relationship:

— I say not *the* first,
  But of the first, our little friend Don Juan
Walked o'er the walls of Ismail, as if nurst
  Amidst such scenes – though this was quite a new one
To him, and I should hope to *most*. The thirst
  Of Glory, which so pierces through and through one,
Pervaded him – although a generous creature,
As warm in heart as feminine in feature.

And here he was – *who upon Woman's breast,*
  Even from a child, felt like a child; howe'er
The man in all the rest might be confest,
  To him it was Elysium to be there;
And he could even withstand that awkward test
  Which Rousseau points out to the dubious fair,
"Observe your lover when he *leaves* your arms;"
But Juan never left them, while they had charms,

Unless compelled by fate, or wave, or wind,
  Or near relations, who are much the same.

(viii. 52–4; emphasis added in 53)

The end of this sequence reminds the reader of Juan's enforced departure
from Julia as well as from Haidée, and the incongruity of echoing Juan's
amorous exploits in the midst of carnage is Byron's means of reinforcing
the fundamental kinship of the opposites. Juan is "nursed" in battle as he
is nursed by Haidée; for Juan to be alone with Haidée "was another Eden"
(iv. 10), and for him to be fighting "was Elysium" (viii. 53). Byron
announces "fierce loves and faithless wars" (vii. 8) as his subject, and the
reversal of Spenser is possible because at one level love and war function
identically. The link between the two actions is passion, etymologically the

root of passivity. Juan's much-remarked passivity might be considered as the annulment of psychological distance, the consequence of an overwhelming presence. The thirst for glory "pervades" Juan, or, to cite the *OED* definitions, it diffuses and spreads through or into every part of him, it permeates and saturates him. Common to the intensity of war and love is an obliteration of detachment, and, as the introduction of the configuration both here and in the Haidée episode insinuates, the prototype of this experience, erasing the outlines of the self, is the fusion of infant and mother.

The fantasy of fusion is situated at two poles: it is a fantasy of origins, of mother and infant, and it returns as a fantasy of prospective conclusions in sexual union, or in war and death. These become prominent in Byron's portrayal of the lustful Empress Catherine whose troops destroy Ismail. Catherine's infatuation with Juan establishes the equivalence of the "oh!" of sexual joy and the "ah!" of misery:

> Oh Catherine! (for of all interjections
>   To thee both *oh!* and *ah!* belong of right
> In love and war) how odd are the connections
>   Of human thoughts, which jostle in their flight!
> Just now *yours* were cut out in different sections:
>   *First* Ismail's capture caught your fancy quite;
> *Next* of new knights, the fresh and glorious hatch;
> And *thirdly*, he who brought you the dispatch!
>
> (ix. 65)

Byron began the description of Catherine by expanding upon Horace's ascription of war to sexual passion: "nam fuit ante Helenam cunnus taeterrima belli / causa" (Satire I. iii. 107–8). The *doubles entendres* of that passage are not more remarkable than its insistence that the gate of life and death is one:

> Oh, thou "teterrima Causa" of all "belli" –
>   Thou gate of Life and Death – thou nondescript!
> Whence is our exit and our entrance, – well I
>   May pause in pondering how all Souls are dipt
> In thy perennial fountain: – how man *fell*, I
>   Know not, since Knowledge saw her branches stript
> Of her first fruit, but how he falls and rises
> *Since, thou* has settled beyond all surmises.
>
> Some call thee "the worst Cause of war," but I
>   Maintain thou art the *best*: for after all

From thee we come, to thee we go, and why
    To get at thee not batter down a wall,
Or waste a world? Since no one can deny
    Thou dost replenish worlds both great and small:
With, or without thee, all things at a stand
Are, or would be, thou Sea of Life's dry Land!

Catherine, who was the grand Epitome
    Of that great Cause of war, or peace, or what
You please (it causes all things which be,
    So you may take your choice of this or that) –

                                                    (ix. 55–7)

Catherine, at once aggression and sexual passion, birth and death, source
and end, is an image of woman as the terrifying and engulfing force who
must be resisted. The light she retrospectively casts alters the impression
made by Juan and Haidée. Their intimacy offers the sole example of
complete communication in *Don Juan*, and Byron's treatment of it, in itself
and as part of the series culminating in Catherine, suggests how the fantasy
union presses toward a lethal silence. Catherine's Russian is as foreign to
Juan as Haidée's Romaic, nor does Catherine speak directly in the poem. If
Haidée and Juan transcend the usual barriers of the self, the poem also
delineates the limitations inherent in their ecstasy. Insofar as their love is
perfect it is finished, incapable of development; "for they were children still,
/ And children still they should have been" (iv. 15). Haidée and Juan reach
a state of atemporal happiness, but from the human perspective such
freedom from time is stasis and death. The narrator observes as Haidée and
Juan join their lives on the beach that she:

                had nought to fear,
    Hope, care, nor love beyond, her heart beat *here*.

And oh! that quickening of the heart, that beat!
    How much it costs us!

                                                    (ii. 202–3)

What the illusion of the all-encompassing *here* costs is the past and still more
the future, the change of the self in time.

The totality of Juan's and Haidée's passion is a fearful exclusion, but the
countervailing claims of the life they sublimely reject are kept before the
reader by the interventions of the narrator. He enables us to perceive that
the fantasy of full speech and full understanding, with its attendant values
of wholeness, presence, and atemporality, is not an isolated ideal: the

thematic networks within which it exists in *Don Juan* expose its connection with silence and the death silence figures. Juan's passion annihilates him on the breast of Haidée, and an ultimate value of silence brings to an end the role of the poet. The narrator and Juan, the poet and the character, are equally endangered: the Latin root of *infant* means "he who does not speak." The episode of Haidée and Juan is Byron's version of the *Ode on a Grecian Urn*: in Byron's meditation on his lovers, as in Keats's, the values of an encompassing symbolic, finally static imagination are set against the humbler commitments and narrative imaginings of the speaker himself. Both poets at last withdraw from the potent ideal they have imagined – the figures on the urn, Juan and Haidée – to face the imperfections of "breathing human passion." But whereas Keats throughout his career remains uncertain what language to put in place of the ennobling fictions of epic and romance that he repeatedly elaborated only to reject, Byron deploys a language that acknowledges and enacts the inescapable facts of absence and loss while affirming human vitality. "You have so many 'divine' poems," Byron vexedly exclaimed to his publisher, "is it nothing to have written a Human one?"[7] The style of *Don Juan* is co-ordinate with the role of speech in the poem: it is best studied through the plot it represents.

II

Somewhat later in his essay on Byron, Eliot turns to "a long passage of self-portraiture from *Lara*" already singled out by Charles Du Bos in *Byron et la fatalité* and declares:

> Du Bos deserves full credit for recognizing its importance; and Byron deserves all the credit that Du Bos gives him for having written it. This passage strikes me also as a masterpiece of self-analysis, but of a self that is largely a deliberate fabrication – a fabrication that is only completed in the actual writing of the lines. The reason why Byron understood this self so well, is that it is largely his own invention; and it is only the self that he invented that he understood perfectly.

Eliot here brilliantly specifies the self-creation Byron wrought in the Byronic hero, but the creation was not wholly uncontingent. If the Byronic hero was no simple transcription of Byron but a fabrication, it was nonetheless a fiction responsive to the fears and desires of its author. The role required of the Byronic hero is displayed in the relationship in *Don Juan* between Juan and Lara's descendant, Haidée's father, Lambro.

At first glance Lambro functions merely as a *senex* who intrudes upon the lovers and puts an end to their happiness. Insofar as Haidée's love imperils Juan, however, Lambro is also a savior who rescues Juan from an absorption he is too weak to withstand. Byron's two heroes are the opposing faces of a single figure (biographically, Juan embodies parts of Byron's childhood, and Lambro, returning to his shattered home, expresses aspects of Byron's response to his broken marriage).[8] *Don Juan* presents in the temporal sequence of drama the continuum of psychological strategy: the stern warrior is the protagonist Byron generates to preserve the passive child from collapsing back into his mother. Alfonso's interruption of Juan's affair with Julia in Canto I operates as a similarly providential occurrence, because Juan risks being crushed by the older women for whom he has become the pawn: his mother, Inez, who contrived the affair for her own reasons, and Julia, suddenly transformed at the end of the canto from a sympathetically self-deceiving lover into a skillfully deceitful intriguer.[9]

As the defense Julia makes on the night the lovers are discovered (i. 145–7) reaches its climax, Byron's rhetoric rises toward the sublime: "pale / She lay, her dark eyes flashing through their tears, / Like skies that rain and lighten" (i. 158). While the tide of Julia's apology breaks over Alfonso and his posse, Juan lies inert, hidden in the bed between Julia and her maid, "half-smother'd" (i. 165), in danger of "suffocation by that pretty pair" (i. 166). Here as elsewhere in *Don Juan*, the powerful speech of others is a menace to the hero.

The erotic triangle in both these episodes bears unmistakable oedipal overtones, and in both the function of the father figure as a principle of difference is apparent. By forcibly separating Juan from the mother whose love overwhelms him, Lambro, like Alfonso before him, makes possible Juan's independence. Moreover, even as the child models his identity on the father whom he cannot supplant, so Juan asserts himself in responding to this older rival. Attacked by Alfonso, Juan is driven to act: "His blood was up; though young, he was a Tartar, / And not at all disposed to prove a martyr" (i. 184). So, too, after his weakness and silence in Canto II and his position in Canto III as Haidée's consort, dependent on her wealth and status, Juan achieves a brief autonomy in his defiance of Lambro: " 'Young man, your sword;' so Lambro once more said: / Juan replied, 'Not while this arm is free' " (iv. 40). This confrontation is virtually the first time Byron presents Juan in direct discourse, and his speech is the proof of his temporary self-sufficiency.[10]

When Lambro overcomes Juan and casts him forth he sets in renewed motion the oscillating and ambiguous journey whose curves shape *Don Juan*. In his passivity Juan falls into a repetitive series at each stage of which he is almost absorbed by a dominating woman – Julia, Haidée, the "imperious" Gulbeyaz, the devouring Catherine, the "full-blown" Fitz-Fulke, and Adeline, "the fair most fatal Juan ever met" (xiii. 12); circumstances free him from her, but only to propel him toward the subsequent lapse. The journey is ambiguous because this potentially deadly woman, mother and lover, is a figure of desire and because Juan's freedom consists only of this endless chain of disruptions and losses.

Two alternatives to this dilemma would seem to exist in *Don Juan*. One is typified by Lambro, whose isolated marauding life and coolly powerful manner show him as the avatar of the hero who fills Byron's earlier works. The absolute masculine will with which Lambro crushes Juan and re-establishes his priority, however, *Don Juan* exposes as no solution at all. His contest is depicted by the narrative as more with Haidée herself than with her love object. Haidée's resistance to Lambro (iv. 44–5) is uncolored by the irony with which Byron tinges Juan's, and the extended pathetic description of her death (iv. 54–71) completes the eclipse of Juan's moment of bravery. In exerting his authority over Haidée, Lambro destroys the peace of his home: the desolate fate he brings on his island and himself (iv. 72) reveals that he too cannot exist apart from the mother figure. The second solution is embodied in the narrator, who is not so much in the story as above it, but whose words are shaped by the same exigencies as those his story witnesses.

Don Juan locates the origin of language in the Edenic harmony of mother and child: Haidée teaches Juan his "alpha beta" (ii. 163). The narrator develops the myth from his own experience:

> 'Tis pleasing to be school'd in a strange tongue
> By female lips and eyes – that is, I mean,
> When both the teacher and the taught are young,
> As was the case, at least, where I have been;
> They smile so when one's right, and when one's wrong
> They smile still more, and then there intervene
> Pressure of hands, perhaps even a chaste kiss; –
> I learn'd the little that I know by this
>
> (ii. 164)

Language here figures as innately sexualized: talk is desire. Byron under-scores the connection in writing of Italy in *Beppo*:

> I love the language, that soft bastard Latin,
> Which melts like kisses from a female mouth,
> And sounds as if it should be writ on satin,
> With syllables which breathe of the sweet South,
> And gentle liquids gliding all so pat in,
> That not a single accent seems uncouth,
> Like our own harsh, northern whistling, grunting guttural,
> Which we're obliged to hiss, and spit, and sputter all.
>
> I like the women too...
>
> (44–5)[11]

Yet the consummation of the desire for women must be resisted, deferred, because it would annihilate the poet's voice. As the puns on death and dying in Elizabethan poetry reveal, orgasm is "the little death." It is also, as a canceled, unfinished stanza of *Don Juan* suggests, a phenomenon literally beyond language:

> But Oh! that I were dead – for while alive –
>   Would that I neer had loved – Oh Woman – Woman –
> <All that I writ> All that I write or wrote can neer revive
>   To paint a sole sensation – though quite common –
> Of those in which the Body seemed to drive
>   My soul from out me at thy single summon
> Expiring in the hope of sensation –[12]

Juan's career and the narrator's reflections thus place language between two equally dangerous termini, both of which are approached with desire yet self-protectively put off. At one extreme looms the power of erotic bliss to annul self and voice, at the other the similar threat of the fusion of infant with mother.

In this schema language exists as the unresolved middle between the states that would abrogate it. Moreover, this middle is a middle of repetitions, for the story *Don Juan* tells is of the loss of the desired object in the necessary separation from her, the yearning for her, and the fresh flight from her. Human existence, as the poem sees it, perpetually re-enacts the primary liberating catastrophe of separation. A repetition is also a re-petition, a re-asking: the repetitions of the poem set forth again and again the mournful questions "How did I become separate?" "Who am I?" Women as much as men exemplify the pattern: once begun, they too must re-enact their initiating gesture:

> In her first passion woman loves her lover,
>   In all the others all she loves is love,
> Which grows a habit she can ne'er get over,
>   And fits her loosely – like an easy glove,
> As you may find, whene'er you like to prove her:
>   One man alone at first her heart can move;
> She then prefers him in the plural number,
> Not finding that the additions much encumber.
>
> I know not if the fault be men's or theirs;
>   But one thing's pretty sure; a woman planted –
> (Unless at once she plunge for life in prayers) –
>   After a decent time must be gallanted;
> Although, no doubt, her first of love affairs

> Is that to which her heart is wholly granted;
> Yet there are some, they say, who have had *none*,
> But those who have ne'er end with only *one*.
>
> (iii. 3–4)

The last stanza illustrates the ever-varying interpenetrations of the story level and the narrative commentary in *Don Juan*, the two aspects Robert Escarpit has distinguished as "le temps fictif" and "le temps psychologique."[13] This interpenetration breaks down any simple distinction between the story and its telling: there is only the modulation of language. The narrator's seemingly unmotivated generalization recalls Julia, banished to a convent a canto earlier, and her imposed constancy is the fate his fluid mode avoids. Juan vows eternal fidelity:

> And oh! if e'er I should forget, I swear –
> But that's impossible, and cannot be –
> Sooner shall this blue ocean melt to air,
> Sooner shall earth resolve itself to sea,
> Than I resign thine image, Oh! my fair!
> Or think of anything excepting thee
>
> (ii. 19)

This protestation is notoriously interrupted by retching, and happily, for Juan's romantic dedication to a single image is the willed counterpart to Julia's unwilling stasis. Juan can go forward because he forgets and because he is prevented from ever looking back. Similarly, Byron's refusal to linger over the episode of Juan and Haidée is a refusal of fixation, a refusal of the seductions of completion and finality. He writes their story not as a self-contained heroico-pathetic romance like his own earlier tales, but as part of an ongoing narrative whose rhythms undo the authority both of its dreams of bliss and of its conclusion. Byron repudiates his own temptation by the totalizing fantasy of Juan and Haidée (iv. 52–3, 74), passionate union or faithful death, to affirm the vital multiplicity of his own independent existence: not for him the diminishing pledge not to "think of anything else, excepting thee." In so doing he restores the intermediate space in which language (and hence his poem) can continue to exist. The space is empty, and marked by absence and lack, but it is an emptiness that invites filling by the imagination of the poet.

III

At the end of the first canto of *Don Juan* Byron threatens to promulgate a definitive set of "poetical commandments": "I'll call the work 'Longinus o'er a Bottle, / Or, Every Poet his *own* Aristotle' " (i. 204). In no respect does Byron differ more greatly from the rules than in his departure from the Aristotelean precept that a work of literature should have a beginning, a middle, and an end: *Don Juan* is all middle. The epic conventionally begins *in medias res*, but at the actual middle point of epic is a stabilizing device, a place about which the story can be organized: Odysseus narrating his adventures, Aeneas describing the fall of Troy to Dido, Raphael recounting the war in Heaven to Adam and Eve as an instructive example. In *Don Juan*, however, the condition of unfinishedness is not merely an aspect of the story, a temporary fiction exposed when the whole is complete, but one that attaches to the poet himself and influences the ongoing creation of his text.

The lines of *Don Juan* which the notion of indeterminacy perhaps first brings to mind are the melodramatic ones at the end of Canto XV:

> Between two worlds life hovers like a star,
>   'Twixt night and morn, upon the horizon's verge:
> How little do we know that which we are!
> How less what we may be!
>
> (xv. 99)

This fundamental unsettledness speaks in other tones as well:

> Of all the barbarous Middle Ages, that
>   Which is the most barbarous is the middle age
> Of man; it is – I really scarce know what;
>   But when we hover between fool and sage,
> And don't know justly what we would be at, –
>   A period something like a printed page,
> Black letter upon foolscap, while our hair
> Grows grizzled, and we are not what we were, –
>
> Too old for youth, – too young, at thirty-five,
>   To herd with boys, or hoard with good threescore, –
> I wonder people should be left alive;
>   But since they are, that epoch is a bore
>
> (xii. 1–2)

This reflection has been prepared for by the allusions to Dante in the previous cantos (e.g., x. 27), but Byron transforms the tradition that thirty-five, as the midpoint of man's allotted span of years, is a moment of decision; the era which in *The Divine Comedy* marks a crisis becomes in *Don Juan* a particularly anomalous stage in which meaningful choice seems impossible. The stanzas connect the uncertainties of middle life directly to the paradoxes of a text – "A period something like a printed page, / Black letter upon white foolscap" – and this odd conjunction recurs at the opening of the fifteenth canto, where Byron opposes the fertile indeterminacy of his text to the brevity of life and blankness of boredom:

> Ah! – What should follow slips from my reflection:
>   Whatever follows ne'ertheless may be
> As àpropos of hope or retrospection,
>   As though the lurking thought had follow'd free.
> All present life is but an Interjection,
>   An "Oh!" or "Ah!" of joy or misery,
> Or a "Ha! ha!" or "Bah!" – a yawn, or "Pooh!"
> Of which perhaps the latter is most true.
>
> But, more or less, the whole's a syncopé,
> Or a singultus – emblems of Emotion,
> The grand Antithesis to great Ennui
>
> (xv. 1–2)

Here is another form of the paradox already noted. The contradiction recurs, for the "syncopé" of emotion which combats boredom itself abolishes consciousness: a syncope is also the loss of syllables and sounds in the middle of a word, hence also the emblem of the cutting-short of the poet's voice. The sexual overtones of the "Oh!" of "joy" and their equivalence to the "Ah!" of "misery" recall the dangerous themes previously developed in the portrait of Catherine (see ix. 65, quoted above).

The intermediate position *Don Juan* occupies thus appears as a positive *modus vivendi*. The repeated suspension of the story functions on two levels. Juan is caught between infantile unconsciousness and sexual self-annihilation, and the poem's interruption of all his affairs corresponds to a refusal to allow passion its obliterating force. The narrator, yearning for both states, is also caught between his lost youth ("No more – no more – Oh! never more on me / The freshness of the heart can fall like dew" [i. 214]), and a future that must ultimately be death. His refusal to treat life according to the familiar pattern of crisis autobiography is a dissent from the notion of a fixed identity, of a life stiffening into shape once and for all, just as his refusal to precipitate a single final meaning is a mode of ensuring the inexhaustible vitality of his text. On both levels he is committed to filling the empty present, to staving off closure at any cost: "the past tense, / The dreary 'Fuimus' of all things human," which "must be declined" (xiii. 40) again links life and language by operating brilliantly in both contexts. The poem's insistence on its own indeterminacy and arbitrariness is its style of freedom: by rejecting the points of fullness – origin and end – Byron devotes himself to a discourse of absences, fragments, and losses which can yet keep the moment open.

The characteristic mode of this discourse is excursive, associative, metonymic, in contrast to the kind of metaphoric, symbolic concentration lauded by Eliot. As we have seen, Byron's resistance to such nodes of convergence is a matter both of substance and of technique: he denies the fatal power of certain meanings by continuing past them, and refuses permanence to identifications and identity. *Don Juan* is thus an anti-sublime poem, a poem that no sooner reaches a point of intensity than it undoes its own effects: the poem advances by negating the obsessions to which it returns, and then moving on, again and again.[14] Insofar as Juan represents aspects of Byron's life, for example, they are admitted only by negation: Juan's crises are Juan's, never acknowledged as the narrator's. Byron, in contrast to Coleridge and Wordsworth, deliberately stays on the surface (as much as he can), and that is why, despite the extravagantly artificial manner of *Don Juan*, he appears as a realist.[15]

The narrative of *Don Juan* seems to be set free of the constraints of purposefulness:

> I ne'er decide what I shall say, and this I call
>   Much too poetical. Men should know why
> They write, and for what end; but, note or text,
>   I never know the word which will come next.

(ix. 41)

Don Juan abounds in this sort of confession, each a protest against a vision of complete authorial control. Byron renounces the goal of a fictitious (and factitious) unity, of a designed poem whose meaning would be thoroughly determinate, thoroughly subservient to an end. In so doing he reinstates the power of language to initiate an endless play of meanings, a range of possibilities unrestricted by the demands of an author obviously shaping, or invested in, his work. Compare, for example, the increasing pressure Wordsworth places on his narrative in the later books of *The Prelude* as he strives to make his lived experience accord with a scheme in which "All [is] gratulant, if rightly understood" (1805, xiii. 385).[16] Byron's structureless habit of proceeding enables him to combat his anxieties by playing them out; it allows him to take on as his own some of the characteristics of the women whom he has placed as the potent other, desired and feared. His characterization of his poem is suggestively similar to that which he gives of women's letters:

> The earth has nothing like a She epistle,
>   And hardly heaven – because it never ends.

I love the mystery of a female missal,
Which, like a creed, ne'er says all it intends,
But full of cunning as Ulysses' whistle,
When he allured poor Dolon...

(xiii. 105)

The digressive manner of *Don Juan* bespeaks a relaxation of will which permits ominous material to surface: instead of repression, whose indefinite force heightens the sublime, the associative chains of *Don Juan* work toward expression and neutralization.[17] Symbolic and metaphoric poetry achieves its richness through compression and ambiguity; *Don Juan*, which, like women's letters, also "ne'er says all it intends," creates its vitality by extended meanings – inexhaustible sequences rather than pregnant points.

Eliot remarks that "if Byron had distilled his verse, there would have been nothing whatever left," but he is uninterested in the positive implications of his witticism. Byron's manner liberates his unconscious; it enables him to write a poem that can continually surprise its author. The long poem for which the romantics strove, only to find their aspirations turn into an onerous task or poignant failure, is for Byron a spontaneous, ceaselessly proliferating process. Novelty, rather than inevitability, marks the growth of *Don Juan*. The result is a poetry of surprising conjunctions and momentary delights. Consider, for example, the last quoted stanza. "The earth has nothing like a She epistle" sounds, apart from the oddity and false literariness of "She epistle," like a cliché, but the weakly descriptive phrase acquires force when a buried comparison is released in the second line: "And hardly heaven." This in turn becomes the starting point of a brief but consistent series of religious terms: "mystery," "missal," and "creed." If, as the drafts McGann prints of this stanza suggest, Byron was trapped into "whistle" by the need to rhyme with "epistle" and "missal," he resourcefully overcame the awkwardness with the allusion to Dolon and Ulysses. The unexpected change of context, from Christian to classical, is found elsewhere, notably in the clash between epic and Christian values which Byron insists that the reader confront with the Siege of Ismail. The poem repeatedly draws on epic tradition: Ismail is the modern counterpart of Troy, and Juan's wanderings are a skewed version of Odysseus's, as the echoes of the *Odyssey* in the Haidée episode make explicit.[18] The linking of female letters to epic craftiness insinuates again the replacement in *Don Juan* of physical adventure by the greater psychological perilousness of "cruizing o'er the ocean woman" (xiii. 40). Moreover, the juxtaposition of religious terms and deception – "you had better / Take care what you reply to such a letter" ends the stanza – connects the seemingly chance allusion to the theme of hypocritical piety running throughout the poem: think of Donna Inez keeping the erotically ornamented "family Missal" for herself (i. 46). It also recalls the elaborate love letter written by the convent-bound Julia in Canto I. Byron drops the allusions at the close of the stanza, but not before they have provoked trains of association that send the reader over the whole poem. To read *Don Juan* is to encounter a succession of such tantalizing occasions, a succession that is not determined by any obvious logic, which is inconsecutive but not therefore inconsequential. The sequences begin with license but as they develop become meaningful; they are justified by what they unfold, and so rise above irrelevance. *Don Juan* is not so much "fortuitous," as Jerome McGann describes it, as it is "overdetermined"; it is because the "fortuitous" happenings can be situated in many overlapping configurations that they possess meaning.[19] The reader may explore each occasion or not, as he chooses, before the flow of the narrator's talk carries him on to the next. The poem, then, is not precisely the "grand poetic riddle" (viii. 139) the narrator once calls it. Riddling is part of its appeal, but – to use a word that in its various forms occurs twenty-three times in the poem – it is rather a multiplicity of "puzzles." *Don Juan* asks less for comprehensive interpretation than for participation.

This range of meaning is possible only when the radically private language of mother and child represented in the relationship of Juan and Haidée is broken by the separation of the child from the mother. The taboos of the Oedipus complex send the son forth on his metonymic career, seeking satisfaction not in his mother but in a surrogate for her, not striving to usurp his father in actuality but to become like him in another setting. The Oedipus complex is thus, as Freud insisted, the foundation of culture, because it is through the Oedipus complex that the child passes from the family to his broader culture. To do so is to pass from the private language of mother and child to the pre-existent terms of the culture, to dream nostalgically of that lost transparency of communication but to feel oneself doomed to speak in the always slightly misfitting words the culture provides; at this level the ever-present allusions of *Don Juan* are the emblem of the pre-emption of the narrator's own voice by the babble of all who have preceded him. "Doomed" but also "enabled": in *Don Juan* Byron exploits this dilemma instead of concealing it by a myth of symbolic plenitude.

To illustrate the strengths of Byron's manner it may be useful to turn once more to Coleridge. Arguing in the *Biographia Literaria* against Wordsworth's assertion that the *Lyrical Ballads* were written in "the real language of men," Coleridge examines the fallacy on which the statement rests:

Every man's languages varies, according to the extent of his knowledge, the activity of his faculties, and the depth or quickness of his feelings. Every man's language has, first, its *individualities*; secondly, the common properties of the *class* to which he belongs; and thirdly, words and phrases of *universal* use. The language of Hooker, Bacon, Bishop

Taylor, and Burke, differs from the common language of the learned class only by the superior number and novelty of the thoughts and relations which they had to convey. The language of Algernon Sidney differs not at all from that, which every well-educated gentleman would wish to write, and (with due allowances for the undeliberate-ness, and less connected train, of thinking natural and proper to conversation) such as he would wish to talk. Neither one or the other differ half as much from the general language of cultivated society, as the language of Mr. Wordsworth's homeliest composition differs from that of a common peasant. For "real" therefore we must substitute *ordinary*, or *lingua communis*. And this, we have proved, is no more to be found in the phraseology of low and rustic life than in that of any other class.... Anterior to cultivation the lingua communis of every country, as Dante has well observed, exists every where in parts, and no where as a whole.[20]

In the Preface to the *Lyrical Ballads* Wordsworth had espoused a view of language as deriving directly from objects; Coleridge exposes the mistake of this "natural" view by maintaining that the "best part of human language ... is derived from reflection on the acts of the mind itself," and is "formed by a voluntary appropriation of fixed symbols to internal acts" (ii. 54). He thus restores language to the distinctively human matrix in which it comes into being, and his formulation permits a recasting of Eliot's critique. To say that Byron "added nothing to the language" is, in Coleridge's more discriminating framework, to indicate the lack of any strongly idiosyncratic "individualities" in his style, but also to throw the emphasis on its "common properties" and "words and phrases of *universal* use."

Byron cherishes the membership of *Don Juan* in the linguistic community to which it ineluctably belongs. The words he speaks have a history of their own, meanings they carry with them from their innumerable uses outside and prior to the poem. They are his only for an instant, loaned to him only briefly for his own purposes, before they return to their larger ongoing life. "If fallen in evil days on evil tongues," Byron writes in the *Dedication* to *Don Juan*, "Milton appeal'd to the Avenger, Time," and he continues: "Time, the Avenger, execrates his wrongs, / And makes the word '*Miltonic*' mean '*sublime*'" (st. 10). Of more interest than Byron's enlistment of Milton to lambaste Southey is his highlighting of the historical process by which words acquire meaning. The allusion to *Paradise Lost* is typical of *Don Juan*, a veritable echo chamber reverberating with phrases, imitations, parodies, and half-heard fragments from Homer, Virgil, Dante, Shakespeare, Milton, Pope, and scores of lesser figures. These shadowy presences augment Byron's voice by locating him within his tradition. Even were it true, as Eliot charges, that Byron added nothing to the language, one might yet reply that through him a whole tradition is summoned and renovated. His contempt for the "insolent . . . wish," as he saw it, of Southey, Coleridge, and Wordsworth "to supersede all warblers here below" (*Dedication*, st. 3) is the corollary of his refusal to give superordinate value to the concept of originality which, given his consciousness of, and commitment to, the public continuities of language, could only seem to him an impoverishing mystification.

Allusion is only a special case of the way in which *Don Juan* continually unmasks the illusion of its own autonomy in order to reap the benefits of acknowledging all that lies outside it. To choose words already invested with significance by their recognizability as literature – allusions – is in one respect to beg the central issue, because one of the fundamental questions raised by *Don Juan* concerns the conventional distinctions between the literary and the nonliterary. Macassar oil, Congreve's rockets, the brand names of ships' pumps, and all the other odd objects that find their way from daily life into *Don Juan*, on the one hand, and the highwaymen's slang, parodied jargons, and the mention of pox and like taboo subjects, on the other, constitute a challenge, less socially radical than Wordsworth's but kindred and no less far-reaching, to the notion of a specialized poetic diction. *Don Juan*, building on the comic precedents of the previous century,[21] demonstrates more thoroughly than does Wordsworth's own work the contention of the *Preface* to the *Lyrical Ballads* "that there neither is, nor can be, any essential difference between the language of prose and metrical composition." The conversation poem that "affects not to be poetry," that undertaking about whose implications Coleridge remained uneasy, reaches a triumphant apogee in *Don Juan*.[22]

Yet to speak, as in the title of Ronald Bottrall's essay, of "Byron and the Colloquial Tradition in English Poetry" is still somewhat to underestimate the ramifications of *Don Juan*, because the poem places itself in relation not only to a tradition *within* literary history but also to what would seem to stand outside it.[23] *Don Juan* could scarcely exist without the conventions Byron manipulates to make his meaning. If his "narration [of her genealogy] / May have suggested" (i. 59) that Julia will be the culmination, that is only because of the expectations of a pattern held by readers and writers within a given culture, their common literary competence. But Byron does not privilege these patterns, or, to put it more accurately, he privileges them by calling attention to their artificiality. To read *Don Juan* is to be made aware of the arbitrary agreements on which the making and maintaining of meaning rest. The relationship between flamboyant literariness and ostentatious anti-, or non-, literariness is a differential one: each throws the other into relief, and both together direct our attention to the functioning of language, to the conventions by which it works and the domains into which historically it has divided itself. By unveiling the artificiality of his own procedures, Byron displays the fictiveness of language generally and the delicate and complex consensus through which it is preserved. The myriad slippages and maladjustments of that social network create the gaps in which his irony and satire operate.

Don Juan, to return to the quotation from Coleridge, can imitate "the indeliberateness, and less connected train, of thinking natural and proper to conversation" because it sees conversation as an exemplary act performed in language, hence different in degree only, not kind, from literature. Byron repeatedly announces a freedom guided only by his own intelligent curiosity: "So on I ramble, now and then narrating, / Now pondering" (ix. 42). By refusing to mark itself off absolutely from everyday life, by denying that it constitutes any sort of special experience, *Don Juan* gains the power to include its opposite within itself. "This narrative is not meant for narration," the narrator comments, "But a mere airy and fantastic basis, / To build up common things with common places" (xiv. 7). Byron had chosen as the motto for the first cantos of *Don Juan* "Difficile est propria communia dicere," a phrase he had translated in *Hints from Horace* as "Whate'er the critic says or poet sings / Tis no slight task to write on common things."[24] He thereby directly connects the difficulty of his art to the prosaic nature of his medium: because his words claim no magic in themselves and because he regularly turns us outward from his words to their uses elsewhere, Byron demonstrates with remarkable clarity the basis of poetry not in "individual words," as Eliot implies, but in the relationship they mutually establish. Though seeing that Byron must be quoted at length to make his effect, Eliot does not recognize the alternative conception of language his practice successfully illustrates: individually colorless counters are transformed into a compelling series by the unexpected but self-validating connections Byron fabricates between them. The aggregative and associative mode of the poem is a virtual paradigm of Coleridge's definitions of the Fancy, but the loss of the intensity Coleridge ascribed to the Imagination only is more than offset by the revelation of the power of language itself, both within and without this particular poem. Despite Byron's evident pride in his achievement, *Don Juan* is almost less concerned with its own status as a unique *parole*, to use a Saussurean distinction, than it is with the overall function of *langue*.[25] *Don Juan* advances its claim to our interest not so much by conveying a meaning as by making its readers aware of the prior conventions on which any sharable meanings whatever depend.[26] Or, to remain with Coleridge, to read *Don Juan* is to be made aware of the characteristics of the "lingua communis [which] . . . exists every where in parts, and no where as a whole."

Despite such declarations as that of Wordsworth in the *Prospectus* to *The Recluse* that he would employ "words / Which speak of nothing more than what we are," the poetics of romanticism habitually resorts to a language of intimation. If the period is one of Natural Supernaturalism, as a magisterial description would have it, that terminology itself betrays the very binary opposition the poetry seeks to mediate. In the *Preface* to the *Lyrical Ballads* Wordsworth sets forth his aims in a fashion that similarly maintains a distinction: he proposed, he says, "to choose incidents and situations from common life" and "to throw over them a certain colouring of imagination, whereby ordinary things should be presented to the mind in an unusual way." To see merely the object is the sign of Peter Bell's imaginative poverty: "A primrose by a river's brim / A yellow primrose was to him, / And it was nothing more" (ii. 58–60). Though he insists on the "real," Wordsworth takes the object as instrumental to the transforming imagination. For Coleridge likewise, the symbol is defined by its embodiment of a realm beyond itself: it "is characterized by a translucence of the Special in the Individual, or of the General in the Especial or of the Universal in the General. Above all the translucence of the Eternal in and through the Temporal."[27] But in poetry there can be only words, and this illusion of depth and timelessness is a linguistic conjuring trick, a sleight of hand performed in language and inseparable from it. Byron's satiric and anti-sublime deconstructions strip away this illusion, insisting that we recognize that it is through our own language that we create the images that enchant us. Byron stresses not the "mystery" putatively residing in the object but the "doubt" caused by our own fallible mental activities. Paradoxically, it is by thus affirming the priority of our constructions that Byron returns us to the object world, but not as an empirical, objective given. To stretch Oscar Wilde, he too knows that it is only shallow people who do not judge by appearances: *Don Juan* shows that "the real" is the totality of our conventions, the agreed-upon social vision of reality. Here, too, Coleridge provides a useful gloss. In a footnote to chapter IV of the *Biographia Literaria*, he discusses the evolutionary process by which synonyms initially "used promiscuously" gradually distinguish themselves from each other: "When this distinction has been so naturalized and of such general currency, that the language itself does as it were *think* for us (like the sliding rule which is the mechanic's safe substitute for arithmetical knowledge) we then say, that it is evident to *common sense*" (i. 86). *Don Juan* continually lays bare the dangers of this "common sense" by correcting delusion, attacking cant, brutally reiterating the brutal "facts" of war and death, but simultaneously calling to our attention the sway of language and social bonds on which it in turn rests. "I write the world" (xv. 60), Byron can declare, because in writing he fully enters the transpersonal medium in which "the world" represents (and misrepresents) itself to itself.

Language in *Don Juan* thus points not to a supralinguistic reality (and hence is spared the agonizing doubt of language characteristic of a Shelley) but to a community of speakers and readers in the world their language builds up. In his influential *Romantic Image* Frank Kermode showed how "inextricably associated" in the romantic-symbolist tradition are the beliefs "in the image as a radiant truth out of space and time, and in the necessary isolation or estrangement of men who can perceive it."[28] These views may be found throughout *Childe Harold* and occasionally in *Don Juan*, but the nature of the latter poem qualifies the statements made within it. Even as he reduced the magical image, Byron restored the poet to his fellow men. Their common habitation in language binds together the two central figures of *Don Juan:* the narrator and the reader his fiction projects. The isolation Byron-as-Juan suffers is recuperated in the affiliation of Byron-as-narrator to his audience.

Though the web of words which is *Don Juan* reveals "the class to which [Byron] belongs" and the aristocratic Whig liberalism of his principles, the poem is remarkably unprescriptive of its reader. Assent, or the maneuvering of the reader into a point of view congruent with that of the author, is only one of the many and successive aims of the poem: the implicitly dramatized responses range from shock and anger to laughter at the author's image of himself, the narrator. The most generous aspect of *Don Juan* is the depth and variety of the experiences it acknowledges: the poem solicits the reader to bring with him all the works of literature he has read, all the political controversies in which he is enmeshed, all the mundane objects through which he moves, all his conflicting passions as child, parent, and lover. The poem functions not so much centripetally, directing attention to its uniqueness (though it does so gleefully), as centrifugally, returning each reader to the complex of private and public experiences that make up his particular life.[29] The comprehensiveness of *Don Juan* and the much debated question of its status as epic are subjects that can be reformulated in terms of the inclusiveness of the response it figures but does not restrict.[30] There is no single perfect reading of *Don Juan:* the text enfranchises all that infinite series of readings, neither idiosyncratic nor stock, which the common cultural context of author and reader empowers. It earns this richness because it is shaped not by the concept of uniqueness but by the concept of difference. The narrator demonstrates that identity exists only through the roles furnished by his culture, and hence is something both his and not his. To avert a threatening alienation, an imprisonment in a role, he must continually repudiate the stances he adopts, defining himself not by fixed points but by the shifting pattern of his movement between them. At one level *Don Juan* is a prolonged elegy for the loss of the union of mother and child represented by Haidée and Juan, but the poem also deploys a tenacious and resilient resistance to the temptations of that fantasy. The attempt to master the conflict perpetuates it: the repetitions of *Don Juan* reiterate the dilemma, revealing Byron's continued subjection to, as well as his conquest of, his desires and fears. The place of language in *Don Juan* is inevitably ambiguous: the situations in which it might be superseded by transparency of communication Byron rejects as self-destructive, and so he remains trapped, his reliance on language the sign of all that he has lost. Language for Byron can never be what it briefly is for Haidée and Juan, private and innocent; every fresh employment of it further implicates him in the continuum of history and society. Caught in words, however, Byron makes the exposure and exploitation of their treacherous wealth serve his ends. By displaying the unavoidable inauthenticity of language, he liberates its fictiveness and sets in motion the self created only through it. He unmasks the illusion of full meaning dear to Eliot and the symbolists, asking us to recognize that poetry can be made not only by saturating the individual word but also by ceaselessly uncovering the paradoxes hid in the use of ordinary words. The contradictions at the center of an existence defined by a language that is creative but inevitably conventional, his but not his, a means of connection but a story of separation, a mode of recovery but an admission of loss, a fantasy of wholeness that is desired but resisted, Byron accepts and makes generate the elaborate play that enlarges the narrator and animates the words of *Don Juan*.

NOTES

1 Eliot (1943) 232–3.
2 I mean only to indicate that this accusation has not been rebutted, not to underrate the excellent studies of Byron's style. In addition to the works cited below, I would single out Ridenour (1960); Joseph (1964); and Robson (1966). Two recent essays of relevance are Beatty (1976) and Berry (1975), which also takes up Eliot's critique.
3 Barth (1977).
4 All quotations of *Don Juan* are from McGann and Weller v.
5 See on this subject Laplanche (1976).
6 The variant for line 4 printed by McGann shows the original contrast to have been between the quiet of the doors and the vitality of Byron's own speaking voice: "The hinges being <oiled / oilier> much smoother than these rhymes."
7 Letter of 6 April 1819 (Marchand vi. 105).
8 Lambro, usually said to be modeled on Ali Pacha, had autobiographical roots, too; see iii. 51–2.
9 To the degree that Inez connives at the affair she and Julia converge. Juan's affair with Julia thereby seems a displacement of maternal incest: Alfonso's intervention is thus punishment for the forbidden act and rescue from a dangerous absorption.
10 Juan first speaks in the poem during the second canto, when his farewell is quickly cut short by seasickness (ii. 18–20), and when he bars the panicky crew from the grog (ii. 36), where Byron takes his speech directly from a scene in his sources. He is unheard during the subsequent 180 stanzas of Canto II and throughout Canto III.
11 Quotation from McGann and Weller iv.

12 Printed in McGann and Weller v. 660.

13 Escarpit (1957) ii. 58.

14 It could not, of course, repeatedly undo the sublime if it did not repeatedly strive for it. This movement is akin to that described as "desublimating" by Weiskel. I have not used the term because the relation between "the sublime" and "sublimation" within Weiskel's otherwise stimulating argument remains problematic.

15 Roman Jakobson proposed the relationships of metaphor to symbolism and metonymy to realism in section 5, "The Metaphoric and Metonymic Poles," of his essay, "Two Aspects of Language and Two Types of Aphasic Disturbances," Jakobson (1971).

16 The notion of free play is taken from Jacques Derrida; see, for example, Derrida (1972).

17 The relationship of repression and the sublime is a theme of the criticism of Harold Bloom; see Bloom (1975).

18 For example, iii. 23, on Lambro's arrival, "An honest gentleman at his return / May not have the good fortune of Ulysses." The allusions are studied in Manning (1978).

19 "Fortuitous" is a word McGann often uses to describe the growth of the poem in McGann (1976). The accretive chains, however, are often generated by the anxieties aroused by certain recurrent subjects, such as women. The motives for the resulting digressions and evasions are partly concealed from Byron himself. These gaps and switches suggest that the meaning of *Don Juan*, to use a Lacanian phrase, is not simply one that Byron speaks but one that speaks him. It is precisely such "arbitrary" links as the one the rhyme forces between epic craft and female cunning that show the connection and inscription of personal and cultural themes in the unconscious. *Don Juan* seems to me a little less rationally experimental, less scientifically instructive and more anarchic (as well as obsessive), than it appears in McGann's presentation. McGann (1976) is nonetheless the most penetrating discussion yet of the mode of the poem; that, starting from such different premises, my conclusions should often coincide with McGann's I wishfully interpret as corroboration of their general rightness.

20 Bate and Engell ii. 55–6. Subsequent page references are incorporated in the text.

21 A. B. England has explored Byron's affinities with Butler and Swift as well as the more commonly cited Pope and Fielding in England (1975).

22 See Schulz (1963) 81, 179.

23 Bottrall (1939), rpt. Abrams (1960) 210–27. Bottrall answers Eliot by arguing that Byron's "interest was rather in the fundamental rhythmic movement of speech than in the word."

24 Given in the variorum *Byron's Don Juan* (1957) iv. 4.

25 Saussure (1966) iii.

26 In an essay of that title, Roland Barthes locates "the structuralist activity" in the reconstruction of an object in order to show its rules of functioning (tr. Richard Howard, *Partisan Review* 34 (1967) 82–8). The structuralist critic Barthes describes focuses not on the content of meanings but on the act of

producing them: he "recreates the course taken by meaning, he need not designate it." A criticism based on these principles reveals virtues in Byron ignored by the still-prevailing organicist or apocalyptic camps.

27 "The Statesman's Manual," *Lay Sermons* 30.

28 Kermode (1957) 2.

29 Ruskin commented long ago on a conjunction between the proselike directness in Byron and the suggestive freedom he grants the reader. Observing that "He is the best poet who can by the fewest words touch the greatest number of secret chords of thought in the reader's own mind, and set *them* to work in their own way," Ruskin chooses as specific example a couplet from *The Siege of Corinth*:

> "Tis midnight: on the mountains brown – The Pale round moon shines deeply down." Now the first eleven words are not poetry, except by their measure and preparation for rhyme; they are simple information, which might just as well have been given in prose – it is prose, in fact: It is twelve o'clock – the moon is pale – it is round – it is shining on brown mountains. Any fool, who had seen it, could tell us that. At last comes the poetry, in the single epithet, "deeply." Had he said "softly" or "brightly" it would still have been simple information. But of all the readers of that couplet, probably not two received exactly the same impression from the "deeply," and yet received more from that than from all the rest together. Some will refer the expression to the fall of the steep beams, and plunge down with them from rock to rock into the woody darkness of the cloven ravines, down to the undermost pool of eddying black water, whose echo is lost among their leafage; others will think of the deep *feeling* of the pure light, of the thousand memories and emotions that rise out of their rest, and are seen white and cold in its rays. This is the reason of the power of the single epithet, and this is its *mystery* [(Quoted Rutherford (1970) 426–7)].

30 See, e.g., Donald Reiman's forceful brief essay, "*Don Juan* in Epic Context," (1977).

10

Byron and the Anonymous Lyric

Jerome J. McGann

Although academic criticism in the twentieth-century has maintained a studied disinterest in Byron's lyric poetry, nineteenth-century attitudes were (as usual) very different. The difference is manifest in Pushkin, Heine, and Poe, but it takes its most startling and perhaps most significant form in Baudelaire. A key figure in the history of the lyric even for those (for instance, T. S. Eliot) who denigrated Byron's importance, Baudelaire took Byron's work as a crucial point of artistic departure. In that (now largely ignored) context the conventional academic view of Byron has to be judged, simply and objectively, mistaken. Profoundly mistaken.

To explain the historical contradiction involved here would require a revisionary critique of the modernist reception of Baudelaire. My object is more simple. I want to sketch certain key points of relation between Byron and Baudelaire in order to describe the general formal character of Byron's lyric procedures. Such a study will also display the peculiar subjectivity of Byron's narrative and dramatic poetry, and hence the remarkable transformation that he worked upon a paradigm romantic form, the lyrical ballad.

The connection between Byron and Baudelaire is most easily traced through the cultural history of dandyism. To study Byron in that context, however, can easily obscure the technical issues to be understood when we try to recover what nineteenth-century writers found so important in Byron's lyrical procedures. So far as poetry as such is concerned, dandyism is important for the rhetorical postures it involves. *Fleurs du Mal* engages an aesthetic of dandyism that Baudelaire studied in Byron's lyric work. This aesthetic is announced in *Fleurs du Mal*'s famous opening poem "Au lecteur," where key conventions of romantic lyricism undergo an ironic meltdown. The sacred interiority of the romantic *rêveur* and his complicit partner, the overhearing reader, is torn open in order to expose (and exploit) its spiritual emptiness.

The text needs no rehearsing. We might recall, however, the important rhetorical move at the poem's conclusion, where Baudelaire addresses the reader directly: "Hypocrite lecteur, – mon semblable, mon frère." Baudelaire turns the monstrous delicacy of the romantic aesthetic – the "overheard" poem, in John Stuart Mill's well-known English formulation – into a weapon. Poet and reader are no longer permitted to imagine themselves saved by imagination. On the contrary, imagination is figured in the poem as hashish, source of illusion. The point of the text is not at all to escape illusion – to acquire an aesthetic redemption through either intense feeling or deeper understanding. Rather, it is simply to confront the reader with his damnation, to plunge him into the hell he has imagined he has *not* chosen and does not inhabit. In this text reader and poet – like Paolo and Francesca – are imagined floating in the dry heat of shared hypocrisies and a culpable linguistic innocence. (As we shall see, Byron read the famous episode from Dante's *Inferno* in precisely that way – as an emblem for a writing that would bring itself as well as its (romantic) readers to a final, terrible judgement).[1]

To write in this style, for Baudelaire, was to write under Byronic signs, as Baudelaire told his mother immediately after the publication of *Fleurs du Mal*.[2] This we have largely forgotten, just as we have forgotten the extraordinary stylistic means Byron developed for releasing that system of signs. Baudelaire understood what Byron was doing, however, and he followed Byron's example in his own poetry.[3]

In this connection, one of Baudelaire's most significant comments appears in his (unpublished) 1862 critical essay "L'esprit et le style de M. Villemain." Baudelaire's essay is an extensive critical survey of Villemain's dull academic work. In his brief abusive dismissal of Villemain's 1859 study of Pindar, *Essais sur le génie de Pindare et sur le génie lyrique*, Baudelaire glances at what he considers most significant in "le génie lyrique." He calls it "*le poésie lyrique anonyme.*" An obtuse academic to Baudelaire, Villemain simply has no grasp of this crucial lyrical style:

> Il a pensé à Longfellow, mais il a omis Byron, Barbier et Tennyson, sans doute parce qu'un professeur lui inspire toujours plus de tendresse qu'un poète.[4]

This "tendresse" is a condition of feeling appropriate to the style of Baudelaire's "anonymous" lyricism. It is a feeling generated from the (paradoxically) cold style of the dandaical poet, who pursues every range of feeling – pain and pleasure, benevolence and cruelty. Baudelaire reads Byron as he reads Pindar, as a poet nearly anonymous. Because Byron is a romantic poet, however, because he inherits the style of romantic self-expression, he becomes for Baudelaire a poet of masks and poses, the manipulator of his own subjectivities. Byron's anonymity lies not in his namelessness – romantic style is inescapably personal – but in his theatricality.

We begin to recover Baudelaire's approach to Byron by starting from a key Byronic text, the once so celebrated "Fare Thee Well!"[5] The academic disinterest in this notorious poem to his wife sounds the hollow echo of a reading that emerged at the moment the text began to circulate. This is Wordsworth's bourgeois reading, a reading generated through the criteria of lyrical sincerity. Wordsworth, who would become a model romantic lyrist for twentieth-century academics, pronounced Byron's poem "doggerel" and the judgement has stuck. Wordsworth saw the poem as a failed and utterly debased effort at romantic sincerity. "Fare Thee Well!" appears to him the emblem of a maudlin and factitious effusion – Byron posing as the sinner candidly self-exposed, confessed, and repentant.[6]

What Wordsworth could not see in this poem – what he probably could not imagine for it – was its deliberate hypocrisy. The sincerity of the poem is a pose, a mask that at once covers and reveals a deeper "sincerity." When Keats later sneered at Byron's theatrical self-displays – "Lord Byron cuts a figure – but he is not figurative" – he followed Wordsworth in turning away from Byron's lyrical rhetoric.[7] In making that turn he seems to have understood – as Wordsworth apparently did not – the choice involved. For Byron *is* a writer who strikes poses in his work; he has only a diminished fancy for Keats's ornamental luxuriance, and a perverse design upon Wordsworth's internal colloquies.

Byron adopts the conventions of romanticism he inherited – spontaneous overflow, internal colloquy – in order to break them apart. His crucial move was precisely a rhetorical one because the key assumption of romantic lyric is that the "true voice of feeling" cannot be studied, is not a matter of rhetorical conventions. A non-artificial paradise (or form of expression) is assumed to exist, and "sincerity" is thereby made the source and end and test of (romantic) art. The drama of the romantic lyric therefore typically traces a sublunary pursuit by the speaking poet for his own deepest and truest self. As a result, the poet *in propria persona*, the poet in what Coleridge and Wordsworth would call his "ideal self," structures the scene of romantic lyric.

Byron did not repudiate his romantic inheritance, he simply traced out the logic of its internal contradictions – what Baudelaire later saw as its hypocrisies. In simplest terms, Byron's poetry argued that "sincerity" *for the poet* has to be a convention, an artifice of language. To write a romantic lyric that will not be utterly self-deceived, the poet must stand as it were anonymously before his own subjective presentations. "Hypocrisy" (or contradiction) will become a poetical issue – a subject for the poet and the poem – as soon as the illusion lying behind the poetical convention of sincerity is exposed. Byron's lyric style, in effect, is a satire upon a normative mode of romantic writing. (As such, it is equally a satire and critique of the moral and social orders implicitly celebrated in that normative mode). Byron's "ideal self" is "born for contradiction," not for (the bourgeois illusion of) balance and reconciliation. Anticipating Baudelaire (and recalling Milton), Manfred would call that illusion of synthesis "The last infirmity of evil" (*Manfred* I. ii. 29).

Byron's critique of romanticism thus argued that a style of art (romanticism) was being transformed into an article of (bad) faith. Coleridge's famous definition of "poetic faith" as the "willing suspension of disbelief" is very much to the point here.[8] As in Coleridge's other technical discussions of poetry, this passage underscores the primacy of "disbelief" so far as poetic artifice is concerned. Coleridge imagines highly self-conscious readers of poetry – readers who deliberately "suspend" their awareness that the poetic scene is a play of language. Problems will arise, however, if the "suspension of disbelief" should lose its hold on the artifice involved – if a reader or poet should slip into a delusion and take the poem for "truth," take it (in its romantic form) as an artistic representation of the poet's inner subjective feelings or state of mind.

As Byron observed the cultural development of romantic ideas, he saw a widespread capitulation to such delusions. Other writers had made similar observations – T. H. Matthias, for example, and William Gifford, and the writers of the *Anti-Jacobin*. Though *English Bards and Scotch Reviewers* follows their critical line on romanticism, it stands apart in one crucial respect. Byron's satire climaxes as an exercise in self-criticism. In making this move Byron's text also raised the troubling (romantic) question: is the self-critique "true," or is it a matter of art? In what sense should Byron (or his readers) "believe" the self-critical representations of a text like *English Bards*? (The question would soon be raised again, even more problematically, in Byron's next published satire, *Waltz* (1813).)[9]

Byron's importance for romanticism lies exactly in his determination to force a confrontation with that question. To do so Byron placed himself at the centre of his work and made a Brechtian theatre of his romantic self-expression and sincerity. In his work these romantic forms are deployed *as if they were real*. Byron's is not merely the poetry of a bleeding heart, it is a poetry that comes complete with bleeding heart labels. Whereas in (say) Wordsworth and Coleridge the question of the truth of poetry remains a theoretical matter, in Byron's work it is the central and explicit subject of the writing.

The manifest sign of this fact about his work remains the biographical obsession that dominates the reading and criticism of his poetry from the outset. The obsession represents a desire to have the textual scene validated by an extra-textual measure of truth (which in romantic terms would have to be a personal, subjective, or psychological measure – the emergence into view of "the real Lord Byron"). That truth, famously, remains elusive – like most romantic forms, "something longed for, never seen." The artifice of Byron's work thereby reinstalls a "primary imagination" of disbelief into the scene of writing and reading. His is an art of seduction in which the seducer is as abandoned (in both senses of that word) as the object of his seduction. Byron's poetry constructs an artifice of the living poet himself, "Byron" (as it were) *in propria persona*. Suspended thus between belief and disbelief, the poetry opens itself to the consequences that follow when a romantic "contract" between poet and reader is put into play. Unlike Wordsworth, Byron is not trying to draw up such a contract – to install the romantic artifice as a style of writing, to create the taste by which his work is to be enjoyed. Byron's relation to romanticism is secondary and critical. Accepting (provisionally and artistically) the power and authority of romanticism's conventions, Byron institutes an anatomy of their world.

To do this meant that Byron had to construct artifices of himself in his work – illusory and theatrical selves that would summon up their necessary reciprocals, an audience of responsive observers. Most famous of these is the figure of the suffering poet, whose (audience) reciprocal is the sympathetic reader. (Poe, Heine, and Baudelaire represent the antithesis of that sympathetic reader; they are all "Byronic" readers, cynical and perverse.) Byron inherited the figure of the suffering poet from his romantic forebears, and especially from Wordsworth and Coleridge. In the benevolent lyricism of those early romantics this relationship comprises a dynamic wherein "feeling comes in aid of feeling." The dynamic operates on the assumption that nature and society are permeated by a spirit of benevolence – in traditional terms, by a loving God. *Lyrical Ballads* and Coleridge's early poetry constructed the model for this kind of poetry. *Lyrical Ballads* is especially important because it tells the story of Wordsworth's and Coleridge's education into the truth and reality of this spirit of benevolence.

Byron's work, on the other hand, tells the story of a poet's education in the demonism of that same spirit. When feeling comes in aid of feeling in the Byronic and Baudelairean world, the sympathetic event is not confined to a horizon of benevolence. Theirs is no mere debunking move, however. Byron, for example, begins with the traditional romantic assumption that the poet is a man like other men but endowed with more lively sensibilities, and so forth.[10] Those heightened sensibilities draw him into a kind of Lucretian perception of nature and society. Love dominates the Byronic world, but – as the Baudelairean Swinburne would later put it –

> Love is one thing, an evil thing, and turns
> Choice words and wisdom into fire and air.

And in the end shall no joy come, but grief,
Sharp words and soul's division and fresh tears.

(Atalanta in Calydon, 209–12)

Love is a destroyer and a preserver, and each function may bring either tears of joy or tears of pain. For the Love that dominates Byron's imagination of the world is not a ruling power, a social force or governor, it is simply (and profoundly, as in Lucretius) the source of all its life and energies. The law of the world is laid down by an interplay of Chance and Necessity, which generate stochastic forms and Chaotic orders. The presiding deity in this dynamic, according to Byron, is "Circumstance, that unspiritual god/ And miscreator" (*Childe Harold* IV. 1122–3).

The inward or psychic equivalent of Byronic Circumstance is the poet's famous chameleonism, or what he later defined as "mobility":

It may be defined as an excessive susceptibility of immediate impressions – at the same time without losing the past; and is, though sometimes apparently useful to the possessor, a most painful and unhappy attribute.

[Byron's n. to Don Juan xvi 97]

Here we see – the event appears throughout Byron's work – the utter translation of Wordsworthian and Coleridgean "feeling." The translation happens because Byron insists upon putting romantic feeling to an absolute test. What do we discover about "feeling" when we explore and pursue it *in every particular of our lives*, and not just in those special moments – for instance, in Wordsworth's "We Are Seven" – that a certain sensibility wishes to define as normative? We discover that such moments are exactly that, momentary. We also discover the illusory impulse to translate those moments into moral and conceptual norms, to generalize from them. For Byron (and later for Baudelaire), the process of generalization will be resisted because its benevolence is inhuman – ultimately, is a betrayal of the romantic commitment to unlimited experience. Pain, evil, despair: these are Byron's crucial "moments in the being / Of the eternal Silence" because, as the reciprocals of romantic pleasure, benevolence, and hope, they reopen the horizon of feeling. When Byron declares that "the great object of life is sensation – to feel that we exist, even though in pain" – he makes a crucial revisionary turn upon his own romantic inheritance.[11]

The force of Byron's lyric poetry comes from his shocking determination– the phrase is not too strong – to use himself to tell this story of the world. We observe his determination very early, even in a juvenile poem like "Damaetas." The strength of this mordant analysis of a wicked youth comes from its poetic deception. Byron publishes the poem in *Hours of Idleness* under a cunning classical heading. The Theocritean name carries a sly homosexual overtone, but that obliquity is merely the sign of a deeper deceptiveness. More important and revelatory is the suppressed title of the work: "My Character."[12] In this poem Byron tells a slant truth about himself, and in slanting the truth he tells a further and more revealing truth: he dramatizes his own hypocrisy.

A master of this style, Byron turns it loose upon all the poetic forms of Europe's cultural inheritance. That fact about his work – the scope of Byron's formal poetic undertakings – explains the immense impact that his poetry had upon later writers. When he takes up the epigram – he wrote many – the same effect appears:

> Tis said *Indifference* marks the present time,
> Then hear the reason – though 'tis told in rhyme –
> A King who *can't* – a Prince of Wales who *don't* –
> Patriots who *shan't*, and Ministers who *won't* –
> What matters who are *in* or *out* of place
> The *Mad* – the *Bad* – the *Useless* – or the *Base?*[13]

"Though 'tis told in rhyme": that conventional gesture of poetic modesty comes as the prolepsis of what the last line names directly. This poem is, in its chosen political terms, a mad, bad, useless, and base piece of work, the moral equivalent of the world it is attacking. It is a small but superb poem, an affront and an offence – quite literally a terrible truth. In a sense Auden's later sentimentality would not have approved, this is a poem that "makes nothing happen." It exposes and exploits the secret hidden within Kant's bourgeois aesthetic of disinterestedness.

But among Byron's shorter poetic forms, the love lyrics illustrate his stylistic achievements most fully. "Fare Thee Well!" is more than a cruel and pathetic piece of hypocrisy; it is a dramatic presentation of the illusion resting at the heart of the romantic lyric, with its commitment to a "willing suspension of disbelief" on the part of poet and reader alike. We do not begin to enter the dangerous space of "Fare Thee Well!" until we see how, in the horizon of romanticism's moral and aesthetic senses alike, it is a *bad* poem. It is bad not simply because it is a cruel poem, intentionally designed to hurt his wife personally and damage her in public. It is bad because, in a sense, it is hardly "poetry" at all, more like a psycho-political broadside in verse. It is also bad because this anti-aesthetic design is pursued in a cunning way, by the manipulation of a mask of romantic sincerity. That pretense of sincerity deepens into an oblique exposure of Byron's own pretences of art. The last infirmity of the poem's evil, then, comes in the failure of its designs. (This failure of the poem takes place on its own anti-aesthetic terms – that is to say, in an immediate and real way, when Byron is expelled from normal society, when he leaves England in disgrace.)

Sincerity that masks a "spoiler's art," poetry that is not poetical: the writing is radically self-contradicted in the context of its cultural inheritance. It imaginatively transcends that historical moment when its immediate failure and disgrace get culturally (re)inscribed, when the poem is (academically) judged a simple piece of factitious romantic trash. That misreading of the poem comes from a culture's determination to cherish a doubled illusion: first, that poetry expresses the best that has been known and thought in the world; and second, that criticism may be confident in its visions of judgement. If the history of critical condescension toward "Fare Thee Well!" registers the collapse of Byron's romantic authority, it equally testifies to the endurance of Baudelaire's hypocritical reader.

Byron's significance as a lyric poet lies in the range of ironizing and critical techniques that he brought to the new lyrical forms of romantic sincerity. These techniques extend from the most sentimental kinds of "romantic irony" (already at work in his earliest poetry, for example *Hours of Idleness*) to corrosive and nakedly self-imploding forms. Though Byron's work shuttles between these two stylistic poles, his originality – and hence his importance for Heine and Baudelaire – must be located strictly at the latter end, in his critical exploration of the conventions of romanticism and the inheritance of sentimentality.

Byron's work has caused great difficulty for many readers, however, because his critical stance so often appears cynical, desperate, or – perhaps worst of all – indifferent. Subjecting Byron's *oeuvre* to a programmatic hope for some kind of social accommodation, Carlyle would later call it "The Everlasting Nay." Thus would he execute upon Byron his middle-class, Victorian version of Hegel's "negation of the negation." Baudelaire's reading is structurally the same as Carlyle's and Hegel's, but politically deviant. Baudelaire has greater sympathy for the devil – he celebrates Byron's satanism – because his politics are resolutely opposed to bourgeois order.

If we are to read Byron well, then, the issue of his satanism – his non-benevolent sympathy and "tendresse" – must hold the centre of our attention. Because Baudelaire did exactly that, his understanding of Byron runs deep. Why, then, would the importance of Byron escape so many twentieth-century readers? The answer, I think, is finally political. While modernists like Eliot could translate Baudelaire's myth of the aristocrat/priest/dandy into a reactionary literalism, it was a move that could not be made on Byron. Baudelaire was appropriated because his satanism – unlike Byron's – remained linguistic, and because a postmodern consciousness had not yet established the spectacular and mordant equivalence between *res* and *verba* that we now take for granted. In Byron, however, that equivalence is – as we shall see – exactly the issue of the work.

II

Thus far I have tried to define the general style and structure of Byron's lyrical dandyism. To understand the originality of this work, we have to inquire further into his relation to certain conventional styles of romantic irony.

As Schiller's famous essay argued, "the sentimental" in literature is a figure of literary self-consciousness. In the analytic dyad naive/sentimental, "naive" is a term generated by the critical power of the idea of the sentimental. "Naive" poetry exists, first, because it has been turned upon by a critical self-consciousness; and second, because that self-consciousness – in a paradoxical move – declares "the naive" to be the primary and generative term so far as poetry is concerned. In this sense, to be sentimental is already to have deployed a form of "romantic irony."

Macpherson's fragments from Ossian, and more especially the subsequent controversies over those works, nicely illustrate the polemic involved in Schiller's position. So far as English romantic poetry is concerned, the project of the *Lyrical Ballads* corresponds to the project of Schiller's essay. In Wordsworth's and Coleridge's work, ballad is to naive what lyrical is to sentimental. Wordsworth's critical formulation of the dialectic came in the Preface to the *Lyrical Ballads* when he distinguished "emotion recollected in tranquillity" from the "spontaneous overflow of powerful feelings." Poetry springs from the latter and depends upon it as a primary source of "feeling." As an artistic and compositional practice, however, poetry for Wordsworth is a recollective and secondary event. It is an act of self-consciousness. It is, in Schiller's sense, "sentimental."

Romantic writing thus involves a negotiation of two kinds of feeling: on one hand, spontaneous and naive feelings (for example, in the poetry of Robert Burns, or in the characters in "The Idiot Boy"); on the other, reflexive and internalized feelings ("the bliss of solitude"). More than anyone else, Wordsworth defined this dialectic for English poetry. It is, as we know, a story of loss and gain – loss of the naive, acquirement of the sentimental:

> We will grieve not, rather find
> Strength in what remains behind;
> In the primal sympathy
> Which having been must ever be...
> In years that bring the philosophic mind.
> ("Ode. Intimations of Immortality," 180–4, 188)

That "mind" is precisely *not* the Enlightenment mind. It is philosophical because it stands opposed to the critical intelligence of the *philosophe*, a figure specifically (and ironically) invoked in Wordsworth's phrase "philosophic mind." Not a contentious and worldly mind, Wordsworth's is a "purer mind," affective and childlike – a mind turned from murderous and socially divisive dissections toward healings, consolations, and "tranquil restoration."

The so-called Greater Romantic Lyric dramatizes the workings of this type of mind.[14] (For the reader of such work, the poems are an educational machinery disseminating the Wordsworthian mind through the culture at large.) The conventions of the form are well-known: a movement into a scene of solitude, typically a solitude in Nature; a meditation on and within that place, which serves as a figure (and map) of lost regions of a more primal self; an encounter with the lost self and its desires, more or less direct; finally, a separation that leaves the mental traveller more deeply attached either through the pain of this (now self-conscious) loss, or through a faith in a suprapersonal order of benevolence that maintains these attachments beyond one's personal will or control. The exemplary romantic form of that conceptual order (which is "sentimental" and self-conscious) was elaborated in Germany by Hegel.

Byron's deviant relation to this romantic programme becomes clear when we study the dynamic of his various natural meditations. For example, as Childe Harold is travelling from Spain to Albania in Canto II of his poem, his maritime solitude becomes the locus for a romantic colloquy (sts 22–7). The Childe's meditation is specially notable because it is a kind of second-order meditation. This is not simply a meditation within a natural solitude, the Childe is meditating upon the idea of such meditations. The thematic core of the passage contrasts the solitude of nature, which appears bountiful, with the solitude of society. Although the latter displays as much energy as the former, it appears a corrosive and destructive energy and hence something to be fled. The idea of taking flight culminates the meditative sequence:

> More blest the life of godly Eremite,
> Such as on lonely Athos may be seen,
> Watching at Eve upon the giant height,
> That looks o'er waves so blue, skies so serene,
> That he who there at such an hour hath been
> Will wistful linger on that hallow'd spot;
> Then slowly tear him from the witching scene,
> Sigh forth one wish that such had been his lot,
> Then turn to hate a world he had almost forgot.

The conclusion deliberately works a shocking inversion of the conventional romantic topos of nature. Structurally the text repeats the Wordsworthian ideas (a) that feeling is primary, and (b) that "powerful feeling" (the naive) is dialectically connected to "tranquil" emotions (the sentimental). Here, however, that dialectic undergoes a reinterpretation of great importance. In simplest terms, Byron's passage through a romantic meditation on nature does not conclude in a Wordsworthian "tranquil restoration" but in a characteristically Byronic turn to passion and savagery. Most startling of all is the presentation of hatred as the emblematic sign of Byron's "naive" poetical condition.[15]

This Byronic structure of feeling – the pursuit of primal and naive spontaneities through an adverse study of memory and sentiment – dominates all his work. Canto III of *Childe Harold's Pilgrimage*, so often read as Byron's "Lakist Interlude," in fact represents his definitive anatomy and rejection of Wordsworth's "philosophic mind." This happens literally in sts 106–7, where Byron pledges his allegiance to the *philosophes* Voltaire and Gibbon, and to their programmes of critical conflict with the conventional world. Furthermore, he takes this position following his conscious pursuit of the meaning of romantic reverie and romantic nature.

The structure of the canto as a whole replicates the structure of the brief passage we just examined from Canto II. Byron (no longer wearing the mask of the Childe) departs "the world" and its scenes of violence and conflict. This violence appears in unmasked political forms early in the canto, when Byron calls back the climactic events of the Napoleonic War. That political scene comprises the emblem of wars that are at once more primal, more personal, and more secret.

Like Manfred, Byron begins by seeking forgetfulness and an escape from the tumult of emotional conflict. His conscious desire is that the strife of his passions might undergo moderated and sympathetic transformations: in the earlier words of the Giaour, "To rest, but not to feel 'tis rest." The famous "Wordsworthian" scenes in the canto, however, which are charged with such transformative powers, barely detain Byron. He engages those scenes as the Childe had engaged them in Cantos I-II, and as Manfred would shortly engage them again: as vehicles for restoring a commitment to elemental passion: indeed, as vehicles for gaining an immediate recovery of such passion.

In this connection, two passages in Canto III are especially significant. The poem climaxes in the famous Jungfrau Storm sequence, where the full force of Byronic passion is exteriorized. Following the logic of Byron's initial conscious desires, the storm breaks only to bring a clear sky and images of peacefulness and love. Concealed within the storm, however, are Byron's deepest and most savage feelings – feelings at once completely personal and wholly elemental:

> Could I embody and unbosom now
> That which is most within me, – could I wreak

My thoughts upon expression, and thus throw
Soul, heart, mind, passions, feelings, strong or weak,
All that I would have sought, and all I seek,
Bear, know, feel, and yet breathe – into *one* word,
And that one word were Lightning, I would speak;
But as it is, I live and die unheard,
With a most voiceless thought, sheathing it as a sword.

(st. 97)

Because the object of Byron's stormy passion is not actually named, this text's true "thought" – the wit here is typically Byronic – remains literally "voiceless." Byron speaks his mind by holding his tongue. The effect is to represent the presence of a psychic force that dwarfs even the Jungfrau's storm. No language is adequate to the enormity of Byron's desire – because that desire must match the enormity of its reciprocal, the righteously inverted betrayal of desire executed by Byron's unnamed enemies. (Readers have always recognized the enemy being imagined here in textual silence: on one hand, the collective Spirit of English moral hypocrisy, on the other the Spirit's immediate avatar, Byron's "moral Clytemnestra.")[16] Byron's savage desire in this passage is therefore literally beyond nature, an *un*natural response to the behaviour and the desire of his antagonists. Theirs is the anti-nature of moral virtue, Byron's is the anti-nature that demands a morality beyond the order of moral virtue.

The demand cannot be met in the normative orders of time and space (traditional nature), history and society (Hegelian Spirit). The sheathed sword of stanza 97 represents an insurgent but hopeless energy:

Their breath is agitation, and their life
A storm whereon they ride, to sink at last,
And yet so nurs'd and bigotted to strife,
That should their days, surviving perils past,
Melt to calm twilight, they feel overcast
With sorrow and supineness, and so die;
Even as a flame unfed, which runs to waste
With its own flickering, or as a sword laid by
Which eats into itself, and rusts ingloriously.

(st. 44)

Exactly forecasting the textual events of the Jungfrau passage, this stanza explains the demonic, Lucretian character of the "Love" figured in the benevolent apparition of Clarens (sts 98–104) following the Jungfrau storm. Byron presents the scene at Clarens as a special moment of clarity, the immediate reciprocal of the deceased storm. Far from an emblem of a universally benevolent Nature, the Clarens passage is exactly that – a mere moment in the being of Byron's ominous Lucretian silence. The wonderful irony of the passage comes from the historical association of Clarens with Rousseau. A Byronic figure of absolute contradiction, Rousseau is at once representative of natural benevolence and the "apostle of affliction" (st. 77): the self-torturing terrorist of freedom, devoured by love (see sts 76–84).

Byron's argument throughout the canto is the same: that no "abundant recompense" (existential or artistic) can accommodate one to the departure of elemental emotional life or naive art. More than this, he argues that the installation of a programme of such recompenses – whether psychological or poetic – installs a secret ministry that, when allowed to run its full course, will ultimately draw one back to the elemental. For Byron, the dialectic of loss and gain is endless, nor does it culminate in any "higher order" or synthesis. According to this argument, death itself, which Manfred deliberately undertakes, puts no period to the dialectic. As Byron says in the fourth canto of *Childe Harold's Pilgrimage*:

> But there is that within me which shall tire
> Torture and Time, and breathe when I expire;
> Something unearthly, which they deem not of...
>
> (st. 137)

To achieve this peculiar kind of immortality requires a perpetuation of resistance and strife, a refusal of what Wordsworth called "primal sympathy." It is to choose instead, with Blake, primal energy, primal conflict.

III

Byron turns all his subjects into lyrical forms. He protested when his contemporaries identified him with Harold, the Giaour, the Corsair, Lara, and so forth. Because these *figurae* are consciously manipulated masks, one has to read them – as Coleridge might have said – in terms of a "sameness with difference." The poetry lies exactly in the relation, in the dialectical play between corresponding apparitional forms: on one side, the spectacular poet – the man cut into a Keatsian figure, the person translated into what the Byronic texts call "a name";[17] on the other, the various fictional and historical selvings. In Byronic masquerade we have difficulty distinguishing figure from ground because the presumptive ground, "the real Lord Byron," becomes a figural form in the poetry.

The anonymous lyric depends upon this stylistic procedure and sets up a hypo-critical contract with the romantic reader. The texts deliver a merciless revelation of a uniform condition – a kind of "universal darkness," but beyond the imagination of *The Dunciad* because Byron's revelatory text has itself been imagined in the darkness.

> I am not of this people, nor this age,
>   And yet my harpings will unfold a tale
> Which shall preserve these times when not a page
>   Of their perturbed annals could attract
>   An eye to gaze upon their civil rage
> Did not my verse embalm full many an act
>   Worthless as they who wrought it: 'tis the doom
>   Of spirits of my order to be rack'd
> In life, to wear their hearts out, and consume
>   Their days in endless strife, and die alone;
>   Then future thousands crowd around their tomb,
> And pilgrims come from climes where they have known
>   The name of him – who now is but a name...
>
> (*The Prophecy of Dante* i. 143–55)

Is this text "about" Byron or is it about Dante, about Italy or about England? Is Lord Byron recollecting the great Tuscan poet, or are we to read it the other way round – with this textual Dante prophecying his future British avatar? Furthermore, this structure of convertibility turns everything into its opposite. Byron/Dante declares "I am not of this people or this age" but his verse "embalms" the "worthless" acts of the age. The word "embalm" is tellingly volatile since it connects the poet's work with corpsed forms – as if he (Dante/Byron) were a literal figure of the nightmare life-in-death that he perceives all about him. To consult such a poet one has to visit his tomb, where one encounters merely his "name." The tombstone's engraved letters enter the text as a sign that even before death the poet lives a postmortem existence.

In his Preface to the poem Byron associates his "prophecy" with the vision of Cassandra, whose prophetic truth shares the doom of Troy. Like Cassandra and Dante – like some utterly bleak democrat of Wordsworth's Preface to *Lyrical Ballads* – Byron is "a man like any other men," but his endowment "with more lively sensibilities" gives him the darkened eye of a seer like Cassandra:

> All that a citizen could be I was;
>   Raised by thy will, all thine in peace or war,
>   And for this thou hast warr'd with me. – 'Tis done:
> I may not overleap the eternal bar
> Built up between us, and will die alone,
>   Beholding, with the dark eye of a seer,

The evil days to gifted souls foreshown,
Foretelling them to those who will not hear ...

(iv. 144–51)

Byron's citizenship – the social and cultural position he sought and achieved – establishes his special identity with his own world. Like the Napoleon of *Childe Harold* Canto III, the Byron of this poem is at once "the greatest [and] the worst" of citizens (st. 36), the literary Alcibiades of his country. The anonymous lyrical style delivers the famous poet over to his text, however, turning him into a symbolic form. As such, the form is both beautiful and ineffectual – the very type of that dead knowledge that Manfred's Faustian quest revealed ("The Tree of Knowledge is not that of Life").

Byronic mobility, like Keats's chameleonism, is therefore "a most painful and unhappy attribute" in virtually every respect – at least if acts are to be measured in functional terms. The Byronic text stands aloof from the dialectic of loss and gain, rewards and punishments, in which it is yet so deeply – so wholly – involved. Its satanism rests ultimately in that posture of aloofness, as if it were indifferent to questions of judgement and valuation. Good and bad, better and worse, are terms to be evaded. Like Byron's Paolo and Francesca, the texts seek (and execute) something beyond our conceptual categories of judgement (whether moral or aesthetic).

> The land where I was born sits by the Seas
> Upon that shore to which the Po descends
> With all his followers in search of peace.[18]

The speaker here is originally Francesca, but through the text's masquerade we translate that name into its immediate equivalent, Teresa. Francesca of Rimini, Teresa of Ravenna: the text applies to both. In his role as poet and as lover Byron is then textually disposed as Dante and Paolo.[19] In truth, however, the "Byron" of this ventriloquist work seeks a gender translation as well, and identifies himself with Francesca as much as he does with her poet and her lover.[20]

As in Byron's equivalent text "To the Po," the river here is a figure of intense and ceaseless passion – Turgenev's "torrent of spring." The Aphrodite of Lucretius dominates the entire scene:

> Love, which too soon the soft heart apprehends,
> Seized him for the fair form, the which was ta'en
> From me, and even yet the mode offends–
> Love, which to none beloved, to love again
> Remits, seized me for him with joy so strong
> That – as thou seest – yet, yet it doth remain.

Damnation itself has not quenched the passion that "Seiz'd him" and "seized me," as the next two lines emphasize:

> Love to one death conducted us along,
> But Caina waits for him our life who ended.

Damned to hell herself, Francesca utters a cold prophetic curse upon her murderer. But the persistence of her passion, and of her love, is only underscored by the curse, which is the emblem of her Byronic satanism.

All these "Souls" are, in Byron's nicely ambiguous translation, "offended." Dante/Byron has "such a sympathy" in these offences of love that he pursues his inquiry and deepens his identification:

> We read one day for pleasure, sitting close,
> Of Lancilot, where forth his Passion breaks,
> We were alone, and we suspected nought
> But oft our eyes exchanged, and changed our cheeks,
> Yet one point only 'twas our ruin wrought.
> When we read the desiring smile of her
> Who to be kissed by such true lover sought,
> He who from me can be divided ne'er
> All tremulously kissed my quivering mouth.
> Accurst the book and he who wrote it were,
> That day no further did we read in sooth.

The real force of this text depends upon our reading it as Byron's – as yet a further event in an eternal story of abandoned love. The book of the tale of Lancilot, Dante's text, Byron's: all are "Accurst" because all are committed, in Byron's view, to the immediate intensities of a mortal life. Paolo weeps as Francesca tells her accurst tale and Dante "swooned as dying" in sympathy with their condition.

Byron finds himself, in 1820, in the same hell as Dante and the damned lovers. As Virgil – who will never achieve salvation – leads Dante through this hell, Byron internalizes the entire transaction. Becoming all the textual characters, Byron invents the myth of the *poète maudit*, whose work now falls under Francesca's curse of love. In Byron's text (unlike Dante's), the poet literally tells the tale of his own damnation, including the damnation of his poetry. What is worse (from a moral and aesthetic point of view), the text does not ask its readers to transvalue the values by which it will be condemned. All is accurst. If a benevolent (and invisible) God watches over all the events in Dante's text, and if this God reigns even in the love-hell of Paolo and Francesca, the children of Byron's text are children of a lesser god. Byron's anonymous and oneiric work takes possession of all its features. Consequently, here there is no God but god, and his name is Byron. (He is also called Dante, Francesca, Paolo, Virgil, Teresa, Gianciotto, and Satan.) He is a god in name only.

In Baudelairean reading of Byron, then, the translation of "Francesca of Rimini" is a key text for the clarity with which it lays out the terms of Byron's lyrical dialectic. The Byronic mode is to *take for its text* Lord Byron's "personal life." Like the "Sun of the sleepless" – Byron's startling term for the imagination – the lunar poem then casts its revelatory light upon its subjects.[21] It is a light, however, "That show'st the darkness thou canst not dispel": "Distinct, but distant – clear but, oh how cold." This is a light that shines in the darkness, but unlike John's salvific light, it *is* comprehended by that darkness. Byron's dark comprehension emerges because his "personal life" is equally his "poetical life" – because a final distinction cannot be drawn between the man who suffers and the poet who sees. Lord Byron's "personal life" is on one hand a fever of passionate intensities, and on the other a cold set of representations: at once a life and a reflection, a self and a text. The work is engulfed in that dissolving, disillusioning ambiguity – an ambiguity which, however, it also embraces.

NOTES

1 See Byron's translation of the episode from Dante (McGann and Weller iv. 280–5). Byron's obsession with this emblematic story is evident throughout his work: several of the poems in *Hours of Idleness* recall the Dante passage (e.g., the "Lines Written in Letters of an Italian Nun and an English Gentleman . . .," ibid., i. 131, as does the love of Selim and Zuleika in *The Bride of Abydos* and Mazeppa and Theresa in *Mazeppa*. Byron puts a quotation from the passage at the head of the first Canto of *The Corsair*, and of course the tale figures in Don Juan's first two affairs, with Donna Julia and with Haidée.

2 See the letters to Madame Aupick of 9 July 1857 and 19 February 1858 (Baudelaire (1973) i. 410–11, 451). The major work of *Les Fleurs du Mal*, "Le Voyage," is an act of homage to Byron, whom Baudelaire defined as the "charactère oriental . . . *le sceptique* voyageur" (Baudelaire (1976) ii. 213). See Baudelaire's letters to Sainte-Beuve, 21 February 1859, and (two days later) to Maxime du Camp (Baudelaire (1973) 553–4 and nn).

3 Heine and Poe also understood Byron's method and imitated his work – and of course Heine and Poe are two of Baudelaire's other early poetical models.

4 Baudelaire (1976) ii. 194.

5 This brief discussion of "Fare Thee Well!" sketches the argument I elaborate more fully in "What Difference do the Circumstances of Publication Make to the Interpretation of a Literary Work?" (1991). For two related discussions, see as well my "The Book of Byron and the Book of a World" (1985), and " 'My Brain is Feminine': Byron and the Poetry of Deception" (1990).

6   Wordsworth's judgement came in a letter to John Scott, who published the first unauthorized printing of the poem in his newspaper *The Champion* (*MY* ii. 204).

7   See Rollins ii. 67.

8   Bate and Engell ii. 6.

9   Katrina Bachinger's brief comments on the extremely complex ironies of this work are the best criticism of the poem that I know; see Bachinger (1991). (*Waltz*, incidentally, was not "published" in 1813, it was privately printed then. Technically, its first "publication" was in the pirated Paris edition of 1821.)

10 See Wordsworth's Preface to *Lyrical Ballads*.

11 See Marchand iii. 107.

12 For the publication history and the titles see McGann and Weller i. 51–2 and 367.

13 See McGann and Weller iii. 91.

14 The phrase is Abrams's, from his celebrated structural study of the romantic lyric: "Structure and Style in the Greater Romantic Lyric," Abrams (1965). Abrams says that "Only Byron, among the major poets, did not write in this mode at all" (p. 527). This is wrong, I think, on two counts at least: first, Blake did not write in this mode (he is, like Byron, a rhetorical poet); and second, Byron did write in the mode, though he took considerable liberties with the form. See, e.g., "Churchill's Grave" and "To the Po"; and *Childe Harold's Pilgrimage* has a number of set-piece passages that correspond to the form.

15 Baudelaire was especially pleased with Byron's sympathetic approach to feelings of hatred. See his letter to Michel Levy, 15 February 1865 (Baudelaire (1973) ii. 462).

16 The classic statement of this reading is in Macaulay's 1831 review of Moore's *Letters and Journals of Lord Byron* (see Rutherford (1970) 295–316).

17 See "Epistle to Augusta," 100 and *The Prophecy of Dante* i. 155.

18 I cite here the first version of the poem, which Byron never saw into print (see McGann and Weller iv. 282–5).

19 The Paolo indentification is made not merely through Byron's relation to the Francesca/Teresa figure, but also through his relation to Dante, whose younger brother (poet) he is (as Paolo was the younger brother of Francesca's husband Gianciotto).

20 For Byron's "feminine" sympathies see Susan Wolfson's two important essays "'Their She Condition': Cross-Dressing and the Politics of Gender in *Don Juan*," (1987); "'A Problem Few Dare Imitate': *Sardanapalus* and 'Effeminate Character'," (1991). See also Hofkosh (1988) and McGann (1990).

21 "Sun of the Sleepless!" is the title of one of the *Hebrew Melodies*; see McGann and Weller iii. 305. At line 4 Byron's poem recollects Dante's Paolo and Francesca passage by echoing one of his favourite texts – the Dante passage he appended to Canto I of *The Corsair*: "How like thou art to joy remembered well!".

Keats

11

The Two *Hyperions*: Compositions and Decompositions

BALACHANDRA RAJAN

I

About September 1818 Keats began the writing of *Hyperion*. On 21 September of the following year he wrote to Reynolds stating that he was "giving up" *Hyperion*.[1] Which *Hyperion* he meant can be a question for dispute but that both were left unfinished is a matter of history. The year that is ushered in and out by these events and that is variously entitled the living year, the fertile year, and Keats's *annus mirabilis*, is described by Walter Jackson Bate as "the most productive in the life of any poet of the past three centuries."[2] As befits a poet, it is a year paradoxical in its structure. The brilliant core of achievement is surrounded by a poem twice abandoned. We might say that the fragmentary circumference directs our attention to the problematics of the centre, displaying its consolidations as unstable and provisional. The inquiry must go on and its continuing imperatives are testified to by the encirclement of the unfinished.

Incomplete poems are not uncommon even if we disregard Valéry's statement that apparently completed poems are not really completed but abandoned. But a poem twice abandoned is relatively rare. *Hyperion* moreover is not simply given up twice but given up twice in mid-sentence. Not finishing a sentence is normally a slovenly act. In the conveyances of a poem it can be an artistic withholding. When the withholding occurs twice something is being intimated. It is not a matter of saying that we have reached the margins of the inexpressible. Keats was fortunately not that kind of writer. Nor is it a matter of considerately handing over to the reader the pleasure of finishing what the poet has begun. The issues negotiated in the two *Hyperions* are too urgent and their sombre weight presses upon the poems too powerfully for such courtesies. It is more a matter of suggesting that the continuing poem of consciousness takes up and discards its vehicles in what Keats himself once called "the grand march of intellect."[3] The fragmentary nature of the individual disclosure and its openness to super-session, side by side with its participation in that revisionary movement to which its own incompleteness both contributes and testifies, are the elements which need to be underlined.

"The grand march of intellect" is too simple a phrase and too blatantly purposive in its connotations. Even Oceanus in the first *Hyperion* has more to say in his cosmic manifesto and his speech seems oblivious to its environment, the immensities of deprivation to which it is addressed. It is radically questioned by the manner in which Keats chooses to "station" his beginning. From the outset the weight of sadness and the possibility of subscription to an objective beyond sadness, the cost of change and its necessity, a necessity which presents itself as biologically demanded rather than creatively understood, seem enmeshed with each other in a manner the literary investigation can only explore and not conclude. Yet the poem twice unfinished makes something important and even haunting, of itself, precisely because it is twice unfinished.

An examination of Keats's œuvre is outside the scope of this study though given a writing span of less than six years, and the persistence of certain critical concerns in the letters, we might expect the œuvre to be tightly drawn together. The brief life, moving with feverish speed from the bucolic to the tragic, exhibits its continuities in accelerated development. Two of these continuities are interestingly characterized by Morris Dick-stein, in his lucid book on Keats, as the Bower principle and the Bildung principle.[4] One should note that the Bower is not quite Spenser's Bower of Bliss. It is the embodiment of a naive rather than a decadent state, of oneness with nature, and of that unified sensibility whose loss was once ritually deplored. The Bildung principle is also not quite the principle of the Quest since its objective is not beyond itself but is rather coextensive with its own self-formation. Because the Bildung principle depends on the supersession or incorporation of a previous state by an emergent state, it entails the destruction of the Bower and is not ultimately compatible with a poetics of retrieval. It can of course be placed in engagement with such a poetics, with the poem itself as the mediating agent. It can also be similarly placed in engagement with a poetics of transcendence, seemingly as in *Endymion*, or with a poetics of historicity, seemingly as in the two *Hyperions*, on the basis of the conversion of the Bower state into the state prevailing in the golden age.

The previous paragraph has proceeded in directions which Dickstein might not endorse and, as will be shown later, the view taken of *Endymion* and the *Hyperions* is not one which can be finally sustained. Nevertheless, the implications of a helpful terminology need to be charted in the abstract. The relevance of the chart to Keats's work is clear. It is also clear that as early as *Sleep and Poetry*, the "nobler life" of the Bildung principle is associated with "the agonies, the strife/Of human hearts" (ll. 124–5). The association at this point is unstable; it is undermined even as it is made. As the chariot of poetry enters the natural world it is attended by shapes of "mystery and fear" but also by shapes of "delight." Weeping may accompany the progress of the chariot but it is also accompanied by murmuring, smiling, and laughing. Finally "a lovely wreath of girls/Dancing their sleek hair into tangled curls" (ll. 149–50) indicates that the "nobler life" has yet to work itself free of the Bower's entanglements. When the chariot passes,

> A sense of real things comes doubly strong,
> And, like a muddy stream, would bear along
> My soul to nothingness.
>
> (ll. 157–9)

Endymion can talk correspondingly of "the journey homeward to habitual self" (ii. 276) but the difference between the real and the habitual is a refinement in formulation that has yet to be achieved. The poetry of repudiation which Yeats writes when he converts the "muddy stream" of the ordinary into "the fury and the mire of human veins"[5] is also not as yet on Keats's horizon. We are still looking at latency, though the latency can form itself into statuesque life when Keats visualizes poetry as

> Might half slumb'ring on its own right arm....
>
> (l. 237)

The reluctance to leave the bower is apparent in the lines which immediately follow

> The very archings of her eye-lids charm
> A thousand willing agents to obey....

As we look at the cluster of relationships, the "agonies and strife," the half-slumbering Apollo first in might and presumably first in beauty, and the finding that poetry "should be a friend/To soothe the cares and lift the thoughts of man" (ll. 246–7), all look forward to the two *Hyperions* but in ways that make evident the distance that must be travelled if these images are to be purged and their interior life intensified. Keats, characteristically, was fully aware of this distance.

> Oh for ten years, that I may overwhelm
> Myself in poesy; so I may do the deed
> That my own soul has to itself decreed.

(ll. 96–8)

He was to receive less than four years, not ten, but tragically curtailed though the time was to be, its duration is less important than the idea that the mind must be overwhelmed in order to achieve its own imperatives. The thought strikingly delineates the interrelationship between the reluctantly eager self and the commitment which, paradoxically, promises destruction in that very purposiveness to which it asks us to subscribe.

Because of its inclusiveness and its elevation, the long poem is the natural vehicle of the "nobler life," that "higher mood" of resolute interrogation heard in Milton's poem before Apollo speaks to Lycidas. *Endymion* is Keats's first essay in this mood. It is tempting to treat it as an adventure in transcendence and even more intriguing to argue that the resurrection of the bower in Endymion's affair with Cynthia proclaims the impossibility of transcendence, the entanglements of a consciousness seeking its shaping principles and yet withheld from them by the very language of its seeking. The text most frequently cited in support of a transcendental reading is the "Fellowship with essence" passage:

> Wherein lies happiness? In that which becks
> Our ready minds to fellowship divine,
> A fellowship with essence; till we shine
> Full alchemiz'd, and free of space.

(i. 777–80)

Keats called for this revision in a letter to Taylor dated 30 January, 1818. *Endymion* had been completed two months earlier. Thus the passage confers upon the poem a retrospective intention which can be treated either as corroborating the poem, or as imposing a stage direction upon it. The view of the poem as fundamentally at odds with a later insertion is not a view we would be eager to sustain unless it is called for by the sheer weight of evidence. If on the other hand, we treat the insertion as an endeavour to clarify rather than to re-orient the text, we have to note that according to the letter the intention of the new lines is not transcendental. Keats speaks of the passage as "a regular stepping of the Imagination towards Truth" and as setting before him the "gradations of happiness even like a kind of pleasure Thermometer." These are figures of continuity, not transcendence, and are fully consonant with Keats's letter of 22 November, 1817 to Bailey in which he argues that a "Life of sensations rather than of Thoughts" is "a Shadow of reality to come." "Sensations" of course is to be read not as sensuality but as experiencing. Happiness in the hereafter, Keats continues, will consist of "Happiness on Earth repeated in a finer tone and so repeated." Adam's dream "seems to be a conviction that Imagination and its empyreal reflection are the same as human Life and its spiritual repetition." The language is uniformly that of continuity and invites us to note that fellowship is a human and social virtue, and that "Full alchemiz'd" can be read as implying the maximum extraction of potentiality from the substance which is alchemized. Indeed the word "full" implies the possibility of partial alchemization even though that is foreign to the nature of the concept. "Essence" can be interpreted platonically but it can also be read as in the Glaucus episode

> If he explores all forms and substances
> Straight homeward to their symbol essences;
> He shall not die.
>
> (iii. 699–701)

Here essence is viewed as kernel rather than as idea, a kernel made accessible to resolute exploration of a symbolic universe. The journey homeward of ii. 276 is now the journey "straight homeward" but to a state more elemental than "habitual self."

The ascent to the finest tone is stated more erotically than in the "fellowship with essence" passage, in a passage which follows almost immediately upon it.

> But there are
> Richer entanglements, enthralments far
> More self-destroying, leading, by degrees,
> To the chief intensity: the crown of these
> Is made of love and friendship, and fits high
> Upon the forehead of humanity.
> All its more ponderous and bulky worth
> Is friendship, whence there ever issues forth
> A steady splendour; but at the tip-top
> There hangs by unseen film, an orbed drop
> Of light and that is love.
>
> (ll. 797–807)

The graduation "by degrees" to the "chief intensity" of love is once again a statement of continuity. But the evolution to a higher self now only seems possible by virtue of the destruction of a lower self. The melting, blending, mingling and inter-knitting with the climactic radiance (ll. 810–14) is, paradoxically, both maximum self-destruction and maximum self-attainment.

Self-destruction cannot always be ecstatic and it is difficult to contemplate without misgiving a pleasure thermometer rising by such degrees. Keats at this point may be too much like Crashaw, and Endymion's encounters with his goddess show singularly little of the finer tone. But Endymion's quest is in more than one direction. It is submarine as well as celestial. The movement to the pinnacle is questioned by the movement to the core. Love as fulfillment confronts love as betrayal. Entanglements and enthralments can be threatening as well as liberating when one enlists in the service of La Belle Dame whose metaphysical sister is the shape all light.

The second book of *Endymion* ends with a startling line – "He saw the giant sea above his head" – that seems to usher us into the world of the interior and the primary. The Glaucus episode, which occupies most of the third book, is the most strongly presented in the poem. The freeing of Glaucus from bondage and of all those he has gathered from similar bondage is at best a rescue, not an exaltation. It assures us that we can overcome our enchantments but it cannot assure us that we will not endure enchantment. Indeed the requirement of endurance is carried further in Book IV where a centre of quietude is to be found in a dark region which is "the proper home/Of every ill":

> the man is yet to come
> Who hath not journeyed in this native hell
>
> (iv. 522–3)

Quietude is attained by wise passivity rather than by protest:

> Enter none
> Who strive therefore: on the sudden it is won
> Just when the sufferer begins to burn,
> Then it is free to him
>
> (ll. 531–4)

The relief makes a "Dark paradise" of the place. It is the other side of the light, not its demonic but its authentic image, a more convincing sisterhood than the identification of Cynthia with the Indian maid.

Endymion it becomes apparent is placed between two coordinates, one delineating, not altogether felicitously, the nature and end of attainment, and the other indicating the necessities which must be passed through to come upon attainment even in its dark mirror. The "suffocation of accidents," as Keats vividly puts it, calls for a recourse but "within the pale of the World."[6] Essence in this image is found not at the top of a ladder but in the grip of a stranglehold. Fellowship with it is companionship in its adversity.

Endymion is not a poem treated with much respect. Keats recognizes its "sentimental cast."[7] More tellingly, in the preface to the poem he affirms that its "foundations are too sandy." A "year's castigation" of it "would not benefit it."[8] He "leaped headlong into the sea" with it, he tells Hessey in October 1818.[9] According to a deleted preface he had "no inward feel of being able to finish" and as he proceeded his "steps were all uncertain."[10] Yet "that which is creative must create itself."[11] A poet makes rather than inherits his language of understanding. The less successful enterprise can be instructive to the critic because it formulates rather than overcomes the difficulties of achieving such a language. It thus can lay bare the problematics which a more fluent accomplishment might have concealed from even its author.

A week before making a crucial revision to *Endymion*, by then with his publisher, Keats had begun to think of his second long poem

> ... the nature of *Hyperion* will lead me to treat it in a more naked and grecian Manner – and the march of passion and endeavour will be undeviating – and one great contrast between them will be – that the Hero of the written tale Endymion being mortal is led on, like Buonaparte, by circumstance; whereas the Apollo in Hyperion being a fore-seeing God will shape his actions like one.[12]

Apollo, here presented as the central character in the coming poem, makes his appearance only in the last book of *Hyperion* and his orgasmic transformation brought about by his "knowledge enormous" (iii. 113) scarcely corresponds with the calm choices which Keats implies in his letter. But some recoil from the ramblings of *Endymion* is justified and the undeviating march of passion and endeavour shifts the intention understandably in the direction of purposiveness. The march, moreover, has its echo elsewhere in Keats's correspondence. The famous letter to Reynolds on the chamber of maiden thought maintains that there is really a "grand march of intellect" and that Milton because of his earlier participation in this "general and gregarious advance," has been unable to see as far into the human heart as Wordsworth. His philosophy Keats suggests reassuringly "may be tolerably understood by one not much advanced in years."[13]

Keats owned an 1807 pocket edition of *Paradise Lost* which he read with a poet's eye, making extensive marginal notes on crucial passages. The comment that follows is on the opening of the third book:

> The management of the poem is Apollonian – Satan first '*throws round his baleful eyes*' [i. 56] the[n] awakes his legions, he consu[l]ts, he sets

forward on his voyage – and just as he is getting to the end of it we see the Great God and our first parent, and that same satan all brough[t] in one's vision – we have the invocation to light before we mount to heaven – we breathe more freely – we feel the great Author's consolations coming thick upon him at a time when he complains most – we are getting ripe for diversity – the immediate topic of the Poem opens with a grand Perspective of all concerned.[14]

Apollonian "management" seeks the overall view, the gathering of "diversity" into a "grand Perspective," as the "grand march of intellect" moves forward to a more inclusive understanding. We can enunciate this programme for a poem, founding it, as is done here, on Keats's views as expressed in his correspondence and yet realize that it is foreign to his temperament. The mind may be attracted to such a programme but in due course it must come to question its attraction. Keats is an exploratory, not a didactic, poet, justifiably hating poetry that "has a palpable design upon us."[15] He is also a poet of the truly exploratory, rather than of the exploratory staging of the didactic, as Donne is sometimes taken to be. Even this note on *Paradise Lost* based as it is on a firm line of thought in Keats's letters, is not without recollections of another view of the nature of poetry: we "breathe more freely" because the consolations come thick, because we are working ourselves free of the "suffocation of accidents." A "grand Perspective" is attained as quietude is attained in *Endymion* only after the darkness has been journeyed through.

If Keats seeks to be the poet of the finer tone and of the overall understanding he also seeks to be the poet of perplexity rather than pattern, of reality proved upon the pulses, of the agony and strife of human hearts, and of whatever labyrinths offer themselves beyond the darkening of the chamber of maiden thought. He may chide himself for looking too far into "the core / Of an eternal fierce destruction,"[16] but a poet looks because he wishes to see, because he knows himself born to have the dream deconstructed. *Hyperion* cannot be simply a study in cosmic purposiveness though Oceanus' speech adheres to such a programme and proclaims, as Tilottama Rajan scathingly puts it, a *Bildungsroman* of consciousness.[17] But Oceanus' speech is subverted by the environment in which it is made, by Keats's "stationing" of it,[18] by the weight of woe it is unable to mitigate. Its status is further reduced by Clymene's vapid endorsement, and since Enceladus' bombastic militarism is no answer to the Titans' predicament, the general futility of the proceedings casts its pall over individual statements. As an argument Oceanus' speech is not demolished and is indeed not even countered, but it is a consolation that is made to struggle against considerably more than a suffocation of accidents.

The beginning *in medias res* works against the tendency of the epic to convert itself into panorama or chronicle, by locating the action in the clenched fist of causality. The hand opens out into future and past, prophecy and history or, more fundamentally, into destiny and origin. In *Hyperion* the beginning seems to initiate us into givenness. The history of dispossession is only dimly charted. There was a golden age "Of peaceful sway above man's harvesting" (i. 110). It has vanished. The enemy cannot be named (ll. 103–5) and the failure cannot be diagnosed (ii. 129–36). Nevertheless the disinherited self is alienated from the real self (i. 112–14) and hopes of reinstating it are couched in a rhetoric which defines those hopes as fictive.

Since dispossession has no cause and since it is to be justified, if at all, only by a future which has yet to be realized and which at this point cannot even be foreseen, we are left with the landscape of deprivation against which Keats assembles the statuary of the obsolete. If the past survives, it survives only as art. More pointedly, it survives as art in ruin. The Titans do not have the consolation of a policy, or even of the pseudo-policies advanced in Milton's hell of Belial's planned inconspicuousness or Mammon's seductive combination of the spirit of capitalism with the Protestant ethic. Acceptance of extinction as the price of a new consciousness may be wisdom but it is not a policy. Little remains but to turn for deliverance to the sole Titan who remains unvanquished and who conveniently manifests himself as soon as his name is spoken by an Enceladus approaching exhaustion of his rhetorical capabilities. Hyperion, however, is already doomed by the striking image which announces him to his fellows as "a vast shade/In midst of his own brightness" (ii. 372–3). The resemblance to Shelley's "shape all light" is striking. As Hyperion confronts the Titans whose misery his own brightness exposes, he also paradoxically exposes his own future to his own depth. The view of light as an envelope surrounding a core of darkness is evidently conducive to a poetics of betrayal, but it would be simplifying the entanglements of the image to see it exclusively as supporting such a poetics. It is at the least also consonant with a poetry of self-formation in which a new self comes into being through its dismissal of a previous self.

Beginnings can sometimes be invested with finality. Hell in *Paradise Lost* is a state that cannot be changed, a demonic extreme that is necessary in cosmic logic. Keats has studied Milton's hell but his own sculptured sublime carves out a place that is irrevocably alienated from itself and not yet capable of attachment to a new self. Nowhere is this differentiation more apparent than in that intensity of dejection and inertness which Keats's opening lines so powerfully convey. They are to be compared to the beginning of the second book of *Paradise Lost* where Milton describes a "throne of royal state" on which

> Satan exalted sat, by merit raised
> To that bad eminence. . . .

In Keats's deprived world one is not allowed even the satisfactions of parody:

> Deep in the shady sadness of a vale
> Far sunken from the healthy breath of morn,
> Far from the fiery noon, and eve's one star,
> Sat grey-haired Saturn, quiet as a stone,
> Still as the silence round about his lair; . . .

Milton, a master of syntactic postponement, takes five lines to arrive at his predicate. Keats, emulating Milton's tactics, arrives in four lines at the same verb, "sat." The word "exalted" separates subject from predicate in Milton's verbal drama. The word "grey-haired" separates predicate from subject in Keats's answering inversion. One is a stationing of pride, the other of defeat. Milton begins his first line with "High" and his second with "Outshone," emphasizing the superlatives of Satan's exaltation. Keats begins his first line with "Deep" and his second and third lines with "Far," a word transplanted from Milton's opening line to suggest not the excess of glory, but the dimensions of its diminution. The careful modelling and the scrupulously regulated intertextuality do not end at this point. In opening Book II, Milton expects us to remember his opening to the whole poem in Book I where an even more imperious syntactic postponement had taken six lines to arrive at the predicate. Keats, withholding from us the promises of design which an invocation can be made to offer, plunges steadfastly into the dejection of things, as Endymion once did in his journey to the core. The denudation increases the force of destitution in Keats's beginning but it also compounds the problematics of that beginning. With the poem so decisively "situated" the risk it must negotiate is that of being trapped in its givenness.

In the "Saturn" movement of Gustav Holst's "The Planets," the brass cries out repeatedly in mounting protest against the mounting dismissal of the drumbeat. It is the claim of an old man's frenzy, of someone who will not go gentle into the night. This, as is obvious, is not at all the mood of the opening lines of *Hyperion*. Here the withdrawal from sustaining natural rhythms, the figure of the grey-haired ex-monarch of the world in its past infancy, the stone he resembles, which could very well be his tombstone, convey a sculpturally frozen numbness of destitution both in the still figure and its answering environment. "Lair" is a word almost cruelly chosen: the one-time ruler is now the hunted animal.[19] We see Chronos bewildered, unable to comprehend that his time is over on the clock of Kairos. A world of natural recurrence, of "peaceful sway above man's harvesting" must give way to a world which at this stage in the mind's elaborations seems to pitch a purposiveness all but crushing in its consequences against an innocence doomed by that unselfconsciousness which seems unavoidably part of its nature. In the forward movement of consciousness this may be an important advance, but it is also one whose exactions are questioned by the very manner in which the advance is delineated.

The weight of dejection presses heavily, "forest upon forest," on the depths of the vale into which Saturn has withdrawn. The consolations of philosophy are obliged to struggle against that weight. Milton too begins in a world of defeat but it is the defeat of those who opposed the *status quo.* Keats studies the victims of a successful and necessary revolution who must learn to reconcile themselves to the indifference of history to its agents. "A mighty providence," Keats observes in language which, unlike Arnold's, makes the man the prisoner as well as the spokesman of the moment, "subdues the mightiest Minds to the service of the time being."[20] Translated into psychic politics the observation means that we must learn to accept dying into life, disinheritance beyond retrieval, the commitment to self-making rather than self-preservation.

Such a programme is not easy to carry into poetry, particularly when the mind that carries it and that is now committed to the sorrow of the actual still clings to the proposition that beauty may be truth. A recent book on Keats suggests that aestheticism is Keats's solution to the problem posed by his scepticism.[21] The argument is persuasive up to a point, but it leaves us with the feeling that aestheticism itself may be the problem or at least a solution which begets its problems. Hartman's essay on spectral symbolism in *Hyperion* helps us to maintain that the poem, for all its monumentality, is the writing large of an interior debate.[22] Indeed, the monumentality may be the means of adequately distancing a debate which it might otherwise be impossible to confront. Apollo's deification – or, more accurately, his transformation from a pastoral state similar to that which Saturn is significantly barred from retrieving – is emblematic of Keats's own willed progress from a pastoral to a purposive world. The change comes about in the third book of *Hyperion* and, not at all accidentally, it is in the third book of *Paradise Lost* that Keats sees the principles of Apollonian management announcing themselves within the world of that poem. His own poem urges itself towards such management while at the same time deeply questioning its possibility. The *Bildungsroman* of consciousness requires to be justified to the reader (if not to the unfortunate Titans) in ways beyond the mere allegation that there is a *Bildungsroman.* The similarity of Apollo's original state to Saturn's and his passive openness to his metamorphosis leave us wondering what he has done to earn his privileges particularly when the Titans remain subjected to a deprivation for which it is hard to find a basis.

If the basis is supersession by a superior state, the state must be shown and not claimed to be superior. Apollo's dying into life is named rather than lived through in a passage which is considerably below Keats's usual standard. It is possible that Keats could do no better but it may be more interesting to conjecture that he decided not to do better and that the poem at this point is entertaining but dismissing its own deliverance. It breaks off poised upon Apollo's shriek, the significantly inarticulate boundary between a superseded past and a future which cannot yet be brought into being, which the imagination can direct itself to but is unable to occupy. The inability admits, in effect, that the poem's actualities have revised its projected balance of forces, that it has contested all too successfully that view of the nature of coming consciousness which it nevertheless continues to underwrite. A real division of allegiance is involved here rather than that familiar undermining of didactic proclamation by imaginative accomplishment in which the authenticity of the latter is assumed and the repressive force of the former is taken to be exposed by it. Oceanus' manifesto is not devoid of eloquence. But it is positioned within a counter-eloquence that confronts it not as argument but, more effectively, as the givenness of deprivation. The result is to bring about a defensive segregation of the aesthetic from the existential. We are introduced to Apollo's realm by an invocation (significantly, the first in the poem) which twice dismisses the world of the Titans and even draws attention to the Muse's inadequacy to sing of such a world. The saving strategy that the poem thus offers itself, the insulation of the poetic from its challenges, is obviously a strategy attended by crucial impoverishments. As might be expected, it is not a course which the main weight of the poem can finally endorse. Oceanus may speak of first in beauty being first in might, but the most haunting statement of beauty in the poem belongs not to Apollo, but to Thea.

> But oh! how unlike marble was that face:
> How beautiful, if sorrow had not made
> Sorrow more beautiful than Beauty's self.

(ll. 34–6)

In a journal letter to George and Georgiana Keats which describes *Hyperion* as "scarce began," Keats says that he can "never feel certain of any truth but from a clear perception of its beauty."[23] In a letter two months earlier he had expressed the hope that the "yearning passion" he had for the beautiful would be "connected and made one with the ambition" of his "intellect."[24] These statements consort with a third one – "what the imagination seizes as Beauty must be truth"[25] – and are quoted because the status of the better-known lines at the end of "The Ode to a Grecian Urn" is likely to remain permanently in doubt. In these and other formulations the implied opposition which is to be overcome (typically by an intensity of perception which makes "all disagreeables evaporate")[26] is between the imaginative and the intelligential, two contraries that contest each other but with a restraint appropriately measured by the term, "disagreement." If the sadness of things is to be admitted into the field of such a relationship its undermining force cannot be indefinitely contained within these moderating limits. Its presence must bring about some revision of the relationship. The movement from Apollonian to tragic beauty is necessary at some stage in Keats's development. It is possible that the first *Hyperion* initiates this movement. If so, the very poem which proclaims Apollo's triumph, is also subversively proclaiming his obsolescence.

In a letter of 8 April, 1818 to Haydon written a few weeks before *Hyperion* was begun, Keats speaks of "the labyrinthian path to eminence in Art." He then goes on to draw attention to

> the innumerable compositions and decompositions which take place between the intellect and its thousand materials before it arrives at that trembling delicate and snail-horn perception of Beauty. I know not you[r] many havens of intenseness. . . .[27]

The allusion here is to Shakespeare's *Venus and Adonis*. Keats had quoted the passage in his letter of 22 November, 1817 to Reynolds.[28] The love of a goddess for a mortal youth which is the dramatic context of the quotation is, of course, the subject of *Endymion*. When Endymion speaks of the rich, yet self-destroying entanglements and enthralments which lead by degrees to the chief intensity he is anticipating the language of Keats's letter and seeing the quest for beauty as mounting aesthetic excitement. *Endymion*, however, has been shown to lie between two co-ordinates. The view of beauty which has so far been outlined is the result of a pursuit along only one co-ordinate. Transferred to the other co-ordinate, the same view becomes the ancestor of the letter on soul-making which is perhaps Keats's most important critical statement.

In the passage just quoted from the letter to Haydon, the intellect seems to be presiding over its "thousand materials." Elsewhere, responsibilities can be differently distributed. Keats can talk of "hovering" between "an exquisite sense of the luxurious and a love for philosophy"[29] and as already mentioned, he can write of "passion" for the beautiful connected and made one with the "ambition" of the intellect. The first wording suggests a necessary vacillation between directed thought and unreflective openness of response. The second suggests an integration of two ways of willing or two directions of pursuit. In the letter on soul-making, the relationship proposed is not between intellect and the beautiful or the luxuriant, but between the mind and the heart. Moreover, it is the heart that is dominant in this relationship.

> I will call the *world* a School instituted for the purpose of teaching little children to read – I will call the *human heart* the *horn Book* used in that School – and I will call the *Child able to read, the Soul* made from that *School* and its *hornbook*. . . . Not merely is the Heart a Hornbook, it is the Minds Bible, it is the Minds experience, it is the teat from which the Mind or intelligence sucks its identity.[30]

The diminution of the mind's claims by likening it to a child who must be taught how to read is striking but is exceeded by that further and telling regression to a state of infancy that is implicitly mindless. The proposition that the mind is constituted exclusively by and through experience is of course respectable and of long standing, but Keats is speaking of the heart and not the senses, and again of the heart and not the imagination. The word is quite new in his lexicon and he did not live long enough to put it to sustained use. It is Yeats who writes of the heart as the soil in which the holy tree grows, the foul rag-and-bone shop from which the ladders reach upward, the sorrow-racked source in which the changeless work originates, and the nourishment of the creative conflagration.[31] The heart, not the imagination, is the natural witness of the journey to the core; and the heart, not the intelligence, is the natural corrective of the journey to the apex. We do not accurately describe *Hyperion* when we describe it as a poem of the journey to the core. It is a poem of the self-achieving consciousness, monumentalized as mythic narrative. But again it is the heart which must authenticate the progress of such a poem, the "innumerable compositions and decompositions" that have to take place in that ongoing self-making to which the poem consents.

Some of the reasons why *Hyperion* cannot be finished will be evident. The Apollonian and Oceanic possibilities are put to school in a world of dejection. The brooding weight of that dejection ushers in the poem and continues to stand unnegotiably in its foreground. Thus the poem is subverted before it is under way and mythic narrative, as becomes apparent, is simply not a form able to absorb the undermining of its postulates. As the poem proceeds we recognize how close it is to conveying the opposite of what it argues and how, even in its segregation of realms, it raises the question of the possible irrelevance of the Apollonian. That a work should convey something other than its thesis in a way made possible only because of the protective blindness offered by that thesis is a proposition Paul de Man has made celebrated.[32] The blindness can sponsor a text that is fundamentally repressive, in which case the critic's task is to disinter and establish that sub-text which is the true text, through the cracks and gaps in the repressive structure.

Alternatively, the blindness can be a chosen fiction, a provocation that elicits in response a sub-text which otherwise would not come to life as vividly. The heart of the poem would then be taken to lie, not in the poem's unifying announcements or in its subversive recognitions, but in the interplay of provocation and retaliation. It is the second alternative which seems applicable to *Hyperion* and, as will be shown later, it also characterizes the poet's relationship to Moneta in the internalized world of the second *Hyperion*. The weight of woe which is the first *Hyperion*'s dominant reality, precedes and by its crushing presence diminishes whatever consolations can be urged against it. It is therefore not an interrogating force which is subversively generated while another understanding is being officially pursued. It would not be repressed if it were directly confronted. In fact it is placed in the poem and given its decisive positioning so that it can question through the immediacies of distress a remote though "mighty" providence which has set aside those whom it has used for the "service of the time being." The "justification" of the ways of that providence is that the setting aside is the unavoidable condition of a crucial advance in consciousness. But the actuality of that advance has yet to be established and must survive against our awareness of the cost. One looks unsuccessfully in the first *Hyperion* for that point of confessional self-disclosure – the magic moment of the deconstructionists – when the poem no longer silenced by its subterfuges,[33] no longer acquiescent in the treason of authorship, betrays itself into its own reality. However if we are unsuccessful it is only because there is no specific "fissure," because it is the poem's entire environment which radically questions its philosophy and indeed the possibility of arriving at a philosophy. The grand march of intellect, a phrase which by now ought to seem reprehensible in its automated overtones, offers us certain blindnesses, or, to put it less starkly, certain Olympian indifferences. The poem resolutely refuses to allow those indifferences. Its very segregation of the realms of Apollo and the Titans underlines the necessity of a dialogue between them. Such a dialogue is all the more desirable because the stated purpose of the progress of intellect is to enable us to see deeper into the human heart. Yet the heart inherits that very dispossession which an advancing consciousness seeks to justify in the name of its advance. Apollonian management, whether viewed cosmically as the dominance of the teleological or psychically as the surrender of sensation to the stern chastenings of thought, must confront the privations which its claims inflict and educate itself into an exchange of understandings that is deeper than the mere appropriation of one term in a dialectic by another.

The deification of history is a widely shared commitment of nineteenth-century thought. *Hyperion* is a poem of deep engagement with that deification, resisting what it also entertains in a response sufficiently pervasive and complex to make the striking of a balance sheet not merely impossible but irrelevant. To understand the accuracy with which Keats identifies a problem which may permit no escape from its constraints it is instructive to turn to a writer of this century making his statement in a quite different context. In 1930 we find the Frankfurt philosopher Horkheimer observing:

> That history has realized a better society out of a worse one, that it can realize an even better one in its course, is a fact; but it is another fact that the path of history leads over the suffering and misery of individuals. Between these two facts there are a number of explanatory connections, but no justifying meaning.[34]

It is the fissure between "explanatory connections" and "justifying meaning" that Keats explores so probingly in *Hyperion*, and it is the impossibility of proceeding from one to the other which leaves the poem unfinished, poised on those interlaced yet divergent affiliations which must remain part of its problem, justly understood. If the exploration is to be carried further (and to carry it further is to be committed more fully to its essential inconclusiveness), it must be in a form more malleable and less sculptural, a form better suited to those compositions and decompositions which a later encounter with Moneta is to chart.

II

Keats's change of mind with respect to Milton is surely the swiftest disenchantment in the history of literature. The time at which he began to annotate his edition of *Paradise Lost* is conjectural, but Stuart Ende's suggestion of the winter of 1817–18 seems plausible.[35] If this date is accepted, the affair came to a climax some eighteen months later. "Shakespeare and the Paradise Lost every day become greater wonders to me," Keats wrote to Bailey on 14 August, 1819. "I look upon fine Phrases like a Lover" he continued.[36] He repeated himself ten days later to Reynolds: "I am convinced more and more day by day that fine writing is next to fine doing, the top thing in the world; the Paradise Lost becomes a greater wonder."[37] No more than four weeks later Reynolds received an altogether different letter: "I have given up Hyperion – there were too many Miltonic inversions in it – Miltonic verse can not be written but in an artful or rather artist's humour."[38] The entry three days later in a journal letter to George and Georgiana Keats is more emphatic:

> The Paradise lost though so fine in itself is a curruption of our Language – it should be kept as it is unique – a curiosity – a beautiful and grand Curiosity. The most remarkable Production of the world. A northern dialect accommodating itself to Greek and Latin inversions

and intonations. . . . I have but lately stood on my guard against
Milton. Life to him would be death to me. Miltonic verse cannot be
written but it [in] the vein of art – I wish to devote myself to another
sensation –[39]

The grounds for dismissal at first seem to be stylistic. There is the adulatory
reference to "fine writing" and the looking upon "fine phrases like a Lover,"
followed by the rejection of Milton's Latinity – a Latinity characterized in a
manner that echoes the findings of Samuel Johnson. But the rejection of a
style is sometimes symptomatic of the deeper rejection of what the style
conveys. *Hyperion* is a Miltonic poem not simply in its cadences but in its
attempt to assert the shape of order against the weight of woe. Both poems
contemplate the defeats of history actual and mythic, and both seek
understandings which will survive those defeats. Milton of course can justify
God's ways by assigning to a freely choosing centre the entire onus of
responsibility for destructiveness. Keats can entertain no such justification.
Indeed, as he proceeds with his poem he raises before himself the inade-
quacies of purposiveness, of final causes or emergent claims. A poem which
seeks to install or even to attain a "grand Perspective" at its centre may be
able to do so only by betraying its own world. To be the poet of "another
sensation" is to learn that one's business is to probe and not to justify.

On the half-title page of his edition of *Paradise Lost* Keats observes that
Milton

> had an exquisite passion for what is properly in the sense of ease and
> pleasure, poetical Luxury – and with that it appears to me he would
> fain have been content if he could so doing have preserved his
> self-respect and feel of duty perform'd – but there was working in him
> as it were that same sort of thing as operates in the great world to the
> end of a Prophecy's being accomplish'd – therefore he devoted
> himself rather to the Ardours than the pleasures of Song, solacing
> himself at intervals with cups of old wine – and those are with some
> exceptions the finest part of the Poem.[40]

Keats mirrors himself in this estimate of Milton. The "luxury" is reflected
in his desire to die a death of luxury, the "ease" in his being "half in love
with easeful death," the "feel of duty perform'd" in the commitment to a
"nobler life," the acceptance of that "flaw in happiness" which cannot but
be admitted into happiness and which "spoils the singing of the nightingale."[41] When Keats describes himself as "hovering between" an "exquisite
sense of the luxurious and a love of philosophy" he reproduces the language
of his comment on Milton. He admires the manner in which Milton's
luxuriance is chastened and kept in place under the pressure of overall

understandings to which the poetry should ideally subscribe rather than submit. In doing so he anticipates relationships later critics were to draw between the poet and the puritan, or the didactic and the imaginative, in Milton's accomplishment. The tempering thus achieved attracted Keats because it spoke deeply to him. It was abandoned because it did not speak deeply enough.

The only way out of the difficulties which the pressing concerns of the first *Hyperion* created was to internalize the conflict which it raised. The poem's increasing resistance to the understandings to which it was expected to testify, its inability to place the Apollonian within its boundaries, call for a different disposition, a fable that is psychological rather than dynastic. When this disposition is made one no longer has to think of the contest between Apollo and Hyperion

> As of a duel or the mortal wounds
> Of head or heel . . .
>
> (*PL* xii. 387–8)

The cruelties of supersession are overcome by an advancing self-understanding which by virtue of what it finds in itself, earns its progress and justifies its cost. We are made conscious of an inadequacy that has been passed through, not of a generation that has been cast aside. The mind does not avoid conversation or merely institute a conversation with the challenge to its structures that is urged upon it by the insistent heart. It is taught by the challenge to decipher itself. Its "strong identity" (*Hyperion* i. 114) is the condition of its future not the pastoral peace which it has left behind.

The second *Hyperion* is entitled "a dream" and it begins by suggesting that dreams are the aberration or privilege of those who stand at the fringes, of the "fanatic" on the circumference of society and the "savage" left behind by the march of progress. The dreaming of poetry is distinguished from the dreaming of dispossessed elites by poetry's ability to "tell" its dreams, its capacity to save imagination from "the sable charm / And dumb enchantment" with the counter-enchantment, the "fine spell" of words. At this point the poet too is a member of an elite the selectivity of which is underlined by "alone." But the potential brotherhood of poetry is now expanded by a reassurance offered to the reader as well as claimed by the author.

> Who alive can say
> "Thou art no poet; may'st not tell thy dreams?"

The emphasis here is not only upon utterance but on the right to utterance. The poet and the reader, recognized as prospective poet, are presumably to be distinguished from the non-poet by the kind of dream they liberate into language and thus expose to scrutiny. It is an emphasis which shifts subtly in the lines that follow:

> Since every man whose soul is not a clod
> Hath visions and would speak, if he had lov'd,
> And been well nurtured in his mother tongue.

The poet here is, as with Wordsworth, a man speaking to men, sharing with all men the gift of vision and the desire for utterance, and differing from them in degree rather than kind. The ambiguous stationing of "lov'd" (it can be either intransitive or take "mother tongue" for its object, with the end-of-the-line position stressing the first possibility) leaves open the question of whether speech is made possible by love of language or by a love that is less particularized. "Nurtured" suggests that more than language is involved, that the mother tongue includes all that has reached expression in it. The text has brought us to the centrality indeed the universality of dreaming and to the vital nature of utterance which is the sustenance of the dream as well as the "fine spell" that liberates it. But the dream may not be the authentic dream which other men recognize in themselves and share with the writer. It may only be the sectarian dream of a fanatic, of a minor tribe the members of which have chosen to call themselves poets.

> Whether the dream now purposed to rehearse
> Be poet's or fanatic's will be known
> When this warm scribe my hand is in the grave.

The dream now depends on survival as well as utterance. Something in it, outlasting the "warm scribe" who reports it, must succeed in declaiming its authenticity.

This passage has been looked at in some slight detail because its tactics anticipate those of the poem's main encounter. The evolving adumbrations proceed as compositions and decompositions that bring us to a tentative understanding. It is not simply a matter of what is affirmed but of how we arrive at what is affirmed. Whatever knowledge we reach is shaped and led into by the history of attainment. The very process of coming to that attainment argues for the necessity of an attainment beyond it.

The poet stands in a place where trees of "every clime" (l. 19) are present, suggesting that the place belongs to every country. He finds in an arbour the "refuge of a meal / By angel tasted, or our Mother Eve" (l. 31). The discovery can be read as an affirmation of belatedness, of alienation from plenitude and from origins. Keats makes a quite explicit statement of belatedness in *Endymion* ii. 723–32, but the march of intellect points in another direction. In any case there is still as much plenitude available as "the fabled horn / Thrice emptied could pour forth" (ll. 35–6). The poet eats liberally and then drinks "pledging all the mortals of the world" (l. 44) in another affirmation of his desire for universality. Having swooned, he wakes before a sanctuary the antiquity of which exceeds even "The superannuations of sunk realms / Or nature's rocks toiled hard in waves and winds" (ll. 68–9). The ways north and south end in mists of nothingness. The way east is dominated by black gates "shut against the sunrise evermore." The way west is the only way available. It is also a way which must be taken since the poet is commanded either to ascend the sanctuary steps or to die on the marble where he stands. The dying into life that follows (ll. 126–7) reproduces Apollo's shriek of transformation in the first *Hyperion* but the survivor does not attain divinity. He merely dates on his doom (ll. 144–5) and secures a position where he can earn his enlightenment.[42]

The poet requests the "High Prophetess" of the sanctuary to "purge off / Benign, if it so please thee, my mind's film" (ll. 145–6). Michael in *Paradise Lost* is described as being of "regard benign" (xi. 336) and in a complex series of operations he removes the "film" from Adam's eyes, purges the "visual nerve" with euphrasy and rue and instills three drops of water from the well of life. In drawing attention to this connection Stuart Sperry persuasively shows us that the movement from the first Hyperion to the second is among other things a movement joining Milton to Dante.[43] Keats, at this time, was reading Cary's translation of the *Purgatorio* and Gittings finds traces of the translation in the second *Hyperion*.[44] Nevertheless Adam's education retains a relationship to the education of the poet by Moneta.

The dialogue with Moneta, a sterner Mnemosyne to the poet's Apollo, is a crucial event in the poetry of self-achieving. The debate within the self is fittingly shown as contentious rather than considerate, with the formative accusations, the understandings attained by defence against the searching over-statement, strongly and authentically conveyed. Twenty-four important lines (ll. 187–210) were, according to Woodhouse, intended to be erased, but editors have wisely let them stand. Their status as a draft within the text simply reminds us that all understanding has to be a draft, overlaid and partly superseded by the further understanding which the draft makes possible. This is the poem of the mind in the act of finding, not what will suffice, but what the frame of the present permits. Language, in the stages of registration of such a movement, is erased by that to which it gives way but reinscribed because that which succeeds it remains informed by a history it cannot efface.

Moneta's status in this dialogue needs to be considered. She is not Dante's Virgil, and though Adam's Michael is, as was pointed out, a distant likeness, Moneta faces a pupil who has survived a test and who will himself, in his contention with his teacher, define the nature of the responsible imagination. Her function is not to expound the vast design against the obscurations of adversity but to disclose the weight of sadness at the centre of things. Whatever understanding the poet achieves must be formed, rather than fractured, by that weight, and cannot be constituted in those evasions or transcendences of it that can at best only announce a preliminary gesture of the fictive capability. Moneta's apparent inconsistencies in performing this function deserve to be studied. She first makes the poet one of an elect minority, one who has the power "to die and live again" before his "fated hour" (ll. 142–3). Because the miseries of the world are misery to him and will not let him rest he has been permitted to "usurp this height" (ll. 167–9). But it is clear that the so-called usurpation was demanded and that the poet would have died if his attempt had failed (ll. 107–17). The initial presumption, the consequent ordeal, and the granting of a status which is nevertheless described as illegitimate, are consistent with the experience but not necessarily with the way in which it is spoken about. Moneta's function, it becomes apparent, is to provoke as much as to expound, to sting her pupil into acts of definition. Thus, having conceded him a position of privilege, she then twice contemptuously speaks of him as a "thing" (ll. 168, 178) and even more scathingly as a "Fever" of himself (l. 169). His ailment is excessive responsiveness to the world's sorrow, an inability to keep pain and joy distinct. He is admitted to the "height" as a protection against his own self-destructiveness (ll. 171–80). It is a criticism the actual poet could urge against himself and which he does urge against himself in the "Epistle to Reynolds." But how then is the dream of the poet to be distinguished on the one hand from the fanatic's dream of paradise and of the bower's resurrection and on the other hand from the sensitive mind's nightmare of sorrow? Keeping a judicious balance is not the answer. When the poet describes his sickness as "not ignoble" (l. 184) he is defending acceptance of the fever; when he describes the poet as "a sage / A humanist, physician to all men" (ll. 189–90) he is implying that the poet himself must heal the fever he undertakes to endure. Apollo, we might remember, is a physician as well as a poet. Moneta's aggressive separation of the poet from the dreamer, thrust forward in no fewer than five variant stylings (ll. 199–202), and her previous association of visionaries with "dreamers weak" (ll. 161–2) seem to undermine these possibilities and even to betray the purpose of the dialogue, which is to arrive at the nature of the poetic dream. Yet, ironically, it establishes the quality of that dream, which is to be tormented by the world without and to be taunted by the voice within. That the poet should describe these observations as "courteous" (l. 215) is perhaps indicative of a wry realism that answers from himself.

Moneta responds to the poet's recognition of her courtesy by undertaking to be kind to him for his "good will" (l. 242). A change in relationship is taking place. The priestess is no longer the mentor, and even if she does not accept the poet as her colleague she seems ready to admit him as her audience. Indeed, the contrast between the "electral changing misery" of vision as experienced and the "wonder" of vision as disclosed strongly suggest the relationship between writer and audience. It is appropriate in these circumstances to note the extent to which Moneta embodies in herself what she has previously castigated the poet for being:

> My power, which to me is still a curse,
> Shall be to thee a wonder; for the scenes
> Still swooning vivid through my globed brain
> With an electral changing misery,
> Thou shall with those dull mortal eyes behold,
> Free from all pain, if wonder pain thee not.

> (ll. 243–8)

It is the poet's stubborn adherence to his calling and his progressive characterization of that calling under assault that entitles him to see Moneta's face unveiled:

> Then saw I a wan face
> Not pin'd by human sorrows, but bright blanch'd
> By an immortal sickness which kills not:
> It works a constant change, which happy death
> Can put no end to; deathwards progressing
> To no death was that visage; it had pass'd
> The lilly and the snow;

> (ll. 256–62)

The "constant change" is not seasonal recurrence, or even the natural movement of life to death, but an eternal onwardness, not caught in time like Thea's tragic dignity, but manifest as an immortal sickness. The poet's own "sickness not ignoble" which Moneta had rebuked in him is now seen to be implacably eternized in her. Yet the terror is not without tranquillity. The eyes "Half-closed, and visionless entire ... Of all external things," their gaze concentrated on inwardness, beam "like the mild moon" in "blank Splendour" (ll. 264–9). The poet, at one time seized by fear, is not reassured by the "benignant light" of these eyes into avoiding flight while keeping a cautious and respectful distance. On the contrary he is consumed by curiosity.

> As I had found
> A grain of gold upon a mountain's side

And twing'd with avarice strain'd out my eyes
To search its sullen entrails rich with ore,
So at the view of sad Moneta's brow,
I ached to see what things the hollow brain
Behind enwombed:

(ll. 271–7)

It is important that the simile is in the first person. A greater distance could have been maintained between the miner's avarice and the poet's compulsive inquiry. But there is avarice, or to put it slightly differently, a creative and therefore exploitative greed, in the inquiry. The explorer is also the would-be possessor. Once again the relationship between priestess and poet is changing. Moneta previously the poet's mentor, is now on the verge of becoming his subject. He aches to see

what high tragedy
In the dark secret chambers of her skull
Was acting, that could give so dread a stress
To her cold lips, and fill with such a light
Her planetary eyes;

(ll. 277–81)

The concerns are literary, but the poet, avid to explore the deep dichotomies that lie behind the "stress" on those "cold lips," is a poet committed to search the mountain's "sullen entrails," to give himself to what the core of fierce destruction yields. Endymion's submarine voyage must be carried on with no assurance that there is quietude at the centre. A different self speaks from the one that first questioned Moneta and the attitude of this new self to Moneta is ambivalent. If the poet invokes the prophetess with "act adorant" he also summons her by his "conjuration" (ll. 283, 291). As "The pale omega of a withered race" (the language is expressive of the shifting relationship in aptly suggesting both reverence and belittlement), Moneta and all that she sees must be brought forward into the imagination's immediacy. The "fine spell of words" does more than simply tell the dream. It raises it into existence out of its darkness. And the poet does not simply search Moneta's consciousness. He appropriates some of her powers. He sees as a god sees, with his "enormous ken" matching Apollo's "knowledge enormous," comprehending the depth of things as the outer eye takes in their size and shape (ll. 302–6). But to see as a god sees is to endure as an immortal endures. It is to take on the unremitting burden of Moneta's deathward progress to no death (ll. 388–99). The poet's dream is certified by its cost.

With the conjuration of Moneta the first *Hyperion* begins again. There are changes in the turns of language, a reduction in the number of Miltonic inversions,[45] an abbreviated description of Thea and a deletion of Saturn's hope (i. 141–65) of forming another universe out of chaos. More important for our purpose are Moneta's attempted guidances. At first she seeks to maintain her status as mentor by insisting on the figural character of what the poet sees:

> "So Saturn sat
> When he had lost his realms"
>
> (ll. 301–2)

Later, she concedes more to the reliability of the representation

> "That Divinity . . .
> Is Thea, softest-natur'd of our brood"
>
> (ll. 332–5)

At the beginning of the second Canto she shifts from vision to narrative much as Michael did in passing from the eleventh to the twelfth book of *Paradise Lost*

> "Mortal that thou may'st understand arights
> I humanize my sayings to thine ear,
> Making comparisons of earthly things,"
>
> (ll. 1–3)

The language also remembers the manner in which Raphael begins his account of the battle in heaven (*PL* v. 571–4). Yet after providing an account of Hyperion's palace, Moneta seems to abandon the pretense that the divine must be accommodated to the human, and with "Thither we tend," transports the poet to the scene of whatever action remains. Thirteen lines farther on the poem breaks off. Moneta's unstable, not to say defensive, view of her status, suggests the extent to which the balance of power has changed, and the extent to which the poet may be disinterring rather than witnessing the "high tragedy" being acted in the "secret chamber" of consciousness. The past is being repossessed but within the guiding interpretative power of a present already constituted by acts of self-formation.

Keats's success in composing the frame dream is authoritative. The internalization re-enacts the mythic-dynastic past, putting the supersessions of the fable into alignment with the self-formative growth of the mind that discovers the fable. A myth of transformational change is surrounded and interpreted by the pre-emptive transformation of the narrating consciousness. The past is obliged to enter contemporaneity. It is remembered and remade in the context of recognition every new author must create in himself.[46] That is why the gates of the temple are barred against the east and barred in that direction only. The point is not that the past must be rejected. Rather it is to be reappropriated on the ground of the present. This too is part of the poet's dream – a dream not of paradise but of the painful passage from paradise to reality.

Paradoxically, the very success of the frame-dream becomes the main reason why the poem must remain unfinished. The difficulties raised by the first *Hyperion* requires its problems to be internalized. The internalization gives access to refinements of composition and decomposition that simply cannot be worked through within the bolder dispositions of the original fable. But with the poetry of self-formation so authentically written into the context there is little for the fable left to do. This is in itself not a fatal objection. The revisionary reading of the fable brought about by its location in the frame might be a matter of interest even if the fable said nothing that was not in the frame. The difficulties lie in the frame and can be adumbrated by pointing out that "frame" is almost certainly the wrong word.

The poem of self-formation is, in its nature, open. The consolidations it brings about are achieved to be superseded. That which is creative must create itself, but in doing so creates its own obsolescence. Placed in its real time of consciousness, such a poem can slight itself by looking forward even to imaginative closures, to the ultimate retrieval or the final attainment. It establishes its objectives out of its onward movement and the objectives are likely to change as the movement proceeds. It is difficult for such a poem to collect itself around a myth of victory and of deification unless, as in Milton's approaches to the problem, that victory is both internalized and placed at the end of time. One might argue that Keats's myth, unlike Milton's, is revolutionary and that a revolutionary myth, if correctly placed and read, can and should be made to subscribe to the permanent revolution of the advancing consciousness. The argument might hold if psychic politics did not radically question the transformations to which it is made to adjust and if the politics themselves were not subject to revision by the continuing dialogue between the change and the cost.

Keats and Shelley might have written more of their unfinished poems if they had lived longer, but we have to ask ourselves what is achieved by their breaking off where they did. The second *Hyperion* does not even proceed as far as the first did. It stops short of the council of fallen Titans, not to mention the deification of Apollo. Significantly it is entitled *The Fall of Hyperion*. Its emphasis is on the environment of defeat with which the world confronts the cry of the heart. It forces the mind to question that vast shade under the brittle surface of its brightness. As the questioning proceeds, the dream changes and the dream that once was can be seen as the dream of the fanatic or the savage. But the deeper dream survives. Hyperion flares on and the brief glory of his transit, a movement which inscribes its own effacement, is one more event in a poem that can only be written, not concluded. The poem, like the encounter with Moneta it depicts, is that individuation of the common utterance by which the utterance is found and named, at once protected and interrogated. But it is also a poem of self-making, erasing itself even as it inscribes itself. It accepts its own nature by breaking off in mid-sentence.

The dignity of a fragment in a poetry of self-formation lies in its finding its place in a process, in its being justified by its own extinction. It makes the truth instead of returning to it. It contributes to a whole which is neither beginning nor end but only history. The unfinished, in such a view, carries with it no natural citizenship, no whole from which it was disinherited, or from which its incompleteness has been made to proceed. Spenser and Milton can situate their poems on generic contests that lead back to real dichotomies surrendered to settlement at the end of time. Byron writes a poem which is additive and which is cumulative only in its openness. Shelley's question mark is the self-definition of a poem unable to pronounce on its own nature. Keats's doubly unfinished effort, the myth of abandonment he himself abandons, is his testimony to the ongoing poem of the heart. The first *Hyperion* is described as a fragment. The second is described as a dream. It is as if the incomplete and the unreal, submitted to "the giant agony of the world," are provinces which the mind must agree to inhabit in search of whatever understanding it can acquire.

NOTES

1   The majority view is that Keats is referring to the second *Hyperion* or to the entire *Hyperion* effort. Aileen Ward is among those who argue that the reference is to the first *Hyperion* (Ward (1963) 434–5 n).
2   Bate 322.
3   Letter of 3 May 1818 to Reynolds (Rollins i. 282).
4   Dickstein (1971), esp. pp. 30ff.
5   Yeats, *Byzantium*.
6   Letter of 3 November 1817 to Bailey (Rollins i. 41).
7   Letter of 23 January 1818 to Haydon (Rollins i. 207).
8   Preface to *Endymion* (Stillinger 102). Quotations follow Stillinger's text.
9   Letter of 8 October 1818 to Hessey (Rollins i. 374).
10 Keats, *Poems* ed. Allott (1970) 755.
11 9 October 1818 to Hessey (Rollins i. 374).
12 23 January 1818 to Haydon (Rollins i. 207).
13 3 May 1818 to Reynolds (Rollins i. 281–2).
14 Wittreich (1970) 558.
15 Letter of 3 February 1818 to Reynolds (Rollins i. 224).

16 "Dear Reynolds, as last night I lay in bed" 95–9, Keats, *Poems* ed. Allott (1970) 244.

17 Tilottama Rajan (1980) 158.

18 Keats, in his comments on *PL* vii. 420–3 (see Wittreich (1970) 559) finds Milton's "perseverance" in pursuing his "imagination to the utmost" most fully exemplified in his *"stationing or statu[a]ry*. He is not content with simple description, he must station."

19 The word may have seemed too cruel since Keats omitted three and a half lines containing it from the second *Hyperion*.

20 3 May 1818 to Reynolds (Rollins i. 382).

21 Sharp (1979).

22 Hartman (1975) 57–74.

23 Journal letter, 16 December 1818 – 4 January 1819 (Rollins ii. 19).

24 Journal letter, 14–31 October 1818 to George and Georgiana Keats (Rollins i. 404).

25 22 November 1817 to Bailey (Rollins i. 184).

26 Letter to 21 December 1817 to George and Thomas Keats (Rollins i. 192).

27 Rollins i. 192–3.

28 Rollins i. 189.

29 Letter of 24 April 1818 to Taylor (Rollins i. 271).

30 Journal letter of 14 February – 3 May 1819 to George and Georgiana Keats (Rollins ii. 102–3).

31 Yeats, "The Two Trees"; "The Circus Animals' Desertion"; "Meditations in Time of Civil War"; "Two Songs From a Play." See also "Vacillation." James Jones (1975) 14–49 discusses soul-making in Keats and Yeats though not with reference to the connections cited here.

32 De Man (1971).

33 See Ragussis (1978), esp. 35–69. For Ragussis the "sceptical underthought and the fragmentation of the Hyperion poems seem Keats's only defenses against the subterfuge of art" (68). The fragmented work is the clearest illustration of the writer's "refusal to close the charmed circle of art around himself and his audience" (9). My account differs in seeing Keats's fictions not as a means of excluding certain awareness, but as a means of confronting awareness which might otherwise be slurred over. The fiction itself undermines the protections it offers and thus makes it impossible not to acknowledge those awarenesses. The subterfuge seems to lie in the smuggling in of subversive forces under the cover of promises of order which cannot be maintained.

34 Max Horkheimer (1930) 44, as translated in *The Origin of Negative Dialectics* by Susan Buck-Morss (Hassocks, Sussex, 1977) 48.

35 Ende (1976) 87–8.

36 Rollins ii. 139.

37 Rollins ii. 146.

38 Letter of 21 September 1819 to Reynolds (Rollins ii. 166).

39 Letter to George and Georgiana Keats, 17–27 September 1819 (Rollins ii. 212).

40 Wittreich (1970) 553.

41 *Sleep and Poetry* 58–159; "Ode to a Nightingale" 52; "Dear Reynolds, as last night I lay in bed" 82–5.

42 The poet's and Apollo's dying into life are to be linked to Lamia's meta-

morphosis (i. 146–70) and to Satan's entry into the serpent (*PL* ix. 179–91), an account by which Keats was, perhaps unduly, impressed: "no passage of poetry ever can give a greater pain of suffocation" (Wittreich (1970) 560). Keats can treat dying into life as ecstatic, as agonizing, as orgiastic, as the highest attainable intensity ("Why did I laugh Tonight?"), as progress to the "chief intensity" by successive enthralments (*Endymion* i. 797–807) and as the death-wards progress to "no death" (*The Fall of Hyperion* 260–1). The antithetical relationship between ecstatic fulfillment and tragic discovery outlined by the last two references suggests not a prospective middle ground but rather a continuing engagement.

43 Sperry (1973) 310–35.

44 Gittings (1962) 178–9.

45 Bate 604 n notes that inversions of noun and adjective decline in frequency from once in fourteen lines in *Hyperion* to once in thirty-three lines in *The Fall of Hyperion*. These figures however include 310 lines before *The Fall of Hyperion* reaches the point where *Hyperion* begins. Only 219 lines are actually shared by the two poems. It may be the difficulty of eliminating Miltonic resonances from these lines which led Keats to make the remarks discussed in the body of this chapter.

46 In Blake's *Milton* a literary figure in the mythologized past has to remake himself in order to enter the creative present. In Keats, the myth involves revolutionary overthrow rather than remaking. The fable Keats chooses makes it extremely difficult to postulate a continuing mythic presence that maintains itself through revolutionary transformations. Internalization makes it possible to combine a transformational view of change with the continuance and constituting of the self through and even because of the transformations. At the same time, internalization preempts the fable not only by transferring it to a psychic theatre, but because self-formation can negotiate the problematics which dynastic supersession is able only to raise.

12

Imagination and Growth in the Great Odes

Leon Waldoff

Keats's great odes are widely and justly regarded as his finest achievement, and, despite our uncertainty about the exact dates and order of composition, there is good reason to treat them not only as a group but as a sequence.[1] They are united by obvious conceptual and stylistic similarities, particularly the presence in each of a dominant symbol and the use in each of a stanzaic form that Keats developed from his experiments with the sonnet and that he apparently continued to perfect in the course of writing the odes. Although the exact shape of the sequence remains conjectural, the change of the long and irregular stanzas of "Ode to Psyche" (the ode for which we have the earliest date – the end of April 1819) into the later, shorter, and regularized stanza of "To Autumn" (almost certainly the last of the odes, written on 19 September 1819) suggests a pattern of progressive refinement in which the other odes can be given a place on the basis of such considerations as the adoption of a ten-line stanza, the regularizing of it (after, presumably, "Nightingale," known to have been written in May), and the apparent movement to a shorter ode form ("Melancholy" and "Autumn" being the shortest, thirty and thirty-three lines respectively). These and other considerations (e.g., allusions to the seasons) are not conclusive evidence, but they are the outward signs of a pattern of inner development, of a gradual deepening and maturing of thought that make the odes not only a unified group but a progressive series of reflections on problems Keats has been concerned with from the beginning, especially the problem of mutability.

Central to any consideration of the odes as a sequence is the question of what unity, if any, is to be found in the five symbols. At first glance they appear to be quite different: one is taken from mythology (Psyche), two from nature (the Nightingale and Autumn), one from art (the Urn), and one from psychology (Melancholy). Yet there is an underlying kinship between them. For one thing, each symbol is conceived as feminine. The goddess Psyche is the most obvious example, but the feminine attributes of "Veil'd Melancholy" and Autumn ("sitting careless on a granary floor, / Thy hair soft-lifted by the winnowing wind" – ll. 14–15) cannot be ignored. The Urn is a more complex and elusive example, but its identity as an "unravish'd bride" is not in question. The case for the Nightingale may seem unclear, but it is addressed as "light-winged Dryad of the trees" (l. 7) – in other words, as if it were a nymph or minor female divinity. For another, each symbol is conceived as immortal, or has immortality attributed to it, even when the immortality seems to be in jeopardy, as in "Ode to Psyche." Although Autumn would seem to be an exception because it signals the approach of winter and symbolic death, it also possesses a kind of immortality by way of its cyclical nature, paralleling a form of immortality shared by the Nightingale as a species. It might be added that if, in his conception of the poem, Keats had the goddess Ceres in mind (perhaps an unavoidable association for the poet who only a month before in "Lamia" had noted "the store thrice told / Of Ceres' horn" – ii. 186–7), then Autumn is simultaneously a natural process, a personification, and a goddess.[2]

Equally important is the relationship the poet establishes with each of the five symbols. Shifts in tone, not only from ode to ode but often from stanza to stanza, serve as a warning against hasty generalization about the nature of all the relationships. But in all the odes the poet assumes a sympathetic understanding between himself and each symbolic object. He either extends his sympathy to it, at times experiencing a sympathetic identification with it or with the figures on it, or he attributes a sympathetic understanding to it. The Nightingale was once a friend to Ruth, and the Urn remains one to man. The exception would seem to be Melancholy. Her association with "Beauty that must die" (l. 21) seems to suggest a figure out of sympathy with the poet's longing for permanence expressed elsewhere in the odes. Yet the image of death is not always fearful. As recently as March 1819 in the sonnet "Why did I laugh tonight?" Keats had written that death is "intenser" than verse, fame, and beauty – "death is life's high meed" (l. 14).[3] The characterization of Melancholy as a figure associated with death is part of an effort to demystify her and reveal the existence of a hidden, primal sympathy with her, an awareness of which intensifies other experiences.

Although each of the five symbols is characterized as feminine, immortal, and sympathetic, the notion that, taken together, they represent related images of a single inner object admittedly risks the charge of reductionism. The critical value of the notion, however, lies in the possibility of relating the symbols to other images in Keats's poetry, from Cynthia and Circe to La Belle Dame and Lamia, from the Indian maiden to veiled Moneta. We are thus able to relate the odes to the narrative poetry more directly than has been done before. The quest of the narrative poems may be seen transformed in the ode sequence into an extended process of symbolization. A subliminal presence haunting the poet finds representation in these dramatic lyrics in a series of discrete but related symbols. The continuation of the quest through symbols gives a bolder and more intense expression of the ancient longing for restoration and reunion than is found in the narrative poems. The imaginative effort devoted to presenting the lost mythological world of Psyche, the pastoral world of the Nightingale, and the Grecian world of the Urn may be seen as part of a deeper effort to restore a lost inner world and to internalize, to perpetuate in the mind, those aspects of each symbol felt to be most self-sustaining. The workings of these two processes of imagination provide important evidence of the psychological development implicit in the sequence. Such rhetorical strategies as apostrophe, personification, questions in a series, elaborate pictorial detail, and aphoristic statement are evidence of the deeper workings of a more personal strategy. "I see, and sing, by my own eyes inspired," Keats says in "Ode to Psyche" (l. 43).

I

"Ode to Psyche" has proved difficult to relate to the other odes. Kenneth Allott once called it the Cinderella of the great odes because it had been so neglected.[4] But at times it seems to be more of a problem child, stubbornly refusing to join the others in any harmonious grouping. Though we naturally tend to think of it as an introduction to the others because it was apparently the first to be written, we are much less in agreement about a unifying theme. Attempts to see it as part of a coherent sequence have stressed its melancholy "mood," its "worshipping of the imagination," its study of what Keats knew as the "creative mood," its celebration of "the timeless beauty of love," and its recognition of the "indeterminacy" of the most important questions facing the modern poet.[5] While each of these concerns can be shown to be present in the poem, none seems to provide a sufficiently strong or convincing link with the other odes. The simple truth is that the tentative probings of the psyche and the human condition in this first ode are not easy to reconcile with the more profound searchings of the odes that follow.

However, since mutability is generally acknowledged as a central concern in Keats's major poems and since the odes in particular seem to be, as Stillinger has remarked, "an investigation of the imagination's ability to cope with time and change," mutability may be taken as the most fundamental theme that "Ode to Psyche" shares with the other odes.[6] Considered as a group, and as an imaginative account of one of the most remarkable attempts ever made to adapt to the mutability inherent in nature and human experience, the odes seem to offer a record of the discoveries Keats made during his exploration of those dark passages seen ahead of him in the letter to Reynolds (3 May 1818) about the "Chamber of Maiden Thought":

> This Chamber of Maiden Thought becomes gradually darken'd and at the same time on all sides of it many doors are set open – but all dark – all leading to dark passages – We see not the ballance of good and evil. We are in a Mist – *We* are now in that state – We feel the "burden of the Mystery." To this point was Wordsworth come, as far as I can conceive when he wrote "Tintern Abbey" and it seems to me that his Genius is explorative of those dark Passages. Now if we live, and go on thinking, we too shall explore them (Rollins i. 281).

Mutability – ultimately, death – was the most fearful and yet compelling passage to ponder, not just because of the all-too-frequent reminders of it in his own life (Tom had died only five months before Keats sat down to write "Ode to Psyche") but because it lay inescapably at the end of every favourite speculation.

"Psyche" was written during the same period (21–30 April 1819) in which he set forth his ideas on the world as a "vale of Soul-making," and the context for both the ode and this section of the long journal letter of February – May 1819 is a deep concern with man's mutability. Keats has in mind King Lear's question, "Is man no more than this?" (II. iv. 105–6) when he observes that "Man is originally 'a poor forked creature' subject to the same mischances as the beasts of the forest, destined to hardships and disquietude of some kind or other" (Rollins ii. 101). In other words, and in essence, "he is mortal". Keats then says that he can imagine "happiness carried to an extreme – but what must it end in? – Death."

> The point at which Man may arrive is as far as the paralel state in inanimate nature and no further – For instance suppose a rose to have sensation, it blooms on a beautiful morning it enjoys itself – but there comes a cold wind, a hot sun – it can not escape it, it cannot destroy its annoyances – they are as native to the world as itself: no more can man be happy in spite, the world[l]y elements will prey upon his nature. (Rollins ii. 101)

This concern with the limited, mortal nature of man, which was so much on Keats's mind in the spring of 1819, finds paradoxical expression in "Ode to Psyche." The poem is concerned with the mutability of an immortal. On the one hand, of course, Psyche cannot be threatened with death because she is an immortal. On the other hand, Keats is very much aware that she is not really an immortal but what he would call a "hethen Goddess" (ii. 106) who represents the soul ("as in the hethen mythology abstractions are personified" – ii. 103), and whose very existence depends on those who believe in her.[7] His awareness that her existence depends on belief appears in the lines "too late for antique vows, / Too, too late for the fond believing lyre" (ll. 36–7). Even if she had not been too late, the poet is aware, belief in her would have been to some extent "fond," both devoted and foolish, not unlike Wordsworth's "fond illusion of my heart" in "Elegiac Stanzas Suggested by a Picture of Peele Castle." As a mythological figure in a shared or cultural imagination, an immortal may very well be threatened with a kind of death through neglect or disbelief.

Keats traces the neglect back to her first appearance in myth. In the letter to the George Keatses in which he copied out the poem for them, he remarked: "You must recollect that Psyche was not embodied as a goddess before the time of Apulieus the Platonist who lived afteir the Agustan age, and consequently the Goddess was never worshipped or sacrificed to with any of the ancient fervour – and perhaps never thought of in the old religion – I am more orthodox tha[n] to let a hethen Goddess be so neglected" (Rollins ii. 106). The irony of her situation is complex. Her existence was originally threatened because the Greeks never believed in her very strongly. She was too late for antique vows. Now whatever claim to existence she may have is in jeopardy precisely because she belongs to the "faint Olympians" (l. 42) and all their "faded hierarchy" (l. 25), and they are no longer believed in. Psyche is thus presented as a fading or dying immortal, and the mutability to which even a goddess and a religion must submit becomes the real subject of the ode.

Another expression of Keats's concern with mutability appears in the gently mournful and somewhat ironic mood of the opening lines, which announce a concern with change and loss:

> O Goddess! hear these tuneless numbers, wrung
> By sweet enforcement and remembrance dear.

Though Keats will not mourn Psyche's faded and nearly lost presence with the high seriousness with which Milton mourned the death of Edward King, he does have "Lycidas" in mind here ("with forc'd fingers rude. . . . Bitter constraint, and sad occasion dear"). Perhaps it would be reading too much into the lines "O latest born and loveliest vision far" (l. 24) and "O brightest! though too late for antique vows" (l. 36) to hear even faint echoes of the more somber mood of Milton's "O ye laurels" and "But O the heavy change, now thou art gone." Yet the very language of the ode invokes a sense of melancholy. Usually when Keats begins a line or stanza with "O" ("O for a beaker full of the warm South," "O Attic shape! Fair attitude!")

he gives voice to a sense of melancholy that derives its intensity and meaning from a pained consciousness of something felt to be absent or lost. In "Ode to Psyche," though the goddess cannot really die, the poet's celebration of her begins in a concern for her fading presence, and the poem's melancholy tone is associated with death.

For example, the "pale-mouth'd prophet" (l. 35) recalls other occasions when the word "pale" is associated with death and mourning: Isabella's "paleness" in mourning the death of Lorenzo (l. 318), the "Pale warriors, death pale were they all" in "La Belle Dame" (l. 38), and the youth in "Ode to a Nightingale" who "grows pale, and spectre-thin, and dies" (l. 26). It might be argued that the poet's tone is only a staged mournfulness appropriate to the story of Psyche, her suffering at the hands of Aphrodite (who is represented in *The Golden Ass*, one of Keats's sources for the myth, as arbitrary and cruel), and what Milton calls "her wandering labours long" (*Comus* 1005). Her abandonment by Cupid every morning might also have been a consideration, for separations, either imagined or experienced, usually induce melancholy states in Keats's heroes and personae. But the real source of the melancholy tone is the poet's inescapable awareness that even a goddess is subject to mutability. And if Leonidas Jones is right that this first ode announces allegorically Keats's intention of becoming a psychological poet, then the melancholy strain in the odes that follow is an appropriate fulfillment of Keats's promise to become the pale-mouth'd prophet of the psyche.

If I have exaggerated the melancholy strain in "Ode to Psyche," it is because I believe that it has never been taken seriously enough. One must acknowledge, however, that readers nowadays tend to disagree about the tone, some feeling that it is melancholy, others that it is happy; there seems to be evidence to support both views. The tone shifts several times. The third stanza is spontaneous and assertive when Keats says "I see, and sing, by my own eyes inspired" (l. 43), and when he begins to reverse Psyche's fate by changing "No voice, no lute, no pipe" (l. 32) to "Thy voice, thy lute, thy pipe, thy incense sweet" (l. 46). Yet at the end of the stanza the tone is identified with that of the "pale-mouth'd prophet" and his "moan / Upon the midnight hours" (ll. 44–5). The tone seems to be a characteristic mixture of contraries, wrung by "sweet enforcement" (l. 2) and "pleasant pain" (l. 52). Even in the happy ending the "soft delight" (l. 64) is to be won for Psyche with "shadowy thought" (l. 65), echoing a common metaphor for melancholy ("For shade to shade will come too drowsily, / And drown the wakeful anguish of the soul" – "Ode on Melancholy," 9–10). No wonder Kenneth Allott suggested that while the poem is a happy one, "its tone is more exactly described if the happiness is thought of as defensive or defiant."[8]

If we extend Allott's fine observation about the tone to other aspects of the poem (the conception of Psyche, the role of the poet, and so forth), and if we take it in a more specifically psychological sense than he intended, other defensive qualities will become apparent. We cannot appreciate the extent of Keats's concern with mutability in this and the other odes until we have seen the lengths to which he goes to defend himself against it.

Apostrophe may be used as a defense against temporality, as Jonathan Culler has pointed out,[9] and this is one of its functions in the odes. But a more specific defense in "Psyche" is the use of paradox in the conception of the goddess. A paradox may be defined as a conception or statement that is simultaneously true and absurd. The paradox here, as I have already suggested, is that Psyche could be immortal, yet also fading, and therefore an object of mourning. The absurd element in the paradox is the defensive (and wish-fulfilling) one: that Psyche is immortal. What would be truly unacceptable would be for her to be mortal (as she was originally) and subject to a real death, for then the poet's grief would be more nearly inconsolable. The paradoxical conception of Psyche as a dying immortal enables Keats to indulge a mournful sensitivity to loss, yet postpone forever the finality of death.

Another defense against the threat of mutability appears in the unanswered question at the beginning of the poem:

> Surely I dreamt to-day, or did I see
> The winged Psyche with awaken'd eyes?
>
> (ll. 5–6)

This question, with only its echo of Spenser and an earlier convention to soften its disarming directness, is strategically placed at the beginning in order to deal with – actually, to dismiss – the doubt that has arisen in the poet's mind about Psyche's existence. He would convince himself that it was not a dream but a real vision, as if the intruding awareness from the letters that Psyche was merely a personification had to be put aside. The question reflects the kind of doubt that in earlier times would have precipitated the disbelief in (and eventual fading of) the Olympian hierarchy, and we can see that the doubt remains in (and on) Keats's mind throughout the first two stanzas and part of the third. But the question is carefully phrased to invite a willing suspension of disbelief and a displacement of the real world by mythology and fantasy.

Keats will often use an unanswered question as a bridge between fantasy and reality. In "Ode to a Nightingale" he concludes by asking, "Was it a vision, or a waking dream?" The question sounds a gentle and somewhat ambivalent note of skepticism toward the vision or dream he has just experienced, suggesting that he returns to reality, but reluctantly. In contrast, the purpose of the question in "Ode to Psyche" is to dispel doubts and, like the unanswered questions in the first stanza of "Ode on a Grecian Urn," it is designed to facilitate rather than conclude a flight of imagination. It is clearly tipped in favor of trusting that the goddess has actually been seen. The blunt and disbelieving "Surely I dreamt to-day" is countered by the longer, more descriptive, and more evocative "or did I see / The winged Psyche with awaken'd eyes?" The poet has already begun to restore Psyche's fading presence.

A full restoration of her presence now quickly becomes the central aim of the first stanza, and the restoration seems to offer a defense against the mutability that a fading immortal so poignantly symbolizes. The "two fair creatures" are described as

> couched side by side
> In deepest grass, beneath the whisp'ring roof
> Of leaves and trembled blossoms, where there ran
> A brooklet, scarce espied:
> 'Mid hush'd, cool-rooted flowers, fragrant-eyed,
> Blue, silver-white, and budded Tyrian,
> They lay calm-breathing on the bedded grass;
> Their arms embraced, and their pinions too;
> Their lips touch'd not, but had not bade adieu,
> As if disjoined by soft-handed slumber,
> And ready still past kisses to outnumber
> At tender eye-dawn of aurorean love:
> The winged boy I knew;
> But who wast thou, O happy, happy dove?
> His Psyche true!
>
> (ll. 9–23)

Keats painted many similar scenes in *Endymion* but none more memorable than this. From his initial hesitation in addressing Psyche, and his self-conscious questioning of how he saw her, he moves quickly to a vivid and detailed recollection of Cupid and Psyche in close embrace. He seems to re-experience his surprise at encountering them and as a result the scene achieves a certain dramatic immediacy, as if the lovers appear before us in all their passion suddenly and unexpectedly.

The relevance of this scene for the rest of the poem is not immediately apparent, but it serves an essential purpose. Though one may object to some of the phrasing (critics have singled out "tender eye-dawn of aurorean love" for its echo of some of the so-called excesses of *Endymion*), the description is sufficiently rich in sensuous detail ("hush'd, cool-rooted flowers," "bedded grass," "Their lips touch'd not, but had not bade adieu") to evoke a convincing image of the lovers before our eyes, and this is its purpose. At the end of the stanza doubts about Psyche's existence are difficult to recall, subtly displaced as they are by the almost palpable sensuality of the scene. When Keats answers his question about her existence ("But who wast thou?") with the short, confident "His Psyche true!" it is clear that she is almost a fully restored, believed-in presence.

Scenes of embracing lovers appear frequently in Keats's poetry. In addition to representing a characteristic quest for permanence, they dramatize a persistent longing for merger with a feminine figure or symbol of beauty, a longing that arises in the mind of a poet possessing a heightened sensitivity to an internal scene of separation and that shapes the internal quest-romance on which so much of his poetry is based. Keats is repeatedly concerned with lovers who fear a separation and strive to avoid it, or strive to overcome the fear. This concern seems to have drawn him to a variety of stories where a separation is threatened ("The Eve of St. Agnes") or actually experienced ("Isabella"), particularly between a mortal and an immortal (*Endymion*, "La Belle Dame," "Lamia"). Venus and Adonis, we recall, had to endure regular separations. Cupid and Psyche did too, and although Keats picks up their story after they have been joined in heaven and after the need for secrecy has passed, he still speaks of "secrets" (l. 3) and he retains that part of the myth in which the lovers are reunited at night, albeit with the aid of a bright torch. Perhaps it was the mortal Psyche caught in "a world of Circumstances" (Rollins ii. 104) and the lovers' experience with separation that first attracted him to the myth. A keen awareness of the ordeal of these separations is what lends dramatic power to the staging of the reunions, with scenes of embracing lovers.

What is the significance of all these separations and scenes of reunion, and why does Keats's imagination return to them so persistently? I would suggest that the desired but always seemingly unexpected encounters with various goddesses and other supernatural figures throughout the poetry may be related to the "pure Goddess" (Rollins i. 341) whom Keats held in fantasy when he was a boy. The scenes of encounter between his mortal heroes, with whom he so often felt an identification, and their goddesses or other feminine immortals, may thus be interpreted as representing wish-fulfilling restorations of an image from the depths of his own psyche, an image that is ultimately related to the shadow of a lost maternal presence. The extensive recreation of the scene of romance ("The stretched metre of an antique song," in the epigraph to *Endymion*) and the elaborate or merely sketched portraits of figures such as Cynthia and Psyche may be seen as part of an unending effort at a permanent reinstatement of that deathless image.

The relation between Keats's narrative poems and the great odes is nowhere more marked than here in the perpetuation of the mode of the quest-romance in the poet's lyrical quest for a symbol of permanence. As Parker says, "It is not difficult to assimilate the trajectory of the Ode to the form of the romance quest; both depend on the separation of subject and object, and on the dialectic of absence and presence this separation begets."[10] Romance is a unifying mode in the Keats canon, linking the various narrative forms (quest-romance in *Endymion*, satirical romance in "Lamia," epic romance in "The Fall of Hyperion") to the romance spirit of the lyrical poems, particularly the odes, especially by the pervasive effort to restore the presence of some feminine figure or symbol of permanence. An important part of the imaginative effort in each of Keats's major poems goes toward working out a defense against a full recognition of irrevocable loss and human mutability. The effort arises from a dual necessity, an old but still pressing psychological need to repair an absence and a more recent but equally compelling intellectual awareness of the complex personal, moral, and philosophical implications of loss and final separations.

One may sometimes wish that Keats's defensive efforts had not been quite so successful in "Ode to Psyche." If he had shown more of the skepticism toward dreams and visions that he shows in the other major poems of 1819, we are tempted to say, and if this ode did not end on quite so happy and confident a note, we could think of it as a more appropriate introduction to the deeper tones of the odes that follow. Yet this first ode is no less serious an effort than the others at the soul-making that all the most mature of Keats's poems have as one of their aims, and it would be a mistake to underestimate the complexity of thought and feeling which, like the "wreath'd trellis" in the last stanza, surrounds the otherwise apparently simple notion of an ode to Psyche.

Consider, for example, the way the erotic scene in the first stanza gives way to a rescue fantasy in the remaining three. Although Psyche was the

> loveliest vision far
> Of all Olympus' faded hierarchy!
> Fairer than Phoebe's sapphire-region'd star,
> Or Vesper, amorous glow-worm of the sky
>
> (ll. 24–7)

she was never properly worshipped. She had no temple, no choir, and no priest, and she was too late for the fond believing lyre. In ancient days she was neglected and now, "in these days so far retir'd / From happy pieties" (ll. 40–1), she may be required to suffer virtual oblivion. She is not quite a damsel in distress, yet she is somewhat like Madeline, an isolated figure in need of a new home. Keats interposes himself between Psyche and the fate imagined for her. Though reference to Cupid is included in the "two fair creatures" of the first stanza (l. 9), and though Keats identifies him as "The winged boy" (l. 21), he is entirely displaced in the remainder of the poem by the poet himself, except for the allusion in the last line ("To let the warm Love in!"). The poet and Psyche become the central couple.

The Oedipal aspirations of the heroic role in which Keats casts himself deserve some attention. We recall that when he was five, as Robert Gittings relates, he "got hold of 'a naked sword'... and held his mother prisoner in the house with it." Gittings goes on to say that this story is "characteristic of all we know later of his possessive and passionate nature."[11] Perhaps this tendency toward possessiveness will help to explain his obvious relish in playing the role of rescuer when he points out to the George Keatses that "the Goddess was never worshipped or sacrificed to with any of the ancient fervour," and then adds, "I am more orthodox tha[n] to let a hethen Goddess be so neglected" (Rollins ii. 106). The tone of this remark may be somewhat playful, but in the poem Keats does quietly change the "No" to "Thy" in lines 46–9 and become Psyche's priest and prophet, rescuer and provider.

The higher mood that now comes to dominate the poem derives from a sense of elation over the achievement of a rescue. Yet when we consider the fact that Keats's way of rescuing Psyche is simply to adopt a new attitude toward her, one that treats her as an inner object ("I see, and sing, by my own eyes inspired"), we realize that the new attitude is really intended as a self-rescue, a rescue of the Keats whose concern with transience and mutability urges him to try to prevent any further fading of the goddess by making her an inner certainty. We earlier saw that Keats could use paradox as a way of denying a full awareness of irrevocable loss, and then an imaginative restoration as a means of replacing what is felt to be lost. Now he uses internalization ("Yes, I will... build a fane / In some untrodden region of my mind" – ll. 50–1) as a defense against the fear of any possible recurrence of the loss. Like Porphyro, he seizes the object of romance and makes a home for her.

Most of the difficulties of interpreting the poem, and especially of relating it to the other odes in a meaningful sequence, now seem to come to a head in the climactic fourth stanza. If we take the view that the poem is a hymn to imagination which ends on a triumphant note, and that Keats means that he can build an inner paradise in which he would be insulated from a world of pains and troubles, then it will be difficult to integrate "Psyche" with the other odes. They hold no such faith in the power of the imagination. We would still be able to see the poem as a kind of introduction to the other odes, especially in the sense that the internalization at the end seems to prefigure Keats's increasing commitment to psychological concerns, as it also seems to mirror an increasing preoccupation in romantic poetry and art with the self and the inner life. But the hope of a more convincing basis for a sequence would have to be abandoned because the optimism in this ode would not square with the profound skepticism toward the imagination in the other odes and major poems of 1819.

On the other hand, if we take Sperry's well-argued view that "the prospect the last stanza unfolds is hardly one of unqualified optimism," and that Keats's emphasis is on "shadowy thought," a "working brain," and an intellectual growth that seem altogether to preclude an unqualified faith in the imagination, then we shall have little difficulty in reconciling the last stanza of "Psyche" with the other odes.[12] But we shall still be left with the considerable task of explaining how the last stanza works as a conclusion. The difficulty is brought home to us when we reflect on how different is the ending of this poem, with its imaginative assertiveness in having Psyche take up residence in the poet's mind, from the more sober return to reality that concludes the odes to the Nightingale and on the Urn. How, we ask, can the self-conscious internalizing of Psyche be supposed to achieve a solution to the problem of mutability as Keats has presented it in the figure and fate of Psyche?

An answer may be found in the fact that the last stanza attempts to provide not a solution to the problem of mutability but an adaptation to it. And this will to adapt, this willingness to accept life, transient and death-bound though it is, is more than anything else what unites "Psyche" to the other odes. The nature of the adaptation is suggested by the region of the mind in which Keats would build a temple for Psyche. It recalls, as various critics have observed, similar bowers in *The Faerie Queene* and *Paradise Lost*. But its deeper affinity, as so often with Keats, is with Wordsworth. It is an "untrodden region" (1. 51), protected by "dark-cluster'd trees" that "Fledge the wild-ridged mountains steep by steep" (ll. 54–5). In its remoteness and its "wide quietness" (1. 58) the region seems to recall the "steep and lofty cliffs" and the "more deep seclusion" of the landscape in "Tintern Abbey" (ll. 5–7), as Bloom has suggested.[13] But, more important, Keats's inner landscape represents a Wordsworthian state of feeling and mind that Keats associates with the presence of Psyche, as Wordsworth had earlier associated a similar state of mind with the presence of Nature. The sanctuary's natural growth, with its "branched thoughts" (1. 52) and "wreath'd trellis of a working brain" (1. 60), is a metaphor for a psychological and intellectual growth that has the Wordsworthian aims of becoming "a living soul" and, as Keats attempts to do in the odes that follow, of seeing "into the life of things" ("Tintern Abbey," ll. 46, 49). If Psyche is not to be exactly the guardian of his heart and soul, of all his moral being, she is nonetheless to be the hallowed presence that will preside over and ensure his growth and its "Soul-making."

This is the healing thought with which "Ode to Psyche" concludes. It brings together two strains of thought in Keats's development. One centers on the notion of soul-making. In the section of the long journal letter of February – May 1819 in which he set forth this notion, he included some reflections on man's potential for happiness in the light of his mortality.

Keats could not forget (and it is worth repeating here) that "a rose . . . blooms on a beautiful morning it enjoys itself – but there comes a cold wind, a hot sun – it can not escape it, it cannot destroy its annoyances – they are as native to the world as itself."

To this reflection on mutability is then joined his view of the world and the use to which it should be put: "The common cognomen of this world among the misguided and superstitious is 'a vale of tears' from which we are to be redeemed by a certain arbit[r]ary interposition of God and taken to Heaven – What a little circumscribe[d] straightened notion! Call the world if you Please 'The vale of Soul-making' Then you will find out the use of the world" (Rollins ii. 101–2). Adversity is not merely a challenge but a call to the quest. As Perkins has remarked, Keats "tended to resolve the large, unanswerable perplexities that afflict us all by constructing myths of process. . . . In the great myth, in the *Letters*, of human life as a 'vale of Soul-making' there is the conception of the gradual forming of a human identity or 'Soul' by means of a 'World of Pains and troubles' [Rollins ii. 102]."[14] In other words, Keats defends against the mutability inherent in human life by trusting in the idea of purposeful growth. If the trust is not a rational answer to the problem, it is a thoroughly natural one, and representative of the romantic poets' situation in an increasingly demythologized modern world. It is also, for Keats, the only path open that "does not affront our reason and humanity" (Rollins ii. 103).

The other strain in his thought, one which goes back to his boyhood daydream that his mind was a nest in which some goddess slept, is his wish for a beneficent presence to oversee the growth. Keats's memory of the daydream suggests that it continues to live in his mind in one form or another. When he was at Margate working on *Endymion*, we recall, he wrote to Haydon of his progress: "Thank God! I do begin arduously where I leave off, notwithstanding occasional depressions: and I hope for the support of a High Power while I clime this little eminence and especially in my Years of more momentous Labor. I remember your saying that you had notions of a good Genius presiding over you – I have of late had the same thought. . . . Is it too daring to Fancy Shakspeare this Presider?" (Rollins i. 141–2). The idea of a presider over his genius enables him to think of the burden of the past as if it were a blessing of the poet and his enterprise, just as the idea of a purposeful growth enables him to think of the burden of the mystery as if it were a dark passage made for our searching.

Now in a year of truly momentous labor he dares to fancy Psyche as the presider over his soul and growth. Her reassuring presence in his mind represents a wish-fulfilling but also adaptive merger of self and object through an act of internalization. The efforts at restoration and internalization here and elsewhere in the ode sequence are not simply an indulgence in pure fantasy or illusion any more than the view and acceptance of reality that emerge in the sequence are independent of imaginative shaping and content. The idea that illusion (or romance) and reality in human perception are always separate and distinguishable is not a very serviceable premise with which to read Keats's poetry, where a psychology of interfusion rather than a logic of distinction so often predominates. In the last stanza of "Psyche" the restored and internalized presence of the goddess enables Keats to transform his concern with mutability, now perceiving it in a different way, shifting the focus from loss to growth. If both human and divine forms are part of a natural process making them mutable and subject to death, the process also ensures change and growth, and these carry with them the hope of fulfillment. In the final moment of the poem, with the image of "a casement ope at night, / To let the warm Love in," the lovers' story is not only recapitulated as desire and fulfillment but perpetuated in the poet's mind as a model for his own anticipated growth and fulfillment.

But the Keatsian acceptance of natural process, in its most mature form in "Ode on Melancholy" and "To Autumn," is more than a wise passiveness. It is an active embrace, an ardent and arduous pursuit of life. Only he who has a strenuous tongue can burst joy's grape. This notion, too, is prefigured in "Psyche." The verbs in the last stanza announce Keats's conviction that he must assume full responsibility for his own growth. He *will build* the fane, *will dress* the trellis, and use his *working* brain to *win* love for the mind. Insofar as it is possible to do so, he would will his own growth. This is the principal reason he felt that the idea of the world as a vale of soul-making was "a faint sketch of a system of Salvation which does not affront our reason and humanity" (Rollins ii. 103), and it is one of the reasons he has had such enduring appeal for modern readers. He does not expect to be redeemed "by a certain arbit[r]ary interposition of God and taken to Heaven – What a little circumscribe[d] straightened notion!" Implicit in the letter and the ode, both crucial in any consideration of Keats's development, is a recognition that a man must be the ultimate presider over his own soul and genius. If Keats has not yet explored all the uncertainties that lie ahead of him, he has at least begun to make his way toward his sole self. And if the last stanza rings a triumphant note, it is due largely to a sense of renewal derived from a fresh commitment to this unending task.

II

In "Ode to Psyche," then, Keats's attempt to restore an image of permanence and internalize it is a means of developing an adaptive attitude that will serve as a defense against the mutability to which even a goddess is felt to be subject. This first ode shares with the others, particularly "Ode to a Nightingale" and "Ode on a Grecian Urn," the impulse to build a psychological or spiritual garden, a bower of enclosed contentment. Yet Keats knew that we cannot "build a sort of mental Cottage of feelings quiet and pleasant ... this never can be" (Rollins i. 254). All of his extended metaphors for psychological or spiritual development (the Mansion of Many Apartments, the mental Cottage, the vale of Soul-making) represent it in terms either of journeying or of natural growth. The fane and garden at the end of "Psyche" form a bower that in its imagery and conception is subject to change and growth. When, at the end of the poem, Keats reverts to a point in the myth when Psyche was still a mortal, waiting expectantly for the arrival of Love, he suggests a note of uncertain anticipation appropriate to the larger theme of mutability and growth.

The principal difference in the handling of the problem of mutability in "Psyche" and "Nightingale" is that in the former Keats's concern with it is so quickly and effortlessly identified with the story and fate of Psyche, the displacement to mythology so complete, and the success of the various strategies (from denial and restoration to rescue and internalization) so convincing in their dramatic context, that the darker aspects of the theme are overlooked and, one might almost say, forgotten. It is as if the problem is too well defended against by the self-inspired seeing and singing. Now in "Ode to a Nightingale" new uncertainties are explored and boldly confronted.

The poem begins in a mood of profound dejection:

> My heart aches, and a drowsy numbness pains
>   My sense, as though of hemlock I had drunk,
> Or emptied some dull opiate to the drains
>   One minute past, and Lethe-wards had sunk.

The aching heart, it is not always easy to remember, is a metaphor for a state of mind, the key to which is the mythological allusion to the river Lethe. The poet feels dead, and as if he were journeying to another world. The drowsy numbness, the dulled consciousness, and the feeling of sinking toward forgetfulness signal a regressive movement that will dominate the poem through stanza 5 and most of 6, culminating in the wish "To cease upon the midnight with no pain" (l. 56). Because of the poet's dejection and his later effort to enter the Nightingale's world, his puzzling claim now that he does not envy the bird cannot be taken literally. The lines " 'Tis not through envy of thy happy lot, / But being too happy in thine happiness" (ll. 5–6) seem to echo the tone of defensive happiness found in "Ode to Psyche." Although the poet appears to deny that his dejection proceeds from envy of the bird, one cannot be certain if the aching heart precedes or follows, if it causes or results from, his awareness of the bird's happiness. The ambiguity must be taken as part of the meaning: the two are uncertainly but inseparably bound up with each other.

The regressive movement and the contemplation of the bird's world thus begin in a complex creative act, one that is doubly defensive, enabling Keats both to escape dejection (and the still unstated reasons for it) and to commence restoring "a sort of Philosophical Back Garden" (Rollins i. 254), or spiritual bower, which he has imaginatively constructed many times before. Much of his attention in the first five stanzas is devoted to the restoration, but this bower is darker and more remote than the one in which the poet first encountered Cupid and Psyche. The "forest" and "whisp'ring roof / Of leaves and trembled blossoms" in the first ode (ll. 7, 10–11) become a "forest dim" of "verdurous glooms and winding mossy ways" in the next (ll. 20, 40). The inner landscape here is far more uncertain. In "Ode to Psyche" the inherited myth provided a means of controlling uncertainty. Keats could, of course, choose to deal with those aspects of the goddess's story that interested him, but her character, her circumstances, and the content of the poem were to a considerable extent already determined. In "Ode to a Nightingale" there is little inherited by way of tradition, perhaps only the melancholy strain in the bird's song, evoked near the end in the mention of the "plaintive anthem" (l. 75), and even less of an individual nature on which to base a characterization. As a result, the poet's entry into the Nightingale's world – in effect, his re-entry into a previously explored but still uncharted inner world – is less structured. Keats has no myth to follow. His encounter with the Nightingale, therefore, involves greater risk and challenge.

The greater freedom offered by the bird as a symbolic object taken from nature results primarily in a bolder, more thoughtful, and deeper response to the problem of loss. Although Keats does not explicitly identify the Nightingale's world as one felt to be lost and needing to be restored, as he had conceived Psyche's, it is clear throughout the poem that he is motivated by a pervasive sense of loss that has deepened into a consuming despair at a world afflicted with greater deprivations than the loss of "happy pieties." The sense of loss is most movingly evoked in the second stanza. The tone is set by the almost breathless "O," with its inextricable mixture of sadness and longing, beginning in the first unit of the stanza, the Shakespearean quatrain ("O, for a draught of vintage!" – l. 11), and repeated in the second unit, the Petrarchan sestet ("O for a beaker full of the warm South" – l. 15). The longing for a lost world also finds expression in two mythological allusions (one to the goddess Flora and the other to Hippocrene) as well as in a surprising evocation of twelfth-century romance and pageantry in the remarkable line, "Dance, and Provençal song, and sunburnt mirth!" (l. 14).

The world for which the poet longs, and which he now restores, is not identical with the one inhabited by the Nightingale and defined for the most part in stanzas 4, 5, and 6. That world is a much darker and quieter imaginary space than the festive one suggested in stanza 2. However, the regressive feelings evoked in the process of thinking of the sensuous world of stanza 2 are not unrelated to those indulged later when the poet believes he is in the presence of the Nightingale. Wasserman interpreted stanza 2 as presenting the first of three proposals by which the poet seeks release from the mortal pains of this world: "the progress [is] from wine to poesy to death – the absorption of the sensuous, the imaginative, and finally the total spiritual self."[15] But since images of wine and physical sensation in Keats's poetry are often a prelude to visionary experience, increased intensity, or new awareness, they seem to function here as a prelude to the intensity and depth of thought in stanza 3. The sensuous world of stanza 2 is in this way less of a separate world, sought and tried for its own sake, than an inner territory through which the poet passes on his journey, as if he were flying back through literary-historical and mythological regions of the mind (Provence and Mount Helicon) toward the midnight-dark and timeless region presided over by the Nightingale.

However we interpret the poem and conceive the two or three (or four) units of its structure, stanza 3 will continue to seem somewhat independent and problematic because of its almost total contrast with the stanzas immediately preceding and following it. Yet it is the most haunting stanza in the poem, containing that core of thought and painful reflection without which this ode, and perhaps the others, would never have been written. As many readers have noted, it represents Keats's boldest exploration so far of those dark passages he had seen ahead of him in the "Mansion of Many Apartments" letter. It brings to mind his conviction "that the World is full of Misery and Heartbreak, Pain, Sickness and oppression" (Rollins i. 281). In that letter, we recall, Keats thought that it was to this point that Wordsworth had come in "Tintern Abbey" in his exploration of the dark passages, where the "burden of the Mystery" is felt most profoundly. "Now if we live, and go on thinking, we too shall explore them" (Rollins i. 281). It is therefore not surprising that now in line 23 – "The weariness, the fever, and the fret" – he should echo "the fretful stir / Unprofitable, and the fever of the world" from "Tintern Abbey" (ll. 52–3). Insofar as his own exploration in this stanza represents the kind of "advance of intellect" (Rollins i. 281), or thinking further into the human heart, for which he praised Wordsworth, it does so because he confronts the real possibility of pointless suffering and ultimate meaninglessness. The exploration begins as an extension of the wish at the end of stanza 2 to "fade away into the forest dim," but quickly deepens into sad reflection:

> Fade far away, dissolve, and quite forget
> What thou among the leaves hast never known,
> The weariness, the fever, and the fret
> Here, where men sit and hear each other groan;

Where palsy shakes a few, sad, last grey hairs,
   Where youth grows pale, and spectre-thin, and dies;
     Where but to think is to be full of sorrow
        And leaden-eyed despairs,
   Where Beauty cannot keep her lustrous eyes,
     Or new Love pine at them beyond to-morrow.

                                         (ll. 21–30)

    To the extent that this poem achieves "the grandeur of the ode" that Keats spoke of in the epistle "To Charles Cowden Clarke" (l. 62), it does so largely because it grows stronger from the load of thought it bears in stanza 3. Almost every line is an axiom Keats had already come to feel on his pulse. The impact of the stanza is no doubt increased by our knowledge of the events and circumstances of his life, especially the recent death of Tom, which Haydon thought, and others since have agreed, Keats was referring to in line 26 ("Where youth grows pale ..."). Nevertheless, much of the power of this stanza is Shakespearean. Echoes of the Duke's "Be absolute for death" speech in *Measure for Measure* have sometimes been heard in the stanza, particularly in Keats's mesmeric use of a series of "Where" clauses, which seem to parallel the Duke's "Thou art" clauses in his strong remarks to Claudio ("thou art death's fool.... Thou art not certain.... Thou hast nor youth, nor age ... thy blessed youth / Becomes as aged, and doth beg the alms / Of palsied eld" – III. i. 5–41). But the real thrust of the stanza has a more basic affinity with the general power of Shakespeare to summarize human experience, or broad aspects of it, in a speech comprised of a succession of fearless, sweeping observations. In stanza 3 Keats expresses so clearly and directly the severest implications of human mutability, and so effectively condenses into a few lines a survey of the darkest aspects of human experience, that he seems close to having become the "miserable and mighty Poet of the human Heart" that he said Shakespeare was (Rollins ii. 115).

    Because stanza 3 is so powerful, its place in the ode appears to be problematic, either because we feel that it will be difficult to continue the poem convincingly beyond this point, or because we sense that the stanza is a break in the movement into the Nightingale's world, a movement begun in stanza 1, advanced in 2, and picked up again in 4. Yet stanza 3 may be seen as the climax of the first section of the poem, which begins in a state of dejection, expresses a longing for a lost world, and concludes (in stanza 3) by uttering a mournful cry and protest at the human condition and the way it is largely defined by an acute sense of loss. In addition, the "Where" clauses in stanza 3 provide not only rhetorical support for the convictions in each line but a psychological intensification of the thought in the whole stanza, one seeming to require some form of release, serving to propel the poet still further into the world of the Nightingale, and making the somewhat artificial exclamation "Away! away!" at the beginning of stanza 4 more urgent and plausible than it might otherwise be.

Stanzas 4, 5, and 6 constitute the second principal section of the poem and define the imaginary space the Nightingale inhabits. In them Keats does not use an image of spatial immensity to evoke a sense of the sublime, as Burke and Kant knew it was possible to do, as Wordsworth often does, and as Keats himself will on occasion do. For example, in the "Chapman's Homer" sonnet he compares the act of discovering Homer to the experience of an astronomer "When a new planet swims into his ken" as well as to the first sight by Cortez and his men of the vast Pacific; in the sonnet "On Seeing the Elgin Marbles" his poet's mortal nature is set in opposition to "each imagined pinnacle and steep / Of godlike hardship" attributed to the artistic achievement of the "Grecian grandeur" and "magnitude" of the Marbles.[16] Instead, in the odes Keats evokes the sublime in the finite but secret or obscure space of a pastoral bower inhabited by the goddess Psyche or the Nightingale, or in the time–space of the lost mythological and historical world of the Urn, or in the mysteries of the psychological and seasonal processes of Melancholy and Autumn. The dark world of the Nightingale thus evokes the sublime less because it is at the threshold of infinity and is presided over by the moon and stars, giving whatever light "from heaven is with the breezes blown" (ll. 38–9), than because it is inhabited by a powerful symbol of the ultimate mystery.

The Nightingale's pastoral bower has the aura of a world that is more than natural. The "Queen-Moon is on her throne" (l. 36), reminiscent of Cynthia, and functions as if she were a benevolent deity presiding over the scene while "Cluster'd around by all her starry Fays" (l. 37). It is true that the bower is flush with flowers, grass, fruit trees, "White hawthorn, and the pastoral eglantine" (l. 46), recalling the embowered world of *Endymion* and the early poetry. Keats also shows an awareness of natural process in his reference to "Fast fading violets," "The coming musk-rose" as "mid-May's eldest child" (ll. 47–9), and the approach of summer. Yet the idea of process here is not the same as that of aging and dying in stanza 3, or of starvation and apparent overpopulation in stanza 7 ("No hungry generations tread thee down" – l. 62), nor is it the simple, natural process discussed in the "vale of Soul-making" letter, where a rose blooms in the morning, then withers in the cold wind or hot sun. Rather, there is a supranatural element in the imaginary space of the Nightingale similar to the idealized pastoral world of silence and slow time in which the Urn exists. The Nightingale's world is almost silent, and only potentially resonant with the bird's song. In the opening line of stanza 6 the poet says, "Darkling I listen," and for this reason we may think that the bird's song is heard throughout the poem, but there is no mention of it in either stanza 4 or 5, nor was there in 3. The only sound imagined in stanzas 4 and 5 is "The murmurous haunt of flies on summer eves" (l. 51).

Even the idea of death is not entirely natural. Although there are funerary suggestions in the imagery of stanza 5 ("flowers ... at my feet," "incense," "embalmed darkness," "fading," "cover'd up," "murmurous haunt") that anticipate the explicit longing for death in stanza 6, as Evert has pointed out,[17] the idea of death is anything but the wretched end of the natural process depicted in stanza 3. On the contrary, in stanza 5 it is closer to the image of Adonis enjoying a deathlike sleep while covered up in leaves in Book II of *Endymion*, or to the image of being "embower'd from the light, / Enshaded in forgetfulness divine" in the "Sonnet to Sleep," written perhaps as little as a week or so before the ode. As E. C. Pettet has observed, death in stanza 5 "is not the doubtful blessing and release of blank extinction but a 'luxury' full of pleasant sensation."[18] In stanza 6, as well, death is "easeful," "soft," "rich," and without "pain." The poet's sense of the beauty of death is so intense that it momentarily "overcomes every other consideration, or rather obliterates all consideration," as Keats had remarked of the experience of intensity in poetry in the letter on Negative Capability (Rollins i. 194). In short, the world restored in these stanzas, while more highly condensed in imagery and thought, is not unlike the luxurious and often mythological world of the early poetry, especially *Endymion*. Keats places the Nightingale in a natural setting, but the impulse to restore a lost, richly sensuous world associated with a familiar goddess of pastoral romance, the Queen-Moon, almost overwhelms his awareness of nature's processes. To the extent that the symbolic Nightingale is defined by this world, it cannot be taken as a wholly natural creature.

At what point the effort at restoration leaves off and the sense of identification with the Nightingale takes over is, of course, impossible to tell. The workings of these two processes do not follow the sequence of the stanzas. The assertion of a sense of identification in the first stanza ("being too happy in thine happiness") comes long before the major effort at restoration in stanzas 4 and 5. The poet's thoughts seem to race ahead, as if he is already with the bird in spirit, then return to the restorative effort of a detailed imagining or pictorializing of the Nightingale's world. When we come to stanza 6, however, the process of identification becomes dominant. This process, through which the poet has so far sought a merger with the Nightingale only by attempting to model his consciousness on its supposed blissful state, now leads him toward the dark immensity of death:

> Darkling I listen; and, for many a time
>   I have been half in love with easeful Death,
> Call'd him soft names in many a mused rhyme,
>   To take into the air my quiet breath;

> Now more than ever seems it rich to die,
> To cease upon the midnight with no pain,
>   While thou art pouring forth thy soul abroad
>   In such an ecstasy!
> Still wouldst thou sing, and I have ears in vain —
>   To thy high requiem become a sod.

Though only "half in love" with death, he says, suggesting a degree of balance or restraint until now, he has in fact "for many a time . . . Call'd him soft names," giving recognition to an old longing that reinforces the present one: "Now more than ever seems it rich to die." Helen Vendler has pointed out that the experiential or psychological beginning of this ode, the actual experience on which it is based, is the profound desire to die revealed in stanza 6.[19] Yet since the image of death here is quite different from the fearful one in stanza 3, we must ask how death is being imagined. If suicide is either a conscious or unconscious intention, what wish or fantasy impels the poet to die? And why is the Nightingale associated with death? The melancholy strain in its song and the mournful character given to it by tradition will hardly account for its dark significance now.

Death here is a metaphor for merger with a symbolic object that the poet has restored imaginatively on the model of an inner object felt to be irrecoverably lost but forever sought nonetheless. I believe that the experiential beginning of this and the other odes must be traced to this sense of loss. The poet attributes to the symbolic object the power to dissolve his anxiety and achieve for him a completion of self in a single, climactic moment of union. His almost irresistible longing is for total resolution and unity; it is a virtually instinctual desire for certainty that had earlier made the counter-conception of Negative Capability (the capacity "of being in uncertainties, Mysteries, doubts" — Rollins i. 193) not only possible but necessary. The longing finds expression in the synaesthetic imagery in stanzas 4 and 5: "tender is the night" (l. 35), "light . . . is with the breezes blown" (ll. 38–9), "soft incense hangs upon the boughs" (l. 42), and "embalmed darkness" (l. 43). What was earlier only a feeling of kinship with the bird has now become an all-consuming desire for fusion.

At midnight, when the poet would "cease . . . with no pain," the Nightingale is imagined presiding over his death. While the bird pours forth her soul in "ecstasy," he would make a final entry into the dark enclosure over which she reigns, a consummation devoutly to be wished. On other occasions, as we have seen, Keats imagines death as climactic. One thinks especially of the "Bright star" sonnet, where he would be pillowed upon his "fair love's ripening breast . . . And so live ever — or else swoon to death." In July 1819, we recall, he wrote to Fanny Brawne, "I have two luxuries to brood over in my walks, your Loveliness and the hour of my death. O that

I could have possession of them both in the same minute." Then he went on to say, "I hate the world: it batters too much the wings of my self-will, and would I could take a sweet poison from your lips to send me out of it" (Rollins ii. 133). Death in these and other similar examples from the poetry and letters is conceived as a dramatic union with an idealized object; it is not a simple wish to die, to cease to exist, but a metaphor for a state of mind in which all anxieties, all tensions, would be dissolved in a moment of luxurious sensation.

But now in "Ode to a Nightingale," and really for the first time, Keats's imagination takes him beyond this moment into the future when, as he says to the bird, "Still wouldst thou sing, and I have ears in vain – / To thy high requiem become a sod" (ll. 59–60). The romance of death ends when he envisions a world continuing beyond his own mortality. This recognition clearly determines the direction of the remainder of the poem, and therefore the source of its reflective and emotional power deserves special attention. Although it clearly includes an awareness that the only possible escape from this world is through death, which would mean an end of the poet's ability to hear the Nightingale's song (hearing is a synecdoche for living), the awareness is anything but a discovery. It is at best a rediscovery, a new awareness of an old truth. Whatever advance in Keats's thought the recognition represents, and whatever power it possesses to impress itself on his mind, derives from its special recasting as an image of mourning. The image is psychologically complex, both wish-fulfilling and fearful. It represents the bird's song as a "requiem" for the poet and it suggests that the bird would mourn his death, perhaps with the same empathy the poet felt in his mourning of the fading of Psyche. But it also presents a scene of final separation. The poet will have ears in vain and become a sod. In this image Keats makes himself an object of mourning but at the same moment recognizes the futility of it. The mourned cannot hear the mourner. Because of the succession of deaths in his brief life, and because of the role of survivor and mourner into which circumstances and a world of pain and troubles had cast him, this recognition of the futility of mourning is one Keats would have felt as an axiom on his pulse. He now makes no further effort to dissolve into the Nightingale's world.

The movement from stanzas 6 to 7, while not abrupt, marks a change in attitude:

> Thou wast not born for death, immortal Bird!
>   No hungry generations tread thee down;
> The voice I hear this passing night was heard
>   In ancient days by emperor and clown:
> Perhaps the self-same song that found a path

Through the sad heart of Ruth, when, sick for home,
　　She stood in tears amid the alien corn;
　　　　The same that oft-times hath
　　Charm'd magic casements, opening on the foam
　　Of perilous seas, in faery lands forlorn.

(ll. 61–70)

The epithet "immortal Bird!" signals an increased distance between the poet and the Nightingale. (The old objection that the bird is not really immortal overlooks its function as a symbol and therefore need not become a consideration.) Distance is also created by the shift of the poet's sense of identification from the Nightingale to the mortal world, to the "hungry generations" and the others who have heard her song. The focus changes from the midnight garden to three scenes from history and literature. In each someone is imagined listening to the Nightingale's voice: an emperor and clown, Ruth, and an unmentioned but implicit figure in a romance, or perhaps a reader of one, looking through an open window "in [or into] faery lands forlorn." The most significant of these scenes from the bird's long existence is, of course, the one involving Ruth. The fact that the biblical Ruth was not sick for home but chose to follow Naomi to Judea is another example of Keats's reinterpretation of inherited material to make it fit his purposes.[20] The homesickness complements the more general longing in the stanza and the poem toward something "forlorn," representing in the figure of Ruth the way the mind maintains a relationship with the past and thereby dramatizing Keats's own determination to preserve the relationship with the inner object for which the bird is a symbol. His emphasis on the bird's immortal and sympathetic nature, on its ancient and still vital potential as a consoling symbol, may be interpreted, of course, as part of the larger restorative effort in the poem. But now a new element is present in his attitude. His placement of the bird in the historical, biblical, and literary imagination (those realms of gold long since held in his mind in fealty to Apollo) is an unexpected and beautifully effective act of internalization, again defending against loss but with greater success than the restorative effort alone, or the effort at identification, would allow. Keats does not say so explicitly, but if the symbolic bird could have been such a friend to Ruth, she may remain one for him.

The internalization here is not so elaborate or outwardly confident as in "Ode to Psyche" and its success may even seem to be thrown in doubt in the final stanza when the bird disappears ("thy plaintive anthem fades / Past the near meadows ... and now 'tis buried deep / In the next valley-glades" – ll. 75–8). But at this point in the poem Keats is no longer referring to the symbolic, immortal bird; he refers instead to the nightingale nesting in Brown's house. By splitting the image of the bird in two, he can retain an

image of the symbolic bird, internalize it, then allow the real bird to fly
away.

It is true that the word "forlorn" at the end of stanza 7 and the beginning
of 8 reintroduces the sense of loss with which the poem began, one that is
an essential part of the poet's "sole self" (l. 72), thus seeming to deny any
notion of gain that an internalization implies. But whatever finality there is
in this word and in the scene of separation in the last stanza, with its
threefold repetition of "Adieu" (ll. 73, 75), is qualified by the poet's
uncertainty at the end of the poem:

> Was it a vision, or a waking dream?
> Fled is that music: – Do I wake or sleep?

While these two lines question the visionary imagination, they also suggest
that the internalized image of the symbolic bird and of the poet's experience
have not disappeared, and are in fact a strong enough part of his state of
mind to make him doubt his powers of perception.[21] This is not to say that
the sense of loss (recalled in the word "Forlorn") has been totally repaired.
On the contrary, the poet has not achieved a merger with the Nightingale;
this is what he means when he says "fancy cannot cheat so well / As she is
fam'd to do, deceiving elf" (ll. 73–4). But the uncertainty with which the
poem ends is due in part to the profound impression the internalized image
of the symbolic bird persists in making on him in contrast to the real world
of which he is now again so aware. The symbolic Nightingale has been
subtly integrated into a cultural imagination in which the poet participates,
and as the poem ends it continues to be a felt presence in his mind.

III

In spite of basic similarities between "Ode to a Nightingale" and "Ode on
a Grecian Urn" (for example, their concern with mutability, the quest for
permanence, and the visionary imagination), several stylistic and conceptual
differences strike us immediately. The greater stanzaic regularity of "Ode on
a Grecian Urn" (achieved by changing line 8 in the "Nightingale" stanza
from trimeter to pentameter) and the reduced length of the poem (from
eighty to fifty lines) suggest a tightening of the ode form, with greater
condensation of thought and economy of expression, as if the exertions of
working through the problems dealt with in "Nightingale" have resulted
here in a more controlled, paradoxical, and epigrammatic mood. The
irregular and somewhat freer structure of "Psyche," already modified in
"Nightingale," has assumed a stricter shape. The principal difference in
symbols is also striking: the Nightingale is a creature of the natural world,
the Urn an object from the realm of art. The bold, explorative, natural

impulse in "Nightingale," most evident in stanza 3, is now under the discipline of a more structured vision. Most noticeable, perhaps, is the absence of any direct expression of the poet's own feelings. As Bate has observed, "with a determined objectivity, the poet — so prominent in the other ode — is now kept as completely out of the poem as possible." [22]

Yet the poet brings to the Urn many of the same thoughts and feelings earlier brought to Psyche and the Nightingale. In spite of his greater objectivity, his self-consuming fascination with the marbled image of a pastoral world, and his restraint on his speculative impulses, a profound sense of loss, scarcely present at the opening of the poem, is almost overwhelming near the end, particularly in stanza 4. While this ode opens with an apostrophe of devotion to the Urn rather than the cry "My heart aches," one cannot avoid the thought that, as Yeats has said, "only an aching heart / Conceives a changeless work of art" ("Meditations in Time of Civil War"). The elegiac tone of the opening lines ("Thou still unravish'd bride of quietness, / Thou foster-child of silence and slow time") is so spontaneous that we may not always hear the darker undertone, but again apostrophe is being used to deny temporality. Keats stresses the Urn's ability to endure rather than any innate permanence: it is "still unravish'd" (taking "still" as an adverb rather than adjective), in part because of its continued protection by the foster parents "silence and slow time." At this point, if the Urn is already conceived as immortal, that quality is not stressed. Instead, the poet is astonished at the Urn's survival, momentarily recalling and dismissing whatever threat was posed to it by twenty or more centuries of change. The role of historian ascribed to the Urn also emphasizes its survival in a mutable world. The poet's longing to discover the "leaf-fring'd legend" haunting its shape (l. 5) arises from his sense of a past ("Of deities or mortals, or of both, / In Tempe or the dales of Arcady" — ll. 6–7) that is felt to be lost and yet, now in the shape of the Urn, is seemingly recoverable.

Therefore, in spite of the opening mood of curiosity, expectation, and excitement, a sense of loss steals across the poem like a lengthening shadow, penetrating its generally confident and at times too cheerful manner. Stanzas 2 and 3 celebrate with almost unreserved ardor the lovers, the unwearied melodist, and the happy boughs that never shed their leaves, but the poet's thoughts are haunted by his awareness of the mutability of his own world and an irrepressible sadness that accompanies it. As Bush observed, "Even when Keats proclaims that the song of the bird is immortal, that the sculptured lover feels an enduring love that is beyond the pains of human passion, his deepest emotions are fixed on the obverse side of his theme." [23] It is against this sense of loss that the poet attempts to establish a relationship with the Urn and restore in this symbol the presence of the inner object.

But the similarity of the Urn to the Nightingale and the other ode symbols is not immediately clear, even though it too is characterized as feminine, immortal, and sympathetic. It seems to possess these qualities in no way that manifests an affinity with the other symbols. Take, for example, its feminine character. Keats calls it a "bride" in the opening line but not again, and the epithet is in any case a puzzling way to characterize an urn. Patterson has suggestively pointed out that the word "shape" in line 5 ("What leaf-fring'd legend haunts about thy shape") "draws attention to the outlines of the urn; and its shape ... bears a haunting resemblance to the lines of the feminine body, a resemblance already intimated, or at least prepared for, in the initial designation of the urn: *unravished bride.*" He goes on to say that "the form of the urn is subtly appropriate to embrace and frame the virile picture of life presented on its surface, for human life unfolds and continues through the body of woman."[24] Despite Patterson's insight, revealing an essential part of the Urn's symbolic potential, the poem provides only one explicit indication of the Urn's feminine character. For this reason the Urn's relation to the other ode symbols and to an inner unifying object or subliminal presence appears difficult to establish. But if we think of the poet's response to the Urn as revealing significant aspects of its character, we will see its affinity with the other ode symbols.

Two features of Keats's response are especially helpful in identifying the feminine character of the shape and presence of the Urn. One is the sense of loss that he brings to the experience. As I have already tried to show, his response arises from an old and deep concern with mutability. Although the excitement of the first stanza includes a sense of discovery, as if he were suddenly encountering the pastoral garden and fane that some other artist had built in an untrodden region of his mind, it is overcast with an awareness of the transience of things. Like Psyche, the Urn is represented as a survivor into days far retired from the happy passions and pieties it depicts, and it is therefore evocative of a nearly lost world. While Keats regards it as immortal, he represents it as more mysterious than either Psyche or the Nightingale ("Thou, silent form, dost tease us out of thought / As doth eternity" – ll. 44–5), and the mystery he feels in its presence reflects the uncertainty of a mortal who, caught in a mutable world, encounters or imagines an eternal shape. The longing in the last stanza, beginning with "O Attic shape! Fair attitude!" (l. 41), is one that can best be understood in the context of his old concern with separations and an unending quest for immortal and mysterious shapes, reaching back to Endymion's quest for his "known Unknown" (Rollins i. 739) and forward to the poet's encounter with the veiled image of Moneta.

In addition to the sense of loss and the related longing for an immortal shape evident in Keats's response, the passion he brings to the Urn is revealing. The series of questions in the opening stanza suggests not only that the poet is interpreting the pictured and/or imagined scene as a sexual one, with "maidens loth," "mad pursuit," and "wild ecstasy" (ll. 8–10), but that the order of the questions mirrors a steadily mounting intensity in him. Keats distinguished himself from Byron with the remark, "There is this great difference between us. He describes what he sees – I describe what I imagine" (Rollins ii. 200). To the extent that the questions at the end of stanza 1 describe a sexual experience, or the anticipation of one, it is imagined by the poet (or, if we assume a real urn, by its creator, and then reimagined by the poet). They capture the excitement of the scene by their rhythm and increased tempo, from the long, slow, first question about the leaf-fringed legend, with its halting syntax and braking repetition of prepositions and conjunctions ("Of deities or mortals, or of both" – l. 6), to the series of short questions, quickly following one another ("What men or gods are these? What maidens loth? / What mad pursuit? What struggle to escape? / What pipes and timbrels? What wild ecstasy?" – ll. 8–10).

His passionate response to the Urn may also be seen in his sympathetic identification with the figures on it. The exact tone with which he addresses them is perhaps impossible to define, but it is in part consoling:

> Bold lover, never, never canst thou kiss,
> Though winning near the goal – yet, do not grieve;
> She cannot fade, though thou hast not thy bliss,
> For ever wilt thou love, and she be fair!
>
> (ll. 17–20)

While the effort to console the fair youth and bold lover indicates Keats's awareness of the disadvantages of life on the Urn (in particular, the absence of any hope of sexual fulfillment, representing that concentration on the obverse side of his theme that Bush has alerted us to), it also suggests a sympathy that overflows into identification. This is especially true in stanza 3:

> Ah, happy, happy boughs! that cannot shed
> Your leaves, nor ever bid the spring adieu;
> And, happy melodist, unwearied,
> For ever piping songs for ever new;
> More happy love! more happy, happy love!
> For ever warm and still to be enjoy'd,
> For ever panting, and for ever young;
> All breathing human passion far above,
> That leaves a heart high-sorrowful and cloy'd,
> A burning forehead, and a parching tongue.
>
> (ll. 21–30)

The dominant strain in these lines is frequently and justly seen as defensive, as if the poet softens his voice to make it more consoling and employs repetition to lend conviction to what he knows is not true. Yet if the strain here is defensive, it is also charged with passion. As Keats contemplates the scene, he seems to participate in the erotic excitement of the bold lover and the maidens overwrought, experiencing it voyeuristically. But his passionate response is to more than a scene depicted or imagined on the Urn; it is also to an inner object long associated with intensity. The "greeting of the Spirit" (Rollins i. 243) brought to the Urn arises in the mind of a poet who earlier imagined Endymion's frequently overwrought response to Cynthia, Porphyro's throbbing, impassioned approach to Madeline, and his own excitement at the vision of Cupid and Psyche "couched side by side / In deepest grass" (ll. 9–10). Now in the "shape" of this "still unravish'd bride" he senses the presence of a figure that, in one form or another, he and his heroes have been pursuing from the beginning.

In responding to the Urn with such intensity, Keats initiates a familiar course of action for his imagination to follow. What the imagination seizes as beauty in the opening lines it seeks to restore through visual elaboration. To call the Urn a "Sylvan historian" that can relate "A flowery tale" (ll. 3–4) is to begin the restoration. As in "Ode to Psyche," where part of the opening question ("or did I see / The winged Psyche with awaken'd eyes?" – ll. 5–6) indicates an implicit, wish-fulfilling answer and an initiation of the restorative process, the series of questions here goes a long way toward a restoration. Before the first stanza ends we have already entered into a world of pastoral romance.

Whatever dull perplexities of the brain might retard progress into this inner world are put aside with a familiar use of paradox:

> Heard melodies are sweet, but those unheard
>   Are sweeter; therefore, ye soft pipes, play on;
> Not to the sensual ear, but, more endear'd,
>   Pipe to the spirit ditties of no tone.
>
> (ll. 11–14)

With a rare combination, even for Keats, of lyrical grace and epigrammatic force, the paradox effectively denies the need to distinguish between the real and the imagined, and almost magically seems to open out to a world of romance. It is a much less self-conscious and far more convincing way of saying, "I see, and sing, by my own eyes inspired." The rest of stanza 2 and most of 3 are devoted to a visual evocation of the imagined world, which is in several important respects far different from the enclosed pastoral world of the Nightingale. Here there is no darkness, or imagery of death, save what is brought with the consoling comment, "yet, do not grieve"

(l. 18). There is also no solitude. The sights and sounds of festive activity (the happy melodist "For ever piping songs for ever new" [l. 24], and the bold lover forever winning near the goal) are in marked contrast to the midnight quiet in "Nightingale."

Yet there are fundamental similarities. Despite the prolongation of sexual excitement on the Urn, which suggests a mounting intensity quite different from the emotional arc of "Nightingale," both poems imagine a world of process halted in a moment of ecstatic intensity. In "Nightingale" that moment is conceived in the sensuous pastoral imagery of stanza 5 and brought to its highest pitch when the Nightingale pours forth its soul "In such an ecstasy" in stanza 6. "Now more than ever seems it *rich* to die" (l. 55, italics mine). In "Grecian Urn" a similar cessation of natural processes is imagined, for the trees cannot shed their leaves, the maiden's beauty will not fade, and love is "For ever panting, and for ever young" (l. 27). The boughs here, like the tree and the brook in "In drear nighted December," are happy because they are imagined as free of any consciousness of time and change. In both odes, therefore, the inner restored world is one of perpetual, idealized intensity that attempts to deny a consciousness of death and natural process.

At the end of stanza 3, however, the mood of the defensive happiness that has prevailed so far begins to alter when the poet compares the immortal passion on the Urn with the "breathing human passion" that, on earth, "leaves a heart high-sorrowful and cloy'd" (ll. 29–30). The fantasy of a perpetual state of intensity is unexpectedly contrasted with love as a fevered condition ("A burning forehead, and a parching tongue" – l. 30), and as a result the mood almost perceptibly darkens, leading to the problematic fourth stanza.

> Who are these coming to the sacrifice?
>   To what green altar, O mysterious priest,
> Lead'st thou that heifer lowing at the skies,
>   And all her silken flanks with garlands drest?
> What little town by river or sea shore,
>   Or mountain-built with peaceful citadel,
>   Is emptied of this folk, this pious morn?
> And, little town, thy streets for evermore
>   Will silent be; and not a soul to tell
>   Why thou art desolate, can e'er return.
>
> (ll. 31–40)

This stanza is perhaps the most difficult of all to interpret. For Bush, it is "the most beautiful in the poem and one of Keats's supreme achievements," but it is also "a total digression from the line pursued so far. The new scene, a sacrificial procession, turns away from the sensuous and erotic to the happy communal pieties treated in the opening pages of *Endymion* and touched on in the 'Ode to Psyche.' "[25] For Bate, on the other hand, "the second and especially the third stanzas have been a digression. ... Hence the primary function of the fourth stanza is to return more concretely to the Grecian urn and to some of the feelings that were present at the start."[26]

Clearly no single interpretation of stanza 4 can answer all the critical questions it poses. It is primarily responsible for evoking the sense of mystery about the Urn that teases us out of thought and for leading us to a larger mystery of which the Urn is only a part. Given the premise, however, that at some fundamental level the poem is concerned with the problem of mutability (and a complementary series of opposites – the mutable and the permanent, the actual and the ideal, the real and the imagined, and so forth), it is possible to see stanza 4 as a logical and natural extension of the development of thought in stanzas 2 and 3, and as an appropriate preparation for the recognition in stanza 5. If stanzas 2 and 3 may be said to have achieved a partial restoration of an old ideal of passion and permanence as a defense against an awareness of loss and mutability, stanza 4 may be seen as continuing the restoration, but, in the course of it, unexpectedly (and ironically) recreating the sense of loss associated with the ideal. In other words, in the very process of seizing on the beauty and marbled permanence of the Urn, entering into its life and restoring the pastoral presence fringing its shape, Keats's imagination suddenly wanders into the silent streets of an emptied town only to experience a sense of absence and loss from which he had sought to escape. The element of surprise is more striking because the town is not even imagined as depicted on the Urn. It is as if the town were a dream within a dream. The mood changes from defensive happiness to that of a more serious inquiry into the identity of the participants in the sacrifice and the little town they are imagined to have left.

The mood change is supported by a grammatical shift from a declarative to an interrogative mode, signaling a new attitude toward the Urn. Following the confident assertiveness of stanzas 2 and 3, the questions now suggest an emotional distance and reflective detachment. There is also a suggestion of a greater spatial distance between the observer–poet and the Urn, if only because the view now implies a wider perspective in order to encompass the almost panoramic vision of the town "by river or sea shore, / Or mountain-built with peaceful citadel." We also note that though the three explicit questions concerning identity ("Who are these . . .?" "To what green altar . . .?" "What little town . . .?") are at least potentially answerable in the same way that the questions in stanza 1 received a partial answer by the imaginative elaboration in stanzas 2 and 3, no effort is made to answer them. Questions of "Who" and "What" are passed over for a more important question of "Why" concerning the emptied town ("Why thou art desolate"). The poet's interest in the Urn has deepened, and questions of identity have given way to more complex questions of origin and cause, anticipating the more philosophical stance the poet takes in the final stanza. Is there some particular image, or something about the general character of the imagined scene in stanza 4, we cannot help but ask, that has the psychological power to so alter the poet's mood? What image or implication in this scene initiates and sustains the disengagement in stanza 5?

One image, more than any other, possesses the power to work as a psychological catalyst, finally moving the poet away from the imaginatively restored pastoral ideal of the scenes on the Urn, and it is an image of an absence: "and not a soul ... can e'er return" (ll. 39–40).[27] There are other images in Keats's poetry that explore the very boundaries of imaginative conception, suspending certainty as they open out onto strange and perilous seas of thought. We recall that in the epistle to Reynolds, Keats was aware that the imagination could be "brought / Beyond its proper bound" (ll. 78–9), where the view extends "Too far into the sea" (l. 94). But no image in his poetry is more suggestive of the ultimate mystery the imagination attempts to explore than that of the empty town and silent streets. Like the poignant image of the Nightingale singing a high requiem to the dead and deaf poet, this image opens out to eternity, evoking the pathos of endless longing while recognizing and stressing the futility of further mournful lingering in the experience of silence and absence. The irony and extraordinary power of the image inheres in its crystallization of a sense of inexpressible grief, "As though a tongueless nightingale should swell / Her throat in vain, and die, heart-stifled, in her dell" ("The Eve of St. Agnes," ll. 206–7). The words "emptied," "evermore," "silent," "desolate," and "return" toll the poet back to his sole self.

The disenchanting power of this image brings with it a shift in mood. The opening apostrophe of stanza 5 ("O Attic shape! Fair attitude!") is the beginning of a farewell. The mood of a sudden awakening from dream to cold reality is not unlike the mood with which Keats begins the sonnet "On Visiting the Tomb of Burns," written the year before:

> The town, the churchyard, and the setting sun,
>   The clouds, the trees, the rounded hills all seem,
>   Though beautiful, cold – strange – as in a dream
>   I dreamed long ago.

Keats copied out the sonnet in a letter to Tom on 2 July 1818 and then remarked, "Burns' tomb is in the Churchyard corner. ... This Sonnet I have written in a strange mood, half asleep. I know not how it is, the Clouds, the sky, the Houses, all seem anti Grecian & anti Charlemagnish" (Rollins

i. 309). The strangeness of the mood and coldness of the dream are part of a deeper melancholy felt in the presence of the dead poet. "His Misery is a dead weight upon the nimbleness of one's quill," he wrote to Reynolds a little more than a week later; "I tried to forget it – to drink Toddy without any Care – to write a merry Sonnet – it wont do – he talked with Bitches – he drank with Blackguards, he was miserable" (Rollins i. 325). The burden of the past includes the fate of poets. Like Wordsworth in "Resolution and Independence," Keats could not help thinking of what had happened to Chatterton and Burns. In the sonnet the town and the churchyard stand in the background of Keats's mood of estrangement from a dream, just as the desolate town in stanza 4 stands in the background of the altered mood of stanza 5. The feeling now is "anti Grecian" and, as in the sonnet, "All is cold beauty."

However, though there is a rejection of enthrallment to the Urn and a somewhat accusatory tone in the climactic lines,

> Thou, silent form, dost tease us out of thought
>   As doth eternity: Cold Pastoral!

(ll. 44–5)

the mood is more accurately described if it is said to include a sense of reluctant detachment and resignation. The powerful image at the end of stanza 4 has dramatized the limits of thought and imagination, and now the phrasing recalls an old axiom from the epistle to Reynolds, "Things cannot to the will / Be settled, but they tease us out of thought" (ll. 76–7). The phrasing in both the epistle and the ode expresses Keats's acute sensitivity to that point in thought at which unceasing aspiration ironically takes the mind beyond a proper bound toward unexpected images of fierce destruction, of becoming a sod, of an emptied town with silent streets. Images of mystery and indeterminacy ("and not a soul to tell...") and symbols of permanence like the Urn remind the poet of his mortal nature.

I have emphasized the darker implications of stanza 4 and the opening of 5 because I believe that a failure to take them into account makes the mood of resignation and reconciliation in the remainder of stanza 5 seem forced and the aphoristic conclusion unearned:

> When old age shall this generation waste,
>   Thou shalt remain, in midst of other woe
>   Than ours, a friend to man, to whom thou say'st,
>   "Beauty is truth, truth beauty," – that is all
>   Ye know on earth, and all ye need to know.

(ll. 46–50)

The controversial last two lines have been discussed more often and in greater detail than many of Keats's poems. If allowance is made for a degree of oversimplification, it can be said that essentially two views of the last two lines have prevailed. One is T. S. Eliot's well-known judgment that they constitute "a serious blemish on a beautiful poem" and the other is Cleanth Brooks's influential defense of them as appropriate and meaningful in their dramatic context.[28] Like many others, I find Brooks's view far more persuasive, and in what follows I assume that Keats intended the last two lines as an appropriate conclusion and that *this* intention, at least, is not in question, however much the meaning of the lines may be.

The intention is evident in the first part of stanza 5, which recapitulates much of the development of the poem so far. The opening apostrophe, though a farewell, recalls the longing and restorative impulse with which the poem began. Then Keats recreates the principal figures and imagined actions in stanzas 2 and 3 in a single, composite image: "brede / Of marble men and maidens overwrought" (l. 42). He also momentarily restores their pastoral world in a beautiful, tactile image, "With forest branches and the trodden weed" (l. 43). But then comes an acknowledgment of the detachment that has resulted from the recognition in stanza 4 that a full restoration of the inscrutable past is impossible: "Cold Pastoral!" (l. 45). The rest of the stanza represents a psychological development new to the ode but familiar to us from its presence in "Psyche" and "Nightingale": internalization. The Urn will survive not simply in a physical sense but as a part of the historical imagination, forming an essential part of the collective wisdom of mankind.

The dramatic significance of this change from a restorative to an internalizing procedure may be seen in the reversal of the poet's attitude toward historical processes. Up to this point the poem has looked backward, and the dominant impulse has been to restore the past. Now the poem looks to the future, and the impulse is to internalize ("Thou shalt remain, in midst of other woe / Than ours"). The principal defensive strategies are set in sharp contrast – restoration, defending against what is felt to be lost; internalization, defending against what in the future might be lost – with the effect of dramatically emphasizing the adaptive nature of the new attitude, not only toward the Urn but toward the inescapable awareness of mutability. The new attitude ensures a permanent continuation of the poet's relationship with the Urn and the inner object of which it is symbolic. In character with the complexity of feeling and thought throughout the ode, the attitude now is richly paradoxical: while it offers consolation for the inevitability of future loss ("old age shall this generation waste"), it also denies future loss in the aphoristic assertion ("Beauty is truth, truth beauty") by suggesting that nothing essential to know is ever really lost ("that is all / Ye know on earth, and all ye need to know").

This enigmatic statement is the rock against which so many interpretations seem to founder. Even if we agree, in spite of the punctuation in the 1820 volume (which Stillinger takes as the standard text and which sets off by quotation marks "Beauty is truth, truth beauty" from the rest of the last two lines), that the entire last two lines are spoken by the Urn to man,[29] we are still left with the staggering problem of defining terms such as "beauty" and "truth." Eliot went so far as to say that they are "grammatically meaningless."[30]

Since the terms can obviously assume various shades of meaning in different contexts, the real difficulty in a particular critical discussion of them is deciding on which context to emphasize. Perhaps the four most commonly invoked contexts are: (1) biographical, in which one relates the terms to Keats's early, seemingly unqualified trust in the visionary imagination, and to his statement in the 22 November 1817 letter to Bailey that "What the imagination seizes as Beauty must be truth" (Rollins i. 184); (2) historical, in which one relates the terms to other romantic assertions such as Shelley's statement in his *Defence of Poetry* that "to be a poet is to apprehend the true and the beautiful";[31] (3) philosophical, in which one relates "beauty" and "truth" to whatever Neoplatonic influences (from Spenser, perhaps) are present in Keats's poetry; and (4) dramatic, in which one stresses the sensuous and sculptured beauty depicted on the Urn, and whatever truth it may be thought to represent. Obviously other contexts could be defined, and it is clear that much of the critical controversy surrounding the last two lines is due to our inability to agree on a single, most appropriate context. The problem is not one of impoverished or canceled meaning, as Eliot suggested, but of unlimited richness of meaning. Since no one context is necessarily more appropriate than another, or will answer all interpretive questions without seeming to jeopardize its integrity as a critical approach, the urge for interpretive certainty needs to be resisted and a sense of critical negative capability encouraged.

The context I have stressed throughout is psychological, and I think it is helpful, in considering the last two lines, to review the direction of feeling and thought in the poem so far. We have already seen how Keats attempts to use denial and restoration as defenses against an imagined or real loss, and then internalization as an adaptive strategy in the face of inevitable future loss. The two strategies are used in sequence. Now he attempts to strengthen the internalization with the force of an epigrammatic statement. Perhaps its most striking rhetorical feature is its circularity. As Hartman has pointed out, "Beauty is truth, truth beauty" is "a chiastic phrase, as self-rounding as the urn . . . . The poet's speculation is circular."[32] However, the grammatical form of the statement also emphasizes balance, representing a desire for synthesis and resolution, and the statement itself must be seen as part of a final effort in the poem to achieve a reconciling, adaptive balance against the burden of the awareness that "old age shall this generation waste." What is longed for now is a means of preserving in memorable form the intensity and essence of the imaginative experience in the encounter with the Urn. The aphorism provides the means. It forever recreates the intensity through a wish-fulfilling, hypothetical fusion of oppositions (beauty and truth, process and permanence) that can never be completed but will never succumb to time and change. It is a radical condensation of the intensity depicted on the Urn into a perpetual dynamic tension caused by ideas forever approaching fusion but never achieving it. The statement is one of being that forever recalls and repeats a process of becoming, a process that Kenneth Burke termed an "eternal present."[33]

In the end, therefore, the poem is not an unqualified rejection or endorsement of imaginative experience. When Keats calls the Urn a "Cold Pastoral!" he seems to give it up and to recognize that his experience has been visionary, and it is true that the epithet is spoken with bold finality. Yet, as Freud would remind us, "we can never give anything up; we only exchange one thing for another. What appears to be a renunciation is really the formation of a substitute or surrogate."[34] What is adopted as a substitute is the aphorism, preserving the poet's experience with the Urn and the inner presence it symbolizes.

IV

"Ode on Melancholy" stands in such obvious contrast to the other great odes that it challenges the conception of them as a sequence. Although Melancholy is personified in stanza 3, she doesn't have the kind of presence or presiding role that Psyche and the Nightingale have. The poem seems to lack a dominant or controlling symbol. It is also addressed not to the goddess, who is referred to in the third person, but to an imaginary auditor, or perhaps to an image in the poet's psyche, as if he were in dialogue with himself. Further, this ode is unique in adopting the imperative rather than the indicative voice. Instead of a sudden encounter with a figure or symbol from mythology, nature, or art, followed by a series of questions or hopeful speculations that would initiate a relationship, the first stanza delivers a series of negative imperatives ("No, no, go not ... neither twist ... Nor suffer ... Make not ... Nor let") in the manner of an urgent protest. The mood of discovery and hopeful inquiry that begins the approach of a symbol in the other odes is replaced by an impatient voice of ironic persuasion and unhesitating confidence:

> No, no, go not to Lethe, neither twist
>   Wolf's-bane, tight-rooted, for its poisonous wine;
> Nor suffer thy pale forehead to be kiss'd
>   By nightshade, ruby grape of Proserpine;

>   Make not your rosary of yew-berries,
>   Nor let the beetle, nor the death-moth be
>   Your mournful Psyche, nor the downy owl
>   A partner in your sorrow's mysteries;
>   For shade to shade will come too drowsily,
>   And drown the wakeful anguish of the soul.

More than anything else, the ironic tone sets this ode apart from the others, making it, in William Empson's words, "a parody, by contradiction, of the wise advice of uncles. 'Of course, pain is what we all desire, and I am sure I hope you will be very unhappy. But if you go snatching at it before your time, my boy, you must expect the consequences; you will hardly get hurt at all.' "[35] However we may wish to qualify Empson's definition of the tone, we cannot doubt that a spirit of ironic reversal is at work in this poem. It largely replaces the symbolization so prominent in the other odes and the effort at restoration that initiates them.

Despite these and other points of contrast, however, "Ode on Melancholy" is usually seen both as a continuation of the sequence and as an advance in the poet's thought, especially since it implies a more open acceptance of the mutability inherent in nature and human experience. Because of the acceptance, it is often thought to have a greater affinity with "To Autumn" than with the other odes,[36] though in fact it forms a bridge between them. It represents a climax of the psychological and meditative development in the sequence so far, but also a preparation of the resolution in "Autumn." For one thing, the irony only thinly veils a continuing concern with quests and an elusive object. But now the quest and its object are viewed with increased ambivalence. The irony is a renewed and refined expression of a skeptical, accusatory impulse that prompted the conception of fancy as a "deceiving elf" and of the Urn's silence as teasing us out of thought. The same impulse now prompts the conception of Melancholy as "Veil'd," seeming to threaten the seeker of pleasure and joy with "the sadness of her might" (l. 29), and suggesting that, like Circe, she will make him captive, for he will be "among her cloudy trophies hung" (l. 30). In a sense, "Ode on Melancholy" is to the ode sequence what "La Belle Dame" and "Lamia" are to the canon of major poems, an expression of a profound mistrust of the inner object the various figures and symbols represent and of the impulse – or compulsion – to pursue it. To be sure, the recognition of Melancholy in the transient nature of existence represents an acceptance of the mutability in human experience, but the characterization of the goddess in stanza 3 suggests an ambivalent acceptance at best, far from the seemingly unqualified embrace of process in "To Autumn."

Also, the very idea of writing an ode on melancholy suggests an effort to examine the psychological processes that render all thought and experience in the shadowy cast of a mournful sense of loss. It is as if Keats turns on himself to confront his own melancholy, to examine the very mourning process that has all along been at the center of his imagination and thought, especially in the odes, even though he acknowledges it only occasionally in his letters. In May 1817 he wrote to Haydon that he had "a horrid Morbidity of Temperament which has shown itself at intervals – it is I have no doubt the greatest Enemy and stumbling block I have to fear" (Rollins i. 142). In January 1819, in another letter to Haydon, he remarked, "I do not think I shall ever come to the rope or the Pistol" (Rollins ii. 32), a remark that was probably an intentional exaggeration but that nonetheless gives some indication of an inner struggle with what on other occasions he referred to as "the blue-devils" (21 September 1819; Rollins ii. 168). In confronting melancholy now in the ode he comes to a new awareness of how "grief [is] contain'd / In the very shrine of pleasure" (*Endymion* ii. 823–4, draft variant). In the other odes the quest for permanence through a union with a symbolic presence led inescapably to a deepened awareness of the transient nature of existence. The sense of an absence or loss with which each renewal of the quest began eventually resulted in a sense of something far more deeply interfused – in the relation between love and the mind, or imagination and reality, or beauty and truth. Now it is this sense of a deeper interfusion of things – pleasure and pain, joy and sorrow, transience and melancholy – that becomes the focus of attention. The consuming interest now is the mystery of sorrow, of melancholy itself, of how the mind changes its state and how "aching Pleasure" turns "to poison while the bee-mouth sips" (ll. 23–4).

In the earlier odes melancholy arose from a sense of loss represented as a longing for a fading immortal and a vanished pastoral world. In this ode there is no figure or object symbolizing a lost presence and providing an occasion to express a sense of loss, suggesting that when the poet's concern with melancholy becomes explicit, when his effort to understand it becomes deliberate and conscious, the sense of loss earlier associated with melancholy is excluded from consideration. We recall that in his essay on the relation between mourning and melancholia Freud points out that the principal distinction between these two states – really processes – of mind is that in the former the loss is known, in the latter unknown. Melancholy, Freud argues, "is in some way related to an object-loss which is withdrawn from consciousness, in contradistinction to mourning, in which there is nothing about the loss that is unconscious."[37] In the first stanza of the ode neither a sense of loss nor a longing for a symbolic object is identified. On the contrary, Keats seems to acknowledge that the cause of melancholy or of a "mournful Psyche" is shrouded in "sorrow's mysteries" (l. 8). "I strive to search wherefore I am so sad," Apollo tells Mnemosyne, "Until a melancholy numbs my limbs" (*Hyperion* iii. 88–9).

The failure to identify any sense of loss in the first stanza, however, is compensated for by the introduction of the notion of a quest, which implies a longing derived from an undefined sense of loss. The seeker after melancholy is warned not to go to Lethe. Melancholy is often linked with, sometimes seems to induce, an indolent or drowsy numbness, causing the poet or one of his heroes to feel as though he "Lethe-wards had sunk" ("Ode to a Nightingale," l. 4). But it is almost never totally paralyzing and is usually associated with a quest, perhaps because Keats felt instinctively that a quest or a renewal of imagination's struggles was the best defense against despair. On one of the few occasions in the letters when he acknowledges a sense of the melancholy that we find in the poetry, he characteristically remarks, "I must choose between despair & Energy" (Rollins ii. 113). To appreciate how essential the quest motif was in the conception of this ode, and how significant it remains, we need to recall the deleted opening stanza:

> Though you should build a bark of dead men's bones,
>   And rear a phantom gibbet for a mast,
> Stitch creeds together for a sail, with groans
>   To fill it out, bloodstained and aghast;
> Although your rudder be a Dragon's tail,
>   Long sever'd, yet still hard with agony,
>   Your cordage large uprootings from the skull
> Of bald Medusa; certes you would fail
>   To find the Melancholy, whether she
>   Dreameth in any isle of Lethe dull.

Interesting though some of the images here may be (e.g., the sail filled out with groans), the stanza is little more than a Gothic extravagance, and Keats was undoubtedly right to delete it. Nevertheless, it reveals a narrative structure in the idea of the quest that underlies the more obviously declamatory and argumentative style of the poem. In the deleted stanza and in the present stanza 1 the quest is conceived as a journey to Lethe; in stanza 2 it is conceived as a series of physical and psychological actions to intensify experience; and in stanza 3 the two quest modes are joined in a conception that approximates allegory: Melancholy becomes a mythological, Circe-like figure and experience is conceived spatially ("She dwells with Beauty . . . in the very temple of Delight" – l. 25), while the quest is conceived experientially and its success measured in terms of sensuous intensity ("Though seen of none save him whose strenuous tongue / Can burst Joy's grape" – ll. 27–8).

The joining of the two quest modes in a single conceptual movement, though not unusual in Keats (it underlies the quest in *Endymion*, for example), is here part of a wider pattern of diffusion and interfusion throughout the poem. No specific object is identified as lost, and yet there is a quest at the end of which the seeker after melancholy encounters a goddess. The sudden appearance of such a figure in Keats's poetry is suggestive of a reappearance, either in the limited context of a particular quest poem, as in *Endymion*, or in the larger context of all the poems, where an inner object reappears as La Belle Dame, Psyche, Lamia, and Moneta. In addition, although in a first reading (or a subsequent one in which we recapture the sense and critical issues of the first) we must wait until we have completed stanza 3 to learn that Melancholy is conceived as a goddess (unless we have read the deleted stanza and recall the last line: "whether she / Dreameth in any isle of Lethe dull"), the fact is that throughout stanza 2 her presence is diffused in the perception–experience of "a morning rose," "the rainbow of the salt-sand wave," and "the wealth of globed peonies" (ll. 15–17). Again, no specific loss is identified and yet all human experience is suffused with it. Significantly, the sense of loss in stanza 2 culminates in a feminine figure, the "mistress [who] some rich anger shows" (l. 18). Commentators generally agree that "She" at the beginning of stanza 3 ("She dwells with Beauty – Beauty that must die" – l. 21) is Melancholy, not the mistress, and certainly the syntax supports this interpretation. Nevertheless, Empson seems justified in making the suggestion that "*She* is at first *thy mistress*, so that she represents some degree of *joy*, however fleeting; then, taking the verse as a unit, she becomes Veiled Melancholy itself."[38] The grammatical question is not one that can be settled. The ambiguity permits the interpretation that "She" is both, as Cynthia and the Indian maiden are one. Indeed, they are all, in their sublime, re-creations of the essential beauty and melancholy of a subliminal figure.

The potential presence of this figure in everything human seems to dispose of the need for a quest, but the poet insists that only a particular kind of experience will lead to Melancholy's "sovran shrine" (l. 26). Intensity, the poem urges, is the quality necessary for the successful conclusion of the quest. It lies at the heart of the exhortation in stanzas 2 and 3. As Sperry has observed, this ode seeks to illuminate "the nature of intensity itself."[39] An important aspect of its nature is its conception primarily as an internalizing experience, especially in stanzas 2 and 3, where it is linked to images of incorporation. There is a richer concentration of gustatory and ingestive imagery in these two stanzas than in any of the other odes or, for that matter, in most of Keats's poems. The seeker after Melancholy is urged to "glut" his sorrow on a "morning rose" (l. 15), and, by means of syllepsis, this verb works silently in the next two lines ("Or on the rainbow of the salt-sand wave, / Or on the wealth of globed peonies" – ll. 16–17). He is also urged to imprison the hand of the mistress and "feed deep, deep upon her peerless eyes" (ll. 19–20). In stanza 3 the moment of greatest intensity comes when the strenuous tongue bursts joy's grape. Only then shall the soul "taste" the sadness of Melancholy's might. The imagery here is more than a celebration of the sensuousness of life and experience. It also represents the seizing, internalizing character of Keats's imagination. Melancholy's "sovran shrine" is not Madeline's "silver shrine," but the seeker of it, like Porphyro, is "After so many hours of toil and quest, / A famish'd pilgrim" (ll. 337–9).

The first irony in the poem, as I have already noted, is that one does not seek melancholy; it comes on the sudden, unexpected, as the poet acknowledges at the beginning of stanza 2 ("when the melancholy fit shall fall"). As the narrator of *Endymion* remarks of the Cave of Quietude, "Enter none / Who strive therefore: on the sudden it is won" (iv. 531–2). A later, more subtle irony, however, is that the very experience recommended as a path to melancholy is one that is simultaneously used to avoid it. To make any moment of intensity last as long as possible ("glut," "Emprison," "feed deep, deep") is to stave off for as long as possible the separation ("Joy, whose hand is ever at his lips / Bidding adieu" – ll. 22–3) and eventual loss that provoke an awareness of the transience of all things and ultimately bring on melancholy itself. Internalization becomes the dominant strategy in the poem, even in the final image, in the notions not simply that boldness and perseverance will enable the seeker after Melancholy to "taste the sadness of her might" (l. 29) but also that he will "be among her cloudy trophies hung" (l. 30), for the effort to "Emprison" and possess results paradoxically in being possessed, in becoming, as Porphyro claims, a "vassal blest" (l. 335). To seize is ultimately to be seized, to experience a fusion of self with the object possessed. The "chief intensity," Endymion states in the "fellowship with essence" speech, is finally a "self-destroying" moment. The Latmian poet–hero, whose efforts to possess Cynthia are repeatedly represented by means of gustatory imagery, defines the experience of love as a fusion ("Melting into its radiance, we blend, / Mingle . . . interknit . . . combine . . . Lif's self is nourish'd . . . And we are nurtured" – i. 810–15).

Keats uses irony and paradox in all the odes, but nowhere with greater force and significance than in "Ode on Melancholy." While "Ode to Psyche" unfolds from a paradoxical conception of the goddess as a fading immortal, enabling the poet to indulge a sense of loss and defend against it at the same time, and "Ode on a Grecian Urn" from a complex image of the contradictions of the death-in-life state of the figures on the urn, "Melancholy" unfolds more directly, without the mediation of a dominant symbol, from a paradoxical conception of experience itself. In the aphorism attributed to the Urn the poet preserves the intensity of perceiving the beauty and truth on the Urn by transforming the experience into an oxymoronic axiom representing a perpetual, dynamic interfusion in which beauty and truth are forever seeking to turn into each other. Now in "Ode on Melancholy" Keats moves toward a bolder, almost allegorical conception of the tensions he has been concerned with. The perception of beauty is again central, but it is more clearly a symbolic act representing all experience. The conception of life as a continual process leading toward death ("aching Pleasure nigh, / Turning to poison while the bee-mouth sips" – ll. 23–4) is an attempt to crystallize a paradoxical notion of the death-in-life quality of experience that has preoccupied him at different times, and particularly this spring. "Circumstances are like Clouds continually gathering and bursting," he wrote to the George Keatses in March; "While we are laughing the seed of some trouble is put into the wide arable land of events – while we are laughing it sprouts i[t] grows *and suddenly bears a poison fruit which we must pluck*" (Rollins ii. 79, italics mine). In Keats's mind and thought, intense or significant experience is repeatedly condensed into metaphors of incorporation. In the images combining pleasure and poison in the letter and in the ode, the rhetorical device of paradox reinforces the idea of a chief intensity, the moment of fusion in which there is a resolution of opposites. Images of paradox represent a figurative equivalent of Keats's sense of a deeper interfusion of things.

If "Melancholy" includes a recognition of an implicit adaptation to mutability and natural process, it also includes a degree of anxiety, one that anticipates an unavoidable encounter with melancholy at the same time that it urges an energetic pursuit of beauty. In "Ode to Psyche," we recall, Keats made a great effort to restore the presence of a once mortal goddess. He built her an imaginary fane from which she could preside over his future growth. Now in "Melancholy" no special effort is made to restore the presence of the goddess Melancholy, for, with an irony that does not escape the poet, her transformed countenance is to be perceived in every desire for beauty, joy, and pleasure. The image recollected from his boyhood of a "pure Goddess" (Rollins i. 341) resting in his mind has assumed the shape of a veiled, haunting figure, no longer a benevolent presider over growth but a melancholy presence in every experience.

In his essay "On Transience" Freud sought to understand this tendency to feel sadness or melancholy in the perception of beauty and he recalled the reactions of two companions on a country walk:

> Not long ago I went on a summer walk through a smiling countryside in the company of a taciturn friend and of a young but already famous poet. The poet admired the beauty of the scene around us but felt no joy in it. He was disturbed by the thought that all this beauty was fated to extinction, that it would vanish when winter came, like all human beauty and all the beauty and splendour that men have created or may create. All that he would otherwise have loved and admired seemed to him to be shorn of its worth by the transience which was its doom.

In the essay Freud reports that he disagreed with his companions and argued that the transience of a beautiful object does not involve any loss. "On the contrary," he says, "an increase!"[40] Keats of course recognizes that an awareness of the transience of a beautiful object will intensify the perception or experience of it, but the recognition cannot free him from a profound sadness felt at the same time. An important meaning in the poem is that melancholy need not be sought; it is unavoidable in the pursuit of beauty. The understanding that Freud reaches of this unavoidable sadness in the experience of beauty relates it to the mourning process. "The idea that all this beauty was transient was giving these two sensitive minds a foretaste of mourning over its decease; and, since the mind instinctively recoils from anything that is painful, they felt their enjoyment of beauty interfered with by thoughts of its transience."[41] Keats does not allow a foretaste of mourning to spoil the experience of beauty. Unlike Freud's companions, he does not try to avoid beauty as a defense against sadness. Indeed, he pursues it more vigorously, with a characteristic assertiveness that continually converts burdens into challenges and dark passages into paths made for our searching. The poem concludes with a recognition of the transient nature of all experience, and to that extent it represents a will to adapt to a world of process and change.

Nevertheless, the search for beauty ends at the shrine of Melancholy, and the searcher will taste the sadness of her might. The recognition, in other words, is itself a foretaste of mourning associated with the veil'd presence of Melancholy immanent in all future experience. The poet has finally found an incarnation of the inner object that will not fade, or leave him in doubt whether he wakes or sleeps, or tease him out of thought, but is forever present – indeed, present with a vengeance. The ode is not, however, a final triumph of a tragic perspective. In this supremely powerful acknowledgment of the transient nature and potentially tragic dimension of human experience, romance makes its inevitable appearance. By representing the consuming nature of the most intense experience in the shape of a goddess, the poem suggests how the imagination employs romance to create an intervenient figure between the perceiving mind and the darkest passage. This is not to suggest that the recognition here is any the less forceful but to call attention to the unavoidable way in which, in a moment of profound insight, imagination shapes the truth the poet sees.

"Ode on Melancholy" is a new and more highly condensed expression of the skepticism expressed in "La Belle Dame," and an advance in Keats's thought, not only in his more explicit recognition of the implications of mutability but in the diffusion of his sense of the presence of an inner object in experience, for in the diffusion is reflected a more profound and mature sense of the nature of things. Keats has gradually moved away from the attempt to restore the subliminal figure in an isolated symbol and toward a deeper perception of her presence in all things, which is itself an unconscious effort at adaptation, at once a loosening of the attachment to the more idealized values associated with Psyche, the Nightingale, and the Urn, and a strengthening of it in the rediscovery of her in a far wider context. "Ode on Melancholy" thus represents a climax in the trend toward internalization begun in "Psyche" at the same time that it is an anticipation of the diffusion in "To Autumn."

V

"To Autumn" was written on 19 September 1819, at least two weeks after Keats had completed "Lamia" and roughly at the same time (give or take a few days) that he ceased to work on *The Fall of Hyperion.* It is the last of the great odes. Although I have made the widely accepted (though admittedly partly conjectural) order of composition of the odes a central premise of my discussion, the concept of an ode sequence is not based solely on chronological considerations. It refers as much to a number of conceptual, structural, and thematic affinities and developments indicative of a general unity and progression of thought as it does to a specific order of composition. Even if the exact order of composition were known, it is doubtful that the kind of psychological growth and intellectual development reflected in a general way in the odes could be charted with such precision and then confined to a notion of linear – almost monthly – progression. Keats's development was not a steady and straight march of the intellect. It is rather to be thought of as a series of movements in which there were hopeful starts, inevitable repetitions, some leavings-off, both advances and setbacks. "To Autumn" seems to represent an almost effortless advance, the fruit of previous labor, as if many of the problems engaged in the earlier odes have been resolved, even if only temporarily. It is a natural culmination of several strains of thought in the ode sequence and, more generally, in Keats's poetry.

One of the most important of these strains is represented by the quest for a feminine and immortal presence in the shape of a dominant symbol. Autumn is identified early in stanza 1 as "Close bosom-friend of the maturing sun" (l. 2) and then is personified in stanza 2:

> Who hath not seen thee oft amid thy store?
>   Sometimes whoever seeks abroad may find
> Thee sitting careless on a granary floor,
>   Thy hair soft-lifted by the winnowing wind;
> Or on a half-reap'd furrow sound asleep,
>   Drows'd with the fume of poppies, while thy hook

> Spares the next swath and all its twined flowers:
> And sometimes like a gleaner thou dost keep
> Steady thy laden head across a brook;
> Or by a cyder-press, with patient look,
> Thou watchest the last oozings hours by hours.
>
> (ll. 11–22)

The opening question recalls the use of an interrogative mood at the beginning of the odes to Psyche and on the Grecian Urn as a means of overcoming the distance between subject and object and initiating a relationship with the presence evoked by the symbol. But the mood now is much less intense, the question so brief and unselfconscious, and the act of restoring a presiding presence in the shape of a feminine personification of autumn so effortless, that an image appears as if it belongs there, integrated into a natural, humanized landscape. In Vendler's beautifully condensed reading of this stanza, "Keats's goddess of autumn, nearer to us than pagan goddesses because, unlike them, she labors in the fields and is herself threshed by the winnowing wind, varies in her manifestations from careless girl to burdened gleaner to patient watcher, erotic in her abandon to the fume of poppies, intimate of light in her bosom friendship with the maturing sun, worn by her vigil over the last oozings."[42] This image appears in Keats's poetry near the end of a season of psychological growth and it represents an integration of imagination and nature, of inner vision and outer reality.

Autumn as another image of an inner object has evolved through a succession of imaginative figures – a goddess too late for antique vows, a bird whose mournful anthems were heard by Ruth, an urn of mystery, and a goddess of melancholy – into a goddess of fruition and plenty. She does not represent the plenty of indulgence and satiation, in spite of the bees' "o'er-brimmed . . . clammy cells" and the fact that "they think warm days will never cease" (ll. 9–11). She represents rich promise as much as teeming fulfillment, for the series of infinitives in stanza 1 ("to load and bless . . . To bend . . . To swell . . . and plump . . . to set budding more" – ll. 3–8) maintains a sense of a process that is still coming to fruition. At the beginning of stanza 3 Keats casts a backward glance at the experience of fresh aspiration in the questions "Where are the songs of spring? Ay, where are they?" In the second question, especially, we hear an echo of old longings now never to be gratified and for that reason put aside. Of the songs of spring, Keats says, "Think not of them, thou hast thy music too" (l. 24). But in the remainder of the stanza can be found variations on a different and more mournful theme in the images of "the soft-dying day" (l. 25), the lambs who "loud bleat from hilly bourn" (l. 30), and particularly the "wailful choir" of "small gnats" who

> mourn
> Among the river sallows, borne aloft
> Or sinking as the light wind lives or dies.
>
> (ll. 27–9)

There are suggestions throughout stanza 3 not only of the end of the day, and of the year, but of death itself.

Unlike the taciturn friend and young poet who were Freud's companions on his summer walk, however, Keats's awareness of the transient nature of existence contributes to rather than detracts from his ability to enjoy the season. This was true of the walk he took on the day he composed the poem, as he reported to Reynolds: "How beautiful the season is now – How fine the air. A temperate sharpness about it. Really, without joking, chaste weather – Dian skies – I never lik'd stubble fields so much as now – Aye better than the chilly green of the spring. Somehow a stubble plain looks warm – in the same way that some pictures look warm – this struck me so much in my sunday's walk that I composed upon it" (Rollins ii. 167). In the poem (in contrast to the letter) Keats gives expression to a keen sense of transience and loss, but it is integrated into an acceptance of a natural process that includes growth as well as decay. As Perkins has pointed out, death in stanza 3 "is neither a pining for an 'easeful' escape nor is it an intensity, a blind, climactic outpouring and release analogous to the song of the nightingale. Rather it is recognized as something inwoven in the course of things, the condition and price of all fulfillment, having like the spring and summer of life its own distinctive character or 'music' which is also to be prized and relished."[43]

Yet to the extent that this ode may be taken to represent a significant advance in Keats's psychological and intellectual development, an implicit reconciliation of old oppositions between the ideal and the actual, presence and absence, and so forth, and an acceptance of the mortal limitations on life, it is an advance in which the restorative processes of his imagination are deeply implicated. While death is not seen as an escape, neither is it seen as the fearful end imagined for the palsy-stricken, gray-haired men and for the spectre-thin youth in stanza 3 of "Ode to a Nightingale." Death in "To Autumn" is presided over not by a grim reaper but by a goddess who gently and lingeringly brings each natural process to fulfillment. She is an intervenient figure, a mediating presence, between the promise in natural process and the death inherent in it, and she enables the poet to see the dying of the day as a kind of falling asleep, "While barred clouds bloom the soft-dying day, / And touch the stubble-plains with rosy hue" (ll. 25–6). Keats's recognition in this ode of an ultimate rightness and harmony in a natural process that leads to death is not any the less genuine or any the less of an advance in his development because it is mediated by imagination.

What needs to be emphasized is that imagination makes the recognition possible.

On the same day that he wrote to Reynolds about the season and reported that he had composed a poem on it (21 September 1819), he also wrote in a journal letter to his brother and sister-in-law in America that he felt "Qui[e]ter in my pulse" (Rollins ii. 209). "Some think I have lost that poetic ardour and fire 't is said I once had – the fact is perhaps I have: but instead of that I hope I shall substitute a more thoughtful and quiet power. I am more frequently, now, contented to read and think" (Rollins ii. 209). Some old truth, or dream of a truth, perhaps represented most clearly by the ode symbols and felt in their presence, had been temporarily or permanently restored, proved on the pulse, and made to seem a part of an altered nature. This is not to make of "To Autumn" the climax of Keats's development, or to suggest that he had achieved a final reconciliation of those oppositions and tensions that were a source of his personal growth and poetic achievement, and are reflected in his frequently ambivalent response to the various figures and symbols in his poetry. But it is to argue that at least twice, in "Ode on Melancholy" and "To Autumn," he achieved an unsurpassed sense of resolution in his rediscovery of an old quest object and the ideals and fears associated with it as a deeply interfused presence in human experience and the very processes of nature. By redirecting the quest for the object toward the processes in which life resides, and is extended, he succeeded in the most fundamental adaptation to the human condition it is possible to make. Ideals with roots deep in his earliest experience, and repeatedly given renewed life in the family romance of the psyche, have been integrated in a self-sustaining way into anticipations of further experience, and of the end of experience. More than any other, the faculty responsible for this adaptation is imagination, with its silent workings.

NOTES

1 The order followed here is that in Stillinger's edition and adhered to by most editors and commentators. Since "Urn" and "Melancholy" cannot be dated more precisely than 1819, however, the positioning of these two odes in relation to the others is uncertain (or, in Stillinger's words, "necessarily arbitrary" – Stillinger 5). But while absolute certainty about the dating of these two odes is lacking, the cumulative effect of the various kinds of evidence (conceptual tendencies, structural and stylistic features, general direction of thought) is to point strongly to the present and now really standard positioning of the odes. Additional evidence tending to confirm this positioning, but not considered before, is Keats's increasing reliance on the imaginative process of internalization, psychological evidence of an adaptive effort reinforcing the growing attitude of reconciliation, especially in "Melancholy" and "Autumn."

For a discussion of the problems of treating the odes as a sequence, see Gleckner (1965).

I do not include "Ode on Indolence" in my discussion primarily because it seems to me greatly inferior to the other odes. But I would at least note that it reflects many of the same concerns as the others, especially the tendency to construct a psychological bower in order to be "for an age so shelter'd from annoy, / That I may never know how change the moons, / Or hear the voice of busy-common sense!" (ll. 38–40).

2   Keats read "Lamia" aloud to Woodhouse on Saturday, 18 September 1819, the day before writing "Autumn." Jack (1967) has interestingly discussed several paintings that Keats may have seen prints of and that in any case indicate that his personification of Autumn in the poem had common analogues, even if not necessarily a specific model. See especially pp. 236–8 and the plate of Giulio Romano's "Psyche asleep among the Grain."

3   In the holograph of this sonnet (see Rollins's transcription, Rollins ii. 81), the last half-line begins "Deaths" rather than "Death is," which Evert reads as a possessive meaning that "life's high meed" is finally claimed by death (see Evert (1965) 291–2, and Stillinger 634). Read in this way, the thought in the last half-line seems to parallel the conclusion of "Ode on Melancholy," where the soul that reaches the "temple of Delight" finally becomes one of Veil'd Melancholy's "cloudy trophies" (ll. 25–30).

4   Allott (1956) 278.

5   See, respectively, Garrod (1926) 97–8; Leonidas Jones (1958) 23; Holloway (1960) 41; Schulz (1960) 56; and Sperry (1973) 244–5, 258.

6   Stillinger (1971) 104.

7   The idea that gods are created by the human mind has been discussed in a different context by Reiman (1971).

8   Allott (1956) 286.

9   Culler (1981) 149–52.

10   Patricia A. Parker (1979) 173.

11   Gittings (1968) 16.

12   Sperry (1973) 256–61.

13   Bloom, *Visionary Company* (1971) 404; the section on "Ode to Psyche" is reprinted Bate (1964) 91–8.

14   Perkins (1959) 197.

15   Wasserman (1953) 196.

16   See Tuveson (1960) 58–68, for a discussion of the concept of "Immensity" ("Usually capitalized, it was like a bell calling the romantic age to devotions of natural religion" – 58), and its typical use for the "deification of space" (67). Keats does not characteristically invoke the sublime as an intimation of a spiritual presence, or as part of a religious experience, but his pastoral bowers and other imaginary spaces are not, strictly speaking, wholly natural, and are often inhabited by a mythological or supernatural figure. The imaginary space in which most of his poetry is set is best thought of as lying somewhere between the natural and the super- or supranatural, with a return to the former a typical ending. The relationship of this natural world to any spiritual beyond is left indeterminate. For a reliable discussion of Keats's religious views,

primarily as they are reflected in his letters, see Ryan (1976). For a different view and a discussion of the poetry, see Sharp (1979). Although Sharp represents Keats as having made up his mind on matters that I think he was not nearly so certain about, he provides a lucid and valuable discussion of Keats's tendency to spiritualize the human world.

17 Evert (1965) 264.

18 Pettet (1957) 268.

19 Vendler (1973) 593.

20 The difference between the biblical Ruth and Keats's representation of her has been noted often. For a useful survey of the criticism and some of the considerations, see the discussion by Lams (1973) 417–20.

21 Hartman makes a similar point, though in another context, when he observes of the last line, "There is no complete disenchantment even here" ("Poem and Ideology: A Study of Keats's 'To Autumn'," in Hartman (1975) 128).

22 Bate 510.

23 Bush (1937) 107.

24 Charles I. Patterson (1954) 211–12, reprinted Stillinger (1968) 48–57 (50–1).

25 Bush (1966) 140.

26 Bate 514.

27 In a lecture on "Ode on a Grecian Urn" given at the University of Illinois in February 1979 Vendler suggestively linked the image here to Hamlet's "undiscovered country from whose bourn / No traveller returns" (III. i. 79–80). Whether or not Keats recalled these lines when he wrote lines 39–40 of the ode, it is interesting to note that the image functions in a similar way, making "us rather bear those ills we have / Than fly to others that we know not of" (III. i. 81–2).

28 "Dante," Eliot (1932) 231; Cleanth Brooks (1947) 140–52.

29 See Stillinger's clarification of the issues in "Who Says What to Whom at the End of 'Ode on a Grecian Urn,'" Stillinger (1971) 167–73.

30 Eliot (1932) 231.

31 *SPP* 482.

32 Hartman (1975) 144.

33 Kenneth Burke (1943–4) 32.

34 Freud (1953–74) ix. 145.

35 Empson (1966) 215.

36 See, e.g., Perkins's influential discussion of "Melancholy" and "Autumn" as an "affirmation of process," Perkins (1959) 282–94, reprinted Stillinger (1968) 85–93.

37 Freud (1953–74) xiv. 245.

38 Empson (1966) 216.

39 Sperry (1973) 279.

40 Freud (1953–74) xiv. 305.

41 Ibid., 306.

42 Vendler (1980) 178. In "Poem and Ideology" Hartman argues that "Autumn" represents a kind of poem, essentially modern, overcoming the epiphanic consciousness and structure that "evokes the presence of a god, or vacillates sharply between imagined presence and absence" (Hartman (1975) 126). I agree

that there is little or no "absence/presence dialectic" (129) in the poem, but would argue that the "spirit" or "figure" Hartman acknowledges is evoked in the poem (143, 146), while markedly different from the god or presence of the traditional epiphanic poem, is not an entirely demythologized image and bears some resemblance to the presences evoked in the other odes.

43 Perkins (1959) 294.

Other Writers

13

Godwin, Burke, and *Caleb Williams*

Marilyn Butler

Where politics appears in English novels, it is commonly at the margins; in *Caleb Williams* it is central. Godwin's most significant creative period was during the political crisis of 1791–6, when a native English radical movement first blossomed, warmed by events across the Channel, and then withered and died in the national crisis of full-scale war with France. He wrote continuously in these years: pamphlets, letters to newspapers, and the two most important books of his career, the treatise *Political Justice* (1793) and the novel *Caleb Williams* (1794). The two books both went into revised second editions by 1796, with *Political Justice* so materially changed that its second edition represents a new political statement.

This body of writing made Godwin the foremost intellectual among English radicals once the post fell vacant with Tom Paine's precipitate departure for France in 1792. Too much knowledge of Godwin's later years makes us pin on him Lamb's tag, "the Philosopher," as though he was always chairbound and anything but practically dangerous. Despite his emphasis on reason and his disapproval of violence, Godwin was no mere bystander in this brief period when revolution seemed a practical possibility. The hue and cry against Priestley in Birmingham in 1791 and the clamour against Paine in 1792 showed how uncomfortable the role of radical spokesman could become. Godwin defined all the unpleasantness of the position, and yet volunteered for it, when he protested against the loyalist hysteria surrounding Paine's trial *in absentia* in December 1792. In one letter to the *Morning Chronicle* he claimed that those of the reform party were reduced to a state of "perpetual fear,"[1] and in a second letter he complained of the hysteria that made a fair trial impossible:

We all know by what means a verdict was procured: by repeated proclamations, by all the force, and all the fears of the kingdom being artfully turned against one man. As I came out of court, I saw hand-bills, in the most vulgar and illiberal style distributed, entitled, The Confessions of Thomas Paine. I had not walked three streets, before I was encountered by ballad singers, roaring in cadence rude, a miserable set of scurrilous stanzas upon his private life.[2]

In the winter of 1793–4, as he was writing *Caleb Williams*, Godwin visited the two condemned Scottish radicals, Muir and Palmer, who were awaiting transportation to Australia on board the prison hulks in the Thames; in April and May he saw his London radical friend Joseph Gerrald in the same circumstances. On 12 May 1794 Thomas Hardy of the London Corresponding Society, and after him eleven other London radicals, including Godwin's close friend Holcroft, were arrested and charged with treason. At the time radicals believed that, if the twelve were found guilty, many others would follow them into the dock. Godwin nevertheless reacted by dating his provocative Preface to *Caleb Williams* 12 May, the very day of Hardy's arrest, and by alluding in it to the newly devised charge of "constructive treason." In October, just before Hardy and the others were brought to trial, Godwin criticized the concept of this offence even more boldly in his *Cursory Strictures on the charge delivered by Lord Chief Justice Eyre to the Grand Jury*, a pamphlet which played a part in obtaining their acquittal.

Godwin was hardly behaving like a theorist though, if he sought martyrdom through the Preface to *Caleb Williams*; he was saved by his publisher, Benjamin Crosby, who would not print it. The opening to the Preface conveys his anxiety that the reader might miss his contribution to current events: "The following narrative is intended to answer a purpose more general and important than immediately appears on the face of it." The novel is designed to explore "the question afloat in the world respecting Things As They Are," a debate inaugurated by Burke's warm defence of the old order, *The Reflections on the Revolution in France* (1790). The case for change which Godwin previously made philosophically in *Political Justice* is now in *Caleb Williams* to be translated into a more popular language. The real oppressiveness of the order Burke idealized

is a truth highly worthy to be communicated to persons whom books of philosophy and science are never likely to reach. Accordingly it was proposed in the invention of the following work, to comprehend, as far as the progressive nature of a single story would allow, a general review of the modes of domestic and unrecorded despotism, by which man becomes the destroyer of man.

The Preface finally appeared in the second edition of 1795, and in July of the same year, responding to an attack on him in the *British Critic*, Godwin wrote a reply which further amplifies the essentially political purpose of *Caleb Williams*:

> [Your correspondent] presupposes that my book was written "to throw an odium upon the laws of my country." But this is a mistake into which no attentive and clearsighted reader could possibly fall. The object is of much greater magnitude. It is to expose the evils which arise out of the present system of civilised society; and having exposed them to lead the enquiring reader to examine whether they are, or are not, as has commonly been supposed, irremediable; in a word, to disengage the minds of men from presupposition, and launch them upon the sea of moral and political enquiry . . . Your correspondent comes nearer the point when he . . . states my object to be: "the laws of this country, and the mode of their execution"; or rather, as he ought to have stated, *the administration of justice and equity, with its consequences, as it exists in the world at large, and in Great Britain in particular.*[3]

In later years Godwin ceased to emphasize what at the time he had boldly insisted on – the dangerous topicality of his book. His later glosses have to do with its novelistic qualities, and with the method of writing that helped to sustain suspense. The celebrated account he wrote in 1832 of the manner in which he composed the novel (beginning with its thriller-sequence, the hunting of Caleb in volume III) indicates that he no longer saw his book as dealing with the social and public perspectives of the Enlightenment. Instead, he reinterpreted his own career retrospectively in the aesthetic and private terminology of romanticism.

Post-romantic critics have tended to concur with Godwin's later view of his 1790s novel. Leslie Stephen influentially remarked that the moral of *Caleb Williams* eludes its author: "How about the wickedness of government? The answer must be that it has passed out of sight"[4]; "the reader, unassisted by the preface, would scarcely perceive Godwin's doctrine between the lines."[5] David McCracken, the book's latest editor, agrees that the Preface has "by no means an obvious connection with the novel itself."[6] A. D. Harvey sums up the majority opinion when he separates Godwin's works from one another and from their context, with the novel "detached from the period of political upheaval in which it was written," so that "*Political Justice* and *Caleb Williams* have very little subject-matter in common."[7]

Karl Popper once protested at the practice of "not taking arguments seriously, and at their face value, at least tentatively, but of seeing in them nothing but a way in which deeper irrational motives and tendencies express themselves."[8] It has been a tendency at least as strong in literary criticism as in other disciplines, and the writers on Godwin's fiction who have attended to his argument[9] have been, for all their weight of evidence, outweighed numerically by irrationalists. Even in the course of a critique sensitively open to nuances from real life and politics, P. N. Furbank insists on the novel's introverted mode. He reads it as "a highly dramatized symbolical picture of Godwin himself in the act of writing *Political Justice*";[10] at its most political, the action is merely "a psychological analogue" to revolution and, thus internalized, nearer to Dostoevsky than to Holcroft.[11] For Rudolph E. Storch, however, the very mention of Holcroft in connection with Godwin is a "critical error";[12] he argues that the novel is a Calvinistic study of the psychology of rebelliousness and the guilt it entails. Falkland comes to stand for Godwin's own father, a Calvinist minister, and for the God of the Old Testament. "Caleb's curiosity means disobedience ... It is in fact the Original Sin"[13]; the action takes place in a stylized landscape of the mind, and "the story of *Caleb Williams* has no place in the society of eighteenth-century England."[14]

Do the proponents of such interpretations realize how extraordinary they are? At the time Godwin insisted on his social meaning, and insisted moreover that the symbolism and stylization of his treatment supported his rational intention, by taking all societies into the critique rather than just England. For Godwin to have written a religious novel, even a novel unwittingly subverted by a religious consciousness, is incompatible with his role in radical politics. The year of *Caleb Williams* was also the year of Paine's anti-clerical *Age of Reason*. Godwin noted in his Journal for October 1793, while he was working on *Caleb Williams*, a plan to write a "treatise on God," which is presumably identical with the project he described elsewhere which would "sweep away the whole fiction of an intelligent former of the world, and a future state."[15] During the next two years, Coleridge's indignation with Godwin, as recorded in his Notebooks, reached its height, precisely because he associated Godwin with the atheism then current among English intellectuals. Anti-Godwin propaganda in *The Anti-Jacobin* and in conservative polemical novels in 1797–8 concurs in portraying Godwin as the atheistical philosopher. His erstwhile friends James Mackintosh and Samuel Parr use his irreligion as the cornerstone of their attacks in 1799 and 1800. No one seems to have sensed any backsliding from the cause of Reason in either *Caleb Williams* or in any other Godwinian writing of the first half of the revolutionary decade.

Storch's notion that Caleb's crime enacts Original Sin is surely a thought that occurs more readily in the late twentieth century than in the late eighteenth: in the post-Freudian era, the idea of the Fall is happily assimilated to a sense of guilt experienced for purely private reasons. It comes as no surprise to find a similar accommodation when a modern critic

of Godwin's great opponent, Edmund Burke, investigates the origins of
Burke's theological pessimism. Isaac Kramnick explains Burke's conviction
of man's fallen nature and the supposed presence in his writing of an
irrational sense of guilt as the product of a youthful trauma due to the
absence of Burke's father, after which one part of Burke's nature found
itself "worshipping the father, or longing for a father to worship."[16]

A more historical type of explanation is available for the theme powerfully
reiterated in the *Reflections on the Revolution in France*, that man cannot hope
to redeem himself through his own efforts and his own fallible reason.
Conor Cruise O'Brien, himself a politically minded Irishman, points to the
legacy of Irish Catholicism which Burke inherited from both sides of his
family. He suggest that Burke's attack on revolution in France was complicated by his suppressed sympathy with resistance in Ireland; in particular,
when Burke urged the English to look with favour upon the Catholics now
dispossessed in France, he subversively made the case for those Catholics
the English themselves had deprived in Ireland.[17] O'Brien's is an analysis
which aims to account for Burke's complexity, for his emotionalism and of
course for a style profoundly indebted to the scriptures. It helps to show
why the *Reflections* were ideologically effective, as history suggests they were.
Kramnick's hypothesis cannot do this for Burke, and Storch's remarks on
Godwin represent the same difficulty in more acute form. How could a
guilt-ridden, God-ridden author make the case for rationalism or radicalism?
If Godwin is a tormented Calvinist, must he not also seem an incompetent
polemicist? Guilt and fear, God and the Old Testament, are notions
necessarily playing a more challenging and difficult part in Godwin's work
than in Burke's, so that they cry out for explanation.

Burke and Godwin, living in revolutionary times, adopted strategies that
would speak to the educated, uncommitted reader. For modern philosophers
writing about *Political Justice*, as for modern critics of *Caleb Williams*, Godwin
is the better for not being political. Yet for Godwin himself, as the Preface
to *Caleb Williams* makes abundantly clear, both his major books were
adversarial, – designed to achieve change and also designed to refute the
case for the *status quo* familiarized, above all, by Burke. *Political Justice* has the
reputation of rising above polemic to seek an objective (if unreal) blueprint
of the just society, but this very appearance of lofty impartiality is dictated
by its role as a reply to Burke's *Reflections*. If Godwin appears passionless, it
is because Burke appears extraordinarily excited; if Godwin casts his eye
forward to a perfect future, it is because Burke has grounded his arguments
in an imperfect past. Burke pooh-poohs the insights of modern individual-
ism ("we know that *we* have made no discoveries"), and sonorously alludes
to the great men of history, the warriors, the leaders and the poets; he
emotively parades such topics as hearth and home, parents, the naturalness
of obedience. Burke casts the reader in the role of a small child, dwarfed by

the scale of the greater world, and he exploits the language in which the child is instructed, the rhythms of Bible, prayerbook and pulpit, to persuade his reader to respond with the child's implicit obedience.

The main theme of *Political Justice* is that all such lessons are pernicious lies. Society is not naturally virtuous at all. It exercises a strong power, previously little understood, over the lives of individuals. This power operates not merely through political institutions and the law, but through prejudice, prepossession and habit. "It [government] insinuates itself into our personal dispositions, and insensibly communicates its own spirit to our private transactions." (I. 4)[18] Obedience to authority is thus not a virtue, even in children; it is only by making us believe in obedience, through exhortation, fiction and other devices of imposture, that our governors maintain their position. The virtuous individual models himself not on the child but on the young adult, who, independent of parents, enquires for himself.

Long ago, in his Whiggish polemic writing of the 1780s (for example in *A Defence of the Rockingham Party* (1783)), Godwin had admired Burke as a man who had risen by merit, as a champion of liberty and a truthteller. His fall was therefore all the greater when, as the author of the *Reflections*, he barefacedly set out to defend and sanctify rule by an oligarchy. In a paragraph in his last chapter (to which he appended an obituary of Burke in 1798), Godwin imitated the rhythms of Burke's own celebrated eulogy of Marie Antoinette in order to evoke a similar regret:

> We know ... that truth will be triumphant, even though you refuse to be her ally. We do not fear your enmity. But our hearts bleed to see such gallantry, talents and virtue employed in perpetuating the calamities of mankind. (II. 545)

Godwin is seldom so directly personal as this. Yet he does devote about two hundred pages of his treatise (a part of the work on which modern descriptions commonly fail to linger) to such topics as the rival social systems, amongst which the aristocratic system advocated by Burke is clearly the most salient. In Books III to V Godwin considers in turn the characteristics of the monarchical, aristocratic and democratic systems, together with the moral influence of each upon the individual citizen, and upon the relations between governors and governed. Under the monarchical system, virtue, he avers, "is, in their conception, arrogant, intrusive, unmanageable and stubborn." (II.56) Monarchy and aristocracy alike have a tendency "to undermine the values and understandings of their subjects ... Implicit faith, blind submission to authority, timid fear, a distrust of our powers, an inattention to our own importance and the good purposes we are able to effect, these are the chief obstacles to human improvement." (II. 119) In the crucial chapter (V. xv), "Of Political Imposture," Godwin again alludes specifically to Burke as an upholder of a system of necessary trickery, by which the population must be duped into obedience. In the *Reflections*, says Godwin sardonically, kings and leaders are represented "independently of their individual character, as deriving a sacredness from their office. They must be accompanied with splendour and veneration" (II. 132). No one should seek to reduce *Political Justice* to the status of mere polemic reply to Burke, but the core of Godwin's book, – the source of its energy and the main determinant of its rhetoric, – lies in Godwin's conception of it as the ultimate answer to the *Reflections*, the only answer to attack the great issues within the same generous frame of reference to man's history, his culture, his morality, and his personal relationships.

Burke and Burkean rhetoric also recur in *Caleb Williams*. The novel is built round the relationship of two men, Caleb Williams and Ferdinando Falkland, who are "servant" and "master" in the words of the first edition, "secretary" and "patron" in the second. Commentators agree that this relationship is all-important, even though the direct conflict between the two is reserved mainly for the second of the three volumes. What is less commonly remarked is the degree to which the two characters are not individuals but stereotypes. Instead of entering into unselfconscious intimacy with either, the reader is kept aloof and made aware of the factors that shape the two characters' views of one another, especially the notions of degree and authority within a paternalistic system.

The theme of the first volume is Falkland's past history, as narrated to Caleb by his fellow-servant Collins. The indirect narration establishes the awe Falkland exacts from others as virtually an element of his character. Though Collins leads the story up to the occasion when Falkland was accused of murder, he himself does not believe the charge; he never sees those implications in his tale which are discreditable to his master. Yet Collins's entire story throws a very harsh light on Falkland's class. Falkland, after all, was the competitor and peer of an unpleasant bully, Squire Tyrrel, who hounded down two victims – his cousin, Emily Melville, who, Clarissa-like, was subjected to an attempt to marry her off to a boor, and a local tenant-farmer, Hawkins, whom Tyrrel ruined. Both these victims began by expressing esteem and love for Tyrrel; when both crossed him and proved obstinate, he used the law to imprison and destroy them. Emily and Hawkins stand for the immediate social inferiors of the squirearchy; what happens to them in the first volume, a prolegomena to the main action, is meant to suggest the variety and range of circumstance in which the power of the upper orders can be felt by other citizens.

As a poor female relation in a system strictly given to male primogeniture, Emily has no economic independence, and her family feels little sense of moral obligation towards her. The imprisonment and attempted rape to which she is subjected is obviously an extreme case, but it follows coarse treatment and coercion which must have been very common. Hawkins first offends by declining to vote as another landlord bids him, but he loses Tyrrel's favour by refusing to let his son Leonard become Tyrrel's servant. Leonard breaks down gates set up on Tyrrel's order, and since he does it at night with his coat turned up, he commits a felony under the "Black Acts" by which the eighteenth-century gentry maintained their absolute property rights in the countryside. Taken together, these offences by the Hawkinses constitute a rejection of the notion of subservience, which Tyrrel angrily sets out to punish.

As Collins's narrative makes clear, Falkland opposed Tyrrel in the latter's bullying both of Emily Melville and of the Hawkins family. If Tyrrel represents the unacceptable face of the English class system, Falkland is apparently its ornament. His refusal to fight a duel, in his youth in Italy, shows that he is critical of the brutish aspect of "chivalry." But in practice Falkland's fastidiousness hardly runs deep. Though he begs Tyrrel to avoid quarrelling with him, he retaliates with interest when Tyrrel strikes him in public. At this insult Falkland reverts to the code of his caste and acts precisely in the manner (so we are told) of the haughtier type of Italian nobleman, when he felt insulted by an opponent he would not deign to meet on the field of honour: he waylays and murders him.

The opening passage of volume II introduces Falkland and Caleb together in scenes which are closely observed and psychologically complex: this is a different quality of writing from the case-studies of the first volume. Nevertheless, Caleb and Falkland are carefully shown to represent their respective orders. Caleb, on hearing the story of Hawkins, does not share Collins's automatic assumption that Hawkins *must* be guilty of murder or Falkland innocent. Caleb is like Hawkins, another commoner, a man of self-respect and independence. It is unthinkable to Collins, the servant of aristocracy, that a gentleman might be guilty, but the possibility remains for the yeoman Caleb.

While Caleb resembles Hawkins, he also resembles Emily. As an inmate and dependent of Falkland's house, he relates to Falkland much as she did to Tyrrel, and he even recalls her artless, inexperienced character. Just as Emily approached Tyrrel direct, so Caleb tries to deal with Falkland: both give offence by not humbly keeping their distance, not observing the obedience due to rank. Caleb's resemblance to the two victims of volume I prepares the reader for the strange, yet convincing, emergence of Falkland, formerly the champion of Emily and Hawkins, as the archetypal tyrant of volumes II and III.

The fascination of the early chapters of volume II, however, has less to do with archetypes than with Godwin's study of the psychology of his two principals within their respective roles. He ventures an exemplary moralistic dialogue in the Holcroft manner about whether Alexander is a great man or not. In the course of this conversation Falkland is tempted into a number of "aristocratical" statements which put his supposed benevolence into a curious new light:

> "Let me hope that you will become more liberal. The death of a hundred thousand men is at first sight very shocking; but what in reality are a hundred thousand such men more than a hundred thousand sheep? . . . It was necessary to the realising his project that he should pass for a God. It was the only way by which he could get a firm hold upon the veneration of the stupid and bigoted Persians."[19]

At times it is hard to see in Caleb's conversational tactics anything but a sort of adolescent slyness, a teasing, knowing provocation of a puzzled older man. Caleb oscillates between maddening Falkland with lower-class cynicism about Alexander's nobility, and buttering him up by pretending to despise the commonalty:

> I replied: . . . "[The world's] affairs cannot be better than in the direction of the genuine heroes; and, as in the end they will be found the truest friends of the whole, so the multitude have nothing to do, but to look on, be fashioned and admire."
> . . . "Williams!" said he, "you instruct me well. You have a right notion of things, and I have great hopes of you" (117).

When after this Falkland accuses Caleb of being a "base artful wretch" who deals in "mystery and equivocation," the charge is unfair without being ridiculous in the reader's eyes. Godwin makes Caleb immature, not merely a social inferior and dependant but the essential type of the son. He "grows" in the course of the novel, without ever being allowed to reach an assured maturity. Godwin maintains his authorial detachment by stigmatizing Caleb's curiosity about his employer's secret as "inquisitiveness," and by having Caleb stress (as Collins did before him), his admiration, even veneration, for Falkland. It is made to seem to the reader, as apparently to Caleb himself, that in the tussle between veneration and inquisitiveness, the latter is a defect or even a transgression (122). Caleb has no vocabulary to justify what he does; even though he knows Falkland to be guilty of murder, he keeps using Falkland's loaded terminology. Indeed, Falkland exercises a powerful spell over everyone in the world of the novel, as a hero, a "beneficient divinity," a human being of special value. Unfortunately, he has also exercised it over most critics, who continue to write of Falkland's greatness and attractiveness as though these were objectively established rather than obliquely reflected in the unreliable narrations of Collins and of Caleb.

As a literary achievement, the character of Falkland hardly deserves our high opinion. Gloomy, guilty, the terror of his subordinates, he derives too plainly from Garrick's celebrated Richard III, or Kemble's Coriolanus, or from the period's veneration for Milton's Satan; a literary cliché, he is about to be outdone by Lewis's Ambrosio and Radcliffe's Schedoni, by Scott's Marmion and Byron's Corsair. What subtleties there are in the writing derive from sociological observation, from generalized character-studies of the manners and morals of gentlemen. Falkland's over-valuing of honour and reputation is the characteristic of a type, and it is bluntly stated rather than traced with much refinement – "This it was to be a gentleman! a man of honour! I was the fool of fame"(135). More delicately drawn is the unconscious aristocratic hauteur which undercuts Falkland's effort to improve his relations with Tyrrel (31). Despite his willed benevolence, his role has taught him to be masterful and coercive. Early in the novel, the dying Mr. Clare, a spokesman for some of Godwin's opinions, expresses the Dissenters' abhorrence of seeking to bind another by an oath. As soon as Falkland discovers that Caleb has found out the truth, he tries to swear him to silence. "I charge and abjure you by everything that is sacred and that is tremendous, preserve your faith!" (136) Thereafter much of Falkland's language is religious – that of a divinity, perhaps, but hardly a beneficent one:

> "You might as well think of escaping from the power of the omnipresent God, as from mine! If you could touch so much as my finger, you should expiate it in hours and months and years of a torment of which as yet you have not the remotest idea! . . . I have dug a pit for you! . . . Be still! If once you fall, call as loud as you will, no man on earth shall hear your cries" (144–54).

David McCracken and B. J. Tysdahl have pointed out that, in using such language, Falkland alludes to Burke twice over.[20] This Old Testament rhetoric certainly resembles that of the *Reflections*, with its hints of the authority of the Church, and the terrors to be experienced by the Church's disobedient sons. But the rhetoric of terror is accounted for more particularly in another of Burke's books that Godwin knew well, and re-read in the early 1790s, *A Philosophical Enquiry into the Origin of our Ideas of the Sublime and Beautiful* (1756). There Burke holds that terror, the source of the sublime, is the strongest feeling of which the human mind is capable, and it is evoked, characteristically, by contemplating power. Power may be invested in a figure of authority, a master or a king, but ultimately it derives from God; and there is no mistaking the fervour with which Burke sketches the terror inherent in the notion of omnipotence:

Whilst we contemplate so vast an object,... we shrink into the minuteness of our own nature, and are, in a manner, annihilated before him ... In the Scripture, wherever God is represented as appearing or speaking, every thing terrible in nature is called up to heighten the awe and solemnity of the divine presence.[21]

This is a concept not to be underrated by Godwin, who had known the rigours of an equally exigent Christian tradition; yet in the second edition of *Political Justice* Godwin was to declare specifically that Burke's aesthetic doctrines were inadequate, the mere pastimes of "a man of taste and refinement":

The sublime and pathetic are barren, unless it be the sublime of true virtue, and the pathos of true sympathy... There is no delightful melancholy, but in pitying distress (i. 447).

Godwin is thus subjecting to critical and satirical analysis the extravagant rhetoric also typical of Falkland.

At the same time, Godwin's own early religious experiences undoubtedly gave him insight into the effect upon an impressionable mind when religious terror of this sort is invoked. Indeed, Godwin never obliterated from his memory the impact religious gloom and rigour had on his adolescence. It is felt in his later novel, *Mandeville* (1817), and most memorably here, in the hold Falkland has over Caleb. Clever and energetic, Caleb longs to become the friend of Falkland and of Falkland's cousin Forester, and is disappointed because both in the end can only think like gentlemen. Yet each relationship is stillborn in any case, because of Caleb's irrational reverence for Falkland, his "master," an awe which makes him guilty, tongue-tied and impotent. Falkland threatens Caleb terrifyingly, invoking an ancient language of dominance, – temporal authority backed by religion, – and the youthful Caleb withdraws in silence, "irresolute, overawed and abashed" (154). It is because he cannot speak to Falkland that he decides to disobey him and run away. Afterwards he comes to see this as a wrong step, because it is dictated by emotion, the rising frenzy in Falkland matched by frenzy in himself (154). In suggesting that Caleb should have been able to master his emotions, Godwin – as frequently happens in his writing – maps out an ideal plan of behaviour for ideal conditions which are not, as he knows, remotely like the actual ones. Everyone, in this study of "Things As they Are," behaves irrationally rather than wisely, driven by prepossession, interest or panic. Where the treatise *Political Justice* both analyses the present system and proposes alternatives, the novel *Caleb Williams* confines itself with intensity to the social conditions men are experiencing.

Thus, the quirks and unconscious compulsions of human nature conspire with social conditions to lead these two men, who originally viewed one another with sympathy and mankind with benevolence, to torment and finally to destroy one another. The leading instrument of their mutual aggression is the law, revealed here as un-justice. The courts can sometimes acquit the innocent, but they do not favour the small man's attempt to challenge, and so claim equality with, the great man. Hawkins went to law to challenge Squire Tyrrel, to the latter's glee (73). Eventually Caleb too challenges Falkland directly in a London magistrate's court, to the indignation of the justice: "There would be a speedy end to all order and good government, if fellows that trample upon ranks and distinctions in this atrocious sort, were upon any consideration suffered to get off" (276). But the absurdity of Caleb's aspiration to achieve personal equality has already been proved by Falkland's easy manipulation of law to punish rebelliousness:

> I was conducted to the same prison which had so lately inclosed the wretched and innocent Hawkinses. They too had been the victims of Mr. Falkland. He exhibited, upon a contracted scale indeed . . . a copy of what monarchs are, who reckon among the instruments of their power prisons of state (177).

The relationship between Falkland and Caleb is, then, a political relationship, unequal despite a cultural tradition ("free and equal in the eyes of the law") that says otherwise; violent and destructive, despite the wish of both men that it should be otherwise.

Most of the characters in the novel are so used to the idea of hierarchy that they only really notice Falkland's behaviour when it is gracious. He can threaten and bully so that Caleb is in danger of his life, but he can also show a lordly compunction to him in prison, for which, absurdly but believably, he expects Caleb to feel grateful. The conventional and virtuous figures in the novel mostly see morality in the same light. Falkland's servants are so convinced of his goodness that they all sincerely abhor Caleb. So does the benign old man who guards him in Liverpool. So, in later editions, does the mother-figure he finds in Wales, Laura.

The last volume indeed becomes a study of the workings of "imposition" at large, rather than a direct duel between Falkland and Caleb. Falkland no longer needs to lurk melodramatically, a Demon King, behind each of Caleb's misfortunes. "Things As They Are," the System, ensures that he is hounded as in real life Priestley and Paine had been, and Godwin's friends, the accused in the Treason Trials, afterwards known in Windham's phrase as "the acquitted felons." If the whole novel is judged as a purely personal drama, parts of volume III are a falling off, because Falkland does not appear in them, but the common reaction to the plot is that it intensifies. The explanation for this lies in real-life politics: it is the last volume which conveys the mood of the beleaguered intellectual minority, the frustration, bitterness and fear of marked men, conscious of their own rectitude, who had become singled out as "constructive" traitors, criminals and outcasts. In its picaresque, unfocused way, less apparently dramatic, yet cumulatively despairing and paranoid, the third volume matches the insight of the other two, while broadening the novel from a closed action which might be read personally to a more open fable of unequivocally political significance.

In general terms, then, *Caleb Williams* is about hierarchy. It shows how the representative relationship of Caleb and Falkland really works, because of the pre-conditioning of the two men and of those about them. More specifically, it re-enacts and even verbally echoes the debate on the merits of the old system conducted since 1790 by Burke and his republican opponents. In *Caleb Williams* the central symbolic moment is the attempt to open the mysterious box, the ark kept in Falkland's private sanctum, an opportunity given to Caleb because of the (revolutionary) fire endangering the house. It is an analogue of the writing of *Political Justice* or the writing of *Caleb Williams*, although the box itself has no literal importance, since there is no one secret, no one piece of evidence, to uncover. Falkland's "secret" is his evil wish to dominate or to be revered, and it is conveyed everywhere in the text's mimicry of Burkean language, its many moments of sardonic parody, like the near-quotation from *both* the *Reflections* and *Political Justice* with which the character of Falkland is introduced – "My heart bleeds at the recollection of his misfortunes as if they were my own" (10).[22] The element of Burke in the portrayal of Falkland has been acknowledged by several of Godwin's most scrupulous and informed critics, including Boulton and Kelly, who do not of course maintain that Falkland "is" Edmund Burke. Godwin himself avoided much direct mention of his opponent in the treatise and he would not have countenanced a personal caricature in the novel. But just as Peacock evoked the published Coleridge in Mr. Flosky of *Nightmare Abbey*, and Shelley surveyed the output of Wordsworth in *Peter Bell III*, in order to discredit their arguments, so Godwin reviews Burke's career as a political writer through having it re-enacted by Falkland. Volume I of *Caleb Williams*, with its sketch of Falkland's courageous liberal past, his opposition to duelling and to petty tyranny, stands symbolically for Burke's early career on the liberal wing of Whiggism. Falkland falls because, like Burke in Godwin's eyes, he proves not to be the corrector of the system but its dedicated servant, the more fraudulent and the more dangerous because he sees through his own lies.

The close correlation in Godwin's mind between *Political Justice* and *Caleb Williams* is demonstrated, finally, by the textual effects of the latter on the former. Soon after he had published the novel in May 1794, Godwin began work on a series of revisions to *Political Justice* which eventually appear in the second edition dated 1796. He lists, in a Preface, the most substantial

of the changes, twelve entirely new-written chapters, and explains some of
his amplifications by the need to bring the earlier chapters into line with his
later thinking. Three of the complete new chapters in Godwin's list, "Of
Obedience" (III.vi), "Of forms of government" (III.vii), and "Of Good
and Evil" (IV.xi), together with a number of passages in this part of
the treatise (e.g., IV.i; IV.vi; V.xi; V.xv) have been little commented on,
probably because they are not readily categorized in terms of politics or
political theory. Here Godwin amplifies his discussion of the relations
between the classes, and especially, the behaviour of the aristocracy or
upholders of existing systems of government.

In keeping with his usual caution, Godwin in contemplating obedience
(III.vi) takes care not to recommend disobedience. "Government is nothing
but regulated force," but it is not wise for the governed to take on a
power too strong for them. The citizen's main duty is to try to secure the
freedom of his own understanding. "Obey; this may be right; but beware of
reverence." Godwin contemplates the notion of civic duty propagated in
existing society, by Burke above all others:

> To a government, therefore, that talked to us of deference to political
> authority, and honour to be rendered to our superiors, our answer
> should be: "It is yours, to shackle the body, and restrain our external
> actions; that is a restraint we understand. Announce your penalties;
> and we will make our election of submission or suffering. But do not
> seek to enslave our minds.... you can have no right to extort our
> deference, and command us not to see, and disapprove of, your
> errors" (I. 236–7).

A kind of violence overtakes the language as Godwin contemplates the very
obedience that to a Burke (or a Falkland) constitutes civic virtue.

> When I make the voluntary surrender of my understanding... I
> annihilate my individuality as a man, and dispose of my force as an
> animal to him among my neighbours, who shall happen to excel in
> imposture and artifice... I am the ready tool of injustice, cruelty and
> profligacy (I. 232–3).

The same force sounds in the paragraphs added in 1796 to "Of Political
Imposture" (V.xv), where Godwin contemplates directly the intellectual
crime of Burke:

> It may not be uninstructive to consider what sort of discourse must
> be held, or book written, by him who should make himself the
> champion of political imposture... By whom is it that he intends his

book should be read? Chiefly by the governed; the governors need little inducement to continue the system. But, at the same time that he tells us, we should cherish the mistake as mistake, and the prejudice as prejudice, he is himself lifting the veil, and destroying his own system. . . . It is not to be wondered at, if the greatest genius, and the sincerest and most benevolent champion, should fail in producing a perspicuous or very persuasive treatise, when he undertakes so hopeless a task (II. 139–40).

Thus Burke, as the author of the *Reflections*, the lapsed liberal, the tool of aristocracy and the propagandist of imposture, recurs again and again as the mystifier, the keeper of secrets in *Political Justice*, and as Falkland in *Caleb Williams*. But the figure, part real man, part emblem of the ideological position Burke was now identified with, is more interesting in the second edition of *Political Justice* than in the first, and more interesting in *Caleb Williams* than in either. The format of the novel, which treats individuals and their relationships, requires Godwin to study "imposition" both as the trait of the aristocrat, and, more interestingly still, as the source of guilt and disturbance in the conditioned, vulnerable common man who is imposition's victim. Instead of generalizing about how society ought to be, and summarizing its present defects, Godwin in *Caleb Williams* enacts coercion, and the impulse to personal liberty, on a private level, and thus uncovers the psychological roots of political behaviour that in the first *Political Justice* philosophic abstraction had tended to conceal. The revisions to the treatise, though more limited, are dictated both by the insights won from the novel and by further thoughtful study of real men suffering actual political oppression. When all Godwin's writing of the 1790s is considered together, including the notebooks, letters and fragments of hard, analytic autobiography, he emerges as a powerful observer of the human psyche, who neither flattered nor simplified his own kind, Caleb's kind. An abrasive, punishing attention to unpleasant realities, rather than utopianism, is the literary characteristic of "the Philosopher."

With all its symptoms of fraught times pressing in upon it, *Caleb Williams* finally emerges as an ambitious symbolic study of a political issue big enough to rise above mere topicality. In the early 1790s radicals like Godwin imaged for themselves an unprecedented power to think and act. To achieve it, they had to divest themselves not merely of the *ancien régime* and its institutions, but of the prepossession within their own minds in favour of those institutions – especially their veneration for hereditary leaders, and their vulnerability to the hypnotic rhetoric of paternal authority sanctioned by religion. *Political Justice*, even in its first version, said as much. The power of fiction to generalize through the particular enables *Caleb Williams* to enact metaphorically the relationship between hereditary government and governed. It shows the psychological traumas, the murdering of fathers, which the establishment of a non-hierarchical system would necessarily entail. It is, therefore, a psychological novel, but a psychological novel set in the special conditions of revolution. As such, it has affinities with the writing of Stendhal, Dostoevsky, or Conrad, when they deal with volatile political situations, but it is unlike most novels which have emerged from relatively stable England. In the heady circumstances, there could be no greater warrant of Godwin's integrity than the acknowledgement in his best writing that revolution will not, after all, easily be won; that even the war in the mind has only just started. The greatest of English literary republicans, Milton, wrote his masterpieces as he adjusted to the political failure of *his* revolution. Perfectibility, said Godwin in the second edition of *Political Justice*, does not mean the attainment of perfection, but only the unending capacity to improve. The gritty redefinition, the scaling down of hope, was worked out step by step in the writing of *Caleb Williams*.

NOTES

1   Godwin (1968) 113.
2   Ibid., 116.
3   Quoted by Dumas (1966) 583.
4   Stephen (1902) 148.
5   Ibid., 140.
6   Godwin (1970) xii.
7   Harvey (1976) 243, 240.
8   Quoted Bogdanor (1978) 1090. I am indebted to this review-article for the comparison between Kramnick and O'Brien on Burke.
9   These include Murry (1938), ch. 19; Monro (1953) 207–49; Boulton (1963) 207–49; Kelly (1976) 179–208.
10 Furbank (1955) 215.
11 Ibid., 234.
12 Storch (1967) 189.
13 Ibid.
14 Ibid., 204.
15 Paul (1876) i. 296.
16 Kramnick (1977) 64.
17 Introduction to Edmund Burke (1969) 34–47; see above, note 8.
18 Godwin (1946); the sentence quoted first appeared in the 2nd ed. (1796). Subsequent references in the text are to volume and page in this edition, though the passage cited appeared in the 1st ed. (1793) unless otherwise stated.
19 Godwin (1970) 111–12.
20 McCracken (1970) 266; Tysdahl (1981) 51–2.
21 Edmund Burke (1826) i. 174–5.
22 Cf. above, p. 348.

14

Murder Incorporated: Confessions of a Justified Sinner
Eve Kosofsky Sedgwick

"Is it as potent as it used to be?"
"What do you speak of, deary?"
"What should I speak of, but what I have in my mouth?"

Dickens, Edwin Drood[1]

James Hogg's *Private Memoirs and Confessions of a Justified Sinner* is a late (1824), and perhaps only arguably, Gothic novel: to classify it as Gothic one has to admit the native (Scottish) scene and vernacular religion into what had been signalized, so far, chiefly as a genre about Catholic Europe. *Caleb Williams* and *Wuthering Heights,* however, neither depending on the overseas picturesque, precede and follow it into the current Gothic canon. Reasons for considering it Gothic are that it is ambiguously supernatural, that it is lurid, that it is "psychological" (i.e., literalizes and externalizes, for instance as murder or demonic temptation, conflicts that are usually seen as internal), that its action seems to be motivated by religious absolutes, and, most importantly, that it richly thematizes male paranoia. Precisely because the novel has such a (not strictly Gothic) grounding in the native and the vernacular, because the characters are racy and textural and the class conflicts exact and anxious, it is a good place to look at some articulations of male paranoia, to test the conjunctions of desire and persecution with gender and empowerment.

Like many Gothic novels, this one begins by seeming to offer neatly demarcated pairs of doubles, whose relationships degenerate under the power pressures of the novel into something less graphic and more insidious.[2] The novel famously offers two distinct narratives of almost the same events; there are two distinct paranoid-style persecutions of one man by another; one character is able to turn into a physical double of other characters; and so forth. But there is also a pairing of opposites, brothers – a less Gothic device – that provides the overtly moral and social engine of the book, and lays out a schema of values by which the Gothic code is, at least provisionally, supposed to be read. But just as in our reading of Sonnet 144 [in Sedgwick (1985)], where the semantic, *ethical* presentation of gender *opposites* undermined and contaminated the supposedly symmetrical, syntactic presentation of *structural counterparts*, so it is in this novel.

The two brothers in the novel may or may not have the same father; their social and familial coordinates are widely different. According to the "Editor's Narrative" that constitutes almost the first half of the book, their mother is a Glasgow woman, "sole heiress and reputed daughter of a Baillie Orde"[3] ("Baillie" is roughly equivalent to "Alderman"), and "the most severe and gloomy of all bigots to the principles of the Reformation" (p. 4). "She had imbibed her ideas from the doctrines of one flaming predestinarian divine alone" – one Robert Wringhim, who goes with her to perform the ceremony when, as a young woman, she is sent off to the country to marry a rich, much older landowner, George Colwan, laird of Dalcastle. The marriage is unhappy – "The laird was what his country neighbours called 'a droll, careless chap,' with a very limited proportion of the fear of God in his heart, and very nearly as little of the fear of man" (p. 4) – and in the face of his wife's persistent sexual refusal, the laird establishes her and later her spiritual guide in a separate set of rooms in the top part of his mansion-house.

The pairing of contrasted values implicit in this marriage, of the landed gentry with the urban bourgeoisie, becomes even more acute and discordant in the next generation. The paternity of each son is mysterious on more than one narrative level: there is an open conjecture, meant to amount to an assumption, that the younger son is Robert Wringhim's, but everyone in the novel including the "editor" assumes that the elder son is the laird's, even though the "Editor's Narrative" offers no significant reasons for differentiating the circumstances in which the two were conceived. Nevertheless, each boy is more or less firmly assigned to one camp. The older one is named "George" after the laird, takes his surname unproblematically, and is brought up in the lower half of the house with the laird. But the second son is not acknowledged by his mother's husband, and finally "Mr. Wringhim, out of pity and kindness, took the lady herself as sponsor for the boy, and baptized him by the name of Robert Wringhim – that being the noted divine's own name" (p. 18).

Thus, without any very secure "genetic" basis, the boys are assigned to class milieux that the novel presents as starkly contrasting; and in a possible triumph of nurture over nature, each one seems ideally suited to his assignment. The narrator describes George in the terms that, in the Victorian novel, will come ever more overtly to denominate the British racial ideal. He is "a generous and kind-hearted youth; always ready to oblige, and hardly ever dissatisfied with anybody" (p. 18); much slower than his brother in "scholastic acquirements," George is "greatly his superior in personal prowess, form, feature, and all that constitutes gentility in the department and appearance" (p. 19).[4] Young Robert Wringhim, on the other hand, "was an acute boy . . . had ardent and unquenchable passions, and, withal, a sternness of demeanour from which other boys shrunk. He was the best grammarian, the best reader, writer, and accountant in the various classes that he attended, and was fond of writing essays on controverted points of theology" (p. 19). His mother's religiosity is re-doubled in Robert. The editor's favorite word for him is "demure": "His lips were primmed so close that his mouth was hardly discernible. . . . His presence acted as a mildew on all social intercourse or enjoyment";[5] he is a physical coward and, according to his own account, a compulsive liar.

In many ways the terms in which class and religion intersect here are familiar from as far back as *Twelfth Night*, via *Hudibras*. Rather than begin with young Robert's sociological and characterological placing, however, I would like to start with an apparently less descriptive comparison: between this dour young Calvinist and Sparkish, the wealthy, puppyish young would-be man about town in *The Country Wife*. In our discussion of Sparkish in chapter 3 [of Sedgwick (1985)], we emphasized his misunderstanding – at least, his fatally partial understanding – of the circuit of male transactions in women. Understanding correctly (in the terms of the play's world) that the ultimate function of women is to be conduits of homosocial desire between men, Sparkish makes the mistake of underestimating the invest-ment that must be made in the fiction of desiring women; and his insufficiently mediated desire to enter into relation with the men he admires results in *his* being feminized, in turn, in relation to them.

Young Wringhim is like Sparkish – like an extreme of Sparkish – in his explicit devaluation of women. For Wringhim, this devaluation has a religious meaning: "In particular," he says in his own account of his life,

> I brought myself to despise, if not to abhor, the beauty of women, looking on it as the greatest snare to which mankind are subjected, and though young men and maidens, and even old women (my mother among the rest), taxed me with being an unnatural wretch, I gloried in my acquisition; and, to this day, am thankful for having escaped the most dangerous of all snares (p. 103).

When we move – temporarily – from Wringhim's overt, "unnatural" devaluation of women to his unmediated bonding with men, we are moving

into the most convoluted and conflicted realm in the novel. To begin
with, the two distinct parts of the novel – the Editor's Narrative and
Wringhim's "Confessions" proper – although covering the same events
from two different perspectives, actually describe two quite different
male-homosocial bonds. The centerpiece of the Editor's narrative is the
intense, persecutory relationship between young Robert and his brother
George – culminating in Robert's murder of George. The centerpiece of
Robert's own narrative of these events, however, is his even more intense,
persecut*ed* relationship with a male character whom the narrator has hardly
even mentioned – one Gil-Martin, apparently the Devil himself. Each of the
two narratives, that is, seems to give an account of a relationship that might
fit fairly readily into the set of psychosocial categories we have been dealing
with so far; but to fit them together as accounts of the *same* events is
complicated.

To begin with Robert's relation to his brother George is to begin in the
(ex post facto) familiar world of Dostoevsky.[6] When the two young men
come together – apparently for the first time – in young adulthood, during
a particularly inflammable political moment in Edinburgh, Robert's strategy
toward his dashing, popular, athletic brother is a maddeningly literal version
of the "feminine" one that we would today call passive-aggressive. When
George and his entourage are at tennis, and "the prowess and agility of the
young squire drew forth the loudest plaudits of approval from his associates," Robert "came and stood close beside him all the time that the game
lasted, always now and then putting in a cutting remark by way of mockery."
Throughout the game, Robert

> stood so near [George] that he several times impeded him in his rapid
> evolutions, and of course got himself shoved aside in no very
> ceremonious way. Instead of making him keep his distance, these rude
> shocks and pushes, accompanied sometimes with hasty curses, only
> made him cling closer to this king of the game. . . . [T]he next day, and
> every succeeding one, the same devilish-looking youth attended him as
> constantly as his shadow (p. 21).

Nothing can be done to shake Robert's attendance on the young
gentlemen's game: asked to keep out of the range of the ball, " 'Is there any
law or enactment that can compel me to do so?' " he asks, "biting his lip
with scorn." "With a face as demure as death," he

> seemed determined to keep his ground. He pretended to be following
> the ball with his eyes; but every moment they were glancing aside at
> George. One of the competitors chanced to say rashly, in the moment
> of exultation, "that's a d—d fine blow, George!" On which the

intruder took up the word, as characteristic of the competitors, and repeated it every stroke that was given (p. 22).

Things get worse. Robert precipitates a tussle with George, in which he is himself bloodied, and makes himself

> an object to all of the uttermost disgust. The blood flowing from his mouth and nose he took no pains to stem, neither did he so much as wipe it away; so that it spread over all his cheeks, and breast, even off at his toes. In that state did he take up his station in the middle of the competitors; and he did not now keep his place, but ran about, impeding everyone who attempted to make at the ball. They loaded him with execrations, but it availed nothing; he seemed courting persecution and buffetings, keeping steadfastly to his old joke of damnation, and marring the game so completely that in spite of every effort on the part of the players, he forced them to stop their game and give it up (pp. 23–4).

However one may read the affect in Robert's "malignant" (p. 21) glances – and it does seem worlds removed from Sparkish's ingenuous admiration for "the wits" – it is nevertheless clear that, like Sparkish, Robert is submitting to feminization in order to get close to – really, get under the skin of – a more powerful and prestigious man of higher class. The bloody nose, especially, is an emblem of a specifically female powerlessness: as Janet Todd points out, it occurs in eighteenth-century novels at moments of sexual threat against women.[7] In a later tussle Robert's nose "again gushed out blood, a system of defence which seemed as natural to him as that resorted to by the race of stinkards" (p. 412), and he again refuses to wash the blood off. Clearly, the tools for advancement he perceives himself as possessing are those belonging to the castrated, to the visibly and even disgustingly powerless. His strength is that of having nothing to lose in the way of prestige: he can be a bad sport, kick his brother when he's down, make an obstructionist stand on the letter of the law – make a pure guerrilla nuisance of himself – through the empowerment of sheer abjection. His very physical presence is flaccid and unresistant: his brother can seize him "by the mouth and nose with his left hand so strenuously that he sank his fingers into his cheeks" (p. 41), and when his dead body is dug up in the Epilogue, "All the limbs, from the loins to the toes, seemed perfect and entire, but they could not bear handling. Before we got them returned again into the grave they were all shaken to pieces, except the thighs, which continued to retain a kind of flabby form" (p. 227). In his abjection, Robert cannot desire women enough to be able to desire men through them; instead, identifying hatingly with them he hatingly throws himself at the man who seems to be at the fountainhead of male prestige. The uncanny "pursuit" of George by Robert that is the subject of the Editor's Narrative offers a portrait of male homosocial desire as murderous ressentiment. It is closer – more shared, more familial, less mediated – than the pristinely stratified ascendancy of cuckoldry in *The Country Wife*, but also far more violent and repressive. The newly virulent, newly personalized element, as we have suggested, is homophobia.

For George, as for his brother Robert, bonds with men are the organizing fact of his social life: he is often seen, and always seen as successful, in groups of young, aristocratic men. Unlike Robert, however, George relates to his male acquaintance as a man, because he has the knack of triangulating his homosocial desire through women. This need be done only in the most perfunctory way. For instance, George on his way to church meets a friend "who was bound to the Greyfriars to see his sweetheart, as he said: 'and if you will go with me, Colwan,' said he, 'I will let you see her too, and then you will be just as far forward as I am'" (p. 35). Or carousing with his friends, he and they "adjourn to a bagnio for the remainder of the night" (p. 48).

In his happy and confident (however minimal) wielding of women as mediators of male transactions, George is merely reproducing as he habitually does the habits of his (at any rate, legal) father, the laird of Dalcastle. The first disagreement between the laird and his bride, at their wedding, had occurred when he "saluted every girl in the hall whose appearance was anything tolerable, and requested of their sweethearts to take the same freedom with his bride, by way of retaliation" (p. 5). Later, on the bride's running home to her father, her status as a worthless, transparent counter for male relationships becomes explicit in what Robert M. Adams calls "a fine scene of folk-humor" (p. xii). Her father, pretending to be outraged by the laird's treatment of her, in turn flogs *her* as her husband's representative:

> "... wi' regard to what is due to his own wife, of that he's a better judge nor me. However, since he has behaved in that manner to *my daughter*, I shall be revenged on him for aince...."
>
> So saying, the baillie began to inflict corporal punishment on the runaway wife.... "Villain that he is!" exclaimed he, "I shall teach him to behave in such a manner to a child of mine...; since I cannot get at himself, I shall lounder her that is nearest to him in life" (p. 10).

Of course, his purpose is to drive her back to her husband, and in this he succeeds.

The first half of the novel, then, has shown us, in the Editor's bluff masculist version, the persecution, the supernatural-seeming pursuit, and ultimately the murder of the attractively masculine George by his sinister, feminized, uncanny brother. The second half, Robert's own narrative, tells a slightly different, redistributed story: George is not a central character, and instead we hear about the courtship, persecution, and eventual entrapment of the rather pathetic, schizoid, feminized Robert by one "Gil-Martin," a glamorous, uncanny male stranger whom he persists in imagining to be the Czar Peter of Russia. In this relationship, we learn, somehow lies the explanation for the peculiar happenings retailed in the Editor's Narrative.

It is in the second half of the novel that a genuinely erotic language of romantic infatuation between men is introduced. The explicit affect is, at least at first, very different from the one that had prevailed between Robert and George in the first half. At the same time, the language that describes the two bonds is curiously echoic. For instance, when Robert first sees the stranger,

> he cast himself in my way, so that I could not well avoid him; and, more than that, I felt a sort of invisible power that drew me towards him, something like the force of enchantment, which I could not resist. As we approached each other, our eyes met and *I can never describe the strange sensations that thrilled through my whole frame at that impressive moment* (p. 106; emphasis mine).

This eye contact is like the glance with which Robert has mysteriously followed George:

> To whatever place of amusement [George] betook himself, and however well he concealed his intentions of going there from all flesh living, there was his brother Wringhim also, and always within a few yards of him, generally about the same distance, and ever and anon darting looks at him that chilled his very soul. *They were looks that cannot be described; but they were felt piercing to the bosom's deepest core* (p. 34; emphasis mine).

When Robert is struck, at the sight of the stranger, by the fact that "he was the same being as myself!" (p. 106), the stranger says, "You think I am your brother...; or that I am your second self. I am indeed your brother" (p. 107). Again, George has felt in the first half of the novel that Robert was appearing to him "as regularly as the shadow is cast from the substance, or the ray of light from the opposing denser medium" (p. 35), while Robert in turn says of Gil-Martin, "He was constant to me as my shadow" (p. 120). When Robert begins – perhaps tardily, having been entangled into committing two murders – to find the stranger creepy and oppressive, he describes the stranger in terms of disgust and fascination that his brother might have used to describe the clinging, bloody, passive rag of a man who tripped him up on the tennis courts:

> I felt as one round whose body a deadly snake is twisted, which continues to hold him in its fangs, without injuring him, further than in moving its scaly infernal folds with exulting delight (p. 175).

Robert's strategy of spooking his brother's circle by parroting their own words back at them is like the strategy Gil-Martin in turn uses toward Robert in theological discussion:

> in everything that I suggested he acquiesced, and, as I thought that day, often carried them to extremes, so that I had a secret dread he was advancing blasphemies. He had such a way with him, and paid such a deference to all my opinions, that I was quite captivated, and, at the same time, I stood in a sort of awe of him, which I could not account for, and several times was seized with an involuntary inclination to escape from his presence by making a sudden retreat (p. 108).

Many of the parallels between the two homosocial relationships are clearly meant to have a literal, rather than a merely echoic, correspondence. For instance, Robert's apparition has not merely dogged his brother, but made a habit of materializing always at a particular point to his right (p. 35). Robert, correspondingly, when he imagines himself haunted, "always beheld another person, and always in the same position from the place where I sat or stood, which was about three paces off me towards my left side" (p. 139). When we go back to Gil-Martin's assertion that he *is* Robert's "brother," we see that that is importantly true in two senses: first, in that scene of their initial meeting, he looks identical to Robert himself; second, later in the events narrated, he looks identical to Robert's actual brother George (p. 76). In fact, Gil-Martin is able at will to take on the exact appearance of anyone (at least, any man) he chooses. We also learn, in Robert's "Confessions," that during much of the time of Robert's supposed persecutions of his brother as described in the Editor's Narrative, Robert was, or imagined himself to be, home in bed in a peculiar trance; and in the latter reaches of the narrative, when "Robert" seems to be carrying on murderous depredations all over the countryside, Robert himself perceives himself as merely being asleep.

In short, the novel's strong suggestion is that Gil-Martin in the shape of Robert is the author of much of the carnage; or, psychologizing that, that Gil-Martin performs these acts as a projection of Robert's unconscious wishes. That much is a critical commonplace. (We should note that at the beginning of the events narrated, it is relatively easy for both us and Robert to keep track of the distinction between Robert and Gil-Martin, even when Gil-Martin is disguised as Robert; later, conforming to the common Gothic pattern, that clarity degenerates rapidly.) What is most striking for our purposes, however, is not the mere presence of Gil-Martin as an eroticized, paranoid double for Robert, but the importance in that context of his slipperiness of identity – and specifically, of the fact that he is Robert's "brother" in two senses: that he can move back and forth between impersonating Robert and impersonating George.

The significance of this is to dramatize precisely the inextricability of identification from desire that makes male homosexuality a necessary structuring term for male heterosexual empowerment. Oedipal schematics to the contrary, there is no secure boundary between wanting what somebody else (e.g., Daddy) has, and wanting Daddy. The protean Gil-Martin represents the fluidity of that bond: Robert both loves and fears Gil-Martin *both* because Gil-Martin mirrors himself in his murderous abjection *and* because Gil-Martin mirrors the empowered male other. A scene that takes place in Robert's bed is the perfect expression of this uncrystallizable, infusory flux of identification and desire. It is during the apparent trance state that occupies him while Gil-Martin seems to be out haunting George in Robert's guise:

> I was seized with a strange distemper. . . . I generally conceived myself to be two people. When I lay in bed, I deemed there were two of us in it; when I sat up I always beheld another person. . . . It mattered not how many or how few were present: this my second self was sure to be present in his place, and this occasioned a confusion in all my words and ideas that utterly astounded my friends . . . over the singular delusion that I was two persons my reasoning faculties had no power. The most perverse part of it was that I rarely conceived *myself* to be any of the two persons. I thought for the most part that my companion was one of them, and my brother the other; and I found that, to be obliged to speak and answer in the character of another man, was a most awkward business at the long run (p. 140).

We might mention that the confusion of identities in this bedroom scene is echoed in two other texts: the attack on John Harmon in *Our Mutual Friend*, and the rape of T. E. Lawrence in *The Seven Pillars of Wisdom*. Steven Marcus, disapprovingly, describes this deliquescence of identity (or identification) in the direction of desire as a feature of sadomasochistic pornography; based on his own examples as well as these, however, I think it would be more accurate to associate it with the conjunction of sexual compulsion and male homosocial desire.[8]

To give a name – "the inextricability of desire from identification in male

homosocial empowerment" – to the slipperiness of Gil-Martin's identity, is
I think to denominate a crucial area of psychological concern in this novel.
At the same time, the sheer confusion caused by this slipperiness – the
proliferation of faces, identities, paranoias, families, overlapping but subtly
different plots – also requires a move away from the focus on intrapsychic
psychology, and back toward a view of the social fabric as a whole. One of
the meanings of the cognitive mess seems to be that the chains of symbolic
transactions in the novel do, after all, take place within a relatively discursive
system, one that is constituted by and offers room for deferral and
displacement.

One of the odd things about this novel is that although the Editor and
the Dalcastles apparently take a cheerful, complaisant view of the oppression of women in the context of male transactive desire, the novel as a
whole and particularly the Editor's Narrative are nevertheless unusually
graphic and explanatory in exploring its mechanisms and effects. We have
already seen, for instance, that the grievances of the laird's wife – in being
treated by both her husband and her father as an exchangeable token of
their own power – are detailed intelligibly, although without any sympathy,
by the narrator. After his wife ceases to cohabit with him, the lusty old laird
consoles himself with the company of a Miss Logan, a "fat bouncing dame"
(p. 12), whom both the laird and the narrator treat with great affection.
Nevertheless, the novel makes plain that she, too, is victimized by him, at
least economically: after years of faithful service in the roles of surrogate
wife and of housekeeper, child-rearer, and nurse, she cannot, in his declining
days, get him to pay enough attention to mere worldly things to settle his
affairs on her behalf (p. 51).

Again, as we have seen, one of the guarantees of young George's
attractive masculinity had been his willingness to romp among his male
friends at a "bagnio." Unexpectedly, however, the Editor's Narrative also
offers at a different moment a much more critical view of the meaning of
that casual use of prostitutes. Lurking – waiting for custom – outside the
bagnio that night, and hence a witness to the murder of George, has been
a prostitute, Arabella Calvert, who becomes an important character in the
Editor's Narrative; telling her story in her own words, she supplies a point
of view very different from the narrator's own. For instance, she "knew" –
"and never for any good," she says (p. 56) – both the old and the young
George, and thinks of them without infatuation. A well-born woman ruined
by a lord, "she had been imprisoned; she had been scourged, and branded
as an impostor; and all on account of her resolute and unmoving fidelity to
several of the very worst of men, every one of whom had abandoned her to
utter destitution and shame" (p. 64). In Edinburgh, on the fateful night, she
solicits a young gentlemen, a friend of George's; during their assignation,
however, he notices that she speaks like a lady, and sentimentally begs her

to "take heart. Tell me what has befallen you; and if I can do anything for you ... you shall command my interest." She continues:

> "I had great need of a friend then, and I thought now was the time to secure one. So I began.... But I soon perceived that I had kept by the naked truth too unvarnishedly, and thereby quite overshot my mark. When he learned that he was sitting in a wretched corner of an irregular house, with a felon, who had so lately been scourged and banished as a swindler and impostor, his modest nature took the alarm, and he was shocked, instead of being moved with pity. His eye fixed on some of the casual stripes on my arm, and from that moment he became restless and impatient to be gone" (pp. 66–7).

The truth of her situation – passed literally from male hand to hand and repeatedly left to be punished "in the place of" the men who have owned her (p. 65) – is far too brutal for the man's intended, Yorick-style pathos and recuperation. Its most memorable emblem is her vision of her death by hanging as a thief: "I think of being hung up, a spectacle to a gazing, gaping multitude, with numbers of which I have had intimacies and connections" (p. 55).

It is not only in the "heterosexual" plot of the two Georges that female sexuality is shown as a corrosive, punishing, and punished commodity, however. In fact, although Robert Wringhim's story condenses into a schema of desire and struggle between masculine men and feminized men, it cannot be understood except through the proscribed sexuality of a woman – his mother. Specifically, it is the *social* forces of religious and class anxiety that are brought to bear on him most acutely through the question of his mother's sexuality.

As usual in this novel, the question of maternal sexuality is displaced every which way including backward: the legitimacy of Rabina, the mother, herself, is treated as dubious (pp. 3, 10, 44). This apparently random animadversion prepares the ground for the question of Robert's own legitimacy (although, as mentioned earlier, the question of George's legitimacy is never raised). The dubiousness of Robert's legitimacy, of his paternity, is, however, the mainspring of his character and homosocial situation. He is brought up in the menage of his mother and Robert Wringhim the elder, to whom he bears a remarkable physical similarity – though as the pastor himself points out,

> "there are many natural reasons for such likeness, besides that of consanguinity. They depend much on the thoughts and affections of the mother; and it is probable that the mother of this boy, being deserted by her worthless husband, having turned her thoughts on me,

as likely to be her protector, may have caused this striking resemblance" (p. 97).

The pastor himself, however, does not seem to feel quite secure about this very plausible explanation. He fires his man for having the temerity to doubt it. Furthermore, it seems likely that a consciousness of his own transgression is the main energy behind his wracking struggles with God for an assurance of the boy's salvation.

"I have struggled with the almighty long and hard. . . . but have been repulsed by him who hath seldom refused my request; although I cited his own words against him, and endeavoured to hold him at his promise, he hath so many turnings in the supremacy of his power, that I have been rejected" (p. 91).

The day on which Wringhim the elder announces that he has finally wrested an assurance of the boy's salvation from God is the very day that young Robert first meets Gil-Martin, and the elements of the murderous plot are finally all in place.

It seems likely, then, that a beginning of young Robert's feminization has been in his father's use of him as a gambling chip in an inexplicit deal with God: forgive my transgression (without my ever having to confess to it), and (to prove that all is forgiven) save my son. This is the Calvinist version of the bargain made by Catholic parents in two other Gothic fictions, Diderot's "La Religieuse" and Maturin's *Melmoth the Wanderer*, who try to pay for the illicitness of their children's conception by donating the children themselves to religious orders. The Protestant, internal siting of the transaction in this case, however, and the tacitness and illogic of its terms even in the mind of the transactor, make its schizogenic effects on the child fully plausible even on the strictly psychological level.

Within the context of this transaction, young Robert's aversion to his mother becomes quite explicable. He himself, professing to find it puzzling, actually explains it:

though I knew her to be a Christian, I confess that I always despised her motley instructions, nor had I any great regard for her person. If this was a crime in me, I never could help it. I confess it freely, and believe it was a judgment from heaven inflicted on her for some sin of former days, and that I had no power to have acted otherwise towards her than I did (p. 104).

There is no explicit indication in Robert's "Confessions" that he believes himself to be illegitimate, but this passage, exercising his characteristic and now compulsive pharisaism on the person who first occasioned it, suggests that his behaviour is at any rate appropriate to that knowledge. Robert seems to grow up, religiously, in the consciousness that only men (Robert the elder, God – if not the old or the young laird) can legitimate him, and that women can only illegitimate him. To the minister he is indebted, he says, "under Heaven," for the "high conceptions" that saved him after the laird disavowed his paternity.

The very first vignette of Robert's home life shows him precociously reaching toward the minister for religious vindication at the expense of his mother: pouncing on her at catechism for responding by rote and with an insufficiently ingenious vengefulness toward sinners, he evokes this delicious version of the Yorickian primal scene:

> "What a wonderful boy he is!" said my mother.
> "I'm feared he turn out to be a conceited gowk," said old Barnet, the minister's man.
> "No," said my pastor, and *father* (as I shall henceforth denominate him). "No, Barnet, he *is* a wonderful boy; and no marvel, for I have prayed for these talents to be bestowed on him from his infancy; and do you think that Heaven would refuse a prayer so disinterested? No, it is impossible. But my dread is, madam," continued he, turning to my mother, "that he is yet in the bond of iniquity" (pp. 90–1).

In this little drama of family constitution, we see the zeal and misogynistic trustfulness with which little Robert takes up his father's ambition to reformulate the family – excluding the mother – in homosocial terms as a transactive bond among God, old Wringhim, and Robert. The lie of Wringhim's claim to "disinterestedness" about the boy's attainments is the foundation of this new male family. Robert's position in it is, however, chronically undermined by Wringhim's ability to turn back toward the mother, who is – however devalued and denied – nevertheless a party to the original transgression that the new family exists to deny. Old Robert understands and to some extent manipulates the lie that excludes the mother; young Robert believes and thus is victimized and himself excluded by it. Hence, old Robert reprobates the mother, while young Robert murders her.

Although old Robert, though a true believer, is nevertheless (through his heterosexuality) in a relatively manipulative position with respect to the received truths of religion, it is interesting that in class and political terms, he in turn finds himself playing exactly young Robert's manipulated, Sparkish-like role: that of the zealot who univocally acts out the essentially cynical, divided ideologies of others. During the congregation of political parties in Edinburgh, the Duke of Argyle and his friends made such use of him as sportsmen often do of terriers, to start the game, and make a great yelping noise to let them know whither the chase is proceeding. They often did this out of sport, in order to tease their opponent; for of all pesterers that ever fastened on man he was the most insufferable: knowing that his coat protected him from manual chastisement, he spared no acrimony, and delighted in the chagrin and anger of those with whom he contended. But he was sometimes likwise *of real use* to the heads of the Presbyterian faction, and therefore was admitted to their tables, and of course conceived himself a very great man (p. 20).

The elder Robert's strategies in the political arena are like the younger Robert's on the tennis court. And of course, the younger Robert inherits his class placement and class ressentiment from his putative father, and they are the building-blocks of his "personal" legalistic, self-righteous, class-marked style. Defending his stand on the tennis court,

he let [Gordon, one of the young gentlemen] know that "it was his pleasure to be there at that time; and, unless he could demonstrate to him what superior right he and his party had to that ground, in preference to him, and to the exclusion of all others, he was determined to assert his right, and the rights of his fellow-citizens, by keeping possession of whatsoever part of that common field he chose."

"You are no gentleman, Sir," said Gordon.

"Are you one, Sir?" said the other.

"Yes, Sir. I will let you know that I am, by G–!"

"Then, thanks be to Him whose name you have profaned, I am none. If *one* of the party be a gentleman, *I do hope in God I am not!*" (p. 33).

Thus, although the novel's paranoid dramas are acted out in "Oedipal" terms, the Oedipal family that frames them is clearly a site whose definition is an object of struggle, not a given. The three-person family of father, mother, child – and then that of God, father, child – is willfully, arbitrarily, in effect violently carved out of the large messy material of too many fathers, too few acknowledgements of paternity, too much female sexuality, two different classes.

An important thematic emblem for the links among the various male figures in the novel's convoluted and finally violent ring of homosocial desire is the two-edged sword. This emblem appears, in addition, braided together with some thematics of anality or of penetration from the rear. For instance, on the morning when Wringhim the elder finally dedicates young

Robert to God's service, intending to bind up the loose ends of the male triangular transaction for good – " 'I give him unto Thee only, to Thee wholly, and to Thee for ever' " – he concludes,

> "May he be a two-edged weapon in Thy hand and a spear coming out of Thy mouth, to destroy, and overcome, and pass over; and may the enemies of Thy Church fall down before him, and be as dung to fat the land!" (p. 111)

When George is murdered by Robert, it is with a two-edged sword, and "both the wounds which the deceased had received had been given behind" (p. 51). The weapon, a gilded one, had been pressed on Robert, "much against my inclination," by Gil-Martin (p. 152). Golden weapons are themselves a related motif: Robert has had an (apparently heaven-sent) vision of "golden weapons of every description let down in [a cloudy veil], but all with their points towards me" (p. 125); and he becomes infatuated with "two pistols of pure beaten gold" that Gil-Martin produces:

> the little splendid and enchanting piece was so perfect, so complete, and so ready for executing the will of the donor, that I now longed to use it in his service (p. 126).

The last golden weapon in the novel is brandished behind Robert during his final degeneration, by Gil-Martin who is using it both to protect him and to prod and subjugate him:

> I was momently surrounded by a number of hideous fiends, who gnashed on me with their teeth, and clenched their crimson paws in my face; and at the same instant I was seized by the collar of my coat behind, by my dreaded and devoted friend, who pushed me on and, with his gilded rapier waving and brandishing around me, defended me against all their united attacks. Horrible as my assailants were ... I felt that I would rather have fallen into their hands than be thus led away captive by my defender at his will and pleasure (p. 211).

A more figurative two-edged weapon, earlier in the book, is Psalm 109, which Wringhim sings in his evening prayers after a legal offensive by the Wringhim has been turned back against them by the laird's party.

> Set thou the wicked over him,
>> *And upon his right hand*
> *Give thou his greatest enemy,*
>> *Even Satan, leave to stand.*

And, when by thee he shall be judged,
    Let him remembered be;
And let his prayers be turned to sin
    When he shall call on thee . . .

Let God his father's wickedness
    Still to remembrance call;
And never let his mother's sin
    Be blotted out at all . . .

As cursing he like clothes put on,
    Into his bowels so,
Like water, and into his bones
    Like oil, down let it go.

                                                      (pp. 31–2)

This scene is clearly the source of the one in *The Mayor of Casterbridge* in which Henchard, cursing the formerly beloved Farfrae musically in the words of the same psalm, initiates a circuit of blight that eventually settles on himself in terms taken literally from the curse.[9] In *Confessions*, some of the terms of the curse alight on both the younger men: *each* has Satan standing to hand; each dies young; each (though in different senses) is given to cursing, and is cursed; since they have the same mother, the ineradicability of her "sin" is exactly what makes their fates inextricable, and makes the different styles of paternal "wickedness" such an explosive combination. Prefiguring *The Mayor of Casterbridge*, however, and also as in the legal proceeding that precipitates the curse in *The Confessions*, the worst consequences fall on Robert himself; the final lodging place of the two-edged sword is in the liquefaction of his own bowels and bones.

It is important and prophetic that even at this relatively early moment in the construction of the modern terms of the homosocial spectrum, "homosexual" thematics appear only in a subordinated yoking with an apparently already-constituted homophobia. Specifically in this case, the bowels and backside as the place of vulnerability to violence, pain, and domination proleptically take the place of any location there of possible satisfactions. Bonds, between men, of fascination and of unmediated power-exchange already take the form of two-edged weapons (in the brother's back, in the Lord's mouth), not of two-edged pleasures. The pleasures may be inferrable, but only from the forms of violence that surround them. Even the charm, for Robert, of Gil-Martin's enthralling society, comes as a reaction against paternal and fraternal denial; and it seems, itself, threatening almost from the first: "he acquired such an ascendancy over me that I never was happy out of his company, nor greatly so in it" (p. 120). "The sexual" itself, in any form – in any genital form – is not a part of young Robert's experience; but the double bind of the structures of sexual repression nevertheless is.

From this apparent disruption of order between homophilic and homophobic thematics, we can learn two things. First, we should be reminded by it that however radically the terms of the homosocial spectrum, and the meanings of homosexual identity, were changing during the two centuries after the Restoration, the thematics and the ideological bases of homophobia were probably the most stable and temporally backward-looking elements of the entire complex: the punitive fate of Edward II, the drama of *Edward II*, and the punitive thematics surrounding Robert Wringhim certainly have more in common than do the actual social or erotic forms in which each was situated.

At the same time, we can, I think, take the priority in this novel – in this period – of homophobic over homophilic thematics as underwriting our speculation about a main function of homophobia in its modern, psychologized form. The internal homophobic pressures on young Robert have the effect, not in the first place of repressing a pre-existent genital desire within him toward men, but of making him an excruciatingly *responsive* creature and instrument of class, economic, and gender struggles that long antedate his birth. As he pushes blindly, with the absurdly and pathetically few resources he has, toward the male homosocial mastery that alone and delusively seem to promise him a social standing, the psychologized homophobic struggle inside him seems to hollow out an internal space that too exactly matches the world around him. Between the conflicted blood- and property-bond to his brother outside, and the far more conflicted bond of narcissistic fascination with the murderous "inner" brother, Robert becomes only the barest membrane of a person: a mere, murderous potential, violent against women and men alike, and capable of being seized and used by and in the service of any social force.

As I have already suggested, I consider it likely that the main subject of the "paranoid" classic Gothic as a whole can best be described in the terms I have been using for Hogg's novel. Some criticism has discussed how close the preoccupation with doubles and with persecution in these novels is to something (today) recognizably like male homosexual thematics.[10] What I wish to emphasize, by contrast, is the focus on homophobia as a tool of control over the entire spectrum of male homosocial organization. This emphasis seems potentially more precise and revealing. Most broadly, it allows us to read these novels as explorations of social and gender constitution as a whole, rather than of the internal psychology of a few individual men with a "minority" sexual orientation. There are several concomitant advantages to this. First, it gives us more, and more interesting, terms for discussing the positions of women in these novels and the societies they portray. Second, the "evidential" questions associated with any literary-critical discussion – never mind a historical one – of individual male homosexuality have most often been couched in peculiarly unilluminating terms, as of accusation and defense.[11] Aside from the inappropriateness of these adversarial terms for the discussion of fictional characters and preoccupations, and apart even from the unacceptably homophobic, and evidentially distorting, assumptions that underlie the treatment of homosexuality as an accusation, the legalistic frame of discussion of ascribed homosexuality disguises or denies the importance of much more fundamental and entirely unanswered questions about the constitution and social meaning of male homosexuality itself.

If there is a loss or a danger in my shift of emphasis from the homosexual to the homophobic content of the Gothic, it would lie in the potential blurring, the premature "universalization," of what might prove to be a distinctly homosexual, minority literary heritage. Feminist critics have long understood that when the male-centered critical tradition has bestowed the tribute of "universality" on a woman's writing, it is often not an affirmation but rather a denial of the sources of her writing in her own, female specificity. The extra virulence of racism in our culture has minimized the danger of this particular spurious naturalization of the work of writers of color, but the ambiguous, prestigious spectre of "universality" has nevertheless exerted a structuring and sometimes divisive effect on the history of at any rate Black American culture. Similarly, a premature recuperation (as being about the entire range of social gender constitution) of a thematic array that might in the first place have a special meaning for homosexual men as a distinctively oppressed group – which, beyond the reach of any unanswered questions, they unmistakably do constitute in our society as it is – would risk cultural imperialism.

Still, it is apt to be a critic able to read and speak as a participant in gay male culture who can recognize and situate such thematic arrays most authoritatively.[12] Obviously, I am not that critic. But also, interestingly, such critics have not so far been much attracted – at least in their writings – to the Gothic paranoid tradition before Wilde, in spite of its obvious focus on hypercharged relationships between men. Their relative neglect endorses, I think, my own contention: that even motifs that might ex post facto look like homosexual thematics (the Unspeakable, the anal), even when presented in a context of intensities between men, nevertheless have as their *first* referent the psychology and sociology of prohibition and control. That is to say, the fact that it is about what we would today call "homosexual panic" means that the paranoid Gothic is specifically not about homosexuals or the homosexual; instead, heterosexuality is by definition its subject.

The writing on the paranoid Gothic that is most closely relevant to this discussion has come, accordingly, not from a gay male but from a feminist perspective. For instance, the history of feminist readings of *Frankenstein*, including particularly Mary Jacobus's sketch of a feminist Girardian reading,[13] makes amply clear several ways in which the kind of analysis I am proposing would find resonances in that text. A remarkable reading of *Caleb Williams* by Alex Gold, Jr., both plots Caleb's story precisely onto Freud's analysis of paranoia (in relation to the repression of male homosexual desire), and then shows how fully Godwin portrays the constitution of *all* desire under the aspect of "the brutal erotics of property,"[14] of class, gender, and generational oppression. Different as it is from mine, Gold's analysis, like mine, locates the node of late eighteenth-century usefulness and misleadingness for twentieth-century readers precisely at the matter of "sexualization." Gold writes,

> The [psychoanalytic] theory of paranoia can account for the emotional patterning in *Caleb Williams* because Godwin is exploring a political theory of passion which contains all the dynamic elements described in purely internal terms in the psychoanalytic account.[15]

Besides (but, as we have discussed, in relation to) their thematization of homophobia, the paranoid Gothic novels, and especially these two, have in common a relation to the family like the one I have sketched in Hogg: in *Frankenstein* and in *Caleb Williams* as in the *Confessions*, the hero intrusively and in effect violently carves a *small, male, intimate* family for himself out of what had in each case originally been an untidy, nonnuclear group of cohabitants. The deforming dominance in the Gothic of an image (however distorted) of the nuclear family household, in novelistic contexts where a much more varied and naturalistic tableau of in-laws, adopted children, unmarried adult siblings, quasidomestic servants, and domestic servants, actually obtained, is a link between the world of the Gothic and the world of *Sentimental Journey*.[16] As in *Sentimental Journey*, too, it is the ideological imposition of the imaginary patriarchal Family on real, miscellaneous, shifting states of solitude, gregariousness, and various forms of material dependence, that rationalizes, reforms, and perpetuates, in the face of every kind of change, the unswerving exploitations of sex and of class.

NOTES

1   Dickens (1972) 206.
2   On this see Sedgwick (1980) 34–40. An especially good account of the form of Hogg's *Confessions* occurs in Kiely (1972) 208–32.
3   Hogg (1970) 3. Further citations will be incorporated in the text.
4   On the high valuation of stupidity in nineteenth-century gentlemen, see Girouard (1981) 166–8 and 269–70.

5   For a suggestive discussion of the psychological meaning of "primmed" lips in relation to paranoid psychosis, see Kris (1953) 128–50.

6   See, for example, Girard's discussion of *The Eternal Husband*, Girard (1972) 45–7.

7   Todd (1980) 404–5. Interestingly, Bradley Headstone in *Our Mutual Friend* has similar nosebleeds.

8   Marcus (1966) 257–62. Marcus himself concludes that the sadomasochistic pornography he is discussing has a male-homosocial basis.

9   Hardy (1912–14), *Mayor*, ch. 33.

10 See, for instance, Praz (1970), and Punter (1980).

11 These critical debates have characteristically occured between "Freudian" critics who locate apparently homosexual material, and "conservative" critics who deny that it "proves" anything. In America, however, psychoanalytic thinking about homosexuality has itself virtually never resisted homophobic recuperation; these critical debates have therefore reinforced, rather than challenged, the homophobic norms of literary scholarship. On this see Abelove, "Freud."

12 Examples can be found in, for instance, Robert K. Martin (1979); Boyers and Steiner (1982–3); and Kellogg (1983).

13 Jacobus, "Is There a Woman . . . ?" (1982–3) 130–5.

14 Gold (1977) 148.

15 Ibid., 153–4.

16 Besides Barrett (1980), especially interesting discussions of the enforcement of the family can be found in Olsen (1983) and D. A. Miller (1983).

15

Bearing Demons: Frankenstein's Circumvention of the Maternal

Margaret Homans

Married to one romantic poet and living near another, Mary Shelley at the time she was writing *Frankenstein* experienced with great intensity the self-contradictory demand that daughters embody both the mother whose death makes language possible by making it necessary and the figurative substitutes for that mother who constitute the prototype of the signifying chain. At the same time, as a mother herself, she experienced with great intensity a proto-Victorian ideology of motherhood, as Mary Poovey has shown.[1] This experience leads Shelley both to figure her writing as mothering and to bear or transmit the words of her husband.[2] Thus Shelley not only practices the daughter's obligatory and voluntary identification with the literal, as do Dorothy Wordsworth and Charlotte and Emily Brontë, but she also shares with George Eliot and Elizabeth Gaskell (and again with Charlotte Brontë) their concern with writing as literalization, as a form of mothering. It is to Shelley's handling of these contradictory demands, and to her criticism of their effect on women's writing, that my reading of *Frankenstein* will turn.

Frankenstein portrays the situation of women obliged to play the role of the literal in a culture that devalues it. In this sense, the novel is simultaneously about the death and obviation of the mother and about the son's quest for a substitute object of desire. The novel criticizes the self-contradictory male requirement that that substitute at once embody and not embody (because all embodiment is a reminder of the mother's powerful and forbidden body) the object of desire. The horror of the demon that Frankenstein creates is that it is the literalization of its creator's desire for an object, a desire that never really seeks its own fulfillment.

Many readers of *Frankenstein* have noted both that the demon's creation amounts to an elaborate circumvention of normal heterosexual procreation – Frankenstein does by himself with great difficulty what a heterosexual couple can do quite easily – and that each actual mother dies very rapidly upon being introduced as a character in the novel.[3] Frankenstein's own history is full of the deaths of mothers. His mother was discovered, as a poverty-stricken orphan, by Frankenstein's father. Frankenstein's adoptive sister and later financée, Elizabeth, was likewise discovered as an orphan, in poverty, by Frankenstein's parents.[4] Elizabeth catches scarlet fever, and her adoptive mother, nursing her, catches it herself and dies of it. On her deathbed, the mother hopes for the marriage of Elizabeth and Frankenstein and tells Elizabeth, "You must supply my place to my younger children" (chapter 3). Like Shelley herself, Elizabeth is the death of her mother and becomes a substitute for her. Justine, a young girl taken in by the Frankenstein family as a beloved servant, is said to cause the death of her mother; and Justine herself, acting as foster mother to Frankenstein's little brother, William, is executed for his murder. There are many mothers in the Frankenstein circle, and all die notable deaths.

The significance of the apparently necessary destruction of the mother first emerges in Frankenstein's account of his preparations for creating the demon, and it is confirmed soon after the demon comes to life. Of his early passion for science, Frankenstein says, "I was . . . deeply smitten with the thirst for knowledge" (chapter 2). Shelley confirms the Oedipal suggestion here when she writes that it is despite his father's prohibition that the young boy devours the archaic books on natural philosophy that first raise his ambitions to discover the secret of life. His mother dies just as Frankenstein is preparing to go to the University of Ingolstadt, and if his postponed trip there is thus motivated by her death, what he finds at the university becomes a substitute for her: modern scientists, he is told, "penetrate into the recesses of nature and show how she works in her hiding-places" (chapter 3). Frankenstein's double, Walton, the polar explorer who rescues him and records his story, likewise searches for what sound like sexual secrets, also in violation of a paternal prohibition. Seeking to "satiate [his] ardent curiosity," Walton hopes to find the "wondrous power which attracts the needle" (letter 1). Frankenstein, having become "capable of bestowing animation upon lifeless matter," feels that to arrive "at once at the summit of my desires was the most gratifying consummation of my toils." And his work to create the demon adds to this sense of an Oedipal violation of Mother Nature: dabbling "among the unhallowed damps of the grave," he "disturbed, with profane fingers, the tremendous secrets of the human frame" (chapter 4). This violation is necrophiliac. The mother he rapes is dead; his researches into her secrets, to usurp her powers, require that she be dead.[5]

Frankenstein describes his violation of nature in other ways that recall what William Wordsworth's poetry reveals when read in conjunction with Dorothy Wordsworth's journals. Of the period during which he is working on the demon, Frankenstein writes,

> The summer months passed while I was thus engaged, heart and soul, in one pursuit. It was a most beautiful season; never did the fields bestow a more plentiful harvest or the vines yield a more luxuriant vintage, but my eyes were insensible to the charms of nature.... Winter, spring, and summer passed away during my labours; but I did not watch the blossom or the expanding leaves – sights which before always yielded me supreme delight – so deeply was I engrossed in my occupation (chapter 4).

Ignoring the bounteous offering nature makes of itself and substituting for it his own construction of life, what we, following Thomas Weiskel, might call his own reading of nature, Frankenstein here resembles William Wordsworth, reluctantly and ambivalently allowing himself to read nature, to impose on nature apocalyptic patterns of meaning that destroy it. Dorothy Wordsworth herself makes an appearance in the text of *Franken-stein*, if indirectly, and her presence encodes a shared women's critique of the romantic reading of nature. Much later in the novel, Frankenstein compares his friend Clerval to the former self William Wordsworth depicts in "Tintern Abbey," a self that he has outgrown but that his sister remains. Shelley quotes (with one major alteration) the lines beginning, "The sounding cataract / Haunted him like a passion" and ending with the assertion that the colors and forms of natural objects (rock, mountain, etc.) were

> a feeling, and a love,
> That had no need of a remoter charm,
> By thought supplied, or any interest
> Unborrow'd from the eye.[6]

If Clerval is like Dorothy, then Frankenstein is like William, regrettably destroying nature by imposing his reading on it.

When, assembled from the corpse of nature, the demon has been brought to life and Frankenstein has recognized – oddly only now that it is alive – how hideous it is, Frankenstein falls into an exhausted sleep and dreams the following dream:

> I thought I saw Elizabeth, in the bloom of health, walking in the streets of Ingolstadt. Delighted and surprised, I embraced her, but as I imprinted the first kiss on her lips, they became livid with the hue

of death; her features appeared to change, and I thought that I held the corpse of my dead mother in my arms; a shroud enveloped her form, and I saw the grave-worms crawling in the folds of the flannel. I started from my sleep with horror (chapter 5).

He wakes to see the demon looking at him, hideous, but clearly loving. The dream suggests that to bring the demon to life is equivalent to killing Elizabeth, and that Elizabeth dead is equivalent to his mother dead. Elizabeth may have been the death of the mother, but now that she has replaced her, she too is vulnerable to whatever destroys mothers.[7] And, indeed, the dream is prophetic: the demon will much later kill Elizabeth, just as the demon's creation has required both the death of Frankenstein's own mother and the death and violation of Mother Nature. To bring a composite corpse to life is to circumvent the normal channels of procreation; the demon's "birth" violates the normal relations of family, especially the normal sexual relation of husband and wife. Victor has gone to great lengths to produce a child without Elizabeth's assistance, and in the dream's language, to circumvent her, to make her unnecessary, is to kill her, and to kill mothers altogether.

Frankenstein's creation, then, depends on and then perpetuates the death of the mother and of motherhood. The demon's final, and greatest, crime is in fact its murder of Elizabeth, which is, however, only the logical extension of its existence as the reification of Frankenstein's desire to escape the mother. The demon is, to borrow a phrase from Shelley's *Alastor*, "the spirit of" Frankenstein's "solitude." Its greatest complaint to Frankenstein is of its own solitude, its isolation from humanity, and it promises that if Frankenstein will make it a mate, "one as hideous as myself.... I shall become a thing of whose existence everyone will be ignorant" (chapter 17). That is, no longer solitary, the demon will virtually cease to exist, for its existence is synonymous with its solitude. But, on the grounds that "a race of devils would be propagated upon the earth," Frankenstein destroys the female demon he is in the process of creating, thus destroying yet another potential mother, and the demon promises, "I shall be with you on your wedding-night" (chapter 20). If the demon is the form taken by Frankenstein's flight from the mother, then it is impossible that the demon should itself find an embodied substitute for the mother, and it will prevent Frankenstein from finding one too.

The demon's promise to be present at the wedding night suggests that there is something monstrous about Frankenstein's sexuality. A solipsist's sexuality is monstrous because his desire is for his own envisionings rather than for somebody else, some other body. The demon appears where Frankenstein's wife should be, and its murder of her suggests not so much revenge as jealousy. The demon's murder of that last remaining potential mother makes explicit the sequel to the obviation of the mother, the male quest for substitutes for the mother, the quest that is never intended to be fulfilled. Elizabeth suggests in a letter to Frankenstein that his reluctance to marry may stem from his love for someone else, someone met, perhaps, in his travels or during his long stay in Ingolstadt. "Do you not love another?" she asks (chapter 22). This is in fact the case, for the demon, the creation of Frankenstein's imagination, resembles in many ways the romantic object of desire, the beloved invented to replace, in a less threatening form, the powerful mother who must be killed.[8] This imagined being would be an image of the self, because it is for the sake of the ego that the mother is rejected in the first place. Created right after the death of the mother to be, as Victor says, "a being like myself" (chapter 4), the demon may be Adam, created in God's image. Indeed, this is what the demon thinks when it tells Frankenstein, "I ought to be thy Adam, but I am rather the fallen angel" (chapter 10). But it is also possible, as Gilbert and Gubar suggest, that the demon is Eve, created from Adam's imagination.[9]

When the demon takes shelter in the French cottager's shed, it looks, repeating Milton's Eve's first act upon coming to life, into the mirror of a "clear pool" and is terrified at its own reflection: "I started back" (chapter 12). Here is the relevant passage from Milton, from Eve's narration in Book 4 of her memory of the first moments of her creation.[10] Hearing the "murmuring sound / Of waters issu'd from a Cave and spread / Into a liquid Plain," Eve looks

> into the clear
> Smooth Lake, that to me seem'd another Sky.
> As I bent down to look, just opposite,
> A Shape within the wat'ry gleam appear'd
> Bending to look on me, I started back,
> It started back, but pleas'd I soon return'd . . .
>
> (iv. 453–63)

But the disembodied voice instructs her, "What there thou seest fair Creature is thyself" (l. 468), and tells her to follow and learn to prefer him "whose image thou art" (ll. 471–2). Christine Froula argues that the fiction of Eve's creation by a paternal God out of the flesh of Adam values the maternal and appropriates it for the aggrandisement of masculine creativity.[11] Frankenstein revises this paradigm for artistic creation: he does not so much appropriate the maternal as bypass it, to demonstrate the unnecessariness of natural motherhood and, indeed, of women. Froula points out that in this "scene of canonical instruction," Eve is required to turn away from herself to embrace her new identity, not as a self, but as the image of someone else.[12] Created to the specifications of Adam's desire, we later learn – "Thy likeness, thy fit help, thy other self, / Thy wish, exactly to thy heart's desire" (viii. 450–1) – Eve is, like Frankenstein's demon, the product of imaginative desire. Milton appropriates the maternal by excluding any actual mother from the scene of creation. Eve is the form that Adam's desire takes once actual motherhood has been eliminated; and in much the same way, the demon is the form taken by Frankenstein's desire once his mother and Elizabeth as mother have been circumvented. These new creations in the image of the self are substitutes for the powerful creating mother and place creation under the control of the son.

That the demon is, like Eve, the creation of a son's imaginative desire is confirmed by another allusion both closer to Shelley and closer in the text to Elizabeth's question, "Do you not love another?" Mary Poovey has argued that the novel criticizes romantic egotism, specifically, Percy Shelley's violation of the social conventions that bind humans together in families and societies. As the object of desire of an imaginative overreacher very like Percy Shelley himself, the demon substitutes for the fruitful interchange of family life the fruitlessness of self love, for what Frankenstein loves is an image of himself. The novel was written when Percy Shelley had completed, of all his major works besides *Queen Mab*, only *Alastor*, the archetypal poem of the doomed romantic quest, and it is to this poem that Mary Shelley alludes.[13] Just before Frankenstein receives Elizabeth's letter, just after being acquitted of the murder of his friend Clerval, Frankenstein tells us, "I saw around me nothing but a dense and frightful darkness, penetrated by no light but the glimmer of two eyes that glared upon me" (chapter 21). This is a direct allusion to a passage in *Alastor* in which the hero, who has quested in vain after an ideal female image of his own creation, sees

> two eyes,
> Two starry eyes, hung in the gloom of thought,
> And seemed with their serene and azure smiles
> To beckon him.

(ll. 489–92)

In *Alastor*, these eyes belong to the phantom maiden, the "fleeting shade" whom the hero pursues to his death, a beloved who is constructed out of the poet's own visionary narcissism. The girl he dreams and pursues has a voice "like the voice of his own soul / Heard in the calm of thought" (ll. 153–4), and like him, she is "Herself a poet" (l. 161). In the novel, the starry eyes become glimmering, glaring eyes, alternately the eyes of the dead Clerval and the "watery, clouded eyes of the monster, as I first saw them in my chamber at Ingolstadt" (chapter 21). This conflation of the eyes of the poet's beloved with the eyes of the demon suggests, even more surely than the allusion to Eve, that the demon is the form, not only of Frankenstein's solipsism, of his need to obviate the mother, but also of the narcissism that constitutes the safety of the ego for whose sake the mother is denied. The monster is still the object of Frankenstein's desire when Elizabeth writes to him, just as its creation was the object of his initial quest.[14] It is this monster, the monster of narcissism, that intervenes on the wedding night, substituting Frankenstein's desire for his own imagining for the consummation of his marriage, just as the visionary maiden in *Alastor* takes the place both of the dead Mother Nature of the poet's prologue and of the real maiden the hero meets, attracts, and rejects in the course of his quest.

That the demon is a revision of Eve, of emanations, and of the object of romantic desire, is confirmed by its female attributes. Its very bodiliness, its identification with matter, associates it with traditional concepts of femaleness. Further, the impossibility of Frankenstein giving it a female demon, an object of its own desire, aligns the demon with women, who are forbidden to have their own desires. But if the demon is really a feminine object of desire, why is it a he? I would suggest that this constitutes part of Shelley's exposure of the male romantic economy that would substitute for real and therefore powerful female others a being imagined on the model of the male poet's own self. By making the demon masculine, Shelley suggests that romantic desire seeks to do away, not only with the mother, but also with all females so as to live finally in a world of mirrors that reflect a comforting illusion of the male self's independent wholeness. It is worth noting that just as Frankenstein's desire is for a male demon, Walton too yearns, not for a bride, but for "the company of a man who could sympathize with me, whose eyes would reply to mine" (letter 2).[15]

It may seem peculiar to describe the demon as the object of Frankenstein's romantic desire, since he spends most of the novel suffering from the demon's crimes. Yet in addition to the allusions to Eve and the "fleeting shade" in *Alastor* that suggest this, it is clear that while Frankenstein is in the process of creating the demon, he loves it and desires it; the knowledge that makes possible its creation is the "consummation" of his "toils." It is only when the demon becomes animated that Frankenstein abruptly discovers his loathing for his creation. Even though the demon looks at its creator with what appears to be love, Frankenstein's response to it is unequivocal loathing. Why had he never noticed before the hideousness of its shape and features? No adequate account is given, nor could be, for as we shall see, this is what most mystifies and horrifies Shelley about her own situation. Frankenstein confesses, "I had desired it with an ardour that far exceeded moderation; but now that I had finished, the beauty of the dream vanished, and breathless horror and disgust filled my heart" (chapter 5). The romantic quest is always doomed, for it secretly resists its own fulfillment: although the hero of *Alastor* quests for his dream maiden and dies of not finding her, his encounter with the Indian maid makes it clear that embodiment is itself an obstacle to desire, or more precisely, its termination. Frankenstein's desire for his creation lasts only so long as that creation remains uncreated, the substitution for the too-powerful mother of a figure issuing from his imagination and therefore under his control.

We might say that the predicament of Frankenstein, as of the hero of *Alastor*, is that of the son in Lacan's revision of the Freudian Oedipal crisis. In flight from the body of the mother forbidden by the father, a maternal body that he sees as dead in his urgency to escape it and to enter a paternal order constituted of its distance from the mother, the son seeks figurations that will at once make restitution for the mother and confirm her death and absence by substituting for her figures that are under his control. Fundamentally, the son cannot wish for these figurative substitutes to be embodied, for any *body* is too reminiscent of the mother and is no longer under the son's control, as the demon's excessive strength demonstrates; the value of these figurations is that they remain figurations. In just this way, romantic desire does not desire to be fulfilled, and yet, because it seems both to itself and to others to want to be embodied, the romantic quester as son is often confronted with a body he seems to want but does not.[16] Thus Frankenstein thinks he wants to create the demon, but when he has succeeded, he discovers that what he really enjoyed was the process leading up to the creation, the seemingly endless chain of signifiers that constitute his true, if unrecognized, desire.

Looking at *Alastor* through *Frankenstein*'s reading of it, then, we see that the novel is the story of a hypothetical case: what if the hero of *Alastor* actually got what he thinks he wants? What if desire were embodied, contrary to the poet's deepest wishes? That Shelley writes such a case suggests that this was her own predicament. In real life, Percy Shelley pursued her as the poet and hero of *Alastor* pursue ghosts and as Frankenstein pursues the secrets of the grave. That he courted the adolescent Mary Godwin at the grave of her mother, whose writing he admired, already suggests that the daughter was for him a figure for the safely dead mother, a younger and less powerfully creative version of her. Yet when he got this substitute, he began to tire of her, as he makes quite explicit in *Epipsychidion*, where he is not embarrassed to describe his life in terms of an interminable quest for an imaginary woman. Mary starts out in that poem as one "who seemed / As like the glorious shape which I had dreamed" (ll. 277–8) but soon becomes "that Moon" with "pale and waning lips" (l. 309). The poet does not seem to notice that each time an embodiment of the ideal turns out to be unsatisfactory, it is not because she is the wrong woman, but because the very fact of embodiment inevitably spoils the vision. Emily, the final term in the poem's sequence of women, remains ideal only because she has not yet been possessed, and indeed at the end of the poem, the poet disintegrates and disembodies her, perhaps to save himself from yet one more disappointment. Shelley was for herself never anything but embodied, but for Percy Shelley it seems to have been a grave disappointment to discover her substantiality, and therefore her inadequacy for fulfilling his visionary requirements. *Frankenstein* is the story of what it feels like to be the undesired embodiment of romantic imaginative desire. The demon, rejected merely for being a body, suffers in something of the way that Shelley must have felt herself to suffer under the conflicting demands of romantic desire: on the one hand, that she must embody the goal of Percy's quest, and on the other, his rejection of that embodiment.

Later in the novel, when the demon describes to Frankenstein its discovery and reading of the "journal of the four months that preceded my creation," the discrepancy between Percy's conflicting demands is brought to the fore. The demon notes that the journal records "the whole detail of that series of disgusting circumstances" that resulted in "my accursed origin," and that "the minutest description of my odious and loathsome person is given, in language which painted your own horrors and rendered mine indelible" (chapter 15). This summary suggests that while Frankenstein was writing the journal during the period leading up to the demon's vivification, he was fully aware of his creature's hideousness. Yet Frankenstein, in his own account of the same period, specifically says that it was only when "I had finished, the beauty of the dream vanished, and breathless horror and disgust filled my heart" (chapter 5). If Frankenstein is right about his feelings here, why should his journal be full of "language which painted [his] horrors"? Or, if the account in the journal is correct, if Frankenstein was aware from the start of his creature's "odious and loathsome person," why does he tell Walton that the demon appeared hideous to him only upon its awakening? If the text of this journal is, like *Alastor*, the record of a romantic quest for an object of desire, then the novel is presenting us with two conflicting readings of the poem – Frankenstein's or Percy's and the demon's or Shelley's – confirming our sense that Shelley reading *Alastor* finds in it the story of Percy's failure to find in her the object of his desire, or the story of his desire not to find the object of his desire, not to find that she is the object.

A famous anecdote about the Shelleys from a few days after the beginning of the ghost story contest in which *Frankenstein* originated lends support to this impression of Shelley's experience. Byron was reciting some lines from Coleridge's *Christabel* about Geraldine, who is, like the demon, a composite body, half young and beautiful, half (in the version Byron recited) "hideous, deformed, and pale of hue." Percy, "suddenly shrieking and putting his hands to his head, ran out of the room with a candle." Brought to his senses, he told Byron and Polidori that "he was looking at Mrs. Shelley" while Byron was repeating Coleridge's lines, "and suddenly thought of a woman he had heard of who had eyes instead of nipples."[17] If disembodied eyes are, in *Alastor*, what are so alluring to the hero about his beloved, eyes in place of nipples may have been Percy's hallucination of the horror of having those ideal eyes reembodied in the form of his real lover. This is an embodiment that furthermore calls attention to its failure to be sufficiently different from the mother, whose nipples are for the baby so important a feature. An actual woman, who is herself a mother, does not fit the ideal of disembodied femininity, and the vision of combining real and ideal is a monster. Mary's sense of herself viewed as a collection of incongruent body parts – breasts terminating in eyes – might have found expression in the demon, whose undesirable corporeality is expressed as its being composed likewise of ill-fitting parts. *Paradise Lost, Alastor,* and other texts in this tradition compel women readers to wish to embody, as Eve does, imaginary ideals, to be glad of this role in masculine life; and yet at the same time, they warn women readers that they will suffer for such embodiment.

It requires only a transposing of terms to suggest the relevance of this reading of *Frankenstein* to the myth of language we traced in chapter 1 in its form as the romantic quest. The demon is about the ambivalent response of a woman reader to some of our culture's most compelling statements of woman's place in the myth. That the mother must vanish and be replaced by never quite embodied figures for her is equivalent to the vanishing of the referent (along with that time with the mother when the referent had not vanished) to be replaced by language as figuration that never quite touches its objects. Women's role is to be that silent or lost referent, the literal whose absence makes figuration possible. To be also the figurative substitute for that lost referent is, Shelley shows, impossible, for women are constantly reminded that they are the mother's (loathed, loved) body, and in any case, "being" is incompatible with being a figure. The literal provokes horror in the male poet, or scientist, even while he demands that women literalize his vision.

That Shelley knew she was writing a criticism, not only of women's self-contradictory role in androcentric ontology, but also of the gendered myth of language that is part of that ontology, is suggested by the appearance of a series of images of writing at the very end of the novel. Once again, the demon is the object of Frankenstein's quest, pursued now in hate rather than in love. Frankenstein is preternaturally motivated in his quest by an energy of desire that recalls his passion when first creating the demon, and that his present quest depends on the killing of animals recalls his first quest's dependence on dead bodies. Frankenstein believes that "a spirit of good" follows and directs his steps: "Sometimes, when nature, overcome by hunger, sank under the exhaustion, a repast was prepared for me in the desert that restored and inspirited me. . . . I will not doubt that it was set there by the spirits that I had invoked to aid me" (chapter 24). He says this, however, directly after pointing out that the demon sometimes helped him. Fearing "that if I lost all trace of him I should despair and die, [he] left some mark to guide me," and Frankenstein also notes that the demon would frequently leave "marks in writing on the barks of the trees or cut in stone that guided me and instigated my fury." One of these messages includes the information, "You will find near this place, if you follow not too tardily, a dead hare; eat and be refreshed." Frankenstein, it would seem, deliberately misinterprets the demon's guidance and provisions for him as belonging instead to a spirit of good: his interpretation of the demon's marks and words is so figurative as to be opposite to what they really say. The demon, all body, writes appropriately on the body of nature messages that refer, if to objects at a distance, at least at not a very great distance ("you will find near this place . . ."). Frankenstein, however, reads as figuratively as possible, putting as great a distance as possible between what he actually reads and what he interprets. His reading furthermore puts a distance between himself and the object of his quest, which he still cannot desire to attain; figurative reading would extend indefinitely the pleasure of the quest itself by forever putting off the moment of capture. Just at the moment when Frankenstein thinks he is about to reach the demon, the demon is transformed from a "mark," as if a mark on a page, into a "form," and Frankenstein seeks to reverse this transformation. One of Franken-stein's sled dogs has died of exhaustion, delaying him; "suddenly my eye caught a dark speck upon the dusky plain"; he utters "a wild cry of ecstasy" upon "distinguish[ing] a sledge and the distorted proportions of a well-known form within" (chapter 24). Frankenstein's response, however, is to take an hour's rest: his real aim, which he does not admit, is to keep the demon at the distance where he remains a "dark speck," a mark on the white page of the snow, his signification forever deferred.[18]

At the same time that *Frankenstein* is about a woman writer's response to the ambiguous imperative her culture imposes upon her, it is also possible that the novel concerns a woman writer's anxieties about bearing children, about generating bodies that, as we have seen with reference to *Jane Eyre* and *Wuthering Heights*, would have the power to displace or kill the parent. Ellen Moers first opened up a feminist line of inquiry into the novel by suggesting that it is a "birth myth," that the horror of the demon is Shelley's horror, not only at her own depressing experience of childbirth, but also at her knowledge of the disastrous consequences of giving birth (or of pregnancy itself) for many women in her vicinity.[19] The list is by now familiar to Shelley's readers. First, Mary Wollstonecraft died eleven days after she gave birth to Mary; then, during the time of the writing of the novel, Fanny Imlay, Mary's half-sister, drowned herself in October 1816 when she learned that she was her mother's illegitimate child by Gilbert Imlay; Harriet Shelley was pregnant by another man when she drowned herself in the Serpentine in December 1816; and Claire Clairmont, the daughter of the second Mrs. Godwin, was, scandalously, pregnant by Byron, much to the embarrassment of the Shelleys, with whom she lived.[20] Illegitimate pregnancy, that is, a pregnancy over which the woman has particularly little control, brings either death to the mother in childbirth (Wollstonecraft) or shame, making visible what ought to have remained out of sight, the scene of conception (Claire), a shame that can itself result in the death of both mother (Harriet Shelley) and child (Fanny).

At the time of the conception of the novel, Mary Godwin had herself borne two illegitimate children: the first, an unnamed girl, died four days later, in March 1815; the second was five months old. In December 1816, when Harriet Shelley died and Shelley had finished chapter 4 of the novel, she was pregnant again. With but a single parent, the demon in her novel is the world's most monstrously illegitimate child, and this illegitimate child causes the death of that parent as well as of the principle of motherhood, as we have seen. Read in connection with the history of disastrous illegitimacies, the novel's logic would seem to be this: to give birth to an illegitimate child is monstrous, for it is the inexorable life of these babies, especially those of Mary Wollstonecraft and of Harriet Shelley, that destroys the life of the mother. Subsequently, as Marc Rubenstein argues, the guilty daughter pays for the destruction of her own mother in a fantasy of being destroyed by her own child.[21]

In *Jane Eyre* and *Wuthering Heights*, we saw that the image of childbirth is associated with the uncontrollability of real things. Once a conception has taken objective form, it has the power to destroy its own source, to transform the mother herself into the literal. In the Brontës' novels, childbirth is structurally equivalent to (and indeed also often situated in) the coming true of dreams, which has, like childbirth, an ironic relation to the original conception. Shelley's 1831 introduction to her novel makes a comparable equation of giving birth, the realization of a dream, and writing. As many readers have pointed out, this introduction to her revised version of the novel identifies the novel itself with the demon, and both with a child.[22] She tells of being asked every morning if she had thought of a story, as if a story, like a baby, were necessarily to be conceived in the privacy of the night. And at the close of the introduction she writes, "I bid my hideous progeny go forth and prosper," and she refers to the novel in the next sentence as "the offspring of happy days." The genesis of the novel, furthermore, is in a dream that she transcribes, a dream moreover that is about the coming true of a dream. One night, she says, after listening to conversation about the reanimation of corpses, "Night waned upon this talk. . . . When I placed my head on my pillow I did not sleep, nor could I be said to think. My imagination, unbidden, possessed and guided me." Then follows her account of the famous dream of "the pale student of unhallowed arts kneeling beside the thing he had put together," the "hideous phantasm of a man" stirring "with an uneasy, half-vital motion," and the "artist" sleeping and waking to behold "the horrid thing . . . looking on him with yellow, watery, but speculative eyes." Waking in horror from her dream, she at first tries "to think of something else," but then realizes that she has the answer to her need for a ghost story: " 'What terrified me will terrify others; and I need only describe the spectre which had haunted my midnight pillow.' . . . I began that day with the words, 'It was on a dreary night of November,' making only a transcript of the grim terrors of my waking dream." Making a transcript of a dream – that is, turning an idea into the "machinery of a story" – a dream that is about the transformation of a "phantasm" into a real body, is equivalent here to conceiving a child. She makes it very clear that her dream takes the place of a sexual act ("Night waned. . . . When I placed my head on my pillow . . . I saw the pale student."), just as the book idea she can announce the next day substitutes for a baby. The terrifying power of the possibility that her dream might be true encodes the terrifying power of conception and childbirth. In Deutsch's language, "she who has created this new life must obey its power; its rule is expected, yet invisible, implacable."[23]

Despite Ellen Moers's delineation of the resemblance of the demon to the apprehensions a mother might have about a baby, it is the introduction that supplies the most explicit evidence for identifying demon and book with a child. Mary Poovey has demonstrated that this introduction has a significantly different ideological cast from the original version of the novel (or even from the revised novel). Written in 1831, fourteen years after the novel itself and following the death of Percy Shelley (as well as the deaths of both the children who were alive or expected in 1816–17), the introduction takes pains to distance itself from the novel, and it aims to bring the writing of the novel further within the fold of the conventional domestic life Shelley retrospectively substitutes for the radically disruptive life she in fact led.[24] Referring obliquely to her elopement with Percy and its effect on her adolescent habit of inventing stories, for example, she writes, "After this my life became busier, and reality stood in place of fiction." Echoed later by Robert Southey's remark to Charlotte Brontë, that "literature cannot be the business of a woman's life," Shelley's busyness refers largely to her responsibilities as a mother and wife. When she describes her endeavor to write a ghost story she repeats this term for family responsibility: "I busied myself *to think of a story*." This echo suggests that her busyness with story writing is somehow congruent with, not in conflict with, her "busier" life as a wife and mother. It makes the novel, "so very hideous an idea," seem somehow part of the busy life of a matron. It is this effort, to domesticate her hideous idea, that may be at the bottom of her characterizing it as a "hideous progeny." If the novel read in this light seems, like *Jane Eyre* and *Wuthering Heights*, to be full of a horror of childbirth, that may only be the result of the impossibility of changing the basic story of the 1817 novel, the result of assembling mismatched parts.

Thus the novel may be about the horror associated with motherhood, yet this reading seems unduly influenced by the superimpositions of the introduction, and furthermore it ignores the novel's most prominent feature, that the demon is not a child born of woman but the creation of a man.[25] Most succinctly put, the novel is about the collision between androcentric and gynocentric theories of creation, a collision that results in the denigration of maternal childbearing through its circumvention by male creation. The novel presents Mary Shelley's response to the expectation, manifested in such poems as *Alastor* or *Paradise Lost*, that women embody and yet not embody male fantasies. At the same time, it expresses a woman's knowledge of the irrefutable independence of the body, both her own and those of the children that she produces, from projective male fantasy. While a masculine being – God, Adam, Percy Shelley, Frankenstein – may imagine that his creation of an imaginary being may remain under the control of his desires, Mary Shelley knows otherwise, both through her experience as mistress and wife of Percy and through her experience of childbirth. Shelley's particular history shows irrefutably that children, even pregnancies, do not remain under the control of those who conceive them.

Keats writes that "the Imagination may be compared to Adam's dream – he awoke and found it truth."[26] In *Paradise Lost*, narrating his recollection of Eve's creation, Adam describes how he fell into a special sleep – "Mine eyes he clos'd, but op'n left the Cell / Of Fancy my internal sight" (viii. 460–1) – then watched, "though sleeping," as God formed a creature,

> Manlike, but different sex, so lovely fair,
> That what seem'd fair in all the World, seem'd now
> Mean, or in her summ'd up.

(viii. 471–3)

This is "Adam's dream." But what of "he awoke and found it truth"? Adam wakes, "To find her, or for ever to deplore / Her loss" (ll. 479–80), and then, "behold[s] her, not far off, / Such as I saw her in my dream" (ll. 481–2), yet what Keats represses is that the matching of reality to dream is not so neat as these lines suggest.[27] Eve comes to Adam, not of her own accord, but "Led by her Heav'nly Maker" (l. 485), and as soon as he catches sight of her, Adam sees Eve turn away from him, an action he ascribes to modesty (and thus endeavors to assimilate to his dream of her) but that Eve, in Book 4, has already said stemmed from her preference for her image in the water. Though designed by God for Adam "exactly to thy heart's desire" (viii. 451), Eve once created has a mind and will of her own, and this independence is so horrifying to the male imagination that the Fall is ascribed to it.

It is neither the visionary male imagination alone that Mary Shelley protests, then, nor childbirth itself, but the circumvention of the maternal creation of new beings by the narcissistic creations of male desire. While Keats can gloss over the discrepancy between Adam's dream and its fulfillment, Shelley cannot. As Frankenstein is on the verge of completing the female demon, it is for her resemblance to Eve that he destroys her. Just as Adam says of Eve, "seeing me, she turn'd" (viii. 507), Frankenstein fears the female demon's turning from the demon toward a more attractive image: "She also might turn with disgust from him to the superior beauty of man" (chapter 20). Also like Eve, who disobeys a prohibition agreed upon between Adam and God before her creation, she "might refuse to comply with a compact made before her creation," the demon's promise to leave Europe. Frankenstein typifies the way in which the biological creation of necessarily imperfect yet independent beings has always been made to seem, within an androcentric economy, monstrous and alarming. Although Mary Wollstonecraft would in any case have died of puerperal fever after Mary's birth, her earlier pregnancy with Fanny and the pregnancies of Harriet Shelley, Claire Clairmont, and Mary Godwin would have done no harm had they not been labeled "illegitimate" by a society that places a premium on the ownership by a man of his wife's body and children. The novel criticizes, not childbirth itself, but the male horror of independent embodiment. This permits us to speculate that the horror of childbirth in *Jane Eyre* and *Wuthering Heights* stems from the Brontës' identification with an androcentric perspective. To a certain extent, as a writer in a culture that defines writing as a male activity and as opposite to motherhood, Shelley too must share the masculine perspective, with its horror of embodiment and its perennial re-enacting of Adam's affront at Eve's turning away. For whatever reason, however, perhaps because of her direct experience of the mother's position, Shelley is able to discern the androcentrism in her culture's view of the relation of childbearing to writing, and thus she enables us to interpret her own painful exposure of it.

At the site of the collision between motherhood and romantic projection another form of literalization appears as well. While it is important how Shelley reads texts such as *Alastor* and *Paradise Lost*, it is also important to consider, perhaps more simply, that her novel reads them. Like the Brontës' novels, whose Gothic embodiments of subjective states, realizations of dreams, and literalized figures all literalize romantic projection, Shelley's novel literalizes romantic imagination, but with a different effect and to a different end. Shelley criticizes these texts by enacting them, and because enactment or embodiment is both the desire and the fear of such texts, the mode of her criticism matters. Just as the heroes of these poems seem to seek, but do not seek, embodiments of their visionary desires, these poetic texts seem to seek embodiment in "the machinery of a story." For in the ideology of postromantic culture, it is part of a woman's duty to transcribe and give form to men's words, just as it is her duty to give form to their desire, or birth to their seed, no matter how ambivalently men may view the results of such projects. In the same passage in the introduction to the novel in which Shelley makes the analogy between the book and a child, between the conception of a story and the conception of a baby, and between these things and the coming true of a dream, she also identifies all these projects with the transcription of important men's words. Drawing on the ideology of maternity as the process of passing on a male idea, Shelley describes her book–child as the literalization of two poets' words:

> Many and long were the conversations between Lord Byron and Shelley to which I was a devout but nearly silent listener. During one of these, various philosophical doctrines were discussed, and among others the nature of the principle of life, and whether there was any probability of its ever being discovered and communicated.... Perhaps a corpse would be reanimated; galvanism had given token of such things: perhaps the component parts of a creature might be manufactured, brought together, and endued with vital warmth.

Directly following this passage appears her account of going to bed and vividly dreaming of the "student of unhallowed arts" and the "hideous phantasm," the dream of which she says she made "only a transcript" in transferring it into the central scene of her novel, the dream that equates the conception of a book with the conception of a child.

Commentators on the novel have in the past taken Shelley at her word here, believing, if not in her story of transcribing a dream, then certainly in her fiction of transcribing men's words.[28] Mario Praz, for example, writes, "All Mrs. Shelley did was to provide a passive reflection of some of the wild fantasies which, as it were, hung in the air about her."[29] Harold Bloom suggests that "what makes *Frankenstein* an important book" despite its "clumsiness" is "that it contains one of the most vivid versions we have of the Romantic mythology of the self, one that resembles Blake's *Book of Urizen*, Shelley's *Prometheus Unbound*, and Byron's *Manfred*, among other works."[30] It is part of the subtlety of her strategy to disguise her criticism of such works as a passive transcription, to appear to be a docile wife and "devout listener" to the conversations of important men. Indeed, central to her critical method is the practice of acting out docilely what these men tell her they want from her, to show them the consequences of their desires. She removes herself beyond reproach for "putting [her]self forward," by formulating her critique as a devout transcription, a "passive reflection," a "version" that "resembles." She inserts this authorial role into her novel in the form of a fictive M. S., Walton's sister, Margaret Saville, to whom his letters containing Frankenstein's story are sent and who silently records and transmits them to the reader.

Now that we have assembled the parts of Shelley's introductory account of the novel's genesis, we can see that she equates childbearing with the bearing of men's words. Writing a transcript of a dream that was in turn merely the transcript of a conversation is also giving birth to a hideous progeny conceived in the night. The conversation between Byron and Shelley probably represents Shelley's and Byron's poetry, the words, for example, of *Alastor* that she literalizes in her novel. That the notion of motherhood as the passive transcription of men's words is at work here is underscored by the allusion this idea makes to the Christ story. "Perhaps a corpse would be reanimated" refers initially, not to science's power, but to that occasion, a myth but surely still a powerful one even in this den of atheists, when a corpse was reanimated, which is in turn an allusion to the virgin birth. Like the creations of Adam and Eve, which excluded the maternal, Christ's birth bypassed the normal channels of procreation. It is this figure, whose birth is also the literalization of a masculine God's Word, who serves as the distant prototype for the reanimation of corpses. And within the fiction, the demon too is the literalization of a word, an idea, Frankenstein's theory given physical form. As Joyce Carol Oates remarks, the demon "is a monster-son born of Man exclusively, a parody of the Word or Idea made Flesh."[31] The book–baby literalizes Shelley's and Byron's words, the words of their conversation as figures for Shelley's words in *Alastor*, just as the demon-baby literalizes Frankenstein's inseminating words. Christ literalizes God's Word through the medium of a woman, Mary, who passively transmits Word into flesh without being touched by it. Literalizations again take place through the medium of a more recent Mary, who passively transcribes (or who seems to), who adds nothing but "the platitude of prose" and "the machinery of a story" to the words of her more illustrious male companions who for their own writing prefer "the music of the most melodious verse." And yet, as we will see again with Eliot's *The Mill on the Floss*, it is precisely the adding of this "machinery," which would seem only to facilitate the transmission of the ideas and figures of poetry into the more approachable form of a story, that subverts and reverses what it appears so passively to serve.

The demon literalizes the male romantic poet's desire for a figurative object of desire, but it also literalizes the literalization of male literature. While telling Frankenstein the story of its wanderings and of its education by the unknowing cottagers, the demon reports having discovered in the woods "a leathern portmanteau containing ... some books. I eagerly seized

the prize and returned with it to my hovel" (chapter 15). The discovery of
these books – *Paradise Lost*, Plutarch's *Lives*, and *The Sorrows of Werther* – is
followed in the narrative, but preceded in represented time, by the demon's
discovery of another book, Frankenstein's "journal of the four months that
preceded [the demon's] creation."[32] Both *Frankenstein*, the book as baby, and
the demon as baby literalize these books, especially *Paradise Lost* – the
demon is Satan, Adam, and Eve, while Frankenstein himself is Adam, Satan,
and God – as well as a number of other prior texts, among them, as we
have seen, *Alastor*, but also the book of Genesis, Coleridge's "Rime of the
Ancient Mariner," Aeschylus's *Prometheus Bound*, Wordsworth's "Tintern
Abbey," William Godwin's *Caleb Williams*, and many others. At the same
time and in the same way, the demon is the realization of Frankenstein's
words in the journal of his work on the demon, a journal that is in some
ways equivalent to (or a literalization of) *Alastor*, since both record a
romantic quest for what was "desired . . . with an ardor that far exceeded
moderation." The demon, wandering about the woods of Germany carrying
these books, the book of his own physical origin and the texts that
contribute to his literary origin, embodies the very notion of literalization
with which everything about him seems to be identified. To carry a book is
exactly what Mary Shelley does in bearing the words of the male authors, in
giving birth to a hideous progeny that is at once book and demon. Carrying
the books of his own origin, the demon emblematizes the literalization of
literature that Shelley, through him, practices.

I pointed out earlier that Mary Shelley, unlike the Brontës, would not see
childbirth itself as inherently threatening apart from the interference in it by
a masculine economy. Likewise, writing or inventing stories is not inherently
monstrous – witness her retrospective account in the introduction of how,
before her life became "busier," she used to "commune with the creatures
of my fancy" and compose unwritten stories out of doors: "It was beneath
the trees of the grounds belonging to our house, or on the bleak sides of
the woodless mountains near, that my true compositions, the airy flights of
my imagination, were born and fostered." Like both Cathys in *Wuthering
Heights* in their childhood, indeed, probably like the young Brontës themselves, Mary Shelley's imagination prior to the fall into the Law of the
Father – in her case, elopement, pregnancy, and marriage – is at one with
nature and also does not require to be written down. The metaphor of
composition as childbirth – "my true compositions . . . were born and
fostered" – appears here as something not only harmless but celebratory. It
is only when both childbirth and a woman's invention of stories are
subordinated to the Law of the Father that they become monstrous; it is
only when such overpowering and masculinist texts as Genesis, *Paradise Lost*,
and *Alastor* appropriate this Mary's body, her female power of embodiment,
as vehicle for the transmission of their words, that monsters are born. When

God appropriates maternal procreation in Genesis or *Paradise Lost*, a beautiful object is created; but through the reflex of Mary Shelley's critique, male circumvention of the maternal creates a monster. Her monster constitutes a criticism of such appropriation and circumvention, yet it is a criticism written in her own blood, carved in the very body of her own victimization, just as the demon carves words about death in the trees and rocks of the Arctic. She is powerless to stop her own appropriation and can only demonstrate the pain that appropriation causes in the woman reader and writer.

NOTES

1   Poovey (1984) 114–42. Hereafter I will refer to Mary Shelley as Shelley (except where her unmarried name is necessary for clarity) and to her husband as Percy.
2   Gilbert and Gubar's reading of the novel focuses on its "apparently docile submission to male myths" and identifies it specifically as "a fictionalized rendition of the meaning of *Paradise Lost* to women" (Gilbert and Gubar (1979) 219, 221). Although my interest in Shelley as a reader of prior, masculine texts, as well as some of my specific points about the novel's reading of Milton, overlaps with theirs, I am putting these concerns to uses different from theirs.
3   For example, Kiely writes that Frankenstein "seeks to combine the role of both parents in one, to eliminate the need for the woman in the creative act, to make sex unnecessary" (Kiely (1972) 164). Rubenstein remarks on "the series of motherless family romances which form the substance of Frankenstein's past" (Rubenstein (1976) 177). The general argument of his psychoanalytic reading of the novel is that the novel represents Shelley's quest for her own dead mother. Knoepflmacher, in the course of arguing that the novel portrays a daughter's rage at her parents, mentions "the novel's attack on a male's usurpation of the role of mother" (Knoepflmacher (1979) 105). Jacobus writes that "the exclusion of woman from creation symbolically 'kills' the mother" ("Is There a Woman in This Text?" (1982–3) 131). Johnson suggests that the novel focuses on "eliminations of the mother" as well as on "the fear of somehow effecting the death of one's own parents" (Barbara Johnson (1982) 9). Froula's argument about the maternal in Milton, although it focuses on the author's appropriation of the maternal for masculine creativity (as differentiated from its circumvention or elimination) helped to stimulate my thinking. See Froula (1983) 321–47.
4   I am following, in this reading, the 1831 revised text of the novel; in the 1818 version, Elizabeth is Frankenstein's cousin. All quotations from the novel will be from the Signet edition (Mary Shelley, *Frankenstein* (1965)), which prints the text of 1831. Future references will be cited in the text by chapter number or by letter number for the letters that precede the chapter sequence. See also James Reiger's edition of the 1818 version, with revisions of 1823 and 1831 (1982).
5   Rubenstein notes the sexual nature of Walton's quest, as well as the maternal associations of those aspects of nature on which Frankenstein carries out his

research (Rubenstein (1976) 174–5, 177). Kiely (1972) 162–3 notes the necrophilia of the passage from *Alastor*'s invocation to Mother Nature, and suggests its similarity to Frankenstein's "penetrating the recesses of nature."

6 Quoted p. 149; Frankenstein quotes lines 76–83 of the poem, altering the original "haunted *me* like a passion" to fit a third person.

7 In the context of arguing that the novel critiques the bourgeois family, Ellis shows that Frankenstein's mother passes on to Elizabeth her "view of the female role as one of constant, self-sacrificing devotion to others," and she suggests that "Elizabeth's early death, like her adopted mother's, was a logical outgrowth of the female ideal she sought to embody" (Kate Ellis (1979) 131). My argument would explain why what created this "female ideal" also determined the interchangeability of mother and daughter.

8 Harold Bloom suggests the resemblance between the demon and Blake's emanations or Shelley's epipsyche, in his afterword to the Signet edition of the novel, 215. The essay is reprinted in *Ringers in the Tower* (1971) 119–29. Peter Brooks makes a similar point when he writes, "fulfillment with Elizabeth would mark Frankenstein's achievement of a full signified in his life, accession to plenitude of being – which would leave no place in creation for his daemonic projection, the Monster" (Peter Brooks (1978) 599). Ellis also suggests, though for different reasons, that the demon is a representative for Elizabeth (Kate Ellis (1979) 136). Jacobus writes that Frankenstein "exchang[es] a woman for a monster," and she discusses Frankenstein's preference for imagined over actual beings (Jacobus (1982–3) 131).

9 Gilbert and Gubar suggest first that "the part of Eve *is* all the parts" and then discuss at length the demon's resemblance to Eve (Gilbert and Gubar (1979) 230, 235–44). However, in describing this resemblance, they focus primarily on the patriarchal rejection of women's bodies as deformed and monstrous, as well as on Eve's motherlessness, but not, as I do here, on Eve as Adam's imaginative projection. Joyce Carol Oates also suggests the demon's resemblance to Eve, also using the scene I am about to discuss (Oates (1984) 547).

10 Quotations from *PL* are from Milton (1957). Other critics have noted Shelley's allusion to this Miltonic scene; see, e.g., Peter Brooks (1978) 595.

11 Froula writes, "Through the dream of the rib Adam both enacts a parody of birth and gains possession of the womb by claiming credit for woman herself." Milton, she goes on to argue, reenacts Adam's solution to his "womb envy" by analogously repressing female power in his account of the origin of his poem: "The male Logos called upon to articulate the cosmos against an abyss of female silence overcomes the anxieties generated by the tension between visible maternity and invisible paternity by appropriating female power to itself in a parody of parthenogenesis" (Froula (1983) 332, 338; and see passim 326–40).

12 Ibid., 326–8.

13 All quotations from Shelley's verse are from *SPP*.

14 Gilbert and Gubar also discuss narcissistic love in the novel, although with reference only to the potentially incestuous relation between Frankenstein and Elizabeth, not with reference to the demon (Gilbert and Gubar (1979) 229). My reading would suggest that Frankenstein's relation to Elizabeth is far less

narcissistic than his relation to the demon; in his descriptions of Elizabeth, he focuses on her difference from him, which is what I believe makes her like the mother and therefore threatening.

15 Jaya Mehta pointed out to me the significance of this aspect of Walton, in a seminar paper at Yale in 1984.

16 Kiely discusses "the sheer concreteness" of the demon, though his concern is with the mismatching between ideal and real in the novel (Kiely (1972) 161).

17 Polidori (1911) 128–9, entry for 18 June 1816. Cited also by Rubenstein, who reads it as a story about "maternal reproach" and connects it with Frankenstein's dream of his dead mother (Rubenstein (1976) 184–5). I am grateful to Marina Leslie for her discussion of this episode in a seminar paper at Yale in 1984.

18 Peter Brooks's (1978) essay on *Frankenstein* also connects the plot of desire with the plot of language in the novel, but to a somewhat different effect. Brooks argues that the demon's acquisition of the "godlike science" of language places him within the symbolic order. Trapped at first, like any baby, within the specular order of the imaginary, the demon is first judged only by its looks; it is only when it masters the art of rhetoric that the monster gains sympathy. But, Brooks continues, despite the promise that the symbolic seems to hold, the monster's failure to find an object of love removes its life from the signifying "chain" of human interconnectedness and makes of it instead a "miserable series," in which one signifier refers always to another with "no point of arrest." Thus Brooks sees the monster as a dark and exaggerated version of all life within the symbolic, where desire is never satisfied and where there is no transcendental signified. Although I agree with much of what Brooks writes, I would argue that in its materiality and its failure to acquire an object of desire, the demon enters the symbolic primarily as the (dreaded) referent, not as signifier. The negative picture of the demon's materiality is a product of its female place in the symbolic, and not of any lingering in the realm of the imaginary (which Brooks, with other readers of Lacan, views as tragic). I would also argue that the novel presents, not a vision of the condition of human signification, but a targeted criticism of those in whose interests the symbolic order constitutes itself in the ways that it does.

19 Moers (1977) 140.

20 Ibid., 145–7.

21 This is the general tendency of Rubenstein's argument, carrying the material Moers presents into a psychoanalytic frame.

22 See Rubenstein (1976) 168, 178–81; Poovey (1984) 138–42.

23 Deutsch (1945) 215.

24 One of the central tenets of Poovey's argument concerns Shelley's endeavour in her 1831 revisions to make the novel more conservative, more in keeping with a proto-Victorian ideology of the family (Poovey (1984) 133–42). Poovey argues, however, that both versions of the novel oppose romantic egotism's assault on the family.

25 Gilbert and Gubar assert as part of their argument that everyone in the novel is Eve, that "Frankenstein has a baby," and that, as a consequence, he becomes female (Gilbert and Gubar (1979) 232). I would argue, to the contrary, that

Frankenstein's production of a new life is pointedly masculine, that it matters to the book that he is a man circumventing childbirth, not a woman giving birth.

26   Letter of 22 November 1817 to Benjamin Bailey, in Keats, *Letters* (1970) 37.

27   I am indebted to Suzanne Raitt for her discussion of this point in a seminar at Yale in 1984.

28   Rubenstein also argues that Shelley deliberately created the impression that she merely recorded Percy and Byron's conversation as part of a project to make her creativity seem as passive and maternal as possible. He discusses at length the analogy she sets up between conceiving a child and conceiving a book, and he specifically suggests that the men's words in conversation are like men's role in procreation, which was, in the early nineteenth century, thought to involve the man actively and the woman only passively: "She is trying to draw for us a picture of her imagination as a passive womb, inseminated by those titans of romantic poetry" (Rubenstein (1976) 181). I would agree with everything Rubenstein says, although I am using this idea for a somewhat different purpose: he is using it to show how the novel is about Shelley's effort to make restitution for her dead mother.

29   Praz (1933) 114. Cited by Moers and also by Rubenstein in support of his argument discussed in note 28 above.

30   Harold Bloom, "Afterword," *Frankenstein*, (1965) 215. It is worth noting that *Frankenstein* preceded *Prometheus Unbound* and was of course written in ignorance of the *Book of Urizen*.

31   Oates (1984) 552.

32   Gilbert and Gubar, who focus much of their argument on Shelley's reading of *Paradise Lost*, connect that reading to the demon's reading of the poem, as well as connecting Shelley's listening to her husband and Byron with the demon's listening to the De Laceys.

16

John Clare in Babylon

TOM PAULIN

John Clare wrote before the long ice age of standard British English clamped down on the living language and began to break its local and vernacular energies. The damage to English liberty for which that change in the cultural climate is responsible has yet to be assessed, but from Tennyson to the poets of the Movement and beyond we can see how a dead official language and a centralizing conformity have worked to obliterate individual speech communities. Now, as the hegemony of Official Standard relaxes, Clare's poetry emerges like a soodling stream. Listening to his unique and delicate sound-patterns the reader is caught in the blow-back of an immense historical suffering, and glimpses what happens when an oral culture is destroyed by the institutions of law, order, printed texts. Clare ought to have been the English Burns, but as John Lucas has remarked he is a great poet who has for a long time "been more or less invisible." He is a non-person, as anonymous as the grass he identified his social class, himself and his language with:

> – So where old marble citys stood
> Poor persecuted weeds remain
> She feels a love for little things
> That very few can feel beside
> & still the grass eternal springs
> Where castles stood & grandeur died

The closing lines of "The Flitting" are partly Clare's reply to those critics who believed he had coined words which were instead "as common around me as the grass under my feet." Though ostensibly a poem about the personal trauma of moving house, it speaks for the experience of being evicted by the economic and legal force of what E. P. Thompson calls, in his account of the effect of Enclosure on the field labourers, "an alien culture and an alien power." We wrong Clare's writing if we regard it as the timeless lyric product of purely personal experience – his language is always part of a social struggle, entangled with and pitched against Official Standard.

Clare emerges for readers in this society as a displaced, marginalized poet whose reputation is being gradually rehabilitated – as Mandelstam's is in the Soviet Union. It may be many years, though, before his name is given the kind of official recognition which is accorded Wordsworth and Keats, and only when social readings of poetic texts have become generally accepted is it likely that his work will be widely read and studied. But it could be that Clare – shy, feral, intensely gifted – will never be redeemed from all the neglect and mutilation he has suffered. Like Mad Sweeney in Seamus Heaney's *Sweeney Astray*, he is a persecuted and derelict figure, a refugee in his own country:

> fallen almost through death's door,
> drained out, spiked and torn,
> under a hard-twigged bush,
> the brown, jaggy hawthorn.

Clare's suffering is both personal and social because he speaks for all those victims of the Enclosure Acts which transformed rural England in the early decades of the last century. He compares Enclosure to a "Buonoparte" intent on destroying everything; like Stalin's collectivization of agriculture, Enclosure was a form of violent and centrally-directed social engineering. It was the Great Displacement – the crushing of a social class by market forces and political interests.

The social forces that were to lift Clare up and then destroy him are prefigured in that flattered sense of alienation he describes five days after the publication of his first book, *Poems Descriptive of Rural Life and Scenery*. Writing to his friend Octavius Gilchrist on 21 January 1820, Clare includes an "Address to a Copy of 'Clares Poems' Sent O. Gilchrist Esqr" – a piece of light verse in which he imagines *Poems Descriptive* being given a gold-tooled binding. The actual volume is "plain & simple" like its author, but the "gilded coat" it may receive will elevate it beyond Clare's social position, rather like an upwardly mobile son leaving his illiterate labouring father behind. Clare's father, like his mother and his wife, was illiterate, but the literate Clare is recognizing here that he is just as trapped as they are. Addressing his printed text, he says:

> L–d knows I couldnt help but laugh
> To see ye fixt among yer betters

Upon the learned shelves set off
& flasht about wi golden letters

and he concludes by saying that if he and this sparky, proud volume happened to meet, the gilded book would "turn thy nose up wi' disdain/& thinkt disgrace thy dad to own." This means that his reputation – symbolized by the notional gold binding – must always run ahead of him while he stays stuck where he is. He is not worthy of his own work and must always be a stranger in the society which has created his reputation. He is therefore writing against himself. (There is a similar recognition in Heaney's "Digging" that the process of writing and publication necessitates a break with the ancestral agrarian society.) Oral tradition enters the metropolitan world of printed texts, but for Clare nothing is changed – the fruit of his labour disowns him, and he exists only as a type of abject advertisement for a commodity labelled *Poems Descriptive of Rural Life and Scenery*. The good, the great and the chic may come to visit him: "they will not let me keep quiet as I usd to be – they send for me twice & 3 times a day out of the fields & I am still the strangers poppet Show what can their fancys create to be so anxious & so obstinate of being satisfied I am but a man (& a little one too) like others." But Clare feels lacerated by their attentions, a puppet knocked about by audience, publishing industry and the reactions of the local community to his sudden fame. His gift has taken him away from that community and he begins to lose his sense of dwelling in the world – that "essence of dwelling" which Heidegger discusses in his essay "Building Dwelling Thinking." It is this ontological theme that Clare shares with Emily Dickinson and Elizabeth Bishop.

As Edward Storey demonstrates in his biography of Clare, the Stamford bookseller Edward Drury helped to initiate the process of Clare's alienation. Drury was among the first people to notice Clare's talent, and he took a bluntly practical view of the commodity-value of his poems. Writing to his cousin, the publisher John Taylor, Drury said in June 1819 that he regarded Clare's manuscript poems "as wares that I have bought which will find a market in the great city. I want a broker or a partner to whom I can consign or share the articles I receive from the manufacturer." Six months later, on 16 January 1820, *Poems Descriptive of Rural Life and Scenery* went on sale and Clare was propelled into polite society. It is painful to watch his spirit being racked by that terrible numbing English deference. Writing letters to the educated and powerful, he concludes, "I am Respected Sir Your Gratful Servant John Clare." He calls himself a "Pheasant" and a "Clown" and trembles under the mind-blowing attentions of bishops and aristocrats: "I send you some of the principal Subscribers which I have procured lately: the first of which is a Baronet!!!"

This is the opening sentence of Clare's first extant letter, and those stunned exclamation marks point to the spiked trap Clare fell into – his success set him apart from his own community, while the system of patronage and publishing which created him could offer nothing but a fitfully marketable public image. The bare, nervous human being experienced this public attention as "all the cold apathy of killing kindness that has numbed me." It is little wonder the strain destroyed him. Like the badger in one of his finest poems, Clare felt hunted, torn and persecuted, a harmless victim of social violence.

To approach Clare's experience we need to see the English class system as a type of apartheid, a form of segregation which made Clare feel like a black slave chained in a plantation. Clare believed that slavery was "disgraceful to a country professing religion," and it would seem that at some level he felt himself to be a slave who had mistaken the brief kiss of fame for a lasting manumission. But Clare was initially no radical – "I am as far as my politics reaches 'King & Country' " – and it is clear that he tried to square his conservatism with the upsetting facts of his social experience. He became obsessed by an episode in which he had addressed a stranger in Drury's bookshop as he might anyone else. The stranger turned out to be the Marquis of Exeter and Clare transformed their terse, equal speech-encounter into a "cursed blunder," a shocking solecism that haunted him like damnation.

The agrarian unrest of the 1830s seriously disturbed Clare, and in January 1831 he praised Viscount Althorp, the leader of the House of Commons and one of the chief supporters of the Reform Bill. Clare hoped that the government might be able to "find out the way to better the unbearable oppressions of the labouring classes," and he was divided between a fear of revolution and his identification with his own class. He tells Taylor that "the 'people' as they are called were a year or two back as harmless as flies – they did not seem even to be susceptible of injustice but when insult began to be tried upon them by the unreasonable & the proud their blood boiled into a volcano & the irruption is as certain as death if no remedy can be found to relieve them." Tennyson was at this time an undergraduate at Cambridge, where he paraded armed with a club and helped put out fires that had been started by rebellious labourers. Yet it would be wrong to see Clare and Tennyson as being politically very far apart – both believed in reform, and they shared a similar patriotism. However, they were thousands of miles apart *socially*, and it is the sense of an absolute social divide which weighs on Clare in his letters. That divide is the real *néant*, a "bottomless" void between the classes which the "clown" stared into and was destroyed by.

Clare lived through and was spiritually damaged by the change from the free space of the open-field system to the reticulated, boxed-in pattern of fields which Enclosure created. Two million acres of wild land were also enclosed, and this seizure of "the common heath" traumatized Clare. It is difficult for us nowadays to register that shock, but a visit to the village of Laxton in Nottinghamshire, the last surviving example of the feudal open-field system, does help towards an understanding of the great change that hit Clare's community. To walk along a wide chalky track through gently sloping, hedgeless ploughland is to step out of the owned space of fenced and protected private property into what feels like a free, almost floating environment. You are in touch with land and space and sky, and that sense of natural freedom depends on the absence of barriers and partitions. Here you can sense what England used to be like – there is a kind of hum or buzz in the place that feels very precious and fragile. Once out of it you are pushed back against that artificially "natural" world of thick hedges and rectangles which our ordinary experience tells us has been there always, eternally. The transition back into the enclosed world brings with it a certain sense of glumness and suffocation that is like the last memory-trace of a deep social trauma.

During his years in Northampton General Lunatic Asylum, Clare saw himself as being locked in the "purgatoriall hell & French Bastile of English liberty," and from his corner of that hell the Ranter convert denounced "English priestcraft & english bondage more severe then the slavery of Egypt & Affrica." For all the tough, desperate moderation of Clare's professed social opinions in the pre-asylum years, his political subconsciousness is a territory of primal hurt and bondage where something wild – some uniquely sensitive spirit – tries to jeuk away from all institutions. With its lack of punctuation, freedom from standard spelling and its charged demotic ripples, Clare's writing becomes a form of Nation Language beating its head against the walls of urbane, polished Official Standard. This is apparent in a letter to Taylor where Clare first strategically praises his publisher's editorial improvements and then adds, "you cross'd '*gulsh'd*' I think the word expressive but doubt its a provincialism it means tearing or thrusting up with great force take it or leave it as you please." Between "gulsh'd" and "gushed" there is a wide social gap that is like the distinction between hollow charm and a real social force, one that desperately wants to burst through all types of barriers and enclosures. Clare's ambition is Joycean – flying through the nets of class, race, religion, monolingualism – and it is a strange coincidence that Clare and James Joyce's daughter Lucia should both have ended their days in that asylum in Northampton.

Ten years after his attempt to protect "gulsh'd" from extinction, Clare wrote to Taylor that he was "astonied" at finding words in "chaucer that are very common now in what is called the mouths of the vulgar." This is the reverse perception of that gold binding which Clare had imagined for *Poems Descriptive* and it shows him beginning to feel a confidence in his own language that Chaucer as literary institution, a well of ethnically pure English, had previously helped rob him of. Clare's identity is created in and through the language he uses, and is then distorted by the changes forced on him by the need to tame that language in order to sell the poems it speaks.

Lord Radstock and other patrons insisted that Clare rid his poems of "radical slang" and ungrateful social sentiments, so the battle between the two nations is fought out in business correspondence about Clare's grammar and use of common speech. Taylor edits, shapes and sometimes rewrites Clare's poems, sends them back, and Clare replies, "your verse is a develish puzzle I may alter but I cannot mend grammer in learning is like Tyranny in government." His identification of this unfettered but precise language with English liberty is sometimes made through the figure of William Cobbett, whose writings Clare admired and to whose *Grammar of the English Language* he often referred. When we consider contemporary reactions to Clare's language we can see that every non-standard word he used could provoke a class anxiety and fear. That sense of threat is apparent in a reviewer's reaction to *The Shepherd's Calendar*:

> We had not, however, perused many pages before we discovered that our self-suspicions were wholly groundless. Wretched taste, poverty of thought, and unintelligible phraseology, for some time appeared its only characteristics. There was nothing, perhaps, which more pro-voked our spleen than the want of a glossary; for, without such an assistance, how could we perceive the fitness and beauty of such words as – *crizzling* – *sliveth* – *whinneys* – *greening* – *tootles* – *croodling* – *hings* – *progged* – *spindling* – *siling* – *struttles* – &c. &c.

Those words have a beautifully intimate quality; each is a unique subversion of the uptight efficiency of Official Standard, and the reviewer rejects them in an angrily institutional manner, crushing them savagely under his heels like so many snails.

This constriction of language was paralleled by the enclosure of the countryside, and several years before mental illness set in Clare is already imagining himself trapped in Babylon. He encloses an imitation of the 137th Psalm in a letter to Taylor:

> By Babels streams we sat & sighed
>   Yea we in sorrow wept
> To think of Sions former pride
>   That now in ruin slept
>
> Our Harps upon the willows hung
>   Cares silenced every string
> Our woes unheeded & unsung
>   No hearts had we to sing

> For they that made us captive there
> & did us all the wrong
> Insulted us in our despair
> & asked us for a song

In Psalm 114 the psalmist begins by remembering how Israel "went out of Egypt, the house of Jacob from a people of strange language," and in the psalm which Clare imitated he asks, "How shall we sing the Lord's song in a strange land?" Although Clare tactically avoids rendering that question in his version of Psalm 137, it is fundamental to the Babylonian experience he underwent. That experience is similar to the historical anger and suffering which beats through the poems in James Berry's anthology of West Indian–British poetry, *News for Babylon*. The common cultural root is Bible Protestantism – that driven, exalted, desperate identification with the scriptures to which Clare gained access through his early interest in Dissenting groups and when he joined the Ranters in 1824. It is hard to convey the intensity of such experience to those nurtured in more "balanced" or more theologically coherent cultures; similarly, the term "culture shock" is inadequate to describe a torn speech struggling in its homelessness against the dead letter.

Clare's madness was therefore nothing less than his manner of living his society's history, and his idea of himself as black slave, prizefighter, Bastille prisoner, captive of the Babylonians, combines images of social injustice with a symbol of individualistic escape from a rural slum (Jack Randall the prizefighter). His oral writing speaks for and to all those who dream of unlocking a frozen language and redeeming an unjust society.

17

"A Revolution in Female Manners"
ANNE K. MELLOR

The Enlightenment ideals of the French *philosophes*, of Voltaire, Diderot and Rousseau, opened up a discourse of equality in which women could participate. On Bastille Day, 1789, Mary Wollstonecraft was living alone in London, working as a staff writer for the pro-Jacobin journal *The Analytical Review* published by Joseph Johnson, and meeting daily with the leading freethinkers of the day. In Joseph Johnson's bookshop she eagerly discussed the progress of the American Revolution and the revolutionary events in France with Thomas Paine, Richard Price, William Godwin, Thomas Holcroft, Thomas Christie, and the painters Fuseli and Blake. Seeing in their demands for liberty and equality against the claims of inherited wealth and aristocratic privilege the possibility for women's liberation as well, she sprang to the defense of Richard Price and Thomas Paine in the pamphlet war concerning the origin of political authority that raged in London in 1790. The war began with Price's heretical speech before the annual meeting of the London Revolution Society in 1789. This anniversary address, historically intended to celebrate the glorious English revolution of 1688, became in Price's hands the opening salvo of a fiery attack on the British monarchy and the established privileges of the English aristocracy. Endorsed by Thomas Paine's *Rights of Man* (1790), which called upon the common Englishman to throw off the shackles of monarchy as both the Americans and the French were doing, these revolutionary ideas inspired a powerful counterattack from Edmund Burke. His rhetorically inspired defense of the French monarchy, of the hereditary principle of succession, of the necessary alliance between church and state, and of the restriction of political power to men "of permanent property" was published in early November, 1790, as *Reflections on the*

Revolution in France, and on the Proceedings in Certain Societies in London, relative to that Event.

Responding to Burke's insistence that we "derive all we possess as an *inheritance from our forefathers*" and that men have equal rights "but not to equal things," as well as to his inflammatory images of revolutionary France as a female prostitute and of Marie Antoinette as an innocent and pure young damsel, forced to flee "almost naked" from her bed, pursued by "a band of cruel ruffians and assassins," from a palace "swimming in blood, polluted by massacre and strewed with scattered limbs and mutilated carcasses,"[1] Mary Wollstonecraft rushed into print in three weeks with *A Vindication of the Rights of Men* (November, 1790). Insisting that all political authority should rest on the grounds of reason and justice alone, she demanded that every person be entitled to enjoy and dispense the fruits of his or her own labors, that inequality of rank be eliminated, and that in place of an exaggerated respect for the authority of "our *canonized forefathers*" be substituted the cultivation of an independent understanding and sound judgment. For Burke's image of the nation as a ravished wife in need of virile protection, Wollstonecraft substituted the image of the nation as a benevolent family educating its children for mature independence and motivated by "natural affections" to ensure the welfare of all its members.[2]

Since she believed that the French Revolution would quickly establish such an enlightened republic, one that would respect the natural rights of every person, Mary Wollstonecraft was appalled when she read in 1791 that the French minister of education for the new Constituent Assembly had proposed a state-supported system of public education for *Men Only*. She immediately composed a lengthy response to the former Bishop of Autun, Citizen Charles Maurice de Talleyrand-Perigord, and his *Rapport sur L'Instruction Publique, fait au nom du Comité de Constitution* (Paris, 1791). That response, *A Vindication of the Rights of Woman*, went through two editions in 1792. Independently of the French feminist thought of the time, Mary Wollstonecraft perceived that the gender inequality at the core of both the revolutionary French nation and of British society threatened the development of a genuine democracy. She recognized that the denial of education to women was tantamount to the denial of their personhood, to their participation in the natural and civil rights of mankind.

Wollstonecraft therefore attempted to initiate her own revolution, what she explicitly called "a REVOLUTION in female manners."[3] In contrast to a masculine romantic ideology that affirmed the rights and feelings of the natural man, Wollstonecraft propounded an equally revolutionary but very different ideology, what we might call the feminine romantic ideology, an ideology grounded on a belief in the rational capacity and equality of woman. Following the lead of Catherine Macaulay's *Letters on Education* (1790), which she had reviewed enthusiastically for the *Analytical Review* two years before, Wollstonecraft explicitly attacked her society's gender definition of the female as innately emotional, intuitive, illogical, capable of moral sentiment but not of rational understanding. Appealing to the Enlightenment rationalists of her day, she grounded her social revolution on a rigorously logical argument, proceeding from the premise that if women are held morally and legally responsible for their sins or crimes (as they were in both England and France), then they must have both souls and the mental capacity to think correctly or ethically. And if women are capable of thinking, they must have a rational faculty. And if they have a rational faculty which is capable of guiding and improving their character and actions, then that rational faculty should be developed and exercised to its greatest capacity.

From this rigorously logical, philosophical argument for the equality of women, Wollstonecraft launched a passionate plea for women's education, for only if women are educated as fully as men will they be able to realize their innate capacities for reason and moral virtue. Calculatedly appealing to male self-interest in order to effect her revolutionary reforms,[4] Wollstonecraft argued that more highly educated women will not only be more virtuous, but they will also be better mothers, more interesting wives and "companions," and more responsible citizens. Wollstonecraft insisted that she was speaking on behalf of *all* women, not just the most talented. As she commented, "I do not wish to leave the line of mediocrity" (p. 50). Therefore she assumed a society in which most men and women would marry, and argued that women would better serve the needs of society, of children, and of their husbands, as well as of their own selves, if they were educated to act more sensibly and judiciously. As Mitzi Myers has emphasized, "the core of her manifesto remains middle-class motherhood, a feminist, republicanized adaptation of the female role normative in late eighteenth-century bourgeois notions of the family."[5]

Because Wollstonecraft assumed a society in which most women would marry, she devoted a large portion of her *Vindication* to describing the ideal marriage, a marriage based on mutual respect, self-esteem, affection and compatibility. It is a marriage of *rational love*, rather than of erotic passion or sexual desire. Wollstonecraft repeatedly insisted in *A Vindication* that sexual passion does not last. She proclaimed,

> one grand truth women have yet to learn, though most it imports them to act accordingly. In the choice of a husband, they should not be led astray by the qualities of a lover – for a lover the husband, even supposing him to be wise and virtuous, cannot long remain. (p. 119)

By identifying the rational woman with the repression, even elimination, of female sexual desire, Wollstonecraft initiated a legacy of female self-denial with which, as Cora Kaplan has forcefully argued, current feminism is still uncomfortably grappling.[6] Yet Wollstonecraft did not sustain an allegiance to a rationality devoid of all sexual or emotional passion, either in her own life or in this very text. As Mary Poovey has shown, the rhetoric and figures of *A Vindication of the Rights of Woman* repeatedly display the tension between Wollstonecraft's effort to deny the idea that women are *essentially* sexual beings and her own conviction that women both desire and need an enduring sexual, as well as emotional, relationship.[7] As we shall see, this very tension between a woman's sexual and emotional needs and her desperate efforts to control, repress or eliminate those desires lest she become a "fallen woman" vibrates through much of the women's fiction of the romantic period.

In addition to advocating a radically new, egalitarian marriage between two rational and equally respected adults, Wollstonecraft demanded even more revolutionary rights for women: the vote (which she insisted should be given to both working-class men and all women), the civil and legal right to possess and distribute property, and the right to work in the most prestigious professions, including business, law, medicine, education and politics. Above all, she demanded for all children between the ages of five and nine a state-supported, coeducational public school system that would teach reading, writing, mathematics, history, botany, mechanics, astronomy, and general science. After the age of nine, the more gifted girls and boys would receive additional education at state expense. If Wollstonecraft's demands now seem self-evidently practical and just (if a bit demanding for nine-year-olds), it is only because the educational reform she demanded actually happened.

Mary Wollstonecraft not only articulated a utopian vision of the rational woman of the future, she also described in detail the errors and evils of the dominant bourgeois gender definition of the female as the subordinate helpmate of the male. Invoking Milton and Rousseau, she sardonically attacked their portrayals of women. When Milton tells us, she wrote with heavy sarcasm,

> that women are formed for softness and sweet attractive grace [*Paradise Lost* iv 297–9], I cannot comprehend his meaning, unless, in the true Mahometan strain, he meant to deprive us of souls, and insinuate that we were beings only designed by sweet attractive grace, and docile blind obedience, to gratify the sense of man when he can no longer soar on the wing of contemplation. (p. 19)

She saved her bitterest attacks for Rousseau, perhaps because she still cherished Rousseau's political and educational doctrines, his emphasis on the development of both reason and the emotions, and his commitment to individual choice, creative thinking, and the social contract. She was particularly disappointed by the sketch of the ideal woman he drew in *Emile*. Depicting Sophy (Sophia, or female wisdom) as submissive, loving, and ever faithful, Rousseau had asserted that:

> What is most wanted in a woman is gentleness; formed to obey a creature often vicious and always faulty, she should early learn to submit to injustice and to suffer the wrongs inflicted on her by her husband without complaint.[8]

Rousseau had further defined women's appropriate education as learning to please men:

> A woman's education must . . . be planned in relation to man. To be pleasing in his sight, to win his respect and love, to train him in childhood, to tend him in manhood, to counsel and console, to make his life pleasant and happy, these are the duties of woman for all time, and this is what she should be taught while she is young. (p. 328).

Much of *A Vindication* is devoted to illustrating the damage wrought by this gender definition of women's nature and social roles as essentially sexual. Late eighteenth-century middle- and upper-class English women were taught to be primarily concerned with arousing and sustaining (but never fully satisfying) male sexual desire in order to capture the husbands upon whom their financial welfare depended. They were obsessed with their personal appearance, with beauty and fashion. Encouraged to be "delicate" and refined, many were what we would now recognize as bulimic and anorexic. As Wollstonecraft commented,

> I once knew a weak woman of fashion, who was more than commonly proud of her delicacy and sensibility. She thought a distinguishing taste and puny appetite the height of all human perfections, and acted accordingly. – I have seen this weak sophisticated being neglect all the duties of life, yet recline with self-complacency on a sofa, and boast of her want of appetite as a proof of delicacy that extended to, or, perhaps, arose from, her exquisite sensibility: for it is difficult to render intelligible such ridiculous jargon. (p. 44)

Worse, women were encouraged to be fundamentally hypocritical and insincere. Forced to be flirts and sexual teases, they were encouraged to arouse male sexual desire by allowing their suitors to take "innocent freedoms" or "liberties" with their person, but were forbidden to experience or manifest sexual desire themselves, a situation that left them blushing in unconscious – yet necessarily fully conscious – modesty.[9]

Since they received no rational education, but were taught only what were known as "accomplishments" – singing, dancing, needlework, painting, a smattering of French and Italian, a "taste" for literature (usually French and Gothic romances) and the fine arts – the upper- and middle-class women of Wollstonecraft's society were kept, she claimed, in "a state of perpetual childhood" (p. 9), "created to feel, not to think" (p. 62). They were – and Wollstonecraft like Catharine Macaulay insisted on the term – "slaves" to their fathers and husbands (p. 167), but, in revenge, cruel and petty tyrants to their children and servants. Forced to be manipulative and sycophantic to their masters, they were "cunning, mean and selfish" to everyone else (p. 141). As a result, they became indolent wives and inconsistent mothers, either overly indulgent (to their sons) or hostile (to their infants, often refusing to nurse them), and directly responsible for the high incidence of childhood disease and infant mortality. Wollstonecraft concluded her *Vindication* with a list of common female follies: the belief in fortune-tellers and superstitions, the excessive fondness for romantic love stories, the obsessive concern with fashion and appearance, the selfish promotion of the members of her own family at the expense of others, the mismanaged households and mistreatment of servants, the overindulgence or neglect of children. While some modern feminist readers have been dismayed by Wollstonecraft's evident dislike of the women of her day, we must keep in mind that she blamed these female follies *on men*, on their failure to provide a suitable education for the women for whom they were financially and morally responsible.

Moreover, insisted Wollstonecraft, the historical enslavement of women has corrupted men. She argued that English men have been forced to assume the social role of the master and thus taught to be demanding, self-indulgent, arrogant, tyrannical. Treating their women as inferior dependants has undermined men's ability to understand the needs of others, to act justly or compassionately, to be good leaders. While Wollstonecraft's attack on men is muted (after all, they comprise the audience whom she must persuade), she nonetheless made it clear that the existence of a master-slave relationship between husband and wife creates evils on both sides. "How can women be just or generous, when they are the slaves of injustice?" she asked rhetorically (p. 189).

The revolution in female manners demanded by Wollstonecraft would, she insisted, dramatically change both women and men. It would produce women who were sincerely modest, chaste, virtuous, Christian; who acted with reason and prudence and generosity. It would produce men who were kind, responsible, sensible and just. And it would produce egalitarian marriages based on compatibility, mutual affection and respect. As Wollstonecraft concluded, we shall not see women affectionate till more equality be established in society, till ranks are confounded and women freed, neither shall we see that dignified domestic happiness, the simple grandeur of which cannot be relished by ignorant or vitiated minds; nor will the important task of education ever be properly begun till the person of a woman is no longer preferred to her mind. (p. 191)

The rational woman, rational love, egalitarian marriage, the preservation of the domestic affections, responsibility for the mental, moral and physical well-being and growth of all the members of the family – these are the cornerstones of Wollstonecraft's feminism, what we would now define as a "liberal" feminism, one that is committed to a model of equality rather than difference. They are also the grounding tenets of the feminine romantic ideology. Wollstonecraft's moral vision diverges profoundly from the ideology both of the British Enlightenment and of the Girondist leaders of the French Revolution in its insistence on the rationality and equality of the female and on the primary importance of the domestic affections and the family. By selecting the image of the egalitarian family as the prototype of a genuine democracy, a family in which husband and wife not only regard each other as equals in intelligence, sensitivity, and power, but also participate equally in childcare and decision-making, Wollstonecraft introduced a truly revolutionary political program, one in which gender and class differences could be erased. While Wollstonecraft shared the Enlightenment *philosophes'* affirmation of reason and wit, of sound moral principles, and of good taste grounded on wide learning, her vision of the egalitarian family, in which husband and wife together serve the interests of the family as a whole, undermines both the traditional affirmation of the father as the final social, political and religious authority as well as the concept of a hierarchical universe or social order grounded on the metaphor of the great Chain of Being. Where Enlightenment thinkers and nonconformist writers such as Defoe, Richardson and Paine, challenged the authority of the father in the name of the younger son or the bourgeois capitalist, she heretically demanded the same rights and status for the daughter, the sister and the common woman.

Wollstonecraft's call for a "revolution in female manners" was not the first feminist tract to be published in England. Throughout the previous century a few intrepid women had argued, in print or by example, for the education of women and the elimination of the sexual double standard.[10] In the late Restoration period, Aphra Behn had promoted the equality of women both in the theater and in the home. Mary Astell had seriously proposed to the ladies in 1697 that they withdraw to a nunnery or seminary to pursue an education in both the classics and Christian doctrine. Lady Mary Wortley Montagu, Hester Chapone, Elizabeth Carter, Mary Robinson

Montagu, and their bluestocking colleagues had publicly proclaimed the intelligence and wit of women. And Mary Hamilton had heeded Astell's call by writing a feminist utopian fantasy, *Munster Village*, in 1778. In this novel, Lady Frances Munster, upon inheriting her father's estate in Shropshire, immediately uses her wealth to found an academy or private university, in which men and women together learn the arts and sciences, medicine and law and business, combining theoretical knowledge with its practical applications. The success of her efforts is marked in Lady Frances herself, who combines a genuine artistic talent for painting, by which she earns an income sufficient to support herself and her brother's family for several years, with a business acumen that enables her simultaneously to found and run her academy while skillfully increasing the productivity of her landed estates by improving her tenants' cottages and training them to use the latest agricultural and practical methods.

In the 1790s Hannah More, Priscilla Wakefield, Catharine Macaulay, Mary Hays and Anne Frances Randall (Mary Robinson) all advocated extensive practical and intellectual reforms in the education and economic condition of women in England.[11] But Wollstonecraft's *Vindication* was the most favorably reviewed, widely read, and — despite the scandal surrounding Wollstonecraft's death and the publication of Godwin's *Memoirs* — lastingly influential feminist tract of the period.[12]

NOTES

1 Edmund Burke (1955) 35, 67, 82.

2 Wollstonecraft (1790), facsimile edition with introduction by Eleanor Louise Nicholes, 41, 52. On the relation of Wollstonecraft's *Rights of Men* to Burke's *Reflections* and the tradition of Commonwealth dissent that Burke opposed, see Guralnick (1977) 155–8 and Barker-Benfield (1989).

3 Wollstonecraft (1988) 192. All further citations from this volume will appear in the text.

   As Raymond Williams reminds us, it was in the 1790s that "revolution" acquired its full modern sense, moving beyond its earlier meanings of "a circular movement of history" or a "rebellion" to take on the additional meaning of "an attempt to make a new social order" (Williams (1976) 226–30).

4 That Wollstonecraft's intended readership was primarily middle- and upper-class men, the men who had the authority and power to institute the educational and political reforms she demanded, has been stressed both by Vlasopolos (1980) and Finke (1987). Wilson has explored, from a contemporary deconstructive perspective, the failure of Wollstonecraft's rhetorical attempt to construct a readership of either men or women, Anna Wilson (1989).

5 Myers (1982) 199–216, 206. Jane Roland Martin reaches a similar conclusion in her chapter on "Wollstonecraft's Daughters", Jane Roland Martin (1985) 70–102.

6 Kaplan (1986) 31–56.

7 On Wollstonecraft's passionate love affairs with Fanny Blood, Gilbert Imlay and William Godwin, see Tomalin (1974) and Sunstein (1975). On the contradictions and tensions in the text of *A Vindication*, see Poovey (1984), ch. 2.

8 Rousseau (1963) 333.

9 On the tensions inherent in nineteenth-century conceptions of female modesty, including Wollstonecraft's, and the significance of the female blush in nineteenth-century fiction, see Yeazell (1991). On the parodic dimensions of Wollstonecraft's invocation of modesty in ch. 7 of *A Vindication of the Rights of Woman*, see Finke (1987) 164–5.

10 For an anthology of eighteenth-century feminist writing, see Moira Ferguson (1985). Ferguson's introduction provides a brief history of eighteenth-century British feminism, 1–50.

11 See Hannah More, *Strictures on the Modern System of Female Education* (1799); Catherine Macaulay, *Letters on Education* (1790); Priscilla Wakefield, *Reflections on the Present Condition of the Female Sex* (1798); Anne Frances Randall (Mary Robinson), *Letter to the Women of England, on the Injustice of Mental Subordination* (1799); and Mary Hays, *Appeal to the Men of Great Britain in Behalf of Women* (1798).

12 Janes (1978). Only More's *Strictures on the Modern System of Female Education* (1799) approached the impact of *A Vindication*; More's tract on the surface seemed more conservative – she advocated restricting women to the domestic sphere – but, as Mitzi Myers has taught us, More's thought was potentially as subversive as Wollstonecraft's, since More allowed women virtually unlimited control over the private sphere, and asserted the equal importance of the private to the public sphere (Myers (1982) 199–216).

18

Jane Austen and Empire

EDWARD SAID

We are on solid ground with V. G. Kiernan when he says that "empires must have a mould of ideas or conditioned reflexes to flow into, and youthful nations dream of a great place in the world as young men dream of fame and fortunes."[1] It is too simple and reductive to argue that everything in European or American culture therefore prepares for or consolidates the grand idea of empire. It is also, however, historically inaccurate to ignore those tendencies – whether in narrative, political theory, or pictorial technique – that enabled, encouraged, and otherwise assured the West's readiness to assume and enjoy the experience of empire. If there was cultural resistance to the notion of an imperial mission, there was not much support for that resistance in the main departments of cultural thought. Liberal though he was, John Stuart Mill – as a telling case in point – could still say, "The sacred duties which civilized nations owe to the independence and nationality of each other, are not binding towards those to whom nationality and independence are certain evil, or at best a questionable good." Ideas like this were not original with Mill; they were already current in the English subjugation of Ireland during the sixteenth century and, as Nicholas Canny has persuasively demonstrated, were equally useful in the ideology of English colonization in the Americas.[2] Almost all colonial schemes begin with an assumption of native backwardness and general inadequacy to be independent, "equal," and fit.

Why that should be so, why sacred obligation on one front should not be binding on another, why rights accepted in one may be denied in another, are questions best understood in the terms of a culture well-grounded in moral, economic, and even metaphysical norms designed to approve a satisfying local, that is European, order and to permit the abrogation of the right to a similar order abroad. Such a statement may appear preposterous or extreme. In fact, it formulates the connection between Europe's well-being and cultural identity on the one hand and, on the other, the subjugation of imperial realms overseas rather too fastidiously and circumspectly. Part of our difficulty today in accepting any connection at all is that we tend to reduce this complicated matter to an apparently simple causal one, which in turn produces a rhetoric of blame and defensiveness. I am *not* saying that the major factor in early European culture was that it *caused* late nineteenth-century imperialism, and I am not implying that all the problems of the formerly colonial world should be blamed on Europe. I am saying, however, that European culture often, if not always, characterized itself in such a way as simultaneously to validate its own preferences while also advocating those preferences in conjunction with distant imperial rule. Mill certainly did: he always recommended that India *not* be given independence. When for various reasons imperial rule concerned Europe more intensely after 1880, this schizophrenic habit became useful.

The first thing to be done now is more or less to jettison simple causality in thinking through the relationship between Europe and the non-European world, and lessening the hold on our thought of the equally simple temporal sequence. We must not admit any notion, for instance, that proposes to show that Wordsworth, Austen, or Coleridge, because they wrote *before* 1857, actually caused the establishment of formal British governmental rule over India *after* 1857. We should try to discern instead a counterpoint between overt patterns in British writing about Britain and representations of the world beyond the British Isles. The inherent mode for this counterpoint is not temporal but spatial. How do writers in the period before the great age of explicit, programmatic colonial expansion – the "scramble for Africa," say – situate and see themselves and their work in the larger world? We shall find them using striking but careful strategies, many of them derived from expected sources – positive ideas of home, of a nation and its language, of proper order, good behaviour, moral values.

But positive ideas of this sort do more than validate "our" world. They also tend to devalue other worlds and, perhaps more significantly from a retrospective point of view, they do not prevent or inhibit or give resistance to horrendously unattractive imperialist practices. No, cultural forms like the novel or the opera do not cause people to go out and imperialize – Carlyle did not drive Rhodes directly, and he certainly cannot be "blamed" for the problems in today's southern Africa – but it is genuinely troubling to see how little Britain's great humanistic ideas, institutions, and monuments, which we still celebrate as having the power ahistorically to command our approval, how little they stand in the way of the accelerating imperial process. We are entitled to ask how this body of humanistic ideas co-existed so comfortably with imperialism, and why – until the resistance to imperialism *in the imperial domain*, among Africans, Asians, Latin Americans, developed – there was little significant opposition or deterrence to empire at home. Perhaps the custom of distinguishing "our" home and order from "theirs" grew into a harsh political rule for accumulating more of "them" to rule, study, and subordinate. In the great, humane ideas and values promulgated by mainstream European culture, we have precisely that "mould of ideas and conditioned reflexes" of which Kiernan speaks, into which the whole business of empire later flowed.

The extent to which these ideas are actually invested in geographical distinctions between real places is the subject of Raymond Williams's richest book, *The Country and the City*. His argument concerning the interplay between rural and urban places in England admits of the most extraordinary transformations – from the pastoral populism of Langland, through Ben Jonson's country-house poems and the novels of Dickens's London, right up to visions of the metropolis in twentieth-century literature. Mainly, of course, the book is about how English culture has dealt with land, its possession, imagination, and organization. And while he does address the export of England to the colonies, Williams does so in a less focused way and less expansively than the practice actually warrants. Near the end of *The Country and the City* he volunteers that "from at least the mid-nineteenth century, and with important instances earlier, there was this larger context [the relationship between England and the colonies, whose effects on the English imagination "have gone deeper than can easily be traced"] within which every idea and every image was consciously and unconsciously affected." He goes on quickly to cite "the idea of emigration to the colonies" as one such image prevailing in various novels by Dickens, the Brontës, Gaskell, and rightly shows that "new rural societies," all of them colonial, enter the imaginative metropolitan economy of English literature via Kipling, early Orwell, Maugham. After 1880 there comes a "dramatic extension of landscape and social relations": this corresponds more or less exactly with the great age of empire.[3]

It is dangerous to disagree with Williams, yet I would venture to say that if one began to look for something like an imperial map of the world in English literature, it would turn up with amazing insistence and frequency well before the mid-nineteenth century. And turn up not only with the inert regularity suggesting something taken for granted, but – more interestingly – threaded through, forming a vital part of the texture of linguistic and cultural practice. There were established English offshore interests in Ireland, America, the Caribbean, and Asia from the sixteenth century on, and even a quick inventory reveals poets, philosophers, historians, dramatists, statesmen, novelists, travel writers, chroniclers, soldiers, and fabulists who prized, cared for, and traced these interests with continuing concern. (Much of this is well discussed by Peter Hulme in *Colonial Encounters*.[4]) Similar points may be made for France, Spain, and Portugal, not only as overseas powers in their own right, but as competitors with the British. How can we examine these interests at work in modern England before the age of empire, i.e. during the period between 1800 and 1870?

We would do well to follow Williams's lead, and look first at that period of crisis following upon England's wide-scale land enclosure at the end of the eighteenth century. The old organic rural communities were dissolved and new ones forged under the impulse of parliamentary activity, industrialization, and demographic dislocation, but there also occurred a new process of relocating England (and in France, France) within a much larger circle of the world map. During the first half of the eighteenth century, Anglo-French competition in North America and India was intense; in the second half there were numerous violent encounters between England and France in the Americas, the Caribbean, and the Levant, and of course in Europe itself. The major pre-romantic literature in France and England contains a constant stream of references to the overseas dominions: one thinks not only of various Encyclopaedists, the Abbé Raynal, de Brosses, and Volney, but also of Edmund Burke, Beckford, Gibbon, Johnson, and William Jones.

In 1902 J. A. Hobson described imperialism as the expansion of nationality, implying that the process was understandable mainly by considering *expansion* as the more important of the two terms, since "nationality" was a fully formed, fixed quantity,[5] whereas a century before it was still in the process of *being formed*, at home and abroad as well. In *Physics and Politics* (1887) Walter Bagehot speaks with extraordinary relevance of "nation-making." Between France and Britain in the late eighteenth century there were two contests: the battle for strategic gains abroad – in India, the Nile delta, the Western Hemisphere – and the battle for a triumphant nationality. Both battles contrast "Englishness" with "the French," and no matter how intimate and closeted the supposed English or French "essence" appears to be, it was almost always thought of as being (as opposed to already) made, and being fought out with the other great competitor. Thackeray's Becky Sharp, for example, is as much an upstart as she is because of her half-French heritage. Earlier in the century, the upright abolitionist posture of Wilberforce and his allies developed partly out of a desire to make life harder for French hegemony in the Antilles.[6]

These considerations suddenly provide a fascinatingly expanded dimension to *Mansfield Park* (1814), the most explicit in its ideological and moral affirmations of Austen's novels. Williams once again is in general dead right: Austen's novels express an "attainable quality of life," in money and property acquired, moral discriminations made, the right choices put in place, the correct "improvements" implemented, the finely nuanced language affirmed and classified. Yet, Williams continues,

What [Cobbett] names, riding past on the road, are classes. Jane Austen, from inside the houses, can never see that, for all the intricacy of her social description. All her discrimination is, understandably, internal and exclusive. She is concerned with the conduct of people who, in the complications of improvement, are repeatedly trying to make themselves into a class. But where only one class is seen, no classes are seen.[7]

As a general description of how Austen manages to elevate certain "moral discriminations" into "an independent value," this is excellent. Where *Mansfield Park* is concerned, however, a good deal more needs to be said, giving greater explicitness and width to Williams's survey. Perhaps then Austen, and indeed, pre-imperialist novels generally, will appear to be more implicated in the rationale for imperialist expansion than at first sight they have been.

After Lukacs and Proust, we have become so accustomed to thinking of the novel's plot and structure as constituted mainly by temporality that we have overlooked the function of space, geography, and location. For it is not only the very young Stephen Dedalus, but every other young protagonist before him as well, who sees himself in a widening spiral at home, in Ireland, in the world. Like many other novels, *Mansfield Park* is very precisely about a series of both small and large dislocations and relocations in space that occur before, at the end of the novel, Fanny Price, the niece, becomes the spiritual mistress of Mansfield Park. And that place itself is located by Austen at the centre of an arc of interests and concerns spanning the hemisphere, two major seas, and four continents.

As in Austen's other novels, the central group that finally emerges with marriage and property "ordained" is not based exclusively upon blood. Her novel enacts the disaffiliation (in the literal sense) of some members of a family, and the affiliation between others and one or two chosen and tested outsiders: in other words, blood relationships are not enough to assure continuity, hierarchy, authority, both domestic and international. Thus Fanny Price – the poor niece, the orphaned child from the outlying city of Portsmouth, the neglected, demure, and upright wall-flower – gradually acquires a status commensurate with, even superior to, that of most of her more fortunate relatives. In this pattern of affiliation and in her assumption of authority, Fanny Price is relatively passive. She resists the misdemeanours and the importunings of others, and very occasionally she ventures actions on her own: all in all, though, one has the impression that Austen has designs for her that Fanny herself can scarcely comprehend, just as throughout the novel Fanny is thought of by everyone as "comfort" and "acquisition" despite herself. Like Kipling's Kim O'Hara, Fanny is both device and instrument in a larger pattern, as well as a fully fledged novelistic character.

Fanny, like Kim, requires direction, requires the patronage and outside authority that her own impoverished experience cannot provide. Her conscious connections are to some people and to some places, but the novel reveals other connections of which she has faint glimmerings that nevertheless demand her presence and service. She comes into a situation that opens with an intricate set of moves which, taken together, demand sorting out, adjustment, and rearrangement. Sir Thomas Bertram has been captivated by one Ward sister, the others have not done well, and "an absolute breach" opens up; their "circles were so distinct," the distances between them so great that they have been out of touch for eleven years;[8] fallen on hard times, the Prices seek out the Bertrams. Gradually, and even though she is not the eldest, Fanny becomes the focus of attention as she is sent to Mansfield Park, there to begin her new life. Similarly, the Bertrams have given up London (the result of Lady Bertram's "little ill health and a great deal of indolence") and come to reside entirely in the country.

What sustains this life materially is the Bertram estate in Antigua, which is not doing well. Austen takes pains to show us two apparently disparate but actually convergent processes: the growth of Fanny's importance to the Bertrams' economy, including Antigua, and Fanny's own steadfastness in the face of numerous challenges, threats, and surprises. In both, Austen's imagination works with a steel-like rigour through a mode that we might call geographical and spatial clarification. Fanny's ignorance when she arrives at Mansfield as a frightened ten-year-old is signified by her inability to "put the map of Europe together,"[9] and for much of the first half of the novel the action is concerned with a whole range of issues whose common denominator, misused or misunderstood, is space: not only is Sir Thomas in Antigua to make things better there and at home, but at Mansfield Park, Fanny, Edmund, and her aunt Norris negotiate where she is to live, read, and work, where fires are to be lit; the friends and cousins concern themselves with the improvement of estates, and the importance of chapels (i.e., religious authority) to domesticity is envisioned and debated. When, as a device for stirring things up, the Crawfords suggest a play (the tinge of France that hangs a little suspiciously over their background is significant), Fanny's discomfiture is polarizingly acute. She cannot participate, cannot easily accept that rooms for living are turned into theatrical space, although, with all its confusion of roles and purposes, the play, Kotzebue's *Lovers' Vows*, is prepared for anyway.

We are to surmise, I think, that while Sir Thomas is away tending his colonial garden, a number of inevitable mismeasurements (explicitly associated with feminine "lawlessness") will occur. These are apparent not only in innocent strolls by the three pairs of young friends through a park, in which people lose and catch sight of one another unexpectedly, but most clearly in the various flirtations and engagements between the young men and women left without true parental authority, Lady Bertram being indifferent, Mrs Norris unsuitable. There is sparring, innuendo, perilous taking on of roles: all of this of course crystallizes in preparations for the play, in which something dangerously close to libertinage is about to be (but never is) enacted. Fanny, whose earlier sense of alienation, distance, and fear derives from her first uprooting, now becomes a sort of surrogate conscience about what is right and how far is too much. Yet she has no power to implement her uneasy awareness, and until Sir Thomas suddenly returns from "abroad," the rudderless drift continues.

When he does appear, preparations for the play are immediately stopped, and in a passage remarkable for its executive dispatch, Austen narrates the reestablishment of Sir Thomas's local rule:

> It was a busy morning with him. Conversation with any of them occupied but a small part of it. He had to reinstate himself in all the wonted concerns of his Mansfield life, to see his steward and his bailiff – to examine and compute – and, in the intervals of business, to walk into his stables and his gardens, and nearest plantations; but active and methodical, he had not only done all this before he resumed his seat as master of the house at dinner, he had also set the carpenter to work in pulling down what had been so lately put up in the billiard room, and given the scene painter his dismissal, long enough to justify the pleasing belief of his being then at least as far off as Northampton. The scene painter was gone, having spoilt only the floor of one room, ruined all the coachman's sponges, and made five of the under-servants idle and dissatisfied; and Sir Thomas was in hopes that another day or two would suffice to wipe away every outward memento of what had been, even to the destruction of every unbound copy of "Lovers' Vows" in the house, for he was burning all that met his eye.[10]

The force of this paragraph is unmistakable. Not only is this a Crusoe setting things in order: it is also an early Protestant eliminating all traces of frivolous behaviour. There is nothing in *Mansfield Park* that would contradict us, however, were we to assume that Sir Thomas does exactly the same things – on a larger scale – in his Antigua "plantations." Whatever was wrong there – and the internal evidence garnered by Warren Roberts suggests that economic depression, slavery, and competition with France were at issue[11] – Sir Thomas was able to fix, thereby maintaining his control over his colonial domain. More clearly than anywhere else in her fiction, Austen here synchronizes domestic with international authority, making it plain that the values associated with such higher things as ordination, law, and propriety must be grounded firmly in actual rule over and possession of territory. She sees clearly that to hold and rule Mansfield Park is to hold

and rule an imperial estate in close, not to say inevitable association with it.
What assures the domestic tranquillity and attractive harmony of one is the
productivity and regulated discipline of the other.

Before both can be fully secured, however, Fanny must become more
actively involved in the unfolding action. From frightened and often
victimized poor relation she is gradually transformed into a directly partici-
pating member of the Bertram household at Mansfield Park. For this, I
believe, Austen designed the second part of the book, which contains not
only the failure of the Edmund–Mary Crawford romance as well as the
disgraceful profligacy of Lydia and Henry Crawford, but Fanny Price's
rediscovery and rejection of her Portsmouth home, the injury and incapaci-
tation of Tom Bertram (the eldest son), the launching of William Price's
naval career. This entire ensemble of relationships and events is finally
capped with Edmund's marriage to Fanny, whose place in Lady Bertram's
household is taken by Susan Price, her sister. It is no exaggeration to
interpret the concluding sections of *Mansfield Park* as the coronation of an
arguably unnatural (or at very least, illogical) principle at the heart of a
desired English order. The audacity of Austen's vision is disguised a little
by her voice, which despite its occasional archness is understated and
notably modest. But we should not misconstrue the limited references to the
outside world, her lightly stressed allusions to work, process, and class, her
apparent ability to abstract (in Raymond Williams's phrase) "an everyday
uncompromising morality which is in the end separable from its social
basis." In fact Austen is far less diffident, far more severe.

The clues are to be found in Fanny, or rather in how rigorously we are
able to consider her. True, her visit to her original Portsmouth home, where
her immediate family still resides, upsets the aesthetic and emotional balance
she has become accustomed to at Mansfield Park, and true she has begun
to take its wonderful luxuries for granted, even as being essential. These are
fairly routine and natural consequences of getting used to a new place. But
Austen is talking about two other matters we must not mistake. One is
Fanny's newly enlarged sense of what it means to be *at home*; when she takes
stock of things after she gets to Portsmouth, this is not merely a matter of
expanded space.

> Fanny was almost stunned. The smallness of the house, and thinness
> of the walls, brought every thing so close to her, that, added to the
> fatigue of her journey, and all her recent agitation, she hardly knew
> how to bear it. *Within* the room all was tranquil enough, for Susan
> having disappeared with the others, there were soon only her father
> and herself remaining; and he taking out a newspaper – the accustom-
> ary loan of a neighbour, applied himself to studying it, without
> seeming to recollect her existence. The solitary candle was held

between himself and the paper, without any reference to her possible convenience; but she had nothing to do, and was glad to have the light screened from her aching head, as she sat in bewildered, broken, sorrowful contemplation.

She was at home. But alas! it was not such a home, she had not such a welcome, as – she checked herself; she was unreasonable ... A day or two might shew the difference. *She* only was to blame. Yet she thought it would not have been so at Mansfield. No, in her uncle's house there would have been a consideration of times and seasons, a regulation of subject, a propriety, an attention towards every body which there was not here.[12]

In too small a space, you cannot see clearly, you cannot think clearly, you cannot have regulation or attention of the proper sort. The fineness of Austen's detail ("the solitary candle was held between himself and the paper, without any reference to her possible convenience") renders very precisely the dangers of unsociability, of lonely insularity, of diminished awareness that are rectified in larger and better administered spaces.

That such spaces are not available to Fanny by direct inheritance, legal title, by propinquity, contiguity, or adjacence (Mansfield Park and Portsmouth are separated by many hours' journey) is precisely Austen's point. To earn the right to Mansfield Park you must first leave home as a kind of indentured servant or, to put the case in extreme terms, as a kind of transported commodity – this, clearly, is the fate of Fanny and her brother William – but then you have the promise of future wealth. I think Austen sees what Fanny does as a domestic or small-scale movement in space that corresponds to the larger, more openly colonial movements of Sir Thomas, her mentor, the man whose estate she inherits. The two movements depend on each other.

The second more complex matter about which Austen speaks, albeit indirectly, raises an interesting theoretical issue. Austen's awareness of empire is obviously very different, alluded to very much more casually, than Conrad's or Kipling's. In her time the British were extremely active in the Caribbean and in South America, notably Brazil and Argentina. Austen seems only vaguely aware of the details of these activities, although the sense that extensive West Indian plantations were important was fairly widespread in metropolitan England. Antigua and Sir Thomas's trip there have a definitive function in *Mansfield Park*, which, I have been saying, is both incidental, referred to only in passing, and absolutely crucial to the action. How are we to assess Austen's few references to Antigua, and what are we to make of them interpretatively?

My contention is that by that very old combination of casualness and stress, Austen reveals herself to be *assuming* (just as Fanny assumes, in both senses of the word) the importance of an empire to the situation at home. Let me go further. Since Austen refers to and uses Antigua as she does in *Mansfield Park*, there needs to be a commensurate effort on the part of her readers to understand concretely the historical valences in the reference; to put it differently, we should try to understand *what* she referred to, why she gave it the importance she did, and why indeed she made the choice, for she might have done something different to establish Sir Thomas's wealth. Let us now calibrate the signifying power of the references to Antigua in *Mansfield Park*; how do they occupy the place they do, what are they doing there?

According to Austen we are to conclude that no matter how isolated and insulated the English place (e.g., Mansfield Park), it requires overseas sustenance. Sir Thomas's property in the Caribbean would have had to be a sugar plantation maintained by slave labour (not abolished until the 1830s): these are not dead historical facts but, as Austen certainly knew, evident historical realities. Before the Anglo-French competition the major distinguishing characteristic of Western empires (Roman, Spanish, and Portuguese) was that the earlier empires were bent on loot, as Conrad puts it, on the transport of treasure from the colonies to Europe, with very little attention to development, organization, system within the colonies themselves; Britain and, to a lesser degree, France both wanted to make their empires long-term, profitable, ongoing concerns, and they competed in this enterprise, nowhere more so than in the colonies of the Caribbean, where the transport of slaves, the functioning of large sugar plantations, the development of sugar markets, which raised the issues of protectionism, monopolies, and price – all these were more or less constantly, competitively at issue.

Far from being nothing much "out there," British colonial possessions in the Antilles and Leeward Islands were during Jane Austen's time a crucial setting for Anglo-French colonial competition. Revolutionary ideas from France were being exported there, and there was a steady decline in British profits: the French sugar plantations were producing more sugar at less cost. However, slave rebellions in and out of Haiti were incapacitating France and spurring British interests to intervene more directly and to gain greater local power. Still, compared with its earlier prominence for the home market, British Caribbean sugar production in the nineteenth century had to compete with alternative sugar-cane supplies in Brazil and Mauritius, the emergence of a European beet-sugar industry, and the gradual dominance of free-trade ideology and practice.

In *Mansfield Park* – both in its formal characteristics and in its contents – a number of these currents converge. The most important is the avowedly complete subordination of colony to metropolis. Sir Thomas, absent from Mansfield Park, is never seen as *present* in Antigua, which elicits at most a half-dozen references in the novel. There is a passage, a part of which I quoted earlier, from John Stuart Mill's *Principles of Political Economy* that catches the spirit of Austen's use of Antigua. I quote it here in full:

> These are hardly to be looked upon as countries, carrying on an exchange of commodities with other countries, but more properly as outlying agricultural or manufacturing estates belonging to a larger community. Our West Indian colonies, for example, cannot be regarded as countries with a productive capital of their own ... [but are rather] the place where England finds it convenient to carry on the production of sugar, coffee and a few other tropical commodities. All the capital employed is English capital; almost all the industry is carried on for English uses; there is little production of anything except for staple commodities, and these are sent to England, not to be exchanged for things exported to the colony and consumed by its inhabitants, but to be sold in England for the benefit of the proprietors there. The trade with the West Indies is hardly to be considered an external trade, but more resembles the traffic between town and country.[13]

To some extent Antigua is like London or Portsmouth, a less desirable setting than a country estate like Mansfield Park, but producing goods to be consumed by everyone (by the early nineteenth century every Britisher used sugar), although owned and maintained by a small group of aristocrats and gentry. The Bertrams and the other characters in *Mansfield Park* are a sub-group within the minority, and for them the island is wealth, which Austen regards as being converted to propriety, order, and, at the end of the novel, comfort, an added good. But why "added"? Because, Austen tells us pointedly in the final chapters, she wants to "restore every body, not greatly in fault themselves, to tolerable comfort, and to have done with all the rest."[14]

This can be interpreted to mean first that the novel has done enough in the way of destabilizing the lives of "every body" and must now set them at rest: actually Austen says this explicitly, in a bit of meta-fictional impatience, the novelist commenting on her own work as having gone on long enough and now needing to be brought to a close. Second, it can mean that everybody may now be finally permitted to realize what it means to be properly at home, and at rest, without the need to wander about or to come and go. (This does not include young William, who, we assume, will continue to roam the seas in the British navy on whatever commercial and political missions may still be required. Such matters draw from Austen only a last brief gesture, a passing remark about William's "continuing good conduct and rising fame.") As for those finally resident in Mansfield Park itself, more in the way of domesticated advantages is given to these now fully acclimatized souls, and to none more than to Sir Thomas. He understands for the first time what has been missing in his education of his children, and he understands it in the terms paradoxically provided for him by unnamed outside forces, so to speak, the wealth of Antigua and the imported example of Fanny Price. Note here how the curious alternation of outside and inside follows the pattern identified by Mill of the outside *becoming* the inside by use and, to use Austen's word, "disposition":

> Here [in his deficiency of training, of allowing Mrs Norris too great a role, of letting his children dissemble and repress feeling] had been grievous mismanagement; but, bad as it was, he gradually grew to feel that it had not been the most direful mistake in his plan of education. Some thing must have been wanting *within*, or time would have worn away much of its ill effect. He feared that principle, active principle, had been wanting, that they had never been properly taught to govern their inclinations and tempers, by that sense of duty which can alone suffice. They had been instructed theoretically in their religion, but never required to bring it into daily practice. To be distinguished for elegance and accomplishments – the authorized object of their youth – could have had no useful influence that way, no moral effect on the mind. He had meant them to be good, but his cares had been directed to the understanding and manners, not the disposition; and of the necessity of self-denial and humility, he feared they had never heard from any lips that could profit them.[15]

What was wanting *within* was in fact supplied by the wealth derived from a West Indian plantation and a poor provincial relative, both brought in to Mansfield Park and set to work. Yet on their own, neither the one nor the other could have sufficed; they require each other and then, more important, they need executive disposition, which in turn helps to reform the rest of the Bertram circle. All this Austen leaves to her reader to supply in the way of literal explication.

And that is what reading her entails. But all these things having to do with the outside brought in seem unmistakably *there* in the suggestiveness of her allusive and abstract language. A "principle wanting within" is, I believe, intended to evoke for us memories of Sir Thomas's absences in Antigua, or the sentimental and near-whimsical vagary on the part of the three variously deficient Ward sisters by which a niece is displaced from one household to another. But that the Bertrams did become better if not altogether good, that some sense of duty was imparted to them, that they learned to govern their inclinations and tempers and brought religion into daily practice, that they "directed disposition": all of this did occur because outside (or rather outlying) factors were lodged properly inward, became native to Mansfield Park, with Fanny the niece its final spiritual mistress, and Edmund the second son its spiritual master.

An additional benefit is that Mrs Norris is dislodged; this is described as "the great supplementary comfort of Sir Thomas's life."[16] Once the principles have been interiorized, the comforts follow: Fanny is settled for the time being at Thornton Lacey "with every attention to her comfort"; Susan is brought in "first as a comfort to Fanny, then as an auxiliary, and at last as her substitute"[17] when the new import takes Fanny's place by Lady Bertram's side. The pattern established at the outset of the novel clearly continues, only now it has what Austen intended to give it all along, an internalized and retrospectively guaranteed rationale. This is the rationale that Raymond Williams describes as "an everyday, uncompromising morality which is in the end separable from its social basis and which, in other hands, can be turned against it."

I have tried to show that the morality in fact is not separable from its social basis: right up to the last sentence, Austen affirms and repeats the geographical process of expansion involving trade, production, and consumption that predates, underlies, and guarantees the morality. And expansion, as Gallagher reminds us, whether "through colonial rule was liked or disliked, [its] desirability through one mode or another was generally accepted. So in the event there were few domestic constraints upon expansion."[18] Most critics have tended to forget or overlook that process, which has seemed less important to critics than Austen herself seemed to think. But interpreting Jane Austen depends on *who* does the interpreting, *when* it is done, and no less important, from *where* it is done. If with feminists, with great cultural critics sensitive to history and class like Williams, with cultural and stylistic interpreters, we have been sensitized to the issues their interests raise, we should now proceed to regard the geographical division of the world – after all significant to *Mansfield Park* – as not neutral (any more than class and gender are neutral) but as politically charged, beseeching the attention and elucidation its considerable proportions require. The question is thus not only how to understand and with what to connect Austen's morality and its social basis, but also *what* to read of it.

Take once again the casual references to Antigua, the ease with which Sir Thomas's needs in England are met by a Caribbean sojourn, the uninflected, unreflective citations of Antigua (or the Mediterranean, or India, which is where Lady Bertram, in a fit of distracted impatience, requires that William should go " 'that I may have a shawl. I think I will have two shawls.' ")[19] They stand for a significance "out there" that frames the genuinely important action *here*, but not for a great significance. Yet these signs of "abroad" include, even as they repress, a rich and complex history, which has since achieved a status that the Bertrams, the Prices, and Austen herself would not, could not recognize. To call this "the Third World" begins to deal with the realities but by no means exhausts the political or cultural history.

We must first take stock of *Mansfield Park*'s prefigurations of a later English history as registered in fiction. The Bertrams' usable colony in *Mansfield Park* can be read as pointing forward to Charles Gould's San Tomé mine in *Nostromo*, or to the Wilcoxes' Anglo-Imperial Rubber Company in Forster's *Howards End*, or to any of these distant but convenient treasure spots in *Great Expectations*, Jean Rhys's *Wide Sargasso Sea, Heart of Darkness* — resources to be visited, talked about, described, or appreciated for domestic reasons, for local metropolitan benefit. If we think ahead to these other novels, Sir Thomas's Antigua readily acquires a slightly greater density than the discrete, reticent appearances it makes in the pages of *Mansfield Park*. And already our reading of the novel begins to open up at those points where ironically Austen was most economical and her critics most (dare one say it?) negligent. Her "Antigua" is therefore not just a slight but a definite way of marking the outer limits of what Williams calls domestic improvements, or a quick allusion to the mercantile venturesomeness of acquiring overseas dominions as a source for local fortunes, or one reference among many attesting to a historical sensibility suffused not just with manners and courtesies but with contests of ideas, struggles with Napoleonic France, awareness of seismic economic and social change during a revolutionary period in world history.

Second, we must see "Antigua" held in a precise place in Austen's moral geography, and in her prose, by historical changes that her novel rides like a vessel on a mighty sea. The Bertrams could not have been possible without the slave trade, sugar, and the colonial planter class; as a social type Sir Thomas would have been familiar to eighteenth- and early nineteenth-century readers who knew the powerful influence of the class through politics, plays (like Cumberland's *The West Indian*), and many other public activities (large houses, famous parties and social rituals, well-known commercial enterprises, celebrated marriages). As the old system of protected monopoly gradually disappeared and as a new class of settler-planters displaced the old absentee system, the West Indian interest lost dominance: cotton manufacture, an even more open system of trade, and abolition of the slave trade reduced the power and prestige of people like the Bertrams, whose frequency of sojourn in the Caribbean then decreased.

Thus Sir Thomas's infrequent trips to Antigua as an absentee plantation owner reflect the diminishment in his class's power, a reduction directly expressed in the title of Lowell Ragatz's classic *The Fall of the Planter Class in the British Caribbean, 1763–1833* (1928). But is what is hidden or allusive in Austen made sufficiently explicit more than one hundred years later in

Ragatz? Does the aesthetic silence or discretion of a great novel in 1814 receive adequate explication in a major work of historical research a full century later? Can we assume that the process of interpretation is fulfilled, or will it continue as new material comes to light?

For all his learning Ragatz still finds it in himself to speak of "the Negro race" as having the following characteristics: "he stole, he lied, he was simple, suspicious, inefficient, irresponsible, lazy, superstitious, and loose in his sexual relations."[20] Such "history" as this therefore happily gave way to the revisionary work of such Caribbean historians as Eric Williams and C. L. R. James, and more recently Robin Blackburn, in *The Overthrow of Colonial Slavery, 1776–1848*; in these works slavery and empire are shown to have fostered the rise and consolidation of capitalism well beyond the old plantation monopolies, as well as to have been a powerful ideological system whose original connection to specific economic interests may have gone, but whose effects continued for decades.

> The political and moral ideas of the age are to be examined in the very closest relation to the economic development . . .
>
> An outworn interest, whose bankruptcy smells to heaven in historical perspective, can exercise an obstructionist and disruptive effect which can only be explained by the powerful services it had previously rendered and the entrenchment previously gained . . .
>
> The ideas built on these interests continue long after the interests have been destroyed and work their old mischief, which is all the more mischievous because the interests to which they corresponded no longer exist.[21]

Thus Eric Williams in *Capitalism and Slavery* (1961). The question of interpretation, indeed of writing itself, is tied to the question of interests, which we have seen are at work in aesthetic as well as historical writing, then and now. We must not say that since *Mansfield Park* is a novel, its affiliations with a sordid history are irrelevant or transcended, not only because it is irresponsible to do so but because we know too much to say so in good faith. Having read *Mansfield Park* as part of the structure of an expanding imperialist venture, one cannot simply restore it to the canon of "great literary masterpieces" – to which it most certainly belongs – and leave it at that. Rather, I think, the novel steadily, if unobtrusively, opens up a broad expanse of domestic imperialist culture without which Britain's subsequent acquisition of territory would not have been possible.

I have spent time on *Mansfield Park* to illustrate a type of analysis infrequently encountered in mainstream interpretations, or for that matter in readings rigorously based in one or another of the advanced theoretical schools. Yet only in the global perspective implied by Jane Austen and her characters can the novel's quite astonishing general position be made clear. I think of such a reading as completing or complementing others, not discounting or displacing them. And it bears stressing that because *Mansfield Park* connects the actualities of British power overseas to the domestic imbroglio within the Bertram estate, there is no way of doing such readings as mine, no way of understanding the "structure of attitude and reference" except by working through the novel. Without reading it in full, we would fail to understand the strength of that structure and the way it was activated and maintained in literature. But in reading it carefully, we can sense how ideas about dependent races and territories were held both by foreign-office executives, colonial bureaucrats, and military strategists and by intelligent novel-readers educating themselves in the fine points of moral evaluation, literary balance, and stylistic finish.

There is a paradox here in reading Jane Austen which I have been impressed by but can in no way resolve. All the evidence says that even the most routine aspects of holding slaves on a West Indian sugar plantation were cruel stuff. And everything we know about Austen and her values is at odds with the cruelty of slavery. Fanny Price reminds her cousin that after asking Sir Thomas about the slave trade, "There was such a dead silence"[22] as to suggest that one world could not be connected with the other since there simply is no common language for both. That is true. But what stimulates the extraordinary discrepancy into life is the rise, decline, and fall of the British empire itself and, in its aftermath, the emergence of a post-colonial consciousness. In order more accurately to read works like *Mansfield Park*, we have to see them in the main as resisting or avoiding that other setting, which their formal inclusiveness, historical honesty, and prophetic suggestiveness cannot completely hide. In time there would no longer be a dead silence when slavery was spoken of, and the subject became central to a new understanding of what Europe was.

It would be silly to expect Jane Austen to treat slavery with anything like the passion of an abolitionist or a newly liberated slave. Yet what I have called the rhetoric of blame, so often now employed by subaltern, minority, or disadvantaged voices, attacks her, and others like her, retrospectively, for being white, privileged, insensitive, complicit. Yes, Austen belonged to a slave-owning society, but do we therefore jettison her novels as so many trivial exercises in aesthetic frumpery? Not at all, I would argue, if we take seriously our intellectual and interpretative vocation to make connections, to deal with as much of the evidence as possible, fully and actually, to read what is there or not there, above all, to see complementarity and interdependence instead of isolated, venerated, or formalized experience that excludes and forbids the hybridizing intrusions of human history.

Mansfield Park is a rich work in that its aesthetic intellectual complexity requires that longer and slower analysis that is also required by its geographical problematic, a novel based in England relying for the maintenance of its style on a Caribbean island. When Sir Thomas goes to and comes from Antigua, where he has property, that is not at all the same thing as coming to and going from Mansfield Park, where his presence, arrivals, and departures have very considerable consequences. But precisely because Austen is so summary in one context, so provocatively rich in the other, precisely because of that imbalance we are able to move in on the novel, reveal and accentuate the interdependence scarcely mentioned on its brilliant pages. A lesser work wears its historical affiliation more plainly; its worldliness is simple and direct, the way a jingoistic ditty during the Mahdist uprising or the 1857 Indian Rebellion connects directly to the situation and constituency that coined it. *Mansfield Park* encodes experiences and does not simply repeat them. From our later perspective we can interpret Sir Thomas's power to come and go in Antigua as stemming from the muted national experience of individual identity, behaviour, and "ordination," enacted with such irony and taste at Mansfield Park. The task is to lose neither a true historical sense of the first, nor a full enjoyment or appreciation of the second, all the while seeing both together.

NOTES

1 Kiernan (1974) 100.
2 Mill (1875) 167–8. For an earlier version of this see the discussion by Canny (1973) 575–98.
3 Raymond Williams (1973) 281.
4 Hulme (1986). See also Hulme and Whitehead (1992).
5 Hobson (1972) 6.
6 This is most memorably discussed in C. L. R. James (1963), esp. ch. 2, "The Owners." See also Blackburn (1988) 149–53.
7 Williams (1973) 117.
8 Austen (1966) 42. The best account of the novel is in Tanner (1986).
9 Ibid., 54.
10 Ibid., 206.
11 Warren Roberts (1979) 97–8. See also Fleishman (1967) 36–9 and passim.
12 Austen (1966) 375–6.
13 Mill (1965) 693. The passage is quoted Mintz (1985) 42.
14 Austen (1966) 446.
15 Ibid., 448.
16 Ibid., 450.
17 Ibid., 456.
18 Gallagher (1982) 76.
19 Austen (1966) 308.
20 Ragatz (1963) 27.
21 Eric Williams (1961) 211; see also Eric Williams (1970) 177–254.
22 Austen (1966) 213.

List of Contributors

MARILYN BUTLER is the author of books and articles on the romantic period, such as *Maria Edgeworth: a Literary Biography* (1972), *Jane Austen and the War of Ideas* (1975), and *Romantics, Rebels and Reactionaries* (1981). She has edited *Burke, Paine, Godwin, and the Revolution Controversy* (1984), the *Collected Works of Mary Wollstonecraft* with Janet Todd (7 vols, 1989), and *Mary Shelley's Frankenstein* (1993). She has been King Edward VII Professor of English Literature at Cambridge, and is now Rector of Exeter College, Oxford.

JAMES K. CHANDLER is Professor of English at the University of Chicago. He is the author of *Wordsworth's Second Nature* (1984) and of numerous essays on topics in post-Enlightenment literature and culture in Britain and America. He has co-edited a volume of essays on method, from *Critical Inquiry*, entitled *Questions of Evidence: Proof, Practice, and Persuasion Across the Disciplines* (1994), and is general editor, with Marilyn Butler, for Cambridge Studies in Romanticism. He is currently completing work on a book called *England in 1819* (after Shelley's sonnet).

VINCENT ARTHUR DE LUCA was Professor of English at Erindale College, University of Toronto. He is best known as the author of *Thomas De Quincey: The Prose of Vision* (1980) and *Words of Eternity: Blake and the Poetics of the Sublime* (1991). He died in 1993.

JAMES A. W. HEFFERNAN, Professor of English at Dartmouth College, has published books and articles on English romantic poetry and landscape painting, and has edited two collections of interdisciplinary essays: *Space, Time, Image, Sign* (1987), and *Representing the French Revolution* (1992). His most recent book is *Museum of Words: The Poetics of Ekphrasis from Homer to Ashbery* (1993).

NELSON HILTON, Professor of English at the University of Georgia, has for many years been review editor for *Blake: An Illustrated Quarterly*. He is the author of *Literal Imagination: Blake's Vision of Words* (1983) and *Lexis Complexes: Literary Interventions* (1995).

MARGARET HOMANS is Professor of English at Yale University, where she also chairs the Women's Studies Program. She is the author of *Women Writers and Poetic Identity: Dorothy Wordsworth, Emily Brontë, and Emily Dickinson* (1980), *Bearing the Word: Language and Female Experience in Nineteenth-Century Women's Writing* (1986), essays on nineteenth-century literature and culture, and essays on contemporary feminist theory. She is currently working on a book on Queen Victoria and Victorian culture.

ALAN LIU is Associate Professor of English at the University of California, Santa Barbara, where he teaches romanticism, postmodernism, and literary theory. Since publishing *Wordsworth: The Sense of History*, he has written essays on the methodology of cultural studies – including "The Power of Formalism: The New Historicism" (*ELH*, 1989), "Wordsworth and Subversion, 1793–1804" (*Yale Journal of Criticism*, 1989), and "Local Transcendence: Cultural Criticism, Postmodernism, and the Romanticism of Detail" (*Representations*, 1990). He is currently completing a book on cultural studies and postmodernism, and another on the "new literary history."

JEROME McGANN is John Stewart Bryan Professor of English, University of Virginia. He is the editor of the standard Oxford English Texts edition of *Byron: The Complete Poetical Works* (1980–93), and has written extensively on the romantic period.

PETER J. MANNING is Professor of English at the University of Southern California. He is the author of *Byron and his Fictions* (1978) and *Reading Romantics* (1990), and is co-editor, with Susan J. Wolfson, of the forthcoming Penguin edition of Byron's selected poems.

ANNE K. MELLOR is Professor of English and Women's Studies at UCLA. Her recent books include *Romanticism and Gender* (1993), *Mary Shelley: Her Life, Her Fiction, Her Monsters* (1988), and an edited collection, *Romanticism and Feminism* (1988). She is currently co-editing a canon-transforming teaching anthology, *British Literature 1780–1840*, for Harcourt Brace Jovanovich, to appear in 1996.

TOM PAULIN is All Souls (G. M. Young) Lecturer in Nineteenth- and Twentieth-Century English Literature at Hertford College, Oxford. His most recent critical work, *Minotaur: Poetry and the Nation State*, was published in 1992. A new collection of poems, *Walking a Line*, was published in 1994.

BALACHANDRA RAJAN is Professor Emeritus at the University of Western Ontario. He was a Fellow of Trinity College, Cambridge, 1944–8, and is an Honoured Scholar of the Milton Society and a Fellow and Medallist of the Royal Society of Canada. His books include *"Paradise Lost" and the Seventeenth-Century Reader* (1947), *W. B. Yeats: A Critical Introduction* (1965), *The Lofty Rhyme: A Study of Milton's Major Poetry* (1970), *The Overwhelming Question: A Study of the Poetry of T. S. Eliot* (1976) and *The Form of the Unfinished: English Poetics from Spenser to Pound* (1985).

TILOTTAMA RAJAN is Professor of English and Theory at the University of Western Ontario. She is the author of *Dark Interpreter: The Discourse of Romanticism* (1980), and *The Supplement of Reading: Figures of Understanding in Romantic Theory and Practice* (1990), and is co-editor (with David Clark) of *Intersections: Nineteenth-Century Philosophy and Contemporary Theory* (1994). She is currently working on two books: *Deconstruction Before and After Post-Structuralism* and *Romantic Narrative*.

EDWARD SAID is Professor of English and Comparative Literature at Columbia University. He is a prolific writer on a wide range of topics, including literature, music, cultural criticism, and Palestinian issues. He is the author of *Joseph Conrad and the Fiction of Autobiography* (1966), *Orientalism* (1978), *The World, the Text, and the Critic* (1991), *After the Last Sky: Palestinian Lives* (1986), *Musical Elaborations* (1991), and *Culture and Imperialism* (1993).

EVE KOSOFSKY SEDGWICK is Professor of English at Duke University. She is the author of *Between Men: English Literature and Male Homosocial Desire* (1985), *The Coherence of Gothic Conventions* (1986), and *Epistemology of the Closet* (1991).

KAREN SWANN is Associate Professor of English at Williams College in Williamstown, Massachusetts. She has published articles on Coleridge, Wordsworth, Keats, and Burke, and is currently at work on a book, *Lives of the Dead Poets*, on death and romantic poetic identity.

LEON WALDOFF is Professor of English and Director of Graduate Studies in English at the University of Illinois at Urbana-Champaign. He is the author of *Keats and the Silent Work of Imagination* (1985), as well as articles and reviews on other romantic writers. He is currently working on a study of Wordsworth's major lyrics.

KATHLEEN WHEELER studied at Ann Arbor, Munich, and Berlin, before completing her doctorate at Girton College, Cambridge. Having taken a BA in philosophy and an MA in comparative literature, she became a Research Fellow at Jesus College, Cambridge, and then a University Lecturer in the English Faculty. She has published on English and German romanticism, her most recent volume being *Romanticism, Pragmatism, and Deconstruction* (1993). She has recently completed *Modernist Women Writers and Narrative Art*.

Bibliography

Abbott, John S. C., *The History of Napoleon Bonaparte* vol. 2 (New York, 1883)

Abelove, Henry, "Freud, Male Homosexuality, and the Americans," *Sexuality in Nineteenth-Century Europe* ed. Isabel Hull and Sander L. Gilman (forthcoming)

Abrams, M. H., ed., *English Romantic Poets: Modern Essays in Criticism* (New York, 1960)

——, "Structure and Style in the Greater Romantic Lyric," *From Sensibility to Romanticism* ed. Frederick W. Hilles and Harold Bloom (New York, 1965) 527–60

Adair, Patricia, *The Waking Dream: A Study of Coleridge's Poetry* (London, 1967)

Addison, Joseph, *Works* (6 vols, London, 1811)

——, *The Spectator* ed. Donald F. Bond (5 vols, Oxford, 1965)

Alford, Henry, *Life, Journals, and Letters of Henry Alford* ed. Fanny Alford (London, 1873)

Allott, Kenneth, "The 'Ode to Psyche,'" *EiC* 6 (1956) 278–301

Ashton, John, *English Caricature and Satire on Napoleon I* (New York, 1968)

Auerbach, Erich, *Mimesis: The Representation of Reality in Western Literature* tr. Willard R. Trask (Princeton, NJ, 1953)

——, *Scenes from the Drama of European Literature: Six Essays* (New York, 1959)

Ault, Donald, "Re-visioning Blake's *Four Zoas*," *Unnam'd Forms: Blake and Textuality* ed. Nelson Hilton and Thomas A. Vogler (Berkeley and Los Angeles, Calif., 1986) 105–44

Austen, Jane, *Mansfield Park* ed. Tony Tanner (Harmondsworth, 1966)

Bachinger, Katrina, "The Sombre Madness of Sex: Byron's First and Last Gift to Poe," *The Byron Journal* 19 (1991) 131–6

Bagehot, Walter, *Literary Studies* ed. R. H. Hutton (2 vols, London, 1879)

Bahti, Timothy, "Coleridge's 'Kubla Khan' and the Fragment of Romanticism," *MLN* 96 (1981) 1035–50

Baker, Carlos, *Shelley's Major Poetry: The Fabric of a Vision* (Princeton, NJ, 1948)

Baker, Jeffrey, *Time and Mind in Wordsworth's Poetry* (Detroit, 1980)

Baker, Keith, *Condorcet* (Chicago, Ill., 1975)

Barker-Benfield, G. J., "Mary Wollstonecraft: Eighteenth-Century Commonwealth-woman," *Journal of the History of Ideas* 50 (1989) 95–115

Barrett, Michèle, *Women's Oppression Today: Problems in Marxist Feminist Analysis* (London, 1980)

Barth, J. Robert, *The Symbolic Imagination: Coleridge and the Romantic Tradition* (Princeton, NJ, 1977)

Barthes, Roland, "Style and Its Image", *Literary Style: A Symposium* ed. Seymour Chatman (London, 1971) 3–10

——, *S/Z* tr. Richard Miller (London, 1975)

——, *Image, Music, Text* tr. Stephen Heath (New York, 1977)

Basler, Roy, *Sex, Symbolism, and Psychology in Literature* (New Brunswick, 1948)

Bate, Walter Jackson, *John Keats* (Cambridge, Mass., 1963)

——, ed., *Keats: A Collection of Critical Essays* (Englewood Cliffs, NJ, 1964)

——, and John Bullitt, "The Distinction Between Fancy and Imagination in Eighteenth-Century English Criticism," *MLN* 69 (1945) 8–15

Baudelaire, Charles, *Correspondance* ed. Claude Pichois and Jean Ziegler (Paris, 1973)

——, *Oeuvres Complètes* ed. Claude Pichois (Paris, 1976)

Beattie, James, *Dissertations, Moral and Critical* (London, 1783)

Beatty, Bernard, "Lord Byron: Poetry and Precedent," *Literature of the Romantic Period 1750–1850* ed. R. T. Davies and B. G. Beatty (New York, 1976) 114–34

Beer, John, *Coleridge the Visionary* (London, 1959)

——, *Coleridge's Poetic Intelligence* (London, 1977)

——, "Influence and Independence in Blake," *Interpreting Blake* ed. Michael Phillips (Cambridge, 1978)

Berry, Francis, "The Poet of *Childe Harold*," *Byron: A Symposium* ed. John D. Jump (New York, 1975) 35–51

Bion, *Greek Bucolic Poets* ed. and tr. A. S. F. Gow (Cambridge, 1953)

Blackburn, Robin, *The Overthrow of Colonial Slavery, 1776–1848* (London, 1988)

Blair, Hugh, "A Critical Dissertation on the Poems of Ossian," in [James Macpherson], *The Poems of Ossian* (2 vols, London, 1773)

Blake, William, *The Book of Urizen* ed. Kay Parkhurst Easson and Roger R. Easson (Boulder, Colorado, and New York, 1978)

——, *The Complete Poetry and Prose of William Blake* ed. David V. Erdman (Berkeley and Los Angeles, Calif., 1982)

Bloom, Harold, ed., *Romanticism and Consciousness: Essays in Criticism* (New York, 1970)

——, *The Ringers in the Tower: Studies in Romantic Tradition* (Chicago, Ill., 1971)

——, *The Visionary Company: A Reading of English Romantic Poetry* (2nd edn, Ithaca, NY, 1971)

——, *The Anxiety of Influence: A Theory of Poetry* (London, 1973)

——, *A Map of Misreading* (New York, 1975)

Blunden, Edmund, *Charles Lamb and His Contemporaries* (Cambridge, 1933)

Bogdanor, Vernon, "Conservatism Psychoanalysed," *Yale Law Journal* 87 (1978) 1083–90

Boothby, Brooke, *Letter to Burke* (London, 1791)

Bottrall, Ronald, "Byron and the Colloquial Tradition in English Poetry," *Criterion* 18 (1939) 204–24

Boulton, James T., *The Language of Politics in the Age of Wilkes and Burke* (London, 1963)

Bowles, William Lisle, *Sonnets, and Other Poems* (Bath, 1800)

Boyd, William, *The Education Theory of Jean-Jacques Rousseau* (New York, 1963)

Boyers, Robert, and George Steiner, eds, "Homosexuality: Sacrilege, Vision, Politics," *Salmagundi* 58–9 (1982–3)

Brett, R. L., ed., *Writers and their Background: S. T. Coleridge* (London, 1971)

Brooks, Cleanth, *The Well Wrought Urn* (New York, 1947)

Brooks, Peter, *The Melodramatic Imagination* (New Haven, 1976)

——, "Godlike Science/Unhallowed Arts: Language and Monstrosity in *Frankenstein*," *New Literary History* 9 (1978) 591–605

Bruce, James, *Travels to Discover the Source of the Nile* (5 vols, Edinburgh, 1790)

Burke, Edmund, *The Collected Works of Edmund Burke* ed. F. Laurence and W. King (8 vols, London, 1826)

——, *The Works of the Rt. Hon. Edmund Burke* (12 vols, Boston, 1865–7)

——, *Reflections on the Revolution in France* ed. Thomas H. D. Mahoney (New York, 1955)

——, *A Philosophical Enquiry Into the Origin of our Ideas of the Sublime and Beautiful* ed. J. T. Boulton (London, 1958)

——, *Reflections on the Revolution in France* ed. Conor Cruise O'Brien (Harmondsworth, 1969)

Burke, Kenneth, "Symbolic Action in a Poem by Keats," *Accent* 4 (1943–4) 30–42

——, *A Rhetoric of Motives* (Berkeley, 1969)

Burton, Sir Robert, *The Anatomy of Melancholy* ed. Holbrook Jackson (New York, 1977)

Bush, Douglas, *Mythology and the Romantic Tradition in English Poetry* (Cambridge, Mass., 1937)

——, *John Keats: His Life and Writings* (New York, 1966)

Butler, Marilyn, *Romantics, Rebels and Reactionaries: English Literature and its Background 1760–1830* (Oxford, 1982)

Butlin, Martin, and Evelyn Joll, *The Paintings of J. M. W. Turner* (New Haven, Conn., 1984)

Byron, George Gordon, 6th Baron, *Byron's Don Juan. A Variorum Edition* ed. T. G. Steffan and W. W. Pratt (4 vols, Austin, Texas, 1957)

——, *Byron's Letters and Journals* ed. Leslie A. Marchand (12 vols, London, 1973–82)

——, *Don Juan* ed. T. G. Steffan, E. Steffan and W. W. Pratt (Harmondsworth, 1977)

——, *The Complete Poetical Works* ed. Jerome J. McGann and Barry Weller (7 vols, Oxford, 1980–93)

Cameron, Kenneth Neill, "Shelley vs. Southey: New Light on an Old Quarrel," *PMLA* 57 (1942) 489–512

——, "The Political Symbolism of Prometheus Unbound," *PMLA* 58 (1943) 728–53

——, *Shelley: The Golden Years* (Cambridge, Mass., 1974)

Canny, Nicholas, "The Ideology of English Colonization: From Ireland to America," *William and Mary Quarterly* 30 (1973) 575–98

Cassirer, Ernst, *The Philosophy of the Enlightenment* tr. Fritz C. A. Koelln and James P. Pettegrove (Boston, 1955)

Chambers, E. K., "Some Dates in Coleridge's Annus Mirabilis," *Essays and Studies* 19 (1933) 85–111

——, "The Date of Coleridge's *Kubla Khan*," *RES* 11 (1935) 78–90

Chandler, David G., *The Campaigns of Napoleon* (New York, 1966)

Chandler, James K., *Wordsworth's Second Nature: A Study of the Poetry and Politics* (Chicago, Ill., 1984)

Chatman, Seymour, *Story and Discourse: Narrative Structure in Fiction and Film* (Ithaca, NY, 1978)

Chayes, Irene H., "*Kubla Khan* and the Creative Process," *SiR* 6 (1966) 1–22

Clairmont, Claire, *The Journal of Claire Clairmont* ed. Marion K. Stocking (Cambridge, Mass., 1968)

Coe, Charles Norton, *Wordsworth and the Literature of Travel* (New York, 1953)

Coleridge, Samuel Taylor, *Poems, by S. T. Coleridge, Second Edition. To which are now added Poems by Charles Lamb, and Charles Lloyd* (Bristol and London, 1797)

——, "On the Philosophic Import of the Words Object and Subject," *Blackwood's Edinburgh Magazine* 10 (1821) 247–50

——, *Literary Remains* ed. H. N. Coleridge (4 vols, London, 1836–9)

——, *Biographia Literaria* ed. J. Shawcross (2 vols, Oxford, 1907)

——, *The Complete Poetical Works of Samuel Taylor Coleridge* ed. E. H. Coleridge (2 vols, Oxford, 1912)

——, *Coleridge's Literary Criticism* ed. J. W. Mackail (London, 1921)

——, *Shakespearean Criticism* ed. T. M. Raysor (2 vols, London, 1930)

——, *Treatise on Method* ed. Alice D. Snyder (London, 1934)

——, *Miscellaneous Criticism* ed. T. M. Raysor (London, 1936)

——, *The Philosophical Lectures of Samuel Taylor Coleridge* ed. Kathleen Coburn (London, 1949)

——, *Collected Letters of Samuel Taylor Coleridge* ed. E. L. Griggs (6 vols, Oxford, 1956–71)

——, *Notebooks* ed. Kathleen Coburn *et al.* (5 vols, New York, 1957–)

——, *Poems* ed. John Beer (London, 1963)

——, *The Collected Works of Samuel Taylor Coleridge*, Gen. Ed. Kathleen Coburn (Princeton, NJ, 1969–)

　I *Lectures 1795 on Politics and Religion* ed. Lewis Patton and Peter Mann (1971)

　II *The Watchman* ed. Lewis Patton (1970)

　III *Essays on His Times* ed. David V. Erdman (3 vols, 1978)

　IV *The Friend* ed. Barbara Rooke (2 vols, 1969)

　V *Lectures 1808–1819 On Literature* ed. R. A. Foakes (2 vols, 1987)

　VI *Lay Sermons* ed. R. J. White (1972)

　VII *Biographia Literaria* ed. James Engell and W. Jackson Bate (2 vols, 1983)

　IX *Aids to Reflection* ed. John Beer (1993)

　X *On the Constitution of the Church and State* ed. John Colmer (1976)

　XII *Marginalia* ed. George Whalley and H. J. Jackson (5 vols, 1980–)

XIII *Logic* ed. J. R. de J. Jackson (1981)

XIV *Table Talk* ed. Carl Woodring (2 vols, 1990)

Collection Complète des Tableaux Historiques de la Révolution Française Vol. 1 (Paris, 1789)

Cooke, Michael, *Acts of Inclusion: Studies Bearing on an Elementary Theory of Romanticism* (New Haven, Conn., 1979)

Crompton, Louis, *Byron and Greek Love: Homophobia in Nineteenth-Century England* (Berkeley, 1985)

Curran, Stuart, *Shelley's Annus Mirabilis* (San Marino, Calif., 1975)

——, "*Adonais* in Context," *Shelley Revalued: Essays from the Gregynog Conference* ed. Kelvin Everest (Leicester and Totowa, NJ, 1983) 165–82

——, "The I Altered", *Romanticism and Feminism* ed. Anne K. Mellor (Bloomington, Ind., 1988) 185–207

Darwin, Erasmus, *The Botanic Garden, Part I. The Economy of Vegetation* (London, 1791)

Dawson, John Charles, *Lakanal the Regicide* (University, Ala., 1948)

Davies, Paul, *Other Worlds: Space, Superspace, and the Quantum Universe* (New York, 1982)

Dekker, George, *Coleridge and the Literature of Sensibility* (London, 1978)

Delson, Abe, "The Function of Geraldine in *Christabel*: A Critical Perspective and Interpretation," *English Studies* 61 (1980) 130–41

De Luca, Vincent Arthur, *Words of Eternity: Blake and the Poetics of the Sublime* (Princeton, NJ, 1991)

De Man, Paul, *Blindness and Insight: Essays in the Rhetoric of Contemporary Criticism* (New York, 1971)

——, *Allegories of Reading* (New Haven, Conn., 1979)

——, "Shelley Disfigured," *Deconstruction and Criticism* Harold Bloom, Paul de Man, Jacques Derrida, Geoffrey H. Hartman, and J. Hillis Miller (London, 1979) 39–73

——, "The Rhetoric of Temporality," *Blindness and Insight: Essays in the Rhetoric of Contemporary Criticism* (2nd edn, Minneapolis, 1983) 187–208

Denham, Sir John, *Poetical Works* ed. Theodore Howard Banks, Jr. (New Haven, Conn., 1928)

Dennett, Daniel C., *Brainstorms: Philosophical Essays on Mind and Psychology* (Cambridge, Mass., 1981)

Dennis, John, *The Grounds of Criticism in Poetry* (London, 1704)

De Quincey, Thomas, *Confessions of an English Opium Eater* rev. 1856 (London and New York, n.d.)

——, *Collected Writings of Thomas De Quincey* ed. David Masson (14 vols, Edinburgh, 1889–90)

——, *Recollections of the Lakes and the Lake Poets* ed. David Wright (Harmondsworth, 1970)

——, *Confessions of an English Opium Eater* ed. Alethea Hayter (Harmondsworth, 1971)

Derrida, Jacques, "Structure, Sign, and Play in the Discourse of the Human Sciences," *The Structuralist Controversy* ed. Richard Macksey and Eugenio Donato (Baltimore, Md., 1972) 247–65

——, *Of Grammatology* tr. Gayatri Chakravorty Spivak (Baltimore, 1974)

——, "White Mythology: Metaphor in the Text of Philosophy," tr. F. C. T. Moore, *New Literary History* 6 (1974) 5–74

——, "Living On: Border Lines," *Deconstruction and Criticism*, Harold Bloom, Paul de Man, Jacques Derrida, Geoffrey H. Hartman, and J. Hillis Miller (London, 1979) 75–176

Deutsch, Helene, *The Psychology of Woman* vol. 2 *Motherhood* (New York, 1945)

DHotel, Yves, *Joseph Le Bon, or Arras sous la Terreur: Essai sur la Psychose Révolutionnaire* (Paris, 1934)

Dickens, Charles, *The Mystery of Edwin Drood* ed. Margaret Cardwell (Oxford, 1972)

Dickstein, Morris, *Keats and his Poetry* (Chicago, Ill., 1971)

Dilthey, Wilhelm, "The Rise of Hermeneutics," tr. Fredric Jameson, *New Literary History* 3 (1971–2) 229–44

Duffy, Edward, *Rousseau in England* (Berkeley and Los Angeles, 1979)

Dumas, D. Gilbert, "Things As They Were: the original ending of *Caleb Williams,*" *Studies in English Literature* 6 (1966) 575–97

Duruy, Albert, *L'instruction publique et la Revolution* (Paris, 1882)

Duzer, Charles Hunter van, *Contribution of the Ideologues to French Revolutionary Thought* (Baltimore, Md., 1935)

Eagleton, Mary, *Feminist Literary Criticism* (London, 1991)

Eagleton, Terry, *Criticism and Ideology: A Study in Marxist Literary Theory* (London, 1978)

——, *Walter Benjamin* (London, 1981)

——, *Literary Theory* (Oxford, 1983)

Easson, Roger R., "William Blake and His Reader in *Jerusalem,*" *Blake's Sublime Allegory: Essays on "The Four Zoas," "Milton," and "Jerusalem,"* ed. Stuart Curran and Joseph Anthony Wittreich, Jr. (Madison, Wisc., 1973) 309–27

Eaves, Morris, *William Blake's Theory of Art* (Princeton, NJ, 1982)

Eco, Umberto, *The Role of the Reader: Explorations in the Semiotics of Texts* (Bloomington, Ind., 1979)

Edwards, Paul, and MacDonald Emslie, " 'Thoughts so all unlike each other': The Paradoxical in *Christabel,*" *English Studies* 52 (1971) 236–46

Eichorn, Johann Gottfried, *Einleitung ins Alte Testament* (3 vols, Leipzig, 1787)

Elam, Keir, *The Semiotics of Theatre and Drama* (London, 1980)

Eliot, T. S., *Selected Essays* (New York, 1932)

——, *The Use of Poetry and the Use of Criticism* (London, 1933)

——, *On Poetry and Poets* (London, 1943)

Ellis, David, *Wordsworth, Freud, and the Spots of Time: Interpretation in The Prelude* (Cambridge, 1985)

Ellis, Kate, "Monsters in the Garden: Mary Shelley and the Bourgeois Family," *The Endurance of Frankenstein: Essays on Mary Shelley's Novel* ed. George Levine and U. C. Knoepflmacher (Berkeley, Calif., 1979) 123–42

Empson, William, *Seven Types of Ambiguity* (New York, 1966)

Ende, Stuart, *Keats and the Sublime* (New Haven, Conn., 1976)

England, A. B., *Byron's Don Juan and Eighteenth-Century Literature* (Lewisburg, Penn., 1975)

Enscoe, Gerald, *Eros and the Romantics* (The Hague and Paris, 1967)

Erdman, David V., *Prophet Against Empire* (Princeton, 1954)

——, "Coleridge, Wordsworth, and the Wedgwood Fund," *BNYPL* 60 (1956) 425–43, 486–507

——, *A Concordance to the Writings of William Blake* (Ithaca, NY, 1967)

——, "*America*: New Expanses," *Blake's Visionary Forms Dramatic* ed. David V. Erdman and John E. Grant (Princeton, 1970) 92–114

Erskine, Thomas, *A View of the Causes and Consequences of the Present War with France* (London, 1797)

Escarpit, Robert, *Lord Byron: Un tempérament littéraire* (2 vols, Paris, 1957)

Everest, Kelvin, " 'Ozymandias': The Text in Time," *Essays and Studies* (1992) 24–42

Evert, Walter, *Aesthetic and Myth in the Poetry of Keats* (Princeton, NJ, 1965)

Ferguson, Frances, "The Sublime of Edmund Burke, or the Bathos of Experience," *Glyph* 8 (1981) 62–78

Ferguson, Moira, ed., *First Feminists – British Women Writers* (Bloomington, Ind., 1985)

Fichte, J. G., *The Vocation of Man* ed. Roderick M. Chisholm (Indianapolis, 1956)

——, *Science of Knowledge* ed. and tr. Peter Heath and John Lachs (New York, 1970)

Finke, Laurie A., " 'A Philosophic Wanton': Language and Authority in Wollstone-craft's *A Vindication of the Rights of Woman*," *The Philosopher as Writer: The Eighteenth Century* ed. Robert Ginsberg (Selinsgrove, 1987) 155–76

Fleischman, Avrom, *A Reading of Mansfield Park: An Essay in Critical Synthesis* (Minneapolis, 1967)

——, *The English Historical Novel: Walter Scott to Virginia Woolf* (Baltimore, Md., 1971)

Fletcher, Angus, *Allegory: The Theory of a Symbolic Mode* (Ithaca, NY, 1964)

Fogle, R. H., "The Romantic Unity of *Kubla Khan*," *College English* 22 (1960) 112–16

Fontainerie, F. de la, ed. and tr., *French Liberalism and Education in the Eighteenth Century* (New York and London, 1932)

Foucault, Michel, *The Order of Things* (New York, 1971)

Fox, Susan, *Poetic Form in Blake's "Milton"* (Princeton, NJ, 1976)

Freud, Sigmund, *The Standard Edition of the Complete Psychological Works of Sigmund Freud* tr. James Strachey *et al.*, ed. James Strachey (24 vols, London, 1953–74)

——, *Jokes and their Relation to the Unconscious* tr. James Strachey (New York, 1963)

Fried, Michael, *Absorption and Theatricality: Painting and Beholder in the Age of Diderot* (Berkeley, Calif., 1980)

Froula, Christine, "When Eve Reads Milton: Undoing the Canonical Economy," *Critical Inquiry* 10 (1983) 321–47

Frye, Northrop, *Fearful Symmetry: A Study of William Blake* (Princeton, NJ, 1947)

——, *Anatomy of Criticism: Four Essays* (Princeton, NJ, 1957)

——, "Varieties of Literary Utopias," *The Stubborn Structure* (Ithaca, NY, 1970) 109–34

Furbank, P. N., "Godwin's Novels," *EiC* 5 (1955) 214–28

Gallagher, John, *The Decline, Revival and Fall of the British Empire* (Cambridge, 1982)

Garaud, Marcel, and Romuald Szramkiewicz, *La Révolution Française et la Famille* (Paris, 1978)

Garrod, H. W., *Keats* (Oxford, 1926)

Gates, Barbara T., "Wordsworth and the Course of History," *Research Studies* 44 (1976) 199–207

——, "The Prelude and the Development of Wordsworth's Historical Imagination," *Études Anglaises* 30 (1977) 169–78

Gerard, Alexander, *An Essay on Taste* (London, 1759)

Gilbert, Sandra, and Susan Gubar, *The Madwoman in the Attic: The Woman Writer and the Nineteenth-Century Literary Imagination* (New Haven, Conn., 1979)

Girard, René, *Deceit, Desire, and the Novel: Self and Other in Literary Structure* tr. Yvonne Freccero (Baltimore, Md., 1972)

Girouard, Mark, *The Return to Camelot: Chivalry and the English Gentleman* (New Haven, Conn., 1981)

Gittings, Robert, *John Keats: The Living Year* (London, 1962)

Gittings, Robert, *John Keats* (London, 1968)

Gleckner, Robert, "Keats's Odes: The Problems of the Limited Canon," *Studies in English Literature* 5 (1965) 577–85

Godwin, William, *An Enquiry Concerning Political Justice* (2 vols, London, 1793)

——, *An Enquiry Concerning Political Justice* ed. F. E. L. Priestley (Toronto, 1946)

——, *Uncollected Writings* ed. J. Marken and Burton R. Pollin (Gainesville, Fl., 1968)

——, *Caleb Williams* ed. David McCracken (Oxford, 1970)

Gold, Alex, Jr., "It's Only Love: The Politics of Passion in Godwin's *Caleb Williams*," *Texas Studies in Literature and Language* 19 (1977) 135–60

Greenblatt, Stephen, *Renaissance Self-Fashioning: From More to Shakespeare* (Chicago, Ill., 1980)

Gregory, Richard L., *Mind in Science: A History of Explanations in Psychology and Physics* (Cambridge, 1981)

Guillaume, M. J., ed., *Procès-verbaux du Comité d'instruction publique* (Paris, 1889)

Guralnick, Elissa S., "Radical Politics in Mary Wollstonecraft's *A Vindication of the Rights of Woman*," *Studies in Burke and His Time* 18 (1977) 153–66

Hampson, Norman, *The French Revolution: A Concise History* (London, 1975)

Harari, Josué V., "Critical Factions/Critical Fictions," *Textual Strategies: Perspectives in Post-Structuralist Criticism* ed. Josué V. Harari (Ithaca, NY, 1979) 17–72

Hardy, Thomas, *Works* vol. 5 *The Life and Death of the Mayor of Casterbridge* (21 vols, London, 1912–14)

Harrison, T. P., Jr., "Spenser and Shelley's 'Adonais'," *Texas University Studies in English* 13 (1933) 54–63

Hartman, Geoffrey H., *The Fate of Reading and Other Essays* (Chicago, Ill., 1975)

——, *The Unremarkable Wordsworth*, Foreword by Donald G. Marshall (London, 1987)

——, *Wordsworth's Poetry, 1787–1814* (2nd edn, New Haven, Conn., 1987)

Harvey, A. D., "The Nightmare of *Caleb Williams*," *EiC* 26 (1976) 236–49

Havens, Raymond Dexter, *The Mind of a Poet* vol. 2: *The Prelude, A Commentary* (Baltimore, Md., 1941)

Hayden, Donald E., *Wordsworth's Walking Tour of 1790* (Tulsa, Okla., 1983)

Hazlitt, William, *Works* ed. P. P. Howe (21 vols, London, 1930–4)

Heffernan, James A. W., *Wordsworth's Theory of Poetry: The Transforming Imagination* (Ithaca, NY, 1969)

——, *The Re-Creation of Landscape: A Study of Wordsworth, Coleridge, Constable, and Turner* (Hanover, NH, 1985)

Hegel, G. W. F., *The Phenomenology of Mind* tr. J. B. Baillie (New York, 1967)

——, *Hegel's Aesthetics: Lectures on Fine Art* tr. T. M. Knox (2 vols, Oxford, 1975)

Henderson, Ernest F., *Symbol and Satire in the French Revolution* (New York, 1912)

Heppner, Christopher, "The Woman Taken in Adultery: An Essay on Blake's 'Style of Designing,'" *Blake: An Illustrated Quarterly* 17 (1983) 44–60

Herbert, Robert L., *David, "Brutus," and the French Revolution: An Essay in Art and Politics* (London, 1972)

Hertz, Neil, "The Notion of Blockage in the Literature of the Sublime," *Psychoanalysis and the Question of the Text* ed. Geoffrey H. Hartman (Baltimore, Md., 1978) 62–85

Hilton, Nelson, *Literal Imagination: Blake's Vision of Words* (Berkeley and Los Angeles, Calif., 1983)

Hobson, J. A., *Imperialism: A Study* (Ann Arbor, Michigan, 1972)

Hofkosh, Sonia, "Women and the Romantic Author – the Example of Byron," *Romanticism and Feminism* ed. Anne K. Mellor (Bloomington, Ind., 1988) 94–114

Hofstadter, Douglas R., *Godel, Escher, Bach: an Eternal Golden Braid* (New York, 1980)

Hogg, James, *The Private Memoirs and Confessions of a Justified Sinner* (New York, 1970)

Holloway, John, *The Charted Mirror* (London, 1960)

Holmes, Richard, *Shelley: The Pursuit* (New York, 1975)

Homans, Margaret, *Women Writers and Poetic Identity: Dorothy Wordsworth, Emily Brontë, and Emily Dickinson* (Princeton, NJ, 1980)

——, "Eliot, Wordsworth, and the Scenes of the Sisters' Instruction," *Critical Inquiry* 8 (1981) 223–41, repr. *Bearing the Word*, Ch. 6

——, *Bearing the Word: Language and Female Experience in Nineteenth-Century Women's Writing* (Chicago, Ill., 1986)

Horkheimer, Max, *Anfänge der bürgerlichen Geschichtsphilosophie* (Stuttgart, 1930)

Houghton, Walter E., Jr., "Lamb's Criticism of Restoration Comedy," *ELH* 10 (1943) 61–72

Hulme, Peter, *Colonial Encounters: Europe and the Native Caribbean, 1492–1797*, (London, 1986)

——, and Neil L. Whitehead, ed., *Wild Majesty: Encounters with Caribs from Columbus to the Present Day* (Oxford, 1992)

Hunt, Lynn, *Politics, Culture, and Class in the French Revolution* (Berkeley, Calif., 1984)

Hutton, Richard H., *Sir Walter Scott* (New York, 1878)

Ingarden, Roman, *The Cognition of the Literary Work of Art* tr. Ruth Ann Cowley and Kenneth R. Olson (Evanston, Ill., 1973)

Jack, Ian, *Keats and the Mirror of Art* (Oxford, 1967)

Jacobus, Mary, "The Idiot Boy," *Bicentenary Wordsworth Studies* ed. Jonathan Wordsworth (Ithaca, NY, 1970) 238–65

——, "Is There a Woman in This Text?", *New Literary History* 14 (1982–3) 117–41

——, " 'That Great Stage Where Senators Perform': *Macbeth* and the Politics of Romantic Theater," *SiR* 22 (1983) 353–87

Jacobus, Mary, "The Art of Managing Books," *Romanticism and Language* ed. Arden Reed (London, 1984) 215–46

——, "The Buried Letter: *Villette*," *Reading Woman: Essays in Feminist Criticism* (New York, 1986)

Jakobson, Roman, "Two Aspects of Language and Two Types of Aphasic Disturbances," *Fundamentals of Language*, Roman Jakobson and Morris Halle (2nd edn, The Hague, 1971) 69–96

James, C. L. R., *The Black Jacobins: Toussaint L'Ouverture and the San Domingo Revolution* (New York, 1963)

Janes, Regina M., "On the Reception of Mary Wollstonecraft's *A Vindication of the Rights of Woman*," *Journal of the History of Ideas* 39 (1978) 293–302

Janowitz, Anne, "Coleridge's 1816 Volume: Fragment as Rubric," *SiR* 24 (1985) 21–39

Jauss, Hans Robert, "Theses on the Transition from the Aesthetics of Literary Works to a Theory of Aesthetic Experience," *Interpretation of Narrative* ed. Mario J. Valdés and Owen J. Miller (Toronto, 1978)

Johnson, Barbara, "My Monster/My Self," *Diacritics* 12.2 (1982) 2–10

Johnson, Samuel, *Lives of the English Poets* ed. George Birkbeck Hill (3 vols, Oxford, 1905)

——, *Johnson on Shakespeare*, ed. Walter Raleigh (Oxford, 1908)

Jones, Frederick L., ed., *Maria Gisborne and Edward E. Williams: Shelley's Friends* (Norman, 1951)

Jones, James, *Adam's Dream: Mythic Consciousness in Keats and Yeats* (Athens, Georgia, 1975)

Jones, Leonidas, "The 'Ode to Psyche': An Allegorical Introduction to Keats's Great Odes," *Keats-Shelley Memorial Bulletin* 9 (1958) 22–6

Joseph, M. K., *Byron the Poet* (London, 1964)

Kant, Immanuel, *The Critique of Judgment* tr. J. H. Bernard (London, 1914)

Kaplan, Cora, *Sea Changes: Essays on Culture and Feminism* (London, 1986)

Keats, John, *The Letters of John Keats, 1814–1821* ed. Hyder E. Rollins (2 vols, Cambridge, Mass., 1958)

——, *Letters of John Keats* ed. Robert Gittings (London, 1970)

——, *The Poems of John Keats* ed. Miriam Allott (London, 1970)

——, *The Poems of John Keats* ed. Jack Stillinger (Cambridge, Mass., 1978)

Kellogg, Stuart, ed., "Literary Visions of Homosexuality," *Journal of Homosexuality* 8, 3–4 (1983)

Kelly, Gary, *The English Jacobin Novel, 1780–1805* (Oxford, 1976)

——, *Women, Writing, and Revolution 1790–1827* (Oxford, 1993)

Kermode, Frank, *Romantic Image* (London, 1957)

Kiely, Robert, *The Romantic Novel in England* (Cambridge, Mass., 1972)

Kiernan, Victor G., *The Lords of Human Kind: European Attitudes towards the Outside World in the Imperial Age* (London, 1969)

——, *Marxism and Imperialism* (New York, 1974)

Kintsch, Walter, "Levels of Processing Language Material," *Levels of Processing in Human Memory* ed. Laird S. Cermak and Fergus I. M. Craik (Hillsdale, NJ, 1979) 211–22

Kittel, Harald A., "*The Book of Urizen* and *An Essay Concerning Human Understanding*," *Interpreting Blake* ed. Michael Phillips (Cambridge, 1978) 111–44

Klancher, Jon P., "From 'Crowd' to 'Audience': The Making of an English Mass Readership in the Nineteenth Century," *ELH* 50 (1983) 155–73

——, *The Making of English Reading Audiences, 1790–1832* (Madison, Wisc., 1987)

Knight, Richard Payne, *An Analytical Inquiry into the Principles of Taste* (3rd edn, London, 1808)

Knoepflmacher, U. C., "Thoughts on the Aggression of Daughters," *The Endurance of Frankenstein: Essays on Mary Shelley's Novel* ed. George Levine and U. C. Knoepflmacher (Berkeley, Calif., 1979) 88–119

Koestenbaum, Wayne, *Double Talk: The Erotics of Male Literary Collaboration* (London, 1989)

Kramnick, Isaac, *The Rage of Edmund Burke: Portrait of an Ambivalent Conservative* (New York, 1977)

Kris, Ernst, *Psychoanalytic Explorations in Art* (London, 1953)

Kroeber, Karl, "Experience as History: Shelley's Venice, Turner's Carthage," *ELH* 41 (1974) 321–39

Krutch, Joseph Wood, *Comedy and Conscience after the Restoration* (New York, 1924)

Lacan, Jacques, *Ecrits* tr. Alan Sheridan (New York, 1977)

Lakanal, Joseph, *Rapport sur J. J. Rousseau, fait au nom de Comité d'instruction publique* (Paris, n.d.)

Lamb, Charles, *Elia and the Last Essays of Elia* ed. Jonathan Bate (Oxford, 1987)

——, *The Collected Essays of Charles Lamb* (2 vols, London and Toronto, 1929)

——, *The Letters of Charles and Mary Lamb* ed. E. V. Lucas (3 vols, London, 1935)

——, *The Letters of Charles and Mary Anne Lamb* ed. Edwin W. Marrs, Jr. (3 vols, Ithaca, NY, 1975–8)

Lambert, Ellen Zetzel, *Placing Sorrow: A Study of the Pastoral Elegy Convention from Theocritus to Milton* (Chapel Hill, 1976)

Lams, Victor J., Jr., "Ruth, Milton, and Keats's 'Ode to a Nightingale'," *MLQ* 34 (1973) 417–35

Laplanche, Jean, *Life and Death in Psychoanalysis* tr. Jeffrey Mehlman (Baltimore, Md., 1976)

——, and J.-B. Pontalis, "Fantasy and the Origins of Sexuality," *International Journal of Psycho-Analysis* 49 (1968) 1–18

Langer, Suzanne, *Philosophy in a New Key* (Cambridge, Mass., 1951)

Leask, Nigel, *The Politics of Imagination in Coleridge's Critical Thought* (Basingstoke, 1988)

——, *British Romantic Writers and the East* (Cambridge, 1992)

Lefebvre, Georges, *The Great Fear of 1789: Rural Panic in Revolutionary France* tr. Joan White (Princeton, NJ, 1982)

Leigh Hunt, James Henry, *Autobiography of Leigh Hunt* ed. Edmund Blunden (London, 1928)

Lemaire, Anika, *Jacques Lacan* tr. David Macey (London, 1977)

Lentricchia, Frank, *After the New Criticism* (Chicago, Ill., 1980)

Levinson, Marjorie, *Wordsworth's Great Period Poems* (Cambridge, 1986)

Lindsay, Jack, *J. M. W. Turner: His Life and Work* (London, 1966)

Liu, Alan, "Towards a Theory of Common Sense: Beckford's *Vathek* and Johnson's *Rasselas*," *Texas Studies in Literature and Language* 26 (1984) 183–217

——, *Wordsworth: The Sense of History* (Stanford, Calif., 1989)

Locke, John, *An Essay Concerning Human Understanding* ed. P. N. Nidditch (Oxford, 1975)

Locock, C. D., *An Examination of the Shelley Manuscripts in the Bodleian Library* (Oxford, 1903)

Lofft, Capel, *Remarks on the Letter of the Rt. Hon. Edmund Burke, concerning the Revolution in France* (2nd edn, London, 1791)

Longinus, Dionysus, *Essay on the Sublime* tr. William Smith (London, 1756)

Lowes, John Livingston, *The Road to Xanadu* (London, 1927)

Lowth, Robert, *Lectures on the Sacred Poetry of the Hebrews* tr. G. Gregory (2 vols, London, 1787)

Luther, Susan, " 'Christabel' as Dream Reverie," *Romantic Reassessments* ed. James Hogg (Salzburg, 1976)

McCracken, David, "Godwin's Reading in Burke," *ELN* 7 (1970) 264–70

Maccunn, F. J., *The Contemporary English View of Napoleon* (London, 1914)

McFarland, Thomas, *Romanticism and the Forms of Ruin* (Princeton, NJ, 1981)

McFarland, Thomas, *Romantic Cruxes* (Oxford, 1987)

McGann, Jerome J., *Don Juan in Context* (Chicago, Ill., 1976)

——, *A Critique of Modern Textual Criticism* (Chicago, Ill., 1983)

——, *The Beauty of Inflections* (Oxford, 1985)

——, *The Romantic Ideology* (Chicago, Ill., 1986)

——, " 'My Brain is Feminine': Byron and the Poetry of Deception," *Byron: Augustan and Romantic* ed. Andrew Rutherford (Basingstoke, 1990) 26–51

——, *The Textual Condition* (Princeton, NJ, 1991)

——, "What Difference do the Circumstances of Publication Make to the Interpretation of a Literary Work?", *Literary Pragmatics* ed. Roger D. Sell (London and New York, 1991) 195–204

MacGillivray, J. R., "The Pantisocracy Scheme and its Immediate Background," *Studies in English by Members of the University of Toronto* (Toronto, 1931) 131–69

——, "The Three Forms of *The Prelude*," *Essays in English Literature from the Renaissance to the Victorian Age* ed. Millar MacLure and F. W. Watt (Toronto, 1964) 229–44

McNeil, Gordon Heath, *The Pantheonization of Rousseau during the French Revolution* (Master's thesis, University of Chicago, 1937)

Maniquis, Robert M., "Lonely Empires: Personal and Public Visions of Thomas De Quincey", *Literary Monographs* 8 (1976) 47–127

——, "The Dark Interpreter and the Palimpsest of Violence: De Quincey and the Unconscious," *Thomas De Quincey: Bicentenary Studies* ed. Robert Lance Snyder (Norman, Oklahoma, 1985) 109–39

Manley, Lawrence, "Concepts of Convention and Models of Critical Discourse," *New Literary History* 13 (1981) 31–52

Mann, Paul, "*The Book of Urizen* and the Horizon of the Book," *Unnam'd Forms: Blake and Textuality* ed. Nelson Hilton and Thomas A. Vogler (Berkeley and Los Angeles, Calif., 1989) 49–68

Manning, Peter J., "Byron's 'English Bards' and Shelley's 'Adonais': A Note," *Notes and Queries* NS 17 (1970) 380–1

——, *Byron and his Fictions* (Detroit, 1978)

——, *Reading Romantics: Texts and Contexts* (New York, 1990)

Marcus, Steven, *The Other Victorians: A Study of Sexuality and Pornography in Mid-Nineteenth-Century England* (London and New York, 1966)

Margoliouth, H. M., "Wordsworth and Coleridge: Dates in May and June 1798," *Notes and Queries* 198 (1953) 352–4

Martin, Jane Roland, *Reclaiming a Conversation – The Ideal of the Educated Woman* (New Haven, Conn., 1985)

Martin, Robert K., *The Homosexual Tradition in American Poetry* (Austin, Texas, 1979)

Masters, Roger D., *The Political Philosophy of Rousseau* (Princeton, NJ, 1968)

Matteson, Lynn R., "The Poetics and Politics of Alpine Passage: Turner's *Snowstorm: Hannibal and His Army Crossing the Alps*," *Art Bulletin* 62 (1980) 385–98

Mellor, Anne K., *English Romantic Irony* (Cambridge, Mass., 1980)

——, *Romanticism and Gender* (London, 1993)

——, *Romanticism and Feminism* (Bloomington, Ind., 1988)

Mercer, Dorothy, "The Symbolism of *Kubla Khan*," *Journal of Aesthetics and Art Criticism* 12 (1953) 44–65

Meyerstein, E. H., "The Completeness of *Kubla Khan*," *TLS* (30 October 1937) 803

Mill, John Stuart, *Disquisitions and Discussions* vol. 3 (London, 1875)

——, *Principles of Political Economy* ed. J. M. Robson (Toronto, 1965)

Miller, D. A., "Discipline in Different Voices: Bureaucracy, Police, Family, and *Bleak House*," *Representations* 1 (1983) 59–89

Miller, J. Hillis, "Ariadne's Thread: Repetition and the Narrative Line," *Interpretation of Narrative* ed. Mario J. Valdés and Owen J. Miller (Toronto, 1978)

——, "The Critic as Host," *Deconstruction and Criticism*, Harold Bloom, Paul De Man, Jacques Derrida, Geoffrey H. Hartman, and J. Hillis Miller (London, 1979) 217–53

——, *Fiction and Repetition: Seven English Novels* (Cambridge, Mass., 1982)

Milne, Fred, "Shelley on Keats: A Notebook Dialogue," *ELN* 13 (1976) 278–84

Milton, John, *Complete Poems and Major Prose* ed. Merritt Y. Hughes (New York, 1957)

——, *The Complete Poetical Works of John Milton* ed. Douglas Bush (Boston, 1965)

Mintz, Sidney W., *Sweetness and Power: The Place of Sugar in Modern History* (New York, 1985)

Mitchell, W. J. T., "Poetic and Pictorial Imagination in Blake's *The Book of Urizen*," *Eighteenth-Century Studies* 3 (1969) 83–107

——, "Style and Iconography in the Illustrations of Blake's Milton," *Blake Studies* 6 (1973) 47–71

——, *Blake's Composite Art: A Study of the Illuminated Poetry* (Princeton, NJ, 1978)

Moers, Ellen, *Literary Women* (New York, 1977)

Moi, Toril, *Sexual/Textual Politics* (London, 1985)

Moniteur universel: Réimpression de L'Ancien Moniteur (Paris, 1863)

Monk, Samuel H., *The Sublime: A Study of Critical Theories in XVIII-Century England* (New York, 1935)

Monro, D. H., *Godwin's Moral Philosophy* (London, 1953)

Moorman, Mary, *William Wordsworth: A Biography* (2 vols, Oxford, 1957–65)

Morkan, Joel, "Structure and Meaning in *The Prelude*, Book V," *PMLA* 87 (1972) 246–54

Murrin, Michael, *The Veil of Allegory: Some Notes Towards a Theory of Allegorical Rhetoric in the English Renaissance* (Chicago, Ill., 1969)

Murry, J. Middleton, *Heaven and Earth* (London, 1938)

Myers, Mitzi, "Reform or Ruin: 'A Revolution in Female Manners,'" *Studies in Eighteenth-Century Culture* 11 (1982) 199–216

Newton, Sir Isaac, *Sir Isaac Newton's Mathematical Principles of Natural Philosophy and His System of the World* tr. Andrew Motte, ed. Florian Cajori (2 vols, Berkeley, Calif., 1934)

Nietzsche, Friedrich, *The Birth of Tragedy* tr. Walter Kaufmann (New York, 1967)

——, *Twilight of the Idols and The Anti-Christ* tr. R. J. Hollingdale (Harmondsworth, 1968)

Nuttall, A. D., *Two Concepts of Allegory* (New York, 1967)

Oates, Joyce Carol, "Frankenstein's Fallen Angel," *Critical Inquiry* 10 (1984) 543–54

Olsen, Frances E., "The Family and the Market: A Study of Ideology and Legal Reform," *Harvard Law Review* 97 (1983) 1497–1578

Ozouf, Mona, *La fête révolutionnaire, 1789–1799* (Paris, 1976)

Paine, Thomas, *The Rights of Man, Part One and Part Two* ed. H. Collins (Harmondsworth, 1969)

Paley, Morton D., *Energy and the Imagination: A Study of the Development of Blake's Thought* (Oxford, 1970)
——, *The Continuing City: William Blake's "Jerusalem"* (Oxford, 1983)
Palmer, Alan, *An Encyclopaedia of Napoleon's Europe* (New York, 1984)
Palmer, R. R., *The World of the French Revolution* (New York, 1972)
Parker, Patricia A., *Inescapable Romance: Studies in the Poetics of a Mode* (Princeton, NJ, 1979)
Parliamentary Debates from the Year 1803, to the Present Time (41 vols, London, 1804–20)
Pater, Walter, *Three Major Texts* ed. William E. Buckler (New York and London, 1986)
Patterson, Charles I. "Passion and Permanence in Keats's 'Ode on a Grecian Urn,'" *ELH* 21 (1954) 208–20
——, "The Daemonic in *Kubla Khan*," *PMLA* 89 (1974) 1033–42
Patterson, Sylvia W., *Rousseau's Emile and Early Children's Literature* (Metuchen, NJ, 1971)
Paul, C. Kegan, *Godwin: His Friends and Contemporaries* (2 vols, London, 1876)
Paulin, Tom, *Ireland and the English Crisis* (Newcastle upon Tyne, 1984)
——, *Minotaur: Poetry and the Nation State* (London, 1992)
Paulson, Ronald, "Burke's Sublime and the Representation of Revolution," *Culture and Politics from Puritanism to the Englightenment* ed. Perez Zagorin (Berkeley, Calif., 1980) 241–69
——, *Literary Landscape: Turner and Constable* (New Haven, Conn., 1982)
——, *Representations of Revolution (1789–1820)* (New Haven, Conn., 1983)
Peacock, Thomas Love, *Works* ed. H. F. B. Brett-Smith and C. E. Jones (10 vols, New York and London, 1924–34)
Peck, Walter E., *Shelley: His Life and Work* (2 vols, London, 1927)
Perkins, David, *The Quest for Permanence: The Symbolism of Wordsworth, Shelley, and Keats* (Cambridge, Mass., 1959)
Pettet, E. C., *On the Poetry of Keats* (Cambridge, 1957)
Pinter, Harold, "Between the Lines," *The Sunday Times* (4 March 1962) 25
Piper, H. W., "The Disunity of *Christabel* and the Fall of Nature," *EiC* 29 (1978) 216–27
Polidori, John William, *The Diary of Dr. John William Polidori* ed. W. M. Rossetti (London, 1911)
Poovey, Mary, *The Proper Lady and the Woman Writer: Ideology as Style in the Works of Mary Wollstonecraft, Mary Shelley, and Jane Austen* (Chicago, Ill., 1984)
Pope, Alexander, *Homer's Iliad* ed. Maynard Mack *et al.* (London and New York, 1967)
Potter, George Reuben, "Unpublished Marginalia in Coleridge's Copy of Malthus' *Essay on Population*," *PMLA* 51 (1936) 1061–8
Pottle, Frederick A., "The Role of Asia in the Dramatic Action of Shelley's *Prometheus Unbound*," *Shelley: A Collection of Critical Essays* ed. G. M. Ridenour (Englewood Cliffs, NJ, 1965) 133–43
Praz, Mario, *The Romantic Agony* tr. Angus Davidson (London, 1933; 2nd edn, 1970)
Price, Martin, "The Sublime Poem: Pictures and Powers," *Yale Review* 58 (1969) 194–213
Punter, David, *The Literature of Terror: A History of Gothic Fictions from 1765 to the Present Day* (London, 1980)

Purves, A. C., "Formal Structure in *Kubla Khan*," *SiR* 1 (1962) 187–91

Quilligan, Maureen, *The Language of Allegory: Defining the Genre* (Ithaca, NY, 1979)

Ragatz, Lowell Joseph, *The Fall of the Planter Class in the British Caribbean, 1783–1833: A Study in Social and Economic History* (New York, 1963)

Ragussis, Michael, *The Subterfuge of Art* (Baltimore, Md., 1978)

Rajan, Balachandra, *The Form of the Unfinished: English Poetics from Spenser to Pound* (Princeton, NJ, 1985)

Rajan, Tilottama, *Dark Interpreter: The Discourse of Romanticism* (Ithaca, NY, 1980)

——, "Romanticism and the Death of Lyric Consciousness," *Lyric Poetry: Beyond New Criticism* ed. Chavia Hosek and Patricia Parker (Ithaca, NY, 1985) 194–207

——, *The Supplement of Reading: Figures of Understanding in Romantic Theory and Practice* (Ithaca, NY, 1990)

——, "The Web of Human Things: Narrative and Identity in *Alastor*," *The New Shelley: Later Twentieth-Century Views* ed. G. Kim Blank (Basingstoke, 1991) 85–107

Rand, Richard, "Geraldine," *Glyph* 3 (1978) 74–97

Randel, Fred V., "Coleridge and the Contentiousness of Romantic Nightingales," *SiR* 21 (1982) 33–55

Rauber, D. F., "The Fragment as Romantic Form," *MLQ* 30 (1964) 212–21

Reed, Mark L., *Wordsworth: The Chronology of the Early Years: 1770–1799* (Cambridge, Mass., 1967)

——, *Wordsworth: The Chronology of the Middle Years: 1800–1815* (Cambridge, Mass., 1975)

Reiman, Donald H., "Keats and the Humanistic Paradox: Mythological History in *Lamia*," *Studies in English Literature* 11 (1971) 659–69.

——, "*Don Juan* in Epic Context," *SiR* 16 (1977) 587–94.

——, ed., *The Romantics Reviewed* (6 vols, New York and London, 1977)

Richardson, Alan, "Colonialism, Race, and Lyric Irony in Blake's 'The Little Black Boy,'" *Papers on Language and Literature* 26 (1990) 233–48

——, "Romantic Voodoo: Obeah and British Culture, 1797–1807," *SiR* 32 (1993) 3–28

Richter, Jean Paul, *Vorschule der Aesthetik* (1804)

Ridenour, George M., *The Style of Don Juan* (New Haven, 1960)

Riffaterre, Michael, *Semiotics of Poetry* (Bloomington, Ind., 1978)

Roberts, Warren, *Jane Austen and the French Revolution* (London, 1979)

Robiquet, Jean, *Daily Life in the French Revolution* tr. James Kirkup (London, 1964)

Robson, W. W., "Byron as Poet," *Critical Essays* (London, 1966) 148–88

Roddier, Henri, *J.-J. Rousseau en Angleterre au XVIIIe siècle* (Paris, 1947)

Roe, Nicholas, *Wordsworth and Coleridge: The Radical Years* (Oxford, 1988)

——, *The Politics of Nature: Wordsworth and Some Contemporaries* (Basingstoke, 1992)

Rorty, Richard, *Philosophy and the Mirror of Nature* (Princeton, NJ, 1979)

Rosen, Michael, *Hegel's Dialectic and Its Criticism* (Cambridge, 1982)

Ross, Marlon B., "Naturalizing Gender: Woman's Place in Wordsworth's Ideological Landscape," *ELH* 53 (1986) 391–410

Romilly, Samuel, *Memoirs of the Life of Sir Samuel Romilly, Written by Himself; With a Selection from His Correspondence, Edited by His Sons* (2nd edn, London, 1840)

——, *The Contours of Masculine Desire: Romanticism and the Rise of Women's Poetry* (New York, 1989)

Rousseau, Jean-Jacques, *The Confessions* tr. J. M. Cohen (London, 1953)
——, *Emile* tr. Barbara Foxley (New York, 1963)
——, *Emile* tr. Allan Bloom (New York, 1979)
Rubenstein, Marc, " 'My Accursed Origin': The Search for the Mother in *Franken-stein*," *SiR* 15 (1976) 165–94
Rutherford, Andrew, ed., *Byron: The Critical Heritage* (New York, 1970)
Ryan, Robert M., *Keats: The Religious Sense* (Princeton, NJ, 1976)
Sagnac, Philippe, and Jean Robiquet, *La Révolution de 1789* vol. 1 (Paris, 1934)
Said, Edward, "Paulin's People," *London Review of Books* (9 April 1992) 11
——, *Culture and Imperialism* (London, 1993)
Salusinszky, Imre, *Criticism in Society* (London, 1987)
Saussure, Ferdinand de, *Course in General Linguistics* ed. Charles Bally and Albert Sechehaye, in collaboration with Albert Riedlinger, tr. Wade Baskin (New York, 1966)
Schapiro, Barbara A., *The Romantic Mother: Narcissistic Patterns in Romantic Poetry* (Baltimore, Md., 1983)
Schelling, F. W. J., *The Ages of the World* tr. F. de Wolfe Bolman (New York, 1946)
Schlegel, August Wilhelm, *A Course of Lectures on Dramatic Art and Literature* tr. John Black (London, 1846)
Schneider, Ben Ross, Jr., *Wordsworth's Cambridge Education* (Cambridge, 1957)
Schneider, Elizabeth, "The Dream of *Kubla Khan*," *PMLA* 60 (1945) 784–801
——, *Coleridge, Opium, and Kubla Khan* (Chicago, Ill., 1953)
Schulz, Max F., "Keats's Timeless Order of Things: A Modern Reading of 'Ode to Psyche,' " *Criticism* 2 (1960) 55–65
——, *The Poetic Voices of Coleridge* (Detroit, 1963)
Sedgwick, Eve Kosofsky, *The Coherence of Gothic Conventions* (New York, 1980)
——, *Between Men: English Literature and Male Homosocial Desire* (New York, 1985)
Shaffer, Elinor, *"Kubla Khan" and the Fall of Jerusalem* (Cambridge, 1975)
Shakespeare, William, *The Riverside Shakespeare* ed. G. Blakemore Evans (Boston, Mass., 1974)
Sharp, Ronald A., *Keats, Scepticism, and the Religion of Beauty* (Athens, Georgia, 1979)
Shaver, Chester L., and Alice C. Shaver, *Wordsworth's Library: A Catalogue* (New York, 1979)
Shaviro, Steven, " 'Striving with Systems': Blake and the Politics of Difference," *Boundary 2* 10 (1982) 229–50
Shelley, Mary, *Frankenstein, Or The Modern Prometheus* (New York, 1965)
——, *Frankenstein, Or The Modern Prometheus: The 1818 Text* ed. James L. Rieger (Chicago, Ill., 1982)
Shelley, Percy Bysshe, *The Complete Works* ed. Roger Ingpen and Walter E. Peck (10 vols, London, 1926–30)
——, *Selected Poetry and Prose of Percy Bysshe Shelley* ed. Carlos Baker (New York, 1951)
——, *Prometheus Unbound: A Variorum Edition* ed. Lawrence John Zillman (Seattle, 1959)
——, *Shelley and His Circle* ed. K. N. Cameron and Donald H. Reiman (8 vols, Cambridge, Mass., 1961–86)
——, *The Esdaile Notebooks* ed. Kenneth Neill Cameron (New York, 1964)
——, *The Letters of Percy Bysshe Shelley* ed. Frederick L. Jones (2 vols, Oxford, 1964)

——, *Shelley: Political Writings* ed. Roland A. Duerkson (New York, 1970)

——, *Shelley's Poetry and Prose* ed. Donald H. Reiman and Sharon B. Powers (New York, 1977)

Silverman, Edwin B., *Poetic Synthesis in Shelley's Adonais* (The Hague, 1972)

Simmons, Robert E., "*Urizen*: The Symmetry of Fear," *Blake's Visionary Forms Dramatic* ed. David V. Erdman and John Grant (Princeton, NJ, 1970) 146–73

Simpson, David, *Irony and Authority in Romantic Poetry* (Totowa, NJ, 1979)

Smith, Barbara Herrnstein, "Afterthoughts on Narrative," *On Narrative* ed. W. J. T. Mitchell (Chicago, Ill., 1980) 209–32

Soboul, Albert, *The French Revolution, 1787–1799: From the Storming of the Bastille to Napoleon* tr. Alan Forrest and Colin Jones (New York, 1975)

Spatz, Jonas, "The Mystery of Eros: Sexual Initiation in Coleridge's 'Christabel'," *PMLA* 90 (1975) 107–16

Spector, Stephen J., "Wordsworth's Mirror Imagery and the Picturesque Tradition," *ELH* 44 (1977) 85–107

Sperry, Stuart, *Keats the Poet* (Princeton, NJ, 1973)

Stephen, Leslie, *Studies of a Biographer* (London, 1902)

Stillinger, Jack, ed., *Twentieth Century Interpretations of Keats's Odes: A Collection of Critical Essays* (Englewood Cliffs, NJ, 1968)

——, *The Hoodwinking of Madeline and Other Essays on Keats's Poems* (Urbana, Ill., 1971)

Storch, Rudolph E., "Metaphors of Private Guilt and Social Rebellion in Godwin's *Caleb Williams*," *ELH* 34 (1967) 188–207

Sunstein, Emily W., *A Different Face – The Life of Mary Wollstonecraft* (Boston, 1975)

Swann, Karen, "Literary Gentlemen and Lovely Ladies: The Debate on the Character of Christabel," *ELH* 52 (1985) 394–418

——, "Harrassing the Muse," *Romanticism and Feminism* ed. Anne K. Mellor (Bloomington, Ind., 1988) 81–92

——, "Suffering and Sensation in 'The Ruined Cottage,'" *PMLA* 106 (1991) 83–95

Sydenham, M. J., *The First French Republic, 1792–1804* (London, 1974)

Tannenbaum, Leslie, *Biblical Tradition in Blake's Early Prophecies: The Great Code of Art* (Princeton, NJ, 1982)

Tanner, Tony, *Jane Austen* (Cambridge, Mass., 1986)

Tayler, Irene, and Gina Luria, "Gender and Genre: Women in British Romantic Literature," *What Manner of Woman: Essays on English and American Life and Literature* ed. Marlene Springer (New York, 1977) 98–123

Thiers, M. A., *History of the Consulate and the Empire of France Under Napoleon, Forming a Sequel to "The History of the French Revolution"* tr. D. Forbes Campbell, vol. 1 (London, 1845)

Thomson, James, *Poetical Works* ed. J. Logie Robertson (London, 1908)

Todd, Janet, *Women's Friendship in Literature* (New York, 1980)

Tomalin, Claire, *The Life and Death of Mary Wollstonecraft* (New York and London, 1974)

Tomlinson, Charles, "Christabel," *The Ancient Mariner and Other Poems: A Casebook* ed. Alun R. Jones and William Tydeman (London, 1973) 235–44

Treisman, Anne, "The Psychological Reality of Levels of Processing," *Levels of Processing in Human Memory* ed. Laird S. Cermak and Fergus I. M. Craik (Hillsdale, NJ, 1979) 301–30

Tuveson, Ernest Lee, "Space, Deity, and the Natural Sublime," *MLQ* 12 (1951) 20–38

——, *The Imagination as a Means of Grace: Locke and the Aesthetics of Romanticism* (Berkeley, Calif., 1960)

Tysdahl, B. J., *William Godwin as Novelist* (London, 1981)

Usher, James, *Clio; Or, a Discourse on Taste* (2nd edn, London, 1769)

Vendler, Helen, "The Experimential Beginning of Keats's Odes," *SiR* 12 (1973) 591–606

——, "Stevens and Keats's 'To Autumn'," *Wallace Stevens: A Celebration*," ed. Frank Doggett and Robert Buttel (Princeton, NJ, 1980) 171–95

Vignery, Robert J., *The French Revolution and the Schools* (Madison, Wisc., 1965)

Vlasopolos, Anca, "Mary Wollstonecraft's Mask of Reason in *A Vindication of the Rights of Woman*," *Dalhousie Review* 60 (1980) 462–71

Voisine, Jacques, *J.-J. Rousseau en Angleterre a l'époque romantique* (Paris, 1956)

Volney, Constantin-François, *The Ruins, or, A Survey of the Revolutions of Empires* (3rd edn, London, 1796)

Waldoff, Leon, *Keats and the Silent Work of Imagination* (Urbana and Chicago, Ill., 1985)

Walzel, O., *German Romanticism* tr. A. E. Lussky (New York, 1932)

Ward, Aileen, *John Keats: The Making of a Poet* (London, 1963)

Wasserman, Earl, *The Finer Tone: Keats's Major Poems* (Baltimore, Md., 1953)

——, *Shelley: A Critical Reading* (Baltimore, Md., 1971)

Watkins, Daniel P., *Social Relations in Byron's Eastern Tales* (London and Toronto, 1987)

——, *A Materialist Critique of English Romantic Drama* (Gainesville, Florida, 1993)

Watson, George, *Coleridge the Poet* (London, 1966)

Webster, Brenda S., *Blake's Prophetic Psychology* (London, 1983)

Weimann, Robert, *Structure and Society in Literary History* (London, 1975)

Weinberg, Steven, *The First Three Minutes: A Modern View of the Origin of the Universe* (New York, 1977)

Weiskel, Thomas, *The Romantic Sublime: Studies in the Structure and Psychology of Transcendence* (Baltimore, Md., 1976)

Wheeler, Kathleen M., *Sources, Processes, and Methods in Coleridge's "Biographia Literaria"* (Cambridge, 1980)

——, *The Creative Mind in Coleridge's Poetry* (London, 1981)

Wildi, Max, "Wordsworth and the Simplon Pass," *English Studies* 40 (1959) 224–32

Wilkinson, L. P., *The Georgics of Virgil: A Critical Survey* (Cambridge, 1969)

Williams, Eric, *Capitalism and Slavery* (New York, 1961)

——, *From Columbus to Castro: The History of the Caribbean, 1492–1969* (London, 1970)

Williams, L. Pearce, "The Politics of Science in the French Revolution," *Critical Problems in the History of Science* ed. Marshall Clagett (Madison, Wisc., 1959) 291–308

Williams, Raymond, *The Country and the City* (New York, 1973)

——, *Keywords – A Vocabulary of Culture and Society* (New York, 1976)

Wilson, Anna, "Mary Wollstonecraft and the Search for the Radical Woman," *Genders* 6 (1989) 88–101

Wilson, Douglas B., *The Romantic Dream: Wordsworth and the Poetics of the Unconscious* (Lincoln, Neb., 1993)

Wittreich, Joseph Anthony, Jr., ed., *The Romantics on Milton* (Cleveland, 1970)

——, *Angel of Apocalypse: Blake's Idea of Milton* (Madison, Wisc., 1975)

Wolfson, Susan, " 'Their She Condition': Cross-Dressing and the Politics of Gender in *Don Juan*," *ELH* 54 (1987) 585–617

——, "A Problem Few Dare Imitate: *Sardanapalus* and Effeminate Character," *ELH* 59 (1991) 867–902

Wollstonecraft, Mary, *A Vindication of the Rights of Woman* ed. Carol H. Poston (2nd edn, New York, 1988)

——, *The Works of Mary Wollstonecraft* ed. Janet Todd and Marilyn Butler (London, 1989)

——, *A Vindication of the Rights of Men* (London, 1790; facsimile edn, Gainesville, Fl., 1960)

——, *A Vindication of the Rights of Men* (Albany, NY, 1975)

Woodings, R. B., ed., *Shelley: Modern Judgements* (London, 1968)

Woodman, Ross, *The Apocalyptic Vision in the Poetry of Shelley* (Toronto, 1964)

——, "Shelley's Urania", *SiR* 17 (1978) 61–75

Wordsworth, Dorothy, *The Journals of Dorothy Wordsworth* ed. Ernest de Selincourt (2 vols, Oxford, 1940)

Wordsworth, Jonathan, "A Wordsworth Tragedy," *TLS* (21 July 1966) 642

——, *The Music of Humanity* (London and New York, 1969)

——, "The Five-Book *Prelude* of Early Spring 1804," *JEGP* 76 (1977) 1–25

Wordsworth, William, *Poetical Works of William Wordsworth* ed. Thomas Hutchinson, rev. Ernest de Selincourt (London, 1936)

——, *The Poetical Works of William Wordsworth* ed. Ernest de Selincourt and Helen Darbishire (5 vols, Oxford, 1940–9)

——, *The Prelude, or Growth of a Poet's Mind* ed. Ernest de Selincourt, rev. by Helen Darbishire (2nd ed., Oxford, 1959)

——, *Lyrical Ballads* ed. R. L. Brett and A. R. Jones (2nd edn, London, 1965)

——, *The Letters of William and Dorothy Wordsworth: The Early Years 1787–1805* ed. Ernest de Selincourt, rev. Chester L. Shaver (Oxford, 1967)

——, *The Letters of William and Dorothy Wordsworth: The Middle Years 1806–1820* ed. Ernest de Selincourt, rev. Mary Moorman and Alan G. Hill (2 vols, Oxford, 1969–70)

——, *The Prelude, or Growth of a Poet's Mind* ed. Ernest de Selincourt, rev. by Stephen Gill (Oxford, 1970)

——, *The Prose Works of William Wordsworth* ed. W. J. B. Owen and Jane Worthington Smyser (3 vols, Oxford, 1974)

Wordsworth, William, *Wordsworth's Literary Criticism* ed. W. J. B. Owen (London, 1974)

——, *The Cornell Edition of the Complete Poetical Works* Gen. Ed. Stephen M. Parrish (Ithaca, NY, 1975–)

The Salisbury Plain Poems ed. Stephen Gill (1975)

Home at Grasmere ed. Beth Darlington (1977)

The Prelude, 1798–1799 ed. Stephen M. Parrish (1977)

The Ruined Cottage and The Pedlar ed. James A. Butler (1979)

The Borderers ed. Robert Osborn (1982)

An Evening Walk ed. James Averill (1984)

Descriptive Sketches ed. Eric Birdsall (1984)

Peter Bell ed. John Jordan (1985)

Poems in Two Volumes, and Other Poems, 1800–1807 ed. Jared Curtis (1985)

The Fourteen-Book Prelude ed. W. J. B. Owen (1985)

The White Doe of Rylstone ed. Kristine Dugas (1988)

Shorter Poems, 1807–1820 ed. Carl Ketcham (1989)

The Thirteen-Book Prelude ed. Mark L. Reed (2 vols, 1992)

Lyrical Ballads, and Other Poems, 1798–1800 ed. James A. Butler and Karen Green (1993)

——, *The Prelude: 1799, 1805, 1850* ed. Jonathan Wordsworth, M. H. Abrams and Stephen Gill (New York, 1979)

Wu, Duncan, ed., *Romanticism: An Anthology* (Oxford, 1994)

Yarlott, Geoffrey, *Coleridge and the Abyssinian Maid* (London, 1967)

Yeats, W. B., *Collected Poems* (London, 1950)

——, *Selected Criticism* ed. A. Norman Jeffares (London, 1964)

Yeazell, Ruth Bernard, *Fictions of Modesty: Women and Courtship in the English Novel* (Chicago and London, 1991)

Young, J. Z., *Programs of the Brain* (Oxford, 1978)

Index